The Meeting of East and West

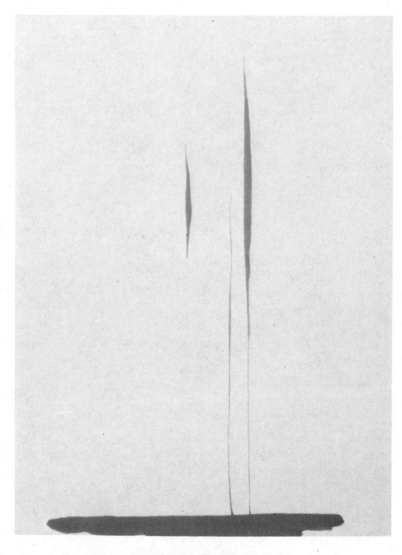

Frontispiece ABSTRACTION, NO. 11. 1916.
GEORGIA O'KEEFFE
Courtesy of An American Place

THE AESTHETIC AND THEORETIC COMPONENTS
IN THEIR UNITY

The Meeting of
East and West

AN INQUIRY CONCERNING
WORLD UNDERSTANDING

BY

F. S. C. Northrop

STERLING PROFESSOR EMERITUS
OF PHILOSOPHY AND LAW
YALE UNIVERSITY

OX BOW PRESS
Woodbridge, Connecticut

First published, 1946

1979 Reprint published by
OX BOW PRESS
P.O. Box 4045
WOODBRIDGE, CONNECTICUT 06525

Copyright Macmillan Publishing Co., Inc. 1946
Copyright renewed 1974 by F.S.C. Northrop

This edition is reprinted by arrangement
with Macmillan Publishing Co., Inc.

ISBN 0-918024-10-2 (Hardcover)
ISBN 0-918024-11-0 (Paperback)
Library of Congress Card Number 79-89839

Printed in the United States of America

TO

J. N. and S. N.

Where standards differ there will be opposition.
But how can the standards in the world be unified?

Mo-ti.

PREFACE

The state of mind following the recent war differs from that subsequent to the previous one. Then everyone supposed there were no ideological conflicts. The war had been fought to "save the world for democracy" and with the defeat of the Kaiser democracy supposedly had won. Only later did disillusionment appear, and even then its real meaning was not understood.

Now ideological conflicts are present everywhere. It is evident to all that the fate of peace depends in considerable part on whether the traditional democracies and communistic Russia can reconcile their economic, political and religious doctrines sufficiently to get on together. But this more obvious ideational issue is by no means the only one. Nor is it the most important one.

Jewish aspirations are at odds with an Arabian culture in Palestine. The Mohammedan version of a good society conflicts with that of the Hindu in India. The medieval Roman Catholic aristocratic conception of moral and social values grounded in naturalistic Aristotelian divine law opposes the modern Protestant democratic and pragmatic concept of an ecclesiastical and civil law which derives its authority solely from the humanistic conventions of a majority of men. Similarly, in the Orient, political institutions and religious observances inspired by Shintoism combat, even in Japan, those which are the fruition of Confucianism, Taoism and Buddhism. And in Pan-America the traditional Latin-American ideals and values conflict with those of traditional Anglo-America. It is literally true in all these instances that, in part at least, what the one people or culture regards as sound economic and political principles the other views as erroneous, and what the one envisages as good and divine the other condemns as evil or illusory.

The time has come when these ideological conflicts must be faced and if possible resolved. Otherwise, the social policies, moral ideals and religious aspirations of men, because of their incompatibility one with another, will continue to generate misunderstanding and war instead of mutual understanding and peace.

It is hardly likely that these sources of conflict can be faced and removed *in practice* within the halls of parliaments and the heated actions of the market place, where slogans are carelessly bandied about, special interests are at work, and passions are easily aroused, unless the problems raised are first traced to their roots and then resolved *in theory* within the calmness of the study where the meaning of words like "democracy" and "communism" can be carefully determined and the issues which they define can be looked at more objectively. It is with this timely, important and difficult undertaking that this book is concerned, as its sub-title indicates.

It happens, however, as Chapter I will show, that the most important ideological conflict confronting our world is the one rendered inescapable by the major event of our time—the meeting of East and West. Within the all-embracing and deep-going issues raised by this momentous occurrence the other ideological conflicts of our world are partial components. Hence, the title of this book.

Because of its subject matter, the contents of this book fall into two major parts: the one, a determination of the differing ideological assumptions of the major peoples and cultures of the West, culminating in Chapter VIII on the meaning of Western Civilization; the other, a similar study of the major peoples and cultures of the East, summarized in Chapter X on the meaning of Eastern Civilization. By combining the ideological assumptions of the traditional West with those of the traditional East, it then becomes possible in Chapter XI to understand, in its barest elements, the behavior of contemporary India, Japan and China. This also permits the fundamental problem underlying the ideological conflict between the traditional East and the traditional West to be determined, just as in Chapter VIII the fundamental problem at the basis of the ideological conflicts of the West is made explicit. It happens by good fortune that the problem in the one case is identical with that in the other. Thus the task in Chapter XII becomes that of solving this basic problem.

The analysis of this problem guides one to its solution. This solution defines a more inclusive truly international cultural ideal which provides scientifically grounded intellectual and emotional foundations for a partial world sovereignty. This ideal defines the criteria also for relating democracy and communism, Roman Catholic medieval and Protestant modern values, and Occidental and Oriental institutions so that they support and sustain rather than combat and destroy one another.

Because the basic problem to which the entire inquiry leads one turns out to be philosophical in character, its solution provides a philosophy of culture. Because it is found to rest on empirical evidence, or on factors inferred from such evidence by logical and scientific methods, this philosophy of culture is also a philosophy of science. In fact, the basic philosophical problem to which the analysis of the ideologies of the diverse cultures of the world leads one is solved in Chapter XII only by means of evidence from an analysis of scientific method and the philosophy of science. Thus the humanities as exhibited in the ideal culture, and the natural sciences grounded in nature are essentially and intimately connected and reconciled.

Also, because Oriental culture and certain elements in Mexican culture turn out to be primarily aesthetic in character, yet aesthetic in a sense different from that of the classical art of the West, the philosophy of culture and of science to which the analysis takes one provides also a rich, more diversified and comprehensive philosophy of art. It is because of this essential connection of art with the problem and its solution that illustrations accompany the text of this book.

So much for the character of its contents. It remains to note certain necessary explanations concerning the form of presentation, especially with reference to quotations.

In any chapter in which a quotation appears it is always accompanied by the name of its author. Any exception to this rule means that the quotation is by the author of the previous quotation.

No footnotes or book or page references appear anywhere in the text. Thus the reader suffers no interruptions to his vision as he reads, and the minimum amount of paper, for a manuscript completed during the paper shortage of war, is required. Nevertheless, the title of any book quoted, its publisher, date, and the page numbers from which the quotation is taken can easily be found by anyone who is interested. Turn to the back of this book and look under the references for the chapter in which you are reading for the name of the author of the quotation. Following the author's name the desired information will be found. The page number or numbers from which the quotation or quotations from a given author are taken appear immediately following the date of publication in the order in which the items, if more than one, are quoted.

Especially in the chapter on the culture of Mexico there are quotations, translated into English, from books printed in Spanish. These translations of the quoted material are by me.

My gratitude and indebtedness for permission to reproduce the paintings which appear in the illustrations and for permission to quote at more than the briefest length from other works is indicated in the specific acknowledgments which follow this preface. Even so, in so varied a subject, aid from others, with respect to the form of presentation or upon specific points, of a character not permitting explicit acknowledgment in the text, is inescapable. In this category are the following, to whom I give most hearty thanks and this acknowledgment of my indebtedness: José Arrom, Leonard Bacon, David Bidney, Harold and Jean Burr, Alfonso Caso, Chan Wing-tsit, Charles E. Clark, Ananda Coomaraswamy, Cecil Driver, Homer H. Dubs, Paul Fejos, Lilian Gill, Frederick A. Godley, Charles W. Hendel, C. Daly King, Francisco Guerra, Everett V. Meeks, Georgia O'Keeffe, Alan Reid Priest, Alfonso Reyes, Alfred Stieglitz, and Louis and Doris Wallner; also individual members of the staffs of the Boston Museum of Fine Arts, the Metropolitan Museum of Art, Gallery of Associated American Artists, and the Museum of Modern Art in New York, and the Sterling Memorial Library in Yale University. For very valuable suggestions after their reading of the entire manuscript I am most grateful to Charles W. Morris and Herbert J. Schneider, and also the readers and editors for the Macmillan Company.

The work of Edith Burnham was of major importance in the preparation of the original manuscript. Words cannot indicate the patience, talent, care and devoted attention which she put into this important part of this book's creation. In the later stages of preparation for the printer, the contribution of Katharine Denison on parts of the final manuscript and of the page proofs is also valued. To Jean Burr I am indebted for a reading of the original manuscript, a reading of the page proofs, and the preparation in considerable part of the index.

With respect to major items of subject matter there is a heavy debt also, gratefully acknowledged: To Justino Fernandez, the expositor of the painting of José Orozco, for many stimulating and illuminating discussions concerning Mexican art and culture and for the encouragement to place on paper the philosophy of art and culture developed in this book. To Junjirō Takakusu, the distinguished Buddhist scholar, for his lectures on Buddhist philosophy and religion and his encouragement in the interpretation which I have placed upon Buddhism and other Oriental doctrines. To Chan Wing-tsit for his lectures on Chinese philosophy. To Shunzō Sakamaki for his objective exposition of Shintoism. To George P. Conger for an appreciation of the flavor of the Indian Vedas and Upanishads. To Charles A. Moore, my former pupil and the executive organizer of the East-West Conference in Philosophy under the auspices of the University of Hawaii, for his emphasis upon the diversity and practical character of Oriental philosophy. And to

Gregg M. Sinclair, present president of the University of Hawaii, and David L. Crawford, its president in 1939, for making available the riches of the aforementioned conference. To my teacher and colleague, Charles M. Bakewell, for an appreciation of the roots of Western civilization in Greek philosophy. To my teacher, H. M. Sheffer, for his emphasis upon postulational technique. To my teachers, William Ernest Hocking and Alfred North Whitehead, and my colleague, Wilmon H. Sheldon, for the realization that no problem in society, science or life is fully understood until its grounds in the metaphysical nature of things are discovered. And to the Fellows of Silliman College, my colleagues in the Department of Philosophy, and my many students in Yale University for countless enriching discussions. It was, for example, James Angleton who, while a senior in Silliman College and an editor of *Furioso,* first elicited, by his probing questions in our conversations concerning contemporary poetry, the analysis of art which this book develops in greater detail.

Finally, there is the inspiration of my sons, who were at war while this book was written and to whom it is dedicated, and the devotion and companionship of my wife, who helped and sustained me at every stage of its construction.

F. S. C. Northrop

New Haven, Conn.
December 2, 1945.

ACKNOWLEDGMENTS

I am grateful to the following publishers for permission to quote at some length from the designated works published by them, as follows:

D. APPLETON-CENTURY COMPANY:
John Locke's *Letter Concerning Toleration*; J. G. Nicolay and J. Hay's *Abraham Lincoln: A History*, published by the Century Company.

ALBERT & CHARLES BONI, INC.:
The Essays of Oscar Wilde.

CHRISTY & MOORE, LTD. (LONDON):
Marco Pallis' *Peaks and Lamas*, published by Cassel & Co., Ltd., London, and Alfred A. Knopf, Inc., New York.

EL COLEGIO DE MEXICO:
Leopoldo Zea's *Apogeo y Decadencia del Positivismo en Mexico.*

P. F. COLLIER & SON CORPORATION:
B. Franklin's *Autobiography*; Voltaire's *Letters on the English*; John Jay's *The Federalist*; George Washington's *Farewell Address*, from Vols. 1, 34, and 43 of the *Harvard Classics.*

COLUMBIA UNIVERSITY PRESS:
Woodrow Wilson's *Constitutional Government in the United States.*

CROWN PUBLISHERS:
Albert Einstein's *The World As I See It*, published by Covici Friede.

THE JOHN DAY COMPANY:
Jawaharlal Nehru's *Toward Freedom*; Lin Yutang's *My Country and My People.*

DOUBLEDAY, DORAN COMPANY:
Muriel Rukeyser's *Willard Gibbs, American Genius*; Emily Hahn's *The Soong Sisters*; Rudyard Kipling's *Kim*, published by the Doubleday, Page Company, with permission also from Mrs. Bambridge, present owner of the copyright.

DUELL, SLOAN & PEARCE, INC.:
Krishnalal Shridharani's *My India, My America.*

E. P. DUTTON & COMPANY:
John Locke's *Of Civil Government*, Everyman's Library; E. R. Hughes' *Chinese Philosophy in Classical Times*, Everyman's Library.

EDUCATIONAL SUPPLY ASSOCIATION, LTD.:
George Carter's *History of England*, Part II, published by Rolfe Brothers.

HARCOURT, BRACE & COMPANY:
E. A. Burtt's *Metaphysical Foundations of Physics*.

IMPRENTA UNIVERSITARIA (Mexico City):
Alfonso Reyes' *Ultima Tule*.

ALFRED A. KNOPF, INC.:
René Grousset's *Civilization of India*, published by the Tudor Publishing Company.

LITTLE, BROWN & COMPANY:
Edwin Arnold's *The Light of Asia*, published by Roberts Brothers; John C. Miller's *Origins of the American Revolution*, published by the Atlantic Monthly Press.

LONGMANS, GREEN & COMPANY, INC.:
George M. Trevelyan's *English Social History*; *The Living Thoughts of Thomas Jefferson*, ed. by John Dewey.

LUZAC & COMPANY:
Sir John Woodroffe's *Shakti and Shâkta*.

THE MACMILLAN COMPANY:
Michael Oakeshott's *The Social and Political Doctrines of Contemporary Europe*, published by the Cambridge University Press; Surendranath Dasgupta's *History of Indian Philosophy*, published by the Cambridge University Press; W. S. Jevons' *The Theory of Political Economy*; Rabindranath Tagore's *Collected Poems and Plays*; Benedetto Croce's *Aesthetic*.

McCOY PUBLISHING COMPANY:
Charles Johnston's *The Great Upanishads*, Vol. I, published by the Quarterly Book Department.

METHUEN COMPANY:
Chiang Yee's *The Chinese Eye*.

OPEN COURT PUBLISHING COMPANY:
J. G. Fichte's *The Vocation of Man*; Lao-Tzu's *Tao-Teh-King*.

OXFORD UNIVERSITY PRESS:
R. E. Hume's *The Thirteen Principal Upanishads*; E. Barker's *Britain and the British People*.

PHILOSOPHICAL LIBRARY:
Ananda Coomaraswamy's *Hinduism and Buddhism*.

PRINCETON UNIVERSITY PRESS:
Philosophy: East and West, ed. by Charles A. Moore.

G. P. Putnam & Sons:
Anita Brenner's *Your Mexican Holiday.*

Random House:
Theophile Gautier's *Mademoiselle de Maupin,* Modern Library; *The Wisdom of Confucius,* trans. and ed. by Lin Yutang, Modern Library.

Charles Scribner's Sons:
Younghill Kang's *The Grass Roof* and *East Goes West*; Sidney and Beatrice Webb's *Soviet Communism: A New Civilization?*

Vanguard Press:
R. B. Perry's *Puritanism and Democracy.*

Viking Press, Inc.:
Rebecca West's *Black Lamb and Grey Falcon.*

Yale University Press:
W. Shakespeare's *Troilus and Cressida* and *Coriolanus*; A. D. Lindsay's *Religion, Science and Society in the Modern World.*

I am grateful also to the following for permission to reproduce the illustrations as indicated:

An American Place for the Frontispiece, *The Two Blue Lines* and Plate XI, *Abstraction Number 3* by Georgia O'Keeffe.

Petroleos Mexicanos for Plate I, *The Ground Plan for the Place of the Gods at Teotihuacan.*

Dr. Alfonso Caso and The Viking Fund for Plate II, *The Terrestrial Paradise at Téotihuacan.*

A. von Wuthenau and von Stetten, Fotocolor, Mexico, for Plate III, *Angel and Side Wall at Tepotzotlan,* and Plate IV, *The Virgin of Guadalupe.*

The Museum of Modern Art for Plate V, *La replica del frésco del Centro Rockefeller* by Diego Rivera, Plate VI, *Man in Flames* by José Orozco, and Plate X, *The Side Show* by Georges-Pierre Seurat.

F. Wilbur Seidoes for Plate VII, *Hands and Flames,* and Plate VIII, *Omniscience,* by José Orozco.

Associated American Artists for Plate IX, *Daughters of Revolution,* by Grant Wood.

The Metropolitan Museum of Art for Plate XII, *Madonna and Child* by a follower of Sandro Botticelli.

The Boston Museum of Fine Arts for Plate XIII, *Sage Contemplating Nature,* style of Ma Yuan; Plate XIV, *Boat at Anchor by Reeds,* Sung dynasty; Plate XV, *Eleven Hydra-headed Kuan-Yin,* Chinese Buddhist, Tibetan style; and Plate XVI, *Seated Buddha,* Indian sculpture, A.D. 150.

CONTENTS

ILLUSTRATIONS

xxi

The Meeting of East and West

THE CONTEMPORARY WORLD

Ours is a paradoxical world. The achievements which are its glory threaten to destroy it. The nations with the highest standard of living, the greatest capacity to take care of their people economically, the broadest education, and the most enlightened morality and religion exhibit the least capacity to avoid mutual destruction in war. It would seem that the more civilized we become the more incapable of maintaining civilization we are.

The paradox appears in a purely verbal, but none the less important, form with respect to the second major war of this century. Strictly speaking, it is *the first world war*. This fact has momentous significance.

To be sure, the previous war claimed this title for itself. Actually, however, it was primarily a Western conflict, in which a few Oriental peoples found it expedient to participate. It began in the Balkans. It was fought for the most part on the European continent. Its peace settlement was determined almost entirely by Westerners and signed at Versailles.

Its successor opened, on the contrary, in the Orient with the Japanese invasion of Manchuria. The implications for the West became evident immediately when Japan demonstrated the impotence of the peace policy of Versailles and of the more isolationist program of the Republican administrations in the United States by withdrawing its delegates from the League of Nations and flouting the Kellogg Pact without penalty. This gave Mussolini his cue and Hitler his courage. Abyssinia followed. Then, as an essential part of the complicated pattern, came the Spanish Civil War with its unresolved conflicts between medieval religious and cultural institutional forms and modern economic, democratic, or communistic values, of which Italy with Germany and Russia took advantage, on opposite sides, to gain invaluable experience in testing their ideological aims and their military instruments. Meanwhile an initially pacifistic England and a fearful, hesitant France attempted, unsuccessfully, to remain indifferent. This was followed by Munich with its dismemberment of Czechoslovakia and the later German declaration of war on Poland, which brought in Great Britain and France and engulfed Denmark and Norway, while Russia, playing for time as she protected her right flank with an invasion of Finland, arranged a pact with Germany. But Germany's ambition and the forces set in motion were not to be withstood. The German attack on Russia followed, thereby continuing a world movement from Manchuria across Europe and through Siberian Asia which came full circle with the Japanese bombardment of Pearl Harbor. It was an attack by an Oriental rather than by a European nation which brought the United States officially into this war.

The global character of the conflict becomes the more evident when one notes its universal accompaniment. Modern Western nationalism has been copied by Japan; it has been established in China; and it has become a world issue in India, even gripping Gandhi and his followers who would prefer the Oriental method of non-action. Everywhere throughout the world, on both sides of the battle line and among neutrals and pacifists as well as belligerents, and in peace as well as in war, this modern Western phenomenon—the positive insistent spirit of nationalism—is abroad and at work. This does not speak well for the peace of the future. It means, unless we are willing to examine and reconstruct the diverse political aspirations and conflicting cultural ideals of our time, learning how to relate them so that they reinforce and sustain rather than combat and destroy one another, that the increasingly intense and destructive wars of the West in every genera- tion are about to engulf not merely Japan but the whole of Asia. No longer will it suffice to watch the Balkans, the Polish Corridor, or the Rhineland. There are danger spots everywhere—in the South Pacific, Northern Manchuria, Outer Mongolia, Burma, Latin America, and even between the Mohammedan and Hindu provinces of India.

This, however, is but half of the story. The East is doing more than merely respond to Western political, economic, military and religious doctrines and influences. It is also for the first time seriously and posi- tively bringing its traditional and contemporary culture and influence to bear upon us, and insisting that we alter our military, political, and economic decisions and even our cultural ideals under the impact of hers. This is part of the meaning of the Japanese bombardment of Pearl Harbor and of Mahatma Gandhi's stand, even in the face of the Japanese invaders, against the British Empire. But it is not only with bombs and passive resistance that the Orient is saying this to the West. It is also saying it more wisely, fortunately, with comradeship and with love. This is the meaning of the visit of Madame Chiang Kai-shek to the United States and to Brazil. China is making herself felt upon America.

All this renders two things clear: First, each part of the Orient has left its traditional, passive, receptive attitude and is coming to impress its existence and values upon the Occident. Second, this coming can be evil and dastardly as well as it can be benign and beneficent. Which it will be in the future depends not merely upon the East but also upon the West, and in particular upon each knowing the other's values and interests as well as its own.

Nor must it be supposed, because of the grace and the charm with which the beneficent influence has come, that China is any less determined than is Japan or Mahatma Gandhi's India to stand on her own feet and insure that the West adjust its ideals as well as its practices to the impact of Oriental cultural values and interests. At the commencement exercises at Yale University in June, 1942, China's Foreign Minister, T. V. Soong—of whom, it is well to remember, President Chiang Kai-shek is the brother-in-law—spoke as follows:

. . . I should like to name the broad objectives for which my country believes it is fighting.

The first is political freedom for Asia. . . . China is fighting for her national independence; she aspires equally for the freedom of all Asiatic nations. There are, of course, here and there certain nations which may not be ready yet for complete self-government, but that should not furnish the excuse for colonial exploitation. . . .

Our second objective is economic justice. Political and economic justice go together; without the one the other cannot flourish. Asia is tired of being regarded only in terms of markets and concessions, or as a source of rubber, tin and oil, or as furnishing human chattels to work the raw materials. The Atlantic Charter, first enunciated by Roosevelt and Churchill and later adopted by all the United Nations, may prove to be the Magna Carta of economic justice, which must be made a living reality.

We now know that political freedom and economic justice are by themselves illusory and fleeting except in an atmosphere of international security. . . . Past failures have not dimmed our hopes that an effective world instrument to dispense and enforce justice will arise. . . . China, with all other liberty-loving nations, will gladly cede such of its sovereign powers as may be required.

. . . Every month of this war has increased the almost unbearable strain on our people and army, but I feel I am justified in assuring you that we shall endure and prevail, and live to cooperate with you in fashioning the brave new world of the future.

These are not the words of a merely passive and receptive Orient. Because of the key position of the Soong family in the New China they are words to be reckoned with in world affairs.

Furthermore, the Orientals generally are a very proud people. With a civilization thousands of years older than that of the West and, as the sequel will show, with aesthetic, religious and social values in many respects superior, as Western values are in other respects superior to theirs, they, like Westerners, have a right to be proud. This pride is such that they will not for always receive values from and make adjustments to the West, without giving as much or more in return. The Orient has shifted from a more passive and receptive to a more active and initiative role in world affairs.

This means that for the first time in history, not merely in war but also in the issues of peace, the East and the West are in a single world movement, as much Oriental as Occidental in character. The East and the West are meeting and merging. The epoch which Kipling so aptly described but about which he so falsely prophesied is over. The time is here when we must understand the Orient if we would understand ourselves, and when we must learn how to combine Oriental and Occidental values if further tragedy, bitterness, and bloodshed are not to ensue.

This is by no means an easy or a perfectly safe undertaking. The recent behavior of Japan is one result of the attempt to put the East and West together. The tragic impasse in India is another. Moreover, much more than the reconciliation of Oriental and Occidental values is involved, since the Western ideological issues between fascism and democracy, democracy and communism, and communism and medieval feudalism are now the issues of the Oriental nations themselves. This shows itself in the world war. It was not a war between the East and the West. Instead, it divided the East as much as it divided the West. Japanese were with Germans; China and part of India are with Great Britain, America, and Russia.

Even within local issues and regions the paradoxes do not cease. A militant Japan or a pacifist Gandhi who would oppose the West uses the Western idea of political nationalism to justify his opposition. A Marx or a Lenin who would bring about the fulfillment of democracy ruthlessly opposes the freedom of belief and speech which is its essence. An Atlantic Charter or Good Neighbor Policy, which would support democracy and the right of each people to choose its own political leaders, seems confronted with a contradiction when in Argentina, perhaps in Italy or in Spain, this policy puts kings or fascists or communists in office, and when in India temporarily, or in the islands of the

Pacific likely to be held by the United States as military bases, it rejects the principle of local autonomy which it affirms. Even within the nation or the individual the situation is not different. In the United States during the 1920's a political policy based on traditionally sound economic and political theory ended in economic collapse and political defeat. It would seem that if we act upon the basis of the traditional Protestant religious individualism and the traditional *laissez faire* economic and political principles we fail to solve or even to face the inescapably social, national, and international problems and dangers of our time. If, on the other hand, we face our problems constructively, through the New Deal or by some other means, admitting the inescapable federal organization and action which this involves, then cross purposes and confusion result, and we seem forced to give up what our pulpits, our press, and our courses in economics have taught us.

Even into morality and religion the paradoxical confusion enters. The Germans who with Luther inaugurated the modern Protestant religion and who with Kant and Fichte created the modern moral idealism, and who have been indoctrinated with these Lutheran, Kantian and Fichtean philosophies for centuries, seem to be the least religious and idealistic in their acts. The British and Americans with their indigenously more empirical, scientific, and pragmatic attitude seem to be the more considerate of others both morally and religiously. Yet many contemporary Anglo-American moral and religious leaders blame science and pragmatism for the ills of our time, and urge that the cure is to be found in a morality and religion independent of science after the manner of Luther, Kant, Fichte, and the Germans. Similarly, the contemporary American conservative charges the leaders of the New Deal with being crass self-seekers, while the New Dealers describe the conservatives as selfish individualists and "economic royalists," devoid of an honest capacity to face facts, and without the guidance of a liberal idealism. Likewise, Protestants and Roman Catholics, Christians and Jews, Jews and Arabs, and Mohammedans and Hindus are suspicious, if not positively antagonistic, toward one another, getting on together if at all more in spite of than because of their religion. Also Western religion often requires its adherents to regard their own gospel as perfect, and, hence, to look upon Oriental religion as false, inferior, negative, or heathen; while, conversely, Oriental sages term their culture superior, in the things of the spirit, to that of the West.

These considerations all remind us that neither war nor the peacetime problems of our world can be diagnosed as a simple issue between the good and the bad. This, to be sure, is the interpretation which each party to the disputes of our time puts upon events. But the very number and diversity of conceptions of what the good and the divine is give the lie to any such diagnosis, and to the ever present proposal that a return to the traditional morality and religion is the cure for our ills. All that such proposals accomplish is the return of each person, each religious denomination, each political group or nation to its own pet traditional doctrine. And since this doctrine (or the sentiments which it has conditioned) varies at essential points from person to person, group to group, nation to nation, and East to West, this emphasis upon traditional religion and morality generates conflicts and thus intensifies rather than solves our problems. This in fact is the basic paradox of our time: our religion, our morality and our "sound" economic and political theory tend to destroy the state of affairs they aim to achieve.

This condition will expectably increase in complexity and intensity, because in addition to continuing conflict between diverse moral, religious, political and economic ideologies in the West, there will be a more direct confrontation of Occidental and Oriental cultural values.

Nevertheless, to become aware of this complicated, dangerous, and paradoxically confusing situation is to have at hand the clue to the way to meet it. Each major nation or cultural group in the war and the peace of our contempary world, both Western and Oriental, must be examined and analyzed to bring out into the open the particular moral, religious, economic and political doctrine from which it proceeds traditionally. In each instance also an attempt must be made to determine the evidence which led its founders to regard its particular ideology as the correct one. When this is done certain nations or cultures will probably be found to rest on different but compatible assumptions and ideals; others, upon diverse and contradictory ideals. In the case of diverse but compatible cultures the task will then be that of correctly relating the compatible elements of the two cultures by enlarging the ideals of each to include those of the other so that they reinforce, enrich and sustain rather than convert, combat or destroy each other. Between diverse and contradictory doctrines, as for example Anglo-American and Russian economic theory, the problem will be to provide foundations for a new and more comprehensive theory, which without contradiction will take care, in a more satisfactory way, of the diverse facts which generated the traditional incompatible doctrines. It is with this complex, difficult but interesting undertaking, including the major task of relating correctly the East and the West, that this book is concerned. The importance of such an inquiry can hardly be exaggerated. The capacity of Russia, Great Britain, China, and the United States to work together harmoniously and constructively in the peace, after the bombs of a common enemy have ceased to give them common cause in war, depends upon achieving some kind of an understanding and working arrangement between the democratic and the communistic ideologies It is very unlikely that this can be achieved in a lasting manner in practice if some way of relating them harmoniously and consistently is not also attained in theory. This is equally important for the internal politics of each nation; as the power of the communist army and party in China, the communistic leanings of the aristocratic Jawaharlal Nehru in India, and the frescoes of Diego Rivera (Plate V) and David Siqueiros in Mexico clearly indicate. Also the power and prestige of Russia will force conservatives as well as liberals and labor leaders to seek for ways of combining the evident virtues of communism with those of traditional democracy.

But there are equally important conflicts in the field of art, religion and the sentiments. No policy of Pan-Americanism, of Regional Europeanism, or with respect to Spain, can hope to become a living reality unless emotional and psychological conflicts are seen to be the heart of the matter. The Mexicans, for example, as the next chapter will show, have a culture extending to the humblest Indian of the villages, rich in things aesthetic and in the religion of passion, beauty, and worship. With respect to these values there is no doubt that their culture is superior to that of the United States. Naturally, the Mexicans cherish it, passionately and rightfully. They have introduced also the more universal and secular education with its power, through scientific technology and medicine, to lessen disease and lighten the physical labor of men. Of the intrinsic human value as well as the practical utility of these things they are not unmindful, as the new village schoolhouses and playgrounds and the contemporary art of Mexico clearly and movingly demonstrate. But they do not want to see these good things, modeled in part upon the United States, come at the price of destroying their own indigenous, traditional values and of taking all the sparkle and individuality of the emotions and the sentiments out of their hearts and their faces. Thus, their desire to be neighborly is tempered with fear. This fear has several sources. There is the vigor and size of the United States and its present all-absorbing zeal in spreading its own valuable democratic, technological, and commercial practices around the world. There is also its emphasis upon the instrumental and pragmatic in its philosophical reflection. Valuable as these traits are, they tend to blind the people of the United States to the aesthetic and spiritual riches of a Latin country. Consequently, the Mexicans, like all Latins, fear that they will be overwhelmed spiritually before they have time to work out the merging of the Latin-American and the Anglo-American values in a manner which will preserve the virtues of both. It is the exclusiveness of the ideals of the United States, rather than its bullets or even its commerce, which Latin America most fears.

There is also the persisting issue within Western civilization between the values of its medieval and modern portions. This issue has increased recently in intensity. It appears not merely in Protestantism and Roman Catholicism, and in the battle over educational policy in the University of Chicago, but also in the way in which, in war and in peace, military and diplomatic decisions on both sides have to reckon with Rome. It was especially acute in the Spanish Civil War. The complex, conflicting values which produced the Spanish struggle exist also in Latin America. The vigor of North American policy, together with the threat of a common danger from Germany, merely sublimated this conflict. With the removal of the danger and the return of peace it will become articulate again. The reason is that the Latin-American countries, like Spain and Portugal and even France and Italy, are confronted with two inescapable sets of values: the one, medieval, religious, aesthetic, Catholic, and classical, made a habit and ingrained in their feelings and emotions by their past; the other, modern, democratic or communistic, reinforced by the pressure of foreign influences—British, North American, and Russian—in the present. Until Spain, Portugal, France, Italy, and Latin America work out the reconciliation of these different values there will be no real peace either in their souls or in their politics. But there is a more fundamental reason, affecting Protestants and the English-speaking as well as the Latin world. As the sequel will demonstrate, the traditional modern world is as outmoded as the medieval world. The major task of our time is to preserve the virtues while avoiding the errors of both. For this, medieval as well as modern doctrine must be understood.

Oriental civilization, similarly, notwithstanding certain important, basic common elements which will be noted later, is not a single thing. Not only are there the different peoples and their countries, but each country is composed of several cultural elements, quite apart from Western influences. China and Korea, for example, are made up of

Confucian, Taoist and Buddhist ideological factors. Japan contains these three, together with Shintoism which is predominant and especially important at the present moment. Tibet is primarily Buddhist, with its own corrupt form, Lamaism, which appears also in parts of China and Mongolia. India and the far southwest Pacific islands are composed of Hinduism (or more exactly Brahmanism), Mohammedanism originally from the Middle East, and Buddhism, in varying proportions.

It appears, therefore, that the character of our undertaking and the nature of its subject matter force us to depart from both the layman's and the scholar's traditional way of looking at things. The layman has tended to regard his own economic and political doctrines and moral, aesthetic and religious values as the only ones, thereby supposing that in so far as other peoples or cultures have ideals they are his own, and that in so far as they are not his own, they are not ideal or valuable. The scholar likewise has been inclined to conceive of scholarship as the meticulous specialization upon some local portion of one of the world's diverse cultures or periods—thereby concluding, consciously or unconsciously, that if there is anything outside his local province, it is like what he studies, or, if it is not, then its character and relation to his own findings will come out merely by adding together the conclusions of other experts like himself. What happens from both of these attitudes is that the basic issues and problems of our time never get faced or understood, to say nothing about being constructively solved by either layman or scholar. For the truth is, as even the above very brief examination of the character of our world has indicated and as the sequel will show in greater detail, the culture of the whole world is not a mere sum of its parts. Moreover, the behavior of any local portion is a function, not merely of its own traits and ideological assumptions and attendant values, but also of an interaction of these with the quite different ones of other cultural elements and nations. Furthermore, the latter relation of interaction between the world's diverse cultures and nations is not one that can be comprehended in terms of the simple arithmetical operation of addition. Thus, the usual outlook of the layman prevents him from understanding his own local practical problems, and the restricted studies of the traditional scholarship, necessary as they are, make it a faulty scholarship even of the local, to say nothing of the civilization of the world as a whole. Nor is this a point of purely academic interest. For it is precisely in this relation between interacting cultural elements grounded in different economic and political doctrines and diverse moral and religious ideals that, in considerable part, paralyzing schisms within the state, and wars between nations, are generated. Consequently, a new kind of attitude and a new type of scholarship are required. We must open our intuitions and imaginations, even our souls, to the possibility of insights, beliefs and values other than our own; and we must bring scholarship to bear upon the world's problems as a whole, seeing local provincial factors in their relation to one another and this whole.

Because of its novelty such a scholarship will make mistakes. But mistakes are not unknown even to the old type of scholarship. One must venture into local domains without all the detailed information of the experts in these domains. The justification for this is that in the present state of the world, when every local province on the earth's surface is affected by what takes place everywhere else, there is greater danger of error from 'seeing the local details while not envisaging the wider issues and relationships than there is in directly facing the world problems and their general characteristics with the knowledge of local details which time permits one to acquire, while being ignorant of many other local factors. The ideal, to be sure, is a combination of the expertness of the local specialist with that of the specialist directing attention upon conflicts and interrelationships. But before this ideal is possible the latter type of expertness as well as the former must be developed. It is this which the subsequent study is attempting to initiate in a preliminary way.

Nevertheless, our method need be neither haphazard nor arbitrary. Its key is the character of the ideological issues of our time. These issues guide us to what must be examined. Starting with the near-at-hand, we are led out first to the hemispherical Pan-American problem, then to the diverse ideological issues of Western civilization as a whole, and finally to the major problem of relating the East and the West, including the examination of Confucian, Taoist, Buddhist, Hindu and Mohammedan elements, necessary for the latter undertaking.

Because it is easier to see the role of ideas in a foreign culture than in one's own, because the conflict of Western economic, political and religious doctrines, both medieval and modern, is more sharply focused in Latin America than in the United States, and because Mexico illustrates the Latin-American component of the Pan-American problem, we begin, in the next chapter, with the ideological manifestations of the culture of the latter country. Its culture, by contrast, sharpens our awareness of the differing and at times conflicting doctrines and ideals of the United States which, in Chapter III, are examined as representative of the Anglo-American portion of the Pan-American problem. But the political, economic and predominantly Protestant beliefs of the traditional culture of the United States arose for the most part in Europe, and are typical of modernism and traditional democracy generally. Thus the United States, apart from its Roman Catholic component, which is treated independently, serves also as an example of the democratic portion of the issue between democracy and communism and the modern portion of the issue between modernism and medievalism. Also, its recent politics, in the issue between conservatives and the New Deal, is typical of the problem confronting the world generally of combining the virtues of individual enterprise with the needs of federal and international action, short of communism. Because British conservatism differs markedly from American conservatism and because of other unique ideological elements in British democracy which must be understood if the British and Americans are not to misunderstand each other, Chapter IV, on the distinctive factors in British culture, follows. A theoretical treatment of German idealism in Chapter V provides the basis for understanding Russian communism in its Marxian orthodox form as analyzed in Chapter VI, thereby permitting the theoretical issue between Russia and the democracies to be sharply focused. It remains in Chapter VII to examine medieval Western culture and its roots in Greek science. Its major contemporary manifestation, orthodox Roman Catholicism, is taken as an example. This completes the analysis of the major significant diverse Western cultures and their underlying ideologies, thereby permitting us in Chapter VIII to define the basic theoretical issue of the contemporary Western world. At the same time, factors common to all the rival doctrines of the West are noted, thus designating the Western component in the major problem of relating the East and the West.

The traditional Eastern component is then examined in Chapter IX, in its four major and most influential manifestations: Chinese Confucianism, Chinese Taoism, Buddhism, and the Hinduism of India. The factors common to these different cultures and doctrines are then noted in Chapter X. By putting these common Oriental factors beside those common to the West, the difference between the East and the West becomes evident and the problem of merging them becomes clearly defined. Also, by combining the traditional indigenous Far Eastern cultural elements with Mohammedanism from the Middle East and modern influences from the West (Chapter XI), the behavior of contemporary India, Japan, and China becomes in part at least explicable.

The final problem then remains (a) of attempting to determine the correct relation between the basic beliefs and values of the East and West and (b) of resolving the theoretical issue underlying the conflicts between democracy and communism, Latin and Anglican values and the medieval and the modern world within the West (Chapter XII). It turns out by good fortune that the theoretical issue in both cases is the same, and that the solution of the fundamental problem underlying the conflicts and issues of the contemporary West provides a criterion of the good also for solving the major problem confronting our world of merging correctly and safely the civilizations of the East and the West.

It is because this problem and its solution necessitate the inclusion of Latin and Oriental intuitive aesthetic values that the illustrations form an essential, rather than merely illustrative, part of this book. It is for this reason also that we come out, in Chapter XIII, with a philosophy of art as well as a philosophy of culture. And because cultures, especially in the West, have their conception of sound economic or political policy and good religious doctrine defined by technical, abstract terms such as those of John Locke, Jevons, Marx or St. Thomas Aquinas, no escape from the consideration of these technical matters is possible in what follows. To do less than this is merely to scratch the surface of things, instead of getting to the heart of the difficulty and to its solution. These technicalities have been kept, however, in contact continuously, as far as is possible, with aesthetically vivid and concrete materials. Consequently, if one stays with the abstract theories they gradually become familiar and one comes out inevitably into the concrete exciting, and at times tragic, world of daily life. For this world in considerable part in its most significant manifestations is but the later reflection of the earlier technical scientific, philosophical, aesthetic and religious beliefs.

Certain cautions are to be noted. This entire inquiry is concerned only with the ideological issues of our time. To be sure, from chapter to chapter concrete materials, facts, and historical events are presented, but this is done solely to illustrate and enable one to discover the theoretical or intuitive economic, political, aesthetic and religious doctrines which predominate in the culture in question, and to penetrate beneath the surface of things to the basic issues and problems around which these doctrines turn. No attempt is made to indicate all the ideological factors. Only those most influential as measured by majority opinion and the more pressing ideological issues of our time are considered. Actually in any culture there are as many different theoretical beliefs as there are different individuals or different opinions of the same individual at different times. Usually, however, certain beliefs capture a majority opinion. It is with these major beliefs only that the worldwide scope of our inquiry permits us to concern ourselves. Consequently, the reader must not expect a complete account of all ideological factors in society or history on the one hand or a consideration of the role of non-ideological factors, such as climate, geography, famine, disease, etc., on the other.

It is not maintained, therefore, that everything in culture and history is determined by the beliefs of men—their specific economic, political, aesthetic, philosophical and religious doctrines. It is maintained, however, with the sociologist Pitirim Sorokin, and with an increasing number of students of society such as Clyde Kluckhohn, B. L. Whorf, D. D. Lee, L. K. Frank and David Bidney, that these ideological factors are very important elements in the total situation—much more important than most people suppose, and that any approach to the issues of war and peace which neglects them does not face the full complexity of the difficulties confronting our world, and to that extent is doomed to failure. As R. B. Perry has noted, "If a factor such as an ideal makes *any* difference, there may be situations in which it makes all the difference."

But it must be noted with equal insistence that an approach which overlooks the non-ideological factors in history and society and the *de facto* state of affairs is equally incomplete and inadequate, even after the final conclusions of our inquiry are obtained. The adequate social ideal for our world must be supplemented with the empirical social scientists' information concerning the actual state of affairs. Only with an adequate ideal for society and a realistic knowledge of the actual state of society can wise practical action be determined.

But this distinction between correct normative social theory and correct *de facto* social theory presents a problem—the final paradox of social thought generally. Since a social ideology defines an ideal or goal toward which we are moving, and hence differs from what is in fact the case realistically, what criterion can there be for determining the validity or invalidity of a given ideology? It is difficult to see how a theory can be tested without appeal to fact, yet in the case of normative social theory correspondence with the social facts clearly is not a decisive criterion. Thus, it is never taken as an argument against the democratic ideal for the state that the factual behavior of Germans is out of accord with it. Nor is the fact that no person is a perfect Christian taken as proof of the invalidity of the Christian ideal. But if correspondence with the social facts is not the criterion of the truth of an ideology, how then can its truth be determined? It would seem that we must have some factual criterion for determining the validity of one social ideal rather than another, and yet that the character of any normative social theory is such that the failure of social facts to conform to it is in considerable part irrelevant to its validity. This is our final and main paradox.

Unless we can resolve it, everything which follows will be arbitrary. For the paradox raises nothing less than the question whether there is any meaning to the statement that one ideal is more correct than another.

Consequently, the problem confronting us is even more difficult than the previous description of its worldwide extent and complexity has indicated. For we not only have to investigate the rival ideological issues of the world, but we have to initiate this undertaking without any clearly accepted conception of what the method is for determining the correctness of one ideology as compared with another. In other words, as we take up one culture after another, we must not merely seek out the theoretical assumptions determining its ideological component, but we must also see if such an inquiry will not reveal to us the method for determining the correctness of one ideology as compared with another in the case of conflicts between them.

It is believed that the following inquiry resolves this methodological paradox and problem of our world as well as its other paradoxical conflicts and confusions. But the time has now come to let the evidence speak for itself.

CHAPTER II

THE RICH CULTURE OF MEXICO

The Sunshine Limited had swerved and twisted through two interrupted nights and a novel but wearisome day from San Antonio to Mexico City. A spirited taxicab had sped by shops and parks reminiscent of Paris, skyscrapers with signs bearing the impress of New York, and past the heavy white marble Palace of the Fine Arts, to stop at the Spanish Hotel Majestic facing the colonial Catholic Cathedral and National Palace, which flank the distinctly Mexican Zócalo, whose lawns and gardens cover the Aztec ruins across the way. There they were. All within one square mile. Five distinct and unique cultures: ancient Aztec, Spanish colonial, French nineteenth century, Anglo-American economic, and contemporary Mexican. Harmoniously yet competitively diverse and at times so tremendous and incredible that again and again one could hardly believe one's eyes.

Within the last of these cultures, painting as expansive and profound as it is vital and arresting. Frescoes with a form and sweep which would take one to Rome to find their equal. The human figure formed at times, as Justino Fernández has shown, with a skill comparable to that of Michelangelo, Tintoretto, and El Greco. Also, there is the music of Carlos Chavez, not to mention the names of notable poets, sculptors, and architects. Such is the rich culture of Mexico. Possessions of the imagination and the sentiments which, when we pursue them, intimate the meaning not merely of Mexico and Latin America but also of all America and Europe, providing even a tie and a bridge to Asia.

Two squares from the Cathedral is a former Encarnación Convent, covering an entire, exceptionally lengthy city block, now a redecorated government building housing the Secretariat of Public Education. This secular public usage of a former seclusive religious compound typifies the influence of the modern democratic and later positivistic French philosophy of Mexico of the nineteenth century upon the Medieval Catholic culture of its colonial period. Passing through its main entrance one finds oneself facing a large, open, primary square patio divided by three levels of open colonnades from a second large, open court beyond.

15

One's attention is caught immediately by the vast expanse of frescoes covering the inner walls of the three levels running entirely around the rectangle formed by the two courts. These frescoes are by Diego Rivera and other contemporary Mexican painters. They depict the history of Mexico, glorifying the native Indian stock and holding up as a human value the application of science to the natural resources of the country freed for the people from both priests and capitalists. Clearly this is the focus into which the culture of the past converges and from which radiates that of the present and the future.

But even this does not exhaust its significance, as the architectural design of the primary patio indicates. The four sides of this square patio with its three levels of colonnades do not meet in visibly right-angled corners. Instead, in each corner a *pan coupé*, or single narrow, vertical, rectangular plane surface running continuously from the stone pavement below to the roof above and facing the center of the court, has been added. These four verticle-plane truncated-corner surfaces of the patio, masking its right-angled corners and focusing upon its center, give a unity to the square court in all three dimensions. Upon these four upright, smooth stone surfaces are cut four world figures, one only in each truncated corner. Their primary location insures that they signify factors which are very important. These four figures are of Quetzalcoatl, Las Casas, Plato, and the Buddha.

In a country such as Mexico in which aesthetic values are primary, and rarely if ever merely decorative, one soon learns to listen carefully when, with architecture, it is said, "These four men are of primary importance." One realizes of a sudden that one is face to face not merely with the roots of Mexican culture but also with its relations to world culture.

But why these four men? To answer this question is to possess the key to the Mexican and even the Spanish soul.

The presence of Quetzalcoatl and Las Casas is easy to understand. Quetzalcoatl, meaning "plumed serpent," was the major deity of the pre-colonial Aztec inhabitants of the valley of Mexico and the founder of their agriculture and industry. He represents the purely Indian portion of the Mexican soul and culture. Fr. Bartolomé de Las Casas is generally regarded throughout the Latin-American world as the creator of the Spanish colonial culture of the New Spain. Some twenty years before Cortés he was in an expedition under Columbus to the West Indies. In 1502 he was in Haiti and in 1511 in Cuba. Later he resided in Nicaragua, Peru, Guatemala, and Mexico, where he was Bishop of

Chiapa. It was he who taught the Indians how to make of the Spanish language, art, and religion, the spontaneous and original creation of their own spirits which we find it to be even today. Las Casas represents the Spanish colonial component of the Mexican spirit.

But why Plato and the Buddha? Were this a building of similar importance north of the Rio Grande or in Europe the Buddha rather than the Christ would be missing. Even the presence of Plato presents a problem. To be sure, Mexico is a predominantly Catholic country, and Catholic theology is rooted in the science and philosophy of the Greeks. But ever since St. Thomas Aquinas was canonized in 1323 it has been Aristotle's philosophy rather than Plato's which has defined orthodox Catholic doctrine. Plato and Buddha present a puzzle, perhaps two puzzles, calling for an explanation. These questions must be kept in mind as one examines the major components of Mexico's culture.

THE MEXICO OF THE INDIANS

The purely Indian pre-colonial civilization of Mexico is not one culture but many; differing as much among themselves as the British, German, French, Italian, and Spanish diversify Europe. Among the more important are the Mayan in Yucatan, the Tarascan in Michoacán, the Mexteco-Zapotecan in Veracruz and Oaxaca, the Aztec in and around Mexico City, and the Toltec to be seen now at Teotihuacán, which existed even before the coming of the Aztecs.

To see the remains of all these types in the National Museum is to be forced to pinch oneself to be sure one is not dreaming, so unbelievably remarkable are they. Immediately before one at its main entrance is the large Aztec calendar stone weighing some twenty-four tons. It was more accurate than anything existing in Europe in its time. Clearly, there was science here as well as art and religion.

To the left and right are sculptured heads and figures, some mammoth in size, which make one think, even when one knows better, that some Egyptian or Greek genius has surreptitiously slipped in, to print misleading labels and to leave behind the very best of his own creations. But to comprehend all these and the many other fascinating things which fill Mexico's National Museum is too much for any one mind. Let us concentrate instead upon the Ancient Toltec in its original setting at one important place, Teotihuacán, some forty-five kilometers north and east of Mexico City.

Leaving the Pan-American Highway, one approaches this Place of the Gods across a flat, dusty plain, broken at occasional spots by village dwellings and green trees. Of a sudden the geometrically regular Pyramid of the Sun stands directly before one. Larger at its base than the Great Pyramid of Egypt, it is not quite so tall. It will be well if this slight qualification causes one to climb it. For only from its top can one immediately experience and come to understand that unique and remarkable achievement of the Indians' aesthetic intuition which we shall find reappearing in quite different forms throughout every historical stage of Mexican civilization.

There it is everywhere below and around one: the sense of the aesthetic form of the whole carried architecturally and geometrically literally over square miles, no one yet knows how far (Plate I). It appears not merely in the perfect yet terraced geometrical form of this Pyramid of the Sun, and in the smaller Pyramid of the Moon to the right at the end of the Avenue of the Dead which one faces directly below, but also in the equally perfect yet varied sense of form, geometrical and conscious in pattern, extending block after block, perhaps mile after mile, binding all together and including the orientation to the rounded hill behind, the contrast of straight and curved lines enhancing each—embracing even the heavens above and the stars in their courses.

For remember, we are standing on top of the Pyramid of the Sun. Upon the very spot which presses against the soles of our shoes it is likely that human sacrificial worship of the astronomer's sun took place. The official publication of the Instituto Nacional de Antropología e Historia informs us:

The City is not laid out according to the cardinal points; that is, the "Avenue of the Dead" does not extend exactly from south to north, nor does the Pyramid of the Sun face exactly to the west, but its center deviates from the west to the north, at an angle of approximately 17°. For a long time the cause of this was not known, but recent investigations have shown that it is due to the fact that the monuments on the ground are oriented, not toward the true west but toward the point where the sun sets on the days when it passes through the zenith, a fact that proves that this pyramid was dedicated to that celestial body.

Consider the significance of this. It means that the scientific, aesthetic, and religious values of the Toltecs functioned together harmoniously, the one reinforcing the other, and that the values of art and religion were oriented and defined with respect to those of geometrical and astronomical science.

This explains the unified, geometrically informed, aesthetic intuition of the whole, infused with human feeling and religious purpose which one experiences from the apex of the Pyramid of the Sun. It explains also the remarkable aesthetic sense of the native Mexicans for the whole field of vision which the informed student of European and Mexican art Alexander von Wuthenau has noted, and which shows in their capacity to extend the form and feeling of the aesthetic intuition over the community as a whole. In the Spanish colonial city of Pátzcuaro not merely the individual churches and other buildings but the community in its entirety is an aesthetic gem. Something quite similar can be sensed in Taxco and also on the approach to Tepotzotlan as one notes its Jesuit monastery located on a rise of ground, lifting it out of the commonplace obscurity of the flat plain, yet at a considerable distance from the mountains forming the background, so that the image of the one does not overwhelm or blot out that of the other. Rarely if ever, von Wuthenau added, does one find the Indians putting up one architectural unit and destroying the independent aesthetic value of any other in its neighborhood when the total effect is apprehended.

The reason for all this we have before us as we look over the Place of the Gods from the top of its Pyramid of the Sun. Obviously the art, sociology, and religion of the Indians were not independent subjects, artificially robbed of their proper vitality by being cut off from each other and their sources in nature; instead, they were defined as to their values and aims as well as to their instruments, by a science which was geometrical and astronomical in its emphasis (Plate I). Because of the central place of the sun in the entire scientific conception, their art and their religion expressed themselves not merely through the edifices and ground plan of the metropolis as a whole, but also in its relation to the heavens above. For such an art, the cultivation of the aesthetic intuition of the whole was inescapable.

Alfonso Caso, in his *Religion of the Aztecs*, writes of Quetzalcoatl that "most important of all, he taught men science, giving them the means to measure time and to study the movements of the planets; taught them the calendar, invented ceremonies, and fixed the days for prayer and sacrifice." It is significant also for religion as well as art that they regarded Quetzalcoatl as "god of life." In short, human values and scientific values coincided.

We are now prepared to pick our dizzy way down the steps of the Pyramid of the Sun in order to proceed along the Avenue of the Dead to the Citadel, which contains the Temple of Quetzalcoatl. There this deity and his subjects have something else to teach us; something which is very important.

Climbing the steps up the outer wall of the rectangular Citadel and descending again onto the flat plain of its interior one finds its rigid geometrical lines and proportions as emotive and moving in their effect as they are unified and simple in themselves. How such elementary straight lines, right angles, and flat surfaces can conjure up such a feeling is hard to understand.

Large enough to enclose the stadium of a university in the United States, with its flat playing ground, this Citadel, when experienced from the center of its paved field within, with the triangular form of the Pyramid of the Sun rising above its north wall, never loses its integrity or its essential geometrical and aesthetic connection with the larger design and intuition beyond. Instead, one feels oneself emotionally taken hold of from without by the vast pattern of the entire geometrically conceived, communal and cosmological system, rather than merely in the role of an isolated spectator looking at a local architectural unit from within.

Even more important is the Temple of Quetzalcoatl hidden behind a smaller pyramid on the far side of the Citadel's inner expanse. Between the persisting horizontal levels and straight lines which enter into the Temple's composition there run the naturalistic curves of the serpents and the petals of flowers surrounding the serpents' protruding heads. Most important of all, the whole was originally in vivid colors. Only fragments of the blues and reds and greens remain, but that everything here and elsewhere throughout the city was ablaze with color seems probable. Although this serpentine theme has a symbolic religious and metaphysical significance, it is important to concentrate attention on the more purely aesthetic quality of this naturalism. It reminds us again that the Aztecs did not separate the geometrical forms or the religious meaning of things from the moving, vivid, aesthetic qualities in which they exhibit themselves to us with immediacy. Evidently the purely aesthetic was a value in and for itself, and not a mere appearance to be dropped as if it did not matter, or added merely as an afterthought.

This second distinctive trait we shall find recurring again and again throughout the entire history of Mexican art and culture. It is not an accident, for example, that the most highly developed and prized of contemporary Mexican arts is painting. Nor is it mere circumstance that Orozco, even when he is condemning science as an evil in conveying man as a gift of Divine Grace, finds it most natural and effective to combine the rigid geometrical forms of modern cubism with the naturalistic forms and the moving, fiery colors symbolizing the human spirit. Geometrical form and naturalistic, human and aesthetic values were inseparably merged by the Mexican Indians.

Their sense of unformalized, naturalistic colors and shapes appears in the reconstruction of the original frescoes of the Temple of Agriculture at Teotihuacán. The name of this temple is significant. One is reminded of the similar presentation of science applied to the soil, as a human aesthetic value, in the frescoes of Diego Rivera and the younger contemporary Mexican painters (Plate V). Nowhere, however, does the Aztec's sense of the free play of naturalistic color and form for its own sake appear in a happier manfestation than in the fresco of the newcomer, singing his way into the paradise of Tlaloc (Plate II), which Alfonso Caso has recently unearthed in the catcus-covered field behind the Pyramid of the Sun.

There are many more things in Indian culture to fascinate one and amply repay a longer study. But we have enough now to take with us to our examination of the Mexican culture of the Spanish Colonial Period in order to appreciate the sense in which it is not a mere copy of imported European forms but an original and spontaneous creation of the Indian spirit.

THE SPANISH COLONIAL PERIOD

Aztec legend had prepared the way for the coming of the Spaniards. Quetzalcoatl, before departing this earth by descending into the West, had promised to come back to earth again by the East. "That is why," Alfonso Caso writes, "when the Spanish conquerors landed at Veracruz in the year 1519 . . . the Emperor Moctezuma never had a doubt that Quetzalcoatl was returning to take possession of his Toltec Kingdom." This accounts for the quickness of the triumph of Cortés. It also enables us to understand why the Spaniards won the souls as well as commanded the bodies of the Indians, even to the extent of enticing them to make the language, art, and religion of Spain their own. But it does not explain why the coming of Cortés resulted in the complete destruction of the very high Aztec culture rather than merely in its enrichment and fulfillment.

The rigidity of the Aztec aesthetic and religious forms has been advanced by many as the cause of their decline. One cannot be sure that the rigidity does not exist largely in the minds of modern observers who have not fully appreciated its moving, aesthetic, human quality rather than in the minds and feelings of the Aztecs themselves. Even if the rigidity for them be admitted, it is hardly sufficient to account for the reduction of their remarkable achievements to pulverized, buried fragments. Only an enemy of the Aztec culture could produce such terrible effects. This enemy appeared in two forms: the conquistador's sword and the Christian religion. Of the two the latter was the more devastating. It is doubtful if anything done to the Jews or the Poles in our time compares with it in the thoroughness and the ruthlessness with which it wiped out Aztec civilization. For, whereas Cortés and his soldiers merely defeated the Indians to place them under the weak political domination of a distant Spain, the Christian priests and their religion remained to bury and well-nigh destroy Aztec culture.

This should reveal the danger in bringing together differing moral ideals and religious values. At their worst the clubs of the savage, the swords of the conquistadors, and the bombs of the Nazis can break only the skulls of some men. It takes ideals and religion to enter into the imaginations and emotions of all and lay waste to their very souls. Not until man's cherished beliefs are captured can his culture be destroyed. This evil aspect of our own highest moral ideals and religious values has been overlooked because, in our blindness to ideals and values other than our own, we see only the new effects which our own provincial goods create and not the equally high values of the old culture which their coming has destroyed. Only a merging of civilizations which proceeds from the knowledge and appreciation of the diverse ideals and values of all parties to the undertaking, can escape evils so terrible and extreme as those wrought by the Christian religion in Mexico.

Fortunately, its destruction of Indian values was not complete. Certain fragments of the native insight, especially in the aesthetic sphere, persisted. To these were added certain superior, more humane religious practices of worship and the ecclesiastical, architectural forms which the Christian Spaniards brought. The product was a second culture in Mexico, termed the Spanish colonial, which, in copying Europe, added Indian elements that make it something precious and unique. It must be emphasized also that even when the Indians copied the Spaniards, by following them in their language, architecture, and religion, they did this at most points with a spontaneous and free movement of their

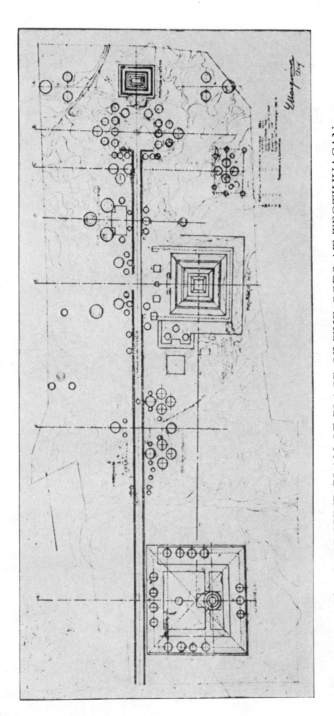

Plate I GROUND PLAN OF PLACE OF THE GODS AT TEOTIHUACAN

Courtesy of the Petroleos Mexicanos

GEOMETRICAL THEORETIC COMPONENT IN TOLTEC CULTURE

Plate II   THE TERRESTRIAL PARADISE AT TEOTIHUACAN

Courtesy of Alfonso Caso and The Viking Fund

THE AESTHETIC COMPONENT IN TOLTEC CULTURE

Plate III ANGEL AND SIDE WALL AT TEPOTZOTLAN
Courtesy of A. von Wuthenau and von Stetten.
Fotocolor. Mexico, D. F.

THE AESTHETIC COMPONENT IN MEXICAN SPANISH
COLONIAL ARCHITECTURE

Plate IV THE VIRGIN OF GUADALUPE.
PHOTOGRAPH BY VON STETTEN
Courtesy of Fotocolor. Mexico, D. F.

THE FEMALE AESTHETIC COMPONENT IN MEXICO'S
ROMAN CATHOLICISM

own spirits, as the care and devotion which they gave to the building of the Catholic churches in Mexico unequivocally indicate.

This shows itself clearly in the Jesuit monastery constructed over the years between 1582 and 1767 at Tepotzotlan, some thirty miles north and a little west of Mexico City. In our exposition of the remarkable aesthetic intuition of the whole embracing even the surrounding horizon and the heavens which the Toltecs exhibited at Teotihuacán, we mentioned the location of this monastery as another example. Clearly the remarkable capacity of the native Mexicans to embrace the entire field of vision within the form of the aesthetic intuition carried over into the colonial period.

When one examines Tepotzotlan at closer range this might seem to mark the end of the Indians' influence. The monastery as a whole, with its surrounding wall, its inner courts, its several chapels, and its principal church of baroque style, is typical of monasteries and churches of this Spanish Catholic type anywhere. In its interior, also, apart from the tremendous amount of Mexican gold that surfaces the extremely rich and complicated interior decoration of its principal church, the same impression prevails.

It is only after one has remained for a time in certain of the smaller chapels to the Virgin and in some of the minor reception rooms and has permitted the general impression of the baroque to wear off, so that the broader spaces within the main lines of the architecture impress one, that something unique and important appears. One finds this novel element first and in its most remarkable form in a little octagonal chapel, the Camarin, located immediately behind the Loretto Chapel dedicated to the worship of the Virgin. It was in the octagonal Camarin, Alexander von Wuthenau tells us, that "the Indians used to clothe the Virgin and delight in the costly vestments she wore for her various feast days of the liturgical calendar of the Roman Catholic Church." He adds that "the style and feeling of the designs of this room are distinctly Indian," and that it is not "to be wondered at that they should decorate it with special care and love." Its dome is broken at the top with an opening which reveals an octagonal cupola extending upward to culminate in a silver dove representing the Holy Ghost, whose reflected light fills the whole room with a cheerful brightness. Everywhere—in the cupola, surrounding its opening, and filling in the open spaces of the dome, even standing out in three dimensions from its surface—are the bright faces and warm, soft bodies of very human angels with their vividly colored wings and their brightly decorated robes. Over all the main supporting and dividing lines of the dome there runs also a slightly formalized but purely decorative naturalistic pattern. Also, as one's eyes move gradually from the dome down the main supporting lines and columns to the floor, one's gaze comes upon partly nude, brown, human figures with naturalistic grass or floral skirts hanging from their waists. It is clear that the aesthetic appreciation of naturalistic color and form for their own sake, which we found in the Temple of Agriculture, on the Temple of Quetzalcoatl, and in the frescoes of the Paradise of Tlaloc at Teotihuacán, are here also.

This becomes even more evident when we enter the larger House Chapel. Over its main altar is a tall, large picture of the Virgin. At its base is a horizontal, rectangular decoration of a purely naturalistic and floral design. Most remarkable of all, however, is the pattern of the decoration on the wider spaces of the side walls. Here one finds tremendous open crimson flowers, each one at least six inches in diameter (Plate III). Obviously the Indians have added items of their own.

The most purely Spanish of all Mexican cities is Puebla de los Angeles. It was founded in 1531 by members of Cortés's army as a purely Spanish city. The same devotion to the Virgin reappears in its El Rosario Chapel of Santo Domingo, in an extreme exaggeration of stucco with gold leaf which testifies again to the Indians' devotion to the female metaphysical principle in Mexico's Catholicism. With it appear, as Anita Brenner has written, "designs dazzling and pagan—fruit, gargoyles, medieval animals and bacchante angels."

This aesthetic sense of the Indians expressed itself in one other way in the churches of the Colonial Period. When the Arabs conquered Spain, after overrunning the entire Middle East and North Africa, they brought with them the tile work of the Persians. This mastery of clay the Spaniards in turn brought to Mexico. It fitted in naturally with the pottery work of the Indians and immediately caught their imaginations. The result appears in the House of Tiles in Mexico City and in dome after dome of the hundreds upon hundreds of churches at Puebla and its neighboring city of Cholula. One of the most spectacular examples occurs in San Francisco Ecatepec, located near Cholula. Anita Brenner has described it accurately as follows:

It is a solid mass of color inside and out. Façade, majolica tile mosaic dating from the seventeenth century, and towers, walls, all majolica too, make the church look like something imagined by a very poetic and patient Chinese.

Again, the native Mexican appreciation of color and form for their own sake made of the Catholic churches of Mexico something unique in the history of art.

It would be a mistake to suppose that the Spanish Catholic influence in Mexico is merely a thing of the past. On the northeastern edge of Mexico City but three miles from its Zócalo, at Villa Gustavo Madero, formerly Guadalupe, is the nation's religious shrine. On a Sunday afternoon, the public square and large church are filled with people of all stations in life but predominantly Indian. Clearly, here is something which has captured the emotions and the souls of the people. Entering the great church one realizes immediately that something more than its colors or its architecture inspires the worshippers. A continuing mass of penitents, dropping to the floor at the first vision of the high altar, moves forward step by step on its knees to the altar railing, where those in the front rank bow and pray, before breaking into two groups slipping out to either side to release the prized position for those behind them. Nothing to be seen in Canada or Europe equals it in the volume or the vitality of its moving quality or in the depth of its spirit of religious devotion.

Wonder arises about the object of this quest. The explanation was evident back in the city: This is the shrine of the beloved Patron Saint of Mexico, the Dark Madonna, Our Lady of Guadalupe. On the windshield of taxicab after taxicab in Mexico City and in the front interior of almost every bus, often with a miniature electric bulb illuminating her presence, one sees her image. Here, in the vast Catholic edifice, illuminated in the high altar, at which all the slowly advancing worshippers have been looking with absorbed devotion, is the original image from which all the others are copied (Plate IV). The official account of its origin is of interest: On December the twelfth, 1531, but ten years after the conquest by Cortés, this Indian Madonna appeared before the humble Indian peasant Juan Diego on the Tepeyac Hill just behind this large national shrine. Previously she had commissioned him to convey to the Bishop in the city her wish that a temple be built in her honor upon this spot. Having completed his mission, Juan Diego now returned with his tilma, or mantle, filled with roses, precisely as the Madonna had instructed. What was his surprise when upon opening it he found that the Madonna, as an expression of her gratitude, had left an image of herself upon it. It is this image upon this peasant's mantle (Plate IV) which captures the gaze of the Mexicans as they worship on bended knees at Guadalupe.

It will be most relevant to our philosophical purposes if we examine in some detail this image, the story of its origin, and the far-reaching trails left by its influence. Those readers who are not accustomed to the artistry of the Roman Catholic Church must not allow a too literal reading of the story of the origin of the image in the high altar at Guadalupe to blind their eyes to the very true and real fact which it symbolizes. The fact is, this image of the Virgin conveys in some direct and effective way a basic, intuitively felt element in the nature of things and in the heart of human experience which is spontaneously natural and convincing to the native Mexicans. In some way, the Virgin of Guadalupe and the story of her revelation, directed especially to the Indians, call forth from the Mexican spirit a devotion and sweeping response not equaled by any other influence in Mexico even today.

The French positivism of the nineteenth century led to the secularization of education and the nationalization of church property. But this positivism is now a dead letter. The frescoes of Diego Rivera are striking and have wrought a far-reaching transformation. But neither they nor copies of them appear everywhere one turns throughout Mexico, as does this image of the Virgin of Guadalupe. Even the democratic ideas of Voltaire and Rousseau were led to their initial victory in the first Mexican Declaration of Independence, of 1810, by the Spanish Indian priest Hidalgo under her banner; and as recently as the second decade of this century the revolution of the Zapatista agrarians was carried forward in her name.

Nowhere does the influence of this Indian Madonna show itself more powerfully than in the Roman Catholic Church itself. As one watches the worshipers moving slowly toward the altar, an official guide steps up to volunteer the information that this shrine is not a cathedral but a basilica, the third church in rank in the whole of Roman Christendom. Even the Church hierarchy has had to rank this village shrine ahead of the more natural claimant, the cathedral over the seat of the Aztec empire in Mexico City, and only two removed from St. Peter's in the entire Catholic world. Nor has this been done entirely of free choice. The first Madonna of the Spanish Catholics, as Anita Brenner informs us, was the Madonna of Los Remedios. Between the latter Madonna and Our Lady of Guadalupe there was intense rivalry, perhaps not yet completely removed. Yet it is the latter whose shrine has been placed by the pontiffs at Rome in a basilica.

Nor is this all. There is something unique about this Madonna, something typical of Mexican Catholicism, and of far-reaching consequences. She is dark of skin and an Indian. When the Indian Juan Diego first met her in 1531 on the hill of Tepeyac, behind the present basilica, she said to him, according to the official account, "I am the Virgin Mary, Mother of the true God." That the Virgin Mary in Mexico should be an Indian is significant. It means that the Virgin has won the Indians' spirit. Having announced her identity, the Lady then added to Juan Diego, "And it is my will that here on this spot a temple should be built in my honor. . . . Go to the bishop and tell him that I send you." In her *Guide to Mexico*, Frances Toor writes of this spot as follows:

> Before the Conquest, the hill immediately behind the present Sanctuary, known as the Tepeyac, was the site of an Aztec temple, in which Tonantzin, Virgin, "Little Mother" and Aztec goddess of the Earth and Corn, had a wide cult. Soon after the Conquest, this shrine and deity were destroyed along with others, and the Indians sorrowed for their "Little Mother." It was on the site of the pagan shrine that the Virgin of Guadalupe appeared for the first time on the American continent, to a humble Indian. She was not the pale Spanish Virgin of the same name, but a *morena* or dark-skinned one, whom, because of her color, the Indians would more readily trust and love. To this day the identity of the Aztec and Catholic Virgins is not very clear in the minds of the Indians. Immediately after her appearance it was so confused, that some of the important missionaries wanted to do away with this shrine. But the *morena* Virgin was so miraculous that she succeeded in establishing herself and is today the beloved Patron Saint of the Republic.

This suggests that Our Lady of Guadalupe is to the Indians not divine mediately, by virtue of being the purely earthly mother of Christ, but is, like the Aztec goddess of the spot in which her spirit first appeared, divine in her own right. Her image in the shrine supports this conclusion. For the churchmen in their artistry did not dare to tamper with the spontaneous movement of the Indians' spirit by even attempting to insure the orthodoxy of the Virgin by placing a Christ-child in her arms. She appears in the shrine of the basilica of Guadalupe alone and in her own right.

That this is what she means to the Mexicans is evidenced again and again throughout the churches of Mexico. To be sure, there are pilgrimages in the church calendar over great distances where the object of the quest is the Christ. Undoubtedly the priests, if pressed on the point, would maintain that her virtue is only mediate through Christ and not immediate in her own nature. But that this is not what she means to the vast majority of Mexicans there can be little doubt. The truth is that it is the Virgin representing what Plato termed the female *éros* (the emotional, passionate, metaphysical principle in the nature of things) and not the Christ representing the male *lógos* (the rational, doctrinal principle, formalized explicitly for orthodox Catholicism by St. Thomas Aquinas) who has for the most part caught the imagination and the devotion of the Mexicans.

This fact shows in countless ways. Anyone who has walked among the mountains or through the fields and orchards of Switzerland, Bavaria, Austria, or France, will recall coming again and again, even in out-of-the-way places, upon little shrines of the Christ hanging upon the Cross. This is the true and natural symbol for orthodox Catholicism. Nevertheless, in journeys covering hundreds of miles radiating from Mexico City in every direction no such image of the Christ located in the countryside or even made very conspicuous in the churches comes to mind; in its place appears instead the Madonna of Guadalupe.

An even more remarkable example appears in the Dominican counterpart of Tepotzotlan and its church of Santo Domingo at Puebla. Here the church proper is plain; it is to the side chapel of San Rosario, dedicated to the Virgin, that one must go to find that portion of the entire monastery to which the Indians gave their real concern and complete devotion. For the Virgin nothing in the way of time, expense, good taste, or affectionate care was too much to offer. That this should appear in a monastery of the Dominican order is especially surprising. For this was the order of St. Thomas Aquinas. He is not merely the author of the present orthodox doctrine of the Catholic Church, but also the proponent *par excellence*, following the metaphysics of Aristotle, of the divine as the purely rationalistic, male, metaphysical principle in the nature of things.

These considerations make it evident that the Spanish Colonial component of the culture of Mexico is something truly original and unique and by no means typical, orthodox Roman Catholicism. This departure from orthodoxy raises queries and calls for further inquiry. Before pursuing it further, examination of the third culture of Mexico is advisable. It exhibits an even more surprising example of the departure of Mexican Catholicism from orthodoxy.

FRENCH NINETEENTH CENTURY

In his illuminating book *El Perfil del Hombre y la Cultura en Mexico*, Samuel Ramos describes the influence of French culture upon

Mexico in the nineteenth century as follows: "The political passion operated in the assimilation of this culture in the same way as the religious passion previously in the assimilation of the Spanish culture." This emphasis upon politics is the key to the nineteenth century in Mexico.

It was a century partially influenced by the United States but dominated by France. The influence from the north appears in the incorporation of the presidency into the legal democracy of Mexico. The French predominance shows itself in the building of the rest of the democracy upon the French model. The talented Mexican scholar and diplomat Alfonso Reyes, in *Ultima Tule*, has summarized the relative contributions to the Latin-American republics in the following manner: "Our constitutional utopias combine the political philosophy of France with the federalist presidency of the United States." In the volatility and frequency of its shifts of personnel and even in its departures from democracy itself with France's Maximilian and the dictatorship of Porfirio Diaz, Latin-American democracy more closely follows its French model in practice as well as in theory.

The adjective "Latin" is the key to this preference. "Between our country and France," Samuel Ramos continues, "exists the affinity of the Latin spirit. Mexico became Latinized by the double influence of the Catholic Church and Roman legislation." He adds that in French culture there exists an intuition of the spirit and "a sensuality, perhaps of Mediterranean origin, which accommodates itself easily with our tropical sensuality." Alfonso Reyes agrees that "in general," without denying affinities "with the other America [*i.e.* the United States], the intelligence of our America encounters in Europe a vision of the human more universal, more basic, more in conformity with its proper feeling."

This is not difficult to understand. The people of the United States, for reasons to be indicated later, are not essentially aesthetic in their interests. For them art tends to be merely a utilitarian instrument or an unnecessary luxury brought in as an afterthought. It is not the substance of human life. On the other hand, the native Indians in Mexico possess a natural and ineradicable aesthetic sense. The Spanish Colonial Period enabled them to express it in their own unique way. The French exhibit a similar appreciation of art, as do the Spaniards. Thus the feeling of the Mexicans for the culture of Paris or Madrid rather than for that of nineteenth-century Chicago or New York is natural.

France is also predominantly a Catholic country. Even though her political forms are modern, the architecture in which they are housed and the religious institutions with which they were associated are medieval or classical. Similarly, her literature extends continuously into the medieval and ancient past. Even as advanced a writer as Anatole France has no sense of leaving his modern cultural homeland in entering into the mind of Abélard or into the thoughts of Cicero or Plato. Mexico also, because of the Spanish Colonial influence, is Catholic and medieval in religious orientation and architectural forms. Her contemporary poet Alfonso Reyes, as his *Crítica en la Edad Ateniense* shows, moves as easily amid the *Dialogues* of Plato and the literary criticism of Aristotle as he does within the embassies of the modern nationalistic states.

The United States, on the other hand, is a purely modern country. Apart from the presence of the Catholic Church, its culture, as the next chapter will show, expresses a purely modern political and religious ideology with no medieval or ancient cultural background to separate it from nature. There are not even the medieval royal ceremonies, largely symbolic and nominal though they be, which one finds in contemporary democratic, predominantly Protestant, Great Britain to remind one of a medieval and ancient heritage. Thus the United States represents but one, instead of several, answers to the basic questions of Western culture; and inevitably must appear to either a European or a Latin American as entirely too simple-minded and emotionally optimistic and undisturbed for a truly informed and sensitive citizen of the Western world. This is at once the key to the particular kind of freedom —the freedom from deep-going cultural conflicts between ancient, medieval, and modern values—which the citizens of the United States enjoy and also the key to their weakness—a weakness arising from a failure to appreciate, as Europeans and Latin Americans do, the conflict between different political, social, aesthetic, moral, and religious ideals which constitutes the very nature of Western civilization. The preference, therefore, of Mexico with its conflicting cultural components, for the similarly complicated culture of Europe instead of for the more single-minded, less critical culture of the United States should cause no surprise.

This root in the medieval and ancient past, which the people of the United States have to seek out first with their minds, bringing their hesitant, untutored emotions along afterward, the Mexicans and other Latin Americans have in the present in their architecture and their native aesthetic and religious sentiments. It was precisely because of this that Mexico in the nineteenth century found democratic French culture, with its roots in the medieval and ancient past, rather more to its liking than the purely modern culture of the United States, even when the Mexicans were in quest of purely modern political and educational values. This French influence led them first to sixty years of democracy, broken by interruptions, some of which also had a French source, and finally to approximately thirty-five years of the dictatorship of Porfirio Diaz in which the idea of the good for the Mexican state was defined by the positivistic philosophy of the Frenchman Comte, supplemented, as Leopoldo Zea has shown, under the leadership of Justo Sierra with the British positivism of Mill and Spencer.

It is difficult to find a more obvious demonstration of the manner in which new philosophical ideas define an entirely new set of personal and social values for a given people and thereby lead to quite radical transformations in, if not the actual destruction of, traditional institutions, and to the creation of new social forms and facts in direct opposition to the old. If in natural science it is the task of theory to follow the facts, in social science there is a real and empirically verifiable sense in which the facts follow the theory. Consequently, in investigating social phenomena one must not merely observe what happens but must also examine the historical background to discover the ideas which have made the facts what they are. In the case of the social institutions and cultural forms of Mexico in the nineteenth century, both the facts and the philosophical ideas behind them are equally evident.

That is the century in which the Mexicans, led by the Catholic Father Hidalgo in 1810, revolted against the medieval political forms and values of the colonial period and instituted a democratic constitution and political organization with its typical, popularly and secularly grounded separation of powers and departments of the modern type. It is the century also in which the monasteries and seminaries of the Catholic Church were closed, parochial schools were not permitted, and the property of the church was nationalized.

These curbs were not, however, purely negative, any more than the very much more thorough confiscation and destruction of the remarkable Aztec civilization by the Spanish Catholic ideology of the colonial period were completely negative. In curbing or eliminating old cultural values and social institutions the modern French influence turned the nationalized and confiscated church property to its own different, but none the less ideal, ends.

Today, in Mexico City, for example, one finds that the building facing the Zócalo, constructed in the reigns of Charles II and Philip V in the architectural style of the colonial period out of actual fragments from the palaces of the Aztec Empire, is now called the National Palace and is used to house the offices of the President, his cabinet, and certain departments of the present constitutionally democratic government. Instead of a king or a royal governor, for whom the building was originally designed, appearing on its main balcony, there now stands each year at midnight on the fifteenth of September before a passionately noisy populace, the President of the Republic, who reaches above his head to toll the same bell which Father Hidalgo rang when he threw down Mexico's first challenge to the political ideals and practices of the Spanish dominion by shouting the Mexicans' first Declaration of Independence: "Long live our Most Holy Mother of Guadalupe! Long live the Republic of Mexico—and death to bad government!"

As we have previously noted, the convent of Nuestra Señora de la Encarnación, rebuilt in the colonial style even as late as 1922, now houses the Government's Department of Public Education. Likewise the simple, beautiful baroque mansion on Ribera de San Cosme, built by the Counts of Orizaba and suggestive in its inner patio of what Aristotle's Lyceum must have been like, is now the home of the Summer School and the Faculty of Philosophy and Letters of the National University. Likewise the former Jesuit Colegio de San Ildefonso, dating from 1618, forms another part of the secularized National University; the Jesuit Colegio de San Pedro y San Pablo near by is decorated in a naturalistic and patriotic theme with the lovely contemporary murals of Roberto Montenegro and is now Primary School No. 7; and the Church of St. Augustine is now the National Library. Another large block of edifices used in the colonial period for religious purposes is today packed in patio after patio with students studying physics, chemistry, and geology in the School of Mines; and, perhaps more appropriately, the Inquisition Building of the Dominican Order is now the School of Medicine.

These social facts are typical of a state of affairs extending over the whole of Catholic Mexico in which church property has been nationalized and turned to modern secular, democratic, political, and educational ends—a secularization which leaves the still virtually and predominantly Catholic Mexicans without the extensive freedom to possess their own parochial primary schools and universities which Catholics enjoy in the predominantly Protestant and very much more secularly minded United States.

Clearly such facts call for an explanation. Why should a Catholic people be so severe with Catholic institutions and property? It is to be emphasized that this severity is not of recent origin or brief duration. The Reform Laws, nationalizing all church property, were passed in 1857. It was these laws that brought English, Spanish, and French troops into Mexico in 1862, to lead in 1864 to the placing of Maximilian on the throne in Mexico City. So great was the reaction which followed that in 1867 Maximilian was shot, democracy was restored under Benito Juárez as President, and immediately the Reform Laws were enforced again. With the positivistically guided dictatorship of Porfirio Diaz the same secularization of education went on, with the Reform Laws still holding, although not so rigidly enforced. When the new democratic revolution occurred during the second decade of this century rigid enforcement returned. This carried on under the more recent regime of Lázaro Cárdenas, to be relaxed considerably only with the advent of the democratic government of Manuel Avila Camacho in 1940.

It is usual to find the explanation in the exploitation of the people by the priests. This seems to be Diego Rivera's thesis in his murals (Plate V). But there is also Guadalupe and the presence everywhere of its image of the Virgin. This does not indicate a Mexican people who conceive of the Church and its priests as evil exploiters. The economic argument seems to be more a pseudo-rationalization after the fact or a bit of propaganda used to bring the fact about, when the real motivation is in other sources, than the motivating cause itself. As Samuel Ramos has indicated, it is another, different set of ideals and values, predominantly political rather than religious or economic in character, not the exploitation of the people by the Catholic priests, which is the real cause of Catholic Mexicans' nationalization of their own church property.

The present visible character of this property confirms this conclusion. It is not the shoddy product of underfed slaves driven under the fear of hell-fire by exploiters. It has entirely too much integrity, it is entirely too original in its derivation and detailed designs, and it has had lavished on it entirely too much labor and devotion, to be anything other than a spontaneous, free creation of the Mexicans' spirit. The number of the churches, and their expensiveness, testify to the fact that most of the gifts of the people went to the religious and aesthetic ends for which the people intended them and not into the pockets of the priests or the coffers of Rome. Instead of complaining because the church took too much money out of their pockets, the real regret of the Mexicans was that they did not have more money to give. Clearly, only different and equally enticing values could win them in such large part away from the accustomed usages of the church's property to its present assignment for such different, purely secular, ends.

As Samuel Ramos and many other Mexicans have shown, these new values were first defined and made known to them by modern French philosophy. This French philosophy came to Mexico in two parts: one, the doctrine of Voltaire, Rousseau, D'Alembert, and the French Encyclopaedists which, during the first three-quarters of the nineteenth century, inaugurated the Mexican revolution and, in spite of interruptions, established and sustained democratic processes; the other, the later positivistic doctrine of Comte which, before coming to power, negatively supported democracy because of its attack upon medieval doctrines of any kind, but which, after coming to power, arbitrarily pushed democracy aside in the dictatorship of Porfirio Diaz between 1876 and 1910. Following the second democratic revolution, led by Francisco Madero in 1910 and completed by 1920, and coincident with the intellectual defeat of positivism achieved during the past thirty years by the philosophers Antonio Caso and José Vasconcelos, positivism and its dictatorship have been eliminated as a seriously considered political doctrine. At the same time, democracy has come back into power with increasing vitality, to be nourished by the paintings of Diego Rivera and David Siqueiros and to be supported in the Cárdenas and Camacho administrations with influences from Russia and especially from the United States.

The appeal of the modern democratic political and secular educational ideals introduced by the French influence is easy for us in the Anglo-American tradition to appreciate. To understand, however, why in a country predominantly Catholic these ideals led to the nationalization and confiscation of church property and a secularization of all education, going beyond anything experienced by Catholics in the United States, requires attention upon factors in the Mexican situation differing from those in the English-speaking democracies.

Before the modern democratic political ideals appeared in Mexico its political and religious philosophy was medieval. In England and the United States, however, before the modern democratic political ideas of Descartes, Rousseau, Locke, and Voltaire appeared, the people had passed through the Protestant Reformation. Although this Reformation was still medieval in its ideology, it none the less freed the religion of its followers from the property and institutions of the Roman Catholic Church. Having made this purely practical economic step away from the buildings which housed their medieval ideas, it was then easier for Protestants, when the new, modern ideas came in with the physics of Galilei and Newton and with the resultant philosophy of Descartes and Locke, to separate their religious feelings from the medieval philosophical and religious doctrine as well, and to associate them at least verbally with the new, modern scientific and philosophical assumptions without too great a sense of conflict. With the Mexicans, however, the medieval philosophical principles defining the monarchical form of government, which the acceptance of democracy forced them to reject, also defined their Catholic religion. Consequently, the acceptance of democracy was coupled in their minds with the repression of their religion.

Also, the fundamental scientific and philosophical ideas of the modern world and their attendant democratic political and secular educational consequences came to the Mexicans in the nineteenth century, instead of the seventeenth and eighteenth centuries, when they became influential in Great Britain and the United States. Had the people of the latter countries received them also at the later date it is by no means certain that modern science and philosophy and modern democracy would not have had the same extreme anti-religious consequences in the English-speaking world which they exhibit in Mexico. For in the eighteenth century the implications of the basic assumptions of the modern world as formulated by John Locke, upon which democracy rests in considerable part, were made explicit first in part by Berkeley and later completely by Hume to reveal their nominalistic and skeptical consequences, thereby making it exceedingly difficult to understand what meaning or justification there can be for the doctrines of the Christian religion. And in the nineteenth century, the natural evolutionary theory of Darwin and the social evolutionary theories of Comte, Spencer, and Sumner appeared, with their extremely positivistic emphases, according to which man's origin, nature, and cultural institutions are natural and secular in character.

The predominantly French source of Mexican democracy is also important. The English-speaking world, as the next chapter will show, received its democratic theory directly from its major original English source in John Locke. It might be thought, since French democracy is largely merely a systematic working out of the Newtonian and Lockean ideas which Voltaire brought to France following his visit in England, that this difference would be minor. But Locke in all his writings gave expression to the conventional religious sentiments carried over by habit from the medieval past, not realizing, as tended to become clear later, that on his own premises they were without meaning. Consequently, except for Thomas Paine, democratic ideas came to the English-speaking people directly from their main source with no disturbing, anti-religious associations.

In the hands of the acute Voltaire, however, Locke's ideas were a different thing. With Voltaire words about God and religion could not pass without having their meanings challenged. Before being admitted as anything more than noises they had quite rightly to be defined in terms of the modern assumptions to which Newton's physics and Locke's philosophy entitled one, just as Catholic, medieval religious concepts were defined, as the sequel will show, in terms of Aristotle's physics and St. Thomas's philosophy. Otherwise, one's religion would be presupposing still the medieval assumptions and Locke's, and the modern democratic, contention that the medieval political doctrine of the divine right of kings had to go would be quite unjustified. In this manner the semanticist Voltaire was led to see that the relation between the basic assumptions of modern democracy and of religion was not the simple, congenial one which Locke's language suggested. Quite the contrary. Consequently, for Voltaire, the acceptance of the scientific, philosophical, and democratic political doctrines of the modern world carried with it skepticism if not atheism, or at best deism with respect to religion.

The Mexicans' association of democracy with Rousseau did not help matters. For this Frenchman, the good life was to be found in "the state of nature." Evil was to be downed not merely by setting man free by means of democratic processes but also by removing the traditional "artificial" institutions which civilization had created. From this standpoint the Catholic religious and the monarchical political institutions and doctrines of the colonial period were on exactly the same footing. If democracy calls for the removal of the one, then it also calls for the removal of the other.

Comte gave to the Mexicans, in the name of modern social science, his law of the three stages of cultural development, according to which the first, theological or fictitious stage, as he termed it, passes over into the second, metaphysical or abstract stage, which in turn culminates in the scientific or positive stage. One has then but to identify the Spanish colonial period of Mexican history with the theological stage, and the democratic period from 1810 to 1876 with the metaphysical stage, to appreciate why the dictatorship of Porfirio Diaz, which took positivism as its model, extended science, secularized education, and felt it necessary to move away from, and curb, not merely the Christian religion but also democracy.

There is another difference between the Mexicans' and the Anglo-Americans' approach to democracy in its bearing on religion. For the Mexicans, art is a necessity of life, not a luxury; religion for them, if it is anything, is a passion, a moving, emotional experience. The culture of the Aztec period and that of the colonial period satisfied both these requirements. Also, Catholic theology, whatever its defects, is rigorously defined and consistently developed. Consequently, the Mexicans know what a doctrinally meaningful, aesthetically adequate, emotionally moving religion is like. For people of the English-speaking world, art tends to be a luxury or an afterthought, or else a hash of souvenirs without integrity because of the use of old art forms for modern institutions and doctrines which deny the theses which the art forms represent. With respect to art, the Protestant Church is scared. At its worst its art is crude; at its best neutral, preferring a pure white in the New England Congregational churches or a dull gray in the Episcopal chapels, which does not commit itself. A church with the diversity of vivid colors which the Indian aesthetic imagination demands would shock a Protestant congregation. But imagine, conversely, how the Protestant religion must appear to the religious Mexicans. Its exceedingly verbal preaching, its aesthetic color-blindness, and its emotional tepidity and coldness must make it look to them like no religion at all. All these considerations should help us to understand why democracy in the Latin-American countries and the complete secularization of life go together.

An even more surprising paradox remains. It arises when one asks how the Mexicans learned of the French ideas which produced their anti-religious, anti-Catholic reaction. The answer is that they were taught these French ideas, every one of which is on the Index, by the Roman Catholic Church itself.

The evidence for this is clear. The French came into Mexico, to be sure, in 1862, but the Frenchmen who came were soldiers, not teachers or skeptical democratic philosophers. They entered, moreover, because of the appeal to Europe to remove the Reform Laws which had nationalized the church property. Hence, the French soldiers did not bring the French philosophical ideas which had produced the supposed evil they came to remove. The Reform Laws were passed in 1857, several years before the French came. Moreover, the democratic revolution occurred much earlier, in 1810. It was led by Miguel Hidalgo. Hidalgo was a Catholic priest. He had read and taught his followers the unorthodox French philosophical doctrines. Because of this, in 1811, he was, as Anita Brenner has written, "unfrocked, excommunicated, and executed." Nevertheless, it is important to remember that he had the support of the Madonna of Guadalupe. Immediately, he was succeeded by José Maria Morelos. The new leader also was a priest, and, as Samuel Ramos indicates, "was prosecuted in the Inquisition for his devotion to the French Encyclopaedists." Nevertheless, he obtained a great following. One of the present states of Mexico bears his name.

That one or two individual priests should do this is perhaps not too surprising, but upon further investigation one finds that they did not read these forbidden books surreptitiously; instead, they taught them openly in official Jesuit Roman Catholic colleges. Nicolas Rangel, in his *Preliminar a los precursores ideológicos de la Independencia, 1789-1794,* writes that "a complete course of modern philosophy" was taught "which relegated Aristotelianism to oblivion, in order to replace it with Cartesianism." He adds: "In this work of preparation and of social transformation it is impossible to forget the Jesuit Creoles—Clavijero, Abad, Alegre, Guevara, and many others—who, in the colleges of the country, spread abroad the new idea in order to get ready for the advent of independence." In fact, Samuel Ramos tells us that "the Royal and Pontifical Seminary of Mexico was a focus of the insurrection."

The second paradox presented by French nineteenth century Mexican culture is now evident. Its official Catholic colleges and seminaries, and in particular the Jesuit branches, taught the unorthodox French philosophical doctrines on the Index at Rome, which produced the confiscation and nationalization of the church property. Additional evidences of unorthodoxy in Mexico's Roman Catholicism appear in the contemporary period.

CONTEMPORARY MEXICO

While preserving and extending the secular development of education, the pursuit of science as a human value, and the principles of French political democracy, contemporary Mexico has modified or departed from its French culture of the nineteenth century in four major ways: (1) the philosophical and political rejection of positivism with the development of a new and creative humanism; (2) the extension of French legal democracy to include Anglo-American economic and cultural values; (3) the suggested combination of Anglo-American democracy with certain Russian economic values; and (4) a reaction against all these secular trends to the Spanish individualistic, or the orthodox Catholic, hierarchical, religious and philosophical values of the colonial period. How these four developments, each one of which is vital, are to be reconciled is the fundamental present problem of Mexico's culture and politics.

The rejection of positivism in the political sphere dates from the second democratic revolution in 1910 which overthrew the dictatorship of Porfirio Diaz. Samuel Ramos informs us that a "revolutionary intellectual movement" with the support of the Minister of Public Education, "antedates by two years the political revolution which broke out in 1910." The intellectual revolution was important. This is shown by the fact that it has persisted, growing in strength and influence up to the present moment, and that the victory of democracy over the dictatorship and positivism was not consolidated in the political sphere until the new constitution of 1917 under Venustiano Carranza and the regime of Alvaro Obregón in the twenties.

The new intellectual movement supported by Justo Sierra, which nursed and sustained the reborn and reconstructed democracy, took two main forms: First, positivism was shorn of its appeal to the imagination by a critique pursued by the philosophers Antonio Caso and José Vasconcelos which revealed its inadequacy in the face of the facts of cultural history and the inescapable, intuitive aesthetic and emotional components of the Indian and the Spanish spirit. Second, a large and distinguished group of philosophically minded creative poets, essayists, and statesmen, including Alfonso Reyes, Pedro Henríquez Ureña, Eduardo Colin and González Martínez, created a richer and more historically enlightened humanism in its place. The two movements were fostered in their earlier period by the intuitive philosophy of the Frenchman Henri Bergson. Recently the defeat of positivism has been made triply secure by the advent throughout Mexico and the whole of South America of the phenomenological and axiological philosophy of Edmund Husserl, Max Scheler, and Nicolai Hartmann.

Introduced by the popular and brilliant writings of the Spaniard Ortega y Gasset, the latter doctrine represents the most vital philosophical movement in the Latin-American world at the present time. Its appeal is by no means restricted to professional philosophers. Legal thinkers, psychologists, essayists, and students of art such as Justino Fernández, have been profoundly and permanently influenced. This phenomenological philosophy of Husserl and his followers is doing for the Latin-American world in the twentieth century what the ethics of Bishop Butler and of Kant did for the English-speaking world in the nineteenth century. One need have no fear of the return of a positivistically oriented dictatorship in Mexico.

The philosophical and political defeat of positivism was a rejection not merely of Diaz and dictatorship but also of the last and culminating French influence. This made it natural for the Mexicans upon their return to democracy to be guided for the first time predominantly by the United States and by Anglo-American rather than French thought in their politics.

In Europe, after Locke and Voltaire, had come Hume's positivistic criticism and the hedonism of Bentham and Mill. This, following the earlier ideas of Adam Smith, gave rise in Jevons to a rejection of Ricardo's theory of value from which Marx's economic communism derives, and, as supplemented by the influence of the Austrian School of economists, led to the psychological theory of value upon which the accepted economic theory of the English-speaking world is now built. Consequently, to the purely political democracy of Descartes, Locke, and Voltaire was added the predominantly economic democracy of Bentham, Mill, Jevons, Marshall, Taussig, and countless other Anglo-American thinkers. Consequently, to take the United States rather than France as her democratic model in this century means that just as Mexico was dominated by "the religious passion" in the colonial period and by "the political passion" in the nineteenth century, so now she is in great part motivated by the economic passion.

It might be supposed that Mexico's long and difficult struggle during the second decade of this century to re-establish democracy, taking the United States rather than France as her model, would receive the wholehearted support of her neighbor to the north. The facts were, however, quite to the contrary. In 1914, during Mexico's struggling democratic revolution, Woodrow Wilson and his country, which a few years later were to fight a "war to save democracy," sent an army into Mexico. To be sure, the situation was trying, but revolutions, even when led by democrats in the United States, England, or France, are rough, upsetting, and erratic things. Also, the disturbances of the revolution were not the sole cause of the military invasion. The truth, as Anita Brenner has shown, is that the regime which all too many in the United States and Great Britain then or since really liked was the dictatorship of Diaz.

This is not an accident. It had its basis in a common ideological factor.

As the next chapter will show, the period in the United States paralleling the Diaz dictatorship in Mexico was characterized by a shift of emphasis from political to economic values. In this shift the statesman gave way to the businessman as the national hero. Freedom became identified less with political liberty and more with economic freedom to accumulate material wealth. Also, sound political action was conceived as requiring the recognition of the laws of economic science. This economic science was grounded in the positivistic empiricism of Bentham and Mill.

Similarly, in his *Apogee and Decadence of Positivism in Mexico,* Leopoldo Zea has shown that the Diaz dictatorship restricted political liberty (hence the dictatorship) in the interests of economic free enterprise, thereby making the political order the servant of the "interests of those individuals who form the bourgeoisie," and that the latter thereby "acquired the great freedom to exploit the economy of the country to their profit." This "sacrifice of political liberty for economic riches" was justified by an appeal to economic and social science. In fact, the Union Liberal Party in Mexico which inaugurated and sustained the dictatorship was called the "Party of the Scientists." "Politics," they said, "should be the object of a special technique. It cannot possibly be the work of all the Mexicans, but only of a specialized group, the technicians of politics, the scientists." It is necessary, they added, "to know the natural laws and their relations in order thereby to be able to establish the conditions of order adequate to the evolution of society." These natural laws were in sociology those of Comte or Spencer and in economics those of Bentham and Mill.

With respect to this community of economic ideals between Mexico and the United States during the Diaz dictatorship, the Mexicans were in no doubt. Leopoldo Zea writes: "The Mexicans of this epoch had great faith in industrial progress as an instrument of social order. The model of this order was the United States."

This admiration was reciprocated. For under Porfirio Diaz North American and British capitalists and their engineers went into Mexico. The Diaz dictatorship is called by them, not untruthfully, "the Golden Age." From the standpoint of the efficiency of the railways, the production of petroleum, the development of the mines, and the pursuit of science and secular education along restrictedly practical lines, they are right. But unfortunately neither the industries nor the government belonged to the people of Mexico. Everything was undoubtedly more efficient and orderly, but the last thing one could say of it was that it was democratic or Mexican.

Nor was the situation under the Good Neighbor Policy installed by President Franklin Roosevelt as completely different as one might suppose. For the exchanges in this century between the Mexican government and former Secretary Hull with respect to the oil and mineral holdings of United States corporations in Mexico have to do with legal titles which go back to the Diaz regime in the late nineteenth century. Furthermore, Secretary Hull's arguments were precisely those of Secretary Kellogg under President Coolidge, Secretary Polk under President Wilson, and Secretary Root under President Taft. What must be realized throughout all these events and exchanges is that we are confronted not with one party which is right and another party which is wrong, but with two conflicting ideas of the economic good.

The crux of the matter will be understood if one notes that in the Spanish colonial period most of the rich agricultural land in Mexico went into the hands of a relatively few Spanish Mexican landowners living in large *haciendas* and that in the Diaz dictatorship practically all of the mineral and oil deposits of Mexico went under the ownership of corporations in Great Britain and the United States. The extent to which this occurred is shown by the fact that at the beginning of the Cárdenas Government in 1934, practically all of the oil resources of Mexico were under foreign ownership.

It happened, therefore, following the second democratic revolution, in 1910, when the Mexican people attempted to take the political democracy of the United States as their model and attempted to reap, in a higher standard of living for their people, what the more universal, secular, scientific, public education of the previous century had sown, that they found their similarity with the United States, notwithstanding all their efforts, remaining more nominal than real. Thus it became increasingly clear to them during the second decade of this century that they could only reap the fruits of their education, scientific training and labor by at least a partial return of the economic natural resources of their country to Mexican ownership.

The Mexicans encountered a second difficulty. When they attempted to regain a reasonable portion of their own national economic resources they found themselves confronted not merely by an international law which had been formulated by Great Britain, the United States, and others during an imperialistic era but also, as examination of the Anglo-

American culture of the United States will show, by a political idealism grounded in the Lockean philosophy of the state, which underlies the Declaration of Independence and the Constitution of the United States. As will be shown in the next chapter, according to this Lockean theory the justification for the existence of government is the preservation of private property. Under these circumstances even the most elementary attempt upon the part of the Mexican Government to establish economic justice within its own country by regaining some of its natural resources would appear to the United States and Great Britain, as it did to Woodrow Wilson in 1916, as a breach not merely of traditional international law but also of the elementary principles of political morality. This international impasse, which is philosophical in its origin and basis, constitutes not merely the fundamental problem of Mexican foreign policy but also one of the inescapable problems in international relations throughout the entire world in the twentieth century.

The first attempt of the Mexican Government to resolve this problem based itself on an appeal to Woodrow Wilson's thesis that "human rights are above property rights." It is an interesting commentary on the impotence of lofty, purely verbal moral sentiments to alter the conduct of even those who utter them, when the basic traditional philosophy which is incorporated in one's national constitution and in international law is to the contrary, that neither Woodrow Wilson's Secretary of State nor Woodrow Wilson himself was impressed by this argument; nor were their successors Secretary Hull and President Franklin D. Roosevelt when the argument was first presented to them in 1933. This is true notwithstanding the fact that President Roosevelt in 1943 at Monterrey reiterated the Wilsonian sentiment, giving it an even more explicit economic content.

The exchange of correspondence between Secretary Hull and the Mexican Foreign Minister of the Cárdenas regime with respect to the attempt of the Mexican Government to get certain natural resources back into Mexican hands is illuminating. It shows that our foreign relations bring us face to face with a conflict of ideological values, fundamentally philosophical in character, which needs to be made explicit and brought out into the open instead of covered up with verbal ambiguities which seem to place the United States on a lofty, noble, and generous plane, but which to the Latin Americans, if taken seriously, can only produce false hopes, followed by later disillusionment and bitterness and which, if not taken seriously, add another fact to support the traditional Latin-American belief that the people of the north "talk big" in terms of the most high and humane principles but do not mean what they seem to say.

The Mexican Government's reply to Secretary Hull's protest concerning the taking over of property owned by United States corporations for a remuneration specified by the democratically elected Cárdenas Government, pointed out two things: (1) In the Pan-American Conference at Montevideo in 1933, all the American nations agreed to extend to aliens all the rights enjoyed by each nation's own citizens. (2) The taking over of the properties of American citizens for a remuneration specified by the duly constituted democratic Mexican Government is an application of the aforesaid Montevideo principle, since the citizens of the United States are treated in precisely the same manner as are similarly situated Mexican citizens. That this is true is shown by what has actually happened to the large Spanish Mexican landholdings. It was clear that the chicks which Secretary Hull had helped to hatch in Montevideo had come home to roost in Washington.

But Secretary Hull was not without a relevant answer. His appeal, like that of the Republican Secretary of State Root in 1910 and the Democratic Acting Secretary of State Polk in Wilson's administration, was to an international law, affecting aliens, known as the "minimum standard." According to this law there are certain limits below which a nation cannot go in international relations without duties and responsibilities under international law. This does not prevent a nation from going beneath these standards in the treatment of its own citizens, but if the nation so acts it cannot make this a basis under an equality of treatment of aliens and citizens principle, such as that agreed upon at Montevideo, for evading the minimum standard treatment of aliens guaranteed by international law. Edwin Borchard in a discussion of this correspondence and in a defense of this principle points out, also, that at the conference at Lima for the codification of international law, the United States Government in accepting the equality of treatment for aliens and citizens "made a long reservation to this convention, reserving its rights under international law."

Nevertheless, this does not dispose of the matter. Edwin Borchard points out that "the existence of the standard and its service as a criterion of international responsibility in specific instances by no means gives us a definition of its content." Consequently, Secretary Hull in order to establish his point had to make one further assumption; namely, that the primacy of property rights is one of the accepted principles of international law falling under the minimum standard. That he made this additional assumption his reply of August 22, 1938, proves since he insisted that international law under the minimum standard protects "both human and property rights." But this assumption rests upon the Anglo-American Lockean doctrine of the primacy of property rights. Now it is precisely the validity of this principle which is the point at issue not merely in this dispute, but everywhere throughout the world today in the problem of the relation between the Lockean, purely political democracy, and the more recent economic democracy, within which the Marxian economic theory is a special case. Thus Secretary Hull's reply, instead of disposing of the matter as it at first seems to do, merely placed our traditional theory of political and economic value over against the Mexican Government's different theory. If taken as resolving the conflict, it begged the point at issue.

Moreover, even on Lockean Anglo-American assumptions under international law the position is none too secure. For according to the modern philosophy of the state, and especially the Anglo-American Lockean one, there are no social laws given by nature or by divine right; there are only laws in so far as they are made and entered into with the consent of the governed. Also, by the same reasoning, these laws can be changed with the consent of the governed. While it is probably true, as Secretary Hull assumes, that the guarantee of property rights has traditionally fallen within the minimum standard, even though this is by no means as explicitly stated as a minimum standard principle itself, this means merely that international law in the past was agreed upon by states which accepted the Lockean philosophy. *Now it is precisely this inclusion of the Lockean principle of the primacy of property rights over human, social, or economic needs which not merely Mexico and other South American countries but also newly constituted democratic republics such as Czechoslovakia and China, and a growing body of public opinion in Great Britain and the United States also, are refusing to accept.* This fact makes it clear that the specific issues in contemporary international relations involve a conflict of economic, political, and philosophical assumptions concerning what is good which can be resolved upon a basis of law and principle without bitterness or bloodshed, only if the differing theoretical assumptions are brought out into the open and some new, more catholic and comprehensive theory for reconciling them is brought forward, upon which a new codification of the minimum standard in international law can be based.

Secretary Hull's reply to the Mexican Government was not decisive even when approached intuitively without regard to theory and legal principles. It is one thing for a country such as the United States to welcome and insist upon the inclusion of the protection of private property rights within the minimum standard principle when, due to the fact that its citizens own practically all of its natural resources as well as large natural resources abroad, the insistence upon such a high minimum standard can bring about no great losses at home and great gains abroad. It is quite a different thing, and one can hardly imagine the Senators from the western silver-mining States acquiescing in it, were their States in Mexico rather than the United States, when the inclusion of the protection of the property rights doctrine in the minimum standard clause means, as it does for Mexico, the taking of the small amount of valuable natural resources owned by Mexicans away from one's own citizens and the leaving of the vastly larger amount of Mexico's valuable assets in the hands of foreigners. Again, to understand Mexico's internal and foreign policy since 1910, it must be realized that Mexico came to the task of extending the values of modern thought from the political to the economic sphere after the Spanish colonial period had placed most of the valuable land of the country in the hands of a relatively few landowners and the Diaz dictatorship had placed a considerable portion of her most valuable oil and mineral deposits under foreign ownership.

We may be sure that this questioning of the inclusion of the Lockean doctrine of the primacy of property rights in the minimum standard principle will persist. Nor should it be identified with communism even though the growing influence of Russia will give it additional impetus. Neither Czechoslovakia nor China was communistic when it took the same stand which the Cárdenas Government of Mexico took in 1933. Nor was the Cárdenas Government a communistic government; it went in and went out of power by a democratic vote and unquestionably represented the opinion of a majority of the people.

China was not troubled by tremendous holdings of her natural resources by a few foreigners. She did want, however, to get rid of the concessions held by Great Britain, France, Japan, and the United States in her own port cities. It naturally did not seem fair to China that she should reimburse these intruding nations for what, to the Chinese, did not belong to them in the first place. Czechoslovakia had been under German domination for three centuries before she became a democracy in the last war. The legal titles to her landed estates and her resources were largely in Austrian or German hands. It did not seem fair to her to be able to confiscate the large holdings of her own citizens which after three hundred years of Austro-German control were negligible, and to be unable to touch the large landed estates which were in the hands of the old German invaders. Yet this is precisely the position in which the insistence on the inclusion of the sanctity of property rights in the minimum standard principle places a nation before international law when it finds most of its economic resources in the hands of foreigners.

The reply of the Mexican Government to Secretary Hull, in its two notes of August 3 and September 3, 1938, makes another point clear. As quoted by Edwin Borchard, it stated that "there is no international obligation to make compensation for the expropriation of property, . . . provided a social purpose is served." Clearly, this refers to the verbal contention of every administration of the United States dating back to Woodrow Wilson, and of the politicians and preachers behind the administrations, that property rights are not sacrosanct in themselves but are justified only by human rights and needs. It is one of the distinct merits of Secretary Hull's reply, which merely repeated what every Secretary of State before him in this century had said in concrete cases, that it brings out into the open the fact that the leaders of the Good Neighbor Policy, for all their suggestive oratory to the contrary, have no more departed in principle from the traditional Anglo-American Lockean principle of the primacy of property rights than did Herbert Hoover's administration or those of Calvin Coolidge and Woodrow Wilson. For when all the public, moral sentiments were brought face to face with a test case it turned out that the policy of the United States still rested on the sanctity of property rights irrespective of human and social needs, regardless of the verdict of the Mexicans expressed through democratic processes to the contrary.

The point of all this is not that the traditional Lockean principle of the primacy of property rights may not be justified at least in internal national policy. It even may be the case, as the contemporary followers of Locke maintain, that the preservation of private property rights is the best way to maintain and preserve human values. This is a question to which we must turn later, one which cannot be effectively discussed until a method is designated for determining the correctness of one philosophical theory of value such as Locke's as compared with another theory such, for example, as the utilitarian, the Marxian, or the Confucian.

These considerations indicate that the time has come when one must either stop talking about the priority of human rights over property rights, and of economic as well as political democracy for every people everywhere, regardless of whether they possess titles to the resources within their national borders or not; or else define the terms carefully and develop a set of principles from which new laws both national and international can be derived which can be used to resolve on a basis of principle the disputes to which the hopes raised by such words give rise. More specifically, we had better stop making general statements in the Fourteen Points, in the Atlantic Charter, at Monterrey, and elsewhere about economic as well as political democratic justice, until we have thought through what, under democratic processes such as those bringing into power the democratic governments of Mexico since 1910, our words may reasonably be supposed to mean, and we are prepared in practice to accept the consequences.

Conversely, there *may* be nothing wrong about the corporations of the United States and Great Britain having property rights in Mexico for which they demand greater legal protection and financial remuneration under international law than the Mexican Government finds it wise in the interests of democracy to accord to its own citizens. But if this is what we mean, then our humanistic, democratic professions should be explicitly presented in these Lockean terms. More specifically, our Presidents and preachers in their public addresses should restrict their "moral leadership of mankind" to the identical principle to which they authorize their Secretaries of State to appeal in carrying out this "moral leadership" in practice.

It must be pointed out also that no policy of the United States with respect to Mexico could have been more effectively designed than was the literal insistence upon the property rights interpretation of the minimum standard international law to persuade the Mexicans that it is impossible to extend democracy in their country from the political to the economic sphere without replacing the Lockean with the Marxian philosophy. This in fact is the point of the frescoes of Diego Rivera and David Siqueiros and their tremendous influence. Nothing was more incongruous than to place a fresco by Diego Rivera—of all places—in Rockefeller Center! Once one goes behind the bare color and form of Rivera's work to the precise conception of one part of the good life which it is conveying, it will not be surprising that the result was unhappy.

The basic human value which Diego Rivera is portraying is that of the imaginations of men freed and fascinated by scientific knowledge, and of their social and economic well-being raised by the application of its principles to agriculture, mining, the harnessing of the waterfalls, and industry. This shows in the Rockefeller Center fresco (Plate V), now in the Palace of Fine Arts in Mexico City, in the scientifically guided hand of man grasping the controls, symbolized in the center of the fresco, by means of which the growing crops and developed industries at its base are generated. It shows also in the ecstasy on the faces of the children located in the lower left hand corner of the painting (not shown in Plate V) when their imaginations are caught by this human ideal, as Darwin, symbolizing scientific knowledge, who is located behind them, whispers his teaching into their ears. All this fits Rockefeller Center as perfectly as it applies to the needs of Mexico.

It is in the remainder of the fresco that the deviations and the conflict appear. To understand these essential, additional items it is necessary to keep three previously noted factors in mind: *First*, the Spanish colonial period, dominated by the aesthetic and religious values and the hierarchical aristocratic social forms of medieval culture, had placed most of the rich agricultural land of Mexico in the hands of a relatively few predominantly Spanish landowners; and the French nineteenth century, with its political democratic, secular, and positivistically scientific values, had allowed most of the mineral and oil reserves to fall under foreign ownership. *Second,* following the coming of the second democratic revolution, of 1910, the failure of the scientific education of the nineteenth century to bring forth the higher standard of living for the entire Mexican people which had been expected convinced more and more Mexicans that all their universal education, their science, and their labors would redound merely to the profit of the Church of Rome and the foreign capitalists, unless the natural resources of Mexico could be returned to the Mexican people. Otherwise, try as they would to copy the United States by extending democracy from the political to the economic sphere, their efforts would be in vain. *Third,* the attempt during the second and third decades of this century to regain these resources inside the assumptions of Anglo-American political and economic theory had been met in 1916–17 with an invasion by the United States Army and continuously by a literal insistence upon the property rights interpretation of the minimum standard principle in international law. Need we wonder, therefore, that Diego Rivera, after he had become acquainted with the Marxian economic doctrine during his study of painting in Paris around 1920, returned to Mexico to portray a new idea of the good in which French and Anglo-American scientifically grounded political democracy is combined with certain elements of Russian economic democracy? The point was that as long as political democracy is combined with the Anglo-American Lockean philosophical insistence upon the primacy of property rights over human needs Mexico's problem is insoluble, regardless of how much universal education she has and how much scientific knowledge she applies. Without the return of the natural resources of Mexico to the Mexican people, all their pursuit of universal education, of democracy, and of scientific technology will merely increase the flow of wealth abroad, in the form either of contributions to Rome or of dividends to Lombard and Wall Streets.

This is why, in the right hand center of Diego Rivera's Rockefeller Center fresco (Plate V), Lenin is shown putting together the hand of scientific control and the hand of the native Mexican; and why, above his head, the workers and peasants are shown marching forward, supporting one of their members with a red flag while the conical domes of Russia show in the background. It is the reason also why in the left center of the fresco, where the alternative is exhibited, a wealthy group of American bridge players, including John D. Rockefeller, Jr., symbolizing the Standard Oil Company, are portrayed beside a Wall Street stock ticker and why, beyond them, appear very healthy priests symbolizing Rome. Nor is this left portion of the fresco purely fanciful. For Anita Brenner, informed resident and student of Mexico, tells us that again and again, when the Mexican people have attempted to make their economic democracy more real and effective, they have found themselves continuously opposed by two institutions in the world: the State Departments of the United States and Great Britain, and the Roman Catholic Church.

Again we must avoid jumping excitedly to a hasty conclusion. What we are confronted with here is not a simple issue between the good and the bad, but a conflict of differing ideas of the good. Neither the Mexicans nor any other people have yet learned how to resolve this conflict of values. It cannot even be understood, to say nothing about being solved, without a knowledge of the differing scientific and philosophical conceptions of the nature of man and the universe from which it stems. This must concern us in the sequel.

Note, however, what Diego Rivera and his colleague David Siqueiros have done. They have provided the world with a new political and economic philosophy in which French and Anglo-American political democracy is combined with certain elements in Russian economic communism. Considering the background of Mexican experience we hardly need wonder at their influence. But unless one recalls the tremendous part which art and particularly painting have played continuously in the culture of Mexico from even its earliest Indian beginnings, one can hardly grasp the magnitude of this influence. Moreover, the frescoes of these two creative and arresting Mexican painters have, since 1920, covered the walls not merely of the patios of the Secretariat of Public Education but also of the National Preparatory School and the National University, even entering into the National Palace and the Palace of Fine Arts and extending to the Cortés Palace at Cuernavaca and to other major Mexican cities. Over the past twenty-five years each Mexican student has had this idea of the good put movingly and arrestingly before him as he walked through corridor after corridor of the higher institutions of learning. In the light of all this the wonder is not that Mexican policy has come at points into conflict with the legal and political doctrines of the United States, but that in her internal and international behavior she has been as restrained and conventional as has been the case.

Two factors have contributed to this state of affairs. One is the unequivocal democracy of the Cárdenas Government between 1934 and 1940 which, coming after fifteen years of influence by Diego Rivera and David Siqueiros, caught the full brunt of their influence. Clearly something had to be done to bring the natural resources of Mexico under Mexican ownership and control. No government could have remained in power which sidestepped this issue any longer. The Cárdenas regime had no alternative, therefore, but to raise the issue in unequivocal terms with the State Department of the United States and the Foreign Office of the British Government. Its hand was strengthened by the fact that it went into office in 1934 and it went out of office in 1940 by thoroughly democratic processes; also, by the fact that during and since its administration the cultural forms of the United States have been more and more incorporated into Mexican life. This is shown unequivocally in the automobiles and buses from Detroit, the moving pictures from Hollywood, the skyscrapers and business practices from New York, the baseball games and horse-racing which are now competing with bull-fighting, and even in the increasingly significant interest in the literature, science, and philosophy of the neighbor to the north.

The other factor is that, thanks to the foundations for understanding between Mexico and the United States constructed by Dwight Morrow and to the Good Neighbor Policy initiated by President Roosevelt and Secretary Hull, the latter—very wisely, in the final stages of the negotiations—did not insist upon the letter of the minimum standard law, as he had previously interpreted it, but instead accepted a compromise. Previously the Sinclair Oil Company had come quite independently of the State Department to the same type of settlement. It is to the great credit of Secretary Hull and the Foreign Ministers of the governments of Cárdenas and Camacho that they have gone so far and so amicably toward such a settlement, especially when the people of the United States, at least, have not appreciated the conflict of economic ideals and cultural values which lies behind the negotiations. The superb achievements of the more recent Chapultepec Conference are also a glorious tribute to the wisdom of the statesmen of the Americas and to the Good Neighbor policy. From these very real and practical beginnings it should be possible to go on to the facing and reconciling of the rival cultural ideals and values, of the different countries, which must occur if Pan-Americanism is to become a deeply rooted and spontaneous movement of the American spirit.

With the advent of the Camacho Government in 1940 one other factor entered into the contemporary Mexican scene. This is a relaxing of the repression of religion which had accompanied the traditional Mexican democracy since 1810, and an attendant revival of humanistic as opposed to merely positivistic, and Spanish colonial in addition to merely French nineteenth century, values.

This vital contemporary development in Mexican culture has many sources. One is the emphasis upon the aesthetic intuition and the individual, mystical, religious passion by the philosopher José Vasconcelos in his critique of positivism. Another is the influence throughout Mexico and the whole of Latin America of the very popular individualistic and socially anarchistic writings of the Spaniard Miguel de Unamuno. A third is the recently growing interest in the works of the German philosopher Heidegger, with their somewhat similar emphasis upon human experience as being laden with care. A fourth is the revival of neo-Scholasticism, as evidenced by the fact that in 1943 both the Rector of the National University and the Chairman of its Department of Philosophy were orthodox Thomists. Even more important, since it is led by humanists with an appreciation of the riches of the whole history of Western civilization rather than by neo-Thomists, with their restriction to the merely Aristotelian and Thomistic Western values, is the rebirth of intense scholarly study of the culture of the colonial period and its historical roots in the European philosophical and literary tradition as evidenced (a) by the Institute for Aesthetic Investigation directed by the scholarly expert in colonial art, Manuel Toussaint, and (b) by the Colegio de Mexico, presided over by the distinguished humanist Alfonso Reyes.

An additional evidence is the moving devotion at Guadalupe and the frank showing of its image of the Virgin everywhere, even on the banners of the democratic reformers as well as in the permanent construction of the most modernistic of contemporary apartment houses. Perhaps most important of all, certainly the most striking in their appeal to "the passion of the Spanish soul" and to the aesthetic intuition of the Indians' spirit, are the frescoes of José Clemente Orozco, especially in the light of the brilliant and profound exposition of them, commending them to contemporary intellectuals, given by Justino Fernández. In fact, José Orozco's art conveys analogically in vivid, emotionally moving, aesthetic materials the philosophical doctrine of this fourth vital movement in contemporary Mexican culture just as Diego Rivera's frescoes function for its third movement.

José Orozco's most striking, important, and universal symbol is fire. Justino Fernández informs us that for Orozco it always symbolizes the human spirit. Its two most notable uses are in the cupola of El Hospicio Cabañas at Guadalajara, and facing the stairway in the House of Tiles in Mexico City. At the former place the fire is seen completely enflaming a human body straining and immersed within it (Plate VI). As Justino Fernández has shown, this expresses the essence of the human consciousness as a tragic yet glorious commitment—tragic because for all man's voluntary, free struggle for specific ideals he is thwarted, even punished, because of the conflict with other, equally human values and impulses, both good and bad; glorious because, notwithstanding the inevitable defeat and failure, man, exercising the freedom of his own spirit, makes his choice and accepts the consequences. Clearly this is no pragmatic philosophy; nor is it a utilitarian hedonism.

The same theme appears in a different symbolism at Pomona College in José Orozco's superbly and classically modeled Prometheus pressing against an arched ceiling which cannot be raised. The virtue of man is all the greater because there is no successful pragmatic reward for his free act at its end. The influence of the Spanish philosopher Unamuno's "Agony of Christianity" and "Tragic Sense of Life" is evident. Why Heidegger's philosophical designation of the essence of human existence as *Sorge*, or care, should also take root in this soil is equally clear. One also understands why it is not a cheap desire to shock people but essential to José Orozco's purpose that he presents the evil, carnal, brutal, and murderous aspects of man's nature as well as the sublime, in all their nakedness, as he does in the large fresco which covers the entire end wall, opposite Rivera's re-creation of the Rockefeller Center fresco, in the Palace of the Fine Arts in Mexico City.

At no point do the values of the Indian and the Spanish spirit stand in greater contrast to those of the Anglo-American people to their north than in these frescoes of Orozco: Spanish America with its conviction that tragedy, brutality, chaos, failure, and death, as well as triumph and compassion, aim at order, and earthly life are an essential part of the glory of man; Anglo-America with its pollyannic tendency, its Christian Science, its life under the elms as if there were no desire there also, its worship of the successful businessman, its formal Kantian idealism empty of empirical content, and its pragmatism making even truth itself dependent upon a successful reward at the end. This opposition must be understood and reconciled if Pan-Americanism is ever to become a spontaneous movement of the spirit.

Orozco is not unmindful of this opposition. This is part of the meaning of his fresco at Dartmouth College of the school teacher with her blank-faced self and pupils, entitled the "Anglo-American Soul." But before we can grasp its full import we must go a little deeper into the artist's Spanish-American philosophy of value and its critique of the differing Anglo-American theory. The criticism is that a philosophy of life which shuts its eyes to the creative fire in man's nature, to the *éros* or frenzy in all its human manifestations so cuts man's soul off from the fresh, warm, bodily, earthly feeling of life and from the emotional, aesthetic and spiritual component of man's nature, that one becomes artificial, stereotyped, without individuality of the feelings, sentiments and imagination, afraid of one's emotions, tense, and often colorless or neurotic. One's Kantian or pollyannic ideals, being so purely formal and artificial, become so separated from one's real, emotional, bodily, and spiritual being that the sparkle goes out of both. The pupils and parishioners become as dull as their teachers and preachers. Moreover, a faulty political idealism is created in which the ideal is so divorced from the actual in human nature or international relations that art becomes empty or vapid and one's political aims become equally unrealistic and ethereal, while one's actual conduct and behavior tend to be left to crass, independent, self-centered opportunism, the reverse of one's idealistic professions. Thus the United States, after 1918, followed Woodrow Wilson in theory and Warren Harding in fact.

Before one concludes that José Orozco's Dartmouth fresco is the

Plate V FRESCO. DIEGO RIVERA. PALACE OF THE FINE ARTS, MEXICO CITY.
Courtesy of the Museum of Modern Art

THE CONTEMPORARY THEORETIC COMPONENT IN MEXICAN PAINTING

Plate VI MAN IN FLAMES. JOSÉ OROZCO.
DOME OF ORPHANAGE AT GUADALAJARA
Courtesy of Museum of Modern Art

THE SUBLIME TRAGEDY OF THE DETERMINATE
FREE HUMAN SPIRIT

Plate VII HANDS AND FLAMES. JOSÉ OROZCO.
THE HOUSE OF TILES, MEXICO, D. F.
Courtesy of F. Wilbur Seideos

THE AESTHETIC MATERIALS SYMBOLIZING
THE THEORETIC COMPONENT

Plate VIII OMNISCIENCE. JOSÉ OROZCO.
HOUSE OF TILES, MEXICO, D. F.
Courtesy of F. Wilbur Seideos

THE FEMALE AESTHETIC OMNISCIENCE

biased view of a foreigner, the reader will do well to recall Grant Wood's "American Gothic" and "Daughters of Revolution" (Plate IX). One other fact must be noted: The initial modern conception of the personality, especially for the English-speaking portion of the modern world, was introduced and defined by John Locke. For Locke, as Chapter III will show, the soul in its essence is a blank tablet. It is precisely this contrast between such an Anglo-American soul and the Spanish and Mexican soul whose essence is passion that José Orozco is portraying.

Orozco also helps one to appreciate Ernest Hemingway's "Death in the Afternoon" and the Spanish bull-fight, which the Mexicans attend with a demand so far exceeding the supply of seats that, despite continuous protests, neither the newspapers nor the government can check the ticket scalpers. Clearly, in this passionately pursued sport of the Spanish and Indian Mexicans, death is very real; but there is very much more in addition. For the aim is not, as in games in the United States, upon the end of the contest—the victory, the killing of the bull; nor is it, as in Great Britain, upon the utilitarian exercise and building of character for some later triumph at Waterloo which one is supposed to achieve in the process. Instead, it is upon living dangerously (and let anyone master the rules within which the matador must operate before he concludes that this sport is not dangerous), and upon the artistry with which the aesthetic ritual is pursued. With complete freedom of action before one of the possible formalized movements is selected, but rigidly fixed, his feet frozen to the ground regardless of what the bull does, once a particular movement is initiated, the matador achieves his dramatic effect, judged by the grace and coolness of the performance within the discipline of his art, considering the degree of danger of the particular movement under the circumstances of the moment which he has chosen and upon which he has wagered his life—a true actor, with his eye as much upon the aesthetic effect of his performance upon the audience as it is upon the one thousand pounds of long-horned, vibrantly healthy, charging flesh in the middle of the ring.

It is not an accident that the one person above all others who comes the nearest to expressing the deepest, most instinctive, and vital values of the Spanish and Indian Mexican soul today, the one of its two most creative spirits, trained wholly within the borders of Mexico—José Orozco—is an artist, or that his symbolism, painted in the cupola of Guadalajara, presents man not as a blank tablet but as a vibrant living flame, a frenzied spirit, an *éros*, living dangerously, making his free choice, and staking his life without compromise upon its consequences. One is reminded of Plato's *Phaedrus* with its account of human frenzy.

José Orozco's second typical use of the flame appears in the symbolism of the hands above the upper left-hand portion of the fresco "Omniscience," which faces the stairway in the House of Tiles in Mexico City. The symbolism exhibits two larger hands cupped to contain the flame, extending down from above toward a smaller hand open to receive it immediately below (Plate VII). Justino Fernández informs us that the larger hands represent God presenting the flame to the smaller hand of man beneath. Thus when the theoretical meaning of the immediately sensed aesthetic materials is correctly read, one finds this painting saying that man does not create his own spirit but that it is a gift of Divine Grace. This is the Christian Catholic doctrine requiring the science and philosophy of the medieval period (or its equivalent) to give it meaning.

The return to the values of the Spanish colonial period is evident. Man is not merely a vibrant frenzy, possessed of free will, living dangerously, and realistically facing death as well as life, and his evil passion as well as his sublime movements; but he is also not his own creator or explanation but a gift of Divine Grace. The irreducible humanism and individualism deriving from the *cogito* or primacy of the human self of Descartes and Locke upon which the Modern World was reared, and the evolutionary optimism and pragmatic instrumentalism in which the Modern World found itself with Hegel and Darwin, have been rejected.

One understands also why José Orozco and Diego Rivera, notwithstanding their opposition on all other points—Orozco's Spanish and Catholic values being Rivera's evils, Rivera's economic and scientific values being Orozco's evils—agree upon one point; namely, the inadequacy of the traditional modern Lockean Anglo-American values. This agreement, to be sure, arises for different reasons—for Rivera, because the Anglo-American Lockean doctrine of the primacy of property rights, like the colonial society which Orozco's Spanish Christian values nourished, has the consequence of drawing off the fruits of the humanistically good science and technology applied to the nation's resources from the people's pockets to the coffers of Rome or the banks of Wall Street; for Orozco because (a) the physical science essentially connected with Lockean Anglo-American democracy leads to scientific technology which, by mechanizing man's life, destroys his soul, and (b) its political and Protestant emphasis, through standardized universal education, starting from the conception of man as an emotionless blank tablet, and aiming at the uniform majority opinion necessary to make democracy function, places the free imagination and the rich warm bodily feelings of men in a straitjacket, so that the individualism, the spontaneity and the freedom of the emotions, necessary for a vital, fresh, aesthetic sense and a deep, personal, religious passion tend to be destroyed.

Put positively, what José Orozco is doing for us is the revealing of a new freedom—the freedom of the aesthetic intuition, the individualistic emotions, and the sentiments. To political freedom and economic freedom, psychological freedom is being added.

But José Orozco's art does more than portray a need of the Anglo-American world. It also provides a key to Spain. Recall the Spaniard Salvador de Madariaga's statement: "The essence of the Spanish soul is passion." Recall also the Spanish Mexican Samuel Ramos's language in writing of the nineteenth century influence of French culture: "The political passion operated in the assimilation of this culture in the same way as the religious passion previously in the assimilation of the Spanish culture." Remember also the worshippers marching forward knee after knee with their devotion fixed upon the Virgin at Guadalupe.

Let one's thoughts go back, as the research of Alfonso Reyes's Colegio de Mexico has done, to the Spanish Christian missionary Las Casas, who showed the Indians how to make the language, architecture, and religion of Spain their own. What does one find? Edmundo O'Gorman in his little but important book *Fundamentos de la Historia de América* has given the answer. Las Casas lived between St. Thomas, who defined the orthodox doctrine of the Roman Catholic Church since 1323, and Descartes, who with Locke laid the primarily humanistic, democratic foundations of the modern world. O'Gorman's study of Las Casas's writings reveals that he departed from the orthodoxy of St. Thomas upon certain very important points and foresaw certain ideas of the founder of modern philosophy, René Descartes. This would explain in part the previously noted, suprising fact that the official Catholic colleges of Mexico "relegated Aristotelianism [the philosophy of St. Thomas] to oblivion for Cartesianism," thereby opening up the whole of modern philosophy to the Mexican Catholics' minds and providing the humanistic and skeptical assumptions of Voltaire and the French Encyclopaedists, which brought in the democratic revolution and led to the nationalization of all the Roman Church's property.

Edmundo O'Gorman's study reveals also that Las Casas returned to St. Augustine's primary emphasis upon the freedom of the human will. St. Thomas, following the science and philosophy of Aristotle, had maintained that the good life is the life completely controlled by reason —in which God himself contemplates his own perfect, pure, rational nature, of which revelation, supplementing man's partial, scientifically determined, rational knowledge, gives man the only completely perfect hint. Accordingly, man is saved through Divine Grace, according to St. Thomas and the current orthodox doctrine of the Catholic Church, not so much by the will or feeling or passion, as by the rational knowledge of God. For St. Augustine, on the other hand, the good life consists as much in the emotional love, the passion for the love of God by the freely acting human will which has indulged in human sin at Tagaste and Carthage, as in the rational knowledge of God.

But Augustine's doctrine goes back to the mathematical science and philosophy of Plato, just as St. Thomas's theology goes back to the physics and methematics of Aristotle. In fact, this Augustinian Platonism was the original Catholic orthodoxy. This is the reason why Abélard was attacked by the Catholic Church in the eleventh century when he proposed the precise Aristotelian doctrine which the Roman Catholics since St. Thomas have used to define orthodoxy.

In Plato's philosophy there are two "ground principles," as his famous lecture *On the Good* specifically stated: one, the rational, mathematical, formal principle; the other, the intuitive, immediately apprehended, emotional, aesthetic principle termed "the indeterminate dyad," or the potentially differentiable aesthetic continuum. The nature of the rational principle is investigated in the *Republic*, the nature of the emotional aesthetic principle, in the *Phaedrus* and the *Symposium*. In the latter books it is called *éros*, which Jowett renders into English as "frenzy" or "love" or "passion." We are now able to understand why, in the square patio of the Secretariat of Public Education in Mexico City, Plato rather than the more recently orthodox Aristotle stands in its Greek corner. Thanks to Edmundo O'Gorman, we know also that Plato would not be there were not Las Casas there also.

But Plato's teaching contains additional, relevant points. In his dialogue the *Timaeus*, which brings together the aesthetic, emotional *éros* principle of the *Phaedrus* and *Symposium* and the rational, scientific *lógos* principle of the *Republic*, he tells us that the former is the female and the latter the male principle in the nature of things. This is the reason why the emotional, passionate person in the Christian Church's symbolism is the female Virgin and why the doctrinal, rational person in its symbolism is the male Christ, representing the unseen, because only rationally known, God the Father.

Failing to make an important distinction, Plato went on quite arbitrarily to brand the aesthetic, emotional female principle as evil and the male rational principle as good. Consequently, it is to this rational factor, termed God the Father, that the Divine is restricted in the orthodox Christian religion of the West, whether Catholic or Protestant.

This is why one destroys orthodox Christianity when one attacks reason, why the Protestant Church does not allow the Virgin in its symbolism at all, why it tends to be afraid of vivid colors, the passions and the emotions, and why the Catholic Church, when orthodox, whether its orthodoxy be that of the earlier St. Augustine and Plato or the later and current St. Thomas and Aristotle, always insists that the Virgin is not divine immediately in her own right, but only mediately because she is the purely earthly mother of the Christ. This is the reason also, as Henry Adams has suggested in his profound *St. Michel and Chartres*, why, during that period when Abélard's attack had wiped out the Augustinian and Platonic theory of ideas, thereby robbing Christ of his traditional divinity, and before St. Thomas had appeared to restore Christ's divinity by defining it in terms of the rational principle in Aristotle's metaphysics, the Church at Chartres had no alternative but to fall back upon the Virgin, divine in Her own right, for whom Christ is important solely because he is Her son. During this important interval the Christian religion, acting more wisely than it knew, became identical, as the later chapters of this volume will show, with the religion of the Orient.

A glimmering of the source of the unorthodoxy of Mexico's catholicism is now beginning to dawn upon us. A few more moments with other relevant events, and it will be clear. Salvador de Madariaga did not say, "The essence of the Spanish soul is passion and reason." He omitted the "reason" entirely; it is nothing but passion. Thus the Spanish soul is not orthodox in the Western religious sense of the word. This answers the major question which anyone who reflects upon the history of Spain in Europe should ask himself: Why is it that in its entire history, until very recently, the Spanish soul has never produced one typical Western scientific or philosophical thinker with a logically formulated doctrine such as Euclid's *Elements*, St. Thomas's *Summa*, Newton's *Principia*, Kant's *Critique of Pure Reason*, or Albert Einstein's *General Theory of Relativity*? The answer is given in Salvador de Madariaga's definition of the Spanish spirit: It has followed the passion principle and neglected the rational principle except in its aesthetic, analogical manifestations.

Consider one other fact. It will be recalled that the Medical School of the National University of Mexico is now housed in what was formerly the Inquisition Building of the Dominican Order. This association between the Inquisition and the Dominicans is not accidental. The Inquisition attacked the unorthodox. The Dominican Order is the Order to which St. Thomas, the definer of orthodoxy, belonged. Studies by Mexican scholars show that the Catholic colleges which openly taught the modern unorthodox doctrines were those of the Order of the Jesuits. This is the one Order in the Catholic Church of purely Spanish origin. Being Spanish, religion for the Spanish Mexican Jesuits was, to use the words of Salvador de Madariaga, "an individual passion like love, jealousy, or ambition." Hence the doctrine, whether orthodox or unorthodox, was irrelevant. Consequently, providing the Church flourished at the time, it was unimportant to the Jesuits whether the doctrine which was taught was that of St. Thomas, Descartes, or Voltaire. This neglect of doctrine accounts also for the frenzied, pragmatic expendiency usually associated with the Jesuits.

The unorthodoxy at Guadalupe and in the greater devotion to the Virgin than to the Christ in the other Mexican churches also gains its explanation: It is in the Indian and the Spanish feeling that the aesthetic intuition and passion are the primary and important factors in human nature and in religion, together with the Spanish Jesuits' resort to pragmatic expediency due to the neglect of the rational principle.

Christians, both Protestant and Catholic, and pragmatists, as well as all others who for one reason or another have neglected theory, will do well to reflect upon this bit of history. Apparently the Catholics have done so, for in the United States and in Mexico today one finds them strictly orthodox in their teaching. Even the Jesuits, having seen their own monasteries and colleges taken away as a consequence of their teaching of Descartes and Voltaire, seem to have learned their lesson. This shows in the present revival of neo-Scholasticism. Throughout the whole of Latin America there is an interest in the writings of its leading contemporary exponent, Jacques Maritain.

It may be safely predicted, however, that this reaction, commendable as it is because of its appreciation of clearly defined and consistently developed religious doctrine, will not go very far. In fact, since this paragraph was first written, popular protest has forced the removal of the Thomist Rector of the University of Mexico. The basis of contemporary religious preaching and practice upon principle rather than upon temporary expediency or the passing and conflicting whims of the moment must be accomplished by determining the basic theoretical assumptions of *contemporary* knowledge and then pursuing them to their theological and cultural consequences, not by attempting to return to the inadequate Aristotelian science and its attendantly inadequate Thomistic theology of the Middle Ages. Authoritative and excellent as it was for the fourteenth century, it will not do for our time, which must include not merely diverse modern as well as medieval Western values but also Oriental insights as well.

But even Mexican Catholicism itself will not sustain neo-Thomism. The vital part of the Mexican religion is that exhibited at Guadalupe and in the artistry dedicated to the Virgin in the Spanish colonial churches. Both of these manifestations, as the previous consideration of them has shown, are unorthodox. They give expression to a religion of passion based on the female *éros* principle in the nature of things, not to the purely male rational principle of the Aristotelian science and the divine revelation of St. Thomas. Moreover, they both insist that the aesthetically immediate, emotionally moving Virgin is not a mere symbol, pointing beyond herself through the Christ-child to God the Father, but is Divine in Her own right. Thereby, they depart not merely from the present orthodoxy of St. Thomas and Aristotle but also from the earlier Catholic orthodoxy of St. Augustine and Plato and from Christianity generally.

Nowhere does this exclusiveness and intrinsic goodness of the female aesthetic component in the nature of things show itself more markedly than in José Orozco's fresco "Omniscience." Since the time of Plato, omniscience, of all things, has been identified with the male theoretical component in human knowledge. Consequently only God the Father, not the Virgin Mary, was omniscient. Nevertheless, in the Orozco fresco in the House of Tiles, omniscience is symbolized by the figure of the human female (Plate VIII).

Again, it is not the mathematically and logically formulated theoretical knowledge itself, but only the passionately felt, aesthetic materials in which the scientific theory is conveyed, that interests the Spanish-Indian portion of the Mexican spirit. To produce a theoretically oriented thinker one must first erect a hypothesis taking one beyond the immediately experienced, passionately felt aesthetic component of the nature of things and then concentrate one's attention upon the abstract, logical, and methematical consequences of its assumptions, returning to the world of aesthetically immediate, passionate experience only later, if at all. That this is uncongenial to the Spaniard, José Orozco has suggested in his painting "The Scientist," in the New School for Social Research in New York City. Conversely, because the Spaniard's attention is absorbed with the passionately felt aesthetic materials which are as much imaginative as sensuous, his genius shows itself in mystics like St. Theresa and the poetic St. John of the Cross, painters like El Greco and Picasso, individual discoverers like Balboa and Cortés, and heroes of the imagination like Sancho Panza and Don Quixote.

One final question remains: Why does the Spanish soul behave in this manner? In doing so, it has adopted as good in itself the emotional, aesthetic female component of things which Plato and the Christian Church following him designated as mere symbol and as evil. This question can be properly answered only when we have examined more in detail the roots of Western civilization and of Eastern culture. Certain points to be demonstrated later may, however, be noted now. Plato, in his famous lecture on the Good, even when designating the female aesthetic component as evil, nevertheless indicated it to be an ultimate, irreducible factor, one of the two "ground principles [ἀρχαί] of all things." As the sequel will show, it is with this female, compassionate, aesthetic component that the good and the divine in the philosophy and religion of the Orient are identified. In fact, it is likely that this female ground principle in Plato's philosophy was not original with Plato but came to him from the East.

It is significant that the medieval culture of Spain was created as much by an Arabian invasion from the East as by indigenous influences within the West. Also, men everywhere, as the Orientals and the ancient Aztecs indicate, begin with the aesthetic emotional principle in the nature of things and come to the rational principle, which is the great discovery of Western science and philosophy and its religion of God the Father, only later, if at all. One feels the beauty of the sunset before one learns of the internal constitution of the stars. The most typical representative in the Orient of this purely intuitive, compassionate, aesthetic view of life is the Buddha.

Thus it is that Quetzalcoatl, Las Casas, and Plato guide us to the reason for the presence beside them of the Buddha rather than the Christ in the fourth truncated corner of the square patio of the Secretariat of Public Education in Mexico City.

These considerations suggest that the contemporary relaxing of restrains by the Camacho Government upon the aesthetic and religious values of the colonial period, the way for which was prepared by the frescoes of José Orozco, and by the hold of the Virgin of Guadalupe upon the sentiments and imagination of the people, represents something very much more permanent than the usual counter-revolution following the secular democratic revolutions of the nineteenth and early twentieth centuries. For it expresses' something so native, spontaneous, and basic in both the Indian and the Spanish portions of the Mexican spirit that never again will it be given up.

Moreover, because of the concern in the West with the theoretical and the technological and the doctrinal, it represents a value which the Anglo-Saxon and logically Latin cultures need. But the present and the future as well as the past are on its side. Rooted as it is, through Spain, in the Arabs of the Near East and in the Buddha beyond them in the Far East, the course of world events bringing about a merging of the Orient and the Occident is also in its favor. We may be reasonably sure, therefore, as Justino Fernández insists, that José Orozco has given expression to an aesthetically and emotionally ultimate, intuitively given component in the nature of man and of things, which deserves to be cherished not merely by Mexico but also by the rest of the world.

But this is not the whole truth nor the end of the story. For one cannot be impressed with Orozco's values without being reminded of Rivera's also. The latter tells us with equal certainty and appeal that scientific knowledge through universal democratic education, freeing the minds of men to accept a more correct theoretical conception of the nature of things, and freeing their bodies from disease and drudgery by means of its technology applied to the nation's resources, is also one of the highest and most perfect human values. Nor can one leave out of account the thousands of students who are studying the modern sciences in Mexico's National Preparatory School and the National University, and the hundreds upon hundreds of students studying physics, chemistry, and geology in the School of Mines. Clearly the youth who will build the Mexico of tomorrow are choosing the modern democratic and scientific values of Diego Rivera also. They have not been misled by José Orozco's unjustified, negative thesis that science and theoretical reflection destroy the human soul, any more than the Mexicans generally have been misled by Diego Rivera's equally unjustified, negative suggestion that the aesthetic and religious interests of the colonial period are entirely evil.

Other considerations support their verdict. There is no incompatability whatever between the intuitive, passionate, immediately apprehended aesthetic values which José Orozco conveys and the postulated, theoretical, and attendant technological, scientific values which Diego

Rivera portrays with equal artistic and human appeal. The ancient Indian culture showed the Mexicans, as it now shows us, how a geometrically informed, aesthetically vivid, astronomically oriented art, religion, and agriculture can function together harmoniously and with human appeal.

The true relation between intuitive, aesthetic, and religious feeling and scientific doctrine is one of mutual supplementation. For we have a conception of the meaning of man and the universe which it is trustworthy for art and religion to convey, only by the aid of scientific knowledge pursued to its basic theoretical assumptions, and then developed with respect to its philosophical and theological consequences. And conversely, we can attain verified scientific knowledge only by observing what is immediately apprehended, and this is always aesthetically vivid and emotionally moving. Furthermore, the whole of mankind, as opposed to a few artists and saints, can obtain the leisure to pursue the aesthetically immediate and the intuitive religion of compassion of the Virgin and the Buddha for its own sake, only if scientific knowledge is applied to the world's resources under legal principles defined by an economic theory which permits the fruits of man's knowledge to redound to the benefit of all men. This is the reason why Orozco's psychological and religious values and Rivera's scientific and economic values are all bound together and equally essential.

The most telling evidence to this end comes from the second generation of contemporary Mexican painters. They have studied the works and grasped the messages of both Rivera and Orozco. Being artists, these younger men cannot be accused of being prejudiced in favor of science or indifferent to human values. In the modern Abelardo Rodríguez Market, but two blocks from the Secretariat of Public Education containing Rivera's most extensive paintings and the National Preparatory School containing Orozco's, the frescoes of the younger painters are to be seen. They follow Rivera in portraying science applied to man's mind and nature's resources as a human value. We must conclude, therefore, that a greater painter than either Rivera or Orozco is coming, called forth by the needs of our time and the direction of world events—an artist who gives expression in sensuously vivid, emotionally moving aesthetic materials to the new comprehensive set of philosophical assumptions which show how the values of Orozco and those of Rivera can be put together.

Before it is possible to designate what these new assumptions are, it is necessary to turn our attention away from Mexico to other fields.

For the basic beliefs of contemporary and traditional modern science are not to be found most easily in the Latin-American world. Their manifestations are more evident in the United States, and their origins are to be found only in Europe. Also, the question whether economic democracy can be realized within the assumptions of traditional Anglo-American political and economic theory, or requires some elements of Russian doctrine, must be faced. This necessitates an analysis of the basic assumptions and factual grounds of the two theories. Such an inquiry takes us to Lockean and post-Lockean British culture and to post-Kantian German and Russian thought. Finally, the basic common denominator underlying the differences in Oriental culture must be sought out and placed over against what is common to the orthodox thought of the West. This also leads us away from Mexico, even though Mexico has given us a hint as to its nature.

As the Sunshine Limited weaves its way back again into the Anglo-American world, one reflects that while the culture of the United States still remains as open, as vital, and as extensive as it was before, nevertheless, from its neighbor to the south there can come into it, if men are wise, a quickening of the imagination and the spirit, a deepening of the sentiments and the emotions, a heightening of the sense of beauty, and a seriousness, vitality, integrity, and realism in architectural, political, and religious forms and practices that are desperately needed. Such is the significance of the rich culture of Latin America, of which Mexico is a representative and perhaps outstanding example, for the United States and the rest of the world—a culture more critical because more complex, varied, and mature, while less proficient in purely modern ways, than that of the United States, and at the same time one in which ideas, life, philosophy and art are more intimately related, a culture moreover which, when traced to its various sources, helps us to see both the strength and weaknesses of Anglo-American values as one never has before, and which at the same time serves as a tie and bridge to Latin Europe and to Asia. Many more things, very important things, such as Alfonso Reyes's definition of the meaning of America, remain to be indicated, but the time for them is later, when America is examined in its relation to Europe, and Europe in its relation to Asia.

CHAPTER III

THE FREE CULTURE OF THE UNITED STATES

"America," writes the Mexican humanist and statesman Alfonso Reyes, "is a Utopia. . . . It is the name of a human hope. . . . From time to time the philosophers divert themselves in outlining the contours of the desired perfect city, and these outlines invoke Utopias, of which the Constitutional Codices—if I may be permitted an observation of actuality—are nothing more than the last manifestation."

The manner in which the medieval aristocratic contour of utopia was replaced in the nineteenth century by the modern democratic form, with the attendant reconstruction of political and religious institutions, has been noted in the case of Mexico. The other Latin-American countries similarly demonstrate the correctness of Alfonso Reyes's observation.

In 1606 the Jesuit missionaries to Paraguay initiated the acceptance of Spanish colonial values by establishing one of the earliest communal utopias in the western hemisphere. In similar fashion the earlier missionaries to Brazil embodied a utopia. More recently, its federal republic, created in the revolt of 1889, bears the official name of the United States of Brazil. The powers of the nation are vested in three branches of government—executive, legislative, and judicial. There are a president and his cabinet, a congress of two parts, and a supreme court. The manner in which the political philosophy of Locke, Jefferson, Hamilton, and Washington has determined the political pattern is evident. Although there are exceptions, due to individual circumstances, the South American nations generally follow the same sequence of Indian, Spanish or Portuguese colonial, French democratic and positivistic, and contemporary values which Mexico exhibits.

THE COLONIAL BACKGROUND

The United States to the north of the Rio Grande also exemplifies the utopian principle. The degree to which the founders of its original colonies were dominated by the desire to escape the restrictions placed upon their religious beliefs and social ideals by the pre-established habits and factions of an older and more conservative England and Holland is well known. Even so, as Charles M. Andrews has shown, they expected to remain under the sovereign powers of the King and within the confines of England's colonial system. With respect to religious freedom, also, they tended initially to conceive of it merely as the setting up of a community at once both political and religious, in which their own particular religious beliefs would dominate. As Harvey Townsend, in his *Philosophical Ideas in the United States*, has written of the New England Puritans, "Their quarrel with the bishops was largely over forms of worship and government within the church. In matters of religious and social opinion, they shared the widespread orthodoxy of the period. They believed in theocracy, in demonology, and in argument as the means of discovering the truth. Their dissent hinged chiefly on ecclesiastical forms, rather than on religious doctrine." It took roughly one hundred and fifty years for ideas to seep down from the earlier modern scientists and philosophers who first formulated them, into the minds of the colonists generally to produce that more enlightened conception of tolerance among the colonial Protestants and that new utopia which expresses itself in the Declaration of Independence.

Also, there were Indians to be met, and forests, rivers, plains, and mountains to be conquered. Even these naturalistic items have made us what we are, primarily a people for whom the deed to be done strikes us first, and the theory for the doing of it comes along afterward, if at all.

Yet this is only part of the truth. For our colonial founders did not come with empty heads, devoid of convictions, or tongue-tied, bereft of speech. They were Englishmen, Dutchmen, Frenchmen. They were Puritans, Cavaliers, Calvinists, and Roman Catholics. They spoke the Englishman's, the Hollander's, or the Frenchman's language. As the early years went by, the Englishmen and the English language came to predominate. The religion became preponderantly Protestant. To be sure, there were strong French and Catholic influences up the valley of the St. Lawrence and across Lake Erie into the upper regions and tributaries of the Mississippi, as there were Catholic influences at Baltimore and among the Indians at Santa Fe and the southerly Far West. But these Latin elements were never sufficient to capture our linguistic habits or religious sentiments or social practices. Thus it has happened that in more recent years, even when the newcomers have been largely Roman Catholics from Ireland or the south of Europe, they nevertheless speak England's tongue and defend freedom of faith for all men and not merely for themselves. As José Orozco and our Spanish-Mexican neighbors to the south of us clearly see, the soul of the United States is basically Anglo-American, just as the soul of Mexico is Spanish-American in character.

Nowhere does this triumph of Anglo-American values show more dramatically than in the association of the names Holy Cross and Notre Dame in the popular mind primarily with the games of baseball and football. Witness, also, the beautiful villages of New England and the Middle West with the village green flanked by the white-steepled Congregational Church in the center of things, much as the Spanish baroque cathedral functions in Mexico. Note, also, Williamsburg or any other small Virginian colonial city with its Georgian native brick, its white trimming, its aristocratic social forms, and its Episcopalian Church.

But this is not all. The early settlers and Indians met. The encounter was one of triumph for English culture and a tragedy for the Indians. The results were even more devastating than in Mexico, for whereas the latter Spanish Catholic culture merely destroyed the high culture of the Indians, the English Protestant influence in the United States, with few exceptions, destroyed the Indians also. It is not inspiring to note how the founders of a republic, which was to give all men freedom, brought even their self-righteous Protestantism to the justification of the slaughtering of the Indians. Benjamin Franklin was not overly pious, yet even he wrote of "the design of Providence to extirpate those savages in order to make room for the cultivators of the earth." Nicolay and Hay, in their *Abraham Lincoln: a History*, state that when the young Lincoln and his parents moved to Illinois in the 1830's "natural and kindly fraternization of the Frenchmen with the Indians was . . . a cause of wonder to the Americans. This friendly intercourse between them, and their occasional intermarriages, seemed little short of monstrous to the ferocious exclusiveness of the Anglo-Saxon." Here as elsewhere Anglo-Saxon values triumphed. The Indians were either exterminated or herded onto reservations. Again one is reminded that nothing can be more evil and tragically devastating in its actual consequence than one's own moral and religious ideals, fine, and justified by certain limited considerations as these ideals may be, when they are accompanied by an ignorance and resultant provincialism and blindness with respect to peoples and cultures acting upon, or proceeding from, assumptions different from one's own.

With the passing of the Indian, his language nonetheless remained. This language merged with England's until words like Winnebago, Pocohontas, Hiawatha, and Mississippi have become the common parlance of all. Gradually the freely flowing pronunciation of these Indian words has smoothed out the precisely articulated, sharply cut syllables of the English speech, until an Englishman in our midst hardly recognizes what he hears. Nor is he in error. As H. L. Mencken and the editors of the *Dictionary of American English* have shown, our language is no longer merely England's language. The Indian, the Negro, the freedom of the frontier, and the vast open spaces away from the confines of sophisticated society have added their components and their spirit.

One Englishman, D. H. Lawrence, believes that the Indian component of this spirit has become, as the poems of Longfellow and the novels of Cooper indicate, a veritable portion of our souls, one cause even of our unrest, forever keeping us from fully giving ourselves to the cultural creations of Europe, even when in grammar and religion and politics they have outwardly converted us. The Indians' forests, rivers, plains, and mountains, which we still designate with Indian names, are at the basis of our history and in the background of our being with all their uncultivated severity and their austere beauty. It is the untamed eagle, at home only on the mountain crag untouched by man, whose "dark, swinging wings of hawk-beaked destiny," Lawrence adds, ". . . one cannot help but feel, beating here above the wild center of America . . . the rudimentary American vision"—the official symbol of the United States.

All these factors have gone into the making of this country and its vision of freedom. Yet none of them nor all of them suffice for the understanding of this land. We are not what we are merely because we, or our forefathers, were set down here with all these natural and cultural heritages. This is not a land of freedom because we were thus left free. Even our freedom had to be defined and guaranteed by rules. These rules in turn had their origin in Europe in a new and purely modern conception of the nature of man and his relation to nature, religion, property, and the state. To be free, as freedom has been interpreted in the culture of the United States, means to believe in and act upon, and defend these rules as basic and axiomatic.

Although there were forerunners of them in *The Fundamental Orders of Connecticut* in 1639, *The Massachusetts Body of Liberties* in 1641, *The Instrument of Government* of Cromwell and his Council of Officers in 1653 in England, and the Charter of Charles II to Rhode Island in 1663, these basic assumptions were first clearly expressed in their purity and simplicity and generally applied without qualification in practice in the Declaration of Independence.

THE DECLARATION OF INDEPENDENCE

The primacy of this document, in defining that idea of the good which is the traditional United States of America, can hardly be over-estimated. It was Lincoln who said:

I have never had a feeling, politically, that did not spring from the senti-ments embodied in the Declaration of Independence. . . . I have often inquired of myself what great principle or idea it was that kept this Con-federacy so long together. It was not the mere matter of separation of the colonies from the motherland, but that sentiment in the Declaration of Independence which gave liberty, not alone to the people of this country, but hope to all the world, for all future time. It was that which gave promise that in due time the weight would be lifted from the shoulders of all men and that all should have an equal chance.

On the Fourth of July in 1943, the *New York Times* reminded its readers of John Adams's statement that there is nothing in the Declara-tion of Independence "but what had been hackneyed in Congress for two years before" and that Thomas Jefferson, at first annoyed with Adams's remark, later admitted that this document "was intended to be an expression of the American mind," adding that "All its authority rests upon the harmonizing sentiments of the day, whether expressed in conversation, letters, printed essays, or the elementary books of public right, as Aristotle, Cicero, Locke, Sidney, etc. . . . I did not consider it as any part of my charge to invent new ideas altogether, and to offer no sentiment which had ever been expressed before."

Two points in this statement by the author of the Declaration of Independence are important: First, its utopian ideal had become the common property of all the colonists; and second, this ideal had not originated with them or even with Jefferson but had been formulated previously by European philosophers. Among these philosophers, as Jefferson was well aware, the most important is John Locke.

Although Jefferson recognized a general contribution by Aristotle, he wrote of Aristotle's more specific ideas concerning politics as follows:

. . . so different was the style of society then and with those people, from what it is now and with us, that I think little edification can be obtained from their writings on the subject of government. They had just ideas of the value of personal liberty, but none at all of the structure of government best calculated to preserve it. They knew no medium between a democracy (the only pure republic, but impracticable beyond the limits of a town) and an abandonment of themselves to an aristocracy, or a tyranny independent of the people. It seems not to have occurred that where the citizens cannot meet to transact their business in person, they alone have the right to choose the agents who shall transact it; and that in this way a republican, or popular government, of the second grade of purity, may be exercised over any extent of country. The full experiment of a government democratical, but representative, was and is still reserved for us. . . . The introduction of this new principle of representative democracy has rendered useless almost everything written before on the structure of government; and, in a great measure, relieves our regret, if the political writings of Aristotle, or of any other ancient, have been lost, or are unfaithfully rendered or explained to us.

Additional weighty considerations support Jefferson in this conclusion. The appropriate political organization for the hierarchical conception of reality which Aristotle's science formulated and his philosophy made articulate is the hierarchical form of society and government which the medieval period, following Aristotle, introduced in both the Church and the State.

But if the generally accepted ideas to which Thomas Jefferson gave expression in the Declaration of Independence did not derive from Aristotle, from whom then did they derive? The answer has been given by John C. Miller in his *Origins of the American Revolution*:

. . . Above all, the political writings of John Locke furnished Americans, whether Carolinians or New Englanders, with an arsenal of arguments against the arbitrary rule of both King and Parliament. If any one man can be said to have dominated the political philosophy of the American Revolution, it is John Locke. American political thinking was largely an exegesis upon Locke: and patriots quoted him with as much reverence as Communists quote Marx today. Indeed, it is not too much to say that during the era of the American Revolution, the "party line" was John Locke. . . . The American mind of 1776 was saturated with John Locke.

It is to the moral, the religious, and the political consequences of John Locke's philosophical conception of man and nature that Thomas Jefferson gives expression in the Declaration of Independence. In short, the traditional culture of the United States is an applied utopia in which the philosophy of John Locke defines the idea of the good.

John Locke was one of the first persons to develop systematically the philosophical consequences of modern science and designate their implications for morality, religion, and politics. Descartes, who lived and wrote much earlier than Locke, also made such an attempt. In fact, there is much in common between the philosophical theories of the Frenchman and those of the Englishman. Both conceived of the nature of things as made up of the material objects of physical science which they termed "material substances," and of persons, whom they termed "mental substances," the remainder of experience being regarded as the product of an interaction of these two types of substances.

Both of them recognized, also, that in the science of physics the Aristotelian philosophy and its attendant Thomistic, medieval conception of the world had broken down. Descartes, in fact, was a mathematician and a physicist. He was the first to attempt to construct a new physics to replace that of Aristotle. Unfortunately he came slightly too early for this task. His knowledge was sufficient to indicate that Aristotelian science and philosophy, and the attendant medieval conception of the good for morals, religion, and politics were inadequate; but he did not possess all the evidence necessary to construct the physics and philosophy which finally replaced them. This was done by Newton, following the investigations of Galilei and Huygens. Consequently, Descartes's physics had a very short life and was rejected following the publication of Newton's *Principia*. The Anglo-American philosophy of Newton's physics is that of John Locke.

Locke was an experimental chemist and a physician and an intimate friend of Newton. He was acquainted with the fundamental ideas of modern physical science. In fact, Locke's theory of the nature of the individual person is, as shall be shown, a consequence of clarifying a distinction which Galilei's and Newton's physics had introduced. Furthermore, French political democracy, like that of nineteenth-century Mexico, derived from Locke by way of Voltaire and the Encyclopaedists. Consequently, if we desire to understand the fundamental assumptions of the modern world, and especially those of French as well as Anglo-American political thought, it is Locke's rather than Descartes's philosophy which we must examine.

Descartes is important, however, for an understanding of the modern French mind, particularly the basic skepticism and the insistence upon rational, logical clarity which distinguish it, as Salvador de Madariaga has emphasized, from Anglo-American or Spanish mentality. Descartes, before he came to his theory of mental and material substances, was a doubter. It is by beginning with a doubt and then applying logical reasoning to clear and distinct data which cannot be doubted that Descartes arrives at his theory of mental and material substances. The source of his doubt was his awareness that every department of knowledge which he had mastered under his traditional Roman Catholic medieval training, except mathematics, had broken down. His confidence in logical reasoning had its basis in the fact that this was the method used by the one branch of traditional knowledge which remained valid; namely, mathematics.

Every modern Frenchman begins with and is grounded in Descartes. The curriculum in the lycées and universities of modern France is prescribed by the government. In this curriculum of both the junior and the senior educational institutions, philosophy and especially modern philosophy stemming from Descartes is required. We need hardly wonder, therefore, why the modern Frenchman's, unlike the Spaniard's, the Englishman's, or the American's, first reaction to any proposal is that of skepticism; and why his second demand is for crystal-clear, logical consistency for any conclusion which is accepted.

This skepticism, combined with a basic respect for, and insistence upon, the rationalistic method of mathematics and formal logic, also explains in considerable part the difficulty which the Frenchman has in getting along with his British and American democratic colleagues. The latter, not starting with initial skepticism, are easily misled by ill-conceived proposals, sugar-coated with a high-sounding moral verbalism. Also, tending to emphasize the practical rather than logical consistency with respect to the theoretical, the British and the Americans continuously put forward proposals according to which they expect to eat their cake and have it too. That these proposals will fail the Frenchman knows, since his respect for logic informs him that the assumptions from which they proceed are self-contradictory. Part of the present despair of the Frenchman, and his present irritation with respect to both the British and the Americans, notwithstanding all that the latter have accomplished for France, stems from this source. The Frenchman knows that the fanciful sentimentality with respect to Germany following Versailles, which a very little initial skepticism would have avoided; and the hit-and-miss, inconsistent, pragmatic bungling which, as Arnold Wolfers has shown, prevented any one policy from being followed continuously—and which a little respect for logical consistency would have avoided—are in great part the cause of the failure of the Allies to prevent the second war of the century.

Descartes is important, also, even for an understanding of British and American mentality. His doctrine of material and mental substances, and his follower Malebranche's theory of mind and matter as an occasion of the activity of God, had a great influence upon Protestant religious leaders, and, as Cecil Driver has shown, upon John Locke. Voltaire, in his *Letters on the English*, reports a conversation which he had with a representative English Quaker. After listening to the Quaker's expression of his faith, Voltaire said, "Why, this... is Malebranche's doctrine to a tittle." Whereupon the Quaker replied, "I am acquainted with thy Malebranche; ... he had something of the Friend in him, but was not enough so." Since the modern democratic conception of morality, religion, and politics turns upon the Lockean theory of the mental substance, and the way for the acceptance of this mental substance was prepared in the minds of Protestants before the time of Locke by Descartes and Malebranche, the relevance of the French philosopher for Anglo-American democracy and for the later French democracy which derived from it is evident. With modern philosophy, first with Descartes and later with Locke, a fundamentally new concept of the nature of the individual arose which entailed in turn a radically new conception of man's relation to nature, religion, and the state.

In constructing his philosophy Locke did not begin with an initial state of skepticism from which he was carried to trustworthy conclusions by logical reasoning. The reason is that, unlike Descartes, he found himself confronted in Newton's physics with an established experimentally verified theory. His task, therefore, was merely that of developing its philosophical consequences.

One thing was immediately clear. According to this physics, which mathematical reasoning applied to its basic assumptions, and controlled experiment had confirmed, nature is to be conceived as a system of physical objects located in a public, infinitely extending, absolute space. It was to these objects guaranteed by Galilei's and Newton's physics that John Locke gave the name material substances. Thus one portion of his philosophy was secure.

One other fact was clear from this physics. In order to carry the theory through in detail and bring it into accord with the factual evidence, it was necessary to identify the material substances of the physics not merely with gross objects but also with unobservable, exceedingly small particles, termed atoms. Pursuing this line of reasoning the later kinetic theory of heat and of gases was developed. Galilei was the first Modern to propose the latter theory and to note its exceedingly surprising and important consequences. The matter is so important for modern philosophy and the modern conception of the individual man and his freedom that we will do well to peruse with care Galilei's own words:

> But first I want to propose some examination of that which we call heat, whose generally accepted notion comes very far from the truth if my serious doubts be correct, inasmuch as it is impossible to be a true accident, affection, and quality really residing in the thing which we perceive to be heated. Nevertheless I say, that . . . I feel myself impelled by the necessity, as soon as I conceive a piece of matter or corporeal substance, of conceiving that in its own nature it is bounded and figured in such and such a figure, that in relation to others it is large or small, that it is in this or that place, in this or that time, that it is in motion or remains at rest, . . . in short by no imagination can a body be separated from such conditions: but that it must be white or red, bitter or sweet, sounding or mute, of a pleasant or unpleasant odour, I do not perceive my mind forced to acknowledge it necessarily accompanied by such conditions; so if the senses were not the escorts, perhaps the reason or the imagination by itself would never have arrived at them. Hence I think that these tastes, odours, colours, etc., on the side of the object in which they seem to exist, are nothing else than *mere names*. . . .
> A piece of paper, or a feather, lightly rubbed on whatever part of your body you wish, performs, as regards itself, everywhere the same operation, that is, movement and touch; but in us, if touched between the eyes, on the nose, and under the nostrils, it excites an almost intolerable tickling, though elsewhere it can hardly be felt at all. Now this tickling is all in us, and not in the feather, . . . and turning to my first proposition in this place, having now seen that many affections which are reputed to be qualities residing in the external object, have truly no other existence than in us, and without us are nothing else than names; I say that I am inclined sufficiently to believe . . . that the thing that produces heat in us and makes us perceive it, which we call by the general name fire, is a multitude of minute corpuscles thus and thus figured, moved with such and such a velocity; . . . and I judge that . . . if the animate and sensitive body were removed, heat would remain nothing more than a simple word.

The important thing to note about this statement by Galilei is that in this conception of nature, which Newtonian particle physics proposed and experimentally verified, the immediately apprehended colors, sounds, odors, and warmth do not belong to the material objects of nature; they are mere appearances projected back upon the material object by the observer.

Newton carried one step further this distinction between apparent factors which we immediately sense and the physical objects of nature. Not only are sensed heat, sensed colors, and sensed sounds mere appearances, but sensed space and sensed time have this same character and status. At the very beginning of his *Principia*, Newton writes, "I do not define time, space, place, and motion as being well known to all. Only I must observe that the common people conceive those quantities under no other notions but from the relation they bear to sensible objects. And thence arise certain prejudices, for the removing of which it will be convenient to distinguish them into absolute and relative, true and apparent, mathematical and common." What Newton was saying here is that the space in which the laws or postulates of his physics locate the colorless, odorless physical objects is not the immediately sensed spatial extension of, and relation between, sensed data (which is a purely private space, varying with the degree of one's astigmatism or the clearness of one's vision), but is instead a single public space of nature which has the same mathematical, geometrical properties always and everywhere and is the same, regardless of the varying, distorted, sensed spaces which appear to different observers. Because the public space is given by postulation mathematically rather than by observation directly, because position in it defines what is public in nature, and because it designates objects of knowledge the same for everybody rather than mere appearance varying from person to person, Newton called it "absolute . . . true and . . . mathematical" space. Because immediately sensed space is relative to the individual observer, even on the same physical frame of reference, and hence different for one person from what it is for another, Newton termed it "relative, . . . apparent" space.

Similarly, time in Newton's physics was postulated as being a public time which "flows equably without relation to anything external," whereas, as everyone knows, immediately sensed time varies from person to person, and even for a single person passes very quickly under certain circumstances and drags under others. Hence, the public time of Newton's physics, upon which the ordinary time of social usage is based, was termed "absolute, . . . true and . . . mathematical" time, to distinguish it from "relative, . . . apparent, . . . sensible" time.

It may be noted, parenthetically, that Einstein has not, as so many people have supposed, departed from the distinction introduced by Newton between the private time and space, varying from person to person, and with circumstances, which we immediately sense, and the public time and space of physics, which is mathematically defined and quite independent of the degree of one's astigmatism or one's sense of time flying or dragging. Einstein has merely changed the mathematical definition of the public time and space, revealing thereby an essential connection between them, and a resultant relativity, the same for everybody, varying not with the sense organs of the observer as do sensed space and time, but with the astronomical, physical objects to which the scientist chooses to refer his measurements. Upon Galilean frames of reference, for example, space for all observers has the same Euclidean properties everywhere for Einstein which it had for Newton. Thus Einstein does not identify the mathematically defined public space and time of physics, from which the public space and time of social usage is derived, with sensed space and time, any more than did Newton. If anything, the discrepancy between the two is even greater, as the shock to common sense produced by the experimental verification of Einstein's theory clearly indicates. The reader must not, therefore, allow the present emphasis upon relativity to prevent him from taking most seriously, just as did John Locke, the fact of the difference between sensed data with their sensed spatial-temporal relations and the objects of physics with their quite different space and time, which Galilei and Newton emphasized.

Modern thinkers, in grasping the meaning and philosophical consequences of Newton's physics, had no alternative, therefore, but to face a question which arose immediately; namely, what is the relation between the relative, private sensed qualities with their sensed spatial and temporal relations and the material atoms in the quite different, mathematically defined public space and time of nature? No error could be greater than to suppose that this question is of purely academic interest. For it is the answer given to it by Galilei and by Newton's physics which necessitated the initial modern scientific conception of the nature of man, which in turn, as the sequel will show, determined the idea of the good for man, the church and the state of the traditional modern portion of Anglo-American culture. Thus although technicalities greater than anything previously encountered in the present inquiry are involved, this question must be pursued. In fact, the further our inquiry into the philosophical and scientific foundations of cultural ideals is pursued the more this particular question will be found to be crucial. So important is it, that it bears repeating: What is the relation between the sensed qualities in sensed space and time and physical atoms in public mathematical space and time?

The physics of Galilei and Newton gave an unequivocal, even though somewhat shocking, answer: The warmth which we sense in the stove, the fragrance which we smell in the rose, and the red which we see on the flag, do not belong to the material objects at all, independently of the presence of the observer. In fact, sensed qualities in sensed space and time are not constituents of nature at all. Instead, nature is composed only of colorless, odorless physical atoms located in a public mathematical space and time which is quite different from the relative private space and time which one immediately senses. Sensed qualities and their sensed spacial and temporal relations are, to use Newton's language, "apparent"; or, to use Galilei's terminology, they are factors such that if the observer "were removed . . . nothing of them" would remain. Put more precisely, what Gililei and Newton assert is that the sensed data in sensed space and time are related to the non-sensuous physical objects in public, mathematical space and time by a three-termed relation of appearance in which the public, colorless, odorless material substances in mathematical space and time are one term, the aesthetic sensed data in their sensed spatial and temporal relations are a second term, and the individual observer is the third term. It is because the mathematically defined space and time with their postulated, unobservable, atomic physical objects are independent of their relation to the observer that there is a public world the same for everybody, regardless of the differences in what different people immediately apprehend. It is because the immediately sensed factors are not intrinsic properties of the public physical objects in the public world but are dependent in part upon the latter and in part upon the observer that they are termed by Galilei and Newton "apparent" rather than "real" things. It is because of the dependence upon the observer also that it follows, as Galilei asserts, that were the observer removed sensed colors, sounds, and warmth would not exist.

The relationship can be visualized as follows:

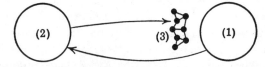

Thus, the sensed qualities in sensed space and time (3) are related to the physical object (1), not directly as common sense supposes, but indirectly by way of the observer (2).

Once this three-termed relation between the sensed and the scientifically objective factors in nature is accepted, another inescapable question arises: What is the nature of the observer which functions as the mediating second term in this three-termed relation? This question does not concern the physicist since his task is to study nature as the object of knowledge, not the observer; it does, however, concern the psychologist, the philosopher and the humanist. But although the

physicist does not pursue the answer to this second question, his speci-
fication of the three-termed relation in which the observer is one of the
terms has unequivocal consequences concerning the nature of man;
and this in fact, both logically and historically determines the answer
which the psychologist, the philosopher and the humanist give to the
question. Failure to note this fact has obscured the scientific foundations and verifiability of the humanistic values of the traditional modern
world. This will become clear through recapitulation and projection of
what has been established.

It has been noted that the experimentally verified physics of Galilei
and Newton joins the sensed to the mathematically defined public
factors in nature by a three-termed relation in which the atoms of
physics in public mathematical space and time are one term, the sensed
qualities in sensed space and time are the third term and the observer
is the mediating second term. The question then arises concerning the
nature of this observer.

The first attempt to answer this question was made by Thomas
Hobbes. Since his answer (and the moral and political theory which it
entails) have been revived in recent times by certain statesmen and
behavioristic psychologists, it merits serious consideration. Hobbes suggested that the observer is merely a collection of the atoms of physics,
like the public table or chair, as either is conceived by the Newtonian
physicist. Thus Hobbes attempted to derive the whole of modern knowledge from nothing but the material substances. Certain facts supported
this conclusion. The observer is a bodily being. There was evidence in
Hobbes's time, which has been multiplied in ours, that the entities of
physics and chemistry function in biology and in human physiology to
a remarkable degree, determining in part at least our emotions, our
states of mind, our moods, and our temperament. Many physiologists
and psychologists with their attention concentrated upon these facts
have concluded with Hobbes that this disposes of the matter.

One has only, however, to take this thesis seriously and to pursue
it to its logical consequences to see that even when all these facts are
admitted it completely fails to meet the difficulty. The truth is that,
were the nature of things nothing but the physical atoms in mathematical space and time, as Hobbes's theory requires, then colors, sounds,
odors, and sensed space and time should not exist even as appearances.
That they do exist as appearances even the physics of Galilei and Newton asserts. The inescapable fact, apart from all theory, is that we immediately apprehend colors, sounds, odors, and sensed spatial and tem-

poral relations. No amount of scientific theory about atoms can remove this fact. Also, it is only by observing these colors, sounds, and odors that we have any basis for verifying the deductive consequences of the postulates of Galilei and Newton's physics concerning unobserved atoms and their unobserved, mathematically defined space and time. Thus this physics presupposes, in its method of experimental verification, the sensed qualities and the sensed space and time. Yet, were there nothing but the public objects of physics acting upon an observer who is nothing but a similar system of physical atoms, as Hobbes's theory requires, there could not be colors, sounds, odors, or sensed space and time at all.

As Galilei and Newton specified, these sensed qualities are not properties of the physical objects. The warmth is not in the atoms of the fire. Furthermore, were the observer merely a system of such heatless, colorless, odorless physical atoms, the action of the atoms of the fire upon the observer would not generate even an appearance of warmth or color; for the sum total of the effect of one physical object or one set of physical objects upon another physical object is specified in Newton's second law of motion, and this effect is merely that of altering the velocity of the interacting objects. Consequently, all that could possibly happen as a result of the physical object acting upon an observer, who, according to Hobbes's theory, is nothing but an aggregation of physical objects, is merely that the atoms of the observer would be accelerated. An acceleration of the atoms of the observer's body is not an awareness of colors, sounds, and odors in sensed space and time. Thus the consequence of Hobbes's theory of the nature of the observer who functions in the three-termed relation of appearance is that the obvious, immediately given facts of experience, which Galilei and Newton specify as existing as appearances and which physics presupposes in its method of verification, should not exist at all, even as appearances.

Locke saw, consequently, that the observer, conceived as nothing but a system of material substances, does not satisfy the three-termed relation of appearance which is required by the physics of Galilei and Newton. He proceeded, therefore, as follows: Instead of attempting to fit the three-termed relation of appearance joining sensed factors to physical objects and the observer to some preconceived theory of the nature of this observer, as Hobbes had done, he used the three-termed relation of appearance to define the nature of the observer.

The following definition resulted: An observer is the kind of entity which satisfies the three-termed relation of appearance. More precisely, it is an entity such that when the material objects in the mathematically defined public space and time of Newton's physics act upon it, it is conscious of colors, sounds, odors, pains, and pleasures, in sensed space and time as appearances. This is precisely what Locke meant by a mental substance. It is a substance capable of consciousness which, when material substances affect it, is aware of qualities in sensed space and time as the content of its consciousness.

In this manner the material substances verified as to their existence by Newton's physics were shown by John Locke to entail the existence of conscious mental substances, in order to account for the existence of colors, sounds, odors and sensed space and time as the appearances which Galilei and Newton had designated them to be. Thus it is that *when Locke made explicit the complete consequences of the physics of his friend Newton, this experimentally verified physics was found to provide a theory not merely of physical nature but also of conscious man.* In fact, once Galilei and Newton's three-termed relation of appearance joining sensed to mathematically designated public factors in nature is admitted, the observer conceived as a conscious mental substance, with precisely those properties which Locke attributes to him, follows necessarily. Not until this was noted were the full philosophical consequences of Newton's physics with respect to both human nature and physical nature made explicit.

Thus, reason in science and the philosophy of science, working as Locke thought with nothing but sensed particulars, provided Locke with a "new state of nature" and a new content for "the law of reason," quite different from that of the Aristotelian Hooker of the King's Party or the medieval Calvin of the Presbyterian majority of the Long Parliament of Locke's seventeenth-century England. Furthermore, this new law of reason and its state of nature prescribed a new idea of the good for religion; namely, toleration rather than the theocratic rule of the Presbyterian magistrate or the divine right of the King's Church of England. It also prescribed a new idea of the good for the State; namely, popular democracy rather than Calvinistic theocracy or the divine right of kings defended by Filmer. In this manner, Locke gave to the individualistic Brownists, Levellers and other Puritan Protestant Independents even better—since more modern—scientific and philosophical foundations for their religious and political actions than the Calvinistic Presbyterians or the Aristotelian Royalists possessed. Furthermore, as we shall see in Chapter IV, he led even the Protestant Independents to regard toleration, not merely as an excellent thesis to which to appeal when one's religious group is in the minority, but also as a good in its own right under any circumstances.

The cultural consequences for religion and politics were indicated immediately by Locke himself. Even though they were foreshadowed in part, as G. P. Gooch has shown, by minority Protestant groups such as the Brownists, Levellers and other Independents and Separatists in Great Britain and the American colonies, they were none the less regarded as extreme if not dangerous by the majority of Protestants of Locke's day who were Calvinists, Anglicans and Episcopalians, as well as by Roman Catholics. And even with the minority groups the affirmation of religious or political doctrines identical with those of Locke was often grounded more in expediency than in principle, as is instanced by the Independents under Cromwell who affirmed these doctrines when they were in the minority in the Long Parliament and repudiated them when they became the majority in the Rump Parliament. Yet for all this the contribution of such Protestant Independents as Brown in England and Roger Williams in Rhode Island to the traditional modern idea of the good in both religion and government is tremendous, and is none the less significant because self-interest of the moment may have prompted it, and inconsistency accompanied it. Such conduct is inevitable where practical decisions and policy are not guided by scientifically grounded philosophical principles. It is precisely such principles that Locke provided.

Forthwith wavering inconsistent actions which all too often, as with Cromwell, looked more like the acts of a dictator than the operations of a lawful government could be brought under philosophically grounded law, and those fighting for religious and political independence, instead of canceling each other's influence out in opposing piecemeal actions, had a single doctrine and policy upon which they could agree and around which they could rally. Moreover, just as the Presbyterians and other Calvinists in the Long Parliament in England and in the New England Colonies believed in a theocratic form of government in which the civil magistrate enforced one religious doctrine upon all and this idea of the good for church and state was grounded by Calvin in a hierarchical, essentially medieval conception of man and nature; and just as the Church of England by way of Hooker, and the Roman Catholic Church by way of St. Thomas, as the sequel will show, are grounded in the scientific philosophy of Aristotle—so John Locke, when he made articulate the theory of nature and human nature of Newton's physics, provided justification in terms of scientifically verified philosophical principles for the otherwise somewhat arbitrary doctrines and actions of the Protestant Independents and Separatists in seventeenth-century England. Thus, it was possible to bring under law a new idea of the good for man and the church and state. Moreover, the further men moved into the modern world and noted how inescapable facts necessitated the replacement of Aristotle's conception of nature and man with that of Newton, the more this Newtonian and Lockean idea of the good was destined to become the guiding principle of the majority rather than of a minority.

The precise manner in which this Lockean articulation of Newton's science provided new meaning and foundations for religion and government must now concern us. According to this theory, the whole of reality is nothing but material substances in public space and time acting upon mental substances to cause the latter to project sensed qualities in sensed space and time as appearances. Consequently, no alternative remains but to identify the soul of man and the political person with the mental substance, since these are the only substances which have consciousness. The person's body on the other hand is an aggregate of material substances or atoms moving under the completely mechanistic laws of Newton's physics. Thus, the person in his moral, religious and political nature as a conscious being and in his subjective scientific status as an observer of nature is a single mental substance, whereas in his bodily nature and in his scientific status as an object in nature he is an aggregate of many atoms of material substances. In Locke's legal theory this group of material substances which is the person's body is his "property," just as much as are the aggregates of material substances which are his land and house. Thus a person though but one mental substance has as his property a body which is many material substances. The content of his mind and consciousness, in the form of sensations in sensed space and time, arises as an appearance when the material substances of his body, either because of their own motion or because of the action of other material objects or propagations upon them, affect his solitary mental substance.

Since a mental substance is an elementary entity, without parts, and quite independent of the material substances, it follows that the soul of man cannot break into parts, as death would require, and is quite unaffected by the dissolution of the human being's body at its death. Thus the distinction between body and soul and the doctrine of the immortality of the soul are necessary corollaries of this modern Lockean scientific and philosophical theory. It is clear, also, that it is with one's mental substance and with this alone, since it alone has consciousness, that religion must be concerned. Since any individual mental substance is a completely self-sufficient, independent thing, in no way requiring the existence of any other mental substances for its own conscious spiritual being, and since it is devoid of any organic relation defined by scientific or philosophical doctrine which makes its well-being dependent upon the existence of other persons, religion tends to become a purely introspective, private thing with respect to which the individual person is far better informed than any professional religious leader and, hence, the only person who is a competent religious guide. As Locke put the matter, in his famous *Letter Concerning Toleration*, "The only narrow way which leads to heaven is not better known to the magistrate than to private persons, and therefore I cannot safely take him for my guide, who may probably be as ignorant of the way as myself, and who certainly is less concerned for my salvation than I myself am. . . . The care, therefore, of every man's soul belongs unto himself, and is to be left unto himself."

Upon this basis the individual man alone, consulting his own mental substance introspectively, is the sole criterion of the correctness of his religion, and the religion of one man cannot be shown to be incorrect by appeal to any other man's doctrine, whether it be that of the Roman Catholic St. Thomas or the Protestant Calvin. This conception of religion differed as much from most Protestant doctrine as it did from Roman Catholic doctrine. In fact, Locke's use of the word "magistrate" refers undoubtedly to the Presbyterian Calvinistic thesis that the magistrate is the preserver of the purity of the Christian faith.

Thus it is that Locke's modern concept of the soul as a supposedly introspected mental substance gave a new, revolutionary, and excessively ego-centric form to the emphasis upon the individual conscience, previously fostered by both Catholics and Protestants, and laid the philosophical basis for the doctrine of complete religious toleration as a positive good which we now take so much for granted in democratic societies. This Lockean idea that the individual man alone, consulting his own private, introspectively given mental substance, or soul, even before the "correct doctrine" has affected that soul, or even before the soul has been "born anew," is the only judge of the religious man, is a very novel thesis in the history of the Western world.

The Brownists and Levellers had, to be sure, foreshadowed Locke in this theory. It is to be noted, however, that they were minority groups and often their conduct, when they found themselves in the majority, indicated that they regarded toleration more as a practical expedient than as a positive good. One has only to examine the practices of our religious colonial forefathers, of Calvin with the citizens and Servetus at Geneva, or of the Presbyterians in the Long Parliament in Cromwell's time, to note that the majority of Protestants initially conceived of freedom of conscience merely as the freedom to impose one's own particular doctrine upon all men in the community.

Of the Colonies of New England, R. B. Perry writes: "Puritanism was intolerant of other creeds—in this resembling its God, who might be merciful, but was not tolerant. It was disposed to make its own creed all-pervasive, and to perfect, after the scriptural model, all the aspects and social relationships of life. To achieve this end it did not scruple to employ the full force of the civil authorities, to limit citizenship to the members of the church, and to identify its religious ideal with public policy. It enjoyed an invincible sense of truth and felt no compunction in saving men from the effects of their own blindness." Most were followers of Calvin. As R. H. Bainton has written: "Calvin . . . tried to achieve a church coterminous with the community and at the same time comprising none but the saints. This could be done only by excluding the unworthy both from the church and the community. . . . In New England the small frontier communities endeavored to recover the pattern of [Calvin and] Geneva, in part by excommunication and banishment, but more largely by restriction of the franchise. Only church members could vote. Church and state thus became one, but not the church and the community. In the New Haven Colony in 1649 the estimate is that out of 144 planters only 16 were free burgesses."

The state of affairs in England in Locke's time is indicated in his *Letter Concerning Toleration:*

No man complains of the ill-management of his neighbour's affairs. No man is angry with another for an error committed in sowing his land or in marrying his daughter. Nobody corrects a spendthrift for consuming his substance in taverns. Let any man pull down, or build, or make whatsoever expenses he pleases, nobody murmurs, nobody controls him; he has his liberty. But if any man do not frequent the church, if he do not there conform his behaviour exactly to the accustomed ceremonies, or if he brings not his children to be initiated in the sacred mysteries of this or the other congregation, this immediately causes an uproar. The neighbourhood is filled with noise and clamour. Everyone is ready to be the avenger of so great a crime, and the zealots hardly have the patience to refrain from violence and rapine so long till the cause be heard, and the poor man be, according to form, condemned to the loss of liberty, goods, or life. Oh, that our ecclesiastical orators of every sect would apply themselves with all the strength of arguments that they are able to the confounding of men's errors! But let them spare their persons. Let them not supply their want of reasons with the instruments of force, which belong to another jurisdiction, and do ill become a Churchman's hands.

The principle of religious toleration for all peoples—Protestant or Catholic, Christian or non-Christian—which Locke specifies and which follows from his philosophy may be put in another way. Since introspective awareness of the deliverances of one's own spiritual nature— that is, of one's own mental substance—is the sole basis of religion, that to which this awareness leads one defines orthodoxy. As Locke adds, "It will be answered . . . that it is the orthodox church which has the right of authority over the erroneous or heretical. This is, in grand and specious words, to say just nothing at all. For every church is orthodox to itself; to others, erroneous or heretical." It follows, also, since force belongs only to the material substances and hence comes only, as we shall see, under the control of the civil authorities, and since religion has its basis solely in the purely spiritual or mental substances, that the influence by religious individuals or ecclesiastical authorities must be purely spiritual, resorting only to verbal persuasion, and never making use of force or of civil law or of the circumstance that a religious person may at the same time be in a position giving him civil power and authority. Thus Locke writes:

No force is here to be made use of upon any occasion whatsoever. For force belongs wholly to the civil magistrate, and the possession of all outward goods is subject to his jurisdiction. . . . But, it may be asked, by what means then shall ecclesiastical laws be established . . . They must be established by means suitable to the nature of such things, whereof the external profession and observation—if not proceeding from a thorough conviction and approbation of the mind—is altogether useless and unprofitable. The arms . . . are exhortations, admonitions, and advices.

Similarly, since religion has to do only with the introspectively given, personal, private mental substance, "the care of souls cannot belong to the civil magistrate, because his power consists only in outward force; . . . Nor can any such power be vested in the magistrate by the consent of the people, because no man can so far abandon the care of his own salvation as blindly to leave to the choice of any other, . . . to prescribe to him what faith or worship he shall embrace."

One other fact is to be noted. The modern Lockean scientific and philosophical theory specifies no relation between the many mental substances. In fact, the theory leaves their relation exceedingly ambiguous. All physical relations between people have to do with their bodies, and the latter are quite independent of their mental substances. In fact, it is very difficult to conceive of what the relation is, on Locke's theory, between one mental substance and any or all other mental substances. They are not related by space, since mental substances are not in space. This is precisely what Leibnitz meant when he described his monads as "windowless." Windows join what is inside a given entity, such as a house, to what is outside that entity. But the terms "inside" and "outside" are spatial terms and are only appropriate to entities in space. On the modern Lockean theory, space refers either to relations between sensed qualities which are items in the awareness of the mental substance or to a public, mathematically defined space independent of the observer in which the material substances are located. Thus it is meaningless and nonsensical to think of mental substances as located, like material substances, in space. But if the relation between the mental substances is not a spatial one, it is exceedingly difficult to imagine what it can be.

This point is tremendously important. It is, in fact, the basis for the entire modern Lockean democratic theory of social organization, whether it be ecclesiastical or civil. Because Locke's philosophical theory of a person as a mental substance prescribes no relation between the persons, or mental substances, making up society, there are no social laws prescribed, either by God or by nature. Hence, no alternative remains but to regard the laws of ecclesiastical or civil government as mere conventions, having their sole authority in the private, introspectively given opinions of the independent atomic individuals and their joint majority consent.

Locke did, to be sure, speak of all people in the state of nature as subject to the law of reason. But this law of reason must not be interpreted as the organic social principle of Hooker and Aristotle. What reason led man to, in the case of Locke, was nature conceived as mechanistically determined material substances and men in the state of nature as individual observers who are mental substances, whose interrelation cannot even be clearly conceived. These mental substances were, however, conscious and hence sensitive to persons and things other than themselves; also their reason did take them to the theory of mental substances, according to which all individuals are absolutely free and independent. Thus, as C. W. Hendel has called to my attention, Locke did not regard the natural state of man as one of warfare, as did Hobbes;

furthermore, this sensitivity of the mental substance develops with his successors Shaftesbury, Hutchinson and Butler into the feeling of sympathy which we shall come upon later in Adam Smith when we examine Anglo-American economic science.

The uniqueness of Locke's conception of social organization, either ecclesiastical or civil, becomes clear if we compare Locke's modern democratic theory of the nature of an individual with the Aristotelian and medieval theory of Hooker and St. Thomas. For Aristotle, man is by his very nature as an individual, a social man. He is, to use Aristotle's language, in his essential nature, and not merely as a result of his free consent expressed through a majority vote, "a political animal." The reasons for this will become clear in our chapter on Roman Catholic culture. Thus, according to Aristotle, political organization is of the nature of man and not something from which he can desist, or into which he may enter, according to the mere suggestion of his purely private, subjective opinion. Similarly, man, to fulfill his own individual nature, must participate in the hierarchical order not merely of society but of nature. Moreover, as Chapter VII will show, this hierarchical order is defined by an empirically determined teleological law of nature existing quite independently of the opinion and social conventions of men.

For Locke, on the other hand, the basis for ecclesiastical or civil laws is quite different. First, nature is made of material substances which, instead of entering into the teleological, hierarchical order of Aristotelian and medieval science, obey the purely mechanistic laws of Newton's physics; thus there is no basis for social laws in nature. Second, the person is, as we have noted, an independent, atomic mental substance, knowable only in one's own self by subjective introspection, and having no conceivable or specified relations to other mental substances or persons. Thus, in the essential nature of the Lockean person, there is no scientifically and philosophically grounded social relation joining him to other persons, with a content sufficient to provide a new law of nature, independent of the private opinions of individual men, for the grounding of ecclesiastic or civil law. Consequently, nothing remains but to regard all laws as mere conventions, having their authority solely in the free consent of the majority.

This applies to divine laws as well as to civil laws. Locke writes:

A Church I take to be a voluntary society of men joining themselves of their own accord in order to the public worshipping of God in such manner as they judge acceptable to Him, and effectual to the salvation of their souls.

. . . I say it is a free and voluntary society. Nobody is born a member of any church; . . . since the joining together of several members into this church-society, as has already been demonstrated, is absolutely free and spontaneous, it necessarily follows that the right of making its laws can belong to none but the society itself; or at least (which is the same thing) to those whom the society by common censent has authorized thereunto.

The difference between this congregational conception and the Anglican or medieval conception of the church is obvious.

The Lockean scientific and philosophical assumptions of the modern world have one other consequence for religion. Locating the sole basis for religion in the introspective awareness of the spiritual nature of one's private mental substance, it frees religion from any recourse to the traditional causal or cosmological arguments from nature to the existence of God. In fact, according to Newtonian science, nature is determined solely by the material substances, which behave according to mechanical causation. Consequently, in the modern world the traditional arguments from nature to the existence of God become untenable. Even the ontological argument from our idea of a perfect being to the existence of such a being, which Descartes as well as St. Anselm accepted, becomes untenable also, since ideas, according to the modern Lockean theory, are of a nature such that their meaning does not entail the existence of what is meant.

The modern scientific and philosophical theory, as made explicit by John Locke, has certain other religious consequences which Locke did not see. Although Locke was a religious man, as were the great majority of the founders of the American Republic who followed him, it is exceedingly difficult to understand, upon the basis of his philosophy, as the acute Voltaire noted, what need there is, or what justification there can be, for the belief in God.

It was suggested that God be introduced as the creator of the material and mental substances. This is Deism. But since the material and mental substances, by their very nature, are conceived as without parts, and hence indestructible and unaffected by time, the need for a creator is quite unnecessary. Furthermore, since God merely creates the material and mental substances, and everything else follows from their properties and interaction, every fact in the universe would be exactly what it is, whether we believe merely in the existence of material and mental substances alone or add on the gratuitous belief in a God who is their creator.

It was a distinguished Western theologian who laid down the principle, which has come to be generally accepted as a sound methodological criterion in any field of inquiry, that one must not multiply one's basic assumptions beyond necessity; one must introduce only the minimum assumptions necessary to account for the facts which we immediately apprehend. This made it clear that the postulation of the existence of God, in addition to merely the mental and material substances in interaction, is not merely a gratuitous but a methodologically invalid procedure. This is precisely what the Frenchman Laplace, follower of Newton, meant when, upon being asked whether he believed in the existence of God, he replied, "I find no need for such an hypothesis." Even modern Protestants have found the deistic hypothesis unsatisfactory.

But what meaning, then, is to be found, on the traditional assumptions of the modern world, for the existence of God? It is no exaggeration to say that modern religion has not succeeded in finding an answer to this question. The recent popular tendency among Protestant preachers to repudiate reason and to blame theology for the ills of the church is a frank confession of this fact. For a religion ungrounded in reason and without theology is a religion which does not know what it means by the words which it uses.

As the British philosopher McTaggart, who accepted the modern theory of the individual as a mental substance or what he termed "a spirit," clearly saw, this conception guarantees the doctrine of the immortality of the soul but leaves the doctrine of the existence of God unfounded. Thus he prided himself upon believing in the immortality of the soul while at the same time being an atheist. This did not leave him without a religion; in fact, he was an intensely spiritual and religious man, although not in a conventional sense. But his religion was one defined in terms of a community of human spirits joined in their essential nature by a certain unique relation. Thus there was, according to his theory of the individual, a meaning for the political community quite apart from anybody's private opinion or consent with respect to the matter. Consequently, as Harold Laski has noted, McTaggart's philosophy would lead to a theory of the nature of the state quite different from Locke's, to which we in the United States have been accustomed.

The traditional modern theory of the individual has another consequence which affects not merely religion but also art. Emotion has nothing whatever to do with the essential nature of the spiritual man. By themselves alone the human spirits or mental substances have nothing but a blank consciousness. To be sure, they have the creative capacity to project the phantasmic, phenomenal world of colors, sounds, odors, pains and pleasures and sensed space and time as mere appearances. But the awareness of even a color or a sound as a determinate item in the private, individual consciousness occurs only when the material substances act upon a given individual mental substance. Unless this action occurs, the individual possesses merely a blank consciousness; hence Locke called the mental substance by itself a tabula rasa, or blank tablet (Plate IX). Furthermore, for such substances, emotions and passions are not intrinsic characteristics of their nature, but merely data like colors and sounds toward which this new, modern man takes merely the attitude of an observer. Hence the modern man, like the cool, contemporary Englishman, avoids enthusiasm.

Clearly, his is a soul quite different from that of the Spaniard, the essence of which is passion. Passion, according to this Lockean Anglo-American theory, is merely an item in one's consciousness, purely phenomenal in character, quite independent of one's essential spiritual nature, which a man who is wise, in the modern Lockean sense of this word, will merely look at coolly and from a safe distance, as he would examine anything else which is an object other than himself, rather than an instinctive expression of his deepest and truest, most vital nature. In fact, emotions and passions, because of their association with pleasure and pain, were given even a lower status in the hierarchy of entities constituting the nature of things than were colors and sounds and odors and sensed space and time. The latter qualities were termed secondary qualities, being secondary to the really primary qualities which were the qualities possessed by material substances. The emotional items were not given even the status of being secondary; they were termed tertiary qualities.

With emotions, passions, and the other aesthetic materials such as colors and sounds given such a second-rate or third-rate status, the traditional modern Anglo-American man who really has his attention upon matters which are fundamental can hardly take art or a religion of passion very seriously. Art works with immediately experienced colors and forms, as in painting; or with immediately experienced sounds and their ordering, as in music; or with the emotions of people, as in medieval religious art or in poetry. But these things, according to the modern theory of Galilei, Newton, and Locke, are mere phenomena; they are merely second-rate or third-rate appearances. The really important things are either the material substances with which the businessman or the engineer "with his feet on the ground" concerns himself during the six workdays of the week; or the blank, purely spiritual, intrinsically unemotional, introspectively given mental substance with which, in a meeting hall, preferably without colors or sounds to disturb him, he communes on the Sabbath. For a religion proceeding from such a conception of the nature of man and the status of the aesthetic and emotional in the nature of things, the beautiful and emotionally moving ritual of the mass is quite unnecessary. In fact, it tends, according to the traditional modern Protestant, to get in the way and to give rise to idolatry, drawing one's attention away from the supposedly real religious object which is within one's own private, introspective self beneath the sensuous appearances. It is not an accident that the early Protestants in England took the color out of the church windows and attacked the theater.

Even the presence of others in worship is quite unnecessary. Thus the Quaker, sitting in silence without a professional preacher in his unadorned meetinghouse, most directly, completely, and perfectly exemplifies the the religion of this modern Cartesian and Lockean man. The Congregationalists almost attain this ideal when the preachers whom they permit are not only elected, but also have what they preach determined for them, by the majority of the laymen, Even with the Methodists, who copy Rome with its organization and its bishops, without taking over the beauty of its ritual, and the Episcopalians, who, with a slight sense of sin, take over an anemic copy of the Roman ritual while often in the United States purporting to be moderns and thereby denying the medieval assumptions which give this ritual its meaning— even with all these Protestants, whose earthly practices fall further and further away from the modern religious ideal, the professional clergy exists largely merely to remind one that one has this private, spiritual self, this introspectively given mental substance, in addition to the material substances of one's body and of nature, and not as in any way necessary to convey the meaning of religion or the means by which it can be actualized in one's life. The latter factors, the really significant things in religion, one can, according to the modern religious notion, really get only by oneself alone without any help from social ceremonies or artistic rituals. As New England's Emerson put it, "The wise man needs no church, for he is the prophet."

One need hardly wonder that a vital religious art or a moving emotional religion such as one finds at Guadalupe in Mexico has not developed in the modern religious world. Nor need one wonder that the preaching of traditional modern Protestantism has tended to become as empty and blank as the mental substance which is its subject matter, giving expression to as many and as varied specific moral and religious precepts in the concrete as there are diverse, contradictory, ill-considered impressions and opinions in the introspectively given consciousness of modern men.

Locke's theory of government was as novel as his theory of religion. Any theory of the state specifies the relation which joins persons to each other and to nature. This relation for any given scientific and philosophical theory depends upon how the theory conceives of a person and of nature. In the modern Newtonian and Lockean theory the conception of these two factors is clear. Nature is a set of material substances located in infinitely extended Euclidean space. A person is a single atomic mental substance. The reason for the latter conclusion is two-fold: first, the material substances of the person's body define only the order of nature, not the order of human society which is a relation between persons. Second, the material substances cannot account for human personality, as the fatal weakness in Hobbes's theory, previously noted, clearly indicates. The relation between a person and nature, or that portion of nature which is the person's body, is interaction. The material substances act upon the mental substance. Free will, which most moderns, apart from the Calvinists, regard as essential for the moral life, would seem to call also for an action of the mental substance upon the material substances. This has tended to be assumed, but it has always presented difficulties for the modern mind, due to the conflict with the laws of the conservation of mass and energy which govern the behavior of the material substances. The relation between a person and other persons is equally clear. There is no specified relation at all. As we have noted, the relation between mental substances is difficult to conceive.

Consequently, the individual person is absolutely free and independent; also, no principle or relation grounded in the nature of mental substances or persons and joining them to each other exists to give the state anything more than a conventional status. Thus the two basic premises of Locke's theory of government and the Declaration of Independence arise: All men are born free and equal, and the origin and basis of government is in "the consent of the governed." Not only is this modern Lockean democratic man in his essential nature as a person absolutely free and independent of all other men, not even requiring other men for the "salvation of his soul" which, Locke adds, "is the exclusive end of religion," but one person is intrinsically and essentially equal to all other persons.

It is to be noted that for Locke, who identifies the person with the mental substance, this is literally true. All mental substances in themselves, before material substances act upon them, are blank tablets. Thus, in themselves, they are equal. Also, mental substances were introduced by Locke in order to account for Galilei's and Newton's sensed colors, sounds, odors, and space and time as appearances. The most ordinary mortal has the same capacity to be aware of colors and sounds as does the genius. Thus in the capacity to project back the world of colors and sounds and sensed space and time all men are equal also. It must be noted that one does not dispose of the Lockean democratic theory to the effect that all men are born free and equal, as many people suppose they have done, by pointing out that an Einstein or a Bach is born with greater capacity than a moron. Locke would admit this to be true but would add that it has its basis in the different structures of the bodies of the two men which have to do with the material substances in the order of nature, and in no way alters the truth concerning the mental substances or persons, to which the legal principles of the state refer. Here lies, in considerable part, the basis of the modern man's conviction that regardless of his brain, his social status, his birth, or his accomplishments—even though, in a given instance, all these be negligible—he is as good as anybody else.

In his essay *Of Civil Government* Locke wrote, "Men being, as has been said, by nature all free, equal, and independent, no one can be put out of this estate and subjected to the political power of another without his consent." But immediately a difficulty arose. A state, even one with a minimum of social organization, restricts the freedom and independence of the individual. Why, then, will men, even by consent as a mere convention, give up some of this ideal, self-sufficient, God-given freedom and independence as they must if they are to have a government? The initial condition of men, before any government is instituted by consent, is composed of the group of unrelated, absolutely free, equal, and independent mental substances in interaction with the material substances, and is termed by Locke "the state of Nature." Again it must be emphasized that this phrase must not be confused, as it has been by many historians and philosophers, with the quite different "law of nature" of Hooker and St. Thomas, which is identified with their hierarchical teleological order of Aristotelian and medieval science. In terms of his "state of Nature" Locke puts the difficulty in his famous essay *Of Civil Government* as follows: "If a man in the state of Nature be so free as has been said, if he be absolute lord of his own person and possessions, equal to the greatest and subject to nobody, why will he part with his freedom, this empire, and subject himself to the dominion and control of any other power?"

The answer is as follows: Man, as a mental substance, by means of his body and other physical objects of nature, cuts down the forests, tills the soil, grows his crops, and builds his home. Other mental substances, with their native freedom and perhaps their more indolent bodies, note this accomplishment and, finding it easier to combine and steal the neighbor's home and crops and perhaps even to destroy his physical body, than to develop and construct their own, take the individual man's property. This is the reason why the modern free and independent man gives up some of his ideal and actual native liberty to submit himself to conventionally prescribed laws of the state. As a free and independent individual he cannot protect his property.

Locke puts the matter as follows:

The enjoyment of the property he has in this state [of Nature] is very unsafe, very insecure. This makes him willing to quit this condition which, however free, is full of fears and continual dangers; and it is not without reason that he seeks out and is willing to join in society with others who are already united, or have a mind to unite for the mutual preservation of their lives, liberties and estates, which I call by the general name—property.

The great and chief end, therefore, of men uniting into commonwealths, and putting themselves under government, is the preservation of their property; to which in the state of Nature there are many things wanting.

Thus it came about in the modern world that the sole justification for the existence of government became the preservation of private property, where property means not merely external material things but also one's material body.

It is to be noted, also, that according to this modern Lockean theory the existence of a government is a lesser evil; it is not the ideal good. The ideal good for man is the initial "state of Nature" devoid of all government in which the individual has complete independence and absolute, unqualified freedom. More exactly, it is this state of freedom without other men possessing bodies of an avaricious nature which leads them to interfere with the free, independent individual's property. Thus the modern man does not enter into the state because organic relations with other men enable one to express more fully one's moral, religious, and political nature and thereby live a richer, more ideal life, as was the case in the medieval concept of the state, or as is the case in the present communistic theory of society. Instead, the state is a necessary evil, forcing one to give up part of the ideal good, which is the complete independence and freedom of the individual, in order to preserve one's private property.

This theory of the basis of the state has one very important consequence. Locke expresses it as follows: "The supreme power cannot take from any man any part of his property without his own consent. For the preservation of property being the end of government, and that for which men enter into society, it necessarily supposes and requires that the people should have property, without which they must be supposed to lose that by entering into society which was the end for which they entered into it." In other words, it would be a contradiction in terms for the state to take property away from the individual, since the sole justification for the existence of the state is the preservation of the property of the individual. One might suppose that the last quotation came from some member of the Supreme Court of the United States who was appointed by Herbert Hoover. Actually, it was written (1690) by John Locke in his *Essay Concerning the True, Original Extent and End of Civil Government.*

We should now be able to understand why, as was noted in our consideration of economic democracy in Mexico, all past attempts of modern liberals within traditional democracy to place human rights above property rights have turned out in practice in the United States to be so purely verbal. Consciously or unconsciously, the Lockean doctrine of the self-sufficient, independent moral, religious, and political person has become so much a common-sense assumption of the vast majority that in a political showdown, when emotions are raised and traditional, instinctive reactions are released, the laissez-faire, individualistic response triumphs over the organic, social principle. Unless and until democracy is reared upon scientific and philosophical foundations different from the traditional ones, and these new foundations are worked out systematically with respect to their national and international legal consequences, and these new assumptions gain the same persuasiveness for us that the Lockean assumptions enjoyed in the past, there can be little hope that the new liberalism will fare any better than its recent predecessors.

It should be clear now also, notwithstanding the emphasis of modern Protestant religion upon the primary importance of man, and notwithstanding the thesis of democracy that man is the source of all political authority, why the seeming paradox arises that the traditional democracy of a predominantly Protestant culture in practice puts property rights above human rights. The reason is that the Protestant emphasis upon the individual conscience tends to locate the source of all good and evil in the individual; thereby attributing any social evils which arise to the fault of the individual rather than to the social, political, and economic circumstances in which he finds himself at birth; and the Lockean democratic thesis that the sole justification for the existence of government is the preservation of private property makes it self-contradictory and hence unconstitutional for even a vote of the majority to place human rights above property rights in any issue between the two.

Thus, whereas one might at first suppose that under American democracy the people are free to do anything they want with respect to private property, providing it is voted by democratic processes, this is in fact not the case because of the Constitution, which, following Locke, guarantees the sanctity of property rights. Consequently, in practice, any democratic vote violating this principle becomes automatically unconstitutional. The fundamental reason why the Constitution is of this character is the one indicated by Locke: The justification for the doctrine of private property is not democratic processes; instead, the preservation of private property is the sole justification for the existence of any government whatever, even a democratic one.

It is to be emphasized, therefore, and never forgotten, that democracy, as it has been conceived traditionally and practiced in the United States, is not a mere political method by means of which the people become the sole source of political authority and express their own wills through a majority vote. It is instead this method subject to constitutional limitations which are defined by and which presuppose a specific theory of the nature of the individual and of the relation of the state and private property to that individual—the specific theory in fact which was formulated by John Locke.

This fact has exceedingly important practical consequences. It makes it likely, first, that when the democratic form of government of the United States is applied to peoples a majority of whom do not believe the philosophical conception of man and his relation to property and his fellow man to be that which the Lockean philosophy prescribes, that democracy may bring forth, as it has recently in Mexico, quite unexpected results. This possibility should make one cautious about pressing for the imposition of democratic processes upon other people without first paying attention to the philosophical assumptions underlying the culture and sentiments of those people. In the second place, it means that the American form of democracy restricted by the constitutional principle of the sanctity of property rights presupposes that the people possess private property. In fact, Locke stated explicitly that "it necessarily supposes and requires that the people should have property." This was the case with the majority of the people of the United States when our democratic government was instituted.

Thomas Jefferson himself saw a danger for democracy in the concentration of great wealth in the hands of a minority of the people, such as existed in the estates along the James River, which the colonial period in Virginia had produced. He writes:

In the earlier times of the colony, when lands were to be obtained for little or nothing, some provident individuals procured large grants; and, desirous of founding great families for themselves, settled them on their descendants in fee tail. The transmission of this property from generation to generation, in the same name, raised up a distinct set of families, who, being privileged by law in the perpetuation of their wealth, were thus formed into a Patrician order, distinguished by the splendor and luxury of their establishments. . . . To annul this privilege, and instead of an aristocracy of wealth, of more harm and danger, than benefit, to society, to make an opening for the aristocracy of virtue and talent, which nature has wisely provided for the direction of the interests of society, and scattered with equal hand through all its conditions, was deemed essential to a well-ordered republic.

Jefferson believed that he met the situation within the processes of democratic procedure by abolishing the law of primogeniture. He continues, "To effect it, no violence was necessary, no deprivation of natural right, but rather an enlargement of it by a repeal of the law. For this would authorize the present holder to divide the property among his children equally, as his affections were divided; and would place them, by natural generation, on the level of their fellow citizens." Consequently, Jefferson adds, "I proposed to abolish the law of primogeniture, and to make real estate descendible in parcenary to the next of kin, as personal property is, by the statute of distribution." Jefferson saw that unless the majority of the people have some share in the natural wealth of their country, which private property widely distributed alone can insure, even democratic government will fail; in fact, the precondition justifying peoples entering into it will not exist.

It is to be noted that this conclusion follows from the Lockean individualistic premises. Since the preservation of private property is the sole justification for free individuals' consent to create or remain in any government, it follows that unless a majority of them possess private property they will not be justified in giving their consent to government, even democratic government. For similar reasons Thomas Jefferson was fearful of the effect upon democracy of the development of an industrial society in the United States and advised his countrymen against it because of the concentration of private property in the hands of a few which it might produce, and the evils of congested city life which it creates.

These considerations suggest additional reasons for caution with respect to insistence upon the literal sanctity of property rights, in the correspondence of our Secretaries of State with a country such as Mexico—where property titles to the nation's resources became concentrated in the hands of a few—if one's interest there is the preservation of a democratic form of government. It also suggests that those political leaders in the United States who are doing the most to insure the preservation of its form of government and its traditional doctrine of the primacy of property rights, may be not those Conservative Republicans and Conservative Democrats who emphasize individual freedom and the minimum of government legislation aimed at keeping property from becoming too completely located in the hands of a minority, but instead those political leaders who work for legislation which insures as far as possible that a majority of people have incomes sufficient to enable them to possess private property.

It also must be emphasized that our traditional association of the democratic method with a specific philosophical doctrine which, as John Adams pointed out, had become the common belief of everybody, is absolutely essential for the working of the method. It need not be the specific philosophical doctrine which Locke formulated; but there must be agreement upon some doctrine.

The reason for this is that if democracy is to function it must give expression to a program which has the support of at least a majority. This does not occur unless there is some political philosophy which has become the common property and belief of at least a majority of the people. The democratic method does not guarantee the existence of this common belief or philosophy of a majority; it merely gives expression to it if it is present. Consequently, if, under the operation of the democratic method, a people come to give up the traditional conception of man and his relation to other men and to nature and to private property, which defines the traditional will of the majority, and no other philosophical conception is put in its place, the people break into so many minority political parties with their diverse and conflicting political policies with respect to these matters that, regardless of who is elected, his policy can represent only the will of an insignificant minority. When this happens it is impossible for the will of the majority to function, there being no majority opinion, and democracy breaks down.

This, it is to be noted, is precisely what happened during the operation of the democratic method in Germany following Versailles. The political philosophy expressing itself in the monarchical government of the Kaiser, which the German people regarded not merely as their own but as having produced the highest *Kultur* in the world, had been smashed by their military defeat in 1918. Consequently, the democratic method, when forced upon the Germans by Versailles, was accompanied by no philosophical theory and attendant political doctrine to define its program which had the support of a majority. Thus German politics in actual practice became a group of little minority political parties at cross purposes with each other, all nurtured, as Arnold Brecht has shown, by the method of proportional representation prescribed by the Weimar Constitution, and the government became an artificial coalition of such conflicting and self-contradictory parties. It must be realized, therefore, that democracy is not a mere method, but requires for its successful operation some philosophical conception of the nature of man and his relation to other men and to nature which has factual grounds such that, by virtue of the scientific evidence in its support, it persuades a majority, at least, of the people to accept it and use it as the criterion of the good for political policy.

If this be true nothing is more important, if democracy is to be preserved in the United States, where we have become accustomed to, and trained in, its method, than that we keep an eye upon the basic philosophical conception of ourselves and the universe and put forth the attention and effort necessary to insure that it is abreast of contemporary knowledge and sufficiently taught to our people so that at least a majority of them freely believe in it and vote and act according to its assumptions.

In his Farewell Address, in which he warned those who were to come after him of the dangers most necessary to guard against if we would preserve our democracy, Washington wrote:

Let me now . . . warn you in the most solemn manner against the baneful effects of the Spirit of Party. . . . This Spirit, unfortunately, is inseparable from our nature, having its root in the strongest passions of the human mind.—It exists under different shapes in all Governments, . . . and is truly their worst enemy.—. . . There is an opinion, that parties in free countries are useful checks upon the Administration of the Government, and serve to keep alive the spirit of Liberty.—This within certain limits is probably true—and in Governments of a Monarchical cast, Patriotism may look with indulgence, if not with favor, upon the spirit of party.—But in those of the popular character, in Governments purely elective, it is a spirit not to be encouraged.—From their natural tendency, it is certain there will always be enough of that spirit for every salutary purpose,—and there being constant danger of excess, the effort ought to be, by force of public opinion, to mitigate and assuage it.

This "force of public opinion" can hardly be expected to exist unless there is a single set of philosophical assumptions defining the public good and transcending party differences which is upheld by at least a majority of the people.

Democracy, therefore, if it is to function and preserve itself, must be accompanied by two conditions. The first of these was emphasized by its founders and is one of the highest fruits of democratic cultures. The other has not received the attention which it deserves. The first requirement is universal education. The second is that this education must concern itself not merely with applied science and literature and art and practical matters but also with man's basic beliefs concerning the nature of himself and his universe. For if the inquiry with respect to the latter matters is not pursued, it is inevitable, as the increase in man's scientific knowledge alters the traditional scientific and philo- sophical doctrines concerning the nature of man and his universe, and thus requires attendant reconstruction in man's psychological, religious, moral, and political theory, that the people will be left without any knowledge or appreciation of the importance of these matters. Then emphasis upon the traditional, outmoded, moral, religious, and political sentiments will become a positive menace, preventing man from making the reconstruction in his sense of values and in his social practices and institutions which new knowledge, technological instruments, and new factual changes in internal national and international affairs may make absolutely essential for the preservation of democracy and the state.

Education, and especially its application of the more objective, dis- passionate method of science, even to the study of religions and the humanities, is an essential instrument by means of which the religious toleration and the democratic, theoretical, political assumptions necessary to make democracy function are propagated. Nothing, therefore, can do more harm to democracy than the thesis, so popular with many contemporary moral and religious leaders, that science is neutral, if not positively evil, with respect to human values. The truth of the matter is that the scientific attitude of mind is one of the highest values, and a primary value in democracy. It is undoubtedly true that religion and the humanities have helped to make men humane. But an examination of the behavior of the Roman Catholics in the Inquisition with respect to Galilei, and of Calvin in the condemnation of Servetus to death because of a difference of religious belief purely within Protestantism, and of countless other similar historical facts, shows that it is even more true that the application of the scientific attitude of mind to the study of religion and the humanities has made individual persons and self-righteous religious groups more tolerant and humane. Also, our analysis of the connection of the modern theory of the good for man in religion and the state with the philosophy of Lockean and Newtonian science, shows that in fact our theory of moral, religious, and political values simply does not have the autonomy and independence from science which so many contemporary moral and religious leaders assert.

The founding fathers were most cognizant of this dependence of moral and political values upon science. Thomas Jefferson wrote, "Science had liberated the ideas of those who read and reflect, and the American example had kindled feelings of right in the people. . . . Science is progressive, and talents and enterprise on the alert." John Quincy Adams added, "The people of this country do not sufficiently estimate the importance of patronizing and promoting science as a principle of political action." As one of our contemporary poets, Muriel Rukeyser, has written:

This country rests more than any other on scientific achievement and the application of scientific law [one might add the scientific attitude of mind] to other fields. . . . The ideas behind [its] growth . . . came from science and a new political theory which rose in interlocking structures whose points meshed so cleanly that the meaning of that delicate triumphant gear was not mistakable in France; and in England, where Newton and Locke had touched the idea with fire, . . . The bloodstream that proved our parentage and stamped its features on us was, more than any other, this double current of political theory and science which gushed up in two fountains: the Declaration and the Constitution.

THE FEDERAL PRINCIPLE

The Declaration of Independence merely "absolved" the colonies "from all allegiance to the British Crown," thereby leaving them "Free and Independent States"; it did not unite them into a federal government possessing a definite form of organization and sovereign powers of its own. The latter achievements were realized with the adoption of the Constitution of the United States. To understand this nation's culture and its particular values and ideals it is necessary, therefore, to examine the conceptions behind the Constitution as well as those behind the Declaration of Independence.

In the case of the Constitution, also, Newton's science and its attendant Lockean philosophy were very important. Nevertheless, they presented difficulties and liabilities as well as assets, as the fears of Jefferson about shifting sovereign powers from the state governments to the federal government, and the efforts of the authors of *The Federalist* who supported this transfer, clearly indicate. Having used his philosophical theory of naturally unrelated, free, and individual men to define the source of all political authority and having made the preservation of their private property the sole justification for their creation of a government, Locke then went on to specify the forms which such a government created by the free consent of a majority would necessarily take. "The majority," he writes, "having . . . the whole power of the community naturally in them, may employ all that power in making laws for the community from time to time, and executing those laws by officers of their own appointing, and then the form of government is a perfect democracy." A page later Locke continues, "The great end of men's entering into society being the enjoyment of their properties in peace and safety, and the great instrument and means of that being the laws established in that society, the first and fundamental positive law of all commonwealths is the establishing of the legislative power, as the first and fundamental natural law which is to govern even the legislative." Similarly, the Constitution of the United States begins by setting up the legislative power and vesting it in the Congress.

Locke immediately adds, however, that "Though the legislative . . . be the supreme power in every commonwealth, yet, first, it is not, nor can possibly be, absolutely arbitrary over the lives and fortunes of the people. For it being but the joint power of every member of the society given up to that person or assembly which is legislator, it can be no more than those persons had in a state of Nature before they entered into society, and gave it up to the community." Consequently, "the obligations of the law of Nature cease not in society, but only in many cases are drawn closer, and have, by human laws, known penalties annexed to them to enforce their observation. Thus the law of Nature stands as an eternal rule to all men, legislators as well as others." Similarly, the Constitution, after vesting all legislative powers in the Congress of the United States, proceeds immediately to designate the specific matters with respect to which it may legislate.

Even these specifications were not enough to put the mind of Thomas Jefferson, and of countless others influenced by the Lockean ideas, at ease with respect to the powers of the democratically adopted Constitution and its federal government. As a consequence, but two years after the new federal government was established ten amendments affecting the rights of the states and the people which the federal government could not touch were duly proposed by Congress and ratified by the legislatures of the several states. The tenth amendment is indicative of the purport of them all. It reads, "The powers not delegated to the United States by the Constitution, nor prohibited by it to the States, are reserved to the States respectively, or to the people." The first amendment also is important. It reads, "Congress shall make no law respecting an establishment of religion, or prohibiting the free exercise thereof; or abridging the freedom of speech, or of the press; or the right of the people peaceably to assemble, and to petition the Government for a redress of grievances." Thomas Jefferson, in writing of Virginia, informs us that a definite attempt was made to restrict freedom of religious belief to freedom of belief in the Christian religion and that this attempt was defeated. Again we see the importance of Locke's philosophical theory in curbing Protestantism and Catholicism to make our humanistic cultural ideals and constitutional safeguards what they are.

With respect to the "legislative or supreme authority," Locke adds that it "cannot assume to itself a power to rule by extempory arbitrary decrees, but is bound to dispense justice and decide the rights of the subject by promulgated standing laws, and known authorised judges." To insure the former requirement the Constitution specifies that:

Every Bill which shall have passed the House of Representatives and the Senate, shall, before it become a Law, be presented to the President of the United States; If he approve he shall sign it, but if not he shall return it, with his Objections to that House in which it shall have originated, who shall enter the Objections at large on their Journal, and proceed to reconsider it. If after such Reconsideration two thirds of that House shall agree to pass the Bill, it shall be sent, together with the Objections, to the other House, by which it shall likewise be reconsidered, and if approved by two thirds of that House, it shall become a Law.

To insure the second requirement, that there be "known authorised judges," the Constitution, in Article III, specifies that the "judicial Power of the United States, shall be vested in one supreme Court, and in such inferior Courts as the Congress may from time to time ordain and establish." Forthwith, it specifies the "Cases, in Law and Equity, arising under the Constitution" to which the judicial power shall extend.

Locke continues:

> The legislative power is that which has a right to direct how the force of the commonwealth shall be employed for preserving the community and the members of it. Because those laws which are constantly to be executed, and whose force is always to continue, may be made in a little time, therefore there is no need that the legislative should be always in being, not having always business to do. And because it may be too great temptation to human frailty, apt to grasp at power, for the same persons who have the power of making laws to have also in their hands the power to execute them, whereby they may exempt themselves from obedience to the laws they make, and suit the law, both in its making and execution, to their own private advantage, and thereby come to have a distinct interest from the rest of the community, contrary to the end of society and government. . . .
>
> But because the laws that are at once, and in a short time made, have a constant and lasting force, and need a perpetual execution, or an attendance thereunto, therefore it is necessary there should be a power always in being which should see to the execution of the laws that are made, and remain in force. And thus the legislative and executive power come often to be separated.

Similarly, the Constitution puts into effect this Lockean doctrine of the separation of legislative, executive, and judicial powers, vesting the executive power in the President.

Locke also assigns to the chief executive two distinct powers, one of which he terms "executive" and the other "federative," the former having to do with internal matters affecting the citizens of the commonwealth alone, the latter having to do with the relation of the commonwealth to foreign nations. Locke noted with respect to the former matters that since they involve only the citizens of the commonwealth and derive from them, the chief executive cannot initiate such powers but can merely execute what the people's representatives in the legislative branch of the government designate. But Locke adds, "What is to be done in reference to foreigners depending much upon their actions and the variation of designs and interests, must be left in great part to the prudence of those who have this power committed to them, to be managed by the best of their skill for the advantage of the commonwealth." The latter powers, which Locke termed federative, consequently could and must initiate with the President himself. Here also our Constitution follows Locke in specifying that "The President shall be Commander in Chief of the Army and Navy of the United States, and of the Militia of the several States, when called into actual Service of the United States" and that "He shall have Power . . . to make Treaties." But with respect to the latter federative power our Constitution is more Lockean than Locke himself, since it specifies that the President's power to make treaties must be "by and with the Advice and Consent of the Senate, . . . provided two thirds of the Senators present concur." However, even Locke himself, immediately after giving the executive initiatory rights with respect to federative powers, adds that "there can be but one supreme power, which is the legislative, to which all the rest are and must be subordinate, yet the legislative being only a fiduciary power to act for certain ends, there remains still in the people a supreme power to remove or alter the legislative, when they find the legislative act contrary to the trust reposed in them."

Clearly, the forms of the federal government of the United States, as specified by its Constitution, are those prescribed by John Locke's political philosophy. Nevertheless, this Lockean philosophy put grave difficulties in the way of the founding of this federal government. Nor are the reasons for this seemingly paradoxical situation difficult to understand. Because of the Lockean theory of persons as absolutely free, self-sufficient, and independent mental substances, the ideal social organization and government, apart from the preservation of private property, is no government at all. As Emerson wrote later, "The less government the better." The degree to which this basic premise of Locke's political philosophy still persists shows itself in the political utterances of Conservative Republican and Conservative Democratic party leaders and the irritations of our friends, especially those with considerable traditional education, at the increased federal powers which the war and its peace make inescapable. So thoroughly has this Lockean philosophical premise become ingrained in the emotions of Anglo-Americans that facts—even the bombardment of Pearl Harbor or the obvious need for a positive national and international federal policy to preserve peace following 1918—have had great difficulty in offsetting it. We need hardly wonder, therefore, that it put difficulties in the way of the formation of a federal government at the time of the adoption of the Constitution, even though this government and Constitution were drawn up specifically in accord with Locke's theory of the end and forms of government.

The reason arose from Locke's implicit assumption that the minimum government is the ideal government and his definition of the sole end of government as the preservation of private property. These basic Lockean conceptions made it difficult for our founding fathers, even after they had accepted the Declaration of Independence and established their local communities as free and independent states, to see what need there was for any more restrictions upon their individual, native liberty than the individual states imposed. Certainly the local constables and the state militias were adequate to keep other mental substances from stealing one's external property or destroying the property which is one's living body. It was hardly necessary to create a federal government if these are the ends of government. It is not surprising, therefore, that Thomas Jefferson and countless others who were so competely dominated by Locke's ideas, regarded states' rights as the ideal, and looked upon the location of sovereignty in a federal government with misgivings and at best as a last resort and a necessary evil.

These considerations also explain why Hamilton and Jay, in *The Federalist*, found it necessary to bring forth quite different arguments for the justification and establishment of a federal government. These arguments rested on two facts, rather than upon the assumptions of Locke's theory, although the agreement of the colonists upon Locke's theory in part constituted one of the facts. These two facts were the cultural agreement and unity of the colonists, and the geographical and physical unity of the country.

Writing in 1787, after the Constitution had been drawn up but before it had been ratified, Jay pointed out that the citizens of the free and independent states were:

. . . one united people; a people descended from the same ancestors, speaking the same language, professing the same religion, attached to the same principles of government, very similar in their manners and customs, and who, by their joint counsels, arms and efforts, fighting side by side throughout a long and bloody war, have nobly established their general Liberty and Independence.

This country and this people seem to have been made for each other, and it appears as if it was the design of Providence, that an inheritance so proper and convenient for a band of brethren, united to each other by the strongest ties, should never be split into a number of unsocial, jealous, and alien sovereignties.

It is to be noted that this argument conceives of government as a positive good called for by certain existing factual, social relations and not as something justified solely because it enables the individual person to protect his private property.

But more than this common cultural heritage was behind Hamilton and Jay's advocacy of the federal principle as a positive good. As Van Wyck Brooks has noted in *The World of Washington Irving,* notwithstanding the revolution from England, Hamilton and his followers "retained the political and social ideas of England"; they wanted none of the equalitarian democratic doctrines of Locke and Jefferson represented in the Society of St. Tammany; they were, in short, "intensely Episcopalian and aristocratic." Also R. B. Perry has reminded us that Washington, Madison, Monroe, Randolph and Lee, and even Jefferson in his social habits, as Monticello shows, were cavaliers "pervaded by the Anglican sentiment." The next chapter will show that this English aristocratic Episcopalian idea of the good society rests upon Aristotle's philosophy as formulated by Richard Hooker and fostered by the regal Tudors, rather than upon the philosophy of Locke. It was precisely for this reason that the socially elite Hamilton and his fellow Federalists believed in the federal as opposed to the more individualistic Lockean principle. For Aristotle and the Tudor Episcopalians following him define man as a political animal and prescribe organic social action at the level of the community as a whole as a positive good. It is not an accident that the Federalists were Episcopalians or that financial New York's Wall Street begins at Trinity Church.

An appeal to the aristocratic philosophical principles of the Episcopalian and Aristotelian Tudor Kings could hardly be used, however, immediately following the revolution from England, to persuade the individualistic Non-conformist Protestant Quakers of Pennsylvania and Puritans of New England and the Jeffersonian democrats to give up even some of their God-given independence in order to provide a federal government with sovereignty. Consequently, Jay used other arguments:

It has often given me pleasure to observe, that Independent America was not composed of detached and distant territories, but that one connected, fertile, wide-spreading country was the portion of our sons of liberty. . . . A succession of navigable waters forms a kind of chain round its borders, as if to bind it together; while the most noble rivers in the world, running at convenient distances, present them with highways for the easy communication of friendly aids, and the mutual transportation and exchange of their various commodities. . . . This country and this people seem to have been made for each other.

Thus, he concludes that the people of this land have been made by both culture and nature "no less attached to Union, than enamored of Liberty."

It is precisely this attachment to Union which adds the social federal principle fostered by Washington, Hamilton and Jay to the individualistic fascination with liberty, primary in the thinking of Locke and Jefferson, that persuaded the framers of the Constitution to go beyond the local state governments to which Lockean and Jeffersonian principles would have tended to restrict them, in founding a federal government and transmitting to it the requisite sovereignty. Even so, this federal government was formulated on purely Lockean lines; and always the Lockean assumption of free, equal, and independent persons was taken as primary, and as the source of any federalistic sovereignty and any principle of unity which was granted. That this is true the many curbs upon federal authority specified explicitly by the Constitution and the Bill of Rights clearly indicate.

Nor was it obvious, even after the Constitution had been adopted and the federal government had been established, that the federal principle was an essential part of the system. In fact, it may be said that it was precisely because of this uncertainty that the Civil War had to be fought. Not until this test case, involving an issue between the individualistic states' rights emphasis of Locke and Jefferson, and the union federal principle in the Constitution of Hamilton and his follower Lincoln, was fought out to determine whether the federal union principle was to stand, or whether the Lockean theory of the origin of the federal government in the consent of the governed gave the states that desired it the right to withdraw their consent from that federal government and depart from the Union, was the issue finally and unequivocally settled.

By the time of Lincoln one other factor, in addition to the federalist principle of Hamilton and Jay, had come into the making of the American concept of the good state. Partially because of his humble beginnings, but also because of his reading of the Bible and his deep musings upon the meaning of the Declaration of Independence, Lincoln had developed a remarkable sympathy and feeling for all men. His settling in Illinois, as has been indicated, near Frenchmen and Indians, made him aware of the possibility and value of understanding and affection for the Indians. His travels down the Mississippi gave him a similar fellow feeling for the Negro slaves. In both these respects he gave expression to a growing feeling and realization upon the part of many of his fellow countrymen. The root of this new fellow feeling was in the Declaration of Independence and John Locke. This document said that *all* men, not merely Anglo-Saxon white men, were by nature free and equal. Certainly, each was a mental substance. Locke also had written, as the first amendment to the Constitution later prescribed, that each individual man, regardless of his creed, is the final and sole trustworthy judge of the divine. The orthodoxy of no faith, not even that of Protestant Christians, could supersede the verdict of the individual man in this regard. Thus, from the standpoint of religion as well as of politics it became evident, as the full consequences of Locke's theory of religion and the Lockean Declaration of Independence were grasped, that even the individualistic roots of modern thought and its democratic form of government placed moral, political, and religious obligations upon that government to use its powers not merely to preserve the private property of the individual but to guarantee freedom of life, work, and religious belief of *all* men. This strenuous achievement of the American spirit is portrayed for us in John Steuart Curry's Kansas mural "The Tragic Prelude," and in Stephen Vincent Benét's *John Brown's Body*. We can understand, therefore, why Lincoln, who defended the federalist union principle in the Civil War against what seemed to be the Lockean democratic principle resting on the doctrine of the consent of the governed expressed in the Declaration of Independence, was nonetheless able to believe quite justifiably that the Lockean democratic principle supported the Union rather than the Southern States, and was able to say, "I have never had a feeling, politically, that did not spring from the sentiments embodied in the Declaration of Independence."

In this manner, with Lincoln, the individualistic principle of liberty of Jefferson and the federal principle of Hamilton became essentially rather than arbitrarily developed and connected. What made the organic federal principle strong enough, even within Lockean assumptions, to restrain the individualistic states' rights principle, was the Lockean doctrine of the equality and freedom of *all* men.

A similar phenomenon occurred in the economic sphere at the same time, with the passage of the Homestead Act of 1862. As Ralph Turner has indicated, this federal action restrained the bitter and unequal competition, between small farmers, speculators and large-scale producers, for property in the public domain, in the interest of the small independent farmers so that as far as possible all might own a home.

Such were the fruits of the science of Galilei and Newton and the attendant philosophy of Locke as the assumptions of the latter worked themselves out at the end of the Civil War in the culture of the United States. Up to this time the leadership of the country had been in the hands of lawyers or others grounded in law, all of whom were statesmen. The difference between a politician, in the bad sense of the word, and a statesman is that both are guided by facts but that only the statesman can understand and act with respect to these facts in the light of a consistent set of philosophical principles. Thus a statesman is a politician who has the intellectual integrity which an articulate and consistent philosophy provides. The philosophy which determined the statesmanship of the United States up to the end of the Civil War was in part aristocratic and distantly Aristotelian, but predominantly that of John Locke.

Following the Civil War a new element entered into American culture. The leadership of the landowner, the lawyer and the statesman was replaced by that of the businessman and his banker. This change also was grounded in modern science and modern philosophical theory.

BUSINESSMAN'S WORLD

The science of the businessman is economics. The science of the traditional American businessman was the Anglo-American economics which was reared in Great Britain by Adam Smith, Bentham, Malthus, John Stuart Mill, Ricardo, Senior, and Jevons. This economic science did not spring into existence without any previous intellectual causes. Adam Smith, who initiated the science, was a philosopher in the University of Glasgow and for the last twenty-five years of his life an intimate, personal friend of David Hume. Jevons, who put Anglo-American economic theory into its final traditional form, was explicit in his insistence that it was grounded upon the utilitarian hedonism of the philosopher Jeremy Bentham. Bentham's philosophy in turn was determined by that of David Hume.

But Hume's philosophy also did not spring into existence without previous causes. Instead, it was the result of pursuing one of the basic assumptions of John Locke's philosophy to its inescapable, logical consequences. This was done in part by Bishop Berkeley and completely by David Hume.

The assumption in question has to do with the nature of the meanings or ideas which a mind can have. The Lockean requirement on this matter is that all our ideas in any field of knowledge whatever must be either names for sensed data such as colors, sounds, odors, pains, and pleasures or for associations of such sensed data.

The reason for this principle in Locke's philosophy is clear. This philosophy conceives of both man and nature as made up of nothing but mental and material substances in interaction. Furthermore, the mental substances, before the material substances act upon them, are blank tablets. Thus no ideas can arise in any human mind until the material substances of the person's body act on that mind. Furthermore, the only effect of such an action is a specific particular sensation. It follows therefore, as Locke affirmed, that the only ideas which a human mind can have on any subject whatever, be it physics, psychology, philosophy, religion, or economics, are either simple ideas which are sense data or complex ideas which are associations of such sense data.

Little did Locke realize the devastating consequences of this inescapable principle in his philosophy. It made his doctrine of material and mental substances meaningless. It is the merit of Bishop Berkeley to have demonstrated this in the case of the material substances, and of David Hume to have shown it for the case of the mental substances.

Bishop Berkeley noted first that these Lockean ideas given through the senses are by their very nature particulars. What one senses is never the class concept referring to all possible "blues" but a specific, particular "blue" of a definite hue and shade. Since all our ideas, according to Locke's philosophy, are merely such simple ideas put together, it follows that there are no class concepts, or universals, and that all the mind's ideas must be particulars. It will be recalled also that Galilei and Newton, who led Locke to his philosophical theory, pointed out that the sensed qualities are "mere names." Thus it happens that the theory of ideas developed by Berkeley and Hume, as a consequence of Locke's philosophy, is called "nominalism."

This consequence of Locke's philosophy being established, Berkeley has no difficulty in showing that the Newtonian and Lockean conception of a material substance then becomes meaningless. Newton, it will be recalled, had defined a material substance as an object located, not in the sensed space which is an association of sense data, but in the unsensed, mathematically defined, postulated space. Galilei, instead of reducing physical objects to mere associations of colors, sounds, odors, pains, and pleasures as Locke's theory of ideas requires, had conceived the atoms of physics as entirely bereft of such sensed qualities. But if Locke's theory of ideas is correct, Berkeley has no difficulty in showing that all this is meaningless nonsense. For if all that one can mean by anything is either a sense datum or an association of sense data, then this is what one must mean by a physical object also; thus the colorless material atoms of Galilei, Newton and Locke, supposedly behind the sense data, become meaningless and hence non-existent; what one must mean by a material object is the directly observed sense impressions themselves. Also, since even Galilei and Newton have said that sense impressions and their sensed spatial and temporal relations exist only for a mind or observer, material objects, if they are nothing but such associations of sense data, must have the same status. Thus, matter becomes a mere appearance for a mind and Berkeley's famous dictum *esse est percipi*, to be is to be perceived, follows.

The important point to note is that if one once accepts Locke's theory of ideas, to the effect that all meanings must derive from sense data or their associations, then Berkeley's conclusion concerning the nature of a material object follows: A physical object is nothing but the association of sensed qualities and their sequence. A second consideration to keep in mind is that Locke's theory of ideas is a necessary consequence of Locke's theory of the self and its relation to the material substances of physics. For if the self is a blank tablet without any meanings in its mind until the material atoms act upon it, then obviously the only meanings a mind can have in it are sense data and their associations since these are the sole effect of the action of material substances upon mental substances.

The full implications of this for every one of us must not be sidestepped. What Berkeley has demonstrated here is that Locke's philosophy, for all its initial plausibility, is self-contradictory. It entails a theory of ideas which, were it true, would render it impossible for any mind to have the notion of a material substance, as other than the associated sensed impressions, which Newtonian physics, common sense, and the Lockean theory itself assume. This conclusion is tremendously important. It means that the fundamental philosophical assumptions to which the physics of Galilei and Newton led the modern world in the philosophy of John Locke, notwithstanding all the important religious and political values to which this philosophy has given rise in the traditional culture of the United States, are faulty and require radical and fundamental reconstruction.

It was precisely the need for this reconstruction, which Bishop Berkeley's analysis first established, that produced the subsequent, modern philosophical theories, of which Bishop Berkeley's own final philosophy is one, and of which Hume's, Bentham's, Kant's, Fichte's, Hegel's,

Marx's, and John Dewey's are others. Unfortunately, even though the reconstruction of Locke's philosophy is inescapable, none of these attempts is adequate to the factual evidence. It must be realized that the attendant disagreement of these modern philosophers and of modern Anglo-American, German, and Russian economists and statesmen who have followed them, is not the result of an incurable, faulty tendency of philosophers to speculate or a faulty method on their part, as so many people assume; it is, instead, the consequence of inescapable difficulties to which the facts of the physics of Galilei and Newton gave rise when it distinguished between sensed data in sensed space and public, physical objects in mathematically defined space, and thereby gave rise to the problem concerning the relation between the two, for which John Locke's philosophy is the first, and, as it turns out, a self-contradictory answer.

The first attempt to make the required reconstruction in the scientific and philosophical foundations of the modern world was made by Bishop Berkeley himself. Retaining Locke's theory of ideas and its attendant principle that to be is to be perceived, he accepted the consequence that we must mean by a material object merely the purely subjectively projected association of qualities which we immediately sense.

It might be supposed that this surprising conclusion of Bishop Berkeley is of purely theoretical and speculative interest, with no practical significance. Quite the contrary is the case. Christian Science is precisely this Berkeleyan theory of matter put into practice seriously as a religion and a technique for treating health and disease. If all that we mean by body is merely the association of sense data for a mind, as must be the case if the Lockean theory of ideas is correct, then the human body is precisely what the Christian Scientists maintain it to be. It is not an accident that Christian Science originated in the New England portion of the United States with its exceedingly modern and Lockean culture. Again we see how alterations in our basic philosophical conceptions define our moral, religious, and medical values and give rise to quite new social facts such as the practices and buildings of the Christian Science Church.

The acceptance of Locke's theory of ideas had one other consequence for Bishop Berkeley's philosophy. The consequence was a devastating one. It entailed that Berkeley's and the Christian Scientist's mental substances or minds, the divine mind as well as the human minds, are as meaningless, and hence non-existent, as the Lockean material substances.

It remained for David Hume to demonstrate this consequence. If nothing has meaning or existence except sense data and their associations, then a mind must be merely an association of sense data also.

In this manner, with Hume, Locke's and Berkeley's mental substances, conceived as the underlying, persisting, immortal projectors of the associated colors, sounds, odors, pains, and pleasures, were shown to be as meaningless, upon the assumptions of Locke's theory of ideas, as Berkeley had shown Galilei's, Newton's, and Locke's material substances to be. Nothing exists but a succession of particular, transitory sense data and their particular, transitory associations; certain of these association are what we must mean by a mind, others are what we must mean by a material object. Thus it happened that the modern world, which began with Galilei, Newton, Descartes, and Locke, with the confident theory that material and mental substances in interaction exist as the sole persisting realities, and that sensed qualities in sensed space and time are "mere names" and "appearances," ends with Hume, as a consequence of its own attendant theory of ideas, with the reverse thesis that particular sensed qualities and their transitory associations alone exist, and that minds and material objects are mere shorthand names for such associations of sensed data.

Clearly, there must be something wrong with a scientific and philosophical theory whose premises, when pursued to certain of their logical consequences, lead thus to their own destruction. Somewhere on this path, from the distinctions and facts correctly pointed out by Galilei and Newton to the conclusion reached in Hume, a mistake in the construction and development of the foundations of the modern world was made which introduced a contradiction into its basic premises. Otherwise, those premises, when developed by Locke, Berkeley, and Hume to their logical consequences, would not have led to their own denial.

The location of this error will be the final problem of this book (Chapter XII). This problem can be fully understood, however, only after completion of the preliminary analyses of the major philosophical and political doctrines of the traditional modern world. These doctrines arose because the Anglo-American economists took Hume seriously and because the German Hegelians and the Russian communists took Kant and the other successors of Hume with equal seriousness. Consequently, we must do the same if we are to understand the ideological issues within and between Anglo-American, German and Russian cultures during the past one hundred and fifty years.

It should have been clear to all in the time of Berkeley and Hume that both common sense and experimentally verified mathematical physics require the distinction between sense data and scientific objects and between sensed space and time and mathematically defined postulated space and time, which Galilei and Newton had noted. Since Hume's philosophy provides meaning only for the sense data and the sensed space and time, leaving the scientific and public common sense objects and the invariant mathematical space and time meaningless, the incompleteness of Hume's and Berkeley's philosophy and Locke's theory of ideas upon which it rests, should have been equally evident. But neither Berkeley nor Hume was intimately acquainted with mathematical physics.

Instead of keeping in mind the scientific evidence pointed out by Galilei and Newton which requires distinctions and meanings which sense data and their associations do not provide, Hume accepted Locke's theory of ideas. Once this is done, Hume's philosophy follows: Nothing exists but particular, transitory atomic sense data and their successive transitory associations.

The consequences are far-reaching. Not merely Locke's and Jefferson's but also the Catholic's and Protestant's conception of the nature of a person must be rejected. Instead of being a mental substance, free, independent, and equal to all other mental substances, or instead of having an immortal soul, a person is a mere temporary collocation of transitory sense data. Forthwith, the Christian doctrine of the immortality of the soul evaporates, as does Locke's thesis that the only end and aim of religion are the salvation of one's immortal soul. Automatically, the association psychology replaces the faculty psychology, there being no substantial self to have any faculties. Similarly, positivism in science arises, since positivism is the thesis that nothing but the immediately apprehended exists. Physics becomes merely a chapter in introspective psychology. The terms table, apparatus, mass, atom, molecule, electromagnetic wave, and electron become mere names for a backhanded, shorthand way of talking about nothing but sense data and their sensed relations. Similarly, the notion of a persisting, immortal Divine Being is equally meaningless, and hence non-existent. Certainly if nothing exists but sense data and their associations, all this follows.

William James, similarly identifying the self with this succession of associated sense data which he termed "the flow of consciousness," made the best makeshift for religion which is possible upon such positivistic premises, by the exceedingly treacherous recourse of grounding the

Divine in an arbitrary decision to insist upon certain imaginatively given desires, very difficult to distinguish from wishful thinking, which he labeled, very honestly, "the will to believe." This course was especially treacherous for James since his "radical empiricism" necessitates, as Hume makes clear, that the belief in an immortal being of any kind is not merely unjustified empirically, but meaningless. Certainly if nothing exists but the factual, transitory sensa and their transitory associations, then that is all that exists. Immortal beings, whether human or divine, are impossible. The followers of Hume, since James, have accepted the latter verdict, as the recent book *Naturalism and the Human Spirit* clearly indicates.

James, however, did make one unique and exceedingly important contribution. He noted that what we immediately apprehend is not limited, as Locke's theory of ideas requires and Hume tended consequently to maintain, to atomic sense data and their relations. Only in the center of the empirically given continuum of immediate experience are there sharply contoured atomic sensa. The remainder of the continuum, what James termed "the periphery of consciousness," is undifferentiated and indeterminate.

This empirical fact is important for two reasons. First, it provides a basis, as the sequel will show, for understanding the Orient. Second, it shows that James was a better empiricist than Hume and, in fact, that Hume was not an empiricist at all. Certainly it is reasonable to suppose that a genuine empiricist would look at immediate experience first and come to his philosophical conclusions by a mere denotation or description of what is immediately given. Had Hume done this, not only would he have noted, as did James and Oriental empiricists long before James, that the immediately apprehended is a continuum, but also that a considerable portion of this continuum is indeterminate in character and undifferentiated by atomic sense data. The truth is that Hume was not an empiricist, but a rationalist, a rationalist who took Locke's theory of ideas for granted and pursued it to its logical consequence. On Locke's theory of ideas, it is true that there should be nothing given empirically but particular atomic sense data and their specific, particular relations.

We need hardly be surprised, now that this Humean doctrine of the eighteenth century has seeped down into the popular mind without any popular realization of what has happened, that there are skepticism and demoralization with respect to the traditional beliefs. What makes the effect so devastating is that the consequences ensue, not because of a departure from our traditional Anglo-American and modern Protestant faith, but because of the pursuit of that faith to its necessary consequences. Thus, it is not to be cured by turning back, except as we go back to root out the initial error in the traditional faith itself, and to put new philosophical foundations for the modern world, differing from those of both Locke and Hume, in the place of the old.

Hume's philosophy had another consequence, a most valuable one, which the French pursued. Locke's theory of ideas, when it reached its final consequences in Hume, completely reversed the relationship between the sensed colors and sounds, which are the aesthetic materials of the painter and the musician, and the mental and material substances, which were supposedly the concern of the Protestant preachers and their businessmen. In Descartes and Locke's original philosophy and in traditional Non-conformist Protestantism, colors, sounds, and pleasures were mere secondary or tertiary appearances masking the supposedly truly real underlying material and mental substances. Thereby, the materials of art were given a superficial, phenomenal status and were enslaved by means of the use of geometrically defined perspective to the handmaid's task of portraying the clear-cut, geometrically proportioned, three-dimensional material object, whether it be the body of a human person in a portrait or the pot with its incidentally colored flowers in a still life. With Hume, following Locke's theory of ideas to its logical consequences, the situation became completely reversed. Since according to Locke's theory of ideas, all one can possibly mean by either a person or an external object is merely an association of sense data, it follows that instead of the immortal, personal selves and material objects being the real things, and the associated, sensuous materials of art being mere appearances, it is the associated sensed aesthetic materials which are the sole reality, and the persisting Protestant persons and the three-dimensional material, external objects which are the meaningless and hence unreal and illusory things. Consequently, instead of making the subject matter of art, by means of the use of geometrically defined perspective, the slave of the three-dimensional bodily person in the portrait or the material substance in the pot of flowers, both the person and the pot must be built out of the associated sense data alone, without the use of the geometrical perspective, which misdirects one's attention away from the aesthetic materials for their own sake to the external material objects and immortal souls supposedly behind them. Thus it is that Locke's theory of ideas, coming to full fruition in the philosophy of David Hume, for almost the first time in Western civilization, made the subject matter of the arts the very stuff of which the nature of things is composed, and valuable in its own right.

The specific consequences were tremendous, as the Spanish, the French, and James Joyce realized. With the geometrical perspective dropped—since it has no point unless one desires to convey the geometrically conceived, three-dimensional external object as something beyond and other than the colors and their associated form—the object, whether a person or a tree, becomes given only two-dimensionally, in so far as the blurred association of sense data constitutes it. Thus one has Impressionism. Automatically, the dropping of perspective in Impressionism frees art from its enslavement to three-dimensional objects. Thereby, the whole introspected content of the aesthetic continuum is opened up to it, and one has Abstractionism. When, in literature, the sense data referring, in the old literature, to a bridge in Dublin, and the introspected data laden with emotional and sexual content are combined, so that one moves from one to the other without any sense of or concern with a supposed dividing line between them, one has the *Ulysses* of James Joyce.

When, furthermore, one conceives of the immediately apprehended aesthetic continuum, as Hume, guided deductively by Locke's theory of ideas, had to conceive of it, as merely an association of atomic sense data, one has not the Impressionism of Cézanne, Renoir, Degas, Rodin, Whistler, Davies, and Prendergast, but the Pointillist Impressionism of Seurat and Pissarro. For in Seurat the total aesthetic continuum is actually constructed by placing separate, independent, isolated sense data on the canvas. The editor of *Modern Masters* describes Seurat's technique as follows: "With scientific precision he took the small brush strokes of the impressionists and made them into dots all of the same size. Each dot is a light or dark shade of one of the six primary colors— blue, yellow, red, green, violet, and orange. With similar logic, he analyzed lines and tones and their emotional effects of sadness, calm, and joy." This is Hume's philosophy *par excellence*. Even the aesthetic continuum, not to mention the physical object or the emotional person, is built up out of independent atomic sense data (Plate X).

Unfortunately, even though Hume was a Scotsman, this novel and rich aesthetic application of his philosophy did not arise in the British or American world. Not until 1929, with David Prall, did an Anglo-American philosopher, largely because of French influence, finally become articulate with respect to the importance of Hume's philosophy for aesthetics. It fell to the glory of France to create this new art. Not until the Paris-trained, American Whistler went to London and until the Revolution of 1908 in New York, led by The Eight, also clearly influenced by France, did this new art appear in either the British or the American world.

These developments in the culture of the United States must concern us later. They are hardly typical of the post-Civil War businessman's world. One question concerning them, however, is of import now. Why did it require all the years from Hume's death in 1776 to Whistler in London in 1878, The Eight in New York in 1908, and to Prall in Berkeley in 1929, for the culture of either Great Britain or the United States to grasp this most important consequence and application of Hume's philosophy?

The answer seems clear. It shows in Prall, as in all the other important British or American followers of Hume. Instead of using the immediately apprehended sense data for what can be built out of them —namely, Impressionistic painting, sculpture, music, and the art of the gourmet—Anglo-American thinkers used them for what they cannot give, namely, mathematical physics; or else Anglo-Americans were interested in them merely instrumentally as the key to the movement of prices in the market place. It is the latter interest which produced Anglo-American economic theory and which gave rise, in the culture of Great Britain in the last half of the nineteenth century and in the culture of the United States up to 1932, to that exclusive identification of the good for man and the state, with the purely instrumental economic values which characterize a businessman's world.

This development shows unequivocally in the British followers of Hume. They were Adam Smith, Bentham, the two Mills, and Jevons. These men were not artists but practical moralists, political thinkers, and economists. The opinion concerning them held by the French artists will be noted later. Their new political and economic doctrines arose when certain ethical consequences of Hume's philosophy were noted. No longer could the good for man be identified, as it was for Locke, with the salvation of one's immortal soul, since, according to Locke's theory of ideas as carried to its consequences by Hume, no such immortal soul exists; the entire person instead is merely a transitory association of sensed or introspected data. Consequently, the good, not merely in religion and personal morality but also in the state and in social morality, had to be defined in terms of these immediately sensed data or their associations. This was accomplished in part by Hume and by Adam Smith, and achieved finally in its most effective form by Bentham, when the latter identified the. good with immediately sensed pleasures, or with happiness which is measured by the quantity of such pleasures. In this manner the hedonistic utilitarianism of Bentham and Mill arose.

Since pleasures were conceived as particular, private, personal things, this tended to leave one with an extremely individualistic and self-centered ethics. Bentham attempted to overcome this weakness by giving it a social formulation in his famous dictum of "the greatest happiness of the greatest number." Thus both for the individual and for society the good became largely a quantitative matter. As Jevons saw, this made it possible to give a science of economics founded upon such premises a mathematical formulation. John Stuart Mill noted also that it provided entirely new philosophical foundations for democracy, not merely replacing those of Locke but also indicating certain evils in the culture which Locke's democracy produces.

One of the differences between political democracy in Great Britain and that of the United States centers in the fact that the British, reacting from the excesses of the Cromwellian revolution and its attendant Non-conformist Protestant intolerance and attack upon art and the theater, all of which became associated in British minds with Locke, have for the last one hundred years followed Mill in their conception of political democracy, whereas the United States up to 1932, in the Republican and Democratic parties, continued to follow Locke. Some of the most unequivocal and weighty lines ever written in support of liberty, individuality, and democratic processes have come from the pen of John Stuart Mill. The general effect of the empirical, utilitarian philosophy of Bentham and Mill is to reinforce and even to carry further the same emphasis upon the primacy of the individual which appeared with Locke.

Nevertheless, the basis for democracy is different. In fact, the new philosophical assumptions of Hume, Bentham, and Mill carry a mild criticism of certain theses of Locke. No longer is the justification for the existence of government the preservation of the private property of the individual. Nor is a government necessarily good, for Mill, merely because it expresses the consent of the majority. The reason is that goodness is no longer defined in terms of the equal, free, and independent mental substances. Instead, goodness refers to the pleasurable, immediately experience *content* of the individual experience, and the universality throughout a people of this immediately apprehended, pleasurable content which is unique for each individual. Consequently, we find

John Stuart Mill, in his famous treatise *On Liberty*, after noting the spread and action of democratic processes according to the Lockean theory, writing as follows:

It was now perceived that such phrases as "self-government," and "the power of the people over themselves," do not express the true state of the case. The "people" who exercise the power are not always the same people with those over whom it is exercised; and the "self-government" spoken of is not the government of each by himself, but of each by all the rest. The will of the people, moreover, practically means the will of the most numerous or the most active *part* of the people; the majority, or those who succeed in making themselves accepted as the majority; the people, consequently, *may* desire to oppress a part of their number; and precautions are as much needed against this as against any other abuse of power. The limitation, therefore, of the power of government over individuals loses none of its importance when the holders of power are regularly accountable to the community, that is, to the strongest party therein.

The reason Mill is thus able to reinforce liberty and individualism and at the same time criticize the Lockean theory of democracy is that Locke, having defined the good for the individual in terms of nothing but freedom of the mental substances, quite apart from any determinate content of their consciousness, has no alternative but to define the good for the state in terms of nothing but the "consent" of a majority of such individuals. When this majority consents to exercise a tyranny over the minority, suppressing individual variations from the group sentiments, there is little on the Lockean premises either to curb this action or to define it as wrong. For Mill, however, the good is not located so much in the mere free action of the individual, important as this is, as in the quantity of pleasure associated with a given type of experience or conduct. Consequently, Mill has a criterion for designating the vote of a majority to be wrong if it fails to produce individual human experiences with the greatest amount of pleasurable content.

Continuing, Mill writes:

Society has now fairly got the better of individuality; and the danger which threatens human nature is not the excess, but the deficiency, of personal impulses and preferences. . . . Thus the mind itself is bowed to the yoke: even in what people do for pleasure, conformity is the first thing thought of; they like in crowds; they exercise choice only among things commonly done: peculiarity of taste, eccentricity of conduct, are shunned equally with crimes: until by dint of not following their own nature they have no nature to follow: their human capacities are withered and starved: they become incapable of any strong wishes or native pleasures, and are generally without either opinions or feelings of home growth, or properly their own.

Whereas Locke, because of the equality of all mental substances, had emphasized the equality of all men, Mill, because of his identification of the personal with the private, immediately sensed experiences and individual preferences, emphasizes in the name of freedom, individuality, and democracy, the uniqueness of each man and differences between men, as the good.

Another fundamental weakness in the previous modern Protestant Christian and the Lockean conception of religion and the good life is emphasized by Mill. In our account of Locke's theory of religion it was noted that it had its basis in an introspective concern with the individual's spiritual nature or mental substance. The Protestant emphasis upon the preciousness of man just because he is a person, and upon his soul which is immortal, fitted in with this thesis. Thus people were led to search within themselves, underneath the sensuous and pleasurable experiences, for the criterion of right and wrong. Since, even on Locke's premises, nothing could be found underneath the introspected sensuous content of one's consciousness but an absolutely blank tablet, either no criterion of right and wrong with specific content was provided by this method, or else, as usually happened, as Mill noted, the old and outmoded, conventional, standardized moral sentiments of the majority were surreptitiously smuggled in, in the name of morality, democracy, and religion, as binding upon everybody. In this manner, according to Mill an evil "censorship" arose, of which he wrote as follows:

> In its interferences with personal conduct it is seldom thinking of anything but the enormity of acting or feeling differently from itself; and this standard of judgment, thinly disguised, is held up to mankind as the dictate of religion and philosophy, by nine-tenths of all moralists and speculative writers. These teach that things are right because they are right; because we feel them to be so. They tell us to search in our own minds and hearts for laws of conduct binding on ourselves and on all others. What can the poor public do but apply these instructions, and make their own personal feelings of good and evil, if they are tolerably unanimous in them, obligatory on all the world?

That Mill, unlike Locke and the conventional Protestants, is able to make this important criticism is due to the fact of his identification of the good not with an appeal to the individual, supposedly persistent, spiritual self beneath the content of his consciousness, but with the specific sensuous, pleasurable content of this consciousness which is unique in each individual.

Thus whereas Locke's philosophy grounds democratic processes upon the equality of all men, and thereby tends to produce a democratic culture in which conformity and like traits upon the part of all individuals are regarded as the good, Mill's Humean philosophical foundation for democracy, which is Lockean in its theory of ideas and its empiricism, but not Lockean in its rejection of the mental substance, grounds democratic processes on the unique, empirically experienced, sensuous, pleasurable content of a certain unique, particular, private association of sense data which, since it varies from one individual to another, tends to produce a democratic culture in which deviation from others upon the part of the individual, and differences between people, are the good. "Where," writes Mill, "not the person's own character, but the traditions or customs of other people are the rule of conduct, there is wanting one of the principal ingredients of human happiness, and quite the chief ingredient of individual and social progress."

Also, whereas for Locke, because of the equality and freedom of the mental substances, government, even the minimum government, is an evil, and something to which the individual contributes only grudgingly in order to preserve his private property, for Mill government is not merely a positive good to which the individual makes his unique contribution, and in return for which he receives the unique contributions of his fellow citizens, but also a necessary instrument for achieving the greatest happiness for the greatest number. "Of good government," Mill says in his essay on *Representative Government,* "its principal element [is] the improvement of the people themselves . . . the ideally best form of government is that in which the sovereignty, or supreme controlling power in the last resort, is vested in the entire aggregate of the community; every citizen not only having a voice in the exercise of that ultimate sovereignty, but being, at least occasionally, called on to take an actual part in the government, by the personal discharge of some public function, local or general." In his treatise *On Liberty* he continues, "It would be a great misunderstanding of this doctrine to suppose that it is one of selfish indifference, which pretends that human beings . . . should not concern themselves about the well-doing or well-being of one another, unless their own interest is involved. Instead of any diminution, there is need of a great increase of disinterested exertion to promote the good of others."

The extent to which this philosophy of Mill, which to be sure is an end-product of Locke's theory of ideas, rather than Locke's initial philosophy of mental and material substances, has determined the British conception of democracy has been indicated by the British authors of the article on John Stuart Mill in the *Encyclopaedia Britannica*. They write, "The influence which Mill's works exercised upon contemporary English thought can scarcely be overestimated. His own writings and those of his successors practically held the field during the third quarter of the nineteenth century and even later. . . . He may, in fact, be regarded as the final exponent of that empirical school of philosophy which owed its impulse to John Locke, and is generally spoken of as being typically English."

It is not an incorrect observation to note of the two great English-speaking cultures that the one in the United States tends to accentuate individual conformity and equality, and to regard all government as an evil, even though a necessary one, rather than a positive good—traits which are fundamentally Lockean in their character; whereas the democratic culture of Great Britain tends to foster individual independence and individual differences even to the point of inequalities, combined with a conception of government as a positive good, not merely contributing and alone making possible the greatest happiness of the greatest number, but also protecting and at the same time giving expression to the unique idiosyncrasies and originality of the individual.

The merits of Mill's and the English form of good democratic culture should not be overlooked. It combines two opposites which in the United States, because of its Lockean and Jeffersonian ideology, tend to combat each other; namely, (1) a premium upon individual idiosyncrasy and deviation from the majority group type, protected not merely by law but also by the native sentiments of the populace, and (2) an appetite upon the part of all individuals for the facing of social questions and a participation in their solution by means of national governmental action, and personal participation therein, as a positive good. It is not incorrect to say that in Great Britain there is, at least in certain respects, a greater appreciation and protection of differences between, and the idiosyncrasies of, individuals combined with a greater sense of, and respect for, social and governmental action as a positive good. In the United States, on the other hand, the attitude tends to be that an individual is queer if he does not conform to type, and that social and governmental action can come only at the expense of the ideal good, which is the complete freedom and independence of the individual.

The Lockean ideology and its culture in the United States have other merits which also should not be overlooked. According to the Lockean theory a man is good because he is a man and not because of the specific pleasurable content of his consciousness. This, especially in the realm of education, has fostered the idea that what is good for one man is good for every man. Thus education is not restricted, even at the higher levels, quite as much here as it has been in England, to the few who are supposed to have particular aptitudes. Also, because a man is good, due to the fact of being a man and not because of the unique content of his immediately experienced nature, there is a general tendency to listen to and respect any opinions whatever, merely because they' are the opinions of a person. This occurs, also, to be sure, in Great Britain in Hyde Park; it does not occur as universally among the British people in their daily judgments of each other and of other nations as is the case in the culture of the United States. For the same reason informed Britishers do not suffer as much as do informed people in the United States from the larger number of obviously absurd and uncritical opinions which the idea of the good of American culture fosters and permits to persist without devastating criticism.

The democratic political theory of John Stuart Mill is exceedingly important, especially to people in the United States, for one other reason. It shows conclusively that the connection which at present exists in American thought between democratic processes and the assumptions of Locke's philosophy is not a necessary one. Although Locke's philosophy entails a democratic theory of government, the converse is not true. It is possible to ground democratic processes in a philosophical theory of the nature of man and the universe which is different from the one specified by John Locke and used by our founding fathers; as Mill's rearing of democracy and representative government upon the philosophy of David Hume and the empirical hedonistic ethics of Bentham unequivocally indicates. This suggests, also, that quite different philosophical foundations for democracy may be possible than those provided either by Mill or by Locke. The inadequacies which we have already come upon in the philosophy of both Locke and Hume, especially the incapacity of either to account for the existence of mathematics and mathematical physics, to be specified in the sequel, tell us that such new foundations for democracy are not merely possible but necessary. This task must concern us later. Now the manner in which Hume's philosophy determined Anglo-American economic theory must be pursued.

To understand the final Anglo-American economic theory which was first developed by Jevons, and also to have the background necessary for a comparison of it with the rival Russian communistic economic theory, it is necessary to acquaint ourselves with the character of modern economic thought before the time of Jevons. This pre-Jevonian economics falls roughly into four parts: (1) the Mercantile School; (2) the doctrine of the French physiocrats; (3) the doctrine of Adam Smith; and (4) the additions and emendations to Smith's doctrine made by Malthus, Ricardo, and John Stuart Mill.

(1) The Mercantile economics was a purely practical one developed by tradesmen as a result of social needs and changes in the time. It was not grounded in a unique philosophical theory; nor was it developed in a systematic, logical manner. It was, however, the product of two Protestant movements in England in the time of Queen Elizabeth, the one Non-conformist and individualistic, the other High Church, hierarchical and exercising marked national social control; both of which, as our later examination of British culture will show, were philosophical in character.

(2) The physiocrats were a group of Frenchmen of whom Quesnay was the leader, and Turgot, D'Alembert, Morellet, Helvétius, and others were members. They proceeded from the Lockean doctrine of the "state of Nature" in which all men are free and independent. Consequently, they rejected the national controls of the early Mercantile Era, regarding governmental controls of business practices and economic transactions as philosophically and scientifically unsound.

(3) Adam Smith (1723–1790) went to Paris in 1765. There he lived for over a year in the society of the physiocrats. It is not an accident therefore that his *Wealth of Nations,* which was published, not inappropriately, in 1776, rests upon the same fundamentally Lockean assumption. Smith, however, went further than the physiocrats by developing systematically and in detail a complete economic science treating labor, capital, production, and exchange upon this Lockean laissez faire basis.

Adam Smith was also, over a period of some twenty-five years, an intimate friend of David Hume. Thus a Humean influence as well as the Lockean influence through the physiocrats, exhibits itself in Smith's moral and economic doctrines. In 1751 he was elected professor of logic at the University of Glasgow, and in the next year he became its professor of moral philosophy, a position which he occupied for the succeeding twelve years. His lectures during this period reveal that he regarded his economic science as essentially connected with moral philosophy. In 1759 he published his *Theory of Moral Sentiments*. In it, the good was not defined in Lockean terms by recourse to the mental substance, but was grounded instead in directly inspected "moral sentiments," the major empirical criterion of which is a feeling of sympathy. This clearly is in accord with a Humean influence.

Also, a purely Lockean influence might have tended to cause Smith in his economic science to identify economic goods with material objects, as they still tend to be regarded by the popular mind, and to treat the value of economic goods as an intrinsic property of these material objects. Hume, however, had repudiated both material substances and mental substances. Both objects and persons became mere associations of immediately apprehended sense qualities. Thus the conception of value as the property of an object was hardly meaningful. Value had to be located instead in the relation between the association of sensed qualities, which is a given object, and something else. Adam Smith gave expression to this consequence of Hume's philosophy, at least partially, in the following manner: The value of an economic object, Smith noted, has two meanings, that of utility and that of purchasing power; the former he termed "value in use" and the latter "value in exchange." It is with value in exchange, Smith emphasized, that economic science is primarily concerned. This conception of value, it is to be noted, is quite in accord with the requirements of Hume's philosophy, since it identifies value with a relation rather than with the property of a thing.

Nevertheless, when Smith went on to specify how value in exchange is measured, he located it in the labor which went into the making of the product, thereby, for all practical purposes, returning to the conception of value as an intrinsic property of the valued thing. This happened and was necessary within the principles of Smith's science of economics because he took the production of labor as a primitive or basic principle in his science, deriving the concept of economic value from this principle, thereby being forced by what may be termed "a labor measure of value" into the attendant conception of value as an intrinsic property of the economic goods. It remained for Jevons to preserve consistently the relational theory of value which Hume's philosophy requires and which Adam Smith achieved in theory, only to lose it in practice when the relational concept became precisely measured.

Adam Smith's system developed roughly as follows: The labor of the people of a given community is the source of all its economic products. The more productive therefore the labor, the greater is the economic wealth of the community. The productiveness of labor is greater with a division of labor. Consequently, the division of labor arises. This, however, gives certain peoples a vast quantity of similar goods, more than they can use, and other peoples similar vast quantities of like goods, greater in amount than they can use. Thus the division of labor gives rise necessarily to the exchange of goods. For this exchange, money is found to be necessary. Thus the necessity for the exchange of goods gives rise to the existence of money. The resultant exchange of goods for each other or for money gives rise in turn to the notion of the economic value of these goods. Since the productivity of labor was taken as the basis of the entire system, the concept of value in exchange coming out as a later derived consequence of this basic assumption, the measurement of value in exchange in terms of the quantity of labor going into the things exchanged followed naturally.

This economic theory of Smith's had one consequence which showed in the different status with respect to prices which labor had as compared with rent. Since, for Smith, the value of goods is measured by the amount of labor going into them, wages are a cause of high or low prices; whereas rent, which does not enter into the definition of value, is a consequence of high or low prices. We shall see that Jevons, when he alters modern economic science to bring it into accord with the moral consequences of Hume's philosophy as developed by Bentham, is necessarily led to deny this difference between the status of wages and that of rent with respect to prices. This indicates again how an alteration in one's basic philosophical conception of man and the universe has exceedingly important consequences not merely for personal ethics and religion and politics, but also for the science of economics.

(4) David Ricardo (1772–1823) and John Stuart Mill (1806–1873) continued the economic ideas of Adam Smith, attempting to fill them in with additional empirical content. Ricardo is often credited with maintaining not merely a labor measure but also a labor theory of value. It is doubtful, however, whether this is the case, and certainly it was not the case with John Stuart Mill, who followed Ricardo's ideas. Adam Smith also had used the amount of labor going into the production of goods as a measure of their value. But we know that Smith did not identify value with labor; on the contrary, ethical value was identified by Smith with an immediately experienced sentiment of sympathy. John Stuart Mill, we know also, followed Bentham in holding an empirical, utilitarian rather than a labor theory of value. It is likely that Ricardo also agreed with Smith, Bentham, and Mill in maintaining the

classical, empirical theory of value, and that he emphasized the labor factor as did Smith, merely in order to find some means of measuring economic values. This suggests that it may be only with Marx and the communists that one finds labor made not merely the measure, but also the meaning, of value in the science of economics and also in ethics.

However, neither Smith and Ricardo, nor John Stuart Mill had grasped the full consequences of their own Humean, empirical assumptions. These Humean assumptions, a necessary consequence of Locke's theory of ideas, restrict the concepts of any department of knowledge whatever, and hence of economics, to immediately sensed factors. John Stuart Mill had realized the consequences of this for personal ethics and for politics, but failed, as did Ricardo, to bring economic science abreast of the new Humean developments. The latter achievement remained for William Stanley Jevons (1835–1882), building upon the hedonistic and utilitarian moral philosophy of Jeremy Bentham.

Meantime, Thomas Robert Malthus (1766–1834) had made his studies of population growth and food supply, upon the basis of which he announced the now discredited law that population increases in a geometrical ratio while food supply increases only in an arithmetical one. Malthus's law gained additional support from Darwin and the Darwinian hypotheses of the struggle for existence and the survival of the fittest. These ideas of Malthus and Darwin gave additional support to a fundamental assumption which Locke, Hume, the physiocrats, Adam Smith, Ricardo, Bentham, Mill, and Jevons held in common; the assumption, namely, that good conduct, not merely from the standpoint of the private individual, but also from the standpoint of the political order and the economic order, is free and independent individual activity, governed by but one social law, and that, the law of free competition.

The reason for this belief as a sufficient basis for adequately facing the political problems of mankind has been indicated in connection with our discussion of the philosophy of Locke. In this philosophy the relation between one mental substance and all other mental substances is not merely undefined but undefinable; consequently, there is no theoretical basis whatever for a more organic social concept of the good communal life. Hume's philosophy and that of Bentham, Mill, and Jevons, which derives from Hume, has the same laissez faire individualistic consequences. A person, according to Humean doctrine, is a mere association of sensed items, and these, as Galilei and Newton first indicated and Berkeley and Hume re-emphasized, are private and personal to the individual. Hume himself also pointed out that between these immediately sensed or introspected items, to which, for Hume, the whole of knowledge is restricted, there are no logically internal, organic relations or, as Hume put it, no "necessary connections" whatever. Consequently, a political philosophy such as Mill's, or an economic science such as Jevons's, which rests upon Hume's philosophical premises, necessarily has the same laissez faire individualistic consequences as a politics or economics derived from the philosophy of John Locke. It is not surprising, therefore, that even Jevons, who departs most sharply from Smith, Ricardo, and Mill in his reconstruction of modern economic science, nonetheless quotes Malthus with favor and is in complete agreement with all his predecessors with respect to laissez faire individualism as the sound and good policy in economic as well as political social relations. In fact, Jevons merely formulates economic science in terms of Bentham's utilitarian hedonism after the manner in which John Stuart Mill had reconstructed democratic political theory in terms of Hume's and Bentham's doctrines.

At the beginning of his classical work *The Theory of Political Economy* Jevons writes:

The theory which follows is entirely based on a calculus of pleasure and pain; and the object of Economics is to maximise happiness by purchasing pleasure, as it were, at the lowest cost of pain. . . . Jeremy Bentham put forward [this] Utilitarian theory in the most uncompromising manner. According to him, whatever is of interest or importance to us must be the cause of pleasure or of pain; and when the terms are used with a sufficiently wide meaning, pleasure and pain include all the forces which drive us to action. They are explicitly or implicitly the matter of all our calculations, and form the ultimate quantities to be treated in all the moral sciences. The words of Bentham on this subject may require some explanation and qualification, but they are too grand and too full of truth to be omitted. "Nature" [quoting Bentham] "has placed mankind under the governance of two sovereign masters—*pain* and *pleasure*. It is for them alone to point out what we ought to do, as well as to determine what we shall do. On the one hand the standard of right and wrong, on the other the chain of causes and effects, are fastened to their throne. They govern us in all we do, in all we say, in all we think: every effort we can make to throw off our subjection will serve but to demonstrate and confirm it. In words a man may pretend to abjure their empire; but, in reality, he will remain subject to it all the while. The *principle of utility* recognises this subjection, and assumes it for the foundation of that system, the object of which is to rear the fabric of felicity by the hands of reason and of law. Systems which attempt to question it deal in sounds instead of sense, in caprice instead of reason, in darkness instead of light."

Locke's theory of ideas and the influence of Hume show themselves in the last sentence. Any concept in the science of economics and in particular the concept of utility or value which does not refer to an immediately sensed item, such as pleasure or pain, is dealing "in sounds instead of sense."

Having thus subjected the concept of utility or value in economic science to the empirically given laws or relations governing immediately experienced pains and pleasures in their associations with other immediately sensed data, Jevons then turns, in his next chapter, on the "Theory of Pleasure and Pain," to the quantitative aspects of these qualities. The connection with the numerical data which make possible a mathematical science of economics is obtained by Jevons by assuming that all the numerical data of the market place are a consequence of individual people attempting to maximize their pleasures and minimize their pains.

Because pleasures and pains are immediately sensed things, as are their relations to other immediately sensed data, we find Jevons asserting that the "ultimate laws" of the science of economics

are known to us immediately by intuition. . . . That every person will choose the greater apparent good; that human wants are more or less quickly satiated; that prolonged labour becomes more and more painful, are a few of the simple inductions on which we can proceed to reason deductively with great confidence. From these axioms we can deduce the laws of supply and demand, the laws of that difficult conception, value, and all the intricate results of commerce, so far as data are available.

It is not, however, until Jevons comes in Chapter 3, on the "Theory of Utility," to his definition of terms, that the break from his predecessors, as a consequence of Hume's positivism and Bentham's hedonistic utilitarianism, makes itself felt.

The chapter opens with a designation of the subject matter of economics and its basic problem. "Pleasure and pain," writes Jevons, "are undoubtedly the ultimate objects of the Calculus of Economics. To satisfy our wants to the utmost with the least effort—to procure the greatest amount of what is desirable at the expense of the least that is undesirable—in other words, *to maximise pleasure*, is the problem of Economics." Pleasures and pains hereby become the primitive or elementary concepts of the science. A "commodity" then becomes "any object, substance, action, or service, which can afford pleasure or ward off pain." Similarly, the concept of "utility" in economics denotes "the abstract quality whereby an object serves our purposes, and becomes entitled to rank as a commodity. Whatever can produce pleasure or prevent pain may possess utility." Jevons immediately adds that this definition of utility was not original with him. For:

> Bentham, in establishing the foundations of Moral Science in his great *Introduction to the Principles of Morals and Legislation* (page 3), thus comprehensively defines the term in question: "By utility is meant that property in any object, whereby it tends to produce benefit, advantage, pleasure, good, or happiness (all this, in the present case, comes to the same thing), or (what comes again to the same thing) to prevent the happening of mischief, pain, evil, or unhappiness to the party whose interest is considered."

Jevons concludes, therefore, that "Economics must be founded upon a full and accurate investigation of the conditions of utility; and, to understand this element, we must necessarily examine the wants and desires of man." His "principal work" then becomes that of "tracing out the exact nature and conditions of utility." It is the taking of this concept of utility as basic in the science of economics and the new definition of its meaning which Bentham's hedonistic utilitarianism provides, that gives Jevons's new mathematical economic science its unique character.

To begin with, "Utility, though a quality of things, is *no inherent quality*. It is better described *as a circumstance of things* arising out of their relation to man's requirements. As Senior most accurately says, 'Utility denotes no intrinsic quality in the things which we call useful; it merely expresses their relations to the pains and pleasures of mankind.'" At last the rejection of the Lockean property-substance concept of utility for the Humean associational or relational concept is achieved. Being a relational concept, Jevons notes that:

> *Utility is not proportional to commodity:* the very same articles vary in utility according as we already possess more or less of the same article. The like may be said of other things. One suit of clothes per annum is necessary, a second convenient, a third desirable, a fourth not unacceptable; but we, sooner or later, reach a point at which further supplies are not desired with any perceptible force, unless it be for subsequent use.

This makes it possible for Jevons to select happiness as not merely the definition but also the measure of utility. Thus he continues, "Utility must be considered as measured by, or even as actually identical with, the addition made to a person's happiness."

Jevons immediately proceeds to give the results of this analysis a mathematical formulation. The degree to which introspectively given feelings of pleasure are regarded by Jevons, in connection with his theory of utility, as amenable to mathematical treatment and formulation is shown by the following statement:

I hesitate to say that men will ever have the means of measuring directly the feelings of the human heart. A unit of pleasure or of pain is difficult even to conceive; but it is the amount of these feelings which is continually prompting us to buying and selling, borrowing and lending, labouring and resting, producing and consuming; and it is from the quantitative effects of the feelings that we must estimate their comparative amounts. We can no more know nor measure gravity in its own nature than we can measure a feeling; but, just as we measure gravity by its effects in the motion of a pendulum, so we may estimate the equality or inequality of feelings by the decisions of the human mind. The will is our pendulum, and its oscillations are minutely registered in the price lists of the markets.

Having thus convinced himself of the possibility of making immediately introspected pleasure or pain not merely the definition but also the measure of utility, Jevons then turns, in Chapter 4, to the "Theory of Exchange." It will be recalled that Adam Smith, rearing economics on the productivity of labor, had derived the exchange of commodities from the fact of the division of labor. Jevons, however, beginning not with the productivity of labor but with Bentham's pleasures and pains must arrive at a theory of exchange in a different manner. Thus he writes, "I find it both possible and desirable to consider this subject before introducing any notions concerning labour or the production of commodities." In connection with exchange and the prices or values of goods associated with it, Jevons agrees with John Stuart Mill's statement that it "implies some theory of Value." Jevons adds immediately, however, that the term "value" has been used in a most "ambiguous and unscientific" manner in the past. Adam Smith, to be sure, had distinguished between value in use and value in exchange; but Jevons maintains that neither usage of the term "value" had been properly defined by either Smith or Mill. Value in use Jevons regarded as properly defined when it is identified with what he termed "utility," for which quantities of pleasure or pain are the criterion. It remained, therefore, for Jevons to clarify the meaning of value in exchange.

Mill had spoken of it as follows: "Value is a relative term. The value of a thing means the quantity of some other thing, or of things in general, which it exchanges for." Of this Jevons writes as follows: "Now, if there is any fact certain about exchange value, it is, that it means not an object at all, but a circumstance of an object. Value implies, in fact, a relation; but if so, it cannot possibly be *some other thing*." What follows is so important for the understanding of the difference between the Anglo-American and the Marxian communistic theories of value in economics that the reader will find it worth while to pursue Jevons's words with care:

> A student of Economics has no hope of ever being clear and correct in his ideas of the science if he thinks of value as at all a thing or an object, or even as anything which lies in a *thing* or *object*. . . . Persons are thus led to speak of such a nonentity as *intrinsic value*. There are, doubtless, qualities inherent in such a substance as gold or iron which influence its value; but the word Value, so far as it can be correctly used, merely expresses *the circumstance of its exchanging in a certain ratio for some other substance*.

In short, value is not a thing, nor a property of a thing, but a ratio. Thus the rejection of the Lockean substance-property notion for the Humean relational concept is carried through by Jevons. He concludes, "Value in exchange expresses nothing but a ratio, and the term should not be used in any other sense. To speak simply of the value of an ounce of gold is as absurd as to speak of the *ratio of the number seventeen*."

This value in exchange of any two commodities, which Jevons prefers to call "the ratio of exchange," is determined by two things: (1) the people's want for the things in question represented by the demand, which in turn is determined by the quantity of pleasure associated with those things; and (2) the scarcity, or what the Swiss economist Walras termed the "rarity," of the commodities, which is represented by the supply. Thus the values of things in exchange are subject to the same laws of supply and demand which Smith, Ricardo, and Mill had formulated.

But between the economic science of Smith, Ricardo, and Mill and the economics of Jevons there is one very radical difference. It shows itself in the differing relations between rent and wages in the two systems. Smith, together with Ricardo and Mill, who followed Smith, it will be recalled, reared their science upon the productivity of labor. This productivity, through its division, gave rise to exchange. Thus labor was a measure of the value of goods in exchange and consequently the cost of labor was a cause of prices; whereas rents were the effect of prices.

For Jevons, however, this difference between labor and rent is removed. "Rates of wages," he writes, "are governed by the same formal laws as rents." This follows because his entire theory of value in exchange and of prices is developed, as we have noted, on a purely empirical, hedonistic basis without any recourse to labor or the productivity of labor. Prices are determined solely by the empirically introspected pleasure associated with the sense data which designate a given commodity and the rarity of such a commodity. Thus, instead of taking labor and its productivity as a basic concept and then using this, through its division, to define the theory of exchange, and to provide a criterion for the measurement of exchange value, Jevons, rearing himself upon Hume's purely sensuous empiricism and upon Bentham's hedonism, makes the concept of value, defined in terms of pleasure, primary, and with this background defines exchange, which, when coupled with the fact of rarity or scarcity, defines prices whether they be of rents or of labor. Smith, Ricardo, and Mill had not used labor to define value, but they had used it to measure value in exchange. Hume's thoroughgoing, sensuous empiricism and Bentham's hedonism required Jevons to reject labor not merely as a theory of value but also as a measure of value.

The assumptions defining the idea of the good of the traditional Anglo-American culture of the United States are now before us. They are: (1) the subjective egocentric religious doctrine of Protestantism and the individualistic political doctrine, grounded in Descartes, Malebranche and Locke's conception of a person as a mental substance, and (2) the laissez-faire economic theory formulated by Adam Smith and Jevons, which rests in turn on Locke, Hume and Bentham.

The Protestant factor tended to make the individual the sole cause of any unfortunate economic or social circumstances in which he found himself. Locke's political philosophy made the preservation of private property the sole justification for the existence of government, thereby rendering unconstitutional any majority legislation which curbed working conditions or business practices in the interest of human rights or social needs. Similarly, the laissez-faire economic theory prescribed it to be unsound to prevent in any way the free play of individualistic action regardless of the social consequences, and required that laborers be treated, not from the standpoint of their value as human beings, but from the standpoint of the exchange value of their labor in a competitive free market. The point to be noted is that this not merely happened in practice between 1866 and 1932 but also was what the traditional religious, political and economic leaders regarded as the good in theory.

We need hardly wonder at the tremendous hold which this exceedingly philosophical and technically economic idea of the good has had upon us. It had behind it a lengthy accumulation of factual and theoretical inquiry in physics, philosophy, and economics covering a period of roughly three hundred years, which began with Galilei in 1590 and reached its climax with the death of Jevons in 1882. This extreme laissez-faire individualism was more marked in the United States than it was in even the purely modern portion of British culture. This happened because our political philosophy was continuously determined by Locke rather than by the social hedonism of Bentham and Mill; and because our economic theory was similarly dominated, as a consequence, more by the extreme laissez-faire individualism of the earlier economists such as the physiocrats and Adam Smith, than it was by the social hedonism of the later economists such as Mill and Jevons. To all this must be added the Protestant preacher's emphasis upon religion as a purely introspective and hence private and subjective thing.

Nevertheless, even in the United States during this period the principles guiding its actual policy were not quite as simple as this statement suggests. A consistent application of the individualistic laissez-faire religious, political and economic doctrine would have uneqivocally prohibited the introduction of tariffs. In other words, it would have placed the Democratic party following Jefferson, rather than the Republican party following Hamilton and Lincoln, in power, most of the time between 1866 and 1932. Yet this is precisely the period in which excessively high tariffs were introduced and in which the Republican party enjoyed its greatest triumphs.

There are several explanations of this apparent paradox. The major one is that the American people, notwithstanding Lincoln's conviction that he had reconciled the organic federal principle of Hamilton and Jay with the laissez-faire individualism of Locke and Jefferson and the Declaration of Independence, have not yet learned how to relate their traditional Lockean and Humean political and economic philosophy with the persisting requirements for a more organic, nationally controlled federal principle. More specifically, we are continuously forced by the inescapable facts arising even in peace time, quite apart from events like the bombardment of Pearl Harbor, to meet problems and determine policy at the national and international level, rather than at the more localized, independent, individualistic level, to an extent far greater than should be the case were our traditional Lockean and Humean, and excessively subjective, private, traditional, Protestant idea of the good for man and the state the whole truth which it purports to be.

These considerations require examination in more detail. For it is the two of them together which produced the administration of Franklin Roosevelt and its New Deal.

THE NEW DEAL

Nowhere does the confusion of the American people and their economic and political leaders, with respect to where they stand on the issue between federal governmental action and laissez-faire, individualistic economic and political activity, show itself more dramatically than in their two major political parties. For, to a limited extent since 1914 and unequivocally since 1932, the Republican party and the Democratic party have reversed their traditional stand upon these matters. Now it is the Democratic party inspired by Woodrow Wilson and Franklin Roosevelt which affirms the federal principle of Hamilton, Jay, and Lincoln to be a positive good and an absolute necessity in the state; and the Republican party which is nearest to Jefferson in being inclined to regard federal action as an evil to be kept at an absolute minimum. This is the ideological reason why Wendell Willkie who tried to return the contemporary Republican Party to the use of the organic federal principle of Hamilton and Lincoln in both international and national affairs was given his walking papers by this party. It is the reason also why the old-line Southern Democrats who take Jefferson as their ideal often find so much more in common with the leaders of the present Republican party than they do with the New Deal Democrats.

But this surprising rejection of Hamilton and Lincoln for a pure and unadulterated Locke and Jefferson is slightly too much for even the old-line Southern Democrats to accept in the twentieth century. They are not fooled by the fanciful current Republican account of American history to the effect that free, independent enterprise devoid of federal governmental interference with the free play of economic forces is what made our country great in the past. The Southern Democrats know very well that the great achievements of American industry in the North between the Civil War and 1914 were to a considerable extent due to the fact that the Northern businessmen, through control of the Republican party and the use of its federal principle, obtained protection and special favors for themselves, while the Southerners followed the laissez-faire philosophy of Locke, Jefferson and Adam Smith. The Southern Democrats know also that since they were converted to the use of the federal principle, not merely in international relations but also in home affairs, by their own Virginia-born Woodrow Wilson with his Presbyterian organic social principle derived in part from Calvin, the economy of the South has proceeded to move sharply upward. This is one of the reasons why the leading proponent of positive legal agreements and cooperation instead of laissez-faire nationalistic independence and isolationism in Pan-American and other international relations has been Cordell Hull from Tennessee.

Aside from his Calvinism, one of the inescapable facts convincing Woodrow Wilson of the necessity of this change in our modern political philosophy was the movement in modern science from Newton to Darwin. Of this Wilson wrote as follows: "The government of the United States was constructed upon the Whig theory of political dynamics, which was a sort of unconscious copy of the Newtonian theory of the universe. In our day, however, whenever we discuss the structure or development of anything, whether in nature or in society, we consciously or unconsciously follow Mr. Darwin; but before Darwin, they followed Newton." Our previous analysis has shown that the connection between Newton and the laissez-faire individualism of Jefferson and Adam Smith is far from unconscious, since John Locke and his successors made it most articulate and consciously explicit. Wilson adds:

Politics is turned into mechanics under his [Newton's] touch. . . . The trouble with the theory is that government is not a machine, but a living thing. It falls, not under the theory of the universe, but under the theory of organic life. It is accountable to Darwin, not to Newton. It is modified by its environment, necessitated by its tasks, shaped to its functions by the sheer pressure of life. No living thing can have its organs offset against each other as checks, and live. On the contrary, its life is dependent upon their quick cooperation, their ready response to the commands of instinct or intelligence, their amicable community of purpose. Government is not a body of blind forces; it is a body of men, with highly differentiated functions, no doubt, in our modern day of specialization, but with a common task and purpose. . . . Living political constitutions must be Darwinian in structure and in practice.

Need one wonder that Wilson faced problems with a positive program, moving away from old conventions as befits a growing, living mind? He left his impress upon the Southern Democrats and upon Franklin Roosevelt.

The manner in which Darwin similarly affected John Dewey and Justice Holmes as well as a vast group of other American sociologists and legal thinkers is equally evident. One of the most brilliant and devoted followers of Justice Holmes is Supreme Court Justice Frankfurter. When the New Deal was initiated, he came very close to being President Roosevelt's major political adviser. One should have no difficulty, therefore, in understanding why the present Democratic party has moved away from the pure laissez-faire individualistic philosophy of Newton, Locke, and Jefferson to the acceptance of federal action and the federal principle of Hamilton and Lincoln which, because of Darwin, is given a dynamic, living content, as a positive good, in home as well as foreign affairs.

The reasons why the Republican party has moved in the opposite direction become equally clear if two main considerations are kept in mind. First, the development of Anglo-American thought following Hume along economic lines tended to make the businessman more important than the statesman, thereby creating the businessman's world. Second, the businessman chose the Republican party because of its federal principle. Had he followed Locke, Jefferson and Adam Smith and the laissez-faire political and economic principle, he would have agreed with the pre-Wilsonian Democratic party in its contention that federal tariffs, due to their governmental interference with the free play of economic forces, are morally, politically, and economically unsound. It was precisely at this point that the Republican party won the businessman's support by offering him the federal principle of Hamilton and Lincoln.

The businessman used this principle to secure federal tariffs and a governmentally controlled and protected market for his products, as well as to receive from the government free lands and funds for the building of his railroads. At the same time, the only economic theory of his culture was that derived from the laissez-faire individualistic philosophy of Locke, Hume, Adam Smith and his early Quaker or Congregational Protestantism. This, he and others used to prevent farmers and laborers and little children in sweatshops from also enjoying the aid and protection of the federal principle. Thereby the rules of the economic game were so arranged that he had for himself the advantage of governmental interference with the free play of economic forces, and the attendant federal protection and aid in scoring, while all the other players were denied these advantages.

One need hardly wonder that the victories were largely his, temporarily. His finished goods were sold in a closed, federally protected and controlled national market. His labor and his agricultural and other raw materials were purchased in an internationally open, truly laissez-faire, freely competitive world market. At the same time the people's religious, political, and moral idealism and even their economic science were so constituted that regardless of the resultant unfairness and abuses for other members of the community, any move to get similar governmental protection in their behalf would be repudiated by the people and their Supreme Court Justices as economically unsound, politically unconstitutional, and morally and religiously evil, doing the proposed benefactors more harm than good in the end. Thus, the businessman was enabled to turn what was initially merely a businessman's world into a businessman's paradise. But like all things reared on a basic inconsistency with respect to principle, it was a paradise doomed to crash. And crash it did—even for bankers and businessmen—in 1929 and 1932 under the leadership, quite fittingly, of a Quaker Republican President.

The remarkable thing is not that the crash came but that it took so long in the coming. The fatigue after war, and the boom which follows the immediate reaction from the ending of a war, were undoubtedly partly responsible. One would have supposed, however, that the game of insisting upon traditional laissez-faire religious, political and economic doctrine for everyone except oneself would have fooled some of the people for a while but would not have fooled so many of the people for so long.

The situation became aggravated for laborers and farmers by one other development. In the nineteenth century, due to the discoveries of the experimental chemists and physicists and the theoretical, scientific investigations of Clerk Maxwell in Great Britain and Willard Gibbs in the United States, modern science established two new theories; one in electrodynamics, the other in thermodynamics and physical chemistry, reared upon basic assumptions different from those of Galilei and Newton. These two new mathematically formulated and experimentally verified scientific theories had far more concrete and novel applications to the materials and practices of man's daily life than did the physics of Galilei and Newton. Out of these theories came the new industrial processes of the steel industry and the chemical industry and, what is even more important, the shifting of a great part of the physical labor necessary to produce man's economic needs from the muscles and shoulders of men to the waterfalls, thereby creating the great public utility corporations. All these tremendous economic, industrial, and social changes involved a development of industrial research laboratories on a large scale, and a construction of plants and an organization of businessmen on a similarly large and far-reaching social scale, all of which were tasks entirely too great for the individual, independent property owner by himself to accomplish. Thus, naturally and inevitably, vast business organizations, fundamentally social rather than individualistic in character, requiring vast organizations of bankers for their financing, arose.

These organizations constituted property, and this property had to be owned by somebody. The traditional laissez-faire philosophy of Locke, Hume, and Adam Smith which arose out of the physics of Galilei and Newton, as we have previously indicated, never having faced such large-scale, fundamentally social developments, provided no adequate theoretical basis for a political policy capable of understanding and consequently of dealing effectively with these social consequences of the new scientific theories of the nineteenth century. It was natural, therefore, that in practice the property as well as the control of these tremendous, fundamentally social organizations should, because of the continued dominance of the Lockean and Humean, Quaker or Congregational philosophy in a world in which it had actually become outmoded, be treated politically, not merely by the businessmen concerned but also by the people generally, in terms of the Lockean and Humean laissez-faire atomistic and individualistic idea of the good, which their Protestant preachers and their editors and orators continued to reaffirm. This resulted in these tremendous social business and banking organizations becoming not merely directed but also largely owned by the few businessmen and bankers who were their organizers. It was not an accident that these same bankers and businessmen were also the pillars of the Protestant churches. The traditional modern Protestant doctrine and the laissez-faire political and economic science rested on the same set of seventeenth century philosophical assumptions.

This control and ownership of these huge, extensive, fundamentally social organizations gave the businessman an advantage over the laborer and the farmer, in addition to that provided by the federal protective tariff of the Republican party. Whereas the tariff had merely protected the businessmen from free competition in the world market, this concentration of ownership and control in a few corporations, interlocked through banking connections, helped also to protect him from the operation of laissez-faire free competition in the home market.

It was precisely this state of affairs which, before the last war, brought in the Sherman Antitrust Act and gave rise to the Bull Moose Republican party and the Big-stick trust-busting activities of the Republican President, Theodore Roosevelt; and which also led to the conception of social controls as a necessary and positive good in Wisconsin, under the Republican governorship of the senior La Follette, whose

Railway Commission became the forerunner of the present, most respected and effective Interstate Commerce Commission. It was also the need upon the part of labor, for at least partially equalizing these advantages of the businessmen which produced the development of the increasingly strong labor union organizations and the increasingly stringent immigration laws which similarly released labor from competition in a laissez-faire world market.

Under these circumstances the farmers in the North and especially in the Middle Western agricultural states, notwithstanding their devotion to the Republican party, because of its associations with Lincoln and their side in the Civil War, found themselves in an increasingly intolerable position. Forced on the one hand to buy their farm machinery and finished goods in a nationally closed market, due to governmental protection and control of the businessman's prices by means of a high federal tariff, and forced on the other hand to pay high wages for labor in a similarly nationally closed market, due to the governmental protection and attendant control of wages by means of stringent immigration laws, the farmer nonetheless found himself forced to sell his goods in a truly laissez-faire world market. The inevitable climax came in the boom of the 1920's when, notwithstanding the incredible profits of everyone else in the community, the farmers of the United States found it increasingly difficult to keep out of bankruptcy. This was too much even for their traditional, sentimental attachment to the party of Lincoln to survive.

But even this was not what finally convinced the majority of the American people that the traditional Lockean and Humean laissez-faire political, economic, and religious philosophy is inadequate and wrong in theory as an idea of the good, and that it can no longer be merely patched up by pressure politics in practice; but must be replaced by a new political philosophy and policy according to which governmental action is conceived as a positive good instead of a grudgingly conceded, necessary moral and political evil, to be kept at an absolute minimum.

The stage was set for the decisive event during the 1920's. Due to Woodrow Wilson's positive facing of international problems at Versailles, the Republicans were led by their own leaders to throw away their federal principle of Hamilton and Lincoln for Lockean and Jeffersonian laissez-faire individualism in foreign affairs. By this time also the businessmen and their Republican leaders saw that the workers had learned, and the farmers were about to learn, the game of using the federal principle of Hamilton and Lincoln to further one's own group interest and that once having learned this game, the laborers and farmers, because of their greater numbers, could beat the businessmen at it. Also, scientific technology, applied to the waterfalls and industry, enabled the businessmen to produce more and more products with fewer and fewer laborers, thereby leaving them with more unsold finished products than the buying power, in the form of wages placed in the hands of the public, could move. Thus more and more, even during the inflationary boom years of the 1920's, they found themselves in need of foreign markets. For this, the tariff policy was a handicap rather than an asset, since foreign nations had no excess gold and could only buy if they could pay here with goods, which a tariff prevented. Thus the businessmen and the Republicans lost their interest in the federal principle even in home affairs. In this manner, under the administrations of Warren Harding, Calvin Coolidge, and Herbert Hoover, the businessmen and Republicans, for the first time in their history, gradually tended to become consistent Lockean and Humean laissez-faire individualists for themselves as well as others, in practice as well as in theory; and the Republican party became the party of Locke and Jefferson. Hamilton and Lincoln must have twitched slightly, in their graves.

With this peculiar about-face two things happened. First, the old laissez-faire individualistic philosophy of Newton, Locke, and Jefferson, which the Democratic party, following Woodrow Wilson, had thrown into the discard, was taken out of the junk pile, dusted off, and decked out with a Republican label by the old-line Republican party bosses. Second, not merely the federal principle of Hamilton and Lincoln, but also the new, more democratic and economic constructive use of it—developed first by the Republicans Theodore Roosevelt and the senior La Follette—were handed over to the new Democratic party as a free gift, to use without any competition whatever.

Meanwhile, during the 1920's, under the boom conditions following the first reaction after the war when stringent federal action should be introduced to avoid inflation, the Republican administrations pursued their new, purely Jeffersonian laissez-faire hands-off policy. A terrific inflation occurred. Stocks went up so quickly that they could not be bought fast enough. Even the imaginations of corporation lawyers and bankers were not fertile enough, in throwing the stocks of old companies together into new permutations, thus, by a miracle, creating absolutely new stocks out of nothing but the old stocks which one had before, to supply the demand. Also, in the rest of the world, again due largely to the pursuit of the laissez-faire individualistic philosophy in international relations, world commodity prices were pursuing their steady, relentless decline. Even in the United States the commodity price index showed a continuous, pronounced decline from 1925 onward. Even so, these practical American businessmen and their Republican leaders "with their feet on the ground" were not satisfied. Notwithstanding the astronomical stock market prices of the inflation there were still surplus industrial products; the American businessman needed foreign buyers.

The problem was solved by loans by the private bankers to Germany. The Germans, at least many, frankly said that they could never pay back the loans. Nonetheless, the loans were fairly thrust upon them. The interest could be paid with a new loan. With this money the Germans built luxurious school buildings and swimming pools and enlarged the museum of science at Munich. They thought the Americans were fools; but if the Americans insisted, well and good. Meantime, the American private bankers passed on these bonds with their attractive 8 per cent coupons to the conservative Republican voters, who were glad that at last an administration was in power run on sound economic principles by practical men.

At the same time that students in the city of Göttingen in Germany were thus enabled to enjoy the most superlative equipment in an oversized high school building, students in the city of New Haven, Connecticut, which is four times the size of Göttingen, were forced to attend school in two shifts—one group in the morning and another in the afternoon—and each group was forced to obey traffic regulations in going from one classroom to another, so congested were the hallways. Yet if one had proposed to build a high school in New Haven one-half as large in proportion to the number of students as the one our loans to Germany helped to build, we would have been told by our professors of economics, our businessmen, and our Republican politicians that it was unsound economically. Finally, however, the bankers and the laissez-faire Washington "Republicans" became a little bit fearful of further loans to Germany even if the loans did help trade. Eventually, the loans were stopped. This meant slightly lower business profits. As stock prices were already discounting increased future profits, the result was inevitable.

In 1929 an American painter was living in Westport, Connecticut. He painted from memory a picture about his native Kansas. The fear and terror, however, which he put into it were not borrowed by memory from the past; they were very real in the present. The painting was called "Tornado over Kansas." It pictures a farmer and his family rushing to the storm cellar. Of this painting the author of *John Steuart Curry's Pageant of America* has written as follows: "The tornado was more than a weather disturbance, for it characterized the terror of the worst economic disaster this country has ever witnessed."

This was but the beginning. The laissez-faire individualistic philosophy had never been particularly satisfactory for laborers or farmers or for families in slums. But in 1932, under the Quaker Republican Herbert Hoover, it failed even for bankers and businessmen. This was the last straw. The climax came when suddenly General Dawes resigned his ambassadorship in London to rush home to receive millions of dollars from Herbert Hoover's federal government in order to save the banks in the city of Chicago from crashing. Even this was not enough. So millions more were added, and the situation was temporarily saved. But the wise Will Rogers saw the point at the time, when he wrote that in the United States the bankers were the first people to go on a governmental dole. The point was not that this action by the federal government was unwise, but that on the traditional businessman's and the Republican party's laissez-faire political and economic philosophy, it should not have occurred.

Meantime, the farmers went more and more into bankruptcy and wondered more and more why bankers were saved by a financial grant from the federal government from having to take their losses, while farmers had to take theirs. Finally their patience became exhausted, and when the sheriff came to foreclose the mortgage on their farms they met him with pitchforks. If Locke's and Hume's and Adam Smith's laissez-faire political and economic philosophy does not work for bankers and businessmen under an administration and under a President who believes in it, both in his religious life and his political philosophy, then it would seem to work for nobody. Moreover, if it is right for a Republican President to step in and prevent the free play of economic forces from pursuing their natural course for bankers, then it is equally right for a different President who believes in governmental action as a positive good in principle, to do this for everybody.

Need we wonder that Franklin Roosevelt and his New Deal were swept into office in 1932 with the support even of the traditionally Republican farmers and thoroughly scared businessmen of the North, or that he was kept there by the longest continuous support of a popular majority ever enjoyed by any President in the history of the United States? Need we wonder also that it is this New Deal Democratic party which is now, with its positive acceptance of the federal principle as a national and international ideal, the true successor of Hamilton and Lincoln, as well as Wilson, while also being, because of its emphasis upon tolerance and the extension of freedom to *all* men, the true successor of Locke and Jefferson in the spirit, if not the laissez-faire letter, of their conception of the law?

Nor should anyone be surprised that each one of us is left disturbed and morally and emotionally uneasy and even moved to inconsistent acts by these developments. One cannot, through Protestant preaching and traditional political and economic teaching over centuries, permit one's emotions and moral convictions to become attached to a set of theoretical, scientific, and philosophical presuppositions which were reasonable and adequate for the seventeenth century, but which have been demonstrated both in theory and in practice to be inadequate for the twentieth, and expect anything else but momentary emotional uneasiness and confusion and even demoralization to result. Nor could one have expected President Roosevelt to escape completely from this past to apply his new positive doctrine consistently and continuously. Such is the price which one must inevitably pay for failing to keep one's religious, moral, political, and economic theory abreast of theoretical reconstructions and advances in philosophy and this philosophy in turn continuously under the control of evidence and verified theory in the mathematical and natural sciences.

Had the Anglo-American world done this we would have learned long ago of the inadequacy of the philosophy of Locke, Hume, Adam Smith, and Bentham, and would perhaps have avoided having the lesson driven home to us now at such a tragic cost. But it is by no means certain that even these recent experiences will be enough to teach us what is required if further catastrophe is to be avoided. Unless we can rid ourselves of our traditional, outmoded, and in part false theoretical philosophical, political, economic, and religious assumptions, and rear our religion, economics, and democracy upon philosophical foundations abreast of unquestioned contemporary scientific knowledge and its attendant philosophical theory, there is grave danger that neither the debacle of 1932 nor even Pearl Harbor and Corregidor, will be able to teach us. It is exceedingly important, therefore, that the layman as well as the expert be aware of precisely why scientists and scientifically informed philosophers know Locke's philosophy to be false and Hume's, Adam Smith's, and Bentham's philosophy to be incomplete and inadequate.

The evidence appeared first in the science of mathematics and mathematical physics. As Chapter V will show in greater detail the technical concepts of these sciences, especially such notions as the square root of two, continuity, and limit in the differential calculus and causality cannot be defined in terms of reds and blues and odors or pains and pleasures or any other immediately sensed factors, as Locke's theory of ideas and the positivism of Hume, Bentham and Mill require. Scientists trained in mathematics, and especially Descartes and Leibnitz, who created the mathematics used in modern physics, recognized from the very outset, this limitation of Locke's theory of ideas which gave rise to Hume's and Bentham's philosophy. Moreover, Newton had pointed out that sense awareness, to which Locke and Hume restricted knowledge, gives only sensed space and time, not the public, mathematically defined space and time of daily life and physical science. Thus it is that under the leadership of Descartes, Spinoza and Leibnitz, each one of whom knew more about mathematics and physics at first hand than did Locke, Berkeley, or Hume, there arose another movement in modern philosophy known as Continental Rationalism, which parallels the British empirical movement from Bacon and Locke, through Hume and Bentham, to Mill and Jevons.

Considerations such as these from mathematics and experimentally verified mathematical physics, together with Hume's demonstration of the limitations to which our knowledge would be restricted were it defined solely as Locke's theory of ideas requires, awoke Kant from his "dogmatic slumbers" during which he had supposed, with Locke and Hume, that even the knowledge of mathematics and mathematical physics derives completely from immediately sensed data. These considerations caused him to seek an additional basis for human knowledge other than sense data, and to construct a new theory of the philosophical foundations of the modern world, a theory moreover which would synthesize the findings of both the British Empiricists and the Continental Rationalists by admitting both the sensuously grounded knowledge for which Locke's and Hume's theory of ideas partially accounts, and the rational, more formal, systematic and mathematical type of knowledge which mathematics and mathematical physics exhibit.

Later we must examine Kant's theory in more detail. Neither German culture and mentality nor contemporary communistic Russia can be understood without doing this.

But Kant must be understood also if we are to understand ourselves. With Hume, as we have noted, the concept of the soul and the doctrine of its immortality became invalid. A person was conceived as merely a transitory association of sensuous data. Consequently, had not different philosophical assumptions than those provided by Locke's theory of ideas and Hume's philosophy actually entered into nineteenth century Anglo-American as well as German and Russian culture, the main tenets of the Christian religion, both Catholic and Protestant, would have been left invalid. It was Kant who came to the rescue of modern Protestantism not merely in Germany but also in Great Britain and the United States. His philosophy proposed an entirely new basis for morality and religion, different from that of the Lockean, Berkeleyan, and Humean modern world or the Greek and medieval, pre-modern and Roman Catholic world. This new Kantian philosophical theory of the foundations of morality and religion was introduced into Great Britain by the Cairds and T. H. Green, to flourish at Oxford as developed by Bosanquet and Bradley.

In Great Britain it had considerable political as well as moral and religious influence, in part offsetting the laissez-faire atomic individualism of the political philosophy of both Locke and Mill and the ethical and economic doctrines of Smith, Bentham, and Jevons and the British Liberal Party deriving from them. As developed in its post-Kantian, more Hegelian form in the hands of Bosanquet and Bradley, because of its basic organic principle and doctrine of internal relations, it taught an organic theory of the state, and fostered the sentiment and practical conviction that man can only justify his own true nature through social relations and action. This is one of the reasons why so aristocratic, able, and distinguished a statesman as the late Lord Haldane, who was impregnated with the post-Kantian philosophy, could, without any sense of inner conflict, take a position in the Cabinet of the Labor Government in Great Britain and work side by side with Socialists for the defeat of the policies of laissez-faire individualism. For the post-Kantian idealistic philosophers and thinkers, as well as the Socialists and Communists, there is no meaning to the individual man apart from internal organic relations with his fellow men; and no possibility of the good life apart from the expression of those social relations in political action on a national scale.

In the United States these idealistic Kantian and post-Kantian philosophical doctrines were introduced by William Torrey Harris (1835–1909) and developed by George Holmes Howison (1834–1916), Josiah Royce (1855–1916), Borden P. Bowne (1847–1910), and in our own day by Charles W. Bakewell, Wilbur M. Urban, William Ernest Hocking, Edgar S. Brightman, Charles Hendel, and Brand Blanshard. It is a peculiar characteristic of this "idealistic" philosophical movement as it has developed in the United States that, until recently, its individualistic, personalistic rather than its organic side has been emphasized, even to the point at times of making the latter difficult to reconcile with the former. Kant's moral philosophy permitted this because, as we shall see, his morality and ethics are so extremely formal, having their basis solely in what is required to have any religious or ethical experience whatever, quite apart from any explicit content which it may possess. This has permitted followers of Kant to fill in the idealistic forms with the traditional individualistic political and economic doctrinal content derived from Locke, Berkeley, Adam Smith and Jevons. Thus, certain of the most extreme of American Kantians have been the most conservative, individualistic, and laissez-faire of politicians.

Josiah Royce and William Ernest Hocking, and more recently, C. W. Hendel and Brand Blanshard because of their less Kantian and more Hegelian emphasis upon the organic unity of the whole or the absolute, rather than upon the atomic individual person, unequivocally in both theory and practice, have been exceptions to this peculiar and paradoxical development. In the case of Royce and especially Hocking, this post-Kantian idealistic influence has taken an aesthetic and intuitive turn, influenced perhaps by Schopenhauer, which renders their final position nearer in many respects to that of the Orient than to that of the traditional, orthodox Kantians and post-Kantians. This is a very important development because it provides a factor, indigenous in our own thought and culture, which is necessary for the basic task of our time of merging the Oriental and Western civilizations.

Kant's philosophy had one other consequence which is important for the understanding of ourselves. As Chapter V will show, he achieved a temporary resuscitation of the Protestant religion and of its traditional, conventional, pietistic moral sentiments, in which he was reared, only by setting up the practical reason as a more trustworthy guide to values and to all humanistic subjects than the knowledge obtained by the scientific methods of what he termed the theoretical reason. With time, however, in the culture of the United States, due to the discovery abroad of non-Euclidean systems of geometry, and the hypothetical rather than the categorical character of the basic formal concepts of scientific inquiry in mathematical physics, the specific content of the Kantian doctrine, although not Kant's basic notion of the synthesis of the empirical and the theoretical components of scientific knowledge, broke down, as did also the early confidence in Kant's purely formal moral philosophy as an adequate basis for either morality or religion. The reason for this breakdown will appear in Chapter V. Thus, at the present moment, many major divinity schools in the United States do not have an idealistic philosopher or theologian on the faculty.

Even though the Kantian moral philosophy has turned out to be unsatisfactory, the weighty considerations which brought it into existence remain and must be met in another way, as Chapters V and XII will show. Also, certain influences from Kant have passed over into the quite different American pragmatic philosophy. Especially, Kant's setting up of practice and practical demands as either a substitute for theory or as something which will give theory automatically as a by-product, or which will release one from uncomfortable conclusions to which empirical evidence and science may lead. William James's "will to believe" is an example of the latter tendency. The popular thesis of businessmen that practice and doing are what matters and that to pay attention to theory is to be impractical is another example. The practice of many Protestants of giving up theory and doctrine to concern themselves with "life's real practical problem," thereby failing to acquire the theoretical knowledge in natural science, philosophy, economics and government necessary to understand these problems, is another instance. In fact, the sweep of the pragmatic philosophy over the United States during the latter portion of its businessman's world owed much of its popular appeal, as well as its specific content, to this same error. People liked to be told in the name of philosophical theory itself that practice would give one trustworthy theory, or, perhaps even better, that experimentation and doing made theory unnecessary. To be sure, John Dewey, in conveying the truth of pragmatism, that the theoretical element in scientific knowledge is given hypothetically with only indirect verification and hence never with absolute certainty—rather than categorically and with absolute certainty as Kant maintained—erred less in this respect than did James; and Charles Peirce erred less than either James or Dewey. But even Dewey's lesser error was not sufficiently slight to prevent his followers in the departments of education and law from getting the erroneous suggestions in his writings and from failing to grasp his less articulate truth.

What Dewey's followers acquired was not his correct thesis that theory and its theoretical problems are as necessary a part of scientific inquiry as empirical evidence and experimental methods—the theory being merely indirectly rather than directly and absolutely confirmed by experiment—but the erroneous assumption that experimentation and an appeal to what happens in practice, without guiding theoretical principles, are alone what matters both in science and in life. Thus the notion got abroad, not without support from Dewey and his associates, that people facing the basic theoretical problems of science, philosophy, and culture were either antiquated old mossbacks or speculative arm-chair thinkers dealing with irrelevant pseudo-problems. The people who found thinking difficult, or who lacked the logical or mathematical training necessary to enable them to pursue it effectively, liked this suggestion, since it lulled them into the complacent fool's paradise in which they were the scientific and effective people; and the theoretically directed, logically disciplined minds were the evil spirits. Professors in departments of education liked it also, because it freed them from the need of knowing any specific subject which they taught; instead they learned the experimental "scientific" method of teaching anything.

Similarly, a new school of jurisprudence arose in the law schools known as "legal realism." Again, theory and principles were irrelevant. One had books filled with individual specific cases; one watched how judges behaved; and, like the Protestant preachers, "one faced the real social problems," again without the knowledge or appreciation of the role of theory in realistic scientific method necessary to understand them. Out of this verbal environment came Professor Thurman Arnold, to write a book upon the meaning of words. From the correct realization that the old Lockean and Humean theoretical principles for economics and political policy had broken down, the conclusion tended to be drawn that all theoretical principles whatever are pseudo-rationalizations and myths. We need hardly wonder that a New Deal based upon such a misguided pragmatism denied in one governmental order what it affirmed at the same time in another. This is precisely what practice and doing, unguided by theory, produce.

But it does not follow from this that the old Lockean laissez-faire theory to which the Republican party has turned is any better guide for policy. An old theory, that of Locke, Hume, and Adam Smith, resting upon a philosophy which we know by scientific evidence from mathematics and mathematical physics to be inadequate, and which we have found to fail in practice, is an even worse guide for political action in a world with the theoretically defined practical issues confronting ours, than is no theory at all. In fact, the leaders of the New Deal had to flounder along pragmatically as best they could, with little consistent philosophical, political, and economic theory to guide them, because in a democracy its leaders merely give expression to the beliefs of the people; and this, if we are honest with ourselves, is precisely the state of mind of most of the rest of us. To suppose that a return to the Lockean and Jeffersonian laissez-faire individualism would not bring even worse bungling and even worse catastrophe into national affairs and international relations is to ignore all that has happened in science and philosophy since the seventeenth century.

What must be realized—even though the noting of it here repeats points previously demonstrated—is that ever since 1710 when Bishop Berkeley revealed a contradiction in Locke's philosophy by showing that its theory of ideas renders its basic concept of a material substance meaningless, as Hume showed later it renders its basic concept of a person equally meaningless, and ever since Leibnitz and Kant in the same century revealed the incapacity of either Locke's or Hume's philosophy to account for mathematics and mathematical physics, it has been clear to scientifically informed philosophers and psychologists that Hume's philosophy, while factually true as far as it goes, is inadequate; and that Locke's philosophy of atomic mental substances, or absolutely independent persons, is self-contradictory and erroneous.

Now it is precisely upon the all-sufficiency of these two scientifically and philosophically rejected premises of seventeenth century thought that the traditional laissez-faire individualism of Jeffersonian old-line Democratic political theory and early Anglo-American economic theory is based. Thus it can be said unequivocally that no hope for a solution of the tragically pressing internal and international problems of our time is to be found in giving up the federal principle of Hamilton, Lincoln, Theodore Roosevelt, La Follette, and Wilson, or of Wendell Willkie, as the Republican party is now proposing, to return at this late date to the laissez-faire individualistic political and economic philosophy of the seventeenth century John Locke and his physiocrats. Even Bentham, Mill, and Jevons knew in the nineteenth century that this political and economic doctrine will not do. Confusing and unfortunate as it is, America's traditionally misconceived pragmatism is a distinct advance over a false and outmoded absolutism. Certainly between a political leadership which bungles along in the right direction and one which would move us efficiently in the wrong, the choice is clear.

But there is no longer any need for us to flounder along at cross-purposes with ourselves, guided by a misconceived pragmatism. For the pragmatists themselves, especially in the "conceptual pragmatism" of C. I. Lewis, have already, for the most part, corrected the errors and the false emphasis in their initial, otherwise true philosophy. Since these errors still persist, however, not merely in the popular mind but also in the teachings and practices of contemporary professors in depart ments of education and in law schools, it is very important to get them out in the open explicitly and to note how they arose.

The initial pragmatic emphasis upon scientific method for all departments of human knowledge, the humanities as well as the natural sciences, was correct, as our previous indication of the connection between religion, economics, ethics, philosophy, and the natural sciences has demonstrated and the sequel will show. But the interpretation of this scientific method operationally and completely in terms of its end-products gave rise in most minds, often even in those of the founders of pragmatism itself, to an over-emphasis on the work of the experimental scientist and the engineer, and to a failure to appreciate the equally important and necessary contribution of the mathematician, the theoretical scientist, and the scientifically grounded philosopher. Thus, in the hands of pragmatists, scientific method itself tended to be pictured as something which made quite unnecessary, if not positively evil, an attention upon basic assumptions, theory, and the systematic, logical formulation of empirically given, experimentally determined facts.

The most elementary knowledge of the history of science or the character of the method of physical science would have corrected this error. Four of the greatest names in the history of modern physics are Isaac Newton, Clerk Maxwell, Willard Gibbs, and Albert Einstein. All of these men made their remarkable and most pragmatically practical discoveries by mathematical analysis and by theoretical inquiries, depending upon others for the factual findings; they were not particularly distinguished as empirical observers or as experimentalists. In fact, Willard Gibbs and Albert Einstein never performed an experiment of any significance in their lives. All these men made their great scientific discoveries by facing theoretical difficulties and problems arising out of the previous scientific concepts and assumptions used in conceiving and relating the known facts; and by modifying or radically changing the traditional theory so as to remove the theoretical difficulties and account for all the facts in a consistent and, what always turns out to be the case, a more pragmatically useful manner. Thus instead of the practical and the pragmatic being the criterion and definition of the theoretical, it is the pursuit of the theoretical problems in their relation to the factual evidence which has not merely produced the great scientific achievements of modern physics but has also turned out to be the most effective method for obtaining the maximum of pragmatically practical and useful results.

Recently, thanks to the analysis of scientific method made by Morris Cohen and H. M. Sheffer and to the logical formulation of mathematics carried through by Bertrand Russell and Alfred North Whitehead, these errors of the earlier followers of pragmatism are being corrected so that at last we are achieving a truly pragmatic philosophy which conveys its original truths without so grossly misleading its followers.

Fortunately, the need for a more critical attitude toward merely practical activity and toward the initial impression produced by the pragmatic philosophy is making itself felt in wider circles. On September 30, 1943, in a review in the *New York Times* of Herbert L. Matthews's *The Fruits of Fascism*, John Chamberlain wrote:

The Fruits of Fascism is filled with a thousand ironies. Fascism attracted a whole generation of "giovinezza," of Italian youth, because it promised idealistic things. It has ended in a caricature of everything that youth could reasonably desire. Fascism got its élan by making a cult of "action." It has ended by drying up the springs of action in the Italian character. By this time it should be apparent that "youth" and "activity" cannot be moral or philosophical touchstones. . . . Mr. Matthews is addressing his book to Americans, who are a pragmatic people. I wonder if they will have the wit to understand it. For what he is saying here is that the pragmatic test is not enough. There must be the test of principle, too.

This comment is profoundly true. But there is nothing in a properly conceived pragmatic philosophy which requires that it produce the effects deplored by Mr. Chamberlain. Only a pragmatism grounded in a partial or a faulty conception of the scientific method upon which it so rightly insists has these consequences. A scientific study of the character of this method will correct these errors, thereby guiding the pragmatists to the theoretical assumptions in the method itself and in the theories which it verifies. These assumptions should provide us with the principles adequate to the problems and empirical knowledge of our time which we so desperately need. This task must concern us in the sequel. Already, important contributions have been made by C. I. Lewis, Morris Cohen, Alfred Whitehead, W. P. Montague, George Conger, Wilmon Sheldon, and others.

Notwithstanding its misconceived legal realism and pragmatism, the New Deal has not been entirely devoid of scientifically grounded theoretical principles. Its economic policy with respect to the problem of unemployment and the control of the business cycle was based, initially at least, upon the theoretical and technical scientific investigations of the British economist Maynard Keynes.

To understand the Keynes theory, it is necessary to note certain exceedingly important developments in the science of economics since the time of Jevons. It will be recalled that Jevons reared economic science upon Bentham's hedonism. Consequently, the movements of prices in the market place and all the laws of economic science were regarded as the result of the attempt of men to maximize their introspected pleasures and to minimize their introspected pains. For Bentham, Mill and Jevons these introspected pleasures defined not merely economic value but also moral and political value. In fact, it was precisely upon this identification of economic value with ethical and political value that the argument of Jevons and his predecessors, from economics to what is good in politics, rested. Only upon the assumption of this identity was it possible ever to make the laws of traditional Anglo-American economic science an argument for laissez-faire individualism in ethics and government.

With the accumulating criticisms of Bentham's hedonism which appeared from many sources, and also from economic considerations alone, economists gradually became aware that the basic assumptions and laws of their science were quite independent of Bentham's hedonism. This discovery was first made on the continent by the famous Austrian school of economists. Instead of identifying economic value, as had Bentham and Jevons, with a specific want such as pleasure, they identified it with any immediately introspected want whatever. This still left economic science in accord with the requirements of Hume's philosophy, since introspected wants are purely empirically given, immediately apprehended data. Thus the current theory of value in Anglo-American economic science is termed not the hedonistic, but "the psychological theory of value." Curiously enough, this shift altered no laws in Jevons's economic science. It merely derived its laws from less restricted psychological assumptions.

The Austrian economists, whose doctrines were introduced into the

United States and Great Britain by John Bates Clarke, Frank Fetter and Lionel Robbins, among others, noted also that this psychological definition of value with which the science of economics is concerned, and to which it restricts itself, is quite a different concept of value from the one which occurs in ethics and in political science. That this is the case the following concrete facts will indicate. The desire for and attendant purchasing of large quantities of opium is a perfectly good value in the economic sense of that term, since it is an introspected psychological want which registers itself in a transfer of money in exchange for the opium in the market place. But it does not follow from this that it is a good in the ethical or the political meaning of that term. Thus both moralists and governments have placed restrictions upon the purchasing and selling of opium.

Curiously enough, although contemporary economic scientists are clearly aware that a calculus of wants or interests does not define ethical value, but gives only economic value, this distinction has not yet entered into the minds of many American philosophers who pride themselves upon being "naturalists" and scientific. For example, Ralph Perry's "interests" are precisely these psychological economic wants. Furthermore, there is no point in his developing a calculus of such interests in the hope thereby of defining a correct theory of the good for man and the state, since such a calculus is already provided in the ordinary registry of people's interests or wants in their daily lives and practices in the market place and in their *de facto* national and international relations.

The separation of ethical and political value from economic value has important implications. It means that there is no justification in economic science for or against a given ethical or political ideal providing it is consistent in its assumptions and applications. With respect to moral and political values, economic science is an instrument rather than an end. It does not define either the moral or the political good. It merely enables one to achieve in the most economical way possible, without inconsistencies which will defeat one's purpose, whatever moral or political ideal knowledge outside the science of economics leads one to accept. Thus, with one stroke all the traditional statements from economists, to the effect that child labor laws or positive governmental action to improve labor conditions or bring about better housing are economically unsound, become spurious.

The moment this was realized it became evident that something positive might be done, using the traditional laws of economic science as a consistent, effective instrument to control the business cycle and mitigate the evils of unemployment. It is precisely this type of thinking which produced the economic theory of Maynard Keynes which the New Deal, when it came into power, put into practice.

This theory depends upon the following analysis of what happens, according to traditional economic principles, when there is full employment. According to this analysis, there will be full employment for all, except those who cannot or will not work under any circumstances. when there is a proper balance in the economy between spending and saving. This balance is disturbed in a boom, according to the analysis, because spending far exceeds earnings and savings. Conversely, a depression sets in when savings far exceed spending.

Thus, put very briefly and in an over-simplified form, the Keynes theory is that wide fluctuations in the business cycle and unemployment can be prevented, quite within the operation of the laws of traditional economic science, if in times of boom the government, by increasing taxation and in every way discouraging spending, builds up savings which the people, enticed by the elusive charm of higher future prices, will not by themselves set aside. Similarly, in times of depression, when saving is overdone and spending is underdone, and the people, by their free activity, refuse to correct the balance, the government must step in and spend until the proper balance between saving and spending necessary for the reasonably full employment specified by the traditional economic science is achieved. It was no fault of the Roosevelt administration, when it came into power in 1933, that it was confronted with the spending rather than with the taxing and saving phase of the business cycle.

Whether this theory of Keynes's will solve the problem of the business cycle and unemployment cannot yet be said. Certain things are, however, unequivocally clear. First, it provides what conservative businessmen have asked for and assert can be realized; namely, a definite theory and policy for meeting the economic problems of our culture in accordance with the laws of economic science, as these laws are now understood, without any recourse to communism. Second, it seems reasonably clear that much of the opposition to it stems from the old identification of economic value with laissez-faire political value, the identification which led pre-Jevonian economists to oppose, in the name of economic science, the governmental action necessary to make the Keynes theory work. Third, the Keynes theory can succeed in the long run without producing terrific government debt and all the dangers of which the businessmen and traditional economists are afraid, only if the theory is correctly understood by everyone and accepted as a principle in the time of a boom as well as in the time of a depression. This means that everyone must not merely accept government spending in the time of a depression, but also increasingly high taxes, higher than normal, in the time of a boom.

Again we see, more specifically, how important it is to reconstruct our moral, political, and economic theory and our traditional sentiments and convictions concerning what is sound practice, in the light of the established advances of recent scientific inquiry. This is especially important if the problem of unemployment is to be solved short of a recourse to communism.

That there are dangers in the Keynes policy, if it is not correctly understood by everyone, cannot be denied. It requires not merely the courage to spend governmental funds comparatively freely in a depression, but also even greater courage to tax businessmen and the public increasingly heavily during the developing stages of a boom. It is customary to say that politicians will not do this. It is to be remembered, however, that we are living in a democracy. Under such a form of government the responsibility for what happens in Congress is with the people. Thus it is unequivocally dishonest to lay upon the politicians the blame for a failure to follow principle. If the politicians in office will not follow principle, then the responsibility is the people's, in a democracy, to put men there who will. There is no reason whatever, providing the people support research and education which provides them with scientifically determined philosophical and economic theory, why this cannot be done. Moreover, there is nothing in the Keynes theory, in particular, which necessarily turns the government into a Santa Claus. It depends upon as realistic a recognition of the fact that one cannot eat one's cake and have it too, as characterized the old, traditional laissez-faire philosophy. This is why the theory prescribes that one must increase taxes in a boom.

The culture of the United States has one other even more difficult problem which our traditional laissez-faire philosophy has shown itself totally incapable of solving. During the pre-Civil War period shipowners and Southern landowners brought to the United States a considerable body of people with a color of skin and cultural values different from those of its other inhabitants. These people soon adopted its language and its predominantly Protestant religion. The victory of the Union in the Civil War and the development of the highly technical and industrialized civilization resulting from the new theories discovered and experimentally verified by modern scientists plunged them into a competitive, mechanized civilization for which they were ill prepared, and thrust them into large cities in segregated areas, among neighbors who did not understand them. Their values are more emotive, aesthetic, and intuitive, placing an emphasis upon the enjoyment of life which the mechanics of trade and of business are supposed to achieve, rather than upon the mechanics itself. This characteristic can become an asset for our culture. For these are values with respect to which Anglo-American culture is weak. The mere reflection upon the nature of this culture suffices to indicate that it has a predominantly political, economic, technological and practical emphasis. In it a religion of the emotions and cultivation of the aesthetic intuition for its own sake have been neglected. Its Negro members have these values instinctively, as Paul Robeson shows in a superlative degree. By the white people, they must be slowly and painfully acquired. The Negroes, similarly, must with equal patience, through education and training, acquire the political understanding and the scientific knowledge and skills necessary for any man to live in the contemporary world.

INTIMATIONS OF NEW VALUES

Certain very important factors have entered into the culture of the United States in the twentieth century. In 1908 in New York City a revolution occurred led by eight painters. These painters, influenced by the French Impressionists, pushed into the background the overstuffed, very rigid leather or plush chairs of the Victorian era and the perfectly proportioned geometrical pots of flowers, and presented the aesthetic continuum and its immediately sensed, emotionally moving colors and forms for their own sake. More recently, Grant Wood in "American Gothic" and especially in "Daughters of Revolution" (Plate IX) made us look at our blankish Protestant souls with all their rigid ethical virtues, but devoid of a hearty, human spontaneous expression of feeling, compassion, and the emotions. Likewise, Thomas Hart Benton in "Persephone" shows what may occur when this traditional Protestant repression of the aesthetic intuition and the emotions in the realm of overt behavior takes place. Also, when the New Deal came into power, upon the advice of Edward Bruce and George Biddle, art was conceived as a necessity and as a positive good which government can and must encourage and sustain, just as the Republican party in the nineteenth century encouraged and sustained business. As a consequence, the Treasury Department's Section of Fine Arts and the Federal Art Project were inaugurated, and the artist was given the place in the community as an essential and creative being in his own right, providing his fellow men with their most elementary and necessary emotional, intuitive, and spiritual requirements. Meanwhile, over recent decades, more and more individual Protestants in New England and the Middle West, unconsciously realizing the failure of their religion to provide them with the necessary aesthetic and emotional sustenance which the spirit of man requires, have turned either professionally, or as an avocation, to the arts and especially to painting. At the same time, under the influence of the Latins—George Santayana, Henri Bergson or Benedetto Croce—other Americans such as DeWitt Parker, Katherine Gilbert, John Dewey, Irwin Edman, David Prall, C. J. Ducasse and Theodore Greene were discovering the primacy and the importance of aesthetics for philosophy.

Important as these movements are, they contain little that is original. The painters tended merely to copy the classical or modernistic art forms of Europe, using them to enable the people of the United States to look at bits of their surroundings, their history, or themselves. Thus, at best, they conveyed an old vision, they did not create a new. The philosophers, similarly, based their theories concerning art entirely upon these European models. Neither to these painters nor to the philosophers did it occur that a new aesthetic approach to the nature of things, different from that of the European West, is possible.

Yet such a new form of art has arisen in the United States—a form indigenously American yet portraying something of universal validity. It appears in the painting of Georgia O'Keeffe (Plate XI), Paul Gill and others.

Like José Orozco in Mexico, Georgia O'Keeffe has developed her talent wholly within her native land. Born in Sun Prairie, Wisconsin, and finding herself driven by an urge to paint, she practiced at the Art Institute in Chicago and in the Art Students' League and the Department of Fine Arts in Columbia University in New York City. And later she has drawn upon the open spaces of Texas and the high plateaus and precipitous mountains of Arizona and New Mexico.

During her formal training there were, undoubtedly, European influences brought to her by her teachers. It is significant, however, that in considerable part, certain of these influences had to be repudiated. For upon looking over her work at the end of her formal training she noted, negatively, that her paintings were second-rate imitations of what one or another of her teachers might have done, and positively, that she was not expressing that something within her which continuously placed a compulsion upon her to paint. From this self-examination there came the resolution that for once in her life she would be herself, stating precisely what was in herself to be said—something, moreover, coming out of her own free and open America, which had never quite been shown before, yet, to use her own words, "so simple and so obvious that it is right before one's very eyes."

First there came the charcoal drawings. These did it in part but not clearly and purely. Then came brush and paint and the lengthy struggle to get the lines and their colors exactly right. Finally, in Abstraction No. 11, *The Two Blue Lines* (Frontispiece), it was done. But this was but the beginning. For the two blue lines are capable of a symbolic meaning; whereas the aim of this new art is to convey the aesthetic immediacy of things without intellectually added references and interpretations; without, at times, even the things themselves being shown. This is achieved in the later paintings of which Abstraction No. 3 is one of the purest examples (Plate XI). Here, although something actually observed in nature is faithfully portrayed, the subject matter is such that the external physical objects, of which this is the aesthetically immediate component, cannot be identified; and one is thereby forced to apprehend the aesthetic component of reality by itself for its own sake. One has pure fact with all its emotive quale and ineffable luminosity, before the inferences of habit and thought have added their transcendent references to the external three-dimensional objects of common sense or scientific belief, to the theological objects of traditional Western religious faith, or to the future pragmatic consequences of reflective action.

And one has also the demonstration that this immediately apprehended portion of reality bereft of the references beyond itself which habit and thought add, is by no means insignificant. Instead, it is superbly beautiful and spiritually sustaining. And for philosophy, there comes the additional demonstration that this purely factual, immediately apprehended component by itself—which we shall henceforth term *the aesthetic component of things*—is its own justification, and the kind of thing which, since it cannot be defined away in terms of anything else, must be taken as primary and ultimate. Here seems to be something self-evident and basic upon which an America and a world fighting their way away from faiths that have failed them can build.

There is another factor of longer and established standing in the culture of the United States, which is equally trustworthy. This is science, especially when it is pursued with respect to its verified theory as well as its technological applications.

Science designates a factor in knowledge and in things at the opposite pole from their intuitive aesthetic component. More and more science becomes essentially and inescapably mathematical. It becomes logically, systematically and deductively formulated, and verified only indirectly by precisely and theoretically defined experiments. It directs attention away from the aesthetically immediate, to the inferred component of things. The astronomer moves from the seen beauty of the sunset to the inferred unseen internal molecular constitution of the sun. Thus, whereas the art of Georgia O'Keeffe exhibits the concrete immediacy of things, devoid of inferred elements and doctrinally designated factors in them, science, and Western common sense and religious belief following science, direct knowledge to the inferred factor devoid of its aesthetic immediacy.

It is well to have a name for this inferred scientifically known factor in things. Because it is inferred from the immediately apprehended aesthetic component and because it is knowable, therefore, only by means of indirectly verified theory, it seems appropriate, as Chapter VIII will indicate in greater detail, to term it *the theoretic component.*

Thus, there is the suggestion, which at the present stage of our inquiry can be little more than a hint, that the culture of the United States is initiating a shift to new philosophical foundations, in which intuitive art conveying *the aesthetic component of things* and experimentally verified theoretical science conveying their *theoretic component* will be basic. A culture rooted in such a philosophy can build with confidence since *the aesthetic component* is immediately apprehensible and *the theoretic component* is scientifically verifiable.

Long ago, Plato in his *Timaeus* identified the mathematically designated *theoretic component* in things with the male principle in the universe and the intuitive *aesthetic component* with the female principle. This is precisely the interpretation which Alfred Stieglitz, the informed student of Georgia O'Keeffe's art, places upon her Abstraction No. 11, *The Two Blue Lines*: the one blue line represents the female aesthetic component; the other, the male scientific component in things. And the common base from which they spring expresses the fact that although each is distinct and irreducible to the other, both are united. It is because this bold intuition of the artist, sensitive to the deeper intimations of her culture, is supported, as the sequel will show, by considerations which are scientific and philosophic in their basis and worldwide in their scope, that *The Two Blue Lines* functions appropriately, both as the Frontispiece of this book and as the concluding topic of this chapter—a chapter which ends with the spirit of a free and adventurous United States turning its attention from the culture of its past to that of its future.

Properly to comprehend this future the major cultures of Europe and Asia must also be understood.

CHAPTER IV

UNIQUE ELEMENTS IN BRITISH DEMOCRACY

Few motion pictures have impressed and moved the people of the United States as did "Mrs. Miniver." This response took the English quite by surprise. To them "Mrs. Miniver" seemed true enough but not outstanding, so much have they always taken for granted what it portrays. To Americans the picture was impressive not merely because Mrs. Miniver exemplified the individualistic self-reliance which people in the United States value and esteem, but also because it portrayed another factor commonplace to the English, which is not so commonplace to the citizens of the United States.

Mrs. Miniver, her husband, their son, and every other person in the film were fighting not merely for themselves and their family, or even for their fellow men, but also for England and Britain. In the individual, independent doggedness, in the calmness and determination, there was something essentially and inescapably democratic. Had this been all that the film portrayed, its impression upon Americans would have been similar to its effect upon the British. But there was something more, a something which gave to the independent actions of the Minivers and their fellow Britons, a communal unity and companionship, cutting across differences of talent and social station, which was tinged with emotion and affection.

It was appropriate that this communal factor in Mr. and Mrs. Miniver's democracy should be portrayed in what was perhaps the final climax of the film by a scene in a parish chapel of the Church of England. Truly it was not merely their private selves, their local community, or the indomitable conviction of their individual consciences for which they were fighting and before which they were worshiping; there was also England, worshiped and beloved in her own right.

In British culture the extreme individualistic conception of freedom and social responsibility, stemming from the scientific, philosophical and religious assumptions of the modern world, is a basic and essential factor. This is the reason why Great Britain like the United States is a democracy, and why the seat of its political sovereignty is located neither in the King nor in the House of Lords, but in the House of Commons. But in contrast to the traditional culture of the United States this is not the whole of the story, just as the individual Englishmen are not the whole of England or the Empire. For there is England itself also, and its Church of England, as well as the many Non Conformist Protestant denominations; and this England, whose Church of England symbolizes even for Non-Conformists the Englishman's love and worship of England in its own right and for its own sake, is a basic factor also, a factor moreover which these modern, individualistic, democratic Englishmen regard as supremely good.

It has been customary, in considering Anglo-American relations, to concentrate only on the individualistic, the democratic, and the linguistic identities. But the differences, such as the organic factor to which the individuals are devoted, are there also in Great Britain and especially in England. It is imperative, if Britons are not to misunderstand their English-speaking fellow democrats in the United States, that they realize the almost complete extent to which the culture of the United States lacks this organic factor, due to its traditional definition predominantly in terms of nothing but the atomic Cartesian, Lockean, and Humean laissez-faire assumptions of modern political and economic theory and Non-Conformist Protestantism; this culture, as thus defined, without any compromise with medieval, hierarchical religious and political forms, being set against a background of nothing but nature. It is equally imperative, if the citizens of the United States are not to misunderstand their British forebears or neighbors, that the presence and affectionate acceptance of the organic social principle in British democracy and the reasons why it is there, be appreciated.

THE ROMAN AND MEDIEVAL BACKGROUND

The primary reason is that England, Scotland, Wales, and Great Britain, unlike the United States, are older than the modern world. Greek, Roman, and medieval ideas combining with a stock composed of natives and invading Norsemen, Romans, and Normans produced a "merrie," medieval, Christian, hierarchical British culture before the modern world was born. This culture initially, like medieval culture generally, was in its social life aristocratic, in its politics regal and in its religion Roman Catholic. From the Romans also the British acquired a respect for law and its governmental institutions not merely as a necessary pragmatic instrument for the achievement of the good life, but also as a positive good in its own right. So much so, that even today the British are often referred to as the Romans of the modern world.

The British have never dropped this heritage and their conviction of its preciousness. It is precisely this which makes the study of Latin by every ideally educated Englishman not the pursuit of a "dead language" or a mere instrument for the disciplining of the human mind but a positive contribution to his present-day conception of the good society and the good life. In an article on "The Place of Classics in Education" the Englishman Alfred Whitehead writes:

> Rome itself stands for the impress of organization and unity upon diverse fermenting elements. Roman Law embodies the secret of Roman greatness in its Stoic respect for intimate rights of human nature within an iron framework of empire. Europe is always flying apart because of the diverse explosive character of its inheritance, and coming together because it can never shake off that impress of unity it has received from Rome. . . . The vision of Rome is the vision of the unity of civilization.

This Roman, medieval, unified, hierarchical conception of the good also determined the structure of medieval British society, with its King, its Archbishop, the King's Privy Council, the dukes and earls, and lords and ladies, the more local gentry, the yeomen, and the craftsmen of the local guilds. According to this social ideal, the good for man is to be found not in the utterance or the realization of his equality with all other men, but in the finding of the particular place in the entire hierarchical social system for which his own peculiar talents best fit him and the achievement of the highest skill which is appropriate to that place. Thus, in medieval England the emphasis was upon man being in "his proper station." In "Mrs. Miniver" it was appropriate that the station-master should convey this medieval value.

For all its emphasis upon unity and hierarchical order both in theory and with respect to one's social station, medieval British culture was extremely individualistic and localized on the economic side. This happened because the physical science of Newton and Maxwell, through its socially organized, technological applications which brought on the Industrial Revolution, had not yet been discovered. Consequently, in the medieval world the production of its economic needs was achieved in the local community through the local guilds by means of purely local social organizations. Thus to the original Englishman, local autonomous social organization in both the economic and political spheres was not an original discovery of the modern world but a practical state of affairs in its otherwise unified and hierarchical form of society. Historically and continuously in the mind of the Briton there is not the supposition of a conflict between the individualistic and local self-government principle and the acceptance of the organic communal principle which tends to exist, in theory and thought at least, for his American cousins.

But there are other reasons for the unique character of British democratic culture. Into the hierarchical social forms and values of medieval England there came the influence of the Protestant Reformation. The power of this Reformation and of Protestantism generally cannot be separated from the movements toward political nationalism and economic mercantile individualism which accompanied it. Luther himself owed his following among the German people as much, if not more, to the release of the nationalistically inclined Germans from the political control of Charles V and the Holy Roman Empire, which his attack upon the Pope fostered, as he did to the popularity of his individualistic justification-by-faith religious doctrine. In England, similarly, the development of Protestantism, political nationalism, and a mercantile economic society of individualistic enterprise went together.

THE TUDORS AND THE CHURCH OF ENGLAND

There the first complete break from the Roman Church came under Henry VIII in 1535 when the Act of Supremacy was passed, making the King the "Supreme Head of the Church of England." The immediate cause of this act, which was of Henry VIII's doing, was to permit Henry to gain the divorce from his wife Catherine which the Pope had refused to grant. His success in achieving this desire by such extreme means was due, however, to the wish upon the part of many of his subjects to see the control of Rome and of the Holy Roman Empire over English religious and political life weakened. In Henry VIII's mind also there was the desire to identify the religious emotions of all Englishmen with England rather than with Rome and to bring his people to the forefront of influence in Europe as a strong and independent nation. To be sure, the general desire for reforms in the practices of the Roman Church in England was also a contributing factor. However, only "very few men," George Carter, in his *History of England,* informs us, "following the teaching of Luther and other continental reformers, wished that the doctrines and services of the Church should be reformed." That this was true also of Henry VIII is shown by his support of the Roman Church in its doctrinal conflicts with Luther. Writing of the translation of the Bible which Henry VIII ordered in 1536, Carter adds, "In granting this privilege it was not his purpose to give any countenance to the Protestants, any more than he did to the Roman Catholics. True it was, that he had severed England from Rome, but he did not intend to forsake the doctrines and practice of the Roman Catholic Church."

It is from these acts upon the part of Henry VIII in the first half of the sixteenth century that the Church of England takes its inception. With its origin, the medieval communal principle of unity and all the traditional religious sentiments attached to it were severed from the Pope and from Rome, and identified with the King and with England. At the same time, between the years 1536 and 1539, Henry VIII dissolved the monasteries and thereby gained funds for himself or his followers which enabled a strong central government to function without too frequent recourses to the conflicting Roman Catholic and Protestant groups which made up the Parliament. At the same time it was exceedingly sound national policy of inestimable value to Great Britain in her competition with continental powers in the centuries to come, since, by initiating a middle course of compromise between the extreme Roman Catholics on the one hand and the extreme Protestants on the other, it set a policy on religious matters carried on by Elizabeth and her successors which enabled Britain to escape the bloody and retarding religious wars which absorbed the energies of her most dangerous continental rivals even into the nineteenth century.

The importance of Henry VIII's policy was demonstrated by the events which immediately followed its temporary abrogation. Before he died, as his health declined and his influence grew weaker, fierce conflicts arose between Roman Catholics and Protestants even within his own council. Upon his death in 1547 his son, Edward VI, a mere boy of ten, succeeded him. By his will Henry VIII had put the young king under the regency of a Council of Sixteen, specifying that Protestant and Catholic members should be equally balanced. Immediately upon the death of Henry VIII one of the members of this council, Hereford, persuaded the other members to make him president of the council, with the title of the Duke of Somerset. Upon being given this power Somerset proceeded immediately to pursue the course of the Protestant reformers, by attempting to wipe out the old religion.

The degree to which the Protestant Reformation was not merely intolerant with respect to the beliefs of Roman Catholics but also blind to aesthetic values is shown by the following events, as recorded by Carter.

Orders were issued that all images of saints should be removed from the churches, that painted glass adorned with figures of saints and angels should be broken, and that frescoes on church walls should be covered with plaster or white-washed. The gross irreverence, with which these orders were carried out, shocked in no small degree the religious feelings of the majority of the people. Many old customs and holy-days were abolished. . . . In 1549 an Act of Uniformity was passed, abolishing the Mass, and enforcing the use of the First Book of Common Prayer. An Act was also passed by the same Parliament allowing the clergy to marry.

These acts, Carter tells us, were followed by general discontent throughout all England.

In 1552 a second prayer book, which is substantially the present Prayer Book of the Church of England, was issued. In the same year the young King Edward VI died. With Mary who became Queen in 1553 the reaction to the beauties and values of the old religion gained expression. She immediately married Philip II of Spain, thereby reconnecting England with the Holy Roman Empire, and in 1554 she restored the Roman Catholic religion and its Mass, depriving the married clergy of their privileges. Even the selectors of the members of Parliament were instructed to send representatives with Catholic sympathies. Carter says: "The people accepted all these changes without opposition. They had opposed the Queen's marriage with Philip, but they did not oppose the restoration of the Old Religion. . . . Toleration in those days was not even dreamt of, and so the persecuting statutes of Henry IV and Henry V . . . were re-enacted. From this moment the burning of Protestants began." Persecution upon persecution followed. Finally popular discontent appeared and Queen Mary died, "hated by her subjects, . . . deserted by her husband," and "on bad terms with the Pope." The policy of the Roman Catholics under Queen Mary had failed, as had the policy of the Protestant reformers under her predecessor, Edward VI.

Into this intolerable and chaotic situation came Queen Elizabeth, acclaimed by both Protestants and Roman Catholics, to break again from the Holy Roman Empire, restore the Church of England, and pursue and consolidate the middle course of her father, Henry VIII, with respect to religion. Again religious sentiments and devotion were attached to England rather than either to Rome or to the private conscience of the individual. Thus it is that George Trevelyan, in his *English Social History*, is able to write of "the joyous sense of nationhood which inspired the Elizabethan English. A man no longer felt his first loyalty owing to his town, his guild, or his 'good lord,' but to his Queen and country." But what began with Henry VIII and even with Elizabeth as little more than a political compromise became under her reign a warm and living reality. The Master of Trinity adds:

Anglicanism had been hardly so much a religion as an ecclesiastical compromise, decreed by a shrewd, learned and moderate young woman, with the consent of Lords and Commons. But at the end of her reign it had become a real religion; its services were dear to many, after more than forty years of use in the ancient churches of the land; and its philosophy and spirit were being nobly set forth in Hooker's *Ecclesiastical Polity*.

RICHARD HOOKER AND ARISTOTLE

The importance of Richard Hooker and his *Ecclesiastical Polity* for our understanding of the unique character of British democratic culture can hardly be overemphasized. His philosophy defines the idea of the good of the Church of England. But since the Church of England is the symbol for all Englishmen, Conformists and Non-Conformists alike and even for all Britons, of the divinely sanctified community of all Britons to which sentiment and religious devotion are attached and personal sacrifice worth the making, Hooker's theological polity is the key to a fundamental portion of British political thought and action as well as to its Anglican religious doctrine. In fact, as Cecil Driver has emphasized, the basic political philosophy of the Conservative party in Great Britain is not, as with conservative Republicans and Democrats in the United States, that of John Locke, but instead, except for recent additions to be noted later, that of Richard Hooker.

This fact is tremendously important and must be understood and fully grasped if the citizens of Great Britain and the United States are not to run grave risk of completely misunderstanding each other. The word "Conservative" has entirely different meanings in the two cultures. In the United States, as analysis of its culture has indicated, a traditional conservative among both the traditional Democrats and the recent Republicans is one whose conception of the good for the individual and the state derives from the laissez-faire individualism of the philosophies of John Locke and David Hume and the economic theory of Adam Smith and the physiocrats. In Great Britain, on the contrary, a member of the Conservative party is one who goes back to and believes in the theologically grounded, anti-laissez-faire, organic, hierarchical conception of the good state and the good individual which arose with Henry VIII and Elizabeth and which was made articulate in the *Ecclesiastical Polity* of Richard Hooker. This is the reason also why the film "Mrs. Miniver," in giving expression to sentiments and responses which were commonplace for all Englishmen and even all Britons, came to its climax in a local parish chapel of the Church of England.

The British authors of the article on Richard Hooker in the *Encyclopaedia Britannica* (11th ed.) tell us that

. . . his influence, so far from being immediate and confined to one particular era, has since the reaction against Puritanism been slowly and imperceptibly permeating and colouring English thought. . . . His theory . . . is the first philosophical statement of the principles which, though disregarded in the succeeding age, have since regulated political progress in England and gradually modified its constitution. One of the corollaries of his principles is his theory of the relation of church and state, according to which, with the qualifications implied in his theory of government, he asserts the royal supremacy in matters of religion, and identifies the church and commonwealth as but different aspects of the same government.

The specific practical consequences of a conservative political party which rests on Hooker rather than, or as well as, on Locke, must not escape our attention. It means in Great Britain that a Conservative regards laissez-faire individualism as a basically inadequate doctrine, giving rise to a policy in action which is quite incapable of meeting the communal problems which are inevitable in human and international relations and at the same time leaving the individual without his proper communal, emotional, and religious nourishment. It means also that the Conservative takes it for granted, in Great Britain, that problems of a social, national, or international character can be met only on the social level by governmental action and regulation. Thus it is not an accident or a mere result of compromise in the face of the rising power of the leftist groups, but because of their own positive conception of the good life for the individual and the state, that most of the major nationally controlled reforms which the Roosevelt administration introduced in the United States after 1932 in the face of the horrified opposition of the American conservatives had been introduced decades previously in Great Britain, not by the Labor party, but by its Conservative party. To be a Conservative in Great Britain means, in part at least, to follow Richard Hooker with respect to the ends and ideals of government and to accept John Locke's democracy merely with respect to the mechanics of government and the concrete instrument of its sovereignty. The party in Great Britain most nearly corresponding to the conservatives in the United States is not the British Conservative party but the very much younger and now almost defunct British Liberal party. For the latter is the party which stems from Hume, Bentham, and Mill. But even the Liberals, while emphasizing retrenchment, took as their slogan the words "Peace, retrenchment, and reform," and accepted John Stuart Mill's definition of a Liberal as one "who looks forward for his principles of government," rather than to the past. They failed because even Bentham's social hedonism, due to its conception of society as a mere sum of private pleasures, failed to put a specific content into these forward-looking principles upon which all Liberals could agree. Thus, in practice they tended to cancel each other, sending their party into eclipse.

Two things remain in our consideration of Richard Hooker and his importance for an understanding of British democracy. The first is the source of Hooker's doctrine; the second, the reasons why British opinion has so consistently and continuously followed it, notwithstanding the influence and instrumental acceptance of Locke and Smith.

Its source is clear. Like Henry VIII and Elizabeth, Hooker preserved the medieval world's philosophical conception of the universe and man. In short, he went back to Aristotle and the latter's organic, hierarchical conception of man and the nature of things. In the Aristotelian theory, as Chapter VII will demonstrate, the individual is by his very nature "a political animal." He is not, as with Descartes or Locke, a purely self-sufficient, independent mental substance. Consequently, for Hooker, neither the basis for religious doctrine nor the source of the sovereignty of the state is in the subjective private opinion of the individual or in a mere convention into which a majority of the many private individuals enter. Instead, it has its source both religiously and politically in the objective organic, hierarchical principle joining individuals to each other in the community and themselves to nature in the universe. This actual order is the basis of law, "whose seat," Hooker writes, "is the bosom of God, whose voice the harmony of the world." Thus the foundation of morality in both the church and the state is the same and is defined by "that law which God from the beginning hath set Himself to do all things by."

Between Aristotle as treated by Hooker and Aristotle as developed by St. Thomas there is, however, a difference. And it is precisely this difference which distinguishes the Church of England from the Church of Rome, as it also differentiates an autonomous and independent England from the England previous to Henry VIII, which was a member of the Holy Roman Empire.

This variation in the development of Aristotle's philosophy arises because Hooker wrote in the sixteenth century, whereas St. Thomas lived in the thirteenth. In the intervening years there had come a great revival of learning, culminating in the latitudinarian mind of the erudite Erasmus. Western man had been able to come more and more intimately into contact with the original Aristotelian and Greek thought. Thus Rome and St. Thomas no longer possessed a monopoly with respect to Aristotle's philosophy. The more these Greek sources of everyone's inspiration were pursued, the more the sense of imaginative freedom came over the minds of men. Greek thought, even Aristotle's thought, was not quite the rigid, cast-iron type of thing which the mold into which St. Thomas had poured Aristotle, within Roman Catholicism, had made it seem to be. Thus Hooker and his Church of England were able to take up the Aristotelian doctrines with a greater lightness of touch. His polity draws freely upon all the Greek and Roman classics and upon all the Hebrew and Christian scriptures. Consequently, while following Aristotle, Hooker gives to the English mind more freedom and latitude, so much so that he has been credited even with inaugurating modern philosophy in England.

The degree to which this freedom and this latitude distinguish the Church of England from the Church of Rome is obvious. Nonetheless, the important agreement remains. The doctrine of Hooker, like that of St. Thomas, goes back to the hierarchical conception of the nature of things of Aristotle. This is why the Throne and Canterbury are intimately related, the Archbishop crowning both the King and the Queen, and why the High Church services of the Church of England are so close to those of the Church of Rome. It is precisely the organic, hierarchical, communal conception of the good individual and the good state which Aristotle's philosophy provides, as over against Locke's or Bentham's, that makes conservatism in the culture of Great Britain something radically different from traditional conservatism in the culture of the United States.

The reasons for the Briton's continued acceptance of this Greek and medieval, Aristotelian conception of the good man and the good government are many and varied, but all easy to understand. Some have already been indicated. The primary one is that each member state of

Great Britain is older than the modern world. British history and culture are ancient, Roman, and medieval as well as modern. England is as proud of Beowulf and Chaucer, of Shakespeare and Falstaff—whose "merrie," hearty, medieval England, as G. K. Chesterton has seen, could not live in the busy, modern, Protestant, utilitarian world—and of Henry VIII and Queen Elizabeth, as she is of Fox, Cromwell, Locke, Wesley, Bentham, Jevons, and Queen Victoria. Naturally, she sees no reason, even if her history would permit her to do so, for repudiating the older values while accepting the modern ones.

There is a second reason, which is part and parcel of the first. It has been noted previously that the peoples of the United States came to the fruits of the Lutheran and Calvinistic portion of the modern Protestant religion and the assumptions of the modern world after the religious battles of Great Britain had been fought for centuries and a sufficient number of heads had fallen to sober the participants from every camp, and after the emphasis upon toleration as a positive good stemming from the philosophy of John Locke had begun to establish its beneficent influence. Thus we, unlike the British, have never known, apart from the burning of witches at Salem, what the initial religious impulses of the uncompromising Roman Catholic and the egocentric Protestant individual, unsobered by the saving control of a strong organic principle in the national government, were like. The experiences, however, of the British under Edward VI and Mary and later under the Puritans, when the organic communal principle pursued by Henry VIII and Elizabeth was set aside, permanently convinced the British, as if by a series of experimental tests, of the necessity and value of a sober national control to protect the people from their own bigotry. Describing English culture of the seventeenth century, G. M. Trevelyan writes: "The principal reason why the English witnessed the return of the old Church establishment with relief, was because it made less constant and obtrusive demands for professions of religious zeal upon the common occasions of life. The Puritans had made men 'eat religion with their bread,' till the taste of it sickened them." Also, "it was lucky for the witches that England was still aristocratically governed. In many rural parts the populace, if it had not been restrained by the gentry, would have continued to drown or burn witches down to the Nineteenth Century." As Alexander Lindsay has written, "Toleration in England was achieved as a combined result of two very different factors—the diversity of the Nonconformist sects—themselves, like the American, often intolerant in spirit—and the comprehensive tolerance of the Elizabethan settlement of the Anglican Church. The price which we had to pay was the dominance in England of a hierarchical social tradition."

Also, the blindness of the Puritans to aesthetic values had led them in their bigotry not merely to the destruction of the beauties and ceremonies of the old Church but also to the repression of the arts and of the theater. Events such as these persuaded the British permanently that, although the culture of the modern world brought with it certain very important values, it was nonetheless blind with respect to others, and driven by a shortsightedness which led it at times even to destroy its own values. Thus the middle course set by Henry VIII and Elizabeth, by means of which a combination of the organic, hierarchical, communal values from the old with the egocentric, laissez-faire individualistic values from the new became the accepted practice of the British.

A third reason for acceptance of the Aristotelian organic conception of the good government and the good state by Conservatives in Great Britain is economic. It also dates back to Queen Elizabeth. In her reign, George Trevelyan informs us, "under the vigorous leadership of Cecil and the Privy Council backed by Parliament, the industrial, commercial, and social system of the country was brought under national instead of municipal control." A citizen of the United States, nurtured in the ideas of Locke and of Adam Smith, might suppose that this intrusion of national control upon the autonomies of the local economic communities would have been resented by the citizens. Actually, however, the response of the citizens was quite the reverse. Professor Trevelyan writes, "Economic nationalism, as interpreted by the Tudors, gave greater liberty to the individual, freeing him from the local jealousies that usually inspired municipal policy."

But there was one other factor causing the local individuals and especially the businessmen to welcome this national control. Previous to the Tudors the local communities had tended to be dominated by the gentry, who favored agriculture and large estates. With the coming of the Protestant refugees from the continent and the protection of the Non-Conformist Protestants, which Elizabeth fostered while maintaining the Church of England, there developed an interest in mercantile trade, and in the support of the larger city traders and merchants against the landed country gentry. Thus national governmental control came first to the British businessmen, most of whom were Protestant Puritans, as a release for their individualistic enterprise rather than as a curb upon it.

Elizabeth went even further by fostering large stock companies in

London and by building up the Royal Navy, which in later years was to make the profits of these stock companies possible through foreign trade. The relationship here was mutual, for the East India Company gunned and manned its own ships, thereby providing the nucleus for a later strong British navy. While doing all this, the Queen's Privy Council, George Trevelyan informs us, "laid down rules" which the businessman in manufacture and trade "had to obey in the interests of the public." Thus it happened that in England the development of individualistic business enterprise and the inauguration of governmental control went hand in hand, the latter making the former possible. In fact, it was because of this governmental control introduced by Queen Elizabeth—which curbed the influence of the landed gentry and thereby released, subject to governmental regulation, the activity of the businessmen—that the mercantile era in British economic history and practice arose.

It was precisely because of this governmental support and control of mercantile organizations such as the Virginia Company and the East India Company, together with the development of the Royal Navy, that England was able to hold off Holland, overcome the Spanish Navy, and eventually dominate the world, economically, because of her foreign trade. In this manner, under Elizabeth, not merely the organically conceived Church of England and the beneficent power of governmental control to release individualistic mercantile activity were envisaged and achieved, but also the American colonies were settled and the Empire was born.

We need hardly be surprised, therefore, if Britons at this moment, even conservative British businessmen, find it not only possible but also natural and good, while insisting upon the Non-Conformist Protestant and individualistic democratic values of the modern world, to value also, and preserve as good, the organic principle of national unity and control in religion, politics, and economics which the Roman world first revealed. Of these two components, in shifting ratios of importance, the culture of Great Britain since the sixteenth century has been constituted. In short, the historical experience of conservative British businessmen since the sixteenth century has been that government regulation and control are valued and necessary accompaniments of effective individual enterprise. Without governmental action in support of manufacturers and merchants against the landed gentry, the businessman in Great Britain would not have received his initial chance; and without this same governmental control in matters of religion, saving Great Britain from the later religious wars which absorbed her continental rivals, he would not have achieved the later advantage in international trade which has been his good fortune.

But the poor and the needy profited also by Hooker's continuation of the Aristotelian philosophy and its attendant support of communal governmental action as a positive good. Guided by this conception, Elizabeth and her Privy Council brought the treatment of the poor as well as the regulation of the businessman under national instead of municipal control. George Trevelyan informs us that "the survival of an effective system of poor relief in England alone of the greater nations of Europe" in the centuries following Elizabeth is attributable to this fact. This acceptance on the part of the national community of relief for the needy became so general that by 1680 one-fifth of the entire nation was "in occasional receipt of alms." It is exceedingly illuminating to note that it was only during the seventeenth century, when the laissez-faire, individualistic, philosophical assumptions of the Non-Conformist Protestants and the Lockean democrats were in the ascendancy, that a "decline of the control exercised by the Privy Council over local magistrates and parishes" in the administration of the Poor Law and other matters occurred; a decline, moreover, described by Professor Trevelyan as "a decay of much-needed central authority which was the heavy price paid for Parliamentary government and constitutional freedom." Nevertheless, he immediately adds that "the Poor Law had taken such firm root in the days of Royal Prerogative that it survived as custom of the country in Parliamentary times."

In legal as well as economic and social matters the medieval organic concept continuously dominates British thought. The great protector of the liberties of the British individual is the law. This law goes back at least to the Magna Carta in 1215 and to the Common Law, which developed following the Magna Carta. It was this triumph of the Common Law, achieved over the centuries, which established the principle that the law is above the king or any other executor of the government. This "victory of the Common Law," G. M. Trevelyan writes, "preserved the medieval conception of the supremacy of law. . . . That mediaeval idea of the supremacy of law as something separate from and independent of the will of the Executive, disappeared in continental countries. But in England it became the palladium of our liberties and had a profound effect on English society and habits of thought." Thus for the British the law, which is one of the most precious protectors of their liberty. is of medieval rather than of merely modern origin. This medieval conception of the supremacy of law was given reformulation in 1765 by Blackstone in his *Commentaries on the Laws of England*. This book was widely read, especially in the United States, becoming its legal Bible. Curiously enough, notwithstanding its medieval origin, Blackstone became more of a Bible for legal thinkers in the United States, up to very recent times, than was the case in England.

The reason for this surprising discrepancy is to be found in Jeremy Bentham and the fact that he was followed in Great Britain by legal thinkers, while being for the most part ignored in the United States. It was Jeremy Bentham who persuaded the British of the inadequacies of Blackstone. The reason for Bentham's opposition centers in his philosophy, which has been previously considered in connection with the development of the democracy of Mill and of Anglo-American economic theory. According to Bentham, who followed Hume, the good is not to be found in any God-given, Aristotelian law of nature such as Hooker claimed. Nothing exists but the immediately apprehended sense impressions. Thus for Bentham the good became identified with pleasure, and the good law became the one which achieved the greatest amount of pleasure for the greatest number of people. With changing social and economic conditions through time, this hedonistic, utilitarian criterion of the good entailed the conception of the good law as a dynamic, changing thing, subject to variations in social conditions. Consequently, as Professor Trevelyan writes,

. . . Jeremy Bentham, the father of English law reform, regarded Blackstone as the arch-enemy, who stood in the way of change by teaching people to make a fetish of the laws of England in the form which they actually bore at the moment, a form dictated by the needs not of the present age but of ages long past. . . . Onwards from that time our laws were rapidly changed in accordance with the commonsense, utilitarian principles that Bentham had laid down.

Bentham died in 1832. It was not until one hundred years later, under the influence of the American pragmatic philosophy, operating through Justice Holmes and his devoted pupil Felix Frankfurter, later Associate Justice of the Supreme Court, that in the New Deal and in President Roosevelt's battle with the enraged American conservatives over his reorganization of the Supreme Court, Blackstone's static conception of the supremacy of law written in the past was seriously and systematically challenged in practice in the United States.

The extent to which British democracy, even its most conservative adherents, conceives of law along Bentham's lines, as a dynamic, growing thing, is shown most emphatically by the absence in Great Britain of any Supreme Court with the capacity, by appeal to a constitution written centuries in the past, to declare unconstitutional any act of the people's representatives in the House of Commons. Again the British, while frankly recognizing their indebtedness to the medieval principle of the supremacy of law, have combined this principle with Bentham's exceedingly modern, utilitarian idea of the good, according to which this law in actual human practice is conceived as a dynamic, changing thing under the control of the people's present legislative representatives.

This combination of the organic, legalistic concept of the Aristotelian, medieval world with the exceedingly modern, social utilitarianism of Bentham should not cause surprise, however. It will be recalled from previous consideration of the democracy of Mill, which stems from the utilitarian hedonism of Bentham, that in Mill's concept of democracy, unlike the Lockean concept, the good is not centered in the utmost freedom and independence for the individual mental substances, but has a positive social definition in terms of the greatest happiness for the greatest number. Thus the social emphasis in Bentham's concept of the good state may combine with the organic social concept of the good individual and the good community of Aristotle and Hooker.

Two respects in which the present democratic culture of Great Britain is to be distinguished from that of the United States have now become evident. One is that the British generally, and especially the members of their Conservative party, looking back upon Henry VIII and Elizabeth as the authors of Britain's greatness, both at home and throughout the Empire, have followed Aristotle and Hooker more than the Non-Conformist Protestants and Locke. The other is that even in their modernity they have tended over the past one hundred years to be influenced and guided, in their conception of the mechanics as well as the ideals of democracy, by Bentham and Mill rather than by Locke and Blackstone.

This does not mean that Descartes and Locke and the Non-Conformist Puritans and other Protestants who came to power contemporaneously with these two philosophers did not have a tremendous if not even a major influence upon modern British culture. It was the philosophical ideas of Descartes, Malebranche, and the Quakers and other Independents, together with the later political and religious philosophy of Locke, which—without destroying the Aristotelian, communal, hierarchical conception of the good life and the good state guiding Henry VIII and Queen Elizabeth and made philosophically articulate by Hooker—nevertheless broke down, during the seventeenth and eighteenth centuries, the absolute authority of the King, his Privy Council, and the House of Lords as the sovereign executors of this medieval, communal ideal, to locate its authority solely in the imaginations and the affections of the individual British subjects and in the symbolic power of the presence of the Church of England and the King, while placing the real control of political power in the democratically constituted House of Commons. The story of this tremendous achievement which transformed Great Britain from a monarchy into a democracy is to be found in a perusal of the famous Putney Debates, recently edited by A. S. P. Woodhouse, in the papers of the Levellers, and in the events associated with Cromwell, the Protectorate, the succeeding Restoration, the Revolution of 1688 and the Whig Party of John Locke. Since the philosophical and religious assumptions underlying this development have been considered in the preceding treatment of the culture of the United States, they need not be discussed here.

THE PURITAN REVOLUTION

Two facts standing out as a result of a perusal of these events must, however, be noted. First, Cromwell and the Non-Conformist Protestants were not especially democratic or tolerant, or motivated by religious toleration, even though the effect of their influence was to break down the power and authority of the king and thereby prepare the way for democracy. Second, toleration *as a positive good* and democracy as an accepted procedure, came with, and in considerable part as a result of, the philosophical doctrines of Locke.

The first fact is made clear by Carter's description in his *History of England* of the events, starting with the rise of Cromwell and leading up through his Protectorate to the Revolution of 1688:

The two great religious parties, which now began to make themselves felt both in the Parliament and in the Army, and played so important a part in the history of the next ten years were the Presbyterians and Independents. The Presbyterians aimed at establishing one great uniform Church on the model of the Church in Scotland. There was to be no toleration; men of all denominations, Papists, Episcopalians, Nonconformists, and Independents were to be driven into the fold of the Church. They wished to make peace with the King, and restore him to at least a nominal power. They formed a strong majority in the House of Commons. . . . The Independents on the other hand, wished that each congregation should be "independent" in itself, and not subject to any outside control. Their name embraced the Anabaptists, Levellers, Fifth Monarchy Men and many other violent Sectaries, and although they differed from each other in many points of their religious beliefs, they were united in opposing the authority of a Church appointed by the State and a compulsory uniformity. They wished to render the war decisive by crushing the King altogether. Of this latter party Cromwell was the acknowledged leader.

Certain points are clear. The Presbyterians represented a majority in Parliament but were intolerant and for the Monarchy. Cromwell's Independents were reasonably tolerant of each other and were for the most part against the King but represented only a minority.

Cromwell made up for the latter weakness by making himself "head of one of the finest armies the world has ever seen," composed of followers "of strong earnest Puritanical convictions." On June 3, 1647, this army, "acting under Cromwell's orders, suddenly appeared before Holmby House, and demanded the person of the King. 'Where is your commission?' asked Charles . . . as he stepped forth on the lawn. 'There is my commission,' answered Cromwell's captain, pointing to his line of soldiers." Thus Cromwell's army, without any authority under law or from the Parliament, took the King captive. In similar fashion, Cromwell and his army dealt with the Presbyterian majority in the Parliament. On October 3, 1648, this army, in what is known as Pride's Purge, "went down to the House with a body of soldiers, . . . and forcibly turned away ninety-six Presbyterian members, warning them not to appear again. The remaining members were Independents and numbered about . . . one-third of the whole House. They took upon themselves the government of the nation, but were in reality mere puppets in the hands of the Army, and were contemptuously called the 'Rump.'" For four years, in name at least, this minority Rump Parliament was the government in England. It became "very unpopular. No reforms had been carried out, justice was disregarded, the members were self-seeking and open to bribery, and secured for their friends and relatives all the most lucrative public offices." Finally Cromwell treated his own Rump Parliament as he had previously treated the Presbyterian majority and the King. One day, continues Carter,

he went down to the House, and leaving the soldiers outside, went in and took his seat as a private member. Just as the last vote . . . was about to be taken, he rose to speak. . . . "The hour is come," he said, "the Lord hath done with you." Some of the members loudly expostulated against the use of such language. "Come, come," he fiercely cried, "we have had enough of this; I will end your prating. It is not fit that you should sit here any longer. Get you gone, and give place to better men; you are no longer a Parliament."

He then stamped with his foot, and in poured the soldiers to clear the House.

For the next seven years, under the Protectorate, Cromwell was virtually in complete command, with a sequence of three futile Parliaments. The First Parliament was selected by him from a wider group of nominees which he ordered his Independent ministers to propose. This "Little Parliament had proved itself a byword and laughing stock to the nation; 'his Second Parliament elected by the people at his command, had questioned his authority and was dismissed without passing a single Act; his Third Parliament, though it recognised him as Protector, and would gladly have him made king, refused to acknowledge his new House of Lords.'"

It is clear that there was very little genuine democracy. Nevertheless, in the *Instrument of Government* drawn up in 1653 certain preliminary and partially democratic principles were formulated, even though under Cromwell they were never seriously followed in practice. With respect to religion, Cromwell, like Henry VIII, in building a strong state, desired to settle the religious question. Thus political expediency rather than the concept of toleration as a positive good dominated his somewhat liberal conduct; even so, his religious liberalism was limited. Carter says:

"Such as profess faith in God," ran the Instrument, "shall not be restrained from, but shall be protected in, the profession of the faith and exercise of their religion, provided this liberty be not extended to papacy and prelacy." . . . No objection was to be made to Presbyterians, Baptists, and Independents, so long as they had the root of the matter in them. Even Episcopalians were to be admitted if they bound themselves by a promise to abstain from using the Book of Common Prayer.

Under his Second Protectorate Parliament in 1656 it was specified that "liberty of conscience in religious matters should be allowed to all, except Papists, Prelatists and blasphemers."

At the time of his death, in 1658, although in foreign affairs he had enabled England "to take her proper place among European nations," and in home affairs he had "caused justice to be administered between man and man with an exactness and purity never known in England before, and gave religious liberty to all except Papists and Prelatists," nevertheless his rule had come to be regarded generally as "quite as tyrannical as that of King Charles himself. 'Every corner of the realm had become dissatisfied with it,'" to such an extent that the populace welcomed the restoration of the King and of a new Parliament composed mostly of Presbyterians favorable to the King, with rejoicing and open arms. It must be added, however, as Professor Trevelyan has written, "Some, though by no means all, of the Puritans' interference with the lives of their fellow citizens, that became so intolerable under the Commonwealth, was common form to all religious sects and all shades of political opinion."

These historical facts make it very clear that the Protestant Reformation and its religion, by themselves, do not necessarily produce democracy and its conception of religious toleration as a positive good. As long as the Protestants' beliefs are those of medieval rather than of modern philosophy they are as likely to favor the Royalist cause, as did the majority of Presbyterians in the Long Parliament, as they are to favor democracy. If one's philosophical beliefs and one's social sentiments are medieval and monarchical, then this is what one's Protestant religious consciousness will reveal. Moreover, if one's beliefs are those of a minority, the tendency of the Protestants' emphasis upon the individual conscience is to make it one's religious duty, in case the majority opinion is not in accord with one's own—as was the case with Cromwell and his minority Independents—to reject the final verdict of the majority which an acceptance of democracy requires, thereby producing a virtual dictatorship in practice. The same must be said for the Protestants' attitude toward religious toleration. For Cromwell and the Protestants associated with him, toleration, even at its best, tended to be used merely as a practical expedient when one was in the minority group, or in order to build a strong nationalistic England. It was not a positive good.

LOCKE'S EMPHASIS UPON TOLERATION AS A POSITIVE GOOD

These considerations make doubly evident the tremendous indebtedness of democracy, both in its religious and in its political aspects in Great Britain as well as the United States, to John Locke. For it was Locke's philosophy which prepared men, after giving expression to their own opinions, to accept the verdict of the majority and which so modified their theory of religious values as to lead them to regard toleration, not merely toward other Protestant sects and even toward Roman Catholic Christians, but also toward all other religious faiths, as a positive good. As George Trevelyan writes, "Locke's argument that Toleration was not merely politically expedient but positively just and right, became generally accepted as the Eighteenth Century went on." The understanding of British democratic culture requires, therefore, as careful a consideration of the philosophy of Locke, and of Descartes before him, as does a similar appreciation of the culture of the United States. This has been done in the previous chapter. The omission of their philosophical doctrines at this point must not, however, cause underestimation of their crucial importance in the British Isles. Great Britain is a tolerant democracy because of the modern philosophy of Locke.

THE NON-LOCKEAN FACTORS

It also must be remembered, however, that this democracy exhibits its unique traits, distinguishing it from the democracy of the United States previous at least to the coming of the New Deal, by the fact that although the philosophical assumptions of Descartes and Locke have made the seat of sovereignty, the mechanics of government and the degree of the religious toleration in Great Britain to a great extent what they are, the aims and ideals of this democracy are defined perhaps in equal part also by the enlightened Aristotelian theological polity of Hooker and the utilitarian hedonism of Bentham. It is the organic social and communal values defined by the philosophies of Hooker and Bentham which, supplementing the Lockean values, made it so spontaneously natural for the British to pursue governmental action and control in both home and foreign affairs as a positive good.

This shows itself unequivocally in the late Archbishop of Canterbury's *Christianity and Social Order*, in which not merely Locke and Adam Smith but also Luther, Wesley, Calvin, and Calvin's Puritans are attacked for their conception of a person as a mere independent individual rather than an essentially social being. Nor does the late Archbishop flinch from drawing the consequences of the early Non-Conformist Protestant philosophy. He charges that its "fundamental individualism . . . undermined the traditional Christian and Aristotelian appreciation of wealth as essentially social and therefore subject at all points to control in the interest of society as a whole." From this it is easy for him to move on, as he does immediately, to agree with Karl Marx that "the *bourgeoisie* [whose most influential members in England, as the Archbishop points out, were Non-Conformist Puritans, in control of the iron, spinning, and weaving industries], wherever it got the upper hand, . . . pitilessly tore asunder the motley feudal ties that bound man to his 'natural superiors' [Hooker and Aristotle again], and left remaining no other bond between man and man than naked self-interest and callous cash payment." It is his social concept of the person held in common by Hooker, following Aristotle, and by Marx, following Hegel, which explains also why the Archbishop often found so much more in common with Marx and the Russian communists than he does with his Non-Conformist Protestant Christian brethren. This is also the reason why the most positive leadership and program for facing the contemporary economic and political problems of our time within the Protestant Church came not from the Non-Conformist Protestants but from the Church of England, under the late Archbishop of Canterbury's leadership.

The late Archbishop's *Christianity and Social Order* is very important for another reason. It shows conclusively how difficult if not impossible it is to speak about Christianity, or a Christian doctrine of the human personality, *per se*; there is only the Christianity of Hooker, Aristotle, or the Archbishop, the Christianity of St. Thomas and Aristotle, the Christianity of St. Augustine and Plato, or the Christianity of Locke or the individual Non-Conformists. In each one of these different conceptions of Christianity the notion of personality has a unique meaning, as the Archbishop has unequivocally indicated in his criticism of the Non-Conformist Christian conception of personality and his defense of the Aristotelian Christian concept. In fact, the Archbishop insists that the Non-Conformist Protestants' neglect of traditional doctrine in their return to the "pure Christ," into which they read modern philosophical conceptions of the nature of a person, is largely responsible for the breaking down of what Hooker and the Archbishop regarded as the correct doctrine, both lay and Christian, with respect to the nature of private property and the necessity of social control of it in the interests of the community as a whole. What must be noted here is that all this follows only if one conceives of a human being and the Christian soul in terms of an Aristotelian philosophy or its equivalent, just as the quite different Christian doctrine, emphasizing the completely free and independent, rather than the social, nature of the human person, which the Non-Conformist Protestants other than the Calvinists, taught, follows only if one formulates Christian doctrine in terms of a non-Aristotelian, traditionally modern type of philosophy. Moreover, until some specific philosophical content and definition are put into the words of Christ, they are left indeterminate and consequently largely meaningless. It is because the late Archbishop of Canterbury realized this that he was one of the few Protestant leaders in the world who had something specific, challenging, and unequivocal to say in the name of Christianity with respect to its bearing on the social and international problems of the twentieth century.

Nevertheless, his specific essentially Elizabethan and Aristotelian doctrine cannot be regarded as a solution of the issues of the contemporary world. For these issues arise, as is already evident and the sequel will make more abundantly clear, because of the conflict between diverse modern and medieval scientific and philosophical doctrines. Clearly a conflict cannot be resolved by reaffirming one of the factors which generate it.

Several influences other than the Elizabethan tradition have given the British an interest in social control and governmental action as a positive good in the state and in the world. One of these is the ethics of Bishop Butler, still taught in the major British universities, which places an emphasis upon duty and a sense of social responsibility, rather than merely upon the independence, self-sufficiency and freedom of the individual person. Another especially important influence in the same direction is the Kantian philosophy introduced into the Scottish universities and into England by the Cairds and developed along peculiarly British lines with marked influence upon a vast company of British statesmen, by T. H. Green, Bradley, and Bosanquet. It is influences such as these which cause A. D. Lindsay, the Master of Balliol, to refer to the conception of freedom "as merely being let alone" as an "antiquated interpretation of freedom," and to add that unless this outmoded negative "freedom from" is replaced by a positive "freedom to," "democracy is put in the dilemma that we have to choose between complete laissez-faire and totalitarianism."

A third, more recent, but tremendously influential, development was the designation in ethics by G. E. Moore, within the empirical tradition of British thought at Cambridge, of what he termed "the naturalistic fallacy." The main point of this fallacy is that the meaning of the word "good" cannot be identified with any empirical datum such as pleasure, as it was by Bentham, since this identification would make the proposition "Pleasure is good" equivalent to the mere tautology "Pleasure is pleasure," which clearly is not the case. It follows that the good for a given individual or a given community cannot be determined by merely an empirical study of what is in fact the case in the behavior of that individual or that community. Recognition of this consequence of G. E. Moore's analysis of the meaning of the word "good" has prevented the vast majority of British social scientists, as H. J. Laski has noted, from falling into the error of the legal realists and other American empirical sociologists who suppose that ideological issues can be resolved and that the principles defining what is good in legal and social action can be found merely by observing what is in fact the case with respect to the behavior of judges and people generally.

G. E. Moore's contribution, to be sure, is a purely negative one. It tells merely what the good is not. Nevertheless, in the errors which it has enabled British legal and social thinkers to avoid, it has been of great importance. Also, because in Great Britain it has destroyed the supposition that the major problems of value in personal and social life will solve themselves automatically if enough factual satistical evidence is gathered, it has forced thought on these problems into its proper, more philosophical sphere. Once in this sphere, the inadequacies of the scientific and philosophical assumptions of Locke and Hume become evident, and the various later philosophical theories of Kant, Fichte, Hegel, T. H. Green, Marx, Alexander, and Whitehead, each of which mediates or replaces the laissez-faire, individualistic values of Locke with utilitarian social or organic communal values, are seen to merit serious consideration. Thus the practical effect of G. E. Moore's emphasis upon the fallacy of identifying the criterion of the good in personal or social conduct with any empirically given factor was to support an organic rather than an ego-centric theory of the state.

Another factor leading Britons to the same conclusion is the experience of their lengthy history. Whenever the extreme laissez-faire individualism of the Non-Conformist Protestants or the Lockean liberals was given unbridled sway, the results in British experience, for all the values, were unfortunate and deleterious. There was the blindness to aesthetic values in the thoroughgoing Protestantism of Edward VI and Somerset and the weak and faulty administration of the Poor Laws during the battle for parliamentary government and constitutional freedom in the seventeenth century. There was also a universal disgust over the intolerance and undemocratic activity of the Non-Conformist Protestants under Cromwell and the Protectorate. This liberal, laissez-faire individualism reached its final condemnation, however, in the nineteenth century, in the slums of Birmingham. There, long before its collapse was demonstrated in the United States in 1932, this same intolerable inadequacy of laissez-faire principles came home to the British people.

So great was the general conviction of the inadequacy of the individualistic Non-Conformist Protestant and the orthodox Lockean philosophical assumptions concerning the good life that the question arose, and has grown in seriousness over the years, concerning whether either the social utilitarianism of Bentham and the Liberal party, or the medieval organic principle of Aristotle and Hooker, accepted by the Conservative party, is adequate to meet the situation arising from the sciences and their technological applications, which have developed since the time of Newton and Locke.

As a consequence, the Liberal party stemming from Bentham and Mill moved into a minor position, being replaced by the socialistic Labor party. Also the Whig party with its Lockean associations became part of the Conservative party, because of the tendency of influential Whigs as they prospered in an industrial society, to participate more and more in the persisting aristocratic ceremonies and hierarchical forms of Elizabethan British society. More recently communism has received sympathetic study and defense from minds as diverse as Sidney and Beatrice Webb, Harold Laski, G. P. Cole, J. B. S. Haldane and William Temple, the late Archbishop of Canterbury.

Communism has a long history in England. The economic portion of its doctrine was developed there by Marx. No doubt his thought was influenced not merely by Ricardo and other British economists but also by the intolerable consequences of laissez-faire individualism which the slums of the large industrial and commercial cities exhibited to him. Moreover, Marx's labor theory of value had a long tradition behind it in British working class circles which, as Cecil Driver has noted, derives from Locke.

It will surprise many to find that the spiritual father of the American Declaration of Independence is also the inspiration in part of the labor theory of value of communism. The likely explanation is that the labor theory of value is rooted, as the sequel will show, in a materialistic philosophy; and whereas American thought defined its idea of the good for man and the state largely in terms of Locke's mental substances alone, British thought in labor circles pursued also the moral and social consequences of a serious belief in the material substances of Locke's philosophy.

In 1939 war tried Great Britain and her Empire as they have never been tested before. Quickly she turned to a coalition government under a Conservative leadership. This was natural because, with the Liberal party of Mill and Bentham a very weak minority, her two major parties believed in social action and governmental control as a positive good.

At the same time, her Conservative Prime Minister and the New Deal President of the United States thoroughly understood each other; since the New Deal in the United States was born of the same conviction of the inadequacy of laissez-faire individualism, arrived at after experiencing it in action in 1932, which the Conservative party in Great Britain has had with respect to it since its inception with John Locke, the physiocrats, and Adam Smith.

But even this is not all. The transformation of Anglo-American economic theory, noted in the previous chapter, has affected British policy also, and Maynard Keynes has become Lord Keynes. Thus, the creator of the economic theory of America's New Deal has been admitted to the hierarchical aristocracy of Conservative England and Queen Elizabeth. Also, even the Liberal party has turned to Sir William Beveridge's leadership, and his social security plan has received an extensive and favorable reception. London's financial weekly, *The Economist*, writes with approval of his program for unemployment. Meanwhile, an Archbishop of Canterbury with unequivocal social and sympathetic communistic leanings has left his impress upon the Church of Henry VIII.

Whether the Conservative party can keep abreast of the demands of peace, as its Winston Churchill kept ahead of those of war, is no longer problematical. The elections of July 1945 have occurred. Furthermore an army of civilian and military Britons, who have seen what positive social and governmental action can do by way of the preservation of the Empire and of Western civilization, have come home from war to harness the same triumphant, frankly governmental social spirit to the defeat of the evils of peace and to the constructive facing of the problems of a twentieth century world. As James B. Reston, writing from London for the *New York Times* on January 16, 1944, has indicated, Britain has learned:

. . . that boundaries do not stop bombers and that buffer States in the middle of the twentieth century do not buff. . . .

The England of Adam Smith is gone forever. When England ceased to be the workshop of the world the doctrine of *laissez-faire* vanished and it won't return. The British are not going to abandon private enterprise, but . . . they are determined to win the peace, and if that means rationalizing industry after the war, if it means scrapping some industries and concentrating on new ones, if it means . . . an embargo on politics; if, in short, it means restrictions on what was looked on in the past as freedom of the individual, she is prepared to do all these things in the interest of peace.

Finally . . . Britain is . . . changed spiritually. Through suffering her people have attained the remarkable unity and discipline which make these other changes possible. . . .

The England of 1944 has rediscovered her Elizabethan youth; she has added change to continuity; she has learned to believe again.

It would seem that the philosophy in which she is believing, notwithstanding the defeat of the Conservative party in 1945, draws more heavily upon Hooker and the Church of England than upon Locke and the Non-Conformists, and incorporates more of Marx and working class socialism than of Bentham and nineteenth century liberalism. Yet in truth Britain is being guided by both the individualistic and the organic doctrines.

DEMOCRACY AS BALANCE

"Non-conformity," writes her historian Ernest Barker, "fostered the notion and the doctrine of the limited State—the State that goes thus far and no farther." The Church of England and many other influences, as he is well aware, sustained the belief in the state going a considerable way if the good for man and society is to be achieved. Thus, he concludes: "We identify democracy with balance."

G. P. Gooch has shown that this characteristically British conception of democracy goes back at least to Halifax and to Harrington in the seventeenth century. Writing of Britons in the twentieth century, Ernest Barker says: "We have shed the antithesis of socialism and individualism," and he quotes the British statesman, Oliver Lyttelton speaking in 1942 as follows: "The essence of democracy should be a balance between the organizing power of the State and the driving force of the free individual. We must foster both." Nor does Ernest Barker hesitate to include the social services, such as those of the Beveridge Plan, within the organizing power of the state. In fact, he emphasizes that "in th[is] act of striking out on new lines, we are still being true to our old tradition of the middle way—the *via media Anglica*: we are still trying to make a reconciliation, and to find a compromise, between conflicting extremes." Evidently it was not an accident that "Mrs. Miniver" gave expression to the modern, Lockean sentiments of independence and self-reliance which the people of the United States so well understand and at the same time moved to its climax and found its meaning for individual sacrifice in the organic

Aristotelian sentiments of Hooker's and Queen Elizabeth's Church of England.

Although the British have envisaged one of the basic problems of the contemporary Western world, that of relating Locke and Aristotle, they have by no means resolved it. For the initial Lockean assumptions of the modern world and the basic Aristotelian premises of the medieval world contradict each other, and contradictories cannot be reconciled by being embraced; they can be resolved only by being superseded by a new philosophy which provides the merits of both without contradiction.

Furthermore, neither Locke nor Aristotle should be accepted, since both have been demonstrated to be fatally inadequate; Aristotle, because of the incapacity of his science and philosophy to account for modern experimental evidence and for the epistemological distinction between sensed and mathematical factors in nature, brought forward by Galilei and Newton; Locke, because of the internal contradiction, previously noted, within his theory, which exhibits itself in the fact that the theory of ideas entailed by his doctrine of interacting material and mental substances renders the notion of material and mental substances meaningless. The elections of July 1945 with their repudiation of the Liberal party derived from Bentham, the Whig Conservatives associated with Locke and the Tory Conservatives stemming from Hooker and Aristotle indicate that the British themselves have reached this conclusion.

It appears that Aristotle and Locke must be transcended if an adequate criterion of the good for the contemporary Western world is to be obtained. It is precisely this which the proponents of traditional German Kultur deriving from the idealism of Kant and of contemporary Russian culture grounded in Marx and Hegelian successors of Kant claim to have achieved.

CHAPTER V

GERMAN IDEALISM

The primary thing to keep in mind about German and Russian thought since 1800 is that it takes for granted that the Cartesian, Lockean or Humean scientific and philosophical conception of man and nature, which defined the foundations of traditional modern French and Anglo-American democratic culture, has been shown by indisputable evidence to be inadequate. This evidence appears in three fields: (1) mathematical physics, (2) the moral life, and (3) the development of historical institutions.

THE NATURE OF SCIENTIFIC KNOWLEDGE

Kant was an expert mathematical physicist before he became a philosopher, and it was the evidence from mathematics and physics which led him to his philosophy. He noted that it is quite impossible to define the technical concepts of mathematics in terms of nothing but colors, sounds, odors, pains, and pleasures and their fainter after-images as Locke's theory of ideas and the attendant philosophy of Hume, Bentham and Mill require. Furthermore, Newton's physics, like Einstein's, requires a distinction between time and space as sensed, and time and space as they enter systematically into experimentally verified scientific theory. Were Hume's philosophy correct only sensed space and time should exist. Nor should causality have the meaning which it has in mathematical physics. Hume himself showed that on his premises causality can mean nothing more than the hope that associations of sense impressions observed today will recur tomorrow. In Newtonian mechanics, or in Maxwell's electromagnetics and Einstein's more recent field physics, causality enters not as a mere hope on the part of the observer, but as a relation of necessary connection joining the present state of a physical system in nature to its future state in a manner such that, given the empirical determination of certain quantities defining the present state of the system, its future state at any specified time is logically implied.

Furthermore, neither the scientist nor common sense means by "physical object" what Hume's philosophy prescribes. Were scientific objects merely an association of sense impressions, then the primitive entities in mathematical physics would be blues and reds and greens and pains and pleasures instead of electrons, positrons, and other directly unobserved, mathematically related, and theoretically designated entities. Similarly, common sense believes that tables and chairs and planets exist independently of the mind's sense impressions of them. Yet Berkeley has shown conclusively that this independent existence is not given in sense awareness. No alternative remains, therefore, but to conclude that our knowledge of both common-sense and scientific objects is composed of two parts, the one given empirically to the senses as Hume affirms and the other given theoretically.

This is Immanuel Kant's great insight. While recognizing the partial truth of the British empirical philosophy, he also saw its inadequacies in the face of mathematics and mathematical physics as well as common-sense beliefs, and forthwith proceeded to provide the first philosophy in the modern world which combines the purely empirical portion of human knowledge which the later British empiricists made all-inclusive, with the formal, theoretical, systematic portion which mathematics and mathematical physics require, and to which Newton referred in his distinction between mathematical and sensed space and time. The philosophy which resulted was a bold one and exceedingly technical in its terminology and formulation.

It was, to be sure, guilty of certain errors, excusable in Kant's time, which subsequent developments have corrected. But these errors in no way obscure Kant's more fundamental and correct insight that not merely our knowledge of mathematical physics but also our knowledge of common-sense objects involves a combination of Humean, purely inductively given sense data with an unsensed, postulated, and theoretically designated element. Kant's only error with respect to the latter theoretic component in human knowledge was that he conceived it falsely as categorical and necessary, rather than, as is the case, merely as hypothetical, confirmed only indirectly through its deductive consequences, as Vaihinger and Dewey have seen, and hence as never final or absolutely certain with respect to its specific content.

The practical importance of Kant's philosophy may be noted immediately, especially since appreciation of it will make us readier to give Kant's technical doctrines the attention and understanding which they deserve. It is because the culture not merely of the communistic Russians but also of the Kaiser's and of Hitler's Germany is reared upon an idea of the good defined by Kant or his philosophical successors, that both the Germans and the Russians regard the democratic cultures of Britain, France, and the United States, grounded in the pre-Kantian philosophy of Descartes, Locke, Hume, Bentham and Mill, as definitely inadequate and outmoded. Precisely, also, because Kant and the post-Kantians take care of formal, rational, mathematical factors in scientific knowledge, and also, as we shall see, offer a new theory of morality and religion, the Germans and Russians regard their culture as scientifically and morally superior to that of their Western neighbors.

This should make it clear also that opposition to the democracies is not limited to twentieth century fascists. It characterized the Germany of the Kaiser and his predecessors as well. In fact, Germany throughout its entire history, in making its transition from the medieval to the modern world, has been a democracy during a total of roughly only fifteen years; and during twelve of these, between the Treaty of Versailles and Hitler's ascendancy, it was a democracy more by compulsion than by spontaneous choice. The reasons for this are two-fold. First, as we have noted, Protestantism does not necessarily produce democracy. Thus the Protestant Reformation, although it came in Germany in the sixteenth century and made the majority of Germans Protestant, left them nonetheless with medieval, monarchical political forms. Luther, by his attack upon the Pope and through him upon the Holy Roman Empire, gave birth to nationalistic sentiments and a German religion for the Germans; but neither he nor his Protestant successors had any marked effect upon the weakening of medieval, monarchical political ideas. In fact, Luther's rigid separation of the authority of the state and that of the church taught his German Protestants to keep their hands off political doctrine.

The second fact is that the German mentality was never thoroughly steeped in the ideas of the Lockean and Humean philosophies. Consequently, the philosophical beliefs necessary to sustain democracy have never been widely held in Germany.

By the time modern democratic liberal ideas had permeated into Germany, as a result of the influences of the British, American, and French political revolutions, Kant's philosophy had been constructed and had captured the German universities and the German mind. It is to be remembered that Kant did his work before the French Revolution and that he died in 1802. The consequence was that the liberal democratic movement, when it came in the German Revolution of 1848, was so feeble that it lasted for a few years only and accomplished little more than to drive most of its devoted adherents to America.

The reasons for the appeal of Kant's philosophy are well grounded. They come in part from common sense but primarily from mathematical physics in which Kant was an expert. Berkeley and Hume had made evident the limited portion of accepted knowledge given through the senses. This portion did not provide meaning for objects or persons existing independently of our sense impressions of them. Kant's professional work as a mathematical physicist also made him aware that sensed space, time and causality as described by Hume are not the powerfully predictive type of causality or the mathematical systematic space and time, extending far into the past and future beyond the reach of our present sense awareness, which are required by Newton's experimentally verified physics. Since these most trustworthy portions of knowledge are not given through the senses, Kant seemed to have no alternative but to conclude that they are brought to the data of sense by the knowing mind itself. It is, Kant affirms, because each one of us, in the act of observing and knowing himself and his world, brings to the data of sense these non-sensuously given meanings, that the accepted beliefs of common sense and the experimentally verified theories of mathematical physics are possible.

Note the logic underlying Kant's conclusion. The argument is that since Hume has shown that these beliefs in external material objects, persistent selves, scientific causality, and the systematic, infinitely extending space and time are not given to the observer through the senses, they must have their basis in the knower or observer himself. Thus the world of things and persons in which both common sense and science with justification believe, is a synthesis or product of (1) Humean data brought to the knower by means of the senses and (2) ordering and regulating concepts brought to the data by the knower. Only with these two types of knowledge—the one contingent and purely empirical, the other, according to Kant, systematic, universal, necessary, and formal— is the knowledge of common sense and mathematical physics possible or to be understood.

This latter type of knowledge—since it is not given empirically, or, as Kant termed it, *a posteriori*, through the senses, but is brought to the data of sense awareness by the observer and is logically previous to the empirical data—Kant termed *a priori*. This *a priori* knowledge, according to Kant, had two characteristics; namely, universality and necessity.

The force of this can be appreciated in the light of the following consideration. Hume had made it clear that there are no logical, necessary relations between purely empirical data. This is the reason why, when we make an observation in our ordinary, daily lives or in science, we can never be absolutely certain concerning what we shall find. Thus the portion of knowledge given through sense awareness is not characterized by necessity or universality; it is a contingent kind of knowledge. Our knowledge, however, of systematic space and time is not, Kant points out, of this character. No matter what observation a scientist makes or when he makes it, there is no contingency whatever about the fact that what he finds will be located in space and time. In other words, we do not at one time observe data located in space and time, and then in another observation find data but no space and time. It is the character of any *a posteriori*, sensuously given, purely empirical knowledge whatever, that it is located not merely in space and time but in the same space and time. In fact, it is only because the latter is the case that we are able to refer facts given in one observation and facts given in another observation to the same time series and the same spatial extension and thereby get a single, public world.

The point to be noted here is that this difference between our knowledge of colors and sounds and odors, and our knowledge of one single spatiotemporal world does exist. It is the merit of Kant's philosophy that it provides an explanation of this difference.

Kant's *a priori* type of knowledge fell into two kinds: the one involving *a priori* space and time which he called "forms of sensibility," and the other involving the *a priori* concepts of substance, relation, causality, etc., which he termed "categories of the understanding." The categories of the understanding were necessary in addition to the forms of sensibility because the latter merely provided a single spatiotemporal relatedness in which to locate and order the colors, sounds, odors, pains, and pleasures given empirically through the senses, and were not sufficient to give also the notion of a physical object or substance and the mathematical physicist's concept of causality. It is because the mind of the observer not only brings to the data of sense in the apprehending and knowing of them the space-time forms of sensibility but also understands these data by recourse to the concepts of substance, relation, and causality that we get not merely a public world of space and time but also a public world of physical objects so related to each other that, given the empirical determination of the location and velocities of these physical objects in a present state of time, it is possible, by the postulates or laws of Newton's mechanics, to deduce logically where that system of objects will be at any specified time in the distant future. It will be recalled that it is this meaning of causality which operates in mathematical physics; and it was precisely this type of causality for which the philosophy of Locke, Berkeley, and Hume did not account.

Kant did not begin his intellectual career as a teacher of mathematics and physics, nor did he use the laws of Newton's mechanics to solve certain problems set by the Berlin Academy of Science and discover the nebular hypothesis, for nothing. For the first time in history the modern man had a philosophy which took care of the empirical sources of human knowledge emphasized by the British empiricists and at the same time accounted for the formal, regulative type of knowledge involved both in common-sense mathematics and in mathematical physics which had been emphasized by the continental rationalists. Need we wonder that this tremendous synthesis and achievement, by one of their own members, took the German intellectuals and through them the German people, by storm? Nor need we be surprised that it captured the Scottish universities and Oxford and moved to the United States, through the influence of W. T. Harris, Josiah Royce, and many others. Unquestionably this is one of the most comprehensive achievements of the Western mind.

Note its immediate consequences. A human person is forthwith presented as something quite different from what he had previously been conceived to be. For Locke, it will be remembered, the person was a mere blank tablet, an undifferentiated mental substance having no ideas, no content to his consciousness whatever, until the material substances of physics acted upon this blank mental substance to bring an awareness of colors, sounds, odors, pains, and pleasures and their relative, private associations and sequences as mere appearances. For Hume the person had been merely an association of such sense data and impressions, simply exhibiting the combinations which the successions of data brought forth. For neither Locke nor Hume was the human person as knower a positively acting, creative being. With Kant the situation is entirely changed. Apart from the knowing person, which Kant termed "the ego," and the *a priori* forms of sensibility and categories of the understanding which this ego brings to the contingent data of sense, there would be no single space-time world whatever, with its public, material objects and knowers. In this fashion Kant transforms the modern man's conception of himself from a merely passive into a systematically active and creative being.

The *a priori* forms of sensibility and categories of the understanding, in terms of which the knower must conceive, order, and understand his world, have one other characteristic. They are the same for everybody. That this is the case, once Kant's account of the basis of knowledge is admitted, cannot be denied. Otherwise, we would not all know the same public world. It is only because every one of us uses the same *a priori* concepts of space, time, substance, relation, causality, that we are able to know the same world. This has a surprising consequence, introducing into the Kantian philosophy an opposition, if not a positive contradiction, giving rise to insoluble problems, bringing forth the post-Kantian philosophers, from which it has never quite been able to escape. Since the *a priori* concepts are the same for everybody and are formal, it is really not the varied, differing persons who are the knowing egos, but instead a single or what might be termed "public ego." It is precisely for this reason that Kant did not call this knowing self which brings the *a priori* concepts to the data of sense an ego; he called it instead "the transcendental ego." It was a transcendental ego because it was an identity, universal to all differing persons. The latter persons Kant termed the empirical selves.

It is the one, single transcendental self which tends, in Hegel's absolute, to so swallow up the individual, personal selves not merely in theory in Hegel's philosophy but also in practice in the Kaiser's German state, which took Hegel as its official philosopher, that little meaning for the independence, freedom, and chance for error of the concrete personality remains. This difficulty appears also in the Kantian philosophy as developed in England by Bradley and Bosanquet. To meet this difficulty Kantians in the United States, especially the personalists Howison and Brightman, probably largely because of the extreme Lockean influence in American culture, have tended to assume many individual, creative egos, adding a theistic God to meet the needs of conventional Protestantism, but thereby running into all the difficulties concerning the interaction between such non-material persons in which Berkeley's philosophy found itself with Leibnitz and which the Kantian philosophy was supposed to remove. This fatal weakness the pluralistic, personalistic Kantians cannot escape. For Kant explains how one person can know a person other than himself only by identifying the *a priori* concepts which make this knowledge possible with the transcendental ego. When this is done, as the development of German thought and culture following Kant clearly shows, the individual person becomes swallowed up in the absolute.

But there is a second point at which the Kantian philosophy begins to fall apart and to give rise to separate notions which cannot be reconciled short of leaving the individual person in the absolute mind or dominated by the evolution of the overpowering state. Kant's moral and religious philosophy of his *Critique of the Practical Reason* has little or no connection with the scientific and natural philosophy of his *Critique of the Pure Reason*. At first this appeared as a great asset, since it seemed to do justice to the moral and religious life, as previous modern philosophy had not done, and to remove any possibility of conflict between science and religion. This brings us to the second factor which caused the Germans and Russians to regard their culture as morally superior to that of the French and English speaking democracies.

MORAL PHILOSOPHY

Kant saw that his scientific philosophy as outlined in the *Critique of the Pure Reason* did not account for morality and religion. In short, it accounted for man as a knower of nature, but not for man as an active, free moral agent. The reason for this is that for Kant morality presupposes freedom of choice. One can hardly be blamed for something over which one has no control. Yet the difficulty of finding any meaning for human freedom in Newton's universe was evident to all. The French mathematical physicist Laplace gave expression to this consequence of the Newtonian physics when he said that if an all-seeing Providence were given information concerning the positions and momenta of all the particles in the universe, he would be able to predict its future to the minutest detail. Thus, eighteenth century man found himself reduced to nothing more than a cog in a vast overwhelming cosmic machine. In Kant's formulation of scientific philosophy in his *Critique of the Pure Reason*, as indicated above, this rigid determinism was increased, since it was applied not merely to nature but to man's knowing of nature. The forms of space and time, and the categories of substance, relation and causality which man used in the knowledge of nature were universal and necessary; moreover they were really the activity of the transcendental ego rather than of the local empirical individual.

One might have supposed under these circumstances that Kant would have taken this as evidence that something must be wrong in his philosophy of common sense and scientific knowledge. This, however, was not Kant's procedure. Instead he took the adequacy of his philosophy of nature and of scientific knowledge for granted and forthwith had no alternative but to set up morality and religion as subjects having no connection with empirical or scientific knowledge. This he did by appealing to what happens in practice—a recourse, it may be noted, to which Hume also turned when his own philosophy led him to conceptions of the self and of material objects to which neither he nor any other modern has been willing to restrict himself.

Kant used the presuppositional method. Without freedom of choice, the moral life is meaningless. Hence, any moral act presupposes the concept of freedom. Freedom in turn presupposes not the transcendental ego, as do the *a priori* concepts of the theoretical reason, but the concrete, local, actual, individual moral agent. Thus it is not until Kant gets to his moral philosophy that he is able to provide any meaning for a real local individual human self.

But even this provision is merely temporary. For if this is not to leave one in sophistry, with each individual person having his own relative idea of the good, the words "good," "freedom," "duty," "God," and "immortality" must be assumed, as they were by Kant, to have the same meaning for all minds. Obviously this assumption is false, as the differing conceptions of all these words in the different cultures of the world noted in this book clearly demonstrate. But if Kant's assumptions were accepted as true, then the same logic which took him to a transcendental scientific ego to account for differing persons having a single concept of a public world would take him to a transcendental moral ego to account for differing persons having the same idea of "good," "freedom," "duty," "God," and "immortality." When this happens, as it did with Fichte and Hegel, the freedom of the individual evaporates as quickly out of Kant's moral and religious philosophy as it did in his scientific philosophy. In fact, the development of classical German thought from Kant through Fichte to Hegel and Marx is the story of this occurrence.

Another element in Kant's moral philosophy has this same consequence. This element he called the moral law. It is exceedingly doubtful whether Kant's rejection of the empirical scientific method in moral philosophy for the presuppositional method of an autonomous ethics warrants the belief in such a law. It would seem that an empirical method appealing to factual evidence—a method which Kant repudiated, with some justification, because of its frequent fallacious identification of the "ought" with the "is"—is requisite for such a conclusion. The probability is that at this point Kant's conservative pietistic background rooted in a traditional ethics determined by an empirical method, and his scientific training with its identification of knowledge with lawfulness, were the decisive factors, giving him a conclusion to which his autonomous presuppositional method in ethics did not entitle him.

But regardless of the origin of the Kantian doctrine of the moral law, it presented a difficulty, if not a contradiction, within his system. For a problem immediately arose: How can a morality rooted in freedom be reconciled with a morality grounded in the necessity of law? For in so far as good conduct consists in obedience to law there is no freedom. The problem was solved by Kant and his followers by identifying freedom in the Anglo-American sense of the word with "freedom from" and describing this as a purely negative kind of freedom, and by identifying positive freedom with obedience to the necessity of the moral law. Thus, a morality which began with freedom ended with the obedient acceptance of determinism. This came out explicitly with Fichte and Hegel.

THE GERMAN CONCEPT OF FREEDOM

In 1790, at the time of the French Revolution, Fichte read Kant. The effect was immediate and stupendous. Two years later Fichte published the *Critique of Revelation,* emphasizing the absolute demands in our human nature of the moral law, and defining religion as the belief in this moral law as divine, such belief being a practical postulate. The Kantian doctrine is evident; but Fichte went one step further, adding that the requirements of the free ego are the justification for any human knowledge whatever, even that concerning nature. By this addition Fichte offered a solution of the problem of the relation between man's knowledge of nature treated in Kant's *Critique of the Pure Reason* and man's knowledge in morality and religion which was treated in Kant's *Critique of the Practical Reason.* According to Fichte the former is secondary to, presupposes, and proceeds from the latter. The justification not merely for our ethical and religious beliefs but also even for our belief in an external world, rests upon moral rather than scientific grounds as given by the needs and inescapable demands of the practical reason.

The release which this thesis gave to the imagination and aspirations of men, especially the Germans, can hardly be overemphasized. Kant's mere placing of moral and religious demands beside scientific knowledge as equally autonomous had been sufficient to let loose the Romantic movement in nineteenth century literature and to stimulate Schelling and the Schlegels to create a free social life in Berlin which shocked Fichte when he went there to live. Assured by Kant that morality and religion had nothing to do with scientific knowledge and stood on their own feet, these romanticists followed their unbridled impulses and imaginations without restraint. But as if this were not enough, Fichte made the practical demands of the free moral agent the grounds not merely for morality and religion but also for nature and science. Thus, the gulf between nature and culture and between science and morals was supposedly removed. The character of the former, according to Fichte, is to be deduced from the demands of the latter.

In the year 1800 Fichte, in his *Vocation of Man*, expressed the accomplishment as follows:

What unity and completeness does this view present!—what dignity does it confer on human nature! Our thought is not founded on itself alone, independently of our impulses and affections;—man does not consist of two independent and separate elements; he is absolutely one. All our thought is founded on our impulses;—as a man's affections are, so is his knowledge. These impulses compel us to a certain mode of thought only so long as we do not perceive the constraint; . . .
But I shall open my eyes; shall learn thoroughly to know myself; shall recognise that constraint;—this is my vocation. I shall thus, and under that supposition I shall necessarily, form my own mode of thought. Then I shall stand absolutely independent, thoroughly equipt and perfected through my own act and deed. The primitive source of all my other thought and of my life itself, that from which everything proceeds which can have an existence in me, for me, or through me, the innermost spirit of my spirit,—is no longer a foreign power, but it is, in the strictest possible sense, the product of my own will. I am wholly my own creation. . . . With freedom and consciousness I have returned to the point at which Nature had left me. I accept that which she announces;—but I do not accept it because I must; I believe it because I will.

This subjection of our scientific knowledge of nature to the demands of the free will is not quite as arbitrary as these statements of Fichte, taken from their context, may suggest. This is shown by the fact that American students of science and scientific method such as C. I. Lewis and Wilmon Sheldon have been markedly influenced by Fichte. In fact, Fichte began with an analysis of scientific method.

This analysis revealed the following factors: There are the data of sense. But these and their sensed associations by themselves are insufficient to give us the notion of a physical object, the infinitely extending space and time, and the causally related states of an external world. For the latter there also must be, in addition to the sense data, the formal, organizing principles and postulates proposed theoretically and formulated deductively by the theoretical scientist. Kant thought the basic concepts of the latter were absolutely certain and would be the same in any kind of scientific theory whatever. We now know, however, that these systematic, formal, theoretical factors are contingent, rather than necessary, as Kant supposed, and that they can be determined only by the method of hypothesis, tested indirectly through its deductive, experimental consequences by trial and error. Furthermore, we now know that the immediately apprehended sense data do not logically imply the theoretical hypotheses. Thus our belief in the external world which our theory postulates is not given necessarily. In short, no scientific theory can be logically deduced from the immediately observed facts alone. Consequently, any conception of nature in common sense or science which involves more than the mere sequence and association of sense data, to which Hume would restrict all human knowledge, is not required necessarily. Its justification instead is that if we so choose to conceive of the nature of things, then it follows by logic from this conception that the observed and experimentally determined data should be what they are. In other words, our theories imply the facts which we observe, but the facts do not imply the theories. Thus, in the nature of the factual evidence and in the scientific method, which relates this factual evidence to the conception of nature which science confirms, there is no necessity requiring us absolutely to believe this conception. Believing the conception, then the facts have to be of a certain character. But accepting only the facts, the theory does not follow necessarily.

It is precisely this characteristic of our scientific knowledge of nature which Fichte noted and singled out. Facts plus logic alone are insufficient to guarantee absolutely the beliefs and theories of natural science. Descartes, for example, had supposed the contrary. He had supposed that scientific and philosophical knowledge consisted merely in restricting oneself to separate, distinct, clear, indubitable, immediately sensed facts and then showing by formal logic that these facts necessitate a given theory, the final conclusion of one's science and philosophy.

Fichte saw, however, as all informed students of scientific method now agree, that such is not the case. One cannot deduce the theories of science from the facts. Instead, the logic of deduction in scientific method runs in the opposite direction. One deduces the facts from the theory;

retaining the theory if its deductive consequences are confirmed by fact, rejecting it if they are not.

Thus in actual scientific procedure there is a third factor; namely, the free act of the scientist in which he postulates the theory. The facts by themselves or the facts plus logical and mathematical deduction are not sufficient to necessitate the scientific theory. There must be, in addition, a free imaginative act upon the part of the scientist, by means of which he conceives and proposes the theory of the character of the world of nature or a certain portion thereof. Thus it is not a mere bit of fanciful, egocentric romanticism upon Fichte's part but a plain statement of fact with respect to the nature of scientific method when he concludes: "I do not accept it [*i.e.* the scientist's conception of nature] because I must; I believe it because I will." In other words, without a free act of postulation upon the part of the scientist, in which the scientific hypothesis is proposed, there is no scientific conception of nature. Thus Fichte concludes that our scientific knowledge of nature as well as our moral demand for a meaning for freedom and personal responsibility presupposes the free act of the human individual.

Fichte immediately saw the implications of all this for the French Revolution. But three years after his reading of Kant, in 1793, he published two political papers, one of them upon the French Revolution. In this paper he defended the Revolution's emphasis upon liberty by maintaining that liberty is part and parcel of the very nature of man as a moral, intelligent agent. Because of this liberty or freedom which is of the essence of man, Fichte also argued for the inevitable change which must accompany political organization and the attendant necessity for reform.

In the intellectual sphere also Fichte insisted upon the implications of his doctrine. In 1794 he was appointed professor of philosophy at Jena. During this period an article was published in the philosophical journal of which he was the editor, against which a charge of atheism was raised. The public clamor was such that the people's electors demanded Fichte's expulsion. Report has it that the Grand Duke of Weimar would have disposed of the matter with a mild nominal warning. But Fichte would not admit even the appearance of an interference with liberty of thought and teaching. Consequently, he was dismissed.

These two influences of Fichte—the one in the political, the other in the educational sphere—are important. They add support in addition to that derived from Locke and Mill for the modern conception of freedom. But they are important for another reason. They mean that in German mentality the concept of freedom tends to be identified with Fichte rather than with Locke and Mill. This fact is tremendously important if we are to understand the attitude of the Germans toward democracy throughout the nineteenth century and in the twentieth century.

In 1807 and 1808, while at Berlin, Fichte delivered his famous "Addresses to the German People." The effect of these addresses upon German political thought has never ceased. It is no exaggeration to say that it is from them that the Germans' conception of the modern state stems.

A few years ago, before the present war, Cecil Driver, Associate Professor of Comparative Government at Yale University, gave an address upon the roots and background of the influence and power of the Nazi party in Germany. In this talk he said that it had been his professional task to study the main German papers of state of the last one hundred and twenty-five years and that what had impressed him as a result of this reading was the identity of demand and policy which had characterized the entire movement. The impression was such that he was led to symbolize the entire development by a continuous curved line, beginning with Fichte's famous "Addresses to the German People" and continuing into the present, in which there was a break only between the Treaty of Versailles and Hitler's advent in 1932. Thus Hitler had merely, in a more crude way, to be sure, taken up the course with respect to expansion without, and to unrestrained self-expression within, which had characterized German policy previous to Versailles.

In the face of Fichte's defenses of freedom, both in the French Revolution and in the German universities, this association of him with Hitler may seem quite unjustified and farfetched. Certain considerations must cause us to hesitate, however, before acquiescing in the latter conclusion. Fichte's defenses of freedom occurred, as we have noted, at the beginning of his intellectual career. In 1820, six years after his death, his *Theory of the State* was published. In this book he outlined his political utopia, organized on the basis of "the principles of pure reason." "In too many cases," write the authors of the article on Fichte in the *Encyclopaedia Britannica* (14th edition), "the proposals are identical with principles of pure despotism." We may with profit ask ourselves why a philosopher and a people who began with an emphasis upon freedom and whose philosophy, to an extent equaled by no other, reared the whole of human knowledge upon this concept, should end with "principles of pure despotism." Two factors are important in answering this question. One has to do with the initial assumption of Fichte's philosophy; the other with what the assumption was used to accomplish.

For all its virtues, with respect to the understanding of moral activity and even of scientific method, the emphasis upon the primacy of the free will of the individual carries with it dangers and liabilities as well as assets. For it identifies the good life not with the fact that man is a man and all men are metaphysically and politically equal, but with the degree to which the individual gives expression to his own will. In fact, for Fichte a man is not a moral creature unless by a completely undetermined and hence essentially arbitrary act he gives expression to his own personal will. Thus, instead of the moral life depending upon the sober influences of knowledge and reason to which the will gives expression, as is the case both in the Aristotelian and in the Lockean or Humean conception of the good and in modern scientific method, the moral life centers in the will itself as primary, unconditioned by anything else; and the character of knowledge of nature or of human relations has its justification solely because it is the creation of, and a necessary condition for, the free and independent action of the will. It does not take very much stretching of the imagination, having accepted this as the idea of the good, to come to value that man as best who most vigorously dominates the situation by the forcefulness of his will and that government as best in which such a dominating will functions. In fact, Fichte's follower Hegel said precisely this. Referring to the great "historical men" who give expression to the "positive freedom" of the moral law of the "World-Spirit," Hegel writes "They are great man because they willed," and speaking of them in the singular he adds: "A World-historical individual is not so unwise as to indulge a variety of wishes to divide his regards. He is devoted to the one aim, regardless of all else. It is even possible that such men may treat other great, even sacred interests, inconsiderately; conduct which is indeed obnoxious to moral reprehension. But so mighty a form must trample down many an innocent flower—crush to pieces many an object in the path."

This type of moral freedom hardly provides the atmosphere in which democratic processes, with their give and take discussion and their weighing of rival interests and rival alternatives for political action, can flourish. When one realizes, however, that Fichte's and Hegel's moral philosophy seeped into the consciousness of the German people to a greater extent even than Locke's philosophy permeated the minds of the American people in 1776, one appreciates, in part at least, why Hitler's impassioned harangue to the German people about their "demands," and his arbitrary ruthless willfulness, together with the presentation of himself to them as the great historical figure who, giving expression to the divine spirit of the German people, would change the course of history for the next two thousand years, brought forth the response which they did. To Anglo-Americans this seemed sheer demagoguery, but to Germans who use Fichte rather than Locke or Bentham as their criterion of the good it might appear as an appeal to the foundations of moral, religious and political action. These considerations suggest that for all its initial promise, the setting up of morality and religion independent of the sobering effects of empirical and scientific knowledge, upon the primacy of the unconditioned will, may be tantamount to the identification of the arbitrary with the good.

But Fichte's philosophy is not exhausted with the mere emphasis upon the primacy of the will. Had he stopped merely with this, its consequences even in his own writings would not have been those which actually ensued. In addition, he went on to attempt to deduce the *a priori* concepts of Kant's *Critique of the Pure Reason* and the world of nature from this solitary, single demand of the unconditioned will. In one sense this was required of his initial thesis and was a merit, since it involved not merely stating that our knowledge of nature derives from the primacy of the free will of the practical reason, but also in showing precisely how this derivation comes about. Yet in this procedure there was an assumption inherited from Kant which had surreptitiously slipped in; the assumption, namely, that what is postulated in scientific knowledge is necessary, even though it cannot be derived from the empirical data. It is because Fichte, like Kant, believed that what the common-sense man and the scientist postulate involves the latter's free act of postulating as well as the empirical data, together with logical inference; and that what this free act postulates is not merely hypothetical, but is instead categorical and absolutely necessary, that he is required to attempt to *deduce* the forms of sensibility and the categories of the understanding of Kant's *Critique of the Pure Reason* dealing with scientific knowledge, from the demands of the moral will of the individual. We now know that the theoretical factor in scientific knowledge which the scientist postulates is not absolutely certain and hence necessary. Thus there is no need nor is there any reason for justifying it by attempting to deduce it from anything.

But Fichte, having supposed the contrary, and as a consequence having regarded this deduction as necessary, is forced on to the systematic construction of a philosophy which, beginning in freedom, ends paradoxically enough in Hegel and the Marxians, and even with the final Fichte himself, in determinism. The reason for this paradoxical result should not be difficult to understand. By reducing the determinism of nature and the *Critique of the Pure Reason* not merely to the free act of will of the individual, but to a free act which is necessary, Fichte merely transfers the necessity which had been previously in nature and in Kant's forms and categories for knowing nature to the determinism of the necessary moral expression of the ego. Thus what begins in freedom ends in determinism; and the good state becomes one in which this supposedly inevitable and necessary development of the moral consciousness comes to expression.

The actual method by means of which Fichte attempted to deduce nature and Kant's *a priori* concepts of scientific knowledge from the demands of the moral will must concern us, especially because in this method pursued by Fichte two new factors appeared, both of which are fundamental in Fichtean and Hegelian Germany and in communistic Russia. The one is the dialectic logic; the other, the primacy of culture over nature.

The dialectic logic arose with Fichte in the following manner. Having assumed correctly that our belief in an external world of nature and in our own selves as persisting beings is not given by immediate apprehension, but depends in addition upon a theoretical postulate which the thinker must add, and having assumed without justification that this postulated factor is necessary and hence in need of being deduced from the free act of the individual, Fichte then went on to ask himself how the practical demand of moral freedom would necessitate such postulates. Postulation of the self is a necessary consequence of moral freedom, Fichte concluded, because it is precisely this assurance of the irreducibility of the free choice of the individual ego which moral freedom requires. In short, it is only if one postulates the reality of the self that moral freedom becomes significant. Thus experience begins with the positing of the ego. For Fichte, as for Hume, this persistent self is not immediately apprehended. For Fichte however, unlike Hume, it exists, but its existence is guaranteed not by immediate apprehension nor even by immediate apprehension plus Kant's theoretical knowledge, but only by the practical demands of moral freedom.

Having thus secured the moral ego as real, Fichte's next task is to derive the external world from the practical demands of the free moral consciousness. Fichte believes that he succeeds in this derivation in the following manner: Moral activity has no meaning apart from opposition. If one's free action could actualize itself perfectly and completely without overcoming handicaps, practical moral life as we know it would be meaningless. Thus morality and the demands of the practical reason presuppose not merely the reality of the self but also the reality of the not-self, or nature, which provides the field within which the moral acts objectify themselves against opposition. (Note how this identifies morality, not with adjustment to objects or people other than oneself, but with the overcoming of them.) The necessary precondition for happenings in nature is the *a priori* forms of sensibility, space and time. Hence, since moral action is not possible without the not-self, or nature, and the *a priori* forms of space and time are a necessary condition for externality which is nature, therefore the moral life requires the oppositing of the not-self, or nature, by means of the *a priori* forms of sensibility and the categories of the understanding, as Kant's *Critique of the Pure Reason* has prescribed.

Now, as a sheer deduction, supposedly, from the demands of the practical reason, Fichte has both the ego, or real moral individual, and the non-ego, or nature—a thesis and its negate, or antithesis, the one limiting the other. In so far as the non-ego determines the character of the ego, the ego is scientific or theoretical; and in so far as the ego determines the non-ego, or nature, the ego is moral or practical. But even the theoretical ego has its basis in the practical, since the origin of nature, or the not-ego, is also in the moral demands of the active, practical ego. Nature, or the non-ego, arises because the moral life requires the ego to be a striving power overcoming opposition. And if it be such, then a limit must be set with respect to which this striving is made possible.

Even so, the Fichtean system is not complete. As has become evident, the human individual is not the free will which does the positing but instead its end product. Thus upon careful analysis, the freedom turns out, even for Fichte, to be not so much in the will of ordinary human individuals as in a transcendental or superhuman will which alone has freedom and which, in positing the ordinary human individual, at the same time limits that individual by its antithesis, the non-human ego, or nature. In fact, Fichte believes that a contradiction would exist in his theory did he not go on to the absolute will as a *synthesis* which embraces the human ego and nature, at the same time removing the contradiction between the latter which would exist were they taken as primary and ultimate in their own right. This absolute will is "pure freedom." It alone is unlimited and unconditioned. Human wills, on the other hand, are the mere expression of its activity. Thus for Fichte, as for Hegel who did little more than work out in detail these later suggestions of Fichte's thought, a post-Kantian philosophy which seems to begin by endowing human beings with the most romantic and unrestrained type of freedom ends by immersing the human individual in a most rigorous, even though divinely sponsored, determinism; human beings existing solely in order that the Absolute may be conscious of his own freedom, and nature existing for human beings solely in order that these human posits of the Absolute may have something against which to strive.

The only difference between this determinism and any other is that this is a determinism of the spiritual life of the individual and the cultural life of humanity, instead of merely a determinism of nature. This follows also from the Fichtean premises, although it was made fully articulate only by Hegel and in an inverted form by Marx. To make the practical reason primary, and to derive the meaning of nature from the demands of the moral ego, was to make nature, like culture, something determined by the dialectical law governing the evolution of self-consciousness. Consequently, everything which happens either in nature or in culture unrolls historically, according to the rules governing the manner in which the absolute ego comes to self-consciousness in constituting the natural and cultural world. The law governing these rules, it has been noted, is defined by the dialectic logic of thesis, antithesis, and synthesis. Consequently, processes in nature as well as culture must unfold according to this logic, and prediction of their development can be made by recourse to it.

THE DIALECTIC THEORY OF HISTORY

In this respect the Hegelian and communistic treatments of history and social institutions are not without a rough analogy to what happens with respect to the laws governing supply and demand and the movement of prices in the market place, according to Anglo-American economic theory. The latter theory also rests upon certain assumptions concerning the nature of human psychology—those, namely, of Hume and Bentham.

These assumptions are that each individual person directly inspects certain wants and also directly inspects their ordering in a series according to the differing degrees to which each of them is wanted or preferred. It is assumed that what each individual thus finds to be true for his own wants holds for every other individual, and that consequently the market and its movements of prices must, since it merely summarizes *en masse* all these individual wants and preferences, obey the laws which such an ordering of private wants by differing degrees of private preference entail. In all this there is no dialectic of thesis, antithesis, and synthesis. But nonetheless, it is being assumed that certain social mass effects in the economic sphere behave as they do because the introspected, psychological nature of the individual is what it is.

The Fichtean, Hegelian, Marxian post-Kantians differ from the Anglo-Americans merely in the fact—and the difference is a tremendous one—that the individual is regarded as being a much more complicated thing than Anglo-American positivistic psychology and philosophy assume him to be. This individual is assumed by both Hegelians and Marxians to be governed in the evolution of his consciousness and also of his historical, social institutions by the dialectic of thesis, antithesis, and synthesis. For Fichte and Hegel at least, the social institutions of mankind evolve as they do because they, like the market place of the Anglo-American economists, mirror and publicly objectify the nature of the individual and the dialectic development of his or the absolute consciousness as it constitutes its world.

With Hegel the final conclusions suggested by Fichte's philosophy were developed systematically and in detail. The dialectic was applied not merely to the ego in constituting its world but to the inter-relations of the concepts of logic themselves, to the philosophy of nature, and to a systematic philosophy of mind including psychology, law and history, and art, religion and philosophy. Having in the final synthesis achieved the Absolute and having regarded both nature and culture as the enrollment in history of its free consciousness coming to self-consciousness and passing over into concrete act, the way was made open for regarding the "idea" not merely as regulative of human knowledge as Kant had done, but also as "constitutive" of the nature of things. Thus Hegel arrived at his famous dictum: "The real is the rational and the rational is the real."

But with this achievement a second paradox in the development of the Kantian philosophy appeared. We have noted how, beginning with freedom, it ended with determinism. We have noted also that one consideration causing Kant to reject the empirical method of science in ethics and normative social theory was the commendable desire to avoid the fallacy in social science of identifying the "ought" for a given culture with the "is" for that culture. Yet here in this famous dictum of Hegel and also, it must be added, in the Marxians who follow him, a post-Kantian philosophy which began in Kant by emphasizing the fallacy of identifying the "ought" for personal or social action with the "is" of that action, ends with Hegel by identifying the ideal with the factually real in history: The good and the divine in culture are the actual writ large, so that the dialectic in history exhibits itself.

For this error the German people have had to pay with tragedy and suffering. It was Hegel who taught them that actual history in its concrete happenings, coming to fulfillment in the German state with its monarchical government, was not merely the expression of the perfectly ideal, but the coming of God or the Absolute Spirit to self-consciousness by means of the dialectic process in the concrete events of history. Need one wonder, after such a moral and intellectual diet taught throughout all their universities over a period of one hundred and fifty years, that the German people took it so easily and naturally for granted, not once but twice in the twentieth century that German *Kultur* was by its nature and merits supreme, and destined by the movement of the universe and the perfect moral activity of God Himself to overcome all opposition and embrace the world? As the philosophically informed German liberal Curt Riess has written: "After all, the German philosophy of history since Fichte and Hegel, though on a very different intellectual level as represented by these two, always saw history as something full of sense, and the Germans as those chosen to administer this sense. The Goebbels idea of dying instead of living in a world not dominated by Germans is really nothing but the same idea turned upside down."

Lest the reader regard this picture of the influence of Fichte and Hegel upon the mentality of the Germans as an exaggeration, let a personal experience be recalled, which happened in Germany in 1922. It was a Sunday evening. The little train, with its usual load of German students and teachers returning from their accustomed Sunday afternoon tramp in the Black Forest, was rumbling down from Titisee to the small university town of Freiburg. Across the aisle and one seat back was a very sensitive, refined, sober, and restrained German school teacher of middle age. It was in the midst of the terrible inflation of German currency, which was wiping out the frugal earnings and savings of those dependent upon fixed incomes. Evidently this, following upon Germany's overwhelming defeat in the war, was weighing heavily upon her mind. In a sad, incredulous mood, she shook her head and said, "I do not understand it all. I simply cannot understand it. Germany, the highest point of the culture of the world, in this terrible condition." To her, in all sincerity, it was as if God and the universe had let her and her people down. Such is the disillusionment and the demoralization through which one must pass if one follows a philosophy which identifies the "is" in actual society with the "ought," and places the supposedly necessary demands of morality and religion behind such an error; thereby giving rise to the romantic and ruthless conviction that the overriding of all opposition in the name of one's own culture is the good, and that such behavior is the actualization in history of a divine perfection.

To understand the Germans of our time is to realize that their culture was built predominantly on Fichte and Hegel, as Anglo-American culture has rested on Locke, Hume and Aristotle. In the war ending in 1918 and in the depths of despair to which the economic inflation following the war plunged the German people, the Hegelian philosophy was smashed. At Versailles democracy was thrust upon them, but without agreement upon the part of at least a majority, with respect to the minimum of philosophical beliefs necessary to make it function. The German people could hardly go back to Locke and Hume, since in the need for, and the initial acceptance of, Kant they had become well aware of the undeniable inadequacies in that earlier philosophy.

Thus they floundered, producing almost as many different political parties as there were groups of individuals with enough cohesion to cling together. Under these circumstances, without a more adequate philosophy which would meet the difficulties that gave rise to the doctrines of Kant, Fichte and Hegel, there were only two alternatives: Either they went forward beyond Hegel to Marx and Russian communism or they achieved some semblance of national unity arbitrarily by force. The latter alternative found in Hitler its leader and, in the greater expression which it gave to purely German sentiments, its popular response.

This popular response was nourished by many items, not the least of which was the identification of morality with the free act of the will and its demands which Kant's *Critique of the Practical Reason* and the initial stages of Fichte's philosophy emphasized. In fact, the culture of the Nazis may be defined as a Fichtean voluntarism which, rejecting the logic of dialectic appropriated by the communists, is developed along Nietzschean and pseudo-Darwinian, rather than Hegelian, lines. This culture has received its rebuttal in its own world of willful, forceful discourse; and the assumptions from which it proceeds are so obviously inadequate before the facts and problems of science and philosophy as to merit no further serious attention.

The tragedy is that, in no small measure due to modern idealistic moral philosophy which, stemming from Kant's *Critique of the Practical Reason,* placed practical demands of the will, in the name of morality and religion, above the sobering influence of empirical facts and experimentally controlled scientific theory, the intelligence of the German people has so frequently become the slave of their wills, instead of their will and energy being made the expression of a factually sobering and scientifically grounded philosophy with its more trustworthy, less hazardous, and nonetheless imaginative and rich cultural implications and values. In fact, the situation is worse than this, for in Kant's *Critique of the Practical Reason* and in Fichte's reduction of even theoretical knowledge to the practical reason, this priority of practical demands and the will over intelligence and the reason was put forward in the name of reason. When reason itself thus sets the will free from the control of a reason sobered by empirical evidence and the experimentally tested theories of natural science one need hardly be surprised that an otherwise intelligent people allows a demagogic appeal to its members' intuitive demands and their wills to cause them to throw their intelligence into eclipse and some of the richest products of their culture into exile or the bonfire. In Germany we see what happens when a people rear morality or religion upon itself alone, and reduce all philosophy to a moral philosophy, grounded in so-called "necessary practical demands," making even the science and philosophy of nature its servant.

CRITIQUE

Having faced German philosophy at its worst and having located its evil cultural consequences in the basic primacy and arbitrariness of the will and its demands of the practical reason, in which it originates, and in the fallacious identification of the historically actual and the ideal in which it terminates, we can, without creating misapprehensions, now examine this philosophy at its best. Even though the solution which it offered is tragically erroneous, the problems with which it wrestled, such as freedom of will, and certain values which it suggested, are real and must be faced and provided for philosophically in some other way.

Foremost is Hegel's indication of the importance of cultural history. It is not an accident that the nineteenth century, at the beginning of which Hegel's philosophy was formulated and throughout which it flourished, is also the century in which the subject of history was pursued with a seriousness which it never enjoyed before.

Hegel's philosophy also made the concept of development of primary importance in science and philosophy. In fact he brought to the German world before 1830 the habit of thinking about everything in terms of the temporal and evolutionary process, which tended to come to the Anglo-American world only later, following the idea of Darwin, derived from natural science. Hegel made it clear also that cultural evolution, unlike evolution in natural science, proceeds by revolution rather than by gradual unfolding, and that the logic of negation is at the heart of cultural revolutions. Thus, Locke and the American Revolution negated the medieval thesis of the divine right of kings. Similarly, the positivism of Comte in the Diaz dictatorship in Mexico in 1870 negated certain Lockean democratic premises of the Mexican Revolution of 1810. Hegel's error, which Marx and the Russian communists have inherited, was in supposing that this negation proceeds in a necessary and absolutely deterministic fashion. That this is not the case is shown by the fact that the philosophy underlying any given culture can be negated in more than one way. To any thesis negation gives more than one antithesis.

This does not mean that the dialectic method is not suggestive and possessive of some predictive power in connection with the sequence of social and cultural changes. That this predictive power is present is shown most markedly by Marx's use of this method in the middle of the nineteenth century to foretell in the economic sphere the coming development of labor unions, the clashes between capital and labor, and the sequence of economic booms followed by severe depressions increasing in intensity with time which characterize the economic world of the twentieth century. However, this suggestiveness and predictive power are only rough at best, and often, as in the case of the rise of Hitlerian Germany, erroneous. What Hegel, and Marx following him, did note, quite correctly, is that insight into the historical development of social institutions is not to be obtained by the mere inductive observation of existent social facts but requires an examination of the philosophical ideology underlying these facts at a given stage of the historical process, and attention upon changes in, or negations of, this ideology in the transition from one stage of history and its form of society to another.

Unfortunately, however, Hegel, in the section "Christianity and the German World" at the beginning of his *Lectures on the Philosophy of History,* identified the final synthesis, achieved by the Divine Spirit as it comes to self-consciousness, according to the supposedly inevitable logic of dialectic, in the actual events of history, with the actual German World. "This," he writes, "is the ultimate result which the process of history is intended to accomplish." Needless to say, it has not been a very happy one.

The evil consequences of this fallacious identification of the "ought" and the "divine" in culture with the historical "is," have been noted. The error goes back to the erroneous separation, by Kant, of the moral ego from the sobering effect of scientific knowledge of man and nature, and the attendant reduction of nature to the "practical demands" of the unconditioned free will, made by Fichte in order to clarify the relation between Kant's natural man and his moral man; thereby leaving nothing but the dialectic development of the Absolute self-consciousness as it reveals itself in actual historical man-made institutions, with which to identify the good and the divine.

Of the two dialectic philosophies, Hegel's, while less realistic than Marx's, in obtaining its unity, was richer in the diversity of its content and in its justice to the different dimensions of human experience. This comes out clearly in the third portion of Hegel's systematic doctrine, his philosophy of mind. It fell into three portions: (1) psychology, which included anthropology, phenomenology, and psychology proper; (2) law and history; and (3) art, religion, and philosophy. Psychology dealt with mind in its subjective, human, individualistic aspect; law and history, with mind in its human, objective, social aspect; and art, religion, and philosophy with the synthesis of these, as exemplifying the absolute mind becoming concrete in history. This philosophy, for all its unbridled romanticism and its fancifulness uncontrolled by the empirical study of natural fact, at least had the merit of setting before man a conception of himself and the meaning of his existence as an ideal, which was not defined primarily either for businessmen alone or for labor leaders alone, but gave expression to every profession in the community and to every aspiration of the human spirit. In the culture of Hegel's Germany the historian Mommsen, the theologian Harnack, the psychologist Wundt, and the musician Wagner, as well as Bismarck and Kaiser Wilhelm, could feel at home.

It is customary at the present moment for many moral and religious leaders, in no small measure influenced by this German philosophy of the primacy of the will and the "demands of the practical reason," to locate the tragic ills of civilization in the pursuit of a philosophy grounded upon scientific knowledge and in the neglect of a moral philosophy, which according to them has nothing to do with science or scientific method. But certainly the Germans and their present behavior give the lie to this diagnosis of the situation. Their conduct is, to put it mildly, no better than that of the rest of us. Yet they are a people who for over one hundred and fifty years have been taught and nourished upon, and have believed in, precisely this autonomous Kantian and Fichtean morality and religion, the neglect of which, according to these Anglo-American "idealistic" diagnosticians, is the cause of our present ills. Judged by its fruits in the culture most unqualifiedly modeled upon it, modern idealistic moral philosophy is a tragic error. For a philosophy which makes the practical and the historical the criterion of value this rebuttal is decisive.

This consideration has been noted by the Mexicans. In 1880 the German idealistic moral philosophy appeared in Mexico as a movement of political and educational reform under the name of Krausism. Its entering wedge was an attempt to replace the empirical logic of Bain with the idealistic logic of Tiberghien as the official text in the National Preparatory School. Its supporting argument, as expressed by Hilario Gabilando, was that a scientifically grounded philosophy leaves the rights of man without protection and destroys the moral foundations of liberty. To this, Leopoldo Zea informs us, Telispero Garcia replied with decisive effect, as the subsequent defeat of Krausism demonstrated, in the newspaper *La Libertad*, as follows: "In the country where positivism is rooted in the national character, where it enjoys its proper status, where the experimental method is applied to all the manifestations of life, in England, in short, there is the more security of liberty and the greater guarantee of right." Whereas, countries such as "Germany, cradle of the absolute idealisms; France, mother of all the absolute rights; Spain, Italy and the other nations which nursed themselves at the breast of those beauties which the Sr. Gabilando is afraid to see disappear from this land, have been victims of every sort of tyranny." Consequently, notwithstanding the decline of positivism, German idealism has not been a seriously considered criterion of social action or educational policy in Mexico.

Much more than the appeal to practice supports this verdict.

The entire inquiry up to this point shows, as the sequel will reconfirm, that the grounds for moral values and cultural ideals simply do not have the autonomy and independence from empirical evidence and scientifically verified theory which the Kant of the second *Critique* and his romantic followers affirmed. This fact has been obscured because the previously noted essential connection between modern physics and modern philosophy, including even that of Kant, has not been appreciated sufficiently, and because most of the histories of Western philosophy have been written or influenced by the German idealistic philosophers who, quite fallaciously, have read the Kantian theory of morality back into Plato and Aristotle. This error has given Greek philosophy and medieval culture a much more arbitrary and speculative cast than they actually had, as Chapter VII will show, and has led to the ignoring of the scientific content and foundations of the Greek and medieval moral and religious doctrines.

But precisely because scientific knowledge is fundamental in moral and cultural issues, certain portions of the Kantian philosophy and of German culture must be taken seriously. Chief among these is the Kantian conception of knowledge as a synthesis of empirically given and theoretically designated components. This is necessitated by the distinction in modern physics between sensed and mathematical space and time, and by many other scientific considerations. Consequently, the pre-Kantian British empirical philosophy of Anglo-American culture and the medieval philosophy of Hooker, St. Thomas and Aristotle of Church of England and Roman Catholic culture, which identify nature as scientifically conceived with nature as sensed, are inadequate, just as is the Kantian and post-Kantian moral philosophy of German culture. Clearly, all these traditional philosophical criteria of the good for culture, while laying hold of certain truths and values, must be superseded.

There are two ways in which this may be done. One way, and, as we shall find later, the correct way, is to go back to the origin of modern science to see if some error was not committed at the very outset of modern culture in passing from its verified scientific theory to the philosophical and ideational consequences of this theory. The other way is to go beyond Kant, Fichte and Hegel, hoping to correct the errors in their philosophy by amendment. This is the procedure of Feuerbach and Marx and the Soviet Russians. Because of the important rôle of Russia in the contemporary world this proposed solution of the ideological issues of our time must receive most serious attention.

CHAPTER VI

RUSSIAN COMMUNISM

At a certain stage of its eastern campaign in 1917 when medieval Tsarist Russia had collapsed and the Russian army showed signs of cracking but before it had actually crumbled, the High Staff of the German Imperial army prepared a train with a sealed baggage car for passage from Switzerland across Germany into Russia, through a pre-arranged opening of the German army on its eastern front. In this sealed baggage car the German military officials had placed two Russian refugees whose business it was to give to the creaking Russian military offensive a final disruptive push from within. These two humble servants of the Imperial German Staff accomplished their mission all too well. Their names were Lenin and Trotsky.

Not only did their work, synchronized with the hammer blows of the German army, destroy medieval Russian culture, but by coming thus to the mind and soul of the Russian people when both were indeterminate and in flux, with a new and extremely modern idea of the good for man and the state, defined by the dialectic, economic philosophy of Karl Marx, it offers one of the most dramatic examples of the way in which an exceedingly technical and systematic theory determines the values, the aims, and the later achievements of a people. The mere coming of Lenin and Trotsky to Russia may have enabled them to help destroy the old culture; but it was the definite philosophical theory brought with them as a blueprint in their minds which enabled them and their coworkers with a minimum of waste effort to build the new one, the culture of Soviet Russia.

The practical consequences are inescapable and astounding. Within two and one-half decades these Marxian communist leaders have transformed a people, the majority of whom were illiterate, into one of the most technically skilled, agriculturally, industrially and militaristically competent people in the world. Within less than thirty years they have moved through the industrial revolution, democratic revolution, and the communist revolution. Their capacity to get where they are so early and with so much, can be explained in only one way: they knew precisely where they were going, and they had a definite policy for getting there. In short, they had a theory to guide them. This theory was provided by the philosophy of Karl Marx.

At the very beginning of his definitive work *The Teachings of Karl Marx*, Lenin informs us that Marx "was the genius who continued and completed the three chief ideological currents of the nineteenth century, represented respectively by the three most advanced countries of humanity: classical German philosophy, classical English political economy, and French socialism combined with French revolutionary doctrines." Among these three factors the classical German philosophy and in particular the Hegelian dialectic, historical conception of the nature of things was basic. Not only was it the initial influence upon Marx but it was a necessary presupposition for the Marxian modifications in and uses of the two other factors. Nor were such primacy and all-pervading influence of the Hegelian dialectic purely theoretical. It determined the concrete acts not merely of Marx and his collaborator Engels, but also of Lenin and Trotsky through the events from 1900 onward which in 1918 culminated in the dictatorship of the proletariat.

At no time does this influence exhibit itself more dramatically than upon the evening of April 4, 1917, in Finlyandsky Station, when, with Trotsky, Lenin stepped off the train in Petrograd at the end of the dramatic journey which had brought them from Switzerland, across Germany, into their native land. Although the Russians and the Russian army were still fighting the Germans, three months previously, in a revolution in which all classes except the aristocrats had participated, the Tsarist regime had been overthrown and a provisional government composed of elected representatives had been put up in its place. In short, the democratic revolution had occurred.

The Menshevik communists and the liberal socialists were elated. They accepted the support which they had received from the middle-class democrats as an asset and certainly as something which should not be alienated and thrown away. Nevertheless, according to the dialectic philosophy not merely of Marx but also of Hegel, the democratic culture stemming from Locke and its attendant skeptical philosophy of Hume is not the final ideal or synthesis, but merely the antithesis to the culture of the Tsarist medieval aristocracy, which stems from what is to Kant and all Hegelians the dogmatic philosophy of the

Middle Ages. Being merely the antithesis, the middle-class democratic culture also must be overthrown before the real revolution has occurred and the ideal synthesis which gets to the root of the problem is achieved.

Consequently, when he stepped off the train, as Trotsky who was present informs us, Lenin, guided as always by this dialectic philosophy of history, did not falter for one moment. Standing on the station platform, he immediately announced, to the great consternation of the Menshevik communists and many others, first, that the bourgeois democratic revolution and its defeat of Tsarism were not enough; second, that the proletariats must arm and strengthen the local Soviets; third, that they must arouse the distrust of the agrarian peasants and country folk generally against the Provisional Government; and finally, that they must seize the supreme political power and use it on a socialistic basis.

Six months later the issue between the Menshevik communists who were fighting for socialism and an improvement of the condition of the working people by gradual, evolutionary, and more opportunistic means without an explicit theory to guide them, and Lenin, with his more revolutionary policy prescribed even to the minutest detail over half a century previously by the dialectic philosophical theory of Karl Marx, came to a head. On October 25, at the opening of the Second Congress of the Soviets, Lenin appeared and directed the fight, demanding an uprising against the Provisional Government. Two days later the revolutionary socialists combined with his Bolshevik followers to win the victory. A small executive committee termed "the Soviet of the People's Commissaries" was appointed and given supreme power with Lenin at its head. Two decrees were passed: one, to make overtures to the Germans for peace; and the other, with respect to the land. By means of the latter decree, Lenin's Soviet of the People's Commissaries won the support of the peasants by giving them the estates of the large landowners. Although this central committee, dominated entirely by the proletariat, was in fact the political power and a virtual dictatorship, a semblance of the democratic processes of the Provisional Government remained for a brief period. In November a Contituent Assembly was elected. But on January 7, 1918, the All-Russia Central Committee, on Lenin's motion, dissolved the elected Constituent Assembly. At last, not merely the Tsar's medieval feudalism but also the traditional modern middle-class bourgeois democracy was liquidated. The dictatorship of the proletariat was a fact.

To be sure, three years more were required for defeat of the counter-revolution from within, which Marx predicted and Lenin expected, and which was supported by the attack of the Czechs on the Volga, with British reinforcements by way of Archangel. Nonetheless, on January 7, 1918, one of the most remarkable illustrations of the Hegelian theory of the theoretical universal becoming concrete in history exhibited itself. For upon this day the specific synthesis of the dialectic process of history was actualized in the precise form and by the precise methods which had been prescribed some seventy-four years earlier in the philosophy of Karl Marx.

If we are to understand the precise form of this historical, dialectic revolution under Lenin, we must pay attention to the French socialistic, and English economic, as well as the Hegelian philosophical elements in Marx's philosophy. Nevertheless, neither his technical economic theory of value, nor his attitude toward the French and other socialists can be understood unless it is realized that Marx comes to the consideration of all these topics, taking the validity of the Hegelian dialectic theory of development for granted. As Marx, Lenin, Trotsky, and the Bolshevik communists have always insisted, the dialectic philosophy is absolutely fundamental to their entire position. Lenin, in his *Teachings of Karl Marx,* is most emphatic upon this point. He writes:

Marx and Engels regarded Hegelian dialectics, the theory of evolution most comprehensive, rich in content and profound, as the greatest achievement of classical German philosophy. All other formulations of the principle of development, of evolution, they considered to be one-sided, poor in content, distorting and mutilating the actual course of development of nature and society (a course often consummated in leaps and bounds, catastrophes, revolutions). . . . Engels writes: "The great basic idea that the world is not to be viewed as a complex of fully fashioned objects, but as a complex of processes, in which apparently stable objects, no less than the images of them inside our heads (our concepts), are undergoing incessant changes, arising here and disappearing there, and which with all apparent accident and in spite of all momentary retrogression, ultimately constitutes a progressive development—this great basic idea has, particularly since the time of Hegel, so deeply penetrated the general consciousness that hardly any one will now venture to dispute it in its general form."

But Lenin is quick to point out that this Marxian concept of development is quite different and involves much more than the evolutionary concept of Darwinian Anglo-American thought. For he continues:

In our times, the idea of development, of evolution, has almost fully penetrated social consciousness, but it has done so in other ways, not through Hegel's philosophy. Still, the same idea, as formulated by Marx and Engels on the basis of Hegel's philosophy, is much more comprehensive, much more abundant in content than the current theory of evolution [*i.e.* the Anglo-American Darwinian theory]. A development that repeats, as it were, the stages already passed, but repeats them in a different way, on a higher plane ("negation of negation"); . . . inner impulses for development, imparted by the contradiction, the conflict of different forces and tendencies reacting on a given body or inside a given phenomenon or within a given society; interdependence, and the closest, indissoluble connexion between *all* sides of every phenomenon . . . —such are some of the features of dialectics as a doctrine of evolution more full of meaning than the current one.

Similarly, when Lenin turns to the exposition of the Marxian concept of value in the science of economics, he adds, "We can understand what value is only when we consider it from the point of view of a system of social production relationships in one particular historical type of society." Since different historical types of society are related by the dialectic law of thesis, antithesis and synthesis, the Marxian science of economics presupposes the Hegelian dialectic philosophy of history precisely after the manner in which the economic science of Jevons was built upon the hedonistic, utilitarian philosophy of Bentham.

Marx's treatment of the socialist thought of the French depended also upon the dialectical theory of history. It is precisely this dependence which caused Marx continuously to attack all socialistic policies based upon "gradualism" or on evolution, and to insist upon revolution.

Marx's early life and intellectual history confirm these conclusions. He was born at Trèves in Western Germany in 1818, thirteen years before the death of Hegel. His father and the entire family became Protestants in 1824, and Karl was baptized. After finishing the schools at Trèves, he proceeded to the University of Bonn and then to the University of Berlin, where he took up the study of law. He turned, however, from law to history and from history to philosophy, receiving his degree of Doctor of Philosophy in 1841. While in Berlin he was not merely immersed in the Hegelianism which dominated the thought of the University, but was intimate with the liberal agrarian circle in which the Bauer brothers were leaders. He was already interested in the working-class movement, but his ideas were too much to the left to permit him to find a place for himself in Berlin. In 1843 he went to Paris to study the socialistic movement which was flourishing there. Thus historically the Hegelian foundations were laid first, and the French socialistic influences came afterward.

FEUERBACH'S REALISM AND MATERIALISM

But in between there was another factor. The German theologian Ludwig Feuerbach had given to the Hegelian philosophy a different emphasis. Instead of conceiving of the content of the dialectic historical process as initiating in ideas which come to concrete material objectivity and fulfillment in nature and culture, Feuerbach sought for the basis and origin of the ideas, locating them in social anthropology. Thus instead of the ideas determining nature and the cultural institutions, the latter tended to determine the ideas. Also, Feuerbach substituted a realistic, for the Kantian idealistic, epistemology. "I do not generate the object from the thought," he writes, "but the thought from the object; and I hold *that* alone to be an object which has an existence beyond one's own brain." The dialectic process as thus determined is called "dialectical materialism," in contradistinction to the Hegelian "dialectical idealism."

Although the difference between these two interpretations is significant, it is by no means as great as it appears to be verbally. There are three major developments in the nature of things with respect to which the logic of dialectic might be applied. They are (1) the self-consciousness of the individual, (2) nature, and (3) culture. Both Hegel and Feuerbach and the Marxians following Feuerbach apply the logic of dialectic to all three. The Hegelians and Marxians also regard the three processes as a single process. Even for Hegel the dialectical development in individual self-consciousness was a mere expression of the dialectical development of culture. Consequently, whether one labels the theory idealistic or materialistic is to a considerable extent largely a verbal matter. The development is completely determined by a dialectic law of the historical cultural process, under either name.

Holding such a common belief, we should have no difficulty in understanding why both the Germans and the communistic Russians find it so congenial to accept extreme regimentation. The only difference between them is that the Germans, paradoxically enough, in accepting regimentation believe that they are getting freedom, because Fichte and Hegel have supposedly shown them that this inevitable dialectic law of history governing human nature is precisely what the practical postulate of complete individual moral freedom entails. Marx and the Russian communists are less sophisticated in their similar acceptance of regimentation, believing merely as an initial assumption of their entire personal, economic, and political philosophy that the inevitable determination of the individual and his institutions by the dialectic law of historical development is a blunt, irreducible empirical fact.

The dialectic materialism of Marxist communism has very little in common with the "materialism" of traditional science or philosophy. The latter materialism did not conceive of nature as a process governed by the logic of thesis, antithesis, and synthesis. Furthermore, it was grounded solely in the theory of nature, and ignored history and the development of cultural institutions. For the Marxians, however, history, and in particular economic history, is the fundamental thing, tending even to determine and define one's scientific theories of nature. Thus even the materialism of Feuerbach and the Marxians is more like the idealism of Hegel than it is like the traditional materialism.

Marx and all his followers accepted this Feuerbachian interpretation of the Hegelian dialectic. During his stay in Paris Marx was in continuous correspondence with Feuerbach. Lenin tells us that by the years 1844 and 1845 Marx's views were completely formed. The materialistic version of the Hegelian dialectic and French socialism had combined.

It would seem as if a slight qualification would have to be placed upon Lenin's report. It is clear that by the years 1844 and 1845 Marx would have absorbed both the Feuerbachian Hegelianism and the revolutionary French socialism. But Lenin tells us also that a third factor went into the Marxian philosophy; namely, classical English economic theory. Marx did not go to England before 1848. It was there that he made his study of English economic science. His own *Concept of Political Economy* was not published until 1859, and it was not rewritten in the form in which it appears in *Das Kapital* until 1867. Thus the contribution of British economic science to Marx's philosophy must have come in considerable part at least much later than the year 1845. Nevertheless, there is undoubtedly a truth in Lenin's statement that Marx's views were definitely formed at this early date. The point is very important because it shows that the word "economic" enters into the Marxian theory with two different meanings and in two different forms, the first of which Marx had in the years 1844 and 1845, and the second of which it is not likely that he had developed until the time of his studies of economic theory in London.

The first view, which rested on the Feuerbachian conception of the dialectical historical process, gives not merely his technical economic theory but also his entire philosophy an economic flavor. This led him to look at social institutions in history. It led him also to look behind the social institutions, to man's relation to material nature. When Marx did this he noted how man works with certain materials of nature to meet his bodily and other needs. It producing these needs, by working upon the materials of nature, man is thrown into certain relations not merely with nature but with other men. These relations, which Marx terms "production relations," are fundamental in the entire Marxian philosophy. It is to these production relations that Hegel's logic of dialectic is applied. In fact, the "totality of these production relations" is what Marx means by "the economic structure of society." But their importance is even greater than this. For it is his theory that the change in these production relations, as they are operated on by the dialectic process of history, "determines, in general, the social, political, and intellectual processes of life." This is true not merely of the life of society as a whole but also, according to Marx, of the consciousness of the individual; and Marx immediately adds, "It is not the consciousness of human beings that determines their existence, but, conversely, it is their social existence which determines their consciousness."

The second and more technical use of the word "economic" in the Marxian philosophy has to do with Marx's "labor theory of value." This theory in its technical, final form he probably did not have until several years later than 1845. But this labor theory of value did little more than bring Marx's treatment of the concept of value and economic science into line with his philosophical theory of the economic determination of history and culture. Thus, since economics in the more technical sense is a requirement of Marx's conception of the primacy of economics in the more historical, philosophical sense, Lenin was in general correct in stating that Marx's philosophy had formed itself by 1845. This consideration re-emphasizes the point that the dialectical theory of history and its Feuerbachian "materialistic" emphasis is fundamental to, and a prerequisite for, the more technical doctrines of the Marxian economic science. The heart of the Marxian philosophy is the Hegelian dialectic applied to the economic production relations. From this, the thesis that socialism must be revolutionary in its policy and the labor theory of value follow.

Again it must be emphasized that even after Marx's singling out of the primacy of the production relations and even after his emphasis upon "materialism" rather than idealism, the dialectical Hegelianism was basic and crucial. While at Paris, around 1843, Marx met Friedrich Engels and joined with him in writing a book directed against the

Bauer brothers in Berlin and their liberal Hegelianism. In this book Hegel was defended against the liberal Hegelianism of the Bauers. Later, in Brussels, Marx and Engels attacked even the German socialists and philosophical radicals who were under the influence of Feuerbach. The reason for all these attacks was that these liberal socialists were emphasizing materialism and a naturalistic reaction against Hegel's idealism, to the neglect of the dialectic. Thus Hegel was superior to them, even to Feuerbach. This neglect of the dialectic caused the Bauers and the followers of Feuerbach to accept evolution and gradual change and cooperation with the middle-class democrats; whereas what was required, according to Marx and Engels, was revolution, and this can be ensured only by basic and unequivocal insistence upon the Hegelian dialectic as the governing principle of all change.

The Hegelian dialectic applied to the production relations is the key also to the Marxian theory of society. For it is the production relations which define the basic classes in society, and it is the dialectic applied to these classes that generates the class conflict which can only be reconciled by revolutionary means, achieving a certain classless social goal. The production relations define two classes: the class of those individuals in society who control the means of production, and the class of those individuals in society who do not control the means of production. Since these two classes are assumed to be controlled by the logic of dialectic, its principle of negation puts the one in opposition to the other. Thus the first class is termed by Marx in the *Communist Manifesto* written in 1848 "The Usurper" and the second class "The Usurped." According to Marx, this antithesis has given rise in history to various attempts at synthesis since primitive times, bringing forth medieval cultural institutions out of the Greek forms and modern democratic, capitalistic, political, and cultural institutions out of the medieval forms. But none of these syntheses has put an end to the class conflict. The form of the production relations has merely undergone a change, but even after the democratic revolutions of the modern world, this change has not been sufficient to wipe out the conflict between the oppressor and the oppressed.

In moden capitalistic society these two antithetical classes are termed by Marx the "bourgeois" and the "proletariat." It is in connection with his study of the precise manner in which the production relations of modern capitalistic society will force the capitalists and their bourgeois class to give rise to their opposite by necessarily driving more and more members of society into the class of the proletariat, thereby bringing on their own overthrow in a revolution led by the proletariat, that Marx's technical labor theory of economic value becomes important.

THE LABOR THEORY OF ECONOMIC VALUE

It is to be noted that Marx lived before Jevons. Consequently, at the time he made his thorough study of English economic science in London, just after the middle of the last century, the most advanced ideas which he encountered were those of Ricardo. It will be recalled from the account of Anglo-American economic science in Chapter III that Adam Smith in his exposition of the concept of value had distinguished between value in use or utility, and value in exchange. Any commodity had value in use or utility if it met some human need. A commodity acquired value in exchange through its relation to other commodities for which it is exchanged. Marx accepted both of these usages of the term "value," using the word "utility" to designate value in use and restricting the word "value" to designate value in exchange. Marx also admitted, as Jevons later emphasized, that exchange value is a relational concept and moreover one expressible in quantitative terms, and so a ratio. It is in fact a ratio joining a certain number of use-values of one kind to a certain number of use-values of another kind. This ratio, moreover, relates quantities designating the values of the different things exchanged.

But these quantities cannot thus be brought into relation with each other in a way that is meaningful unless they are built up out of units referring to something in common between all the different things which are exchanged. This factor in common, the exchanged things in themselves do not exhibit. For example, a painting by Rembrandt is in itself quite different from an automobile; yet we may speak of the Rembrandt as having twice the value of the automobile. Since this quantitative comparison of these two things does not find in the two commodities themselves the common denominator which makes the comparison possible, where, then, is this common denominator of the exchange values of these commodities to be found?

Both the Marxians and the Anglo-American economists recognize the need for answering this question. The difference between them centers in the fact that they answer it in different ways. This difference in their answers has its basis in turn in the radically different philosophical conceptions of the nature of things with which they approach the construction of their technical economic science.

The Anglo-American economists, it will be remembered, came with Jevons to their present theory of value from the positivistic, philosophical theory of Hume, Mill, and Bentham. According to this theory the whole of reality is to be conceived as nothing but the contingent association and succession of private sense data and the introspected pleasures, pains, and wants associated with them. Consequently, Jevons and his followers must find the meaning for the common denominator relating the quantities designating the relative exchange values of different commodities within the set of psychological data which this philosophical theory provides. They have little choice, therefore, but to identify the common factor either as did Jevons, following Bentham, with the amount of introspected pleasure associated with the commodity, or as more recent Austrian and Anglo-American economists have done, with the degree of preference for the different introspected wants. Thus, according to the contemporary classical Anglo-American economic theory, what all economic goods, notwithstanding their intrinsic differences, have in common in exchange is that they are all introspectively and psychologically wanted. Thus the differing prices or values which attach to the different commodities give expression to or measure the relative quantities or degrees of preference attached to the different goods. For this reason the Anglo-American theory is called the psychological theory of value.

The merit of this theory is that it explains the autonomy of economic science, making it completely independent of historical circumstances and cultural or social institutions and permitting it to apply to any society whatever. This is true because it rests upon immediately introspected individual wants ordered by a relation of introspected preference, factors which hold for all people under any form of government at any stage of the historical process. However, for this merit a certain price has been paid. As the writer has shown elsewhere, the rearing of economic science upon such restricted philosophical foundations makes it logically impossible to obtain a theoretical economic dynamics; that is, to predict the future state of an economic system by means of the postulates of this theory from a knowledge of the present state of the system. With respect to predictive power, the Marxian economics is far superior to this Anglo-American theory, even though the Marxian theory, as the sequel will show, falls far short of having the predictive certainty and validity which its followers claim for it.

The relative superiority of the Marxians, with respect to the prediction of the course of economic events, arises from the fact that they come to their technical definition of the common factor underlying the quantitative ratio between commodities in exchange, with a totally different philosophy. According to them, as we have indicated, reality is to be conceived as the dialectical process of historical development in which the production relations joining individuals to each other in their wresting of their physical needs from physical nature are the crucial and fundamental factor. Consequently, for the Marxians, what all commodities entering into exchange have in common is that they are the product of physical human labor applied to an objective physical nature. This physical human labor, as Maurice Dobb has emphasized in his *Political Economy and Capitalism*, is "conceived objectively as the output of human energy." Dobb also points out that this was the way in which Ricardo and all his predecessors had measured the basic common factor in economic activity.

But with Ricardo, value in itself, apart from exchange value, was something quite independent of human labor and physical nature. Thus for Ricardo the labor theory of value was probably merely a theory of the measure of value rather than a theory of the nature of value itself. But for Marx the situation is different. Following Hegel in identifying the "ought," or good, for culture with the actual, historical, dialectic development of cultural institutions, value itself became automatically identified with the historical cultural process. Also, when the key to the content of this historical process became identified with the material production relations resulting from the labor expended by men in securing their needs from material nature, then the labor theory became not merely a measure of value but also its very essence or ideal meaning. One has, in the strictest sense of the term, not merely a labor measure but also a labor theory of value.

One other factor distinguishes the Marxian from the present Anglo-American theory of economic value. In the latter theory, because the psychological wants and preferences of the atomic individuals merely aggregate in the market, organic social relations and the historical structure of a given society are quite irrelevant to the laws of economics. For Marx, on the other hand, neither an individual preference nor an individual economic transaction has any meaning apart from the systematic production relations characterizing and determining organically the whole of society at a given stage in the historical process. Thus the value of a given commodity in exchange, for Marx, is not determined by the individual in isolation by himself, nor merely as an effect of the public aggregation of individual preferences; but is instead arrived at the other way around, by first taking the total amount of physical labor of all the people in society involved in producing all the products of men's labor and then taking the portion of the total amount of human labor which went into the production of the particular commodity. Thus, as Lenin, in his exposition of Marx's doctrine, writes: "the element common to all commodities is not concrete labour in a definite branch of production, not labour of one particular kind, but *abstract* human labour—human labour in general. All the labour power of a given society, represented in the sum total of values of all commodities, is one and the same human labour power. . . . Consequently, each particular commodity represents only a certain part of *socially necessary* labour time."

Given this organic, social labor theory of value, Marx is then able to designate precisely how he believes the bourgeois class in capitalistic society exploits the laborer and thereby generates the antithesis of itself and the attendant class struggle which only a classless society under the dictatorship of the proletariat can synthesize and resolve. The heart of the matter centers in the treatment of labor as a commodity by those who control the means of production and the taking out, by the capitalist, in the finished product, of more value for himself than the laborer was paid in the making of that product.

On the labor theory of value, the value of the commodity is determined not by the total demands for it or the sum total or aggregate of psychological preferences for it in the free market, but by the amount of physical energy and labor which went into its production. Thus, that portion of the total labor of society which the particular commodity took for its making is the actual value of that commodity and the value for which the capitalist, when he sells it, is paid. But because the laborer, under capitalism and also according to Anglo-American economic theory, is treated as a mere commodity in the free market and consequently is paid only what his isolated bargaining power in competition with that of his fellow laborers will bring in such a market, he actually receives for his labor a value less than the value of the commodity which his labor produces. This difference between the labor value of the laborer's product and the value which he receives in wages Marx calls "surplus value." No harm would be done or injustice rendered if the capitalist who owns the means of production put this surplus value back into wages. Actually, however, he does not do this. He puts only a part into wages and the rest into the means of production which he owns and controls. Thereby, according to Marx, augmentation of the capitalist's capital occurs, at the cost of the exploitation of the workingman, and the tremendous differences in wealth in these two different classes of modern capitalistic society occur.

Having all these things in mind, we should be able to appreciate what Marx means when he says of the Anglo-American economic theory, "It has resolved personal worth into exchange value," and "It has drowned the most heavenly ecstasies of fervor in the icy waters of egotistical calculation." The latter statement brings to mind Bentham's and Jevons's counting of degrees of pleasure. The Marxian theory of "exploitation" may be summarized, therefore, as follows: The essential condition for the existence and power of the bourgeois class "is the formation and augmentation of capital." Its necessary condition is wage labor, which rests essentially on free competition between laborers.

With the discoveries of science and the development of machinery, the laborer is stripped of his tools and also more and more of his technical skills, thereby weakening his competitive power. Thus the means of production pass more and more into the hands of the few capitalists, and more and more people become crowded into the class of the proletariat. But this high social organization of industry upon a larger and larger scale brings all laborers more and more into communication with each other. Thus, "The advance of industry, whose involuntary promoter is the bourgeoisie, replaces the isolation of the labourers, due to competition, by their revolutionary competition, due to association. The development of modern industry, therefore, cuts from under its feet the very foundation on which the bourgeoisie produces and appropriates products." The way is thus prepared by the development of capitalism itself and the action of the capitalists for the antithetical class organization and growing power of the proletariat and their subsequent revolutionary capture of the means of production as a dialectically necessary synthesis and consequence of the entire previous historical development. This capture of the means of production by the proletariat is accomplished not by economic but by political means. Thus the Marxian philosophy entails not merely a philosophical theory of history and a technical theory of economic value but also a theory of the state.

THE COMMUNISTIC THEORY OF THE STATE

In considering the Marxian theory of the state a clear distinction must be drawn between "society" and the "state," as the communist uses these terms. Society always exists. It is the organic system of individuals determined by the production relations in the dialectical process of history. On the other hand, the state, according to Marx, is a more restricted social organization within society, arising out of the dialectical conflict of class interests by means of which those who control the means of production oppress those who do not. At the modern capitalistic stage of the dialectical development of history, the state, according to Marx, becomes more and more a power "standing above society and increasingly alienating itself from it." This power consists of "special bodies of armed men which have prisons at their disposal" and "the right to collect taxes." Thus the modern capitalistic state, whether it be of a monarchical, aristocratic or democratic, middle-class, "bourgeois" form, has within it the same dialectically controlled class conflict leading to the triumph of the proletariat as does the modern economic system.

Once these identifications between the state and the dialectical process of history are made, the remainder of the Marxian and communistic theory of political policy and the inevitable, dialectically controlled political goal follows. The conflict will be resolved only by wiping out all classes. This occurs when the proletariat captures the means of production to become the only class in society. Since this process is determined by the dialectical development of history, and dialectical development is revolutionary rather than evolutionary, this goal can be achieved by the proletariat only by revolutionary action. Moreover, since this revolutionary action takes the political power located in the control of the means of production out of the hands of the ruling class and of the modern state, and since the modern state had its basis, according to Marx, in the irreconcilable antithesis or conflict between the capitalists and the proletariat, the state automatically disappears when the triumph of the proletariat wipes out the class conflict. Automatically also the dialectical process of history comes to its end. This occurs because to go on would require a class conflict, and since the triumph of the proletariat removes all class conflicts, only one class—the whole of society—remaining, no such conflict is possible.

The revolution required by the dialectical logic of the historical development which is to bring about this final, stable, ideal social condition thus involves two things: first, the seizure of the state power by the proletariat and the transformation of the means of production into state property; second, the "destruction of the apparatus of state power." Thus the first consequence of the communistic revolution will be the substitution of state capitalism for private capitalism. Only later will the "apparatus of state power" be destroyed and the final ideal communistic society be achieved. This second stage in the appearance of the fruits of the revolution Lenin described as the "withering away of the state."

These two stages in the historical appearance of the communistic ideal as a consequence of the revolution are inevitable, according to Marx, because of the time required to consolidate the securing of power by the proletariat majority and to remove the old capitalistic and bourgeois mentality and social habits from all the members of society. Because many people, even after the revolution, will still persist in thinking and acting in terms of the values and from the standpoint of the old, outmoded, prerevolutionary stage of the historical process, the power of the state controlled by the proletariat must remain for a time. But gradually and finally, when the mentality and the habits of each and every member of society become that of the whole of society, as defined by the postrevolutionary communistic synthesis and ideal, then the power will go automatically to all the people of society itself, and the state will "wither away."

These two distinct historical stages following the revolution are distinguished economically as well as politically. In the first stage, in which the proletarian state has replaced the bourgeois capitalistic state, the revolution will have succeeded in destroying exploitation of laborer by capitalist because it will have placed the control of the means of production in the hands of the proletarian state instead of in the hands of the capitalist. But, according to Marx, it will not have destroyed the distribution of economic goods according to the amount of work performed instead of according to human needs. This happens again because the old bourgeois conception of "right" in terms of equality of distribution will persist. Gradually, however, the new communistic conception of "right" will spread through the whole of society. This involves an elimination of all "enslaving subordination" due to the division of labor and more specifically the vanishing of the "antithesis between mental and physical labor." Also, the free release of the "productive forces" will have increased meanwhile the full development of the individual. And the socially produced total wealth of society will be flowing freely to all the individuals in society. Then the new conception of right, "from each according to his ability, to each according to his needs," will have become not merely an ideal universal but also a concrete particular in each individual of society, and the state will have "withered away."

All this was specified by Marx some three-quarters of a century before Lenin proceeded to put it into practice in Russia following the Revolution of 1917. But there was an additional complexity in Marx's specifications, about how the revolution must proceed, which Lenin also followed to the minutest detail in his leadership of the proletariat. These specifications have to do with the relation between the leaders of the Communist party and the very much larger growing class of proletarians. The proletariats generally will be in sympathy with the inevitable dialectical development which comes to a climax in the revolution; but, untrained in the Marxian philosophy and, unlike the leaders of the Communist party, not fully understanding its theory, they will be in no position to foresee future developments or to direct the revolution wisely. Consequently, in the actual carrying through of the revolution, control cannot be entrusted even to the triumphant proletarian majority expressing their will through democratic processes, but must be instead in the hands of the few leaders of the Communist party who thoroughly understand the Marxian philosophy. Consequently, when the revolution actually occurs, government will not take on the form of a proletarian democracy; instead, as Marx specifically stated, it will take on a form of dictatorship; the dictatorship, namely, of the proletariat or, more accurately expressed, the dictatorship of the few proletarian leaders who thoroughly understand and literally follow the Marxian philosophy.

We are now able to understand not merely why Lenin, when he stepped off the train at Finlyandsky Station in Petrograd in 1917, refused to accept the democratic revolution as the real revolution, but also why, after the real proletarian revolution of October had occurred, he put the small executive committee of the Communist party in complete command, locating in it all the power of the state, and wiped out any semblance of even a democratic control by the proletariat, by liquidating their elected Constituent Assembly. We should be able to understand also why the leaders of a state, taking the Marxian philosophy as their ideal, should deem it good to liquidate all opposition to their power, and to oppress and discourage as far as possible all people holding philosophical beliefs contrary to the one specified by their Marxian theory. If the latter theory is correct, only thus can the old class mentalities be "dialectically synthesized," and the communistic ideal be achieved.

THE COMMUNISTIC ATTITUDE TOWARD DEMOCRACY

In connection with this detailed account of the policy of the revolutionists and their resolute aim, Marx in several connections uses the word "democracy." It is tremendously important that the leaders and people of democratic countries know precisely what these references mean and precisely what the communistic attitude is toward democracies of the traditional French and Anglo-American type.

Of one thing we can be sure: The leaders of communistic Russia are unequivocal realists. We must be realists also. But their realism is of a very peculiar and trustworthy type. It is a realism with respect to the theories underlying the different stages of historical development and the existing world states. For a realism based on an opportunistic power politics, uncontrolled by a specific philosophical, economic, and political theory, or for a so-called realism which does not take into account the ideological theory of rival nations, they have no respect or use whatever. Marx, Lenin, and Trotsky continuously referred to such unrealistic realism as eclecticism and opportunism, and for it they had the utmost contempt.

In a similar manner, in our association with Russia, we must be realistic, becoming perfectly clear in our minds concerning precisely what their theory is, avoiding at all costs opportunistic reactions based on a sentimental mood of repulsion at one moment or of brotherly love and attraction at another moment. The leaders of communistic Russia thoroughly understand the Lockean, Humean, and Jevonian philosophy, interspersed with Church of England or Roman Catholic, Aristotelian philosophical assumptions, which underlies the traditional French and Anglo-American democracies. Knowing this, they are in a position to predict roughly how, in a given set of circumstances, we will act. Also, being perfectly clear about their own philosophy, they know precisely where they are going and are not at cross-purposes with themselves in getting there. This stark realism, not with respect to the eclectic opportunism of power politics, but with respect to the philosophical assumptions underlying the different peoples and governments of the contemporary world, gives them a tremendous advantage in their dealings with the rest of us. Unless we can match their kind of intellectual realism with a similar realism grounded in a philosophical, economic, and political theory which defines what we stand for, and a clear conception of the Marxian philosophical theory which defines what they stand for, we are not merely going to be at a tremendous disadvantage in our relations with Russia, but we are also going to waste our power and influence in the contemporary world. Precise understanding, therefore, of the communistic Russians' use of the word "democracy" in connection with communism and of their attitude toward democracies of the Franco-Anglo-American type is exceedingly important.

In connection with the communistic ideal, Marx uses the word "democracy" or the word "freedom" at two points: One is in connection with the dictatorship of the proletariat, the first stage following the revolution; the other is at the end of the second stage, following the revolution, when the state has "withered away." In the first usage, he writes that the dictatorship of the proletariat is necessary in order "to win the battle of democracy." This is somewhat paradoxical. For what it means in actual practice, as we have previously noted and as Lenin's conduct unequivocally indicates, is that democratic processes must be done away with and a dictatorship of the communistic party leaders must be put in their place. On this point Lenin, in his exposition of the Marxian philosophy, is unequivocal, quoting Engels as follows: ". . . the proletariat . . . does not use [its power] in the interests of freedom but in order to hold down its adversaries. . . ." The Marxians justify this peculiar procedure in order "to win the battle of democracy" on the ground that in the democratic state the democracy is really only a democracy for the capitalistic owners of production, and not a democracy for all the members of society. But, even if this were true, to take democracy away from everybody today in order, at some distant future time in history, to win the battle for democracy seems an unnecessarily roundabout and regressive way to achieve one's purpose. In any event, this is precisely what the communists' first usage of the term "democracy" means.

The second usage of the term "democracy" in the postrevolutionary period of communistic society refers to its second stage, when the dictatorship of the proletariat's leaders, guided by the Marxian philosophy, has destroyed all opposition. Lenin speaks of it as follows:

Only in communist society, when the resistance of the capitalists has been completely broken, when the capitalists have disappeared, when there are no classes . . . [*i.e.* when every member of society spontaneously accepts the Marxian philosophy], only then does "the state . . . cease to exist," and it "becomes possible to speak of freedom." Only then will really complete democracy, democracy without any exceptions, be possible and be realized. And only then will democracy itself begin to wither away. . . . Communism alone is capable of giving really complete democracy, and the more complete it is the more quickly will it become unnecessary and wither away of itself.

It would seem, therefore, that in neither of the two stages following the communistic revolution, not even in the future second state, are there to be democratic processes. For in the first stage democracy is replaced by an unequivocal dictatorship of the proletariat's leaders, and in the second stage "democracy itself [will] . . . wither away" and "become unnecessary." Such is the status of democracy under communism in the ideal state of affairs following the bloody revolution, as conceived by Marx and by Lenin, the founder of communistic Russia.

The attitude of the communists with respect to a democracy grounded in the Lockean or Humean rather than the Marxian philosophy is also definite. The primary thing to remember here is that the Marxian attitude is precisely that of the post-Kantian Hegelians. For both, democracy is an expression of the pre-Kantian, British empirical, philosophical movement from Bacon, Newton and Locke to Adam Smith, Hume, Bentham, Mill and Jevons. With Kant this philosophical movement was definitely superseded, and with Hegel and Marx modern society passed on to a higher synthesis in which democratic societies grounded in the philosophy of Locke and Hume are definitely outmoded.

For the Marxians they are outmoded, in addition, because this dialectic development is grounded in a cultural development, fundamentally economic in character, in which the production relations arising from man's physical wresting of his physical needs from physical nature are crucial; and these production relations are such, as controlled by the dialectic law of their development, that the modern democratic culture defined by Locke's political philosophy and Jevons's economic theory must necessarily negate and destroy itself. In this dialectic development, before the revolution, the communists will make use of the traditional democratic processes. But the ideal of the communistic state can never be achieved by means of them. Only a revolution which replaces democratic processes by "the dictatorship of the proletariat" can initiate this ideal state. As Lenin put the matter, "Democracy is of great importance for the working class in its struggle for freedom against the capitalists. But democracy is by no means a boundary that must not be overstepped; it is only one of the stages in the process of development from feudalism to capitalism, and from capitalism to communism."

A first reading of the new Russian Constitution of 1936 might lead one to suppose that the Russians have left this appraisal of democracy of Marx and Lenin, for that of the traditional democracies, in considerable part at least. Supporting such a conclusion are the wide extension of the franchise, regardless of sex, race, creed, color or nationality, to some 55 per cent of the population as compared with 40 per cent in Great Britain and the United States; the direct or indirect election of all officials from the local Soviets to the Presidium of the Supreme Soviet and the Council of the People's Commissars in Moscow; and the detailed Bill of Rights specified in Articles 1 to 12 and 118 to 133, guaranteeing freedom for work, rest, education, speech, press, assembly, and religious worship and "freedom of anti-religious propaganda" to all citizens. However, certain other less obvious but none the less real elements in the Constitution should give one pause. They are: (1) the unique character of the Soviet Bill of Rights; (2) the qualification upon the freedoms apparently guaranteed, because of Article 131; and (3) the manner in which the candidates for office are nominated, referred to only near the end of the Constitution in Article 141.

The Soviet Bill of Rights is unique, in a commendable way, in the manner in which it combines the duties of the citizen with the guarantees to him by the government, which are specified even as to the material means by which they are to be implemented. Article 12 is typical of the citizen's duties; it reads: "Work in the USSR is a duty and a matter of honor for every able-bodied citizen, on the principle: He who does not work shall not eat." These words come direct from Karl Marx; not from John Locke, Jeremy Bentham or Richard Hooker. The difference from the conception of individual rights of the American Declaration of Independence is marked. According to the Lockean theory of the person underlying the latter document, man has his rights inalienably and automatically; the function of government, therefore, is largely negative, to see that they are not interfered with. For Marx, on the other hand, the person is a physiological being using his body in material or mental labor to wrest sustenance from material nature, without which life, liberty and the pursuit of happiness are "an idle dream"; consequently, the rights of man are not something that man has automatically but something which by his labor he has to acquire. With respect to the guarantees of the citizen's rights by the government, the situation for Marx is the same; they have to be achieved by definite specified instruments. Thus, in Article 125 the government does not merely guarantee freedom of speech, press and assembly; it also places "printing shops, supplies of paper, public buildings . . . and other material requisites" at the disposal of the workers in order to make the guarantee real. Similarly, Article 123 does not merely guarantee equal rights for citizens "irrespective of their nationality or race, in all spheres of economic, state, cultural, social and political life"; it also specifies that "any propagation of racial or national exclusiveness or hatred and contempt, shall be punished by law." In the same manner, Article 118 not merely asserts "the right to guaranteed employment and payment for work in accordance with its quantity and quality," but also this "is ensured by the socialist organization of the national economy, the steady growth of the productive forces of soviet society, the elimination of the possibility of economic crises, and the abolition of unemployment." This is done as specified in Articles 1 to 10 by what Beatrice Webb has described as "the substitution, for profit-making manufacturing, of planned production for community consumption." Nor does the difference in financial reward for differences in "quantity and quality of work," referred to in Article 118, in any way indicate a compromise with capitalism, for as Beatrice Webb adds: "The entire net product of the community is, in fact, shared among those who cooperate in its production, in whatever way they themselves decide." Never has there been any deviation from "the liquidation of the capitalistic economic system, the abolition of private ownership of tools and the means of production, and the abolition of the exploitation of man by man" prescribed at the very beginning of the new constitution in Article 4. Thus, notwithstanding the machinery of popular elections and the emphasis upon the rights of man, the government of contemporary Russia is still one in which the Marxian thermodynamic concept of a person and the nature of his rights, and the Marxian socialistic theory of economics and politics define the idea of the good.

The second factor giving one pause before concluding that Russia is moving away from the Marxian toward the French or Anglo-American concept of democracy appears in Article 131. It concludes as follows: "Persons making attacks upon public socialist property shall be regarded as enemies of the people." We may assume that in Soviet Russia it is a very serious thing to be branded as an enemy of the people. It is important, therefore, that we realize in practice what this sentence in Article 131 means. The sympathetic and informed student of Soviet Russia, Beatrice Webb, gives the answer: "No criticism of the living philosophy of the Communist party is permitted in the Soviet Union. . . . [There is an] absolute prohibition within the USSR of any propaganda advocating the return to capitalist profit-making, or even to any independent thinking on the fundamental social issues about possible new ways of organizing men in society, new forms of social activity, and new developments of the socially established code of conduct." This has the consequence of making the government a one-party government; there is no opposition or minority party in the elected legislative bodies. Here the erroneous Hegelian and Marxian confusing of the "ought" for society with the supposedly inevitable historical "is," identified by Marx with "the dictatorship of the proletariat" directed by the Communist party leaders, again shows its evil consequences. Thus most of the important guarantees of the Soviet Bill of Rights are nullified by one sentence in Article 131. Complete freedom of speech, press, assembly and demonstration is guaranteed providing one speaks, writes or demonstrates about nothing but the merits of the Communist party doctrine. This is quite a different concept of freedom and of human rights from that in the traditional democracies where the opposition can speak its mind. It is a conception also, which in the long run will become stultifying to the people who adopt it, for as Beatrice Webb has noted, "It is upon this power to think new thoughts, and to formulate even the most unexpected fresh ideas, that the future progress of mankind depends."

It must be added though in all honesty, as she also indicates, that this "disease of orthodoxy in a milder form is not wholly absent in the capitalist political democracies." Also, as the Webbs have amply demonstrated, within the Marxian orthodoxy, Joseph Stalin in no way has the power or the behavior of a dictator. All decisions made in the legislative or the executive branches of the Soviet Government occur only after debate and discussion, often only after being referred to the people, and with the entire executive cabinet, and not merely its president or chairman, entering into and taking responsibility for the result. Thus, Joseph Stalin has less personal independence of decision and action than the President of the United States is allowed by the American Constitution. Also, the fact that there is a prescribed and unquestioned orthodoxy tends to result in decisions being made upon the basis of principles which are known to all.

A third caution with respect to the democracy of Soviet Russia arises when one asks how the candidates for whom the people vote are nominated. Article 141 gives all that the Constitution has to say upon this point. It reads: "Candidates for elections shall be nominated by electoral districts. The right to nominate candidates shall be ensured to public organizations and societies of working people; Communist party organizations; trade unions; cooperatives; organizations of youth; cultural societies." In short, nominations are made by the Communist party and other workers' organizations. The Webbs in their classic study of Soviet Russia have shown, as the Communist party leaders and Karl Marx before them frankly affirm, that the party men are the key men, "the vanguard of the proletariat" in these other organizations. Stalin himself, who is head of the Communist party, has written: "In the Soviet Union, in the land where the dictatorship of the protelariat is in force, no important political or organizational problem is ever decided by our soviets [the elected legislative bodies] and other mass organizations, without directives from our party. In this sense, we may say that the dictatorship of the proletariat is substantially the dictatorship of the party, as the force which effectively guides the proletariat."

Important as this makes the Communist party, the Constitution tells nothing about its character or the rules under which it must or does operate. Nor is this an oversight. For the Webbs inform us that the Communist party "is literally outside the legal constitution of the secular state, and professedly independent of it." Like the Roman Catholic Church it "repudiates any national boundaries, and claims a sphere that is worldwide, and independent of nationality, race or colour." Also, it is "pyramidal in form, broadly democratic in its base, but directing its self-management from the top downwards."

Although the Communist party is in no way regulated by any article of the Constitution, it is nonetheless protected by the Constitution. For Article 126 guarantees the right of "the most active and politically conscious citizens from the ranks of the working class and other strata of the working people [to] unite in the All Union Communist party." But the uniting in this party is not optional, as its two and one-half million members in a Russian population of one hundred and ninety-two millions clearly indicate. Instead, the Communist party is, the Webbs add, "self-selective in its recruitment" and its "test for membership is fundamentally that of acceptance of an ideology of the nature of a creed"—the creed, namely, of Karl Marx.

This creed the Webbs describe in part as follows: "The Communist

Party flatly rejects, not only Christianity and Islam, but also every form of Deism or Theism." This places another qualification upon the Soviet Bill of Rights. It appears that Article 124, which affirms that "freedom of religious worship and freedom of anti-religious propaganda shall be recognized by all citizens," is, so far as the beliefs and influence of the Communist party are concerned, taken advantage of only with respect to its second portion. The Webbs continue: The Communist party "will have nothing to do with the supernatural. It admits nothing to be true which cannot be demonstrated by the 'scientific method' of observation, experimentation, ratiocination, and verification." To this the query arises whether the Marxist doctrine itself passes this test. Its origin throws considerable light upon this question.

COMMUNISM AND SCIENCE

When Lenin was in exile from Russia during the years between the abortive Russian Revolution of 1905 and the successful Revolution of 1917, he founded in Munich a paper called *Iskra* (*The Spark*), the motto of which was "From Spark to Flame." The spark he would undoubtedly have identified with the formulation of the Marxian philosophy in the mind of Karl Marx in the years 1844 and 1845. For us, however, the spark goes back much farther, not merely to Hegel and to Fichte, who first brought forward the logic of dialectic, but also to Kant's setting up of the demands of the practical reason as in its own right a trustworthy criterion of philosophical theory. For it is this placing of the demands of practice, out of control of philosophical theory arrived at by the methods of science applied to the empirical facts concerning nature and man, which produced the gulf between moral and scientific knowledge and thus prepared the way with Fichte for the reduction of all knowledge, even that of nature, to the "demands" of practice, thereby making everything subject to the dialectic law which all practically grounded knowledge following Fichte is supposed to embody and entail.

Furthermore, when these practical demands seemed, with Fichte and Hegel, to presuppose the free will not of the local, human beings, but of the absolute spirit coming to concrete expression in the dialectical, historical development of culture, then, instead of the theory of man and nature discovered by a factually controlled scientific study determining man's beliefs and evolving historical, cultural institutions, the process of history itself became the determining factor; and the human being who started out with Kant and Fichte in the name of genuine freedom of choice, found himself, with Hegel and Marx, caught in an absolutely deterministic cultural development. It was a very slight change, and it makes little difference to the individual when, with Marx, man's socially determined beliefs, acts, and cultural institutions were conceived as conditioned by the physical production relations instead of the absolute self-consciousness. In both instances everything is supposed to be absolutely determined and the dialectic law of the development of culture is the key to, and condition of, everything else. When, in addition, this entire philosophy was presented, as it was by Fichte, as a necessary requirement for the meaningfulness of the moral life, a fallacy occurred which exhibits itself in both the Hegelians and the Marxians—the "is" of the inevitable, dialectically determined development of culture is identified with the ideal and the good for culture. In short, the "ought" for human institutions and conduct is fallaciously identified with the historical "is" of either the present or the inevitable future.

The Marxians have attempted to cover up this fallacy by making a virtue of it, a virtue to be sure which gives the Marxian or the Hegelian doctrine a certain appeal to minds which overlook its fallacious identification of the "ought" for culture with the "is." This occurs when the Marxians present themselves as having no concern with a utopia and as being purely empirical scientists. The following statement from Lenin is typical. Speaking of the Marxian approach to the development of social institutions, he writes: "There is no trace of an attempt on Marx's part to conjure up a utopia, to make idle guesses about what cannot be known. Marx treats the question of communism in the same way as a naturalist would treat the question of the development of, say, a new biological species, if he knew that such and such was its origin, and such and such the direction in which it was changing."

This is very appealing as thus stated. But its plausibility depends upon several presuppositions. One is the identification of the ideal for the state and for man with the historical development of the actual. This unequivocally commits the fallacy of identifying the "ought" for history and culture with the "is." There is also the presupposition that the actual does follow the dialectic law; and that the dialectic law does entail, by its principle of negation and subsequent synthesis, that present events and institutions in the historical process must necessarily go only to the final state which Marx's description of the postrevolutionary communistic state prescribes. The slightest examination, however, of the nature of the logic of dialectic shows that there is in it no such inevitability relating present conditions to future ones. From the negation of a present thesis one does not get one specific antithesis but at least a finite and probably an infinite number of antitheses. And from a specific antithesis standing over against its prior thesis there are at least several theories which might provide a synthesis. Thus the claim that the communists are not concerned with a utopia but are realistic, scientific empiricists looking objectively at the historical process and merely reporting what is happening to it as a whole is a sheer pose, a pose by means of which they have succeeded with a vast mass of people in smuggling in their own particular utopia not merely, because of Fichte's influence, in the name of the demands of morality, but also in the name of empirically grounded truth and logical necessity.

Russia is what it is today not because there was any necessity that it be that way, but largely because, for the reasons indicated, the leaders of the Russian revolution took the speculative philosophical theory of Marx, and by persuasive and forceful means brought others to its acceptance, and built political action and cultural institutions in terms of it. Consequently, instead of establishing the point that the physical production relations in the dialectic development of cultural institutions determine the beliefs of the individual and man's political and social institutions, the Marxian philosophy as embodied in the practices and social forms of contemporary communistic Russia is one of the most spectacular examples in human history of the manner in which a philosophical theory, and a most speculative one, first formulated by a single individual—Karl Marx—has determined later social facts and institutions, and in part conditioned the character of the economic structure of society.

Another item essential to the Marxian doctrine is devoid of the necessity which the philosophy presupposes and explicitly assumes. This is the step from Hegel to Marx by way of Feuerbach's materialism. In this step four different things, each of which, independently, in its respective specific context possesses a partial or complete validity, were combined and muddled. The four things were: (1) an anti-positivistic, realistic epistemology, termed by Marx and his followers "materialism"; (2) the Hegelian dialectic theory of development; (3) the physical relation between realistically conceived bodily men and realistically conceived physical nature, as both are known by physical and physiological science; and (4) the economic structure of society which is constituted by what Marx termed the "material" or "physical production relations."

Plate IX DAUGHTERS OF REVOLUTION. GRANT WOOD

Courtesy of Associated American Artists

LOCKE'S THEORETIC COMPONENT: THE TABULA RASA

Plate X THE SIDESHOW. GEORGE-PIERRE SEURAT
Courtesy of the Museum of Modern Art

HUME'S ATOMIC SENSE DATA AS ASSOCIATED
BY A FRENCHMAN

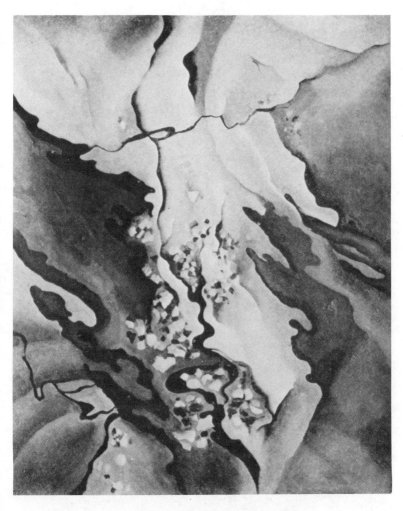

Plate XI ABSTRACTION NO. 3.
GEORGIA O'KEEFFE. 1924
Courtesy of An American Place

THE AESTHETIC COMPONENT — THE DIFFERENTIATED
AESTHETIC CONTINUUM

Plate XII MADONNA AND CHILD
Courtesy of the Metropolitan Museum of Art, New York City
By a follower of Sandro Botticelli

ART IN ITS SECOND FUNCTION

Let us consider these four different senses of Marx's use of the word "materialism" in turn. (1) Materialism in the sense of the anti-positivistic, realistic conception of nature refers to a relation joining man as knower to nature as known, which is of a character such that nature exists independently of our consciousness of it. That this is the Marxian thesis the following statement from Lenin shows, "For the sole 'property' of matter—with the recognition of which materialism is vitally concerned—is the property of being *objective reality*, of existing outside our cognition." That this thesis is justified our later analysis of scientific knowledge, in terms of what we term concepts by postulation, will show in part. But if this is what we are to mean by the word "materialist," then Plato, Aristotle, and countless others besides Marx are materialists. (2) The dialectical theory of development has been analyzed already. It is a process in which the logic of negation operating between a thesis and its antithesis gives rise to a synthesis. (3) The relation between physiological man and physical nature is equally clear. This is a physical relationship. The word "materialistic" may be used to designate it, but such a usage is quite different from that of either (1) or (2). Items (1) and (3) are in accord with the content and nature of the knowledge of natural science. Were this the meaning of "materialism," then practically all scientists and philosophers except Berkeley and Hume and the old-fashioned positivists would be materialists.

The confusion begins to enter when (1) and (3) are combined with (2). This is precisely what it means to combine Feuerbach's materialism, (1) and (3), with Hegel's dialectic, (2). When this was done by Marx, a dialectic process of development was attributed to nature, quite contrary to anything indicated by the precisely postulated, experimentally verified theories of the natural scientists. Certainly in none of the theories of the natural scientists—Newton, Maxwell, Gibbs, Einstein, or Max Planck—is nature exhibited as obeying Hegel's dialectic. Thus at this basic point, as Sidney Hook has shown, communistic philosophical theory is unequivocally false. Yet unless this false conception of nature is insisted upon as the truth, one does not have the basic thesis of the Marxian philosophy; namely, dialectic materialism.

The error increases and the confusion becomes worse confounded when (1), (2), and (3) are combined by Marx with (4), *i.e.* when the dialectic materialism of nature is combined, if not even identified, with the dialectic development of cultural legal conventions and institutions as constituted and controlled by the economic production relations. This happens when the materialistic dialectic is applied to "the totality of production relations which constitutes the economic structure of society."

Without the false identification of the dialectic with the basic ontological character of nature, Marx's dialectic would not be a materialistic dialectic rather than the old Hegelian idealistic one; and without the identification of his materialistic dialectic with the dialectical development of the economic structure of society, Marx would not obtain his economic determinism. Thus, the somewhat dialectical transition from one form of legal and social convention in man's thinking and in his social institutions to another form is muddled with the quite different and false dialectical materialism of a dialectically conceived nature— so much so in the end that the economic determinism of culture threatens to swallow up nature, even to the point of causing certain recent communists to attempt to find the meaning for the basic concepts of Newton's physics in the dialectically controlled class struggle between the bourgeoisie and the proletariat.

The reasons for these errors and this muddled confusion, which the failure to note Marx's different uses of the word "materialistic" has obscured, is clear: The old *Naturphilosophie* of Hegel, in which nature is arbitrarily fitted into a dialectic philosophy of culture and history, to which Fichte's reduction of natural science to moral philosophy gave rise, still persists in Marx and his communists. Otherwise, when Marx, following Feuerbach, turned, as he did in part, to natural scientists for his theory of man and nature, he would have left the theories of both just as they stand as experimentally verified by the scientists, instead of arbitrarily, like Fichte and Hegel, insisting upon making nature march through the paces of the dialectic.

Thus there are many very weak links and many unequivocal gaps in the supposed "necessity" which joins the spark to the flame. This means that the final solution for the cultural problems of the contemporary world is no more to be found in Russian communism than in the philosophy of Locke and Hume. Both have certain facts and attendant philosophical considerations in their support, but neither is adequate to all the evidence; and least of all is either absolutely necessary.

Hence, the solution of our problem must begin by going back to the fundamental factual and scientific discoveries of the modern world to review in detail the elements, and to discover the error which brought into existence these diverse inadequate, traditional, modern philosophical theories.

The need for the latter inquiry and the failure of the Kantian, Fichtean, and Marxian, as well as the Lockean and Humean, philosophies to give an adequate philosophical answer to the inescapable philosophical problems arising out of the scientific knowledge of the modern world does not alter the fact, however, that the Marxian philosophy, no less than the Lockean, has come upon certain insights and truths, and contributed certain exceedingly important attendant values to the total store of values of the modern Western world. These contributions must be noted.

The first is the demonstration that, for all the weaknesses of the dialectic, the approach to the history and development of cultural institutions and their forecasting is to be most effectively pursued by paying attention to the manner in which one set of theoretical assumptions underlying the economic, political, aesthetic, and religious institutions of a given stage of Western history is in part or wholly negated by the advent of some later, basic philosophical theory. This negation and the resultant specific later theory by no means possess the inevitability or the logical necessity which the Hegelians and the Marxians maintain. But that a later theory always does negate at least one assumption of the previous theory is the case. And that this negation and the advent of the new theory do entail, at least to some extent, a revolution and reconstruction in all cultural institutions and in one's scale of human values cannot be denied.

Such a reconstruction occurred within medieval culture and the Catholic Church itself when Thomas Aquinas shifted its philosophical foundations from those of Augustine and Plato to those of Aristotle. It was instanced again when the discoveries of Galilei and Newton in physics necessitated a shifting of the philosophical foundations of the culture of the Western world from the philosophy of Aristotle and St. Thomas to that of Descartes and Locke. It is quite clear that in any one of these shifts, given the previous philosophy and the principle of negation, one could not have deduced the succeeding theory. Thus, there is not a determinism in history, having its basis either in economics or in the self-consciousness of the absolute. Nevertheless, that the succeeding theory does negate certain fundamental assumptions of the preceding theory is true. And attention upon its novel premises—when the character of the new factual evidence, rather than the mere dialectical logic of negation, tells what they are—is of tremendous importance in understanding the development of cultural institutions, and the reconstructions and revolutions in human valuations.

A second contribution of the Marxians is their emphasis, following Feuerbach, upon the empirical, factual, physical, and physiological character of nature and man in its effect upon a correct philosophical theory of the criterion of the good for culture and the character of adequate economic and political institutions. It was high time that economic and political theory in its concept of a person treated man as a creature with a body, having continuous energy requirements in the form of food in order to maintain even his human existence. For Locke, as we have noted, man, as a legal person, was identified fundamentally not with the material substances of his body but only with the mental substance. For Hume and Mill and Bentham the person was nothing but an association of sense data or introspected wants rather than the complex, sensuous, bodily physiochemical creature requiring energy from without, of which the sense data are mere suggestive signs. Into our thought about economics and politics Marx brought a naturalistic realism which is nonetheless good because it is true.

It may seem as if, in pointing out the latter fact, we are overlooking the fallacy of identifying the "ought" for culture with the "is" for culture, of which we have rightfully accused the Marxians and the Hegelians. This, however, is not the case. It only seems to be so because of the complexity of the situation at this point, and the failure to note all the distinctions which this complexity involves. The difficulty is, so far as it affects the Marxians, that they did not seriously develop the consequences of their own naturalistic thesis. Had they done so, they would have put aside for a moment the Hegelian dialectic, which was primarily a theory of the development of historical, cultural institutions, and allowed nature to speak for itself through the factual findings and attendant experimentally verified theories discovered by the natural scientists who are experts with respect to the knowledge of nature.

Such a procedure would have given them, in the time of Marx, Galilei's and Newton's physics, and a little later the field physics of Faraday and Maxwell; and at the present moment the generalized Newtonian and Maxwellian mechanics of Einstein, together with the quite different quantum mechanics of De Broglie, Schroedinger, and Dirac. In none of these theories, nor in nature as conceived by these theories, is there any logic of dialectic. It would also, in the study of development as it occurs in nature, have led Marx, as it has led the natural scientists who are experts in this matter, to the evolutionary rather than the revolutionary theory of development for biological nature. Certainly in the process of biological development the advent of a new species does not involve the wiping out of the preceding species by a logic of negation after the manner in which the proletariat is supposed to wipe out the bourgeoisie. Even with the presence of man, the chimpanzees, birds, fishes, reptiles, paramecia, and most of the other earlier species in the evolutionary development—not to mention all the living organisms of the entire vegetable world—are still here. None of these earlier biological classes has been wiped out after the manner in which Marx, misguided by the Helegian identification of the dialectic with nature, insists.

Again, the basic assumptions of German philosophy, which Marx took as axiomatic, misled him. In this instance there was the influence of Kant as well as the influence of Hegel. The Kantian thesis was that the character of the object of knowledge must conform to the concepts and laws governing the development of consciousness and of thought in the knowing mind. Unwittingly, this thesis, as well as the Fichtean and Hegelian logic of dialectic, became basic in the Marxians' thinking. For it is this Kantian assumption which leads them to attribute to nature itself the antithetical type of relationship joining the sequence of theories in the human mind and the sequence of cultural institutions formed upon the basis of such human theories. Having done this, the Marxian theory, which started out quite correctly by noting man's bodily, naturalistic character as well as the revolutionary development of Western culture, ended by making the former obey the revolutionary form of development of the latter.

Thus the dialectic evolution of culture, with its economic production relations singled out as the crucial and only genuinely causal factors, became the whole of philosophy and of reality, nature being merely a minor, incidental exemplification, in the background, of the basic dialectic law of the cultural process. As a consequence, nothing remained but to identify the "ought" for culture with the inevitable future "is" in which the dialectically determined cultural process was supposedly necessarily and inevitably to terminate, and nothing existed outside of this cultural process to provide an empirical criterion, apart from culture, for the correctness of such a theory of utopia.

Had the difference between the character of man's body and nature, as revealed by expert natural scientists, and the character of the sequence of the theories of nature in human thought and the attendant sequence of cultural institutions in cultural history been maintained, the Marxians would not only have had the much more exact and trustworthy expert natural scientist's rather than the Hegelian dialectical philosopher's conception of nature, thereby adding greater content and practical effectiveness to their initial emphasis upon the naturalistic character and basis of at least a part of man's nature and his cultural, economic, and political institutions, but they would also have had in the empirically given facts of nature, which are quite independent of culture, a test for the validity of the philosophical theories which define the idea of the good for culture. In this manner the fallacious identification of the "ought" for culture with the "is" for culture would have been avoided. At the same time the initial emphasis of the Marxians upon the necessity of paying attention, in one's theory of economics and politics and ethics, to men's bodies as well as their thoughts and to nature as well as to the sequence of human ideas in culture would have been more effective.

Notwithstanding this failure to capitalize on Feuerbach's important insight, the value of this insight still remains and has made itself felt not merely in present-day Russia but in the influence of the Marxian doctrine upon the rest of the world. Marx has made it forever impossible hereafter for anyone to pretend to have an adequate economic or political theory or moral philosophy which does not pay attention to man's bodily as well as his ideational nature; and to the physical universe as well as to purely cultural institutions. To political democracy with its freedom to choose one's own political leaders, there has been added economic democracy with its vision of freedom from physical want.

Of one thing we can be certain. Thanks to a great extent to Karl Marx and to the incontestable achievements of contemporary communistic Russia—but not entirely to these factors—either the people of the modern democratic cultures are going to develop a new philosophy underlying and guiding their democratic processes and defining an attendant new idea of the good which, because of its adequacy to the bodily and theoretically scientific, as well as to the sensuous and the Humean positivistic aspects of man's nature, directly and with dispatch, applies the scientific knowledge which is at hand to the materials of nature which are also present, to meet bountifully the needs of men generally, as is obviously possible, or else Marx's communists are going to do it for us. Mankind, once having caught this vision of science and nature put together to lift the well-being of men generally in time of war, with work and better food for all while also producing tremendous quantities of materials for fighting, is not going to wait indefinitely for similar achievements in time of peace, merely because of social inhibitions arising from charges of unsoundness put forward in the name of traditional religion, economic science, and politics, especially when the philosophy of Locke, Fichte or Hume, underlying these traditional doctrines is now known to be either false or inadequate.

Nevertheless, inadequacies and errors of a different kind which are present in the Marxian philosophy show with equal certainty that its program is not the only one, nor the adequate one for achieving these important ends. What is needed and what the evidence calls for is a philosophy grounded in science and reared upon new assumptions, which provides new meaning for the freedom and individual creativity which the traditional modern philosophy, religion, and social science of Locke, Hume, Bentham, and Jevons, to their everlasting credit, fostered, and which at the same time escapes their inadequacies, errors and attendant evil inhibitions upon social action, by so joining nature and man, as they are conceived and instrumented by theoretically formulated, experimentally verified science, that the potentialities of both are realized as a positive good for all men.

To the designation of such new philosophical foundations for both democracy and communism this inquiry must turn. But before this can be done properly other cultures must be understood. For Protestant Anglo-American and communistic Russian values are not the only ones for which an adequate philosophy for our time must provide.

CHAPTER VII

ROMAN CATHOLIC CULTURE AND GREEK SCIENCE

For many reasons analysis of the philosophical foundations of Roman Catholic culture is exceedingly important at the present moment. Not only are there the growing influence and numbers of Roman Catholics in the culture of the United States, and the persisting influence of the Pope in the predominantly Roman Catholic countries of the south of Europe and in Latin America, and upon policy in the remainder of the Western world; but there is also a recent revival of interest in the orthodox Catholic philosophy on the part of some of the most acute of modern non-Catholic philosophers and thinkers. In addition, there is the neo-Thomism of which the French Catholic philosopher Jacques Maritain is perhaps the most wise and systematic spokesman.

In the United States there has been the quite independent return to the Thomistic and Aristotelian philosophy as a measure for legal theory and educational policy, under the leadership of President Stringfellow Barr and Dean Scott Buchanan in St. John's College; and of Professor Mortimer Adler and President Robert M. Hutchins at the University of Chicago. This indigenous American development is the more impressive because all of its leaders are exceptionally informed, influential and original thinkers; and also because none of them was initially a Roman Catholic. A similar phenomenon appears in England in the growing influence of the leadership of the Church of England, with its philosophy formulated by Richard Hooker which goes back, as does that of St. Thomas, to Aristotle. The American-born poet T. S. Eliot in his *Idea of a Christian Society* aligns himself with this movement. There are signs of it also in the recent writings of Aldous Huxley. This is all the more surprising in the author of *Point Counterpoint*.

THE CONTEMPORARY REVIVAL OF INTEREST IN MEDIEVAL VALUES

We may well ask ourselves what lies behind these spontaneous developments. The reasons are many, but the major one is easy to understand. The truth of the matter is, as previously noted, that each of the traditional modern attempts to give philosophical expression and meaning to the facts of nature and human experience has led to insoluble difficulties and to inescapable inadequacies. Disillusioned by the modern world, men have turned to the Middle Ages. In short, the contention is that in order to solve modern problems it is necessary to go back to medieval philosophical assumptions.

Other and more specific factors have contributed, especially in the case of President Hutchins and Mortimer Adler. Both are acute students of law. President Hutchins, at least when he was the Dean of the Yale School of Law, was impressed by the "legal realism" which still dominates the thinking of so many of his colleagues. According to this philosophy the norms which legislation defines are to be found by applying the empirical methods of natural science to the facts of existing social practices. This commits, of course, with different content and in a different way, the same culturalistic fallacy of identifying the "ought" for society with the "is" of that society, which occurred in the case of the Hegelians and the Marxians.

Dean Hutchins soon noted, however, as he and his colleagues enthusiastically piled up the empirical social data, that this fallacy was occurring and that the philosophy and method of "legal realism," in which he initially had put so much trust, was actually in practice, whenever it reached a conclusion significant for the law, surreptitiously smuggling in value judgments in the name of science, which its *empirical method applied to social facts* could not give. Instead of being the empirical, scientific, hard-boiled realists which they thought themselves to be, the legal realists were merely fooling themselves and their followers by allowing value judgments, smuggled surreptitiously into the empirical evidence, to determine their legal opinions and prescriptions, all of which they were quick to urge upon the officials in Washington. Never had the application of the empirical method of science to facts, with the crudest of controls and in the briefest spaces of time, given such remarkable results. By the time Dean Hutchins had become President Hutchins of the University of Chicago, he had seen through all this. The philosopher Morris Cohen undoubtedly helped, for in his writings upon legal matters he had continuously pointed out the fallacy in legal realism.

The heart of this fallacy is grasped when one notes that social science is distinguished from natural science by the fact that it is confronted by problems of value as well as problems of fact. This occurs because we ask of society not merely what the facts are but also how we can alter them to produce a more ideal state of affairs.

NORMATIVE VERSUS FACTUAL SOCIAL SCIENCE

Thus it happens that in social science two fundamentally different kinds of scientific theory arise. There are social theories, like those of natural science, which attempt to give a systematic and correct conception of precisely what is, in fact, the case in a given society at a given instant or period of time. Such social theories may be termed "factual social theories." For these factual social theories, the well known empirical and formal methods of natural science applied to social facts, after the manner of the legal realists, are appropriate. Such theories, however, although necessary, are not sufficient. They do not give one the laws with which the lawyer, the judge, and the statesman are concerned. This is the case because the latter laws do not merely record what is in fact the case in society; otherwise there would be no need of passing them and putting police force and financial penalties behind their enforcement. Instead, the laws passed by legislatures and applied by judges are introduced not because they accord with existing social facts but because their aim is to remove or modify certain existent social facts. These considerations make it clear that in social science, and especially in legal social science, social theories different from factual social theories are also present; theories, namely, which set up a specific norm for human and social behavior differing at certain points at least from what is in fact the case in society apart from the introduction and enforcement of this norm. Such social theories are appropriately termed "normative social theories."

It is to be noted that their relation to empirical social facts is precisely the opposite from that of a factual social theory. Since the purpose of a factual social theory is to give one a correct conception of what is in fact the case in society—just as the purpose of a theory in astronomical natural science is to give one a correct conception of precisely how the heavenly bodies do in fact move—a factual social theory, when correctly determined, must correspond to the facts at every point. This is why the empirical and formal method of natural science, of the legal realists, applied to social facts, is the appropriate and correct method for determining factual social theory. For precisely this reason, however, it is only in part the correct method for determining the quite different normative social theory with which lawyers, judges, and statesmen are primarily concerned. By use of a method which tells merely that certain social facts exist as thus conceived, one cannot arrive at a theory which, instead of adjusting itself to these facts, outlaws them and attempts to remove them. Nevertheless, this is precisely what every law passed by a legislature and applied by a judge does.

It is interesting that not merely the student of law President Hutchins, but also the scientific foundations and the public generally, have at last come to the realization that the methods of natural science applied to social facts leave the most vital problems concerning man and his social relations to a considerable extent untouched. By a wise instinct also, President Hutchins, the scientific foundations, and the public generally have sensed the correct method for determining normative social theory. All three individuals or groups have turned recently to philosophy. This is the point of the grant of the Rockefeller Foundation to the American Philosophical Association for the investigation of the place of philosophy in society.

That their instinct is correct all the previous analyses of the cultures of the West have demonstrated. Each one of these cultures as a whole and in its different parts exhibits a normative social theory. It has become clear also that none of these normative social theories arose as a result of a mere description of existent social facts. Had the latter method of the legal realists been pursued in Mexico at the beginning of the nineteenth century, the normative theory at which the Mexicans would have arrived would have been the Spanish Catholic one of the colonial period, since this was the normative theory which the cultural facts in Mexico in 1800, to a considerable extent, embodied. Mexico had its Revolution of 1810 because of the introduction of a new philosophical theory of the nature of man and his universe; the theory, namely, of Voltaire and the French Encyclopaedists. In a similar manner the normative social theory embodied in the Declaration of Independence and the Constitution of the United States was determined in considerable part by the philosophy of John Locke. The manner in which the culture of the Church of England goes back to Richard Hooker and to Aristotle, and in which the culture of communistic Russia rests upon the philosophy of Karl Marx, is equally obvious. Thus analysis of diverse cultures shows that whereas the formal and empirical method of natural science applied to social facts is the correct procedure for determining trustworthy factual social theory, it is the method of philosophy applied to the verified theory not of social science but of human and natural science, to make articulate one's philosophical conception of man and the universe which constitutes the correct method for determining trustworthy normative social theory. This is the reason why a people becomes demoralized in its judgments concerning the value problems of social science when it neglects philosophy which is grounded in natural science.

It is to be emphasized that it is not merely the legal realists who have committed the fallacy of confusing the "ought" for society with the "is," but also most of our contemporary humanists and moral philosophers, who would attempt to find the good for man by studying the humanities. The humanities merely exhibit intuitively how men now behave, or at best they merely embody the *old* traditional normative social theories. All the major demoralization of our time and all of its vital political, moral, religious, aesthetic, and other issues arise from the fact that these old traditional normative social theories which our humanities still convey have turned out to be inadequate either to merit the loyalties of men or to solve the problems of our time. Thus an attempt to take contemporary man out of his present moral confusion by feeding him more of the traditional humanities merely makes his demoralization the more confounded. What is needed—and there will not be any cure for our present troubles until it is provided—is a philosophical articulation of the conception of man and the universe which contemporary empirical knowledge of man and nature entails, and the creation of a new humanism in terms of the new idea of the good which this more adequate scientifically grounded philosophy defines.

It is because President Hutchins, as a result of actually pursuing the method of the legal realists during his deanship in the Yale Law School, became aware of the validity of the scientific method of the legal realists for factual social theory and its inadequacy for normative social theory that his subsequent insistence upon a systematic philosophy relating social science to philosophy and philosophy to natural science and logic, after the manner of Aristotle, arose. We need hardly be surprised therefore that in an address given before the American Bar Association in Chicago, soon after he became the President of the University of Chicago, he attacked the existing theory of law in the major American law schools; and, when pressed for his positive proposal, replied that legal thinkers need an "idea of the good." This shocked his auditors because they did not understand it, due to their failure to distinguish problems of fact from problems of value in the social sciences. As a consequence, it seemed to most of them to be a return to obscurantism. All that Dr. Hutchins was saying, however, was the plain, elementary truth that there are in social science problems of fact with their factual social theories and problems of value with their normative social theories; and that it is with the latter primarily that the lawyer, as opposed to the empirical sociologist, is concerned.

It is to be emphasized that the legal realists did not gain even factual social theory. They were too much concerned with advising the Administration in Washington, and dealing with the inescapable normative social problems of our time which their own methods, had they seriously pursued them, could not have touched. That this is the case is shown by the reaction of the legal realists to the genuinely scientific factual type of social theory of their colleague in the Yale Law School, Underhill Moore. For his laborious, genuinely empirical, and abstractly formal, truly scientific application of the method, which the legal realists talked about but never actually used, the legal realists tend to have only a humorous indifference, charging, with considerable justification, that it does not solve the pressing social problems with which lawyers and social scientists should concern themselves. But what this proves is not that the factual social theory, which is Underhill Moore's sole aim, is not tremendously important even for lawyers, but merely that the legal realists are unable to recognize either the character or the consequences of their own method when it is actually used.

All these considerations do not explain, however, why President Hutchins has tended to identify the required idea of the good for our time with the one defined by Thomistic, Aristotelian philosophy. With respect to this second step the influence of Mortimer Adler was undoubtedly important.

There were, however, other factors. These show themselves clearly in President Hutchins's articles and books upon education. As the president of a university he was forced continuously to make value judgments about the relative worth and attendant financial support to be assigned to different subjects and departments. Was this judgment to be determined largely by the pressure politics of competing departmental chairmen, or was there some more objective principle which would at least introduce some semblance of consistency into what one did? Clearly, such a guiding principle is possible only if there is some way of determining the relation of the subject matter of one department to the subject matters of other departments. Modern philosophy and culture, as they exhibit themselves in the organization of contemporary American universities, do not seem to give any such correlating theory. The departments, after the manner of Kant's faulty conception of moral philosophy, tend to be intellectually autonomous entities, treating each subject matter as if it stood entirely upon its own feet and could be understood apart from its relation to anything else. Perhaps such considerations contributed to President Hutchins's final decision to seek for these interconnecting relations, which would define a consistent guiding principle for educational policy, in the medieval rather than in the modern or postmodern world. In any event, these interconnections do become very vivid when one considers medieval scholastic culture and philosophy; and the use of them at least as a model has had a vital and stimulating influence upon American education, as President Conant of Harvard University has noted, even if it has not captured the minds of even a large minority of American educators as the definitive idea of the good for contemporary cultural institutions and practices.

Another reason exists for considering Roman Catholic culture. There is Russia. Russian culture is determined not merely by the Hegelian philosophy of Marx, but also by that of the traditional Russians. The Russians are a very old people who existed long before the advent of Marx and Lenin. They were steeped, by way of Tolstoy and the other Russian dramatists and novelists, in the moral problems of the Kantian philosophy. One has but to read the autobiography of Trotsky to realize that all the Russian leaders of the communistic revolution were brought up in a Russian culture which was predominantly Kantian and Hegelian in its character. But before they were Kantians and Hegelians they were also medieval Tsarist Russians, absorbed in the intuitive and mystical religion of the Greek Orthodox Church. No amount of dictatorship by the proletariat will ever succeed in removing completely from the nature of the Russian people all these aesthetic and religious influences and sentiments. This Greek orthodoxy, as its name signifies, goes back by way of the Eastern Church at Constantinople, as Roman Catholicism goes back by way of the Western Church at Rome, to the philosophy and the science of the ancient Greeks and to the aesthetic intuitive philosophy of the Orient. Thus it is necessary to understand Aristotle and Plato and the Greek science to which their philosophies gave expression, not merely if we are to understand Roman Catholic culture and the revival of and interest in Aristotle upon the part of acute and competent non-Catholics in the United States, but also if we are to have a comprehension of the full background and nature of Russian culture in its entirety. Current happenings in Russia may be accentuating the importance of this consideration. There are reports and rumors that Stalin in his remarkable rallying of the patriotism and fighting spirit of the Russian people has appealed to the old Russian sentiments and emotions. The more recent lenient attitude toward the

Orthodox Church is another straw in the wind. Nobody outside Russia knows how far these influences have gone or how permanent they may be.

The present orthodox doctrine of the Roman Catholic Church was formulated in the thirteenth century by St. Thomas Aquinas. Taking the scientific conception of the universe and of man which was accepted at that time as it had been formulated technically in the philosophy of Aristotle, St. Thomas identified the objects and doctrines of Christian religious belief with certain items and their hierarchic relations in this Aristotelian universe. To be sure, he also distinguished between the contribution of reason, which Aristotle's science provided and precisely expressed, and the contribution of divine revelation, of which the Church of Rome was the earthly custodian. But even revelation, as we shall see, gave the kind of religious knowledge with which Aristotle had identified the divine, merely presenting it more completely and fully than human reason alone could do. Thus for St. Thomas even revelation itself was defined in Aristotelian terms. Present Roman Catholic doctrine can be best understood, therefore, if one follows the actual course of St. Thomas by beginning with Greek science and its Aristotelian philosophy, and then finding the meaning for the Thomistic, Catholic Christian doctrines within this Greek and medieval scientific view.

THE SCIENCE AND PHILOSOPHY OF ARISTOTLE

The first thing to realize about the science and philosophy of Aristotle is that it specified the conception of nature and man generally accepted by scientists in the later Greek period and throughout the whole medieval world following the coming of the Arabs to Spain. These later Greek, Arab and medieval scientists took for granted the physics and philosophy of Aristotle, precisely in the manner in which modern scientists have accepted the physics of Newton. There were, to be sure, certain scientists during these centuries who accepted the atomic physics of Democritus or the mathematical, geometrical physics of Plato; but up to the time of Kepler these scientists were in the minority. Similarly during the modern era there have been a few scientists, especially in biology, who have been Aristotelian and some, especially in recent times, who are Platonists.

The second thing to realize about Aristotelian science is that it was thoroughly scientific in character. It was excessively inductive. This, in fact, was its final weakness. It reared itself too excessively upon the deliverances of mere observation, description, and classification and was as a consequence, in its laws of motion, misled. It had behind itself a tremendous accumulation of factual evidence. Moreover, this evidence was not restricted to any one branch of science. It covered arithmetic, geometry, physics, astronomy, biology, and psychology.

Nor was the Aristotelian science the first scientific theory of man and the universe at which the Greeks arrived. Democritus—in developing the science of acoustics in an initial form which it still retains—had discovered the atomic theory and formulated a particle physics not unlike that of the Newtonian particle physics which dominated the initial scientific outlook of the modern world. This physics broke down in Greek times because it could not satisfactorily take care of incommensurable magnitudes in mathematics. It was succeeded by the mathematical physics of Plato's scientific Academy. This physics also assumed an atomic theory but conceived of the three-dimensional atoms as having the geometrical shapes of the five regular solids, termed the Platonic bodies, which appear in the thirteenth book of Euclid's *Elements*. This Platonic mathematical conception of nature and man also broke down in Greek times, again for mathematical reasons, because it could not take care of the Greek equivalent of the modern calculus, the method of exhaustion, which was rigorously formulated by Eudoxus, who was a member of Plato's Academy.

This method of exhaustion presupposes for its validity Proposition I of Book X of Euclid's *Elements*. This proposition is necessary in order to prove several of the later propositions of Euclid. It affirms that given *any* two unequal magnitudes, say two lines of different length, it is possible by a specified procedure to remove part of the larger magnitude and thereby arrive at a remainder which is smaller than the lesser of the two original magnitudes. The affirmation seems obvious enough. Nevertheless, as Aristotle points out again and again in his physical and mathematical treatises, this proposition is invalid if either the Democritean or the Platonic science is true. The point is that Proposition I, Book X of Euclid requires for any magnitude whatever, no matter how small it may be, that there be a smaller magnitude. (See T. L. Heath, *The Thirteen Books of Euclid's Elements*, Vol. III, pp. 14–16.) Both the Democritean and the Platonic science, because of the belief in atoms or, as the Greeks termed them, "indivisibles with magnitude," had been forced to affirm smallest magnitudes and thereby to deny Proposition I of Book X of Euclid or its earlier equivalent, thereby becoming incompatible with Eudoxus's method of exhaustion. As Aristotle expressed it, "a view which asserts atomic bodies must needs come into conflict with the mathematical sciences." (*De Caelo*, 303a21. See also *De Caelo*, 306a27 and 271b12, and *De Gen. et Cor.*, 325b25.) Thus it was that the Greek scientists were led to reject the Democritean and the Platonic physical and mathematical theories of the universe and man.

It was the great merit of the science of Aristotle that it met these difficulties while also accounting for everything for which the Democritean and Platonic theories were adequate. At the same time it gave a reasonable solution of certain other scientific problems, particularly those concerning the organization of living organisms. These are the decisive reasons why the later Greek scientists were Aristotelians, and why the Arabian scholars who came into Spain in the tenth century, were convinced Aristotelians also. This point is important, for these scholars were Arabs and Jews and consequently their conclusions cannot be attributed to a desire to support the doctrines of Roman Catholic theology. They were convinced Aristotelians because of the factual evidence from mathematics, physics, biology, astronomy, and psychology, and because of the capacity of the Aristotelian science to account for all this evidence.

In addition to their acceptance of an atomic theory, the Democritean and Platonic Greek scientists whose scientific theories of man and nature were replaced by that of Aristotle held one other doctrine in common. Because the atoms were not immediately observed, Democritus and Plato were led to introduce the exceedingly important distinction, which reappeared at the beginning of modern times with Galilei and Newton, between the world as immediately sensed and the world as designated by the mathematically formulated and experimentally confirmed theories of science.

The importance of this distinction can hardly be overemphasized. It is the origin and the basis of the Platonic and Augustinian Catholic doctrine to the effect that the sensed world is not the real world, and that the sensed self is not the real self but merely the symbol or sign of a more real and immortal self beyond. In fact, it was the Platonic formulation of this distinction between the "sensed world" and the "real world," coming through Plotinus and Augustine, which in considerable part defined the original orthodoxy of the Roman Catholic Church. Thus even the Roman Catholics themselves did not originally hold their present Aristotelian Thomistic doctrine. In fact, when Abélard first proposed it, not only was he vigorously attacked by the Church, but his Aristotelianism was damned as the rankest heresy.

Nevertheless, as the centuries following the coming of the Arabs to Spain passed and European scholars generally, such as Albertus Magnus, became more and more acquainted with the original Greek scientific and philosophical treatises, and were thereby brought face to face with the fact that the Platonic science had broken down in Greek times before indisputable mathematical evidence and had been replaced by the Aristotelian science, even Catholic scientists and theologians and the Church itself were forced to give way to the Aristotelian scientific influence. Thus with St. Thomas, who studied under Albertus Magnus, the meaning of Roman Catholic Christian doctrine was shifted from the science and metaphysics of Plato to the science and metaphysics of Aristotle. Even so, in the Fourth Gospel and in the writings of St. Paul, as well as in the persisting influence of St. Augustine, the distinction between things as sensed and things as scientifically conceived, first introduced by the Democritean and Platonic Greek scientists for purely mathematical and physical reasons, still brings its influence to bear upon the entire thought of Christendom in Protestant as well as Roman Catholic cultures.

ARISTOTELIAN SCIENCE AND THE THEOLOGY OF ST. THOMAS AQUINAS

The reason why the Roman Catholics at the time of Abélard were so shocked by the Aristotelian doctrine is easy to understand. With Aristotle's rejection of the atomic theory, because of its incompatibility with the mathematical method of exhaustion, the reason for the Democritean and Platonic distinction between the sensed world and the more real world of atoms vanished. Thus Aristotle found himself forced to say that the real world is the sensed world, and that there are consequently no ideas in the intellect which are not first given through the senses. Since pre-Aristotelian Christianity had identified the divine, and that to which the divinity of Christ refers, with the unsensed and unseen, scientifically and philosophically postulated factor, which could only be known by means of indirectly verified scientific theory and not by direct observation through the senses alone, this Aristotelian thesis seemed to the churchmen in Abélard's time tantamount to pulling God and Christ's divinity down into the gutter. Accustomed as they were to take the Platonic scientific and philosophical doctrine of the unseen, theoretic component in scientific knowledge as the real and the ultimate, we need hardly wonder that this Aristotelianism shocked them.

Nevertheless, with time, the Church, guided by Albertus Magnus and Thomas Aquinas, saw that the Aristotelian science and philosophy provided, within its more inductive and very empirical epistemology, an equally adequate meaning for the traditional doctrines, and even an element of the eternal, the immortal, and the timeless, sufficient to dignify and save both the perfection of God as well as the immortality of the human soul and the divinity of Christ. Thus, approximately fifty years after his death, Thomas Aquinas was canonized as a saint of the Church, and forthwith and up to this very moment his Aristotelian theology has been the predominant official Roman Catholic orthodoxy.

This historical shift by the Roman Catholics themselves from one orthodoxy to another should give us hope for the much-needed liberalism and progressivism and originality in the immediate future, which the present intellectual state of the world requires. That the present Roman Catholic Aristotelian and Thomistic orthodoxy is as inadequate for the twentieth century as its original Platonic and Augustinian orthodoxy was inadequate in the thirteenth century A.D., has been proved conclusively by the investigations in mathematical physics of Galilei and Newton at the beginning of the modern world and by all the developments in modern physics, biology, mathematics, and mathematical logic since the time of Descartes and Newton. One cannot expect to find a philosophical solution for the inadequacies of the theories of modern philosophy by going back to the medieval Aristotelian and Thomistic science and philosophy, whose breakdown in the sixteenth century brought these modern philosophical theories into existence.

The theories of man and nature to which the scientific experts in the study of man and nature have been led today simply are not those of Aristotle and St. Thomas, scientific though the latter theories were, considering the empirical evidence known at the time they were formulated. Instead the scientific experts' conceptions of nature and man are those of Maxwell and Darwin, Einstein and Mendel, Planck, Schroedinger, and Dirac. *It is in terms of these present experimentally verified scientific theories and an analysis of the relation between sensed and theoretical factors in the scientific method used in their formulation and verification that an adequate philosophy for the culture of our time is to be found.* Just as Eudoxus' rigorous formulation of the method of exhaustion forced Greek scientists and philosophers, and later the Roman Catholic Church itself, on from the scientific philosophy of

Plato and St. Augustine to that of Aristotle and St. Thomas; and just as Galilei's theoretical and experimental analysis of the laws governing the motion of the projectile forced modern scientists and philosophers on from the scientific philosophy of Aristotle and St. Thomas to that of Newton and Locke, so the Michelson-Morley experiment and Planck's study of black-body radiation—together with the unsolved problems, previously noted, to which Locke's philosophy gave rise—force the thinkers of our day on to a new philosophy. This philosophy must be adequate to the totality of present empirical evidence, and do for our time what the Aristotelian science and philosophy of the Thomistic theology did for the final stage of Greek science and the later Middle Ages.

Even so, the Aristotelian and Thomistic, like the Newtonian and Lockean science and philosophy had their merits. It is wise, therefore, for us to examine the Aristotelian science and philosophy in greater detail.

Aristotle's rejection of the atoms of the Democritean and Platonic science forced him to hold a continuous or field theory, rather than a discontinuous or atomic theory, of matter and to identify this continuous matter with the immediately apprehended manifold of stuff given through the senses. Because it was a field or continuous manifold, and because there were no atoms to put an end actually to its division, the requirement of the Eudoxian method of exhaustion, of divisibility without limit, was satisfied.

Greek science in Aristotle's time, like contemporary science in Einstein's theory of the finite universe, also had been led to conceive of the universe as a whole, as being finite in its magnitude and diameter. Thus Aristotelian science affirmed that the continuous field of matter, which —apart from the qualities differentiating it, Aristotle termed "prime matter"—is limited in the dimension of the large and unlimited in the dimension of the small. If one sets this finite extension or diameter of the continuous prime matter of the universe equal to unity, designating it by the natural number one, and then conceives of this unitary magnitude as divided into parts in thought because of its potential divisibility without limit, one then generates the sequence of natural numbers and thereby explains why this sequence has a first number but no last one. Consequently, we find Aristotle saying that magnitude, the finite continuum of immediately apprehended matter, is limited in the dimension of the large and unlimited in the dimension of the small; whereas number, arising from the potentially unlimited division of this magnitude, actually is limited in the dimension of the small, by the initial natural number one, and unlimited in the dimension of the large. (*Physica*, 207b.) Thus Aristotle's capacity to account for the method of exhaustion in geometry, and for the natural number series in arithmetic, was accomplished in an empirically grounded and exceedingly neat manner.

As many historians of mathematics have emphasized, Aristotelian as well as all previous Greek science regarded mathematics as an empirical science. Its two parts were geometry and arithmetic. Geometry was the science of the extension of the immediately sensed empirical world; and arithmetic was the science of the potential divisibility and resultant numerical character of this extension. It was only in the nineteenth century, after modern physics had returned to an atomic theory and thereby forced science to give an entirely new account of the basis and meaning of arithmetically incommensurable magnitudes, that the contemporary conception of mathematics as a deduction from the primitive assumptions of formal logic arose. For Greek and medieval science mathematics was an empirical natural science just like physics, astronomy, and biology. The only difference was, in its Aristotelian formulation, that mathematics was concerned only with prime matter, that is, with the extension and *potential* divisibility of the immediately observed material continuum of nature, with the qualities which differentiate this continuum neglected; whereas physics, astronomy, biology, and psychology are concerned with the immediately sensed continuum and its qualitative differentiations, as given by empirical observation and description and the attendant hierarchic system of scientific classification.

Thus mathematics was the natural science of most complete generality. The next science was physics. Physics was concerned with the elementary constituents of "secondary matter," that is, of qualitatively differentiated prime matter. Greek science, in its observation of different materials, had come to but five, instead of the present ninety-two, elementary chemical materials. These five were earth, air, fire, water, and the ether. They roughly correspond, apart from the ether or cosmic body, to solids, liquids, gases, and fire (which was conceived by all scientists, even modern ones, as a substance, until the investigations of Lavoisier at the end of the eighteenth century). With Plato these five sensed materials were identified with unobserved, postulated atoms having the regular geometrical shapes of the five regular solids of Book XIII of Euclid. Thus the atom of fire, for example, in the Platonic science, had the shape of the tetrahedron, and the atom of earth had that of the cube.

It is an interesting fact that these Platonic regular, solid, geometrical forms do appear in crystallography and in contemporary stereochemistry. In fact, had stereochemistry turned out to be the whole of chemistry, the Platonic science would be the science which we should all be holding at the present moment. When Aristotle was forced, because of the requirements of the method of exhaustion, to reject the theory of atoms, it became necessary to define the four elementary chemical constituents of all things—earth, air, fire, and water—in a different way. The thesis that the real world is the sensed world, and its attendant doctrine that there are no ideas in the intellect and hence no concepts in science which are not given first through the senses, prescribe this way. By fire, for example, we must mean sensed fire; by water, sensed water. Sensed fire is hot and dry. Thus by the chemical element fire, Aristotle meant any portion of the whole field continuum of prime matter of the whole of nature which is sensed as hot and dry. Earth, air, and water were defined in the same way, using one or the other of the two qualities hot and dry, or their negates, or "opposites," wet and cold. The ether was identified with the continuum of prime matter of which earth, air, fire and water were the sensed differentiations.

Thus the theory of chemistry and physics in Aristotelian science was purely descriptive, empirical, and qualitative. One meant by earth, air, fire, and water the qualified bits of the total manifold of nature which one immediately senses. Since all objects in the universe were merely permutations or compounds of earth, air, fire, and water, and since earth, air, fire, and water are defined in terms of prime matter together with the four qualities hot, cold, wet, and dry, Aristotle had a qualitative atomism.

The four basic atomic qualities—hot, cold, wet, and dry—have certain relations to each other. They fall into two pairs: hot-cold, wet-dry. Thus the doctrine of opposites, fundamental in the Aristotelian physics, arose.

This doctrine of opposites played an essential role in the Aristotelian theory of development and fitted in very neatly with other considerations. When one puts one's hand upon a cold window pane one senses the differentiated prime matter as possessing the attribute cold. This immediately sensed attribute of the prime matter Aristotle terms the "positive form." The positive form is a sensed quality which is immediately sensed as the attribute of some portion of the extended prime matter. There is, however, a remarkable thing about our scientific knowledge of this empirical fact. Upon the basis of it we are able to assert not merely one scientifically true proposition but two. We are able to assert not merely, "The window pane is cold," but also, "The window pane is not hot." How is this verification of these two propositions possible in terms of nothing but the empirical sense of coldness?

Again the doctrine of opposites provides the answer. It is the character of any positive form or quality which we immediately sense that it is logically related to its opposite. It is because the immediately sensed qualities or positive forms are not mere bare data, but are logically connected to their opposites by the relation of opposition, that in sensing the window pane to be cold we are also able to assert that the window pane is not hot. To be sure, in another experience we may sense the hot directly as positive form, but in this case we are then able to assert that the object is not cold. In this instance, the cold is given logically rather than by sensation. When a given quality is thus given logically as an opposite of the sensed positive form, it is called by Aristotle "the form by privation." (*Physica*, Bk. I.)

Now it is because of this fact, that there are not merely positive forms but also forms by privation related to them by negation or opposition, that change is possible. To be an actual thing is to possess not merely the positive form which it exhibits at the moment to the senses but also to possess potentially, but not actually, its opposite form by privation. Thus, what happens in becoming is that a potential form by privation, or combination of forms by privation, shifts to the status of positive form, the previous positive forms shifting to the status of forms by privation. Thus the becoming and change and novelty which we immediately sense are real and possible without getting into the difficulty of having them come out of nothing. What happens in change and becoming, which involves novelty, is that qualities which are merely subsistent as mere potentialities in the status of forms by privation become actualized in concrete prime matter as immediately sensed positive forms. Thus, for anything to be, is not merely to possess certain sensed properties but also to have logically within itself the potentiality of becoming something else.

This doctrine of opposites and its attendant doctrine of potentiality and forms by privation has one other exeeedingly important consequence. It is this consequence which saved the dignity and divinity of the Western man's conception of God and Christ in the Thomistic shift from the science and philosophy of Plato to that of Aristotle.

In sensing the coldness of the window pane, we are also getting knowledge that the window pane is not hot. The hotness in this instance is not known as a particular, directly sensed warmth at a given moment and place in space and time, but is known in its purely logical character as a possible predicate. Thus it is known not as a particular but as a logical universal. It is in this thesis that the sensed particulars, because of their capacity to operate as forms by privation, are also universals, potentially present and required to make becoming and the truth of negative propositions possible, that the unique character of an Aristotelian "idea" consists. Aristotelian "forms" or ideas are only given to human knowledge through the senses as particulars. Yet they have, because of their logical character as forms by privation, a universal, immortal meaning and status.

As will be shown later, in the Aristotelian and Thomistic science, philosophy, and theology, the soul of man is identified with the rational form of the living body, and God is identified with the rational form of the universe. Once the logical character of the Aristotelian forms as immortal universals is admitted then the eternity of God's being and the doctrine of the immortality of the human soul follow by definition. All that happens in human death is that the soul of the individual passes from the status of positive form to that of form by privation. Only its material particularity, not its formal individuality, dies.

The general outlines of the Aristotelian science and philosophy and of Thomistic theology are now complete. The remainder consists in little more than working out these basic ideas in terms of more complicated subject matters and situations. It will be worth while, however, because of certain problems which Aristotelian science solved and the acceptance of modern science unsolved, to pursue these additional factors in the Aristotelian system in detail.

The extremely inductive, very descriptive, natural-history approach to science and nature required by the Aristotelians' rejection of the distinction between the sensed and the postulated, had one other consequence. One observes physical objects going to different natural places. Having admitted becoming with real novelty, one is forced to reject the complete determination of the final place by the initial state. Thus, mechanical causation becomes invalid. Even inorganic objects and processes can be understood only teleologically in terms of their final state or goal.

In this manner, even in his physics, Aristotle was led to his fourfold theory of causes. These are the material cause, the efficient cause, the formal cause, and the final cause. The material cause is the sensed thing with its determinate qualities in the initial state. The efficient cause is the activity moving the sensed thing from its initial to its final state. The formal cause is the ordering or organizing relation governing the change and defining the form of the process at the middle stages of its development. The final cause is the final form which the changing thing exhibits or toward which it approximates at the end of the development. But because this final form exhibits characteristics which cannot be deduced from the sensed form of the initial state, it is, in the status of form by privation, an irreducible cause operating from the very beginning of the process and not a mere effect present only at the end. In short, the final form or final cause exists initially as form by privation controlling the direction which the development takes, even though it only exhibits itself actually as positive form at the end of the process and even then only approximately. This is why Aristotle says that the final cause, although it appears last to the senses, is present initially and is first logically. (*De Partibus Animalium*, 639b12.)

In no part of the Aristotelian science does this doctrine of the four causes exhibit itself more pointedly than in biology. Biology was Aristotle's own science. It is not an exaggeration to say that he initiated biology as a science. Before him to be sure there were such men of genius as Hippocrates of Cos. Very important scientific work had been done. Yet most of this work was pursued from the standpoint of the understanding of disease and for the utilitarian purpose of gaining an effective, practical medicine. As the distinguished Scotch physiologist Sir D'Arcy Thompson has said of Aristotle, "There was a wealth of natural history before his time; but it belonged to the farmer, the huntsman, and the fisherman—with something left over (doubtless) for the schoolboy, the idler, and the poet. But Aristotle made it a science, and won a place for it in philosophy."

For twenty years Aristotle had studied in the mathematical Academy of Plato. Following his great teacher's death he left the Academy, undoubtedly convinced of the inadequacy of the Platonic science on mathematical grounds because of the method of exhaustion; and took up the study of the subject in which his boyhood rides with his father, who was a doctor, had undoubtedly interested him. There can be no doubt that in these studies he allowed not merely the living organism but a tremendous number of different kinds of living creatures to speak for themselves. Before anyone falls into the all too prevalent modern error of supposing that Aristotle was a mere armchair thinker, given to fantastic philosophical speculations, he should read Aristotle's *Historia Animalium*. In this work there are, to be sure, errors—errors which, in the light of the accumulation of factual information since the time of Aristotle, may seem somewhat unnecessary and silly. But nevertheless, when the work is read as a whole, what must impress one is not the errors into which Aristotle fell, but the tremendous, diversified, detailed range of his empirical, scientific knowledge. Nowhere in the work is there any reference to his philosophy or to any of the doctrines and technical scientific concepts of his physics. It is a faithful, detailed attempt to accumulate, describe, and classify a wide range of observable, factual information about an exceedingly large number of different living organisms. It is with this classification that modern biology began, when, with Linnaeus, Buffon, Cuvier, the de Jussieu family, and countless others, it continued the natural history description of living creatures which Aristotle had so brilliantly inaugurated. So inductive was Aristotle's approach that an exceedingly large number of the classificatory concepts and distinctions which Aristotle introduced still remain. It is undoubtedly from this scientific method of classification that Aristotle obtained the concepts of genus, species, difference, quality, and accident, which function so significantly as the "predicables" in his logic.

In the *Historia Animalium* one will find also the serial ordering of life, from the simplest forms up through the more and more complicated forms. Nor is there any dogmatic, rigid, cast-iron fixity of types about his classificatory system. Aristotle, from empirical experience, knew very well, for he explicitly states, that any classification in this field, when pressed far enough, breaks down. Certain individual organisms will be found which because of certain observed qualities should go in one class, and because of other qualities should go in another class.

This fact also had a tremendous influence on his philosophy. It led him to the thesis that it is the concrete individual, embodying in itself both the prime matter and the abstract, logical universal which is the real thing. It is this irreducibly concrete individual which Aristotle designates by the term "substance." Thus, substance for Aristotle is not an abstract concept but a term designating the most concrete, individual particularity, involving not merely the stuff or material cause which prime matter contributes and the universal form which the final cause contributes, but also the life history within which the final form becomes more and more actualized in the otherwise raw matter.

Undoubtedly his acquaintance with individual living organisms would have convinced Aristotle of the validity of the doctrine of the four causes even if his knowledge of Greek mathematics and physics had not previously done so. When one passes on from Aristotle's designation of the empirical evidence in the *Historia Animalium* to his *De Partibus Animalium* and his other biological treatises, one finds these scientific and philosophical doctrines of the earlier physics and the later metaphysics coming out of the biological materials and evidence. Here the Aristotelian theory seems to fit the facts in a far more remarkable and convincing way than it did even in the physics. Hippocrates of Cos, before Aristotle, had pointed out the distinctive characteristic of a living organism; namely, its organization. Empedocles, following Democritus, had been forced to conceive of this organization as the mere effect of the motion of the moving atoms. But living organisms, as directly observed, seem to give the lie to this theory. The matter in a living creature is continuously changing with time. Yet we have no difficulty in identifying it as the same individual. This identity has its basis in the form. Moreover, as Hans Driesch, Spemann, and many other experimental biologists have re-emphasized for us, the fertilized egg of the living creature, as it develops and differentiates itself, seems to be controlled by the final type of creature which it eventually produces. Thus, the form as well as the matter and the final form as well as the intermediate form seem to be genuine causal principles and not mere effects.

This fact was explained by the Aristotelian scientific theory of the four causes. The fact that living organisms maintain a formal identity through changes in the matter passing into and out of the formal structure is intelligible if the form of things as well as the raw stuff within them is a causal principle. The fact that living organisms grow, generate, and reproduce themselves provided equal evidence for the validity and importance of the efficient cause. Thus biology, as well as mathematics and physics, added its impressive evidence to the support of the Aristotelian scientific theory.

When Aristotle turns to the study of human beings his philosophy becomes equally effective. Its doctrine of the nature of any individual thing or substance as being the actualization in matter of the potentially present final cause, existing initially in the status of form by privation, enables him to draw a distinction between plants, animals other than men, and those animals which are human beings. All have form, and since Aristotle identifies the word "soul" with "the form of a natural body having life potentially within it" (*De Anima*, 412a20), all living creatures have souls.

There is nothing esoteric about this, since the word "soul" means the final form of the organism conceived as a causal principle determining its growth, development, and characteristics. In his psychology, Aristotle explicitly states that "the study of the soul must fall within the science of Nature" (*De Anima*, 403a28.) Vegetables are organized living material substances in which the final form by privation has become sufficiently actualized in matter to give the resulting concrete individual substance sensitivity to other substances. Animals other than men are concrete substances in which this actualization has gone further to include locomotion. In both plants and animals there is the capacity through sense awareness to know the form of another thing as an immediately sensed particular. In short, what the knowledge of vegetables and animals gives them as a result of their relation to other things in the universe is merely the positive form of those things. What distinguishes human beings from all other animals is that their final form and the final form of other things is sufficiently actualized in them so that they grasp the sensed form of other things in its logical, universal character as form by privation, as well as a mere particular in its status of positive form. It is this ability to grasp the sensed forms of things in their universal, logical character which, according to Aristotle, distinguishes human beings from all other creatures in the universe with the exception of the Unmoved Mover, or God.

It is precisely because of this ability also that science is possible for human beings. For without the forms considered as universals grasped in their logical connection, the universality and generality which every scientific law expresses, extending in its range far beyond the particulars actually observed, would not be possible. The evidence which Aristotle might bring forth in support of this unique distinguishing trait of human beings is the fact that only human beings, not even the most sophisticated chimpanzees, have the capacity to construct scientific theories, and to gather to read papers at scientific meetings. It is this unique capacity of man to grasp his world in terms of scientific law in its aspect of generality as well as a mere, otherwise chaotic aggregation and succession of particulars that Aristotle has in mind when he defines man as a "rational animal." An animal is rational if it has the ability to grasp the form by privation; to grasp the sensed particular in its logical character, as it functions in the expression of general propositions in scientific and philosophical theory.

Aristotle's science and philosophy and their attendant psychology and epistemology have one other merit. They avoid the insoluble epistemological problem to which the physics of Newton and the philosophy of Descartes and Locke led the modern mind, with its distinction between the knower conceived as a mental substance and nature conceived as a collection of material substances or atoms. On the basis of the latter theory it became impossible to understand, as Berkeley, Leibnitz, and Hume made clear, how such a knower could ever have in his mind the knowledge of the form of the material object. On the Aristotelian theory this presents no problem. The material object, like the knowing subject and the intervening medium, joining the two, is a union of matter and form. Before the knower knows the object he has the form of the object in him only as a potentiality. It is the indeterminate prime matter which in part constitutes his nature, together with the notion of form by privation, that makes possible this initial ignorance of the knower combined with the potentiality for knowledge. What happens when the knower knows the table is that, in a completely naturalistic manner, the form of the table becomes actualized first in the form of the intervening medium; and then, by way of the medium, becomes actualized in the form of the material body of the knowing subject. When this occurs the knower has the form of the objective table in him. As only the form of the objective table has come to the knower, and the formed matter of the table still remains in the table, there is a meaning both for the fact that the knower has the form of the table in his mind and that the table exists apart from the knower's knowing of its form. In the Aristotelian psychology and epistemology there is no need for the form of the object to have to jump an impassable metaphysical gulf between the material substance and the mental substance in order to get to the knowing subject. This should help us to appreciate why contemporary Roman Catholics, and other followers of Aristotle, believe that in Aristotle we have the solution of the basic unsolved epistemological problem of modern philosophy. This is no mean merit. It would be fortunate were the Aristotelian science and philosophy as adequate on all other points as they are with respect to this one.

THE ROMAN CATHOLIC CONCEPT OF A PERSON

We are now prepared to note the difference between the Roman Catholic and the traditional modern Protestant theory of the doctrine of soul and body. In the modern Protestant theory based upon Descartes and Locke an individual human person is not, as he is for Aristotle and the Thomistic Roman Catholics, one substance, his body and soul being merely the material and the formal components of this one substance. Instead, according to the modern Protestant theory, the individual human being is an interacting aggregate of a tremendous number of substances, one of which, the mental substance, is his soul, the remaining substances being the many material atoms making up his body. Thus it must be emphasized that when both Catholic and Protestant Christians talk about a human being as having both a body and soul they mean quite different things. It is to be emphasized also that the Catholic or Church of England conception of the human being is very much closer to the Marxian conception than is that of the traditional Protestants. The reason for this is that for the Roman Catholics following Aristotle, the soul is the form and organization and final cause of the body as actually determined by scientific observation and inquiry conducted by means of the senses. There is nothing esoteric about it. Thus a human being for the Roman Catholics, as well as for the Marxians, is a person who, by his very nature, has material, physical needs of a definite, formal, material kind. Nor is an inquiry by scientists which shows human beings as well as other individual substances to be material in character quite the bugaboo and moral horror for the Roman Catholics that it tends to be for the Protestants. For to be a concrete substance on earth is to be composed of a material as well as a formal principle. The soul is the form of the material body. It is not a completely independent mental substance of a purely immaterial kind having nothing to do in its own nature either with the atoms of the body or with the form and organization of the body. For modern Protestant thinkers following Descartes and Locke the form of the body is in no way conditioned by the soul but has its basis solely in the material substances and their mechanical causal laws; the only relation which the soul has to the body and the form of the body is the capacity, by some unexplained means, to became aware of sense data when the material substances of the mechanically determined body act upon it.

The Aristotelian science indicates not merely that every concrete substance has a form, but through its scientific method of classification according to the rule of species being included within the larger classes which are genera, it shows also that the formal and final causes of all individual things fit together organically into a hierarchic unity and pattern. This hierarchic pattern again is nothing esoteric but something quite specific and definite given in the relation joining species to genera in the scientist's observation, description, and classification of all natural objects.

This system of classification specifies that anything, as scientifically known, carries within itself as part of its essential nature not merely the unique form which differentiates it from other specific things, but also the wider generic forms and the entire hierarchic classificatory formal system within which its unique form has a specific place and with respect to which it has a scientifically specifiable organic relation. Thus in the Aristotelian Thomistic theory not only is the concrete individual one substance, whether he be a human being or anything else; but by his scientifically prescribed nature, he also involves in his own being and definition, or "essence," the whole organic, classificatory system of forms of all things in the universe. Thus man alone fully actualizes and satisfies the generic portion of his own essential nature when he participates in the nature of other things, and when, in rational self-consciousness in scientific and philosophical theory, the knowledge of this organic, formal pattern of the whole becomes actualized in him as not merely a potential form by privation but as a positive form. Furthermore, good conduct, or what Aristotle termed "practical wisdom," occurs only when man acts upon the basis of this scientifically verified hierarchical conception of his own nature.

This will occur perfectly and completely, however, only for one who has a complete and perfect scientific knowledge of everything in the universe. No human being possesses this knowledge. By his science and his reason man has found that such a vast organic formal cause of reality as a whole exists; but in his specific, incomplete, human science he has been able to fill in concretely only a portion of its specific content. It is precisely at this point in the Aristotelian system that St. Thomas and his followers are able to express the distinction between reason and revelation completely in Aristotelian scientific terms. It is the function of revelation to make us aware continuously of the existence in perfection of the whole rational system or final cause of nature, which human beings, through science with its reason, know only in part.

REASON AND REVELATION

Just as the final, formal cause of the human being's body is the human being's soul, so the organic pattern of all the final, formal causes of all things, which is the first and final cause of the determinate universe as a whole, may be termed the soul of the universe. This final, formal cause of the whole of reality, within which the final cause of the human being's body is a part, and to which it has the organic, hierarchical relation prescribed by the scientific method of classification is termed by Aristotle "the Unmoved Mover," and it is with the Unmoved Mover of Aristotle's scientifically grounded philosophy that St. Thomas identifies the God the Father of Christian doctrine.

The extent to which the rational principle, or final formal cause, in Aristotle's philosophy has defined the present Thomistic Roman Catholic orthodoxy with respect to (a) the nature of the human soul, (b) the nature of God, and (c) the nature of divine revelation is shown by the following quotations from the recent, very precise and concise exposition of St. Thomas's theology by J. C. Osbourn of the Dominican House of Studies in Washington, D. C.: (a) With respect to the nature of the human soul, Osbourn writes, "According to St. Thomas, man is a substantial composite of body and spirit," adding that, "the central and superior region of man's nature [is] his intellectuality," and that the "divine likeness in man is the term or end [final] cause of the production of man." (b) With respect to the nature of God, Osbourn adds that "the entire human soul informs the whole body and all of its parts just as God is present in the whole universe and all of its parts." Thus God is the final cause of the scientifically discovered order of nature just as man's soul is the final cause of the observed generation and growth of the living human body. (c) With respect to revelation, after indicating that it is with this final cause of things considered in its universal, logical character as form by privation, that intellectuality in God or man is identified, Osbourn adds that "no other conceivably higher perfection than intellectuality has been manifested either by nature or revelation." Thus the final cause or rational principle in Aristotelian science defines not merely the content of human reason and the nature of the human soul and the divine perfection, but also even that divine perfection as it is known by revelation.

Thus, according to contemporary Catholic doctrine, it is quite erroneous to suppose, as do so many Protestant Christians, that by independent, purely religious modes of information and knowledge one knows what the words "soul," "God," "grace," and "revelation" mean. Clearly none of these items is given with self-evident immediacy in experience. It is precisely because this is the case that Christ had to come into the world, the point being that God himself, immediately, in his own nature, is not here. Thus St. Thomas and the Roman Catholics see very clearly that the traditional words of Christian doctrine are by themselves quite meaningless noises unless they are identified, or by the accepted methods of logic, connected with the specific content of scientific knowledge. Thus, what St. Thomas did was to take the conception of man and nature precisely in the form which Greek science, as made philosophically articulate by Aristotle, indicated it to possess, and to identify the traditional words of Christian doctrine such as "soul," "God," "perfection," "grace," and "revelation" with certain factors in this generally accepted and, for its time, scientifically verified theory. Thus there is no justification whatever, even in the doctrine of revelation in Roman Catholicism, for the contemporary, erroneous supposition that the doctrines of the Christian religion and one's moral ideas of perfection can be validated independently of systematically developed philosophical theory that is grounded in the empirical content of our knowledge of man and nature, as this content is specified by the methods of natural science. Again the reader must remind himself that Aristotle explicitly says that even "the soul must fall within the science of Nature."

This becomes even more evident when one examines the Aristotelian and Thomistic conception of God and perfection in more detail. The all-embracing first and final, formal cause, the rational principle of the universe, is called "the Unmoved Mover" because it produces its effect by merely being itself without itself moving. Just as the living organism comes into mature being because it is guided by its final cause, as its aim and pattern, so the universe is created out of otherwise undifferentiated prime matter because reality, composed of both prime matter and the rational principle, which is the Unmoved Mover, is so attracted by the latter principle as its aim and goal that the ideal form of the Unmoved Mover becomes gradually and approximately but never completely actualized in the matter.

The reason for the failure of the material universe perfectly to actualize God, or the rational principle, which is its final cause, is that matter is the source of contingency. The nature of prime matter is to become anything and everything instead of one specific thing, and thereby to oppose the imposition of the final form upon itself. In this irascibility and contingency of prime matter, human evil and the free choice of human beings has its ultimate metaphysical source and basis according to Aristotle. Thus in his metaphysics, which merely states in general terms, applying to all sciences and fields of knowledge, what his previous investigations in the specific sciences had demonstrated independently for each one, Aristotle's philosophy summarizes itself by reducing the original four causes to two, *i.e.* prime matter and the Unmoved Mover. The efficient cause is accounted for by these two, since the attraction of the Unmoved Mover is the source of the activity involved in imposing form upon recalcitrant matter. The formal cause also reduces, because every form of a developing system in the different stages of its development is the effect of the final form acting upon the material component of the substance. The material cause and the final cause enter into a unity also. This unity, because it designates reality to be a materially grounded activity, guided by a final, formal cause, Aristotle terms "entelechy."

By means of this system and the different types of substances which it contains, Aristotle gets a theory of value. Certain of these substances are more perfect than others. There is nothing precious or autonomously moral about this criterion of perfection. No appeal to a practical reason independent of the methods of science is required. A substance is perfect to the extent that it most completely actualizes the final form of itself and all things. Upon this basis vegetables and animals are less perfect than human beings because in the latter the final cause of all things is actualized in its universal, logical character as form by privation in addition to being given to the sense organs merely as a particular, as is the case in plants and animals other than men. Human beings can not merely sense that the window pane is cold but also at the same time assert the proposition that the window pane is not hot. They can also formulate and verify the general propositions of scientific theory. But since the presence of matter in any substance prevents the final cause from being completely actualized, it follows that the only completely perfect substance is one in which there is no matter. The only thing in the universe which has this character is the formal principle of the universe itself. Consequently, Aristotle is entitled to call this soul, or being, the only completely perfect being. Thus, without any reference to morality at all, in the modern Kantian, supposedly autonomous sense of the word, but merely by attention upon the notion of the different degrees of actualization of the final cause which different substances in the universe exemplify, Aristotle is able to arrive at the theological doctrine of the perfection of God's nature by means of nothing but scientific concepts and distinctions—scientific concepts moreover which were derived solely from natural science. In fact, there is not a solitary principle in the Aristotelian philosophy and theology which is not required by and does not appear in Aristotle's physics. Thus Aristotle illustrates the method for solving the problem of the criterion for ethical and normative social judgments which so much perplexes contemporary modern thinkers. He illustrates the solution to this problem offered by Plato in the middle books of the *Republic*.

Plato resolved the relativity of moral judgments which had broken loose in his day in the teachings of the Sophists by locating a criterion for the good which we have a right to say holds for everybody, not varying from man to man, in one's theory of the philosophically true for nature, as arrived at by scientific method applied to the empirical data of nature, and made articulate in the resultant empirically verified philosophical theory of nature. This theory we have a right to say defines an idea of the good which holds for everybody because it states conclusions which anybody can check against empirical evidence; and these conclusions are determined by a scientific method which gives the same result for everybody. Thus with Aristotle, as with Plato, one's idea of the good for culture was identified with one's theory of the scientifically and philosophically true for nature.

This is the reason why Socrates in Plato's *Republic* (533) affirms that "the idea of the good" can be revealed "only to one who is a disciple of the previous sciences," every one of which as previously specified by Socrates was a mathematical natural science. It is the reason also why in *Education at the Crossroads* the contemporary neo-Thomist Jacques Maritain, in his outline of an ideal university curriculum, specifies that the course in the philosophy of natural science must come ahead of the course in moral philosophy and theology. Without a scientifically grounded natural philosophy provided first, the basis and validation of humanistic values which may be said to be confirmed for everybody will not be at hand, and humanistic sophistry and ethical relativism will not be avoided.

It is precisely because this is the correct criterion of the good for personal conduct and normative social science that we are now forced to regard the Thomistic and Aristotelian conception of the Divine and the Good as outmoded and incorrect. The latter conception rests upon a theory of nature and of man which was justified by empirical evidence and scientific method in the medieval period, but which has turned out since then in the face of additional, similarly determined empirical scientific evidence, to be false at certain points to an extent sufficient to invalidate its basic assumptions. Were nature and man what Aristotelian science claims, then certain facts and experimental findings discovered first by Galilei would not be what they are. It is scientific, not moral or religious considerations which force us to reject the Aristotelian.

Thomistic philosophy and theology as the correct and adequate idea of the good to be taken as a model for solving the scientific, philosophical, and cultural problems of our time. Put more concretely, as Galilei shows, were the Aristotelian science correct, projectiles should not move as they do, and Newton's rather than Aristotle's laws of motion should not be empirically valid. Also, the non-Aristotelian basic concepts of mathematics and logic which modern analysis of the fundamental concepts of mathematics has revealed should not be what they are.

THE ROMAN CATHOLIC ATTITUDE TOWARD DEMOCRACY

This attitude has been expressed officially by Pope Leo XIII in his Encyclical, *Immortale Dei*, of 1885.

That fatal and deplorable passion for innovation which was aroused in the sixteenth century, first threw the Christian religion into confusion, and then, by natural sequence, passed on to philosophy, and thence pervaded all ranks of society. From this source, as it were, issued those later maxims of unbridled liberty which, in the midst of the terrible disturbances of the last century, were excogitated and proclaimed as the principles and foundations of that new jurisprudence, previously unknown, which, in many points, is out of harmony, not only with the Christian law, but with the natural law also. Amongst these principles the chief one is that which proclaims that all men, as by race and nature they are alike, are also equal in their life; that each is so far master of himself as in no way to come under the authority of another; that he is free to think on every subject as he likes, and to act as he pleases; that no man has any right to rule over others. In a society founded upon these principles, government is only the will of the people, which, as it is under the power of itself alone, so is alone its own ruler.

That this judgment concerning the Lockean democratic theory of government follows from the Aristotelian Thomistic assumptions can hardly be denied.

In one particular, however, Pope Leo's statement must be qualified. It was not in a "fatal and deplorable passion for innovation," as Pope Leo suggests, that modern political theory had its origin. Instead, inescapable experimental evidence forced Western scientists in the seventeenth century to replace Aristotle's conception of nature as a hierarchic system governed by final causes, with Galilei's and Newton's conception of nature as a system of physical objects governed by mechanical causes. This physics, as we have previously noted, entailed the distinction between mathematical space and time and sensed space and time, thereby repudiating the basic thesis of Aristotelian epistemology which identified the content of nature with sensed nature. This scientific distinction in turn gave rise to the question concerning the relation between the colorless, odorless atoms in postulated, mathematically defined public space and time, and the sensed colors, sounds, and odors in relative, private, sensed space and time. When this relation was suggested by the scientists to be a three-termed relation of appearance in which the observer is the mediating second term between the sense qualities and the material atoms, then the Lockean modern concept of a person as a mental substance became defined. It is upon this modern concept of a person that Locke's, and the traditional modern democratic theory of the state is based, with its novel concept of human equality and freedom. Thus sober scientific and philosophical considerations produced the traditional democratic theory of the good state, just as centuries previously different equally sober scientific and philosophical considerations had produced the Thomistic theory of theology and government. The one is no more the result of a "fatal and deplorable passion for innovation" than was the other.

Moreover, the modern theory was in accord with the physics of Galilei and Newton, which took care of inescapable experimental evidence for which Aristotle's physics and philosophy cannot account. Since the time of Galilei the amount of such evidence in logic, mathematics, chemistry, and biology as well as physics has accumulated. Consequently, it is not by a return to the science and philosophy of Aristotle and the theology of St. Thomas that a solution for the basic scientific, philosophical, and cultural issues of our time is to be found. A science and an attendant philosophy which were shown by factual evidence to be wrong in 1590 are not shown to be right by the fact that the Lockean, Humean, Kantian, and post-Kantian modern philosophies which succeeded them have revealed other inadequacies.

MERITS AND INADEQUACIES

Those brought up in the Protestant modern tradition may wonder what place the Hebrew background of Christianity and Christ Himself have in this exceedingly Greek and Aristotelian Roman Catholic Christianity. Obviously Christ is included, as is also the doctrine of the creation of the universe by God, in Genesis. More than this, the specific texts of other portions of the Old Testament, as well as those of the New, are given explicit, empirical scientific and philosophical content in terms of the Aristotelian philosophy, by St. Thomas. The interested reader will find an excellent, brief indication of precisely how this is done in the previously mentioned article by J. C. Osbourn. Christ Himself, moreover, set against this Aristotelian background, takes on a unifying power and a richness of divinity which He cannot possibly possess if He is stripped of all meaning except that provided by the few statements which modern biblical exegesis leaves in His mouth. The heart of the doctrine of the divinity of Christ is the thesis that Christ has an origin in and a reference beyond Himself to a God the Father who is not merely the creator of the human soul but also the creator of the natural physical universe. If this thesis is to have content and to mean anything this creator, this God the Father, must find identification not merely in the introspective feelings of the individual and the ethical statements of the earthly, historical Christ, but also in the empirically and scientifically and philosophically investigable character of man and nature itself. Only if this is the case can the basic themes of the book of Genesis and the rest of the Old Testament, and the claims of Christ that He represents a divine creative Father other than and greater than Himself, be either meaningful or substantiated. It is precisely this meaningfulness and scientifically grounded, theoretically formulated substantiation which Greek science and philosophy contributed to the Hebrew prophetic religious tradition and to the otherwise merely human and earthly Christ Himself, to constitute Christianity and create the original Western Christian civilization.

The Hebrew tradition alone was not enough to produce a Western Christian civilization, as the cultural products of the religion of the Jews clearly shows. Nor is Christ alone, stripped by modern higher New Testament criticism of all reference to Greek philosophy, sufficient either, as the egocentric, introspective isolation and the aesthetically, socially, and emotionally barren condition in which such Protestantism has left the Christian religion demonstrate, eloquently and tragically. A Christ by himself, stripped of all scientifically and philosophically grounded empirical content in nature and man for his statements, has no power to save either man or society. He represents merely an isolated, historical item in human knowledge or at best a very private, personal, introspective item of experience which, instead of pulling the whole of man's knowledge and experience together into one meaningful whole, thereby saving his life and defining an idea of the good for ordering all the diversified interests of society, merely leaves man with the problem of reconciling this item with the other facts of his knowledge and experience by some other means.

As a consequence, the modern Protestant man, instead of being saved and having his society saved from demoralization by his religion, is merely presented with more items of knowledge which he finds it difficult to reconcile with the other facts of his experience. Thus more and more Protestants have increasingly found their religion and the sustaining of it. more of a worry and a liability and a load of troublesome baggage than an asset in meeting the emotional, the spiritual, the social, and the intellectual difficulties of an already sufficiently disorganized, confused, and demoralized world. The Christ of the medieval Catholic Christian civilization was of no such character. He pulled Western men from the depths of a moral and social confusion and despair perhaps greater than, but not totally unlike, that of the contemporary world; having His referential roots initially in the Greek science and philosophy of Plato, as it was mediated and developed theologically through Plotinus and St. Augustine, He integrated man's empirical knowledge, his emotional and religious intuitions, and the highest and most sober reflections of his intellect into one meaningful and triumphant whole.

It is a tragedy that such a Christianity, both in the Platonic form in which it was expressed by Plotinus and St. Augustine, and in the later Aristotelian mold in which it was embodied by St. Thomas, has broken down. But this is the fact. Even so, the contribution of Roman Catholic culture to the contemporary world is tremendous, for in the scientific and philosophical content of its doctrine, even though outmoded, and the artistry of its ritual it reveals to us what a truly adequate religion of the Western type is like. It makes us aware, quite independently of the breakdown of the traditional modern scientific and philosophical theories at the basis of modern Protestantism, what an intellectually empty, emotionally tepid, morally and socially inadequate, aesthetically blind religion so much of modern Protestant Christianity has become, notwithstanding all its indispensable values with respect to freedom of thought.

This reference to the aesthetic factor in religion and culture calls attention to another remarkable trait in Roman Catholic Christianity. Our exposition of the science and philosophy of Aristotle has forced us into technical and abstract matters. But they are as nothing in comparison with the technicality and dry abstractness of the theology of St. Thomas. This theology in its French edition comprises some nine tremendous volumes. Each one of these volumes is written in a language which is most technical. All terms are carefully and precisely defined by means of the technical terminology of Aristotle's logic. The reasoning moves forward step by step syllogistically and systematically. It has been said that only five men understand Einstein's theory of relativity. Yet Einstein's theory of relativity is simple in comparison with the abstractness, the technicalities, the distinctions, and the ramifications of the theology of St. Thomas. Nevertheless, the Roman Catholic Church, using it rigorously and without compromise, insisting in its orthodoxy on the modification of not even a comma, has captured the devotion and the support of the humbler, the more uneducated and untutored members of society to a degree far surpassing that of modern Protestantism, which, with the hit-and-miss extemporizing of its preachers, has tried unsuccessfully to express the meaning of Christ's divinity, of God, and of the other Christian doctrines in the common-sense language which anybody should be able to understand. One may well ask how this has been possible.

The modern and the Protestant will be inclined to answer that it is by dropping the doctrine in practice and by appealing with idols and by esoteric hocus-pocus to the ignorance and superstitions of men. This is in part true. But it is a truth that does not apply to Roman Catholics alone. The Protestant preacher, in repeating the old Christian doctrines of the immortality of the soul, the divinity of Christ, the Fatherhood of God, and the Trinity, has been even more guilty of the use of hocus-pocus and of idolatry. For hocus-pocus and idolatry consist in using the word and the symbol and repeating and worshipping it instead of referring to and worshipping that which it symbolizes. When modern Protestant preachers utter these traditional Christian doctrines, which they have really inherited from the Roman Catholic, medieval world, and suppose that their statements will take on meaning if they are merely repeated often enough, without going on to develop a theology and an empirically grounded scientific philosophy which gives them content and meaning in terms of present-day knowledge, it is they who are the real idolators. For they are giving us the symbols without specifying anything for them to symbolize. This is idolatry, pure and unadulterated; it is also hocus-pocus. Fortunately, many Protestant thinkers, such as Robert Calhoun and Paul Tillig, now appreciate this, and are returning to a study of philosophy and theology. But even these do not realize that a philosophy and a theology pursued in isolation and out of connection with science (because of the many philosophical and theological theories) are likely to produce confusion and skepticism or an arbitrary dogmatism rather than salvation and faith.

Only a philosophy and a theology which find meaning for their concepts in terms of the specific content of the verified theories of contemporary science, after the manner in which Aristotle and St. Thomas did
this with respect to Greek science, will meet in part the religious and
other cultural needs of our time.

But to suppose that Roman Catholic practices owe their success
completely to an appeal to man's superstitions and his ignorance is to
overlook the relation which exists between the aesthetic symbols of the
church and the theology of St. Thomas Aquinas. Keeping the doctrine
precise, technical, and uncompromising, the leaders of the Roman
Catholic Church have realized that it is impossible to convey this
doctrine literally to the whole of its congregation. For those, however,
who have the capacity and the logical training to grasp the definitions
of the technical terms and to follow the logical course of the argument,
the doctrine is available—and it is clear. The problem then remains of
making the doctrine, or the practical and emotional and religious attitudes which it entails, available as far as is possible to those who cannot
literally comprehend its full, complete, technical meaning. Here again
Plato and Aristotle provided the answer, with their aesthetic theory of
the analogical relation between the sensuous, emotional, aesthetic data
which every mortal immediately experiences and the technical, logical,
rational principles analogous to them, or embodied in them.

Guided by this suggestion, the leaders of the Catholic Church took
vivid, aesthetically and emotionally moving symbols and materials
which even the humblest person can feel and see, and they identified
these vivid materials with certain factors specified by the technical doctrine and moved these symbolic materials about in the ceremonies of the
Church, after the manner in which the technical doctrine prescribes the
symbolized factors to be related. Thus by the means of art, in what
will later be called its second function, the Roman Catholic Church
brought into the experience and emotions and attitudes of the masses
an abstract, technical doctrine which only the most expertly and
logically trained can literally understand. This was done by means of
aesthetic analogy (*e.g.* Plate VII). It is for this reason that Roman
Catholicism provides not only a scientifically and philosophically technical but also an emotionally moving and aesthetically vivid and rich
religion. Dante did the same thing by means of the aesthetic images
and materials of the poet. First he read St. Thomas's *Summa Theologica.*
He then expressed certain portions of the technical meaning of man's
life and his destiny, which this theological work defines precisely, in

terms of vivid ordinary experiences, ordering these earthly human analogies as St. Thomas's doctrine indicated. The result was the *Divine Comedy*.

As President Hutchins has clearly seen, Roman Catholic culture illustrates in terms of Greek and medieval materials, the manner in which the present disorganized and departmentalized portions of human knowledge might be related providing the implications of contemporary science for philosophy and the potentiality of such a scientifically grounded philosophy for theology were thoroughly pursued. It exemplifies how mathematical and natural science, as its facts are made theoretically systematic and articulate, gives rise to philosophy; and how this philosophy, when certain identities are made, gives technical meaning and—since it is scientifically determined—publicly valid empirical justification to the claims of Western religion and morality; and how these in turn and the science and philosophy from which they stem, when applied, then generate the Western arts of poetry, painting, music, sculpture, architecture, and governmental and ecclesiastical polity in their normative character, as well as engineering and technocracy, thereby defining not merely the instruments by means of which ends can be achieved but also the good end itself. In short, Western philosophy, when pursued according to the method of its Greek founders, is natural science made articulate with respect to its basic assumptions on the theoretical side. Conversely, natural science is, with respect to philosophy, the anchor to windward which prevents philosophy from degenerating into idle, futile speculation, and which through philosophy prevents humanism from degenerating into moral relativism and sophistry. Ethics is such a scientifically articulated philosophy taken as the definition of the nature of man and the universe, and thereby usable as a verified criterion of the good for the determination of human conduct and human cultural institutions. Religion is such an idea of the good, such a philosophy accepted with enthusiasm and embodied in one's emotions and one's conduct. The arts, both fine and applied, are, in part but not wholly, as their names signify, the practical means by which the ideal, emotionally accepted, philosophical theory is made actual in every phase of personal and cultural experience in practice.

The tragedy of the modern world with respect to these saving, organizing interconnections between the different portions of human knowledge is that as its initial scientific theories went over into philosophy with John Locke, insuperable problems arose which seemed to make it necessary to set up ethics and religion and many other subjects as independent, autonomous units, thereby leaving man with no basis for relating one part of his knowledge to any other, and inevitably producing not merely the hodge-podge which characterizes the present university graduate's state of mind but also the present demoralization of the purely modern Western cultures. With respect to religion the tragedy is even worse, for as this initial Lockean philosophy and its problems and their successive inadequate solutions appeared, more and more the nature of man and his universe, as thereby revealed, failed to provide the factors and relations necessary to make the claims of the Western theistic religions valid. Thus as Protestantism developed and moved further and further from its initial medieval beginnings into the modern world, its preaching became more and more purely verbal and devoid of meaning in terms of the content of modern science and philosophy which it purported to accept.

But as the previous studies of the successive major cultures and philosophies of the modern world have indicated, all of these modern philosophies have revealed their inadequacy and broken down. Also, modern science itself moved on in the nineteenth century with Faraday and Maxwell, and in the twentieth with Einstein and Planck, to experimentally verified theories of nature quite different from those of Galilei and Newton. Thus it appears that we must leave the modern world; that we have already moved on to a new science; and that quite apart from the inadequacies of the old modern philosophies and their attendant traditional modern cultures this new science requires that we also move on to a new philosophy.

Furthermore, contemporary science, as well as that of Galilei and Newton, requires the distinction between nature as theoretically conceived and nature as immediately sensed. It will be recalled from the consideration of the scientific and philosophical foundations of the culture of the United States, that it was the question of the relation between these sensed and theoretically known factors in knowledge, which constituted the basic problem of modern philosophy and its culture. This problem remains to be solved and must be faced in the sequel. Perhaps when its solution is designated, a scientifically grounded philosophy for our time will be at hand, which after the manner of the Greek founders of Western civilization but in terms of present content, restores the old connection between science and values by way of philosophy, and thereby gives the virtues without the inadequacies and evils of both the Protestant modern and the Roman Catholic medieval worlds.

But more even than this is involved in the issues of our time. We are experiencing world events and not merely local events within Western civilization. This means that before turning to the sketching of the new philosophy which recent developments in the West entail, the culture of the Orient must be examined. With this in view it will be well to look at the basic philosophical theories of the medieval and the modern West in their unity, noting the identities underlying them. For curiously enough, notwithstanding all its inner conflicts Western civilization has a continuous identity and a single predominant meaning.

CHAPTER VIII

THE MEANING OF WESTERN CIVILIZATION

"America is a utopia." This, it will be recalled, is Alfonso Reyes's definition of the meaning of America. Expanding this meaning he writes, "Before being discovered America was presented in the dreams of the poets and in the investigations of the scientists." But these poets and scientists were Europeans. Hence, this must be the meaning of Europe also.

AMERICA IN ITS RELATION TO EUROPE

This utopian urge has exhibited itself in the case of both the Latin and the Anglo-Saxon Americas. Originally these different portions of the Western hemisphere were either uninhabited by man or else the physical basis for the culture of the Indians. Into this naturalistic and Indian world of the continent to the south of the Rio Grande came the conquistadors with their European Roman Catholic religion and their missionaries, bringing with them the traditional Latin hierarchic political and religious forms and the novel utopian ideals of a Las Casas or a Sir Thomas More, obtained by way of St. Thomas, St. Augustine, Aristotle and Plato from the conclusions of Greek science. These or similar ideal visions of a new and more perfect city forthwith became actualized in the Indian social institutions of the religious foundations of Vasco de Quiroga and Las Casas in Mexico and in the first missions to Brazil and the Jesuit Rule (Imperio) of Paraguay. In a similar manner the different religious and political utopia of John Locke, derived from the scientific investigations of Galilei and Newton, became embodied in the duly constituted Republic of the United States. Later, in the nineteenth century, in the Latin Americas, this Lockean utopia, brought by way of France through Voltaire and the Encyclopaedists, caught the imagination of the Jesuit priests and the people, and forthwith crowded out the old medieval, monarchical, and Roman Catholic religious forms of the Spanish colonial period to bring in the democratic revolutions and the attendant nationalization of church property

and secularization of education. This in turn was interrupted temporarily by the actualization, in dictatorial government and the extension
of education in applied science, of the utopia defined by the scientific
positivism of the French social philosopher Comte. Truly the meaning
of the Americas is the embodiment in brick and clay and stone and the
social habits of the people, of previously conceived, essentially European,
scientific philosophical and social ideas.

In every instance these utopian personal and social ideals, after the
manner of Aristotle's Unmoved Mover, by the sheer fascination which
their contemplation creates in the minds of men, have moved things
and men about to constitute what Reyes has aptly termed "the American
exoticism." This American exoticism, he adds, "gives new relish to literature. Different from the Oriental exoticism, which was purely picturesque or aesthetic, this American exoticism carries a meaning political
or moral; it affirms, what the literature hopes to prove with the spectacle
of America, as image proposed *a priori*," or, to use the language of the
Spanish Mexican Edmundo O'Gorman, *"un supuesto a priori,"* a
hypothesis *a priori.*

But the analyses of the cultures of Europe have shown that this also
is true of them. For America existed not merely as a vision but also as
a necessity of the European imagination before it was discovered in fact.
To use again the language of Alfonso Reyes, "America felt itself prom-
inent because of its absence." Moreover, this prominence is not a purely
modern phenomenon of the European imagination. It goes back behind
Marx and Hegel, Hume and Locke, Descartes and Las Casas, St.
Thomas and St. Augustine, and even behind Aristotle, to Plato and
Democritus. Full-born, it shows itself in the vision of the "New Atlantis"
in the *Dialogues* of Plato. Here we find the meaning of Western
civilization, both in its European origin and in its American manifestations, in its roots. From these roots in ancient Greece comes forth first,
negatively, the break from that "purely picturesque or aesthetic" exoticism which, as the sequel will show, is the civilization of the Orient;
and then, positively, that great trunk growing and resuscitating itself
through time to give birth in its different seasons and through its different branches to those varied and diverse utopian fruitions of the Western
scientifically grounded, philosophically articulated, and aesthetically and
institutionally applied images and activities of the human spirit and its
body, which constitute in such great part the content and history of
Western civilization.

Back to these Greek and Platonic roots Samuel Ramos, Edmundo

O'Gorman, Alfonso Reyes, and many of their Mexican colleagues have traced that particular branch and its flowering, of this great trunk, which is the culture of Latin America. Its democratic nineteenth century manifestations return, as has been indicated, through Comte, the French Encyclopaedists, and Voltaire into the main trunk by way of Locke and Descartes. The Spanish and Portuguese colonial elements similarly trace back in major part, by way of Las Casas, through St. Thomas, St. Augustine, and Seneca into their Greek sources, and in lesser part by way of the utopias of Sir Thomas More and other lesser philosophical creators of the ideal for culture to which their reflections upon the actual character of man and nature had led them.

In the Spanish and Portuguese cultures, whether on the European mainland or on the American continent, the importance and persisting influence of Seneca must not be overlooked. Even today Spanish or Portuguese translations of his works hold their place conspicuously in the windows of the bookshops of Cuba, Mexico, the South American countries, and the Iberian peninsula of Europe. It is to be noted that Alfonso Reyes takes from Seneca the title for the book, *Ultima Tule*, in which his general conception of the meaning of America is outlined. The reason is that Seneca revived the study of Greek philosophy in Latin literature and in this revival gave expression anew to Plato's vision of the "New Atlantis," the place where, unhindered by the traditional cultural institutions and practices of the previous outmoded utopias, that fuller, richer, more scientifically adequate philosophical conception of the nature of man and his universe can be given the most perfect expression.

Those branches of Western civilization which are the more purely modern cultures of the United States, France and Great Britain and of post-Kantian Germany and communistic Russia also trace back by the main branch to the early Greek Democritean and Platonic roots. It was because the old medieval conception of this "New Atlantis" broke down with the physics of Galilei and Newton that the new utopia defined by the Newtonian philosophy of John Locke came into existence. It was because this utopia in turn and the Lockean and later Humean philosophy underlying it showed inconsistencies or inadequacies (not merely in practice but before the concepts, facts, and experimentally verified principles of mathematics and mathematical physics) that Kant pursued his investigations, giving rise in turn to inadequacies and difficulties which brought into being the Hegelian and the Marxian ideas of the good for society. Thus, although these modern utopias differ from their medieval and Greek predecessors in content, they are nonetheless mere additional manifestations of the root and basic unique meaning of Western civilization to which Plato initially, and Seneca later, gave expression. Through all the changes the form is the same; only the content is different.

THE CHARACTER OF WESTERN KNOWLEDGE

Confronted with himself and nature, Western man arrives by observation and scientific hypothesis at a theoretical conception of the character of these two factors. This theoretical conception, even when determined by empirically and experimentally controlled scientific methods, always affirms more, as Democritus and Plato were the first to see, than bare facts by themselves provide. In short, scientific theory always asserts more than observation gives, and is not verified directly, as Aristotle and the Humean and modern Positivists supposed, by mere observation; instead, it is a hypothesis proposed *a priori*, verified in part at least indirectly through its experimentally checked deductive consequences. As the contemporary Spanish philosopher Ortega y Gasset has put it, "Physics is a knowledge *a priori*, confirmed by a knowledge *a posteriori*." This *a priori* is, however, as the previous critique of Kant has shown, a hypothetical *a priori*, subject to change in its formal as well as its empirical content; not a categorical and immortally certain *a priori*, even with respect to its formal concepts. Albert Einstein has given expression to the same characterization of Western scientific and philosophical knowledge in the following way:

Since . . . perception only gives information of this external world or of "physical reality" indirectly, we can only grasp the latter by speculative means. It follows from this that our notions of physical reality can never be final. We must always be ready to change these notions—that is to say, the axiomatic substructure of physics—in order to do justice to perceived facts in the most logically perfect way. Actually a glance at the development of physics shows that it has undergone far-reaching changes in the course of time.

Western religious knowledge has precisely this same changing character, as is clearly demonstrated by the shift of Roman Catholic orthodoxy from that of Plato, St. Augustine and William of Champeaux to that of Aristotle, Abélard and St. Thomas, and the reformations and denominations of Protestantism. Christ Himself said, "My Kingdom is not of this world." This being its character, knowledge of it cannot be gained or justified directly by mere factual observation or direct introspection. Similarly St. Paul adds that "the things which are seen are temporal; but the things which are not seen are eternal." Now unseen things cannot be given by observation. They can only be given by a hypothesis, proposed postulationally and *a priori*, and checked only indirectly through its deductively designated, empirical consequences.

An examination of the specific doctrines of the Western Christian religion confirms these statements by Christ and St. Paul. We do not by direct sense awareness or introspection observe as an immediately given datum either the existence of our souls or their immortality. At best such mere direct inspection or observation could give us merely our soul while we are looking; it could not guarantee the belief that this soul will exist immortally for the infinite future. Thus by no stretching of the imagination can the Christian doctrine of the immortality of the soul be justified or guaranteed by mere sensed or introspected inspection.

The doctrine that there is a divine reason which is the creative origin of the universe, the unseen God the Father, is equally obviously not a direct deliverance of bare fact apart from any postulationally proposed hypothesis. The Christian doctrine of the Trinity is even more obviously incapable of justification upon the basis of observation and introspective factual data alone. Like the experimentally verified theories of physics and, as has been made evident in the case of the theology of Aristotle and St. Thomas, because of them, Western religious knowledge, like Western scientific and philosophical knowledge, is only in part factually given, and always involves in addition a hypothesis "proposed *a priori*." It is precisely for this reason that the Western conception of religion, like Western science and philosophy, is subject to reconstruction and alteration in its fundamental premises with time and the appearance of new factual evidence.

It is exceedingly important to understand why the doctrinal content of Western knowledge in philosophy and religion as well as science, has in part this lack of finality and absolute certainty, and the tentativeness—like the railway timetable, "subject to change with further notice"—which Ortega and Einstein have correctly attributed to it. The reason is two-fold. First, as has been noted, Western scientific, philosophical, and religious knowledge always asserts more than immediate apprehension conveys. Thus it is knowledge proposed as a hypothesis and not knowledge fully guaranteed as a bare fact or an accumulation of bare facts, given by mere sense awareness or introspection. Second, this being its character, it can be checked only indirectly through its deductive consequences. Thus we believe our Western scientific, philosophical, and religious theories to be true not because we directly introspect or sense what they assert, but because, assuming them by hypothesis to be true, it follows by logical deduction or mathematical calculation that the empirical facts which are directly sensed or introspected should be what they are. Consequently, when, having scientifically established a given scientific and philosophical theory, such for example as that of Aristotle, and having made its appropriate theological identifications, as with St. Thomas; and when, having deduced from the basic assumptions of this theory certain empirical consequences, which are contrary to the observed or experimentally determined facts; then there is no alternative but to reject the proposed traditional theory, regardless of its ability to account for all other facts and experiences, and to put a new theory in its place.

THE THEORETIC BASIS OF THE REVOLUTIONARY CHARACTER OF WESTERN CIVILIZATION

This reconstruction in theory has happened again and again throughout the entire history of Western civilization. When it has occurred not merely science and philosophy but also religion and all the values and institutions of society have been affected. It is precisely because the utopian ideals of the different stages and branches of Western thought have been identified with these successive scientifically grounded, philosophically articulated hypotheses concerning the nature of man and his universe, proposed *a priori* and verified only indirectly and *a posteriori*, that the culture of Western civilization has had the diversity and the revolutionary reconstructions in time which it exhibits historically.

One other consequence of the character of the method used in gaining Western knowledge, and an attendant cultural manifestation in Western civilization, must be noted. One fact incompatible with the traditional doctrine, such as the method of exhaustion in Greek science, the experimental analysis of the motion of the projectile by Galilei, or the Michelson-Morley experiment at the end of the nineteenth century, is sufficient to demonstrate that the traditional scientific and philosophical doctrine proposed *a priori* and the conception of morality, politics, economics and religion formulated in terms of it, are incorrect, and must be succeeded by a new theory reared on different basic assumptions. A similar certainty is not present, however, if a given Western theory, through its deductive consequences, takes care of all the known facts. This follows because of the indirect method of verification.

The logic of the verification, even when it is empirical and experimental, is as follows: The theory is proposed; logic is applied to its basic assumptions and to their operationally determined empirical content. By means of this application of logic and its more technical instrument, mathematical calculation, the consequences of the theory are deduced. These consequences are then put to the test of ordinary or experimentally controlled observation. Thus it is to be noted and emphasized that it is not the assumptions or postulates of the theory itself, but merely certain of its localized, deduced consequences which are verified in even the most meticulous and quantitatively precise experiment.

Thus the logic of the verification, even when all facts are in accord with the deductive consequences of the theory, is as follows: If the theory is true, then these specified facts follow. The facts are what is specified; therefore, the theory is true. Even the most elementary examination of this argument, which defines the logic of the verification of all doctrines, such as those of Western science, philosophy and religion, which refer to unseen factors, is sufficient to show that it does not give absolute certainty. The mere fact that the proposed theory is confirmed factually in every one of its deductive consequences does not establish the conclusion that it is the only theory which can meet this test. Thus it may very well be the case—and history has in fact often shown it to be the case—that some other theory will also take care of all the known evidence. Furthermore, there is nothing in the method to guarantee that tomorrow some new facts may not arise, with which the proposed theory, when developed logically with respect to its deductive consequences, is incompatible. This also Western history has demonstrated again and again.

These characteristics of the typical scientific, metaphysical, and religious doctrines of the West are tremendously important. They have exceedingly important moral and social implications. They mean that no Westerner is ever entitled to be cocksure about that portion of his moral, religious, and social ideals which refers to or derives its justification from unseen, inferred factors not given with immediacy. Samuel Ramos, Edmundo O'Gorman, and Alfonso Reyes have emphasized, as the preceding analyses of the specific cultures and cultural ideals of the

West have confirmed, that any one of our Western utopias is a hypothesis proposed *a priori*. Any such hypothesis, moreover, is identified in each instance with a specific philosophical theory arrived at by man's observation of and theoretical reflection upon the available facts concerning the natural man and nature, at different stages in the accumulation of empirical knowledge throughout Western history. These philosophical theories defining their attendant utopias are known and confirmed by che indirect scientific and logical methods indicated. Consequently, all the tentativeness and the liability to change with further information which these methods indicate for the hypotheses they confirm, apply to Western personal and social moral, political, and religious ideals also.

Such a conception of the nature of Western moral and religious knowledge is not merely one which is completely adequate for Western moral, religious—and political—needs, but also one which should be welcomed. It is adequate to meet Western needs because all that is required to end the present demoralization is a philosophy specifying the nature of ourselves and the universe, thereby defining the meaning of human existence, which is adequate to the present stage of knowledge of ourselves and this universe. "Sufficient unto the day is the evil thereof." If new facts appear tomorrow, this is a problem with which tomorrow alone can be intelligently or wisely or necessarily concerned. The trouble which constitutes the contemporary demoralization of Western culture is not that there is a present scientifically grounded philosophical theory adequate to all contemporary knowledge which some future discovery might render inadequate; but that we do not know how to relate and thereby give meaning to even contemporary factual knowledge. The immediate need is not for some theory which will remain adequate for all future time but merely for a theory which is adequate to the present accumulation of Western scientific knowledge. Certainly if there were a philosophy integrating twentieth century empirical information with the degree of trustworthiness with which the scientific philosophy of Aristotle gave expression to Greek and medieval scientific knowledge we would have all that any age of philosophical and religious faith of the West in the past has ever had in fact, and we would also possess everything that is immediately needed.

This conception of the character of Western utopias and ideals should also be welcomed. For it means that there is opportunity to improve the conception of the good life and to enlarge and expand and make more comprehensive the sense of values, precisely in the same manner as, and to the degree that, we improve our scientific theories. Were it not for this character of moral and religious as well as mathematical and physical knowledge, the Western idea of progress in the moral and ethical sense of the word would be illusory. It is precisely in the reconstruction and attendant increasing adequacy of the scientifically grounded philosophical theories of the nature of man and the universe, rather than in an inevitable, automatic evolutionary development, that part of the meaning for human freedom and for genuine human progress in the moral, political, and religious as well as in the mechanical and physical sphere has its real basis and its justification. It is in the proposal of imaginatively conceived theoretical hypotheses that we in part have our freedom; and it is in the keeping of them under the control of the methods which science has devised for such indirectly confirmed knowledge that these proposals can merit trust. Similarly, it is in the transition to new possibilities which this procedure entails, these new proposals in turn becoming new utopias for the reconstruction and ideal pattern of society, that the moral progress of Western mankind expressing itself through the historical diversification and sequence of Western cultures has its origin and its exemplification.

It is in this "adventure of ideas," as Alfred Whitehead has so aptly termed it, that the originality, the genius, and the glory of the West consist. Furthermore, it is in the wider freedom of the imagination which this great Western virtue requires for its sustenance and its progressive life, rather than in the restricted and outmoded philosophy of Locke and Hume that the democracy of the future must find its scientific and philosophical foundations. In this philosophically enlarged and comprehensive concept of freedom mankind will have the vision of a "New Atlantis" for the twentieth century in which freedom will be conceived as involving not merely the Lockean political freedom to choose one's own lay and ecclesiastical representatives, and the Marxian economic freedom to have enough to eat, but also the Latin and especially the Spanish psychological freedom of the emotions and the sentiments. This wider concept of freedom is not purely negative; it is instead the positive adventure in achieving a scientifically grounded philosophy adequate to the present accumulated total of factual knowledge and all sides of human nature. Consequently this freedom can justify itself or save itself only if it fills in with content the idea of the good for the twentieth century which it proposes *a priori* and verifies indirectly *a posteriori*. What is this content?

A complete answer to this question would require an examination of the basic concepts and postulates of the several experimentally verified theories of natural science of the time, bringing out as did John Locke the conception of man as observer as well as the concept of nature which it entails. It may be necessary, before the conclusion of the present inquiry, to enter into certain aspects of this very difficult task. Nevertheless, much can be specified already upon the basis of the results of our present analysis. The conclusion will be all the more convincing, comprehensive and trustworthy because it derives not merely from the more technical content of present Western knowledge, but also from what is a common denominator running through practically all of the scientific and philosophical theories which the Western world has proposed in its entire history.

These common elements, as Ortega and Einstein have indicated and this analysis of the nature of Western knowledge has expanded, are two-fold: There is (1) an immediately apprehended factor and (2) an inferred theoretically designated component. Without the latter theoretical factor, Western knowledge in all fields would not have its hypothetically *a priori*, indirectly verified character, subject to change with new information, nor would Western civilization exhibit its sequence and conflict of rival ideologies or utopias. Without the immediately apprehended component, functioning sometimes *a posteriori*, the theoretical hypotheses proposed *a priori* could not be tested empirically with respect to their truth or falsity, and what is equally important, there would be no aesthetically luminous world to apprehend with immediacy. Each factor merits independent examination.

THE AESTHETIC VERSUS THE THEORETIC COMPONENT

The purely empirical component comprises a very much smaller portion of common-sense, scientific, philosophical, and religious knowledge than most people suppose. Much of what many regard as guaranteed as pure fact by direct inspection alone is contributed by the theoretic component in knowledge as an indirectly verified hypothesis added to and combined with pure fact. The lasting importance of Bishop Berkeley consists in his having demonstrated this to be true even of knowledge of a common-sense object, such as a three-dimensional table conceived as existing in public space independently of human awareness of it. He shows that even when one is directly inspecting the impressions correlated with one side of the three-dimensional table, this direct inspection does not by itself give either the back side of that table, which is not directly inspected, its constant right-angled corners, or its public status in a public, external world.

Similarly, the lasting importance of David Hume is not to be found in his purely empirical and positivistic philosophy; this is utterly inadequate to account for Western mathematical, physical, historical or religious knowledge. Hume's importance instead consists in his having demonstrated that even knowledge, not merely of other persons but even of one's own self conceived as a being who exists and persists when one is not inspecting oneself or when one is sleeping, is not guaranteed by purely direct inspection alone, but depends in addition upon a hypothetically proposed, a priori, theoretical component, only indirectly confirmed through its deductive consequences. This is attested by the fact that the concept of a person is different in every scientific, philosophical, political, and religious doctrine. As the previous analyses have indicated, Locke's concept of a person is different from Aristotle's, as the Protestant concept of the soul is different from the Roman Catholic concept. Similarly, Hume's concept of a person is different from that of James or of Freud, as all three are different from that of Berkeley or Descartes or Karl Marx or St. Thomas or Plato or Democritus.

It was Kant, in modern times, who saw, following Berkeley and Hume's demonstrations of the limited amount of human knowledge given with immediacy, that not merely Western knowledge of obviously unobservable scientific objects like atoms and molecules, but even common-sense knowledge of tables and chairs and persisting persons involves the synthesis or combination of the empirical component of knowledge given a posteriori with the theoretical component given a priori. Kant's major mistake was that he conceived of the specific formal content of the latter theoretical portion of knowledge as necessary, and as final. His other error was that he never completely eliminated the preconceived Lockean mental substance or ego from the background of his thinking, as a necessary presupposition for the synthesis of these empirical and theoretical components in any trustworthy knowledge of the Western type. This led him, following Locke, to thrust his transcendental ego outside of nature and the moral life, and to give rise to the dichotomy, in the distinction between the theoretical reason and the practical reason, which the later excesses of Fichte, Hegel, and Marx attempted—without success—to resolve. Kant was right, however, in maintaining that in any instance of complete Western knowledge, whether it be in science or common sense, or, it must be added, even in religion, there is a theoretical factor given by postulation *a priori*, as well as the empirical factor given by observation *a posteriori*. This theoretic component is, however, a hypothetical, not a categorical, *a priori*. It is, however, none the less real and objective because of this fact.

All these considerations enable us then to summarize the situation with respect to the components of present Western scientific philosophy as follows: The nature of things, including both the observer and the observed, is composed of two factors or components, the one given immediately and purely empirically with certainty; the other having existence known with equal certainty, but known as to its specific formal as well as empirical content only hypothetically and postulationally. This second factor is not immediately observed, but is instead theoretically postulated *a priori*, and is only indirectly verified through its deductive consequences. One is thus led to conceive of the nature of things—himself, the object of knowledge other than himself, and the intervening medium—as composed of two ultimate and irreducible components; the one purely empirical and directly inspectable in its character, the other unobservable and designated only by theory proposed *a priori*, and then later given the status of existing when this proposed, *a priori* theory is verified empirically and indirectly through its deductive consequences.

In so far as Western knowledge in any field is based on the purely empirical component in it, it is final and not subject to change with time except as the empirical data alter; and in so far as it is based, as it always is in part, upon the theoretic component, it is not absolutely certain, and with the advent of new evidence, incompatible with the traditional formulation, is subject to change with time. It is because the idea of the good in the Western world has been identified almost exclusively, as the previous discussion has shown, with *the theoretic component*, proposed *a priori*, that Western theories of value in politics, economics, religion, and the arts, and the cultures based upon them, have undergone so many diversifications and reconstructions during the history of the Western world.

The purely empirical, positivistic component must now be considered with respect to its characteristics and nature. As Galilei and Newton noted, it is made up of colors, sounds, odors, flavors, pains, and pleasures and their immediately sensed spatial and temporal relations. These are not the things out of which electrons, electromagnetic fields, or the equations of mathematics are built; instead, they are the materials with which the painter, the musician, the poet, and the epicure work. When these immediately experienced items are conveyed as they are by the artist under certain circumstances, in and for themselves, there is art for its own sake (Plate XI). It is appropriate, therefore, as suggested in Chapter III, to call this purely empirical, positivistic, immediately apprehended *a posteriori* factor in human knowledge *the aesthetic component* in the nature of things. It is not to be concluded from this usage that all art is to be understood solely in terms of this aesthetic component. In fact, traditional Western art involves reference to the inferred factor in things also. This will become clear in the sequel.

Since the other component in things is not immediately experienced or felt, but is known only by means of theory proposed *a priori* and confirmed only indirectly through its deductive consequences, it is equally appropriate, as has been suggested previously, to term it the *theoretic component.* The reader must not conclude from this usage that the *theoretic component* is a mere idea or subjective construct. It is a part of any real thing with precisely the characteristics which the verified theory designates. It is, however, convenient at times to use the expression "theoretic component," especially when referring to knowledge, to designate the theory rather than the component in things which the verified theory designates. We trust that the context in each instance will make clear which usage is intended.

David Hume regarded the empirically given aesthetic component as nothing but the particular sense qualities and the succession of their inspected associations. It will be recalled, however, from Chapter III, that Hume did not arrive at this conclusion empirically. Instead, he came to it deductively as the result of carrying Locke's theory of ideas to its logical consequences. Had he approached the purely empirical component in knowledge directly and empirically he would have obtained, as William James, Henri Bergson, Alfred Whitehead and the gestalt psychologists have indicated, a much more complete description of its nature. For what is immediately apprehended is not merely a disjunctive aggregate of atomic sensa or qualities and their contingent associations, but also the all-embracing aesthetic continuum in which these are local, determinate differentiations. As James noted, it is only in its center that it is differentiated and determinate; at what he termed its periphery, this aesthetic continuum is indeterminate. It seems appropriate, therefore, to designate and describe the aesthetic component in its totality as "the differentiated aesthetic continuum." It is the great achievement of Georgia O'Keeffe in certain of her paintings that she has given us this differentiated aesthetic continuum in its purity with all suggestion of the theoretical component in the nature of things, of which it is the sign, omitted (Plate XI).

This aesthetic component or any part of it has one other characteristic. It must be immediately experienced to be known. Unlike that factor in the nature of things which is designated by theory, the aesthetic component cannot be conveyed syntactically and deductively by the postulational, formalized technique of a Newton or a St. Thomas Aquinas. This is the reason why no amount of verbal description will enable one to convey the sensed color blue to a person born blind. This is also why neither mathematical calculation nor logical deduction can ever take one from the theoretically known number of the wave length for blue in electromagnetic theory to the sensed blue of the differentiated aesthetic continuum. For this reason both components must be regarded as elementary, irreducible the one to the other—and hence ultimate.

This characteristic of being immediately experienced in order to be conveyed or known is precisely what one means by the ineffable. This ineffability of the given, this characteristic of being unknowable to one who has not experienced it, is precisely the trait attributed by the mystic to the character of his peculiar type of knowledge.

It has been usual to suppose that mysticism refers to the purely speculative, and to that type of speculative theory for which there is no specified criterion of verification. This, as subsequent study of the culture of the Orient will show, and as the above designation of the character of the immediately given has indicated, is erroneous. The factor in the nature of things which has the ineffability and the indescribability to one who has not immediately experienced it, upon which the mystic insists, is the immediately apprehended factor—the factor which is not given as a speculative hypothesis confirmed only indirectly.

Moreover, it is this immediate aesthetic component of human nature which gives essential emotional and aesthetic character. This is one of the reasons why the modern Lockean, Galileian, Newtonian, Protestant, Anglo-American West which threw this emotional, aesthetic component of both the natural object and the observing person out of the essential nature of both, to turn it into a mere projected, phantasmic, transitory appearance, has tended to leave the modern Anglo-American man in the state of aesthetical and emotional blankness and starvation which Grant Wood and José Orozco have portrayed.

The situation was aggravated further when Kant went on to put the theoretic component of the self and nature in one compartment, and the equally theoretic component in morality and religion, muddled with the aesthetic component in nature, psychology, and art, in another compartment, with an absolute gulf between the two. Need one wonder that such a disrupted and muddled modern man has been utterly confused morally, and completely incapable of getting himself integrated into a consistent, single, comprehensive human being?

But even in the medieval world the situation was not so much better. For even there the aesthetic component in the nature of things was not revealed to man as a good in itself for its own sake, but tended to be used instead merely as a handmaid or sign of the theoretic component of the nature of things beyond, with which the totality of goodness both in morality and religion tended to be identified. Even with Aristotle it was with the universal logical character of the sensible that the Divine was associated. Thus it is that not until the French Impressionists in the nineteenth century, and until Georgia O'Keeffe in this century, did Western art have an aesthetics which conveyed the aesthetic component in the nature of things for its own sake. Before these two recent developments, the differentiated aesthetic continuum was being used by means of geometrically defined perspective to convey the theoretically conceived, perfectly geometrically proportioned external material object or the doctrinally defined divinity of the Christ-child and His unseen God the Father (Plate XII).

In fact, it is precisely in this use of the aesthetic component in the nature of things to convey the theoretic component that the uniqueness of Western art before the Impressionists consists and that the genius of Western civilization exhibits itself. What the West discovered is the existence of a factor in the nature of things, not immediately apprehended, which only theory can designate, and which only indirect verification through its deductive consequences can confirm or deny. What has happened throughout our history is that the West became so fascinated with this theoretic component and with the quest for a more and more adequate theory of its nature, that it (the West) has tended to turn the equally primary, real, and basic aesthetic component into a mere appearance and a mere handmaid, whose sole value is the conveying of the theoretic component.

The point to be noted here is not that art of this traditional Western type and theoretical knowledge of this Western kind are not the most excellent of art and knowledge of that kind, but merely that they are but one type of art and one type of knowledge. Or, to put the matter positively, there is also the equally important and scientifically, philosophically, and religiously basic, aesthetic component in the nature of things which is genuine knowledge in its own right, quite apart from its usefulness in verifying the theoretically designated knowledge of the theoretic component; and similarly, there is another kind of art which dropping the use of geometrically and hence theoretically defined perspective, restricts itself to the purely given, non-theoretically conceived, differentiated aesthetic continuum in and for itself, and conveys this component in the nature of man and in the nature of all things for its own sake.

THE TWO TYPES OF ART

Elsewhere the present writer has termed these two types of art, art in its first function, and art in its second function. Art in its first function is to be defined as art, such as that exemplified in Georgia O'Keeffe's "Abstraction" (Plate XI), which uses the immediately apprehended aesthetic materials of the differentiated aesthetic continuum to convey those materials and that continuum in and for themselves for their own sake. Art in its second function, on the other hand, by the use of theoretically controlled and defined techniques such as perspective, uses the aesthetic materials and the aesthetic continuum not merely in and for themselves for their own sake, but also analogically and symbolically to convey the theoretic component of the nature of things of which they are the mere correlate or sign.

Most traditional Western art is of this second kind (Plates I, V, VI, VII, XII). As Charles de Tolnay in his recent *History and Technique of Old Master Drawings* has written of Michelangelo: "He postulated the white paper as in itself a kind of matter, into which he penetrates with his lines by successive planes as though working on marble." Similarly, de Tolnay quotes Ghiberti to the effect that "Art must be based on optics, theory of proportion and perspective," and adds that "Leonardo unified the Northern faculty of observation with the Southern conception of art as science." Likewise, A. Hyatt Mayor in *Jefferson's Enjoyment of the Arts* refers to "Jefferson's 'trinity' Bacon, Newton and Locke," and quotes Fiske Kimball as follows: "The inevitable mathematical processes, instead of coming last, came first. He [Jefferson] gave expression to mathematical over graphical methods of deriving his designs." This is the typical art of a Western civilization which grounds its use of the aesthetic component in the scientific principles of the theoretic component. The essential connection between aesthetic values and science is evident.

Even Hume, who attempted to reduce the whole of reality to nothing but the atomic aesthetic qualities and their sensed associations, omitting not merely the theoretic component but even the field character of the aesthetic continuum within which the atomic sensed qualities appear as differentiations, failed to reap the fruits for aesthetics of his own true but partial positivistic insight. For Hume and his followers Bentham, Mill, and Jevons used these aesthetic qualities not for what they can do; namely, provide the materials of pointillist Impressionistic art (Plate X), but for what they cannot do; namely, account for the theoretically designated, mathematically defined, public space and time and their unobserved, scientific objects of mathematical physics. Not until David Prall were the full implications of Hume's philosophy for aesthetics appreciated; and even then Prall's great insight was obscured and confused because he, like Hume, overlooking Newton's distinction between sensed space and time and mathematically defined, postulated space and time, identified the latter with the former, thereby confusing the relatedness of the theoretic component in the nature of things with the quite different, immediately inspected relatedness of the differentiated aesthetic continuum. So far was this confusion carried by Prall that he fell into the error of attempting to define the logical relation of implication in terms of sensed space and time.

Hume, Bentham, Mill and Jevons also used the aesthetic qualities and their introspected relations to define the economic laws governing the movement of prices in the market place. Nowhere does the persistent Western tendency to pursue the theoretic factor in knowledge show itself more pointedly. For although Hume and his positivistic followers deny the existence of the theoretically inferred component in things, affirming only what the senses deliver to exist, they none the less use the latter aesthetic materials not for their own sake but in order to construct mathematical deductively formulated theory in the science of economics. For all their verbal restriction of knowledge to the purely empirical aesthetic component in things, it was the theoretic component which they pursued, and because this theoretic component is always used in the West as a utopia to improve society, they were not artists but moral and political reformers. Thus, it happened that one of the major Western defenders of the portrayal of the purely empirical aesthetic factor in things for its own sake, Théophile Gautier, in the

Preface of his *Mlle de Maupin*, finds no group with less sense for the empirical, emotional aesthetic immediacy of things than the followers of Hume:

> Poor fellows! Their noses are too short to admit of their wearing spectacles, and yet they cannot see the length of their noses.
>
> If an author threw a volume of romance or poetry on their desk, these gentlemen would turn round carelessly in their easy chair, poise it on its hinder legs, and balancing themselves with a capable air, say loftily:— "What purpose does this book serve? How can it be applied for the moralisation and well-being of the poorest and most numerous class? What! not a word of the needs of society, nothing about civilisation and progress? How can a man, instead of making the great synthesis of humanity, and pursuing the regenerating and providential idea through the events of history, how can he write novels and poems which lead to nothing, and do not advance our generation on the path of the future? How can he busy himself with form, and style, and rhyme in the presence of such grave interests? What are style, and rhyme, and form to us? They are of no consequence (poor foxes! they are too sour). Society is suffering, it is a prey to great internal anguish (translate—no one will subscribe to utilitarian journals)."
>
> No, fools, no, ... a book does not make gelatine soup; a novel is not a pair of seamless boots; . . . There are two sorts of utility, and the meaning of the vocable is always a relative one. What is useful for one is not useful for another. You are a cobbler, I am a poet. It is useful to me to have my first verse rhyme with my second. . . . To this you will object that a cobbler is far above a poet, and that people can do without the one better than without the other. Without affecting to disparage the illustrious profession of cobbler, which I honour equally with that of constitutional monarch, I humbly confess that I would rather have my shoe unstitched than my verse badly rhymed, and that I should be more willing to go without boots than without poems. . . . I know that there are some who prefer mills to churches, and bread for the body to that for the soul. To such I have nothing to say. They deserve to be economists in this world and also in the next.
>
> For my own part, may it please these gentlemen, I am one of those to whom superfluity is a necessity—and I like things and persons in an inverse ratio to the services that they render me. I prefer a Chinese vase, strewn with dragons and mandarins, and of no use to me whatever, ... and of my talents the one I esteem the most is my incapacity for guessing logogriphs and charades.

It should be noted, however, that Gautier is restricting himself to art in its first function, which conveys the aesthetic component of things in and for its own sake; and that it is not merely economists, but even artists themselves, who have made this aesthetic component the handmaid of theoretical doctrine. In fact, most of Western art has done this. Consider the artist whom the West has ranked as the first of its poets.

He has Menenius, in *Coriolanus*, say to the citizens who, "in hunger for bread," would revolt:

> I tell you, friends, most charitable care
> Have the patricians of you. For your wants,
> Your suffering in this dearth, you may as well
> Strike at the heaven with your staves as lift them
> Against the Roman state, whose course will on
> The way it takes, cracking ten thousånd curbs
> Of more strong link asunder than can ever
> Appear in your impediment. For the dearth,
> The gods, not the patricians, make it, and
> Your knees to them, not arms, must help. Alack!

Shakespeare is using the artistry of his verse to convey the Aristotelian, medieval, hierarchic conception of the theoretic component in the nature of things, with its doctrine of the Divine right of the Roman patrician rulers. It must be emphasized also with respect to Gautier's ridicule of the utilitarian economists that there is nothing in their economic science which requires that its basic concept of "utility" be restricted to eliminate the aesthetic object in the manner which he has suggested. The Chinese vase is as much an "economic good" as is a jar of mustard or a ton of coal.

Nevertheless, in their actual handling and use of the emotional and aesthetic materials given in the purely empirical component of human knowledge, the modern British empirical philosophers and economists did actually neglect the aesthetic and emotional values, which these empirical materials, pursued in and for themselves for their own sake, provide, and did tend to turn them into mere counters, entering them into theoretical scientific relations, for understanding and computing the course of prices in the market place. Thus the equally important aesthetic values which their purely empirical knowledge could have given modern Western mankind were lost, and the modern Western world fell into the very serious fallacy, to which the Marxians as well as the Anglo-Americans are heirs, of tending to identify the whole of human value with nothing but restrictedly utilitarian economic value. Thereby the traditional modern Anglo-Americans who took Locke and Mill as their philosophical ideal not merely lost an understanding and appreciation of the theoretic component in Western scientific, philosophical, common-sense and religious knowledge, being forced as a consequence into short-sightedly pragmatic, hit-or-miss fumbling and bungling; but also they missed the aesthetic and emotional riches of an art for its own sake and a religion of the emotions as well as the intellect. These the aesthetic component to which Hume restricted human knowledge could have given them. Such has been the tendency of the traditional Western mind to pursue the theoretic component, even when in Hume's, Bentham's and Mill's positivism the purely empirical aesthetic component is asserted to be all that exists.

THE SOURCE OF THE TRADITIONAL CHARACTER OF WESTERN CIVILIZATION

This tendency goes back to the beginning of Western science and philosophy when Parmenides and the physicist Democritus distinguished the sense world from what they termed the real world and branded knowledge of the former as illusory and spurious. It was carried on and consolidated by Plato, when in his famous lecture on the good he identified the idea of the good with the theoretic component given only as idea, and branded the immediately apprehended aesthetic component as a "bastard" kind of knowledge and the principle of evil in man and nature. This doctrine entered into Judaism through Philo and into Christianity through the Fourth Gospel, St. Paul, Plotinus and St. Augustine. Aristotle's restriction of the divine to the rational principle continued this tradition. Galilei and Newton, with their distinction between the sense qualities in relative, apparent sensed space and time and external physical objects in "true, real and mathematical" space and time, follow Democritus. In fact, it is precisely this distinction which, as demonstrated in Chapter III, led to Locke's philosophical foundation of the traditional democratic modern world, and which, because of the contradictions in Locke's philosophy revealed by Berkeley and Hume, gave rise on the one hand to the subsequent inadequate but partially valid philosophical doctrines of Hume, Kant, Fichte, Hegel and Marx, and on the other hand, to the revival of Aristotelian Thomism, thereby creating the ideological issues of the contemporary Western world. Even with the followers of Hume this identification of the good with the scientifically and theoretically formulated continues, since these traditional Anglo-American empiricists measure sound business and political policy by the deductively formulated economic and political science of Jevons and his successors. To realize that, for the most, the good in the West has been identified with the inferred theoretically and scientifically formulated factor in knowledge and that our conception of this factor changes, because of the indirect method of its verification, with the advent of new empirical information, is not merely to grasp the meaning of Western civilization and to understand the revolutionary character of its evolution but also to appreciate the reason for the conflict of utopias which constitutes the ideological problem of our time.

CONTEMPORARY DEVELOPMENTS

Even so, Ortega and Einstein remind us that the theoretic component presupposes the aesthetic component, in its own verification. The previous analysis shows that the one cannot be derived from the other. This suggests that the aesthetic factor is as primary and hence as justified a criterion of trustworthy knowledge and of the good and the divine in culture as is the theoretic component. But this, as the sequel will show, is to affirm the basic insight of the Orient. Thus, it appears that not merely because of the course of world affairs, but even to attain a correct comprehension of its own knowledge and a correct solution of the issues of its own culture, the West must understand the East.

CHAPTER IX

THE TRADITIONAL CULTURE OF THE ORIENT

The traditional culture of the Orient is extremely complex—so much so that many persons would urge that it is a large number of different cultures. The reasons for such an emphasis are evident. The Orient comprises many countries. These countries are separated by the highest of the world's mountain ranges, by vast expanses of land and water, and by great differences of climate. The peoples also, even if they came from a common stem, branched off from this stem countless ages ago. It would be strange indeed if such naturalistic differences did not generate cultural diversities. This they have done. The dominant contemporary religion of Japan, Shintoism, is purely Japanese in origin. Two of the Chinese religions, Taoism and Confucianism, are Chinese in origin. Buddhism and Hinduism arose in India. Mohammedanism came into India and the Pacific Islands from the Middle East. There are other religions, important but less influential, of purely Indian origin. Within each of these religions there are many forms. In Buddhism and Hinduism these forms are so technically and highly developed and so different that at the extremes they seem to Westerners to be almost self-contradictory.

THE UNITY OF ORIENTAL CULTURE

Nevertheless, to specify these facts which distinguish one country or culture from the others is at the same time to indicate the equally evident interconnections and identities which tie them all together to constitute a single civilization of the East. Confucianism and Taoism are religions of Korea and of Japan as well as of China. Buddhism is as influential in China, Korea and Japan as are Confucianism and Taoism. Buddhism and Hinduism occur in India, Ceylon, the Malay Peninsula, and the Southwest Pacific islands. Confucius, for all his originality, continuously insisted that he obtained his wisdom from a laborious study of the ancient classics. Lao-Tzu, the founder of Taoism, went back to the ancient classics also. Moreover, as will be shown, what he found there is precisely what the Buddha found in the ancient classics of the civilization of India. Similarly, the founder of Buddhism claimed no originality, but insisted instead that he was returning a corrupted or overlaid Hinduism to its original source in the poetry of the early Upanishads and the even earlier Vedic hymns. As Franklin Edgerton has written, "Every idea contained in at least the older Upanishads, with almost no exceptions, is not new to the Upanishads but can be found set forth, or at least very clearly foreshadowed, in the older Vedic texts." Thus, to specify the philosophical and religious differences entering into the constitution of the cultures of the East is at the same time to possess inescapable interconnections and identities. It is the unity provided by these essential relations and identities which merges the cultures of the Oriental countries into one traditional culture of the Far East.

This traditional culture is exceedingly old. This turns out also to be a bond of unity. Indian culture both Hindu and Buddhist has its present roots in the Upanishads and the even more ancient songs of the Vedas. Of the antiquity of the Vedas and of their present influence, Surendranath Dasgupta in his *History of Indian Philosophy* writes as follows: "When the Vedas were composed, there was probably no system of writing prevalent in India. But such was the scrupulous zeal of the Brahmins, who got the whole Vedic literature by heart by hearing it from their preceptors, that it has been transmitted most faithfully to us through the course of the last three thousand years or more with little or no interpolations at all." Dasgupta adds that certain scholars have placed their origin as far back as 4000 B.C. The date, however, is unimportant. The significant fact is that "the Vedas were handed down from mouth to mouth from a period of unknown antiquity." Thus even if one goes back to the earliest date at which they may have been set down the "people had come to look upon them not only as very old, but so old that they had, theoretically at least, no beginning in time. . . ."

Confucius and Lao-Tzu, similarly, went back to the most ancient classics and tradition, and in particular to the "Eight Trigrams." The date to which the Chinese tradition attributes the invention of these trigrams is 2852 B.C., when Fu Hsi is supposed to have founded Chinese civilization.

Contemporary Korea is distant from the origins and locus of Confucius, Lao-Tzu, and Buddha, in space as well as in time. Nevertheless, in his beautifully written autobiographical novel *The Grass Roof*,

Younghill Kang, after describing the rather elementary economic conditions of his native Korean village and home as they existed at the opening of the present century, writes as follows:

Our home was not exempt from this miserable dependence upon the elements, but my family did not seem to mind their helpless poverty, since most of them were indulging in the mystical doctrine of Buddhism, or in the classics of Confucius, who always advocated that a man should not be ashamed of coarse food, humble clothing, and modest dwelling, but should only be ashamed of not being cultivated in the perception of beauty. The sage said: "Living on coarse rice and water, with bent arm for pillow, mirth may yet be mine. Ill-gotten wealth and honors are like to floating clouds." A man has no place in society, Confucius teaches, unless he understands aesthetics.

Similarly Marco Pallis, in *Peaks and Lamas*, notes this same appreciation of the aesthetic upon the part of the humblest Tibetan peasant, taught him by his Buddhism, which Confucianism still achieves in present-day China, Korea, and in a momentarily submerged traditional Japan.

Younghill Kang adds:

My grandmother . . . was a true Oriental woman. The quietism of Buddha, the mysterious calm of Taoism, the ethical insight of Confucianism all helped to make her an unusually refined personality. Because of her lonely life . . . and because she was a woman, she was most attracted by the emotional elements of Buddhism. No one else in our house was a Buddhist. My father was a Confucian; my crazy-poet uncle was mostly a Taoist; only my grandmother loved best the stories and sayings of the pitying Buddha. . . .

Similarly, Surendranath Dasgupta writes:

Even at this day all the obligatory duties of the Hindus at birth, marriage, death, etc., are performed according to the old Vedic ritual. The prayers that a Brahmin now says three times a day are the same selections of Vedic verses as were used as prayer verses two or three thousand years ago. A little insight into the life of an ordinary Hindu of the present day will show that the system of image-worship is one that has been grafted upon his life, the regular obligatory duties of which are ordered according to the old Vedic rites. Thus an orthodox Brahmin can dispense with image-worship if he likes, but not so with his daily Vedic prayers or other obligatory ceremonies. Even at this day there are persons who bestow immense sums of money for the performance and teaching of Vedic sacrifices and rituals. Most of the Sanskrit literatures that flourished after the Vedas base upon them their own validity, and appeal to them as authority. Systems of Hindu philosophy not only own their allegiance to the Vedas, but the adherents of each one of them would often quarrel with others and maintain its superiority by trying to prove that it and it alone was the faithful follower of the Vedas and represented correctly their views. The laws which regulate the social, legal, domestic and religious customs and rites of the Hindus even to the present day are said to be but mere systematized memories of old Vedic teachings, and are held to be obligatory on their authority. Even under British administration, in the inheritance of property, adoption, and in such other legal transactions, Hindu Law is followed, and this claims to draw its authority from the Vedas. To enter into details is unnecessary. But suffice it to say that the Vedas, far from being regarded as a dead literature of the past, are still looked upon as the origin and source of almost all literatures except purely secular poetry and drama. Thus in short we may say that in spite of the many changes that time has wrought, the orthodox Hindu life may still be regarded in the main as an adumbration of the Vedic life, which had never ceased to shed its light all through the past.

These ancient, intuitive insights and sentiments exhibit themselves in countless other ways throughout the entire Orient in all the specific, practical activities, family relations, and social institutions of the peoples. Having thus grasped these temporal and religious bonds of unity which merge the diverse cultures of the East into a single civilization of the Orient, thereby permitting approach to each part with an appreciation of its essential connections to the whole, it is now in order to examine the more specific instances of Oriental culture with respect to their concrete content and to determine the specific ancient Oriental doctrines which have to so great an extent made the empirical content what it is.

ITS INTUITIVE AESTHETIC CHARACTER

This content must be experienced to be known. This is true in a certain sense of any culture. But it is true of the East in a unique and much more fundamental way. For the genius of the East is that it has discovered a type of knowledge and has concentrated its attention continuously, as the West has not, upon a portion of the nature of things which can be known only by being experienced. The West, to be sure, begins with experience in the gaining of its type of knowledge and returns to experimentally controlled portions of experience in the confirmation of that knowledge. But the Western type of knowledge tends to be formally and doctrinally expressed in logically developed, scientific and philosophical treatises. The syntactically constructed sentences of these treatises, by the very manner in which they relate the key factors in their subject matter, enable the reader, with but incidental references to items of his imagination or bits of his experience, to comprehend what is designated. Consequently, in the West, although appeals to experience are necessarily present and continuously made by the scientific, philosophic and theological experts who verify and construct its doctrine, nevertheless, providing the reader has an elementary acquaintance with the rules of grammar, and masters the Western technique for understanding things in terms of their verbally designated relations to each other, it is not necessary for the Western reader to squat upon his haunches, like a sage in an Indian forest, immediately apprehending and contemplating what is designated. Being concerned, as the West tends continuously to be, with the factor in the nature of things which is not immediately apprehended, but is instead merely suggested as a possible hypothesis by the immediately apprehended, the Westerner, trusting the reports of his scientific experts, supplemented with the ordinary, immediately apprehended items of his own direct experience, is enabled to a great extent by his books and texts alone to gain the type of knowledge which the West values, and to know the factor in the nature of things which this Western type of knowledge designates.

The Easterner, on the other hand, uses bits of linguistic symbolism, largely denotative, and often purely idiographic in character, to point toward a component in the nature of things which only immediate experience and continued contemplation can convey. This shows itself especially in the symbols of the Chinese language, where each solitary, immediately experienced local particular tends to have its own symbol, this symbol also often having a directly observed form like that of the immediately seen item of direct experience which it denotes. For example, the symbol for man in Chinese is 人, and the early symbol for house is 介. As a consequence, there was no alphabet. This automatically eliminates the logical whole–part relation between one symbol and another that occurs in the linguistic symbolism of the West in which all words are produced by merely putting together in different permutations the small number of symbols constituting the alphabet.

Sentences, furthermore, in Chinese are constructed by setting such purely individual symbols the one after the other in columns in the order in which the items which they denote in immediate experience are associated. Similarly, Chinese painting is often on scrolls which are several yards in length, the immediately apprehended aesthetic items being connected in the sequence in which they occur in the immediate experience of the artist. The need of bringing everything together into a geometrically balanced and theoretically conceived pattern, after the manner of the classic works of the great Western painters, is absent.

Even the written texts of prose writers and poets use a symbolism which is fundamentally merely miniature painting. Each character is literally painted with a brush, and the mastery of the various strokes of this brush, used in constructing the individual Chinese characters of the entire Chinese language, is the first thing which any Chinese painter of landscapes or of any other visual aesthetic materials must acquire. As Chiang Yee has written in his book *Chinese Calligraphy*, "The earliest inventors of handwriting modelled their characters upon actual objects, . . . and although the later forms develop further and further away from direct pictorial representation, it is still possible to trace in them common visual links."

Consequently, instead of beginning, as does a student of painting in a traditional Western art school, with the laborious copying of the three-dimensional, geometrical casts of Greek statues, and then passing on to the three-dimensional living human figure in the nude, to master the use of perspective which the Western postulationally formulated science of geometrical optics has defined, the Oriental painter starts with the elementary brush strokes used in the writing of the countless symbols of the Chinese language. Since these symbols often merely put on paper in an immediately apprehended form certain characteristics of items of direct experience, it is an easy and natural transition for the painter to pass from the mastery of the strokes used in constructing the symbols of the Chinese language to the painting of the richer, more complete, immediately experienced aesthetic materials which these symbols frequently denote and from which, often, they had been abstracted.

It is to be emphasized that in the entire process no knowledge or application of theoretically formulated, scientifically verified, postulationally prescribed theory, either in itself or in its applications, is required. Nor is there necessity for even the common-sense conception of the subject matter which one is painting, as a three-dimensional, external, physical object. In fact, the first thing which the Chinese painter must acquire, aside from the mastery of the brush strokes used in writing the Chinese linguistic symbols, is the capacity to grasp the immediately apprehended aesthetic factors in the immediately experienced, aesthetic continuum in their purity and all alone, without any reference to the postulated three-dimensional, common-sense, external object of which they are the sign. It is precisely this factor which causes the Oriental painter, even after he has mastered his technique, to put his brushes and his easel aside and to go off alone into nature to sit and contemplate it for hours and even days until he grasps it, in its pure, aesthetic immediacy by way of the immediately apprehended aesthetic continuum of which he is a part, from within, instead of as a partially postulated, geometrically proportioned, common-sense external object from without (Plate XIII).

It is this concentration of attention upon the all-embracing, immediately apprehended aesthetic continuum, rather than the direction of thought and of Western art following this thought upon the three-dimensional, postulated, common-sense object in the theoretically conceived, geometrically defined space of the external world, which lies at the basis of Lin Yutang's incisive remark that to an Oriental, a Western painter always seems to have painted the object from the outside, whereas the Oriental paints it with feeling and with identification of the artist with it from within.

That such a difference between Chinese and Western art is possible becomes clear if one realizes two things: first, what we experience directly as pure fact, apart from speculatively constructed, indirectly verified theory, is the differentiated aesthetic continuum, not the external, three-dimensional object or the persisting individual self; second, the Chinese artist, like the Oriental generally, has tended to restrict himself and his conception of the nature of things to the immediately experienced aesthetic continuum and its aesthetic objects in and for themselves for their own sake. As Lin Yutang has written, "Chinese thought . . . always remains on the periphery of the visible world, and this helps a sense of fact which is the foundation of experience and wisdom."

The idiographic symbolism of the Chinese language has one other consequence. Each stroke and character having its own independent, purely denotative, immediately experienced referent, and these strokes and their compounded characters being associated merely as direct experience in a given particular instance happens to associate them, the Chinese language gains a superlative degree of fluidity, a capacity to convey the unique particularity, nuance, and precisely refined richness of the specific, individual experience which probably no other mature language in the world today achieves. This shows itself also in the Chinese psychology. It is doubtful if any other people have such capacity as have the Chinese, having visited, lived with, and immediately experienced the culture and psychological reactions of another people, to put themselves in the intuitive standpoint of that people. A Chinese student, after living a brief period upon the Left Bank in Paris, becomes often more French than the French. In the United States, similarly, he shows a capacity to catch the exact shade of American humor and American slang to a degree which no Englishman, even though he is supposed to speak our language, can ever hope to achieve. But there is more than their linguistic symbolism behind this capacity of the Chinese. It goes back to, and is supported and sustained by, their ancient philosophical and religious intuitions. Unless we of the Occident find in our own immediate experience the factors to which their remarkably denotative philosophical and religious terminology refers, we can never hope, regardless of our information, or our observation, to understand either the Chinese or any other Oriental people.

But this fluidity of the Chinese language carries with it certain consequences. Since the symbols tend to be related merely as the items in the concrete, individual aesthetic experience are associated, the rules of grammar are less definite. Thus Lin Yutang points out that while this type of symbolism results in especially good poetry, it cannot compare with the language of the West in producing excellent prose. The reason is clear, as he has emphasized. In poetry the premium is upon rearing, in the immediately introspected imagination of the reader, with a minimum of symbols, the maximum amount of rich, subtly related, immediately felt aesthetic content. In prose the premium is upon a grammatical and logical ordering of the subject matter. Here the Chinese language, because of its fluidity, is at a disadvantage.

The spoken symbols of the Chinese language have the same immediate aesthetic quality. A Chinese who does not have a good ear can hardly speak his own language. Literally, the words have to be sounded as in choral training in the West. In the Cantonese dialect, for example, a sound which to the untrained English ear would seem to be continuously identical in its different repetitions actually is twelve different sounds, each of which has a unique meaning, depending upon slight differences in pitch or inflection, with which the otherwise similar sounds are uttered. As a consequence, if a person speaking Chinese becomes emotionally excited, thereby throwing his voice into a higher key than that required for the meaning which he desires to convey, he automatically says something having nothing to do with what he intended.

But it is not merely the visual and auditory symbols themselves which have this inseparable, insistently immediate aesthetic content. More important still, the totality of the nature of things which this symbolism denotes throughout almost the entire range of Chinese, and even Oriental knowledge, has this primarily aesthetic character also.

This is the reason why the Oriental, from one end of the East to the other, is continuously telling us that one can never understand what he is saying or writing by merely listening to or studying his spoken statements or published works alone and that one must in addition directly apprehend and experience, and then take time to contemplate, that to which they refer. This is the unique sense and the much deeper sense in which it is true to say that the Orient, to be known, must be immediately experienced.

For a Westerner, however, even this is not enough. One can experience the Orient by going there. Yet after doing this while studying the language for months or even years, it is possible to come away with certain basic, key, inescapable, intuitive impressions, yet possessing not even the slightest comprehension of what these experiences mean. Again and again individual Western religious leaders, with the most kindly and tolerant dispositions, men who are the most generously minded in their valuations of cultures other than their own, have gone to the Orient and especially to India and have come back to say that they found the religion "positively loathsome." These supposed value judgments, while having a certain superficial justification, can arise only in a mind which has no comprehension of what the religion in question has discovered and is proclaiming.

Again and again one meets missionaries, businessmen, and diplomats who have had immediate experiences of the specific empirical content of Oriental culture lasting through a major portion of their lives, who nonetheless come away seeing nothing in the religion and in the practices of the East that they do not regard as having been achieved in greater perfection in the religion and the practices of the West. It can be safely said that whenever this happens, for all the lengthy, immediate experience of the Orient which they have enjoyed, they have nevertheless failed completely to comprehend even the most elementary points concerning what it all means. Correctly to know and to understand the East entails not merely the having of immediate experiences of its concrete cultural forms and practices, but also the viewing of these immediately experienced facts from the Oriental rather than from the Western standpoint. For this, experience alone, essential as it is, is not enough. The basic Oriental premises which have made these experiences what they are, and which have defined the standpoint from which the Orient views them, must also be grasped. Otherwise the Westerner is merely fitting his factual information concerning the East into Western theories and assumptions and evaluating it from his standpoint rather than its own, in a manner which will never enable him to see its virtues or to appreciate its riches.

The premises which define the Orient's standpoint are to be found in its great traditional philosophical and religious classics. As Chiang Yee has written, "The course our painting has followed in China, in contrast with yours in Europe, can only be ascribed to our traditional philosophy." Only if one comes to the concrete empirical content of Oriental culture from the standpoint and by way of these classical Oriental doctrines can he hope to know the East or to discover its unique values.

Paradoxical as it may sound, it is nevertheless true that if one understands the basic theses of the traditional Oriental classics he can experience the East without going there. This seems at first sight to be an exceedingly self-confident Western attitude. A little reflection shows, however, that if the Oriental classics are saying something which is true, then this must be the case. For the immediately apprehended factors of experience to which the Oriental classical texts refer must be immediately apprehended facts, not merely within the experience of the Oriental, but also within the experience of anybody else in the world who takes the trouble, by a direction of his attention, to seek them out. When one has located in his own immediate experience the factors which the traditional Oriental doctrines designate as primary, he should then find himself automatically in the standpoint of the Oriental and able to share the concept of life from the point of view which takes these factors as primary. Just as one places oneself in the viewpoint of the communists by grasping the basic conception of the nature of things defined by the philosophy of Karl Marx, or just as one achieves the outlook of a traditional modern Anglo-American by viewing the nature of things and the meaning of human existence in terms of the doctrine of interacting material and mental substances of the philosophy of John Locke; so one should find oneself in the place of the Oriental when, by examining immediately apprehended experience under the direction of the classical Oriental treatises, one notes those factors in the nature of things which those treatises designate to be primary and ultimate, and then forthwith proceeds to conceive of the meaning and end of human existence from such a point of view.

It will be well to enter upon this undertaking, however, by way of the concrete materials, coming through them inductively and naturally to the traditional Oriental philosophical and religious doctrines. To this end it will be wise, also, to begin with Chinese culture and with but the Confucian factor in it, since the Confucian component stays the nearest to common sense, is the most concrete in its teachings and imagery, and is the nearest of any of the doctrines of the Orient to certain empirical philosophical doctrines and moral teachings of the West.

CONFUCIANISM AND TAOISM

Certain characteristics of the Chinese language call for further consideration. Its signs themselves, whether visual or auditory, are, as has been noted, heavily laden with aesthetic content quite apart from what they denote. In many cases, however, the content of the sign itself, that is, the actual shape of the written symbol, is identical with the immediately sensed character of the factor in experience for which it stands. These traits make the ideas which these symbols convey particulars rather than logical universals, and largely denotative rather than connotative in character.

Certain consequences follow. Not only are the advantages of an alphabet lost, but also there tend to be as many symbols as there are simple and complex impressions. Consequently, the type of knowledge which a philosophy constructed by means of such a language can convey tends necessarily to be one given by a succession of concrete, immediately apprehendable examples and illustrations, the succession of these illustrations having no logical ordering or connection the one with the other. This is the precise character of the writings of Confucius. He ambles along in an informal conversational style with concrete, common-sense examples. There is little of the technical terminology, the formal definitions, or the logically connected reasoning which characterizes practically all of the scientific and philosophical treatises of the West. Moreover, even the common-sense examples are conveyed with aesthetic imagery, the emphasis being upon the immediately apprehended, sensuous impression itself more than upon the external common-sense object of which the aesthetic impression is the sign. Nowhere is there even the suggestion by the aesthetic imagery of a postulated scientific or a doctrinally formulated, theological object. All the indigenously Chinese philosophies, Taoism as well as Confucianism, support this verdict. Even when expounding one of his more abstract teachings concerning the emptiness and yet the profundity of "reason," Lao-Tzu, in the *Tao-Teh-King*, resorts to poetry:

> It will blunt its own sharpness,
> Will its tangles adjust;
> It will dim its own radiance
> And be one with the dust.

This concern with the aesthetic object rather than the external physical object, shows also in the poetry of Li Po:

> I lift my wine-cup to invite the bright moon,
> With my shadow beside me, we have a party of three.

In the *Sayings of Confucius,* this restriction to ordinary common-sense objects and to these in their aesthetic immediacy is even more evident. "There is pleasure," he says, as translated by Lin Yutang, "in lying pillowed against a bent arm after a meal of simple vegetables with a drink of water. On the other hand, to enjoy wealth and power without coming by it through the right means is to me like so many floating clouds." A conversation with Kunghsi Hua proceeded as follows: " 'It doesn't matter,' said Confucius, 'we are just trying to find out what each would like to do.' Then [his friend] replied, 'In late spring, when the new spring dress is made, I would like to go with five or six grown-ups and six or seven children to bathe in the River Ch'i, and after the bath go to enjoy the breeze in the Wuyi woods, and then sing on our way home.' Confucius heaved a deep sigh and said, 'You are the man after my own heart.' "

But it is also with family and wider social conduct that Confucius is concerned, and especially with these in their moral aspects. Nevertheless, even in these matters the approach is step by step from concrete particulars.

The achieving of true knowledge depends upon the investigation of things. When things are investigated, then true knowledge is achieved; when true knowledge is achieved, then the will becomes sincere; when the will is sincere, then the heart is set right (or then the mind sees right); when the heart is set right, then the personal life is cultivated; when the personal life is cultivated, then the family life is regulated; when the family life is regulated, then the national life is orderly; and when the national life is orderly, then there is peace in this world. From the emperor down to the common men, all must regard the cultivation of the personal life as the root or foundation. There is never an orderly upshoot or superstructure when the root or foundation is disorderly. There is never yet a tree whose trunk is slim and slender and whose top branches are thick and heavy. This is called "to know the root or foundation of things." . . . I greatly admire a fellow who goes about the whole day with a well-fed stomach and a vacuous mind. How can one ever do it? I would rather that he play chess, which would seem to me to be better. I have seen people who gather together the whole day and never talk of anything serious among themselves, and who love to play little tricks on people. Marvelous, how can they ever do it! . . . Education begins with poetry, is strengthened through proper conduct and consummated through music. . . . In this matter of rituals or ceremony, rather than be extravagant, be simple. In funeral ceremonies, rather than be perfunctory, it is more important to have the real sentiment of sorrow. . . . If a man loves honesty and does not love study, his shortcoming will be a tendency to spoil or upset things. If a man loves simplicity but does not love study, his shortcoming will be sheer following of routine. If a man loves courage and does not love study, his shortcoming will be unruliness or violence. If a man loves decision of character and does not love study, his shortcoming will be self-will or headstrong belief in himself. . . . The young people should be good sons at home, polite and respectful in society; they should be careful in their conduct and faithful, love the people and associate themselves with the kind people. If after learning all this, they still have energy left, let them read books.

All these practical moral precepts are presented as if they were mere descriptions of what is immediately apprehended to be the case. Very few reasons and no arguments are given for their validity. It is quite clear, however, that a mere description of human conduct might lead to quite different precepts. Thus, while all that has been said concerning the common-sense aesthetically immediate character of the sayings of Confucius remains true, there is in them another factor. This factor is the influence of the ancient classics. Upon the importance of this influence Confucius is emphatic:

The earlier generations were primitive or uncouth people in the matter of ritual and music; the later generations are refined . . . in the matter of ritual and music. But if I were to choose between the two, I would follow the people of the earlier generations. . . . Let us go home! The scholars of our country are brilliant but erratic, but they are anxious to go forward, and have not lost their original simplicity of character. . . . Give me a few more years to finish the study of the *Book of Changes,* then I hope I shall be able to be free from making serious mistakes. . . . I'm not born a wise man. I'm merely one in love with ancient studies and work very hard to learn them. . . . In every hamlet of ten families, there are always some people as honest and faithful as myself, but none who is so devoted to study.

All these quotations, and especially the last one, lie at the basis of a second concrete characteristic of Chinese society. This is its placing of the scholar at the very top of the social scale. Even in this century when one traveled far from a large city, past the smallest of country villages, one would often see, rising out of their midst, one or two tall wooden poles, similar to the telephone poles of the West. Attached to them, however, were no wires. They stood alone in their solitary splendor with no utilitarian purpose. Instead, they testified to the fact that the village had one or two sons who had passed the examinations on their studies of the classics in Peiping. In these examinations the premium was upon the memory, a literally exact repetition of the texts, and an appreciation of them in their felt, aesthetically immediate, vitally moving content. Not only must the person who is to be regarded as the leader in his community have a highly developed perception of beauty, but he must also surpass all others in his study of the classics.

Lin Yutang describes this study, as it was applied to the *Analects* of Confucius himself, as follows:

The abrupt, jumpy style of the *Analects* requires of course some hard thinking on the part of the reader. . . . The full participation of the reader is necessary and the truths must be apprehended by personal insight; the reader must draw upon his own personal experience. . . . Chu Hsi said, "Read the *Analects* first. Just take one or two sections a day. Never mind whether the passage is difficult or easy to understand, or whether it is a profound passage or not. . . . If you don't get the meaning by reading, then use some thinking, and if you don't get the meaning by thinking, then read again. Turn it back and forth and try to get its flavor."

So varied and diversified are the sayings of Confucius that one might suppose there is no ordering principle in his outlook or his life. Confucius asserted the contrary: "I have a system or a central thread that runs through it all." This principle applies to the social as well as the personal life. He called it *li*:

In the art of government, *li* comes first. It is the means by which we establish the forms of worship, enabling the ruler to appear before the spirits of Heaven and Earth at sacrifices on the one hand; and on the other, it is the means by which we establish the forms of intercourse at the court and a sense of piety or respect between the ruler and the ruled. It revives or resuscitates the social and political life from a condition of disgraceful confusion. Therefore *li* is the foundation of government.

When one attempts to determine precisely what this ordering principle in society is and what the single thread is which runs through all the sayings of Confucius, the task is by no means easy. In the actual arrangement of the sayings of Confucius himself in the *Analects*, as these sayings appear in the Chinese texts, there does not seem to be any ordering principle. Much of order of Confucius' remarks has been put there by translators who have taken the Chinese symbols out of the order in which they appear in the manuscripts, and have thrown together those groups referring to similar matters. Moreover, even when this is done the *Analects* of Confucius do not define this guiding principle. Even the later Confucian treatises convey the reports on the great sage's teaching given either by his grandson, Tzu Ssu, or by even later scholars such as Mencius. It is likely also that the portion of the Confucian teaching which seeps down into the sentiments and consciousness of the general populace is the more disconnected influence of the *Analects* rather than the more systematic doctrine.

In even the later Confucian classics the meaning of the unifying element which Confucius affirmed to be present in his exceedingly common-sense and aesthetically vivid philosophy must be approached with extreme care and caution, especially when one is attempting to convey it in the language of the West. It has an unequivocally ethical character. What must be realized, however, is that if we designate this Confucian ethics with the Western ethical terms, there is the danger that we will surreptitiously read into these terms the Western, rather than the Confucian or Oriental, ethical meanings. For this reason, all translations of Oriental texts by Western moral or religious scholars, or even by Chinese who have come under Western philosophical or Christian influences, or who are anxious to commend the Orient to the West by establishing an identity between Oriental and Western doctrines, must be approached with a slight degree of skepticism. The best way to ensure that we get the Chinese rather than the Western meaning is to keep ourselves continuously aware of the character of the Chinese symbolism—the excessively heavy aesthetic content of the symbols themselves as well as of what they denote, and the lesser amount of grammatically rigid lawfulness governing the ordering of the symbols. If one continuously keeps in mind this intuitive, denotative, primarily aesthetic approach to immediate experience, he will not go wrong.

Consider now the Confucian conception of the ordering principle in society. According to the sage's grandson, Tzu Ssu, it involved the establishment of five relationships: (1) between ruler and subject; (2) between father and son; (3) between husband and wife; (4) between the elder and the younger brother; and (5) between friend and friend equally. These five relationships, however, are not upon the same level. Some of them depend on others and cannot be established until the other relations are first achieved. Thus there is a specific hierarchic order defining the unifying relation which joins these five relations to each other. Roughly, this hierarchic order is as follows: There can be no trust in government, no proper relation between sovereign and subject, without a trust of friend in friend. Thus the first of the five relations depends upon the fifth. But there can be no trust of friend in friend unless men are dutiful to their parents. There is no point more important than this for the understanding of Chinese culture, both traditional and contemporary. A proper filial relation in the family is prior to, and the necessary prerequisite for, any wider social organization in the business world or in the government.

So powerful is this conception in Chinese culture that even as late as 1920 most business organizations tended to be family business organizations, and any attempt to found business corporations on the Western model, involving partnership of men from different families, tended to break down. Later analysis of contemporary nationalistic China will show this primacy of the family relation to be at the heart of what is happening. The reason for this primary, crucial, central position of the family in Chinese culture centers in the Chinese belief that cooperation and unity cannot hope to exhibit themselves in the wider relations of man to man in the community, if they are not first achieved in the more intimate and warmly affectionate, biologically and naturalistically grounded unit of the family. Here again a common-sense, this-worldly, emotionally warm, aesthetically intimate immediacy and intuitive realism is defining the idea of the good of the Chinese. As a consequence, they have not expected to find too much social idealism beyond the reaches of the family. They would welcome it if it came, but the tendency has been, in practice at least, to regard it as expecting too much of human nature for anyone to hope that it will be continuously achieved. This attitude is one of the sources of the strength of the Chinese bandits.

Nevertheless, Confucius, and the Chinese following him, had a definite conception of how good government in the community as a whole is to be attained. And throughout their history, considering the character of their feudal sovereigns and the artistic products of their culture and the humane wisdom of their people, they have not fared so badly. This way of achieving the good life in society depended not merely upon the primacy of the relation between father and son with respect to the four other relationships mentioned above, but also upon the means by which the basic filial relation and the four other social relations were to be achieved. These means were three in number: *chih, jen,* and *yung.* In designating them with English words, we must be exceedingly careful. Lin Yutang translates the three Chinese idiographic symbols designating these three means of obtaining the five social relations as "wisdom, compassion, and courage." E. R. Hughes translates them, "knowledge, human-heartedness, and fortitude."

The second of these two virtues, *jen*, is the one to which the most careful attention must be given, not too hastily taking it in its Western meaning. But even the two others of the three means must be grasped in their intuitive Chinese sense. Wisdom or knowledge is treated by Tzu Ssu as follows, as translated by Hughes: "The Master said, 'To love to learn is to be near to having knowledge.'" It must be remembered that this knowledge consisted of a study of the Chinese classics and of Chinese history with an insistent emphasis upon poetry; upon immediately given, common-sense experiences and aesthetic impressions such as those which one finds in the disconnected sayings of the *Analects*. Always, for the Chinese, knowledge and the Chinese ethics which is rooted in this knowledge have to do with warm, vivid, personal experiences filled with aesthetic content, such as the crunching of bamboo sprouts between one's teeth, the enjoyment of the flavor of sharks' fins, or the quiet aesthetic intuition of the fragrance and the flavor of a cup of tea, together with a feeling for and an appreciation of the beauty and the ritual of all the ceremonies associated with the drinking of it.

For the Chinese, the ethical is grounded in the aesthetic. Instead of using the aesthetic as the West tends to do, merely as an instrument for conveying moral teachings the meaning of which has some non-aesthetic, more purely doctrinal source, the Chinese find the meaning for their ethics in the immediately apprehended aesthetic materials themselves. This is why Younghill Kang, in describing his humble Korean home and village, was led to say that Confucius teaches that "a man has no place in society unless he understands aesthetics."

The third of the three Confucian means by which the five relations in the good society are to be achieved has also an emotional aesthetic content given with immediacy. This third means is translated as fortitude or courage. It is not to be conceived, however, as the fortitude or courage of the soldier, least of all as the free will of a Fichte, grounding morality upon the supposedly logical demands of the freedom of the human will. It is instead something immediately apprehended, full of emotional content, at which words can merely hint or point. Thus Tzu Ssu has his grandfather, Confucius, say, "To know the stings of shame is to be near to fortitude."

The second of the three Confucian means for obtaining the good

social life is *jen*. Lin Yutang translates it "compassion," Hughes translates it "human-heartedness." Hughes adds, however, that were the
expression not so clumsy for continued use, it might better be translated "man-to-man-ness."

It is the precise meaning of this word *jen* which is the heart of and
the unifying principle in the entire Confucian philosophy. It has been
noted that all the five relations involved in establishing the good society
rest upon the filial relation in the human family, as basic. But Confucius
teaches that this relation in turn goes back to an immediately felt factor
in the nature of the individual man himself. This factor is *jen* or the
quality of "compassion" or "man-to-man-ness." Thus *jen* is the key to
and prerequisite for everything else.

Now *jen*, this immediately experienced compassion or man-to-man-
ness, is not a mere attitude. Instead, the word *jen*, according to Tzu
Ssu, denotes something in the nature of the natural human being which
is true (*ch'eng*). Thus it must be emphasized that the good for Confucius is cognitive in character. It designates a factor in the nature of
man which is actually there; it is not a mere attitude, even though its
presence and the recognition of that presence give rise to an attitude.

Moreover, this factor actually existing in human nature is in the
universe as a whole as well as in man. It is precisely at this point that
Confucianism fits in with the other Chinese philosophy, Taoism, and
with Buddhism, which have equally captivated the Chinese spirit and
outlook. The Chinese tradition affirms that Confucius visited and con-
sulted Lao-Tzu, the founder of Taoism. Recent scholarship indicates
that this is the result of the Taoists' later attempt to give Lao-Tzu
priority in time with respect to Confucianism, and to connect Confucius
with Taoism. But there would have been no point in doing this unless
both Lao-Tzu and Confucius had a basic doctrine in common. Moreover, according to Confucius' grandson, Tzu Ssu, the second of the
three Confucian means for achieving the good society, namely *jen*, also
defines the "way" or central path. Thus Tzu Ssu says (as translated
by Hughes): "Man-to-man-ness (*jen*) and knowledge (*chih*) are spiritual powers (*te*) inherent in man, and they are the bridge bringing
together the outer and the inner." Hughes adds that the word "bridge"
in the latter translation means literally *tao*, *i.e.* way. Thus, not only are
the basic virtues *jen* and *chih* in Confucianism said by Confucius' own
grandson to be the basic *tao* of Taoism, but the latter reference to the
"bringing together of the outer and the inner" is clearly reminiscent of
the aim of the Taoist and Buddhist landscape painting (Plate XIII).

Thus the connection between the basic factor underlying everything else in Confucianism and the basic insight of Taoism is clear. Therefore, if we are going to grasp correctly what Confucius meant by *jen*, by the compassion or man-to-man-ness in human nature and the universe, which defines the unity running through his entire outlook, we would do well at this point to go back to Taoism, as Confucius himself did—according to the tradition, if not in fact—in the earlier days of his life.

In the seventeenth century A.D., when Taoism captivated the Chinese sentiments and imagination by becoming the state religion, it was accompanied by what is usually referred to as "The Great Period" of Chinese painting. It is to be emphasized that the painting to which Taoism gave rise was not subjective, egocentric, or excessively humanistic in its emphasis. The painters took nature as their subject matter (Plates XIII and XIV). Moreover, as Lin Yutang and Chiang Yee have emphasized, these artists approached nature in a manner different from that of the landscape painters of the West. Before taking up brush and pigments, they went out into nature, and immersed and lost themselves, becoming one with the all-embracing continuum which is nature in its aesthetic immediacy. Approaching nature in this way, in their paintings they portray the aesthetic manifold primarily, and the external three-dimensional objects, which Westerners tend to seek for in these paintings, only incidentally, if at all (Plate XIII). Thereby, the aesthetic immediacy of what the Westerner would term the cloud or mist between the subjective Western painter and his external object receives the same attention as the aesthetic qualities of the external object itself. Thus the immediately apprehended aesthetic manifold, rather than the external objects located in an inferred, postulated public space, external to the observer, is what the Chinese painter is portraying. Since Taoism gave rise to an aesthetic interest of this character it is reasonable to suppose that the factor in the nature of things which Taoism singles out as of primary importance and as real must be aesthetic in character.

A second characteristic of Taoism confirms this conclusion. This characteristic is the mysticism which the Westerner usually attributes to the Taoist doctrine. That it is in a certain sense mystical cannot be denied. But it is a mysticism which is fundamentally empirical, realistic, and positivistic; the mysticism arising out of the ineffability which attaches to anything, such as a color or a sound or the all-embracing aesthetic continuum, which is immediately apprehended. Nevertheless, the immediately apprehended, emotionally moving, aesthetically vivid factor in purely empirical experience which the basic symbol of Taoism, *tao*, is trying to denote, is not an immediately sensed color or flavor or sound. In fact, it is nothing determinate or definite which any adjective referring to a specific quality can designate. It is nonetheless immediately experienced.

Thus the Taoist finds himself in a paradoxical position when he attempts to make men aware of this factor in their immediate experience. It is immediately experienced; yet not being one of the local, specific, sensed qualities such as a determinate color, sound, or fragrance, it cannot be revealed by any specific sense or designated by any specific adjective referring to what is immediately sensed. Nevertheless, one finds it not merely, as Lao-Tzu and Confucius emphasized, with immediacy within the self, but also, as Lao-Tzu emphasized, with equal immediacy in nature. In fact, it is an all-embracing immediacy including both (Plate XIII).

What then can be this *tao*, this all-embracing something given with aesthetic immediacy, yet not given by any specific sense quality alone? Obviously, since it is immediately apprehended, it can be but one thing; namely, the immediately apprehended aesthetic continuum or manifold within which the introspected images associated with the self, or the sensed qualities associated with natural objects other than the self, are mere local differentiations. The Western reader can prepare himself for the understanding of this Taoist aesthetically immediate manifold in the totality of immediate experience if he avoids certain confusions. First, he must not confuse the immediately apprehended aesthetic continuum with the postulated external space of Western science and philosophy. Second, he must not confuse the theoretically given, external object in the postulated external scientific space of the West, with the immediately apprehended sense qualities in the immediately apprehended aesthetic continuum which embraces sensed nature and the introspected self. Between the aesthetically given self and the aesthetically given natural object there is one-ness or identity, as well as difference, due to the fact that the immediately apprehended aesthetic self and the immediately apprehended aesthetic object are not merely different from each other, but also differentiations of the one, all-embracing, immediately apprehended aesthetic continuum. Thus the aesthetic self and the aesthetic object are the one aesthetic continuum. It is only with respect to the relation between the persisting, postulated self known by Eastern common sense and Western scientific and philosophical theory, and the persisting, postulated external object known in the same manner, that a relation of other-ness between the knowing subject and the known object exists. In the aesthetic continuum the blueness of the sky is sensed with the same immediacy and simultaneity as the introspected pain of the observer. What Lao-Tzu and Confucius are saying is that the "true self" is something given with aesthetic immediacy and is not merely a purely local association of atomic sensed or introspected data, but is also the whole aesthetic continuum of the entirety of immediate experience, embracing aesthetic nature as well as aesthetic man. This is why both Lao-Tzu and Confucius say that the true self is not merely in the local human being but also in nature in its aesthetic immediacy.

Another thing which the Westerner must keep in mind if he is to understand Taoism and Confucianism is that the Orientals are more thoroughgoing empiricists than even a Western empiricist such as Hume. What the Chinese and in fact all the Orientals have noted is that one immediately apprehends not merely the specific local association of determinate atomic data of the senses, such as colors, sounds, fragrances, and flavors, but also these in an all-embracing continuum or manifold. This manifold is as much the content of self-consciousness and the content of immediately experienced nature as are the differentiations within it.

It is the one-ness provided by this immediately apprehended aesthetic continuum common to all men and to all aesthetically immediate natural objects, which gives the Confucian and Taoist man his compassionate fellow-feeling for all men, and his man-to-man-ness (jen) with all men. It is this also which Confucius affirmed to be necessary for a proper relation between man and man in the good society; and which Lao-Tzu emphasized and the Taoist and Buddhist artists portrayed in man and nature (Plates XIII and XIV).

Nothing is more foreign to the Chinese psychology or to Confucian and Taoist philosophy and religion than a technical terminology; nor is anything more dangerous, when introduced by a Westerner. Nevertheless, precisely because Western words tend to refer beyond the aesthetically and empirically immediate to the theoretically designated, whereas Chinese terms tend to concentrate attention upon the aesthetically immediate itself, it is necessary, in order to avoid false identifications and confusions, to have different names for these two different things. Let the immediately experienced aesthetic continuum in its totality with all its differentiated, specifically sensed colors, sounds, fragrances, and flavors be called "the differentiated aesthetic continuum" (Plates XI and XIII). The danger inherent in using this technical name for the immediately apprehendable, aesthetically moving, emotionally charged fact which it denotes can be avoided provided one realizes, as the Oriental always insists with respect to his terminology, that its meaning can be grasped only by immediately experiencing and contemplating what it denotes. Thus although the expression, the complex differentiated aesthetic continuum, is technical, what it denotes is charged with emotional content everywhere in nature as well as in man and is aesthetically vivid and emotionally moving. To use the language of contemporary philosophy, it is known only semantically and with immediacy, and not syntactically by means of the postulational technique of grammar and logic.

The complex differentiated aesthetic continuum is ineffable and indescribable and unconveyable to anybody who does not turn away from words and language to experience it and contemplate it with immediacy. It is to be emphasized that this aesthetic continuum is not to be confused with the logically defined mathematical continuum of modern experimental physics in which three-dimensional external common-sense and scientific objects are located. As Newton emphasized, sensed space and time are not to be identified with mathematical space and time. The latter continuum, because it is part of the theoretic component in things, and because it is theoretically designated and verified as to its existence only indirectly, rather than by direct apprehension, has been termed the theoretic continuum, to distinguish it from the immediately apprehended aesthetic continuum.

It must be emphasized also, as Berkeley has taught and the Buddhists in the Orient will affirm, that any object in nature, whether it be a table or a chair or a person of common-sense belief, or a chemical atom, a molecule, or an electron of experimentally verified Western science, is not in its character as an external, theoretically conceived object completely in the aesthetic continuum; only its aesthetic component, not its theoretical component, is there. Neither is the *determinate*, persisting human person, as Hume has shown and the Buddhists reaffirm, in the aesthetic continuum; only the determinate, transitory, successive assosions of sense data are there.

Within the aesthetic continuum there is no distinction between subjective and objective. The aesthetic continuum is a single all-embracing continuity. Moreover, the aesthetic person or self, like the aesthetic natural object, is the all-embracing aesthetic continuum plus the local introspected differentiations which distinguish the self from any other aesthetic natural object. Furthermore, the same all-embracing aesthetic continuum which is an essential part of the self is also an essential part of the aesthetic object. Thus with respect to the field portion of his immediately apprehended aesthetic nature, the person is identical with the aesthetic natural object; only with respect to his differentiations is the self other than the aesthetic natural object. This is the point of the Taoist and Cha'n Buddhist landscape paintings in which the sage is shown immersed in the naturalistic aesthetic manifold (Plate XIII).

Conversely, since the aesthetic continuum is the aesthetic object of nature as much as are the qualities of that aesthetic object, it follows that the aesthetic object is also, through the aesthetic continuum, or the field portion of itself, in the aesthetically given person or observer. It is necessary, therefore, merely to view another person or natural object from the standpoint of the indeterminate aesthetic continuum common to both the observer and the object, in order to grasp the immediately apprehended root meaning of the *tao* or way in Taoism, and of the man-to-man-ness, creature-to-creature-ness, compassionate "central path" or "central harmony" of Confucianism. At the same time one understands what the Chinese means when he says that his painters "become bamboo" and paint the aesthetic object from within.

What Taoism did was to pursue this all-embracing, immediately experienced, aesthetically vivid, emotionally moving aesthetic continuum with respect to its manifestations in the differentiated sensed qualities of immediately apprehended objects in nature. What Confucianism did was to pursue the all-embracing aesthetic continuum with respect to its manifestations in human nature and its moral implications for human society. The Taoist claim is that only if man and the artist conceive of the empirically given objects of nature, as constituted of the immediately experienced, emotionally moving, all-embracing aesthetic continuum common to all things and all persons; and only if one takes the aesthetic continuity in its all-embracing-ness as ultimate and irreducible, will one properly comprehend the meaning of the universe or properly understand nature, or properly appreciate the message and the significance of art. The Confucian claim, similarly, is that only if one takes the same standpoint, recognizing this all-embracing aesthetic manifold to be an ultimate and irreducible part of man's nature, will man have the compassionate feeling in himself for human beings other than himself which is necessary to build correct relations within the family and, through them, a good order in the state.

Once these considerations are grasped, it should become evident that for the Orient, art is not a mere handmaid of ethics or religion; but is instead the sole source and fountainhead, the conveyer in its own right and for its own sake, of the aesthetic materials apart from which the claims of both Oriental morality and Oriental religion would be empty and meaningless. As Chiang Yee, indicating the relation between religion and painting for the Chinese, has written, "religion [in the sense of something *sui generis*] has never been a natural instinct with us as it seems to have been with most other nations of the world." It is because art is the sole means of conveying the immediately apprehendable, the ineffability of sounds, colors, fragrances, and feelings, and because art is the best means of directing man's attention to the aesthetic component in the nature of things with which the good and the divine in the Orient are identified, that aesthetics is of the essence of the moral and religious life for the Taoist and the Confucianist Chinese.

It will help tremendously in appreciation of this standpoint and in future consideration of the Buddhist element in Chinese culture if two factors are distinguished within the complex differentiated aesthetic continuum. These two factors have already made themselves evident. One is the all-embracing, immediately apprehended unity and continuity apart from the sensed or introspected differentiations and qualities within it. It is appropriate to call this the indeterminate or undifferentiated aesthetic continuum (Plate XIV). The other is the aggregate of differentiations and qualities apart from the continuum in which they appear. These may be termed the aesthetic differentiations (Plate X, were the pointillist dots so large one could see them more clearly).

The philosophy of David Hume may be defined as one which restricts the whole of reality to nothing but the aesthetic differentiations. The *tao* of Taoism, which is also identical with the source of the compassionate man-to-man-ness of Confucianism, may be defined as the undifferentiated aesthetic continuum (Plate XIV). Again the reader must be warned that these technical terms in no way completely convey their own meanings. They merely point toward immediately apprehendable factors in direct experience. Consequently, to grasp their full emotional and aesthetic content one must locate, within the totality of immediate experience, that to which they refer.

Consider the undifferentiated aesthetic continuum. Actually, we never experience it by itself. We always experience it as at least partially differentiated (Plate XIV). This is why Chiang Yee describes Chinese poetry as "an inexplicable mixture of the apparently concrete and definite with the thoroughly elusive and intangible." Krishnalal Shridharani notes this same indefiniteness in his own Indian culture. Nevertheless, just as we can consider a color such as an immediately sensed blue apart from the manifold in which it is sensed, so, by a similar direction of attention upon one factor of the totality of the immediately apprehended, to the neglect of another, we can consider the aesthetic continuum or manifold apart from its particular, limited, local, determinate sensed qualities. But when we do this and attempt to describe what remains we inevitably find ourselves in a paradoxical situation. Its character cannot be described. For description is possible only by having recourse to words denoting local, specific qualities or differentiations; and since the undifferentiated aesthetic continuum is the all-embracing, immediately apprehended unity apart from any differentiations, the recourse to descriptive terms always brings out the differentiations rather than the undifferentiated aesthetic continuum. Nevertheless, in sensing any specific differentiation such as a specific fragrance, one immediately apprehends at the same time the entire aesthetic manifold. Thus in speaking of *Tao* the Taoist in the *Tao-Teh-King* writes as follows:

Look for the Tao, and it is not enough to be seen,
Listen for the Tao, and it is not enough to be heard.

There was Something, without form [and yet] all complete.
Silent! Empty!
Sufficient unto itself! Unchanging!
Moving everywhere, but never exhausted!
This indeed might well be the mother of all below heaven.

The object you look at and cannot see is called "invisible";
The sound you listen to but cannot hear is called "inaudible";
The thing you try to grasp but cannot get hold of is called "intangible";
These three it is impossible to investigate to the end;
And thus it is that they blend and make One.

Thus it is called the "form of the formless," the "image of the non-material."
Thus it is called "indistinguishable."

Go on to the limit of emptiness:
Hold fast to the stability of stillness.

. . . the sage embraces oneness (Plate XIII).

Consider now the relation of the aesthetic differentiations, given with immediacy through the different senses, to the undifferentiated aesthetic continuum. It is clear that every differentiation comes and goes. Thus the differentiations are mortal and transitory. Moreover, the all-embracing continuum gives rise to all the differentiations everywhere and throughout the whole of time spontaneously. The beautiful shade of color appears on the aesthetic landscape and then is gone. Another differentiation comes in its stead and so on, without end. Thus the *Tao-Teh-King*, in speaking of the differentiations, continues:

> And, as our eyes demonstrate to us, they
>   all turn back.
> They may flourish abundantly,
> But each turns and goes home to the root
>   from which it came.
> Home to the root, home, I affirm, to the
>   stillness.
> This means, to turn back is destiny;
> And the destiny of turning back, I affirm,
>   can never be changed.

But the *tao* does not turn back. The undifferentiated aesthetic continuum is not mortal. Only the differentiations in it come and go and are transitory.

> To be of the Tao is to continue—
> With a mortal body to be free of danger.

Consequently, according to the Taoist and the Confucian, it is because the self is in part the non-transitory, indeterminate aesthetic continuum that it has any immortality. It follows from their doctrines that there is no immortality of the concrete, local, determinate personality. For the determinate, local personality is the indeterminate aesthetic continuum common to all things, together with the transitory, immediately introspected differentiations of it which are local and private to the individual. Since the latter differentiations are all transitory, the full, rich, differentiated, aesthetically immediate personality is not immortal. Only the undifferentiated aesthetic continuum common to all persons and all natural aesthetic objects, to use the language of the Hindus, "escapes the ravages of death."

It is precisely for this reason that the worship of ancestors is so important in the Chinese religion and culture. Only by putting up tablets which preserve the memory of their differentiated, unique, local, private personalities and by carrying on ceremonies associated with these tablets which keep the memory of their presence and one's sense of indebtedness to them continuously in mind, can a continuity of their full personality beyond the time of death be preserved. Conversely, in the Christianity of the West, in which immortality of the individual personality in its unique differentiations is guaranteed by doctrine, the use of symbols to preserve their memory and of religious ceremonies associated with these symbols is not encouraged, since according to the Western doctrine it is provided for by God Himself.

Having turned, as did Confucius, according to tradition, to the earlier Taoism, to discover the source of his compassionate man-to-man-ness in the immediately apprehendable factor in the nature of all things which has been termed the undifferentiated aesthetic continuum, one may recall Tzu Ssu's description:

> Man-to-man-ness and knowledge are spiritual powers [*te*] inherent in man, and they are the bridge [literally *tao*, way] bringing together the outer and the inner. . . . The result is that entire realness never ceases for a moment. Now if that be so, then it must be extended in time: if extended in time, then capable of proof: if capable of proof, then extended in space-length: if extended in length, then extended in area: if extended in area, then extended in height-visibility.

The word "visibility" shows that its continuity is immediately apprehended. Tzu Ssu continues:

> And this quality of extension in area is what makes material things supportable from below: this quality of extension in height-visibility is what makes things coverable from above: whilst the extension in time is what makes them capable of completion. Thus area pairs with earth, height-visibility pairs with heaven, and space plus time makes limitlessness. This being its nature, realness is not visible and yet clearly visible, does not (deliberately) stir things and yet changes them, takes no action and yet completes them. . . . It is only the man who is entirely real in his world of men who can make the warp and woof of the great web of civilized life, who can establish the great foundations of civilized society, and who can understand the nourishing processes of heaven and earth.

Here the naturalism so evident in Taoism appears also as an essential part of Confucianism.

It is a characteristic trait of the Chinese that they are persistently and unequivocally concrete. Even the indeterminate *tao*, or *jen* is sought not for its own sake, but in its manifestations either in aesthetic nature or in aesthetic human nature in society. Thus the attention in the two religions of purely Chinese origin is always upon the concrete differentiations in the immediate world of experience, with undifferentiated aesthetic experience the key to good conduct with respect to determinate acts, arts, and institutions.

This approach will suffice when one's concrete experience is successful and when at times other than death one is enjoying the concrete determinate experiences rather than suffering their inevitable loss. Buddhism identifies the divine also with this same immediately apprehendable, determinately indescribable, ineffable aesthetic factor; but unlike Taoism and Confucianism it concentrates attention and human conduct upon this continuum for its own sake.

The Chinese spirit, because of the fact of death, found it necessary to accept the imported Buddhist religion along with its own indigenous Taoism and Confucianism. Thus Chiang Yee and Lin Yutang indicate that the Chinese tend to be Confucianists and Taoists when they are successful and to become Buddhists or to practice their Buddhism when they are confronted with tragedy and death. This is as it should be. For the Oriental, the emotional, aesthetically immediate, hedonistic, sensuous differentiations are real and good for their own sake. Were this not true, aesthetics would not have the central place which it enjoys in both of the Chinese religions and in Buddhism and Hinduism. But the Chinese and the Orientals generally, with their unqualified realism and empiricism, see that all immediately sensed and felt determinate characteristics, all differentiations, whether they be those of the beloved personality or of the aesthetically beautiful natural landscape, are transitory. Thus hedonism as a complete philosophy of life is inadequate—not because it is naughty or because sensed things are not real, but merely because determinate things are transitory; and a philosophy which treats determinate pleasures as if they were a basis for living under all circumstances treats pleasure as an immortal law rather than the actual transitory thing which it is. Thus for religious solace, for the sustenance necessary to face the loss of the aesthetically and emotionally dear, as well as for its presence and its enjoyment, the cultivation of the indeterminate aesthetic continuum for its own sake is also necessary.

But it is necessary not because man needs it, but because by paying attention to it we can bring our lives into accord with the complete content of the purely empirically given, immediately apprehended character of the nature of things. Both the individual person and nature are in part this indeterminate aesthetic continuum as well as the cherished aesthetic differentiations within it. Thus if one is going to act in accord with his own true nature and the true nature of all natural things, there must be a philosophy and a religion which pursue the continuum of immediate aesthetic experience for its own sake. This philosophy and this religion are found by the Chinese in Buddhism. It is as important and continuous a part of Chinese culture as are Confucianism and Taoism.

Other characteristics of Chinese culture remain to be noted. One is its nominalism and positivism, its essentially aesthetic character. For the *tao* and for the *jen* of Confucianism, as well as for the more determinate, differentiated, sensed qualities which appear within the aesthetic continuum, the symbol of language is a mere name denoting an immediately apprehendable fact. None of the concepts of these two Chinese philosophies are universals. Even the all-embracing, undifferentiated aesthetic continuum is a concrete particular. As Hu Shih has said, in his *Development of the Logical Method in Ancient China*, Lao Tzu was "the greatest of all the Sophists," and Confucius was a Positivist. This is to affirm that all concepts are names for immediately apprehended particulars. In the more technical language of Chapter VIII, it is to assert that there is no reality except that which is denoted by concepts by intuition, and that there is no real component in the nature of things except the aesthetic component.

This view shows also in the primarily aesthetic character of the Taoist and Buddhist emphasis upon the undifferentiated, indefinite aesthetic continuum (Plate XIII), as well as in the Confucian attention upon its more humanistic, sensuous differentiations. When the American, Helen, in Younghill Kang's *East Goes West*, said to the very wise Chinese, Kim, "Tell me more about Oriental art, I am so ignorant about it," Kim replied:

Its simplicity sometimes escapes the Western eye. The inspiration is usually nature. That, the artist admires with simplicity. It was said of Yu-K'o that when he painted bamboos he forgot his own body and became transformed into bamboo. He saw bamboos, not mankind. So when you paint a horse, a cat, a butterfly, a stream, you must become all these, not see them in terms of utility to man, nor as part of some mystical scheme to human advantage (not like the praying cows of Italian primitives, that is). He who succeeds in setting down the soul of bamboo, of stone, of old trees, that man must feel serene and divine. (He is in union with nature, as they say.)

Kim is clearly portraying how this art attempts to exhibit with immediacy (Plate XIII) the identity of the self of the painter with the aesthetic natural object which the immediately apprehended and felt aesthetic field concept of the self makes possible.

Such a self can be one with bamboos, a stone, or old trees because the self is the whole, all-embracing aesthetic manifold with all its emotional and aesthetically vivid content, and this manifold is as much in the aesthetically immediate tree or stone as it is in the painter. Moreover, a painter who conceives of himself and of nature from this standpoint can set down the "soul of bamboo," because soul exists when emotionally laden aesthetic immediacy is in anything; and this is precisely what the single aesthetic continuum common to the aesthetically immediate bamboo and the aesthetically immediate self provides. One is conscious and spiritual, a soul, not because he is a local, atomic, mental substance with respect to which all aesthetic colors, sounds, tastes, fragrances, and feelings are purely discrete, subjective data projected by this mental substance as mere appearances, but because everything, man as well as other natural objects, is made up of an all-embracing aesthetic field, the essence of whose nature is feeling and aesthetic vividness. Upon such a view reality has a character which only art, or a philosophy using purely nominalistic, idiographic symbols handled in the non-logically ordered associations of the poetry of the *Tao-Teh-King* or the disconnected conversations of Confucius, can convey. Such is the importance of that factor in the purely positivistically given nature of things which is denoted by the purely nominalistic symbol which is termed the concept of the undifferentiated aesthetic continuum.

But reality for the Oriental is not merely the indeterminate aesthetic continuum but also the determinate differentiations, equally aesthetic, given through the senses, which appear within it. There is a fundamental difference between the aesthetic differentiations and the indefinite aesthetic continuum. The former are local, here-now, determinate data. By a determinate datum is meant any factor-in-fact which has a definite character different from some other factor-in-fact. It is also a limited or finite rather than an unlimited or all-embracing, infinite factor. Thus the immediately sensed red does not cover the whole of the aesthetic continuum but a limited portion of it, and is different in its character from a similarly limited immediately sensed blue. The undifferentiated aesthetic continuum is, as its name indicates, the same everywhere. It is precisely for this reason that this continuum in the immediately apprehended self of the painter is identical with what it is in the equally immediately experienced aesthetic bamboo, or stone, or old tree.

That there is such an undifferentiated aesthetic continuum is known in three ways, notwithstanding the fact that what is immediately experienced is this continuum with its differentiations. First, the whole of the immediately experienced continuum is not differentiated. As William James pointed out, and Alfred Whitehead has recently re-emphasized, its periphery is undifferentiated and indeterminate. Secondly, the differentiated aesthetic continuum can be known even where it is differentiated, by merely abstracting it from the local limited differentiations, just as the shape of a sensed color can be abstracted from the color, or the color from the shape. Thirdly, we can, by certain specific methods, attempt actually to remove the sensed or imagined differentiations from the otherwise completely indeterminate undifferentiated aesthetic manifold. This is a perfectly straightforward scientific procedure, and one the success of which only actual empirical experimentation can determine. It is precisely this experimentation which the retreats of the Buddhists and the methods of Yoga attempt to put into actual practice. Westerners who have gone to this experimentation with cool, sober minds and with no prejudices in favor of Oriental philosophy and religion, report not merely that these methods, when pursued, confirm the existence of the completely undifferentiated, emotionally and aesthetically moving continuum, but also that the product of the experiment not merely wipes out the theoretically postulated self, the theoretically postulated external object, and the gulf between them, leaving merely an unlimited, imaginatively and sensuously undifferentiated immediacy; but also that this indeterminate immediacy, instead of being nothing, as it seems at first to a Westerner, is, though indeterminate and hence indescribable, one of the most emotionally rich and moving, and one of the most aesthetically ineffable, of all experiences.

Once this point is grasped one is prepared to consider the second factor distinguishing the abstracted undifferentiated aesthetic continuum from its concrete differentiations. Out of it the differentiations come, and back into it they go. Now it is precisely this coming into existence of the differentiations and their passing away again, to be replaced by new transitory qualities, that gives rise to the sequence of associated sense data, which Hume in the West so correctly described. And it is precisely this sequence of associated differentiations which is the sensed arrow of time. But the undifferentiated, all-embracing, indeterminate aesthetic continuum is not in this arrow-like temporal sequence; instead it embraces within itself this sequence and the coming and going of its associated sense data. Thus the undifferentiated aesthetic continuum is timeless. This is the reason why this component in the self, although a particular and not a logical universal with postulated immortal subsistence, is nonetheless immortal.

In this different status of the aesthetic continuum as compared with its differentiations, with respect to time, the difference between the

Western and the Oriental metaphorical image for time has its basis. As the anthropologist Paul Fejos first pointed out to me, the Westerner represents time either with an arrow, or as a moving river which comes out of a distant place and past which are not here and now, and which goes into an equally distant place and future which also are not here and now; whereas, the Oriental portrays time as a placid, silent pool within which ripples come and go. Because it is thus the source of all differentiations, giving rise to them when they are born and receiving them back when they die, the aesthetic continuum is the great mother of creation, giving birth to the ineffable beauty of the golden yellows on the mountain landscape as the sun drops low in the late afternoon, only a moment later to receive that differentiation back into itself and to put another in its place without any effort.

As the *Tao-Teh-King* expresses it:

> The spirit of a valley is to be undying.
> It is what is called "the Original Female,"
> And the Doorway of the Original Female is called
>   "the root from which heaven and earth sprang."
> On, on goes this spirit for ever, functioning
>   without any special effort.

It is precisely this effortless, infinitely diversified creativity of this "female," aesthetic continuum, giving rise to anger and avarice and the emotions of the murderer and the warrior as well as to the affection and charity of the saint, which the religious art both of India and of Mexico, picturing the divine in all these different aspects, attempts to convey. Nonetheless, the good life is the life of the more passive, human-hearted, underlying, all-embracing "silence," since this is the part of man's nature and the nature of all things which can be counted on always as a guide for life at any time or place under all circumstances, because it alone is neither partial nor transitory.

The realization of the ultimacy and irreducibility of this undifferentiated aesthetic continuum has one other consequence. A genuine basis for human freedom is provided. It is not by a spurious invention of a so-called practical reason, which places the supposed demands of the earthly, temporary, local human being above all factually grounded, scientifically verified or positivistically given principles that a meaning for freedom in human nature is to be found. Instead, as the Orient noted long ago, freedom has its basis in that part of the nature of man and things which is indeterminate and thus a potentiality for a determinateness that is not yet. As the Orient has seen, and as the Westerner, by the failure of his attempts to derive freedom from the behavior of determinate entities, has demonstrated, if all reality is determinate, then no meaning for human freedom can be found. This is precisely what the Oriental means when he asserts that if man gives expression only to the differentiated, specifically sensed, determinate portion of himself and of things, then he is caught in the remorseless wheel of fate. It is what he has in mind also when he affirms that it is only by recognizing the indeterminate, all-embracing field component of his nature and by giving expression to the creativity which it permits, that man attains freedom, while also gaining equanimity with respect to the coming and going of the transitory, differentiated portion of the self and all things.

The hold which this conception of man and the nature of things as indeterminate and indefinite has upon even such a concrete mind as that of the Chinese, showed itself in even so westernized an Oriental city as Hong Kong, when in 1920 one talked with even the most lowly of coolies. Again and again, when one asked them if they could do such and such a specific thing, the Cantonese word "*wock-jeh*" was given in reply. The dock might be five minutes away, and the boat which one wanted to catch might be leaving fifteen minutes later. Nevertheless, if one asked the ricksha boy whether he could get one there in time, the reply would be "*wock-jeh*." Again and again, to all sorts of queries, this expression kept coming back. Its meaning is "Perhaps." What he was saying was that the nature, not merely of human affairs but of all things, is in part indeterminate, and that consequently a wise man, an informed man, will never absolutely commit himself. It is likely that this is what lies behind the intense shame which comes upon an Oriental if he "loses face." One loses face when one has committed himself to a specific, determinate future course of events from which one cannot gracefully retreat if the events turn out to be otherwise than was anticipated when the commitment was made. A person in the Orient who put himself in such a position is covered with shame because he has disregarded what the Orient teaches man to believe is one of the most elementary facts about human experience and the nature of things generally; namely, their indeterminateness and contingency.

This belief also makes the traditional Oriental suspicious of moral codes that lay down determinate, specific lines of conduct which must hold under all circumstances. Determinate things in the world are transitory. Hence, any rules based upon them can never be expected to hold under all circumstances; and consequently the dying of man or the sacrifice of human beings for determinate, concrete moral precepts shows a lack of religious as well as philosophical and scientific wisdom. To the Oriental it is a sign rather of sophomoric human conceit than of the judgment of a wise man who, by long and more mature experience, has a more correct conception of the transitory nature of all determinate things.

This does not mean that the Chinese and the other Orientals do not insist upon certain types of moral behavior to which a man must be true under all circumstances; but, as has been noted, this constantly valid moral type of conduct has its basis in the indeterminate, all-embracing, undifferentiated aesthetic continuum, and the common bond of emotionally felt sympathy for all persons and all things which it provides, rather than in laying down of one's life for a specific, determinately differentiated line of conduct. It is this which has given to Oriental religion a charity, an open-mindedness, a disinclination to force itself upon other peoples' attention, and a fellow-feeling not merely for all men but for all aesthetic natural objects of any kind whatever, which Western religion either in theory or in practice cannot claim for itself. But precisely for this reason it is not an effective religion of reform. It tends to produce a people who find peace of mind and equanimity of the spirit by facing realistically and with aesthetic sensitivity the transitoriness, the attendant suffering, and the undeniable relativity of sensed things, thereby fitting one to accept circumstances as they are, rather than to transform them in ways other than those which a cultivation of one's intuitive fellow-feeling for all creatures elicits.

This attitude shows itself in the tendency of the traditional Chinese, when he has a sharp, determinately defined, concrete issue with his neighbor or his adversary, to maintain that it is the part of wisdom to compromise. It appears also in Confucius's disinclination to enter government, and in his suggestion that the best legal rules are no legal rules at all. The wise man knows that determinate things are transitory and hence that they should not be elevated into immortal principles. He realizes also that the differentiations in the aesthetic continuum vary from person to person, being at times direct opposites; hence, the introspectively felt determinate convictions of one person cannot be made the basis of moral judgments holding for all. Consequently, instead of pressing his determinate thesis in a law court to the limit and to the death, he takes his adversary out to lunch where, after a good wine and artistically prepared food have put the two in a more indeterminate compassionate human-hearted state of mind, some kind of a compromise will be attempted in which each will gain something of his point without "losing face." To be sure, such wise conduct did not always occur, but it was, nonetheless, the traditional ideal.

Buddhist culture is a major and persistent component of traditional Chinese culture. Nevertheless, if one wishes to note the type of empirical cultural institutions which Buddhism produces, it is better to examine it in a country in which it is largely the only factor. Such a country is Tibet. Here, to be sure, Buddhism takes but one of its many forms, that one known as Lamaism. Nevertheless, the basic philosophical and metaphysical doctrines of Tibetan Lamaism operate also in other Buddhist cultures.

It must be constantly kept in mind, however, that there are many different Buddhist doctrines. Philosophically, there are four major forms, and each one in turn has many different applications and manifestations. Nevertheless, underlying all these differences and running through them there is one fundamental principle providing a common identity and agreement. Thus the differing forms of Buddhism owe their differences to the additions to the basic common doctrine. This common doctrine in Buddhism must be of primary concern, even though incidentally in arriving at it the four major philosophical forms in which it presents itself will appear.

The approach to it may best be made by way of certain concrete characteristics of Tibetan life and culture. Marco Pallis, in his sensitive and profound *Peaks and Lamas*, describes the Tibetans as a "people who have shown so much taste, and who delight in all that is beautiful. . . . Even ordinary farmers possess many objects which do not differ in any essential respect from those of the aristocracy, though naturally they are rougher in execution and employ less costly materials. This is perhaps conclusive evidence of how real and universal Tibetan culture has been, and how thoroughly it has permeated the whole society." Thus the same appreciation of the aesthetic which is found in traditional China, Korea, and Japan exists also in Buddhist Tibet. Marco Pallis points out also that this "diffusion of artistic knowledge from the aristocracy downwards into the peasantry is doubtless due to the . . . great monasteries and their dependent houses, where, though the domestic life may be Spartan in respect to food and dress, the highest level of refinement is attained, not only in the furnishing of temples but in the apartments of the higher prelates." The perception of the beautiful is at the heart of the Buddhist philosophy and religion.

Nevertheless, there is a marked difference between Buddhist art and Taoist or Confucian Chinese art. The Buddhist art is very much more symbolic in its character. It does not restrict itself, except in the Zen or Cha'n form, as much as does Chinese art to the painting of the aesthetic landscape in its more non-symbolic aesthetic immediacy. Instead, figures of the Buddha in the form of three-dimensional external common-sense objects appear (Plate XVI); and even when, in painting, the wall decoration is two-dimensional, the aesthetic forms or differentiations are not purely naturalistic in character but are arranged in ordered patterns almost every part of which has some symbolic meaning (Plate XV).

At first sight it appears that one is confronted in Buddhism with an art which is identical with that of the West. The immediately apprehended aesthetic materials are used with undeniable symbolic references which are theological in character. But that these references are, as in the traditional West, to something beyond the reach of immediate apprehension, which only syntactically and postulationally formulated theory can designate, does not follow. The symbolic reference in Buddhist art may be from certain factors which are immediately apprehended and aesthetic in character to other factors equally immediate and aesthetic in their nature. It will be well to examine the technical, philosophical doctrines of Buddhism and then come back to Buddhist art with these possibilities in mind, before interpreting its symbolism.

The four major Buddhist doctrines were developed by three Indian philosophers—Nagarjuna (c. A.D. 100–200), Harivarman (c. A.D. 250–350), and Vasubandhu (A.D. 420–500). All four doctrines attempt to convey the earlier, more intuitive insight of the Buddha (c. 600 B.C.). Nevertheless, they are exceedingly technical, involving the theoretical distinctions and complications typical of Western philosophy. In fact, three of the four Buddhist philosophical theories are very similar to certain Western philosophical doctrines. This has led many Western and Oriental scholars to conclude that Buddhist philosophy is like Western philosophy in its use of syntactically designated, logically formulated concepts by postulation. But again, before assuming hastily an identity between Oriental and Western thought, it will be well to examine the Buddhist doctrines and the Buddhist dialectic of negation which relates them.

One thing must be noted at the outset. None of these Buddhist philosophers pretended to be formulating anything novel. Each was merely giving doctrinal expression to basic philosophical truths which the Buddha had revealed. The Buddha's teachings were not syntactically formulated. His method was the intuitive one of immediate apprehension, similar to the philosophical approach of Lao Tzu and Confucius. This suggests that even though the later Buddhist philosophers formulated their Buddhism logically and systematically, nevertheless, what they were trying to designate is something which is immediately apprehended.

Another fact supports this conclusion. The final system resulting from the application of the Buddhist dialectic of negation was the nihilistic Mahayanistic Buddhism of Nagarjuna. This system unequivocally affirmed the nature of things to be something which neither logical reasoning with its systematically formulated theory, nor words denoting sense data, could convey. Moreover, although this system is the end-product of the Buddhist logic of dialectic, it was the first of the four systems historically, as the date of its author Nargarjuna unequivocally indicates. Consequently, what it conveys must be known quite independently of the logical method.

An examination of the precise manner in which the four systems of Buddhism arise out of the dialectic of negation makes this clear. One begins with the ordinary belief of common sense, that man and the universe are to be conceived as a collection of persisting persons acted upon by external objects independent of these persons. Applying the logical principle of negation to this common-sense belief, the later Buddhist scholars first negated the common-sense notion that a persisting self exists. This was equivalent to what Hume did for the philosophy of Berkeley. Hume, it will be remembered, pointed out that if one is going to believe only in what is given with immediacy through the senses, then there is no such thing as a persisting self; all that one can mean by the self is the mere association and sequence of introspected pleasures, pains, colors, sounds, etc. This negation of the notion of a persisting determinate personality, or mental substance, underlying the immediately introspected association of sense impressions, produced the first system in the dialectic of negation, the realistic Hinayanistic Buddhism of Vasubandhu. According to this theory, external material objects are real, but the concept of a persisting, substantial, determinate self does not designate anything real.

To this system of Vasubandhu the logical principle of negation is applied again, this time to the common-sense belief in an external three-dimensional material object with an existence independent of one's awareness of it. This produces the nihilistic Hinayanistic Buddhism of Harivarman. It is to be noted that this application of the principle of negation does for the common-sense belief in a material object what Berkeley did for the similar belief in Locke's philosophy. As a consequence, in the Buddhism of Harivarman neither the mental nor the material substances of common sense exist. All that one means by a material substance is a given association of sense impressions; and all that one means by a self is a similarly transitory succession of immediately introspected data in the aesthetic continuum. The similarity to the philosophy of David Hume is obvious.

To this system of Harivarman the logical relation of negation was applied again, giving rise not to the negative thesis that material substances and mental substances are not real, but to the positive thesis that ideas—meaning thereby nominalistically denoted data of the senses in the aesthetic continuum—are alone real. This is the second system formulated by Vasubandhu, termed semi-Mahayanistic Buddhism. It is a great testimony to the intellectual integrity of these Buddhist philosophers that one of them should formulate two different philosophical theories. This shows that they were being guided not by wishful thinking but by a genuine intellectual curiosity and by a definite, logical method.

Again, to this second system of Vasubandhu, the logical relation of negation was applied, producing as its final consequence the nihilistic Mahayanistic Buddhism of Nagarjuna. A Westerner might at first wonder, after having negated the reality of persisting personal selves and of external objects, to leave nothing apparently but the immediately inspected data of the senses and introspection, what would remain after all the latter data are negated also. It would seem that this final negation would leave one with absolutely nothing. Now this is precisely the way this remainder—the Nirvana of Buddhism—impresses Westerners initially. Nonetheless, this impression is quite misleading. The Buddhist insists that the contrary is the case.

He explains, however, that in order to convey this positive remainder, which is Nirvana, he is confronted with a paradox, the same paradox, in fact, which confronts one with respect to the *tao* of Taoism. He can tell what it is not; but he cannot tell what it is. The reason for this is that in order to state what a thing is, it is necessary to specify certain determinate properties. Now it is precisely this absence of determinateness which is the characteristic of that which remains after the dialectic of negation has been applied to the limit. The Buddhist tells us also that for the same reason no grammatically constructed sentences, no postulationally prescribed deductive system, can convey it. It is something which must be immediately experienced to be known. But these two considerations give us all that we need in order to find it. If it is immediately experienced, it must be a factor in the aesthetic continuum of immediate experience; and since it is not a determinate sensed or introspected factor, nothing remains but for Nirvana to be the undifferentiated or indeterminate aesthetic continuum. Thus, the basic factor in the nature of things denoted by the word Nirvana, or "thusness," in Buddhism is identical with the basic *tao* of Taoism which was also the root of the basic compassionate man-to-man-ness of Confucianism. With this in mind reconsider the first three Buddhist doctrines. The one which seemed to be similar to the philosophy of Hume was in fact not completely similar. Although it had rejected external, postulated, material objects, and persisting, subjective, substantial, determinate selves, it did not restrict itself to nothing but the atomic data of sense and their associations as did Hume. Instead, there still remained not merely these data and their transitory associations but the entire aesthetic continuum in which they exist. Otherwise, the indeterminate aesthetic continuum would not have remained when, in the final application of the dialectic, the first differentiations were negated. Thus there is a difference between the first three Buddhist systems and the somewhat similar Western philosophies of Hobbes, Berkeley, and Hume.

These considerations make it clear also that none of the systems of Buddhism is concentrating its attention primarily upon postulated objects or upon the theoretic component of things. Even the first system of Vasubandhu, which admitted the existence of external material objects, while denying the existence of a subjective, substantial self, had its attention primarily on a partial movement from common sense toward the irreducible, undifferentiated aesthetic continuum, which appears in its purity only in the final product of the dialectic of negation, the nihilistic Mahayanistic Buddhism of Nagarjuna.

Furthermore, in the semi-Mahayanistic, almost Humean, philosophy of Vasubandhu there clearly is no symbolic reference by postulation to anything beyond the immediately apprehended; both subjective, persisting, substantial selves and objective, independently existing, external material objects, having been denied to be real. Yet even the two Mahayanistic systems, which have no reference to postulated, theoretically designated objects, nonetheless make use of the Buddhist painting in which aesthetic materials have a symbolic reference beyond themselves.

All these considerations should make it clear, therefore, that the symbolic character of Buddhist art is not an exception to the general Oriental rule that art and the most real in knowledge are concerned primarily with the immediately apprehended aesthetic experience, not with a symbolic reference from the aesthetic materials to postulationally prescribed entities beyond the aesthetic component of the nature of things. Put positively, the symbolic reference of Buddhist Oriental art is from the formalized, determinate, differentiated aesthetic qualities in their sensed immediacy to the equally immediately apprehended indeterminate aesthetic continuum (Plates XV and XVI). In short, the symbolic reference is from one item in the totality of immediate experience to another indeterminate item. It is a symbolic reference, not as in traditional Western art, from the aesthetic component to the theoretic component in the nature of things, but from one factor in the aesthetic component to another in the same aesthetic component.

All the emotionally and aesthetically moving figures of the Buddha are symbolically conveying this reference. The Buddha sits in quiet contemplation, his eyes half open, half closed (Plates XV and XVI); half open to give the cosmic naturalistic component of the all-embracing aesthetic continuum; half closed to keep the differentiations in it from being clearly and determinately sensed and also to give the so-called subjective or introspected portion of this continuum; but with the eyes nonetheless half open so that the images even in the introspected portion of the continuum will also be indeterminate, indefinite, and unclear. Thus immersed in the all-embracing aesthetic continuum, with all its emotionally moving, ineffable content, one gets its ineffable immediate unity in the very midst of its transitory, determinate differentiations. Thereby the common denominator running through the distinction between the subjective and the objective is found; and the one-ness of the aesthetic field portion of the real self with the field portion of all other things is achieved. Having found the all-embracing unity and identity that exists in all differences and having given expression to the calm aesthetic feeling which it is, one has the Buddha-nature; one is Nirvana (Plate XVI).

The achievement of this indeterminate ineffably emotional, aesthetic field factor in oneself and all things, alone and in its purity is difficult for natural human beings whose attention is normally fixed upon its differentiations. Only by practice can it be attained. Also, most people, even when they recognize its immediately factual presence, will be able to grasp it only with at least some additional differentiated content. It is precisely this which produces the four major systems of Buddhism rather than merely the nihilistic Mahayanistic system of Nagarjuna.

Furthermore, it is not necessary that the Buddhist, even the followers of Nagarjuna, deny the reality of the differentiations or the reality of theoretically known, postulated factors, such as the objects of common sense, or the more sophisticated and deductively adequate scientific objects of Western mathematical physics. Buddhism permits one to admit in addition to the undifferentiated all-embracing Nirvana the existence of whatever else similarly empirical scientific inspection or postulational technique operating in conjunction with experimental confirmation, may validate The only essential contention of the Buddhist is that one of the ultimate factors in terms of which the scientist and the philosopher must conceive the world to be constituted is the indeterminate, undifferentiated aesthetic continuum. The differentiations within it are effects of its presence, not the irreducible atomic qualities out of which it is constructed as a mere aggregate.

Even though the determinate inspected data of the specific senses and specific introspections are effects rather than causes, and transitory, mortal things, they are nonetheless real because of this fact. Nor are they mere phantasms or projections of a purely subjective local ego, as Galilei, Newton, Hobbes, Locke, and Berkeley, and the other scientific and philosophical thinkers of the modern world have supposed. In fact, for the Buddhist and the Oriental generally this modern Western, and even the medieval Christian notion of a determinate personality, soul, or mental substance which is both differentiated in its nature and immortal, refers to nothing which exists. For this reason also, the modern Western notion of the aesthetic data which one immediately inspects as supposed projections of an underlying, determinately substantial, persisting, immortal personality or self, is untenable. In short, in Buddhism as in Taoism and Confucianism, and also, as shall be seen, in Hinduism, there is no immortality of the full, *differentiated,* immediately apprehended, or postulationally conceived, personality. Only the immediately apprehended aesthetic field component which is common to all persons and all aesthetic things is immortal.

This conclusion has its basis in a fact already noted: All differentiated, determinate things are transitory. Any immediately apprehended, specifically sensed differentiation of the aesthetic continuum, such as a specific blue characterizing a local, limited portion of the aesthetic manifold, is temporal and temporary. It arises out of the undifferentiated continuum and fades back into it again. Thus the Buddhist arrives at his basic thesis that all determinate things, even the determinate portion of the personality, that which differentiates one personality from another, is mortal and transitory. In fact, one of the most insistent contentions of the Buddhist, and of the Oriental sages generally, is that the emphasis on the immortality of the determinate portion of the self is not merely a conclusion to which the immediately apprehended facts of experience give the lie, but also a positive source of selfishness. Thus the Oriental sage is continuously insisting that one must become self-less. Put more positively, what he is saying is that the self is composed of two components, one a determinate, differentiated, unique element, distinguishing one person from any other person; the other the all-embracing, aesthetically immediate, and emotionally moving compassionate indeterminate, and hence indescribable, field component. The former is temporary, transitory, and not immortal; furthermore, the cherishing of it, the desire for its immortality, is a source of suffering, selfishness and evil. The part of the self which is not transitory and immortal is the aesthetic field component of the self. Because it is identical not merely in all persons, but in all aesthetic objects throughout the entire cosmos, the cherishing of it, instead of making men selfish, gives them a compassionate fellow-feeling for all creatures. The way to secure peace of mind and religious contentment is, according to the Buddhist, not to go on, as the Western Christian does, optimistically assuming and cherishing the immortality of the complete, differentiated, determinate, unique personality. Such a procedure is false to the immediately apprehended fact that all differentiations, all determinate things in the complex, differentiated aesthetic continuum, are transitory. At this point the Buddhist—and the Oriental generally— is as realistic as the most hard-boiled Western materialist or contemporary relativistic naturalist.

In fact, this utter realism and positivism is at the basis of the initial principle in the Buddhist philosophy of religion. This principle is termed "the principle of suffering." With respect to religion and to life this is the elementary and primary fact which one must grasp, according to the Buddhist. The determinate, differentiated portion of all things, personal selves as well as natural objects, is transitory, exactly as the senses and specific introspections indicate. It is precisely because these determinate transitory factors in man's nature and in the nature of all things are, to use William James's language, in "the center of consciousness" that man is naturally attached to them. Thus man in his natural state rightly and of necessity cherishes the determinate immediately felt qualities of his parents, of those who are dear to him, and of himself and of natural objects to which he has devoted his attention. But all these determinate things being transitory, man inevitably must suffer. The realization and unequivocal acceptance of this conclusion is, according to the Buddhist, the first step in ethical, philosophical, practical, or religious wisdom.

Nevertheless, there is a way to obtain peace of mind. There is a way to obtain contentment or what the Buddhist terms "salvation." This "way" is characterized by all the unequivocal positivism and stark realism which characterize the Buddhist acceptance of the principle of suffering. The Buddhist merely reminds one of the equally realistic and positivistic, immediately apprehended fact that the self and all things are not merely the many distinguishable and different transitory differentiations, but also the all-embracing, indeterminate aesthetic continuum of which the transitory factors are the temporary differentiations. This immediately apprehended indeterminate aesthetic manifold, since it contains the temporal, arrow-like sequence of transitory differentiations within itself, instead of being itself within this arrow-like passage of time, is timeless and hence immortal; or, put more exactly, it is outside the death-delivering "ravages" of time and hence escapes its consequences. It embraces time as one of its determinate differentiations, instead of time embracing it. Since the self is as much this undifferentiated aesthetic continuum embracing the temporal process as it is the transitory, determinate differentiated factors caught within the death-delivering ravages of time, it is possible for human beings to take the standpoint of the former, which the Buddhist terms Nirvana, while also being in the standpoint of the latter. It is precisely this which the Buddha, sitting amid the transitory, death-doomed, determinate things which are here and now, with his eyes half closed, half open, is doing. This all of us can do. And once having thus shown us the way, Buddha informs us that even Buddha himself is unnecessary.

In this statement also the Buddha is right. For there is nothing in his teaching which one's immediate experience does not contain. Hence, having pointed out the factors which are there and having revealed the potentialities which they offer in practical living, for facing the stark transitory realities of life as they are; and even so finding it possible to gain an emotional, aesthetic, and hence essentially spiritual contentment, thereby preparing us for the death not merely of those who are dear to us but also of all other determinate things; and giving us a deep, even tragically deep, fellow-feeling for all creatures, vegetables and animals as well as men, he has taught us how to stand upon our own feet. Then he can go his way.

There is no transcendental hocus-pocus breaking into our lives from without in some manner which we can never understand, thereby always making us its slave. There is no claim that one cannot attain the perfect moral and religious life without the Buddha. There is no charge of sin loaded upon us of an origin so far in the distant past that obviously, by its very nature, we can have no responsibility for it. There is as a consequence no over-righteous sense of self-sacrifice nor any claim upon the part of the Buddha that he is suffering or dying for us, thereby making us permanently his chattels by putting us permanently in his debt. The Buddha's claims upon the lives of men are merely those of a mortal man—he never claimed to be anything more—who, with the utmost realism and the most sober reasonableness, merely calls man's attention to, and with him has a compassionate feeling for, the sufferings of human and natural things which the inevitable death that overtakes all determinate creatures entails; while at the same time pointing out another factor in the nature of things and the practical consequences with respect to aesthetic appreciation, spiritual sustenance, and emotional equanimity, which the awareness and cultivation of its existence engenders. Need one wonder that this Buddha in spirit if not entirely in name has won the hearts and the affection of more of the earth's inhabitants than any other religious leader in the world?

Moreover, he has won this allegiance tolerantly by combining amicably with, and even losing himself in, other religions rather than by replacing or destroying them. The Hinduism of India since 660 B.C. has been in considerable part what it is because of the Buddha's reform movement within it. The cultures of China, Korea, and Japan and Mongolia are as Buddhist as they are Confucian, Taoist or Shintoist.

In his enlightened followers there has also come an appreciation of things intellectual as well as aesthetic, an open-mindedness—in fact, a positive welcoming of religious and philosophical doctrines other than one's own, and, as Marco Pallis has noted, an attendant spirit of tolerance such as befits one who maintains that the divine component of the nature of things is truly and literally not merely in all persons, but in all aesthetic natural objects. Madame Alexandra David-Neel's statement (in *Magic and Mystery in Tibet*) of the Buddhist Padmasambhava's six prescriptions for the most perfect, practical, and moral religious conduct makes this clear:

1. To read a large number of books on the various religions and philosophies. To listen to many learned doctors professing many different doctrines. To experiment oneself with a number of methods.

2. To choose a doctrine among the many one has studied and discard the other ones, . . .

3. To remain in a lowly condition, humble in one's demeanour, not seeking to be conspicuous or important in the eyes of the world, but behind apparent insignificance, to let one's mind soar high above all worldly power and glory.

4. To be indifferent to all. Behaving like the dog or the pig that eat what chance brings them. Not making any choice among the things which one meets. Abstaining from any effort to acquire or avoid anything. Accepting with an equal indifference whatever comes: riches or poverty, praise or contempt, giving up the distinction between virtue and vice, honourable and shameful, good and evil. Being neither afflicted, nor repenting whatever one may have done and, on the other hand, never being elated nor proud on account of what one has accomplished.

5. To consider with perfect equanimity and detachment the conflicting opinions and the various manifestations of the activity of beings. To understand that such is the nature of things, the inevitable mode of action of each entity and to remain always serene. To look at the world as a man standing on the highest mountain of the country looks at the valleys and the lesser summits spread out below him.

6. It is said that the sixth stage cannot be described in words. It corresponds to the realization of the "Void," which, in Lamaist terminology, means the Inexpressible Reality.

With respect to the word "Void," Madame David-Neel adds the footnote: "In a general way, one must understand here, the realization of the non-existence of a permanent *ego*, according to the Tibetan current formula: *'The person is devoid of self; all things are devoid of self.'*"

The reference to the viewing of "the world as a man standing on the highest mountain of the country" is illuminating, since it shows the identity underlying the differences in Buddhism, Taoism, and Confucianism. The Chinese have described the difference between the Orient and the Western landscape painting in precisely this way. Lin Yutang, in *My Country and My People*, writes:

. . . the artist should convey to us the spirit of the scenery and evoke in us a sympathetic mood in response. That is the highest object and ideal of Chinese art. We remember how the artist makes periodic visits to the high mountains to refresh his spirit in the mountain air and clean his breast of the accumulated dust of urban thoughts and suburban passions. He climbs to the highest peaks to obtain a moral and spiritual elevation, and he braves the winds and soaks himself in rain to listen to the thundering waves of the sea. He sits among piles of wild rocks and brush-wood and hides himself in bamboo groves for days in order to absorb the spirit and life of nature. He should convey to us the benefit of that communion of nature, and communicate to us some of the spirit of the things as it is instilled into his soul, and recreate for us a picture, "surcharged with moods and feelings, everchanging and wonderful like nature itself." He might, like Mi Yujen, give us a landscape of nestling clouds and enveloping mists which entwine the rocks and encircle the trees, in which all details are submerged in the general moistness of the atmosphere, or, like Ni Yunlin, he might give us a picture of autumn desolation, with the country a stretch of blank whiteness and the trees so sparse of foliage that only a few dangling leaves affect us by their loneliness and their shivering cold. In the power of this atmosphere and this general rhythm, all details will be forgotten and only the central mood remains.

Notwithstanding this identity between the art of Confucianism (and especially of Taoism) and that of Buddhism there is also the difference which gives Buddhist art in certain respects much more in common with Western art; namely, its more evident highly symbolic character. The beauty of the Buddhist works of art is not merely in the differentiated aesthetic materials for themselves, conveying, as do the Chinese landscape paintings, the feeling of the aesthetic manifold in and for itself, the external objects appearing only incidentally; it involves also a much larger symbolic reference depending upon a doctrinal element. This symbolic reference is, however, to the equally aesthetic and immediate Nirvana factor, the undifferentiated aesthetic continuum. Thus it distinguishes itself from the symbolism of Western painting. The symbolic factor expresses more than the all-embracing "Buddha-nature." It is also attempting to convey the infinite fertility of this "nature," as the source in birth, and the receiving receptable in death, of the transitory differentiations which appear within it. The Buddhist symbolism is also trying to direct the aims of the observer along the practical way or "mystic path" to the pure Nirvana; depicting the life of the Buddha to this end. Consequently, the Buddhist art is attempting to accomplish, in aesthetically immediate moving terms, what the Buddhist dialectic logic of negation attempted to do theoretically, when it moved from one of the four major systems of Buddhism to another.

Thus Buddhism uses all the arts to convey, denote, and guide man to the intuitive, aesthetic component in things with which it identifies the divine (Plates XV and XVI); much as Roman Catholicism in the West has used all the arts to direct man's thought to and bring his emotional practical life into conformity with the different logically given, doctrinally designated, theoretic component in the nature of things with which it identifies the divine. So successful have the Buddhists been that Marco Pallis is moved to describe the largely Buddhist culture of Tibet as follows:

There is no phase of Tibetan life which is exempt from the all-leavening doctrinal influence, nor is it easy to pick out an object of which it could be said that its inspiration is purely secular. . . . The aim of ritual—and ritual must be regarded as a synthesis of all the arts, acting as the handmaids of Doctrine and collaborating towards one end—is to prepare the mind for metaphysical realization, to spur it on to pierce the veil of the finite and to seek Deliverance in Knowledge, that is, in identification with the Supreme and Infinite Reality. The latter is devoid of every determination whatsoever, even unity or goodness; that is why the least misleading title that the human mind is capable of inventing for It, is the Void Itself. No symbol can stand for It save only vacuity. The Jewish Holy of Holies, enclosing nothing except an empty space, must be saluted as a triumph of art. Apart from this special instance, all art must concern itself with forms; it is there where its sphere lies. Once it has helped to pilot the mind up to the frontier between Form and the next stage, the world of Non-form, its task is over—. . . . Even ritual is not efficacious in its own power— . . .

Another quite significant commentary upon the effect of Buddhism, coming as it does from a Westerner, is Marco Pallis's following remark: ". . . deification of race, or the nation, now so prevalent in many Western countries, is a serious and destructive form of idolatry. To read eternal qualities into things so utterly temporal is a symptom of low intellectuality." The Buddhist thesis that all sensed or introspected determinate things are transitory, is evident.

TRADITIONAL INDIA

Even before the impact of the West, traditional India was an exceedingly diversified and complicated culture. Western influences have made it more so. In 1940, India had a population of roughly 350,000,000. Of this total 239,000,000 were Hindus, 77,000,000 Mohammedans, approximately 13,000,000 Buddhists, 8,000,000 Animists, 6,000,000 Christians, 4,000,000 Sikhs, and a little more than 1,000,000 Jains, with roughly 100,000 Parsees or Zoroastrians. There remain slightly more than 2,000,000 representing minor religions.

These figures give the proportions of the various components of

India's kaleidoscopic culture. They are misleading in only one respect. Buddhism has a greater influence in India than these figures indicate, because it has determined in part the character of Hinduism as well as being the guiding pattern of its own adherents. Since the basic doctrine and insight underlying Buddhist culture has been determined, the main task which remains in order to understand the culture of India is that of analyzing Hinduism and Mohammedanism with respect to their overt character and their underlying conceptions of the nature of man and the universe. One need add merely that the Buddhism of Tibet represents but some of the several forms of Buddhism, whereas in India are found all its many forms which the analysis of its philosophical doctrines has indicated. Roughly, the Buddhism of the Southern school is Hinayanistic; that of the Northern school, Mahayanistic. As Ananda K. Coomaraswamy has indicated in his *Buddhism and Hinduism*, "The two schools originally flourished together in Burma, Siam, Cambodia, Java and Bali, side by side with a Hinduism with which they often combined." The Southern, Hinayanistic Buddhism survives today not merely in India but also in Ceylon, Burma, and Siam. The Mahayanistic Buddhism of the Northern school is not merely the Buddhism of Tibet, but also passed over into China, Mongolia, Korea, and Japan, to exist side by side with Taoism, Confucianism, and Shintoism and to become fused with them. In the latter countries the "greatest influence was exerted by the contemplative forms of Buddhism; what had been Dhyana in India became Cha'n in China and Zen in Japan." Thus India is the home of Buddhism as well as of Hinduism and Jainism.

When one first compares Buddhism, Hinduism, and Jainism, as they exhibit themselves in the concrete art, both painting and architecture, of India, what most impresses one is the difference between them. Instead of the serene calmness of the Buddha, interspersed at many points and times, to be sure, with manifestations of frenzy and fury, one finds in the wall paintings and the sculptured figures of the Hindu temples an overwhelming burst of differentiated passion and fury with a frank and most realistic emphasis upon sexual passion and erotic relations, which in the artistic symbolism and the ritual of the Hinduism of the Tantric doctrine becomes to Westerners not merely religiously incomprehensible but positively shocking.

Here, however, as at other points in Oriental culture, one must be cautious before allowing oneself to be driven suddenly to a conclusion. Many considerations warrant this caution.

The major one is that the Buddha himself, who lived, according to tradition, around 600 B.C., continuously affirmed that there was nothing original in his teaching. Just like Hinduism in all its different forms and branches, the Buddha went back to the early Upanishads and the Vedic hymns and literature which were the Scriptures of the Hindus. In fact, the Buddha maintained that he was merely leading a Hinduism, which in time had become formalized, back to its own basic and initial insight and wisdom which even in the Buddha's time was in Hinduism and had been merely obscured by its practitioners. This requires one to examine Hinduism and especially its early sources before coming to the conclusion that it is radically and fundamentally different from Buddhism.

HINDUISM

The initial impression, when one examines the non-Buddhist, indigenously Indian philosophies and religions, as C. A. Moore has recently indicated, are their tremendous differences. Roughly, the early Hindu tradition and literature, that known as the Vedic, falls into four parts. These are termed the Samhitas, the Brahmanas, the Aranyakas, and the earlier Upanishads.

The first of these four, the Samhitas, are, as the literal meaning of the word indicates, "collections" of verses. These collections, as Surendranath Dasgupta indicates, are four in number; "namely, Rg-Veda, Sāma-Veda, Yajur-Veda and Atharva-Veda." Of these the Rg-Veda is the most important, since the others are either repetitions of parts of it or its spirit, or applications in prayers or rituals. These Samhitas are largely in verse form and were sung, being memorized and transmitted from generation to generation. Note again this presence and importance of the aesthetic.

The Brahmanas were ritualistic and more theological in character and written in prose. They dealt with the diversified symbolism of the rituals and were exceedingly imaginative in character. The result, as Surendranath Dasgupta has written, was "the production of the most fanciful sacramental and symbolic system. . . ."

The Aranyakas, or "forest treatises," were meditative in character; but meditative, as their name indicates, in a naturalistic setting. These forest treatises had the effect of breaking the more intelligent members of the religious tradition away from the Brahmanic emphasis upon ritual. Surendranath Dasgupta notes that forthwith philosophical speculation arose. To a Westerner, however, such a description must inevitably be misleading. One merely has to consider the character of these meditations, which their name indicates, to note that it was a meditation and a "philosophical speculation" arising in connection with an immediate apprehension and contemplation of nature, when one is immersed in an overwhelming Indian tropical forest. Out of these forest meditations which revived the original basic intuition of the Rg-Veda the philosophy and religion of the Upanishads arose.

In these Upanishads the philosophy and religion of Hinduism came to expression. Again it must be noted that the Upanishads are in verse form, and, as we shall see, these verses are heavily loaded with aesthetic content.

According to the orthodox Hindus the attendant distinctions of Indian philosophy and religion fall into two main portions: (a) the nastika, the unorthodox, and (b) the astika, the orthodox. The basis of this distinction, according to the orthodox Hindus, is that the unorthodox group, made up of the Buddhists, the Jainists, and the Carvakian materialists, does not accept the infallibility of the Vedas; whereas the orthodox group does. This claim of the orthodox Hindus must be taken with certain qualifications: First, the leaders of the three unorthodox groups maintain the contrary, insisting that they still retain and in fact only properly give expressioin to the original Vedic wisdom. This has been noted also in the case of the Buddhists. Surendranath Dasgupta, and Sir John Woodroffe in his mature and profound *Shakti and Shākta,* make clear that it is equally true for the Jainists.

In the case of the Carvakian materialists, who affirmed the existence of material atoms, it is well to keep in mind the realistic Hinayanistic Buddhism of Vasubandhu to which reference has been made. This system, it will be recalled, was also materialistic, since it denied the existence of persisting substantial selves, while affirming the existence of external material objects. It might very well have affirmed also that these material objects were atomic as well as gross in character. It is well known, however, that in this materialistic Hinayanistic Buddhism of Vasubandhu there was no rejection of Nirvana. Perhaps the Carvakian materialists among the Hindus were like Vasubandhu among the Buddhists. Democritus in the West held a similar theory, affirming the existence not merely of the unseen, material atoms but also the existence of the immediately apprehended continuity of the sense world. The Russian scholar S. Luria has shown recently that it was by this means that Democritus reconciled the discovery of incommensurable magnitudes in Greek mathematics with the atomic theory called for by early Greek physics.

Moreover, the Chandogya Upanishad, whose doctrine is attached to Vedic sources, was materialistic in the sense that it regarded everything including "the mind" as "consist[ing] of food" as "the breath consists of water [and] the voice consists of heat." These three atomic materials, food, water, and heat, as R. E. Hume's translation shows, were the elements from which all things, persons as well as the sun, the moon, and lightning, are made. When one inquires concerning what is meant by "food, water, and heat," one finds, as the name of the last suggests, that they are defined after the manner of Aristotle, Berkeley, and Hume in the West in terms of their immediately sensed qualities. Furthermore, there is no substantiality to the lightning apart from the three sensed forms which are its sensed qualities. Moreover, the sensed qualities are, as Galilei, Berkeley, and Hume maintain, "mere names." Thus the Chandogya Upanishad specifies, "Whatever red form the lightning has, is the form of heat; whatever white, the form of water; whatever dark, the form of food. The lightninghood has gone from the lightning: the modification is merely a verbal distinction, a name. The reality is just 'the three forms.'" Thus, the Carvakian materialists may have been materialistic merely in the positivistic and nominalistic sense of this Chandogya Upanishad. In any event, the matter is not important with respect to analysis of Indian culture, since this school of Indian thought never succeeded in gathering about itself a sizable group of followers. It has had very little effect upon either traditional or present Indian institutions.

The astika, or orthodox indigenous Indian philosophy, falls into six systems. These are called orthodox precisely because they are in basic agreement. Consequently, their differences and even their names are of no concern here. One may merely note that they range over almost all subjects, from the nature of the "true self," through the Upanishads and the principles governing rituals to logic, metaphysics, law, and physics, including even semantics. One of these systems is sufficient for present purposes; namely, the Vedanta, since it treats of the basic philosophy of the Upanishads, especially as commented upon by Sankara; and it is this form of orthodox Hinduism which largely defines and determines the culture of most of the Hindu portion of traditional India. This philosophy of the Vedanta exhibits itself in the Upanishads and in the many different orthodox Hindu philosophies and religious practices which ground themselves upon the Upanishads, which in turn, as Franklin Edgerton indicated, express little not in the early Vedas.

In the examination of this orthodox Hinduism there are many advantages in selecting for investigation that specific one of the orthodox Hindu rituals and doctrines which is known as the Tantric Shakta. First, it is a form of orthodox Hinduism which is apparently not merely different, but most shockingly different, from Buddhism and Jainism, and even from other forms of orthodox Hinduism. If there is an identity of this extreme form of Hinduism with Buddhism, then the proof of agreement is established for all the other Hindu systems, since they differ less obviously from Buddhism than does the Tantric form. A second advantage is that attention concentrates upon a specific, concrete example, making it possible to study something definite with care, rather than to have attention dissipated and made superficial by an incomplete attempt to examine everything. The third is that we have at our disposal in the English language the translations of the main Tantric treatises and the product of a lifetime of immediate acquaintance with them in India and of mature reflection upon their meaning, by Sir John Woodroffe in his detailed, systematic, and profound *Shakti and Shâkta*. In this instance the translation and study by an Englishman who has lived his life in India, rather than by a native Indian is an advantage, for if an Englishman, coming to the East with all the assumptions of the West, finds this apparently most shocking form of Hindu culture not merely identical in its main tenets with other forms of Hinduism and with Jainism and Buddhism, but also religiously profound and of unquestionable moral value, then the verdict is all the more impressive.

A few general considerations and references to the Upanishads will prepare the way for an appreciation and correct understanding of Sir John Woodroffe's conclusions. The first thing which the Hindu continuously emphasizes and impresses upon anyone who would understand the basic philosophical and religious insight of India is that it refers to something which must be immediately experienced to be known, and which cannot be attained by the logical methods of Western science, philosophy, and theology or described in any determinate way.

The first question to be asked in the light of this fact is why, then, the Orientals, both Hindus and Buddhists, as has been noted, have developed so many logically formulated philosophical systems in so many respects similar to if not identical with many systems of the West. The answer to this query is to be found in two considerations: First, even when the Easterner formulates such logically subtle and systematic systems, the words in these systems for the most part, although not always, tend to refer to immediately apprehended factors. They are thus concentrating on differentiated, transitory factors in the aesthetic continuum rather than logically inferred, theoretically formulated, external, common-sense, scientific, or philosophical structures of the Western type having to do with the theoretically known component in things. Second, even if, in the cases in which it occurs, the logical formulation of an Oriental system does involve reference to external common-sense or scientific objects of the Western type, these systems tend to be used not as in the West to show what the most important factor in the nature of things is, but instead to show what it is not. Consequently, for the Easterner, even when he develops logically formulated systems containing most subtle distinctions and technical concepts, his aim tends to be to direct the reader away from the persisting, postulated, determinate theoretical component in the nature of things in which the West believes, toward the indeterminate, indescribable, ineffable, and immediately apprehendable aesthetic factor, which neither logical methods nor philosophical or scientific theory can convey.

This shows itself throughout all the Oriental philosophies. In China, for example, as Hu Shih has made us aware, Mo Tih developed logical and scientific methods not unlike those of the West. An examination of his writings will show, however, that this logical reasoning was applied only to immediately apprehendable factors. Mo Tih writes, as translated by Hughes, "The universally true way of learning by investigation whether a thing exists or not is, without question, by means of the actual knowledge (on the evidence) of everybody's ears and eyes. This is the criterion of whether a thing exists or not. If it has been heard and seen, then it undoubtedly is to be taken as existing." When one moves on, however, to note how Mo Tih applies this empiricism, he finds that what he uses this method to verify is this same immediately experienced "all-embracingness," the same indeterminate "all-inclusiveness" common to all persons and all aesthetic objects, which we noted to be at the heart of Confucianism and of Taoism. The manner in which the logically formulated systems of Buddhism functioned also, by means of the logic of negation, to direct man's attention to this same immediately apprehended, indeterminate aesthetic continuum as the primary factor, has been previously noted. Thus both Mohism in China and Buddhism suggest the answer to the query. The Oriental asserts the primary factor in human nature and the nature of all things to be something which neither the formal methods of science and philosophy nor, determinate qualities can convey; and uses logically formulated doctrines, without contradiction, either positively to lead one toward the primary indescribable factor or else negatively to designate what the primary factor in the nature of things is not.

Hinduism itself supports this conclusion. Charles Johnston, in his commentary on the Kena Upanishad, summarizes the Hindu attitude as follows: "All rationalistic philosophies end, and inevitably end, in agnosticism. This is the one logical conclusion to the search for knowledge in that way by that instrument . . . having been inspired and set in motion by intuition, . . . the rationalistic philosopher instantly turns his back upon intuition. . . . Having begun with intuition, he should go on with intuition." As the Katha Upanishad expressed it, "Nor is this mind to be gained by reasoning; . . . It is to be apprehended . . . by direct experience." Surendranath Dasgupta, in his description of the logical, scientific, and rationalistic method of the West when used by the Indians as a negative method, adds: "We cannot describe [the positive factor toward which this negative method is guiding one] by any positive content which is always limited by conceptual thought."

Turning to this positive factor in the Hinduism of the Tantric Shakta, one finds Sir John Woodroffe writing that it "is actual immediate experience . . ." He makes it clear, however, that the factor in knowledge which the treatises of this particular Hindu teaching are attempting to point out to men is not any specific immediate experience or the totality of immediate experience, but a factor in this totality which requires a definite practical method and procedure for its discovery by itself. He adds, furthermore, that the Orientals generally, Buddhists as well as Hindus, insist that this method is thoroughly scientific, different to be sure from the scientific methods of the West, but even more completely empirical and positivistic than the latter methods because no use of abstract, mathematical equations or formal, logical reasoning is involved. In fact, the Tantric, or other treatises describing this Eastern method, Sir John Woodroffe continues, "were regarded," as a Tibetan Buddhist once explained to him, "rather as a scientific discovery than as a revelation." Consequently, these treatises describe "a practical philosophy, . . . a philosophy which not merely *argues* but *experiments*. . . . All that exists is *here*. There is no need to throw one's eyes into the heavens for it. . . . The claim of the Agama [the Tantric treatise on method] is that it provides such means and is thus a practical application of the teaching of the Vedānta."

This method falls into two parts, the one the method of the ritual which takes one part of the way to the basic factor in immediate experience; the other the method of the Yoga, which takes one the rest of the way. "In order to understand the ritual," Sir John Woodroffe continues, "one must know the psychology of the people whose it is; and in order to know and to understand their psychology, we must know their metaphysic." The use of the word "metaphysic" here must not be allowed to lead anyone astray. In the Western sense of this term these Easterners are not metaphysical at all; instead they are the most extreme positivists, since they insist that no reality exists except that which is immediately apprehended. The inferred, postulated type of knowledge of the West designating unobserved electrons, electromagnetic propagations, or the unseen God the Father they tend traditionally to deny. Thus they are metaphysical only in the sense that they claim to have noted an immediately apprehended factor in experience in addition to the data given through the specific senses.

Sir John Woodroffe writes of this factor: "As the Varāha Upanishad says it is 'The Reality which remains after all thoughts are given up.' What it is in Itself is unknown but to those who become It. . . . It is [the] . . . boundless substratum which is the continuous mass of experience . . . [the] primordial extensity of experience . . .'" It is termed "primordial" because "if it be not positive at the beginning, it cannot be derived at the end." What the Hindu is saying here is that this indeterminate boundless factor in immediate experience must be taken as an irreducible element in scientific and philosophical knowledge. It cannot be defined in terms of, or deduced from, anything else, whether this something else be its immediately apprehended differentiations given through the senses or the inferred, syntactically designated, indirectly and experimentally verified theoretic component in things.

From this it follows that all things, whether they be non-human or human natural objects, must be conceived as made up of this boundless indeterminate aesthetic factor as one of their irreducible, elementary components. It follows also that the individual, local, determinate, conscious self is not to be conceived as a postulated, persisting, mental substance which, by means of some mysterious faculty, projects out of itself the emotionally moving, aesthetically vivid, immediately apprehended differentiated aesthetic continuum. The logical and the causal order is precisely the reverse of this. Instead of the undifferentiated or the differentiated aesthetic continuum being projected and known by faculties of the postulated substantial self, or modern Western mental substance, the emotionally laden aesthetic self and the emotionally laden aesthetic object must be conceived as constituted of the irreducible aesthetic continuum. We are conscious, emotional, aesthetically luminous creatures not because we are a purely spiritual or purely mental, reflexively presupposed, or postulated, substance; but because we, like all other aesthetically immediate determinate things in the universe, whether they be the knowing subject (*purusha*), or the known object (*prakriti*), are constituted of the emotionally moving, aesthetically ineffable, indeterminate aesthetic continuum. As the Tantric doctrine puts it, Chit, the "unchanging formlessness" is the source of consciousness in the self.

Of Chit, Sir John Woodroffe writes:

There is no word in the English language which adequately describes it. It is not mind: for mind is a limited instrument through which Chit is manifested. It is that which is behind the mind and by which the mind itself is thought, . . . The Brahman [which is identical with Chit] is mindless. If we exclude mind we also exclude all forms of mental process, conception, perception, thought, reason, will, memory, particular sensation and the like. We are then left with three available words, namely, Consciousness, Feeling, Experience. To the first term there are several objections. For if we use an English word, we must understand it according to its generally received meaning. Generally by "Consciousness" is meant self-consciousness, or at least something particular, having direction and form, which is concrete and conditioned; an evolved product marking the higher stages of Evolution. According to some, it is a mere function of experience, an epiphenomenon, a mere accident of mental process. In this sense it belongs only to the highly developed organism and involves a subject attending to an object of which, as of itself, it is conscious. . . . If then we use (as for convenience we do) the term "Consciousness" for Chit, we must give it a content different from that which is attributed to the terms in ordinary English parlance. Nextly, it is to be remembered that what in either view we understand by consciousness is something manifested, and therefore limited, and derived from our finite experience. The Brahman as Chit is the infinite substratum of that.

Furthermore, Chit "is immediacy of experience." But it is "undifferentiated (Abhinna), all-pervading (Sarvatravastha), . . . pure (Shuddha) experience. . . ." In short, Brahman in Hinduism is the same immediately apprehended, undifferentiated aesthetic continuum which was found to be Tao in Taoism, *jen* (human-heartedness) in Confucianism, and Nirvana in Buddhism.

Mind, on the other hand, is a localized, differentiated limited portion of the otherwise undifferentiated boundless Chit or Brahman. Thus whereas Chit is unchanging and formless, mind is transitory, changing, and limited or formed. Hence, mind arises as does an immediately sensed, differentiated natural object, when Chit, or the undifferentiated aesthetic continuum, becomes limited and in certain parts determinate, because of its differentiations. Consequently, mind, or the full, determinate personality, is for the Hindu as for the Buddhist no more immortal and able to escape the death which overtakes all determinate, differentiated things than is the determinate natural object. Only the portion of mind and the object which is Chit, the undifferentiated aesthetic continuum, is timeless and escapes "the ravages of death."

But Chit, or Atman, the undifferentiated aesthetic continuum, is in the immediately apprehended natural object in its empirically given aesthetic character as much as it is in mind. As R. E. Hume's translation of the Svetasvatara Upanishad expressed it,

> The Soul (Atman) which pervades all things
> As butter is contained in cream, . . .
> This is Brahma, . . .

Thus, both mind or the determinate personality and the natural object are constituted of (a), Chit or Brahma, common to all things, and (b), the qualities (*guna*) differentiating one determinate part of Chit from another determinate part. As Sir John Woodroffe writes, "This appearance of Consciousness [in mind] is due to the reflection of Chit upon it." Similarly, all determinate natural objects, whether they be persons or flowers, or mountains, or streams, are made up of two aesthetic factors which the Tantric Hinduism terms the Chit-Shakti and the Maya-Shakta. The former is the undifferentiated aesthetic continuum which is in all objects in their purely empirically given, immediately apprehended component as well as in all persons; the latter is the limiting principle, or the sensed differentiations distinguishing one object in the complex aesthetic continuum from another, and the determinate self from its determinate object.

It follows from this that if it may be possible, by some experimental technique, to eliminate the Maya-Shakta differentiations from the complex aesthetic continuum, so that only the emotionally moving, aesthetically ineffable, indeterminate field factor in it remained, then all distinction between the knowing subject and the known object, and between the personal self and the non-personal natural object, would be escaped. The knower would be identical with its object, and the object would be identical with the knower.

It is precisely this which the Oriental method known as the Yoga attempts to achieve. It is to be emphasized that the method is perfectly definite and practical. It is a straightforward matter of experimentation as to whether or not it is possible to eliminate all differentiation from the totality of immediately apprehended fact, and whether anything positive remains when this is done.

One technique for doing this is as follows: The experimenter goes into the mountains, usually up a high valley, and sets up a laboratory. This laboratory consists of a small, thick-walled building completely tight on all sides. The man puts himself in this small building and in certain cases has the doorway completely filled in except for one small opening sufficient to permit entrance of a minimum of food and air. Outside of this opening he also may have a lean-to with a small doorway, just large enough to let some attendant enter with the necessary food. This entrance is placed on a side of this lean-to which is not directly opposite the opening into the main experimental chamber. By this technique the experimenter eliminates from the immediately apprehended differentiated aesthetic continuum all differentiations which arise from the sense of sight. The location, high up a mountain valley, and the thick walls help also, especially when there is not a heavy wind outside, to eliminate all differentiations due to the sense of hearing. By keeping food at a bare minimum and by avoiding all exercise as far as health will permit, one also cuts to a minimum the differentiations arising from the bodily senses. Even this, however, is not enough. One must remain in this state until one also eliminates from the immediately apprehended aesthetic continuum, all differentiations due to thought and imagination. Not until all these differentiations are eliminated does the crucial experiment give a decision with respect to the question it is devised to answer.

Westerners as well as Orientals who have performed this experiment report that the outcome is precisely what the Oriental philosophical and religious doctrines maintain. Instead of being left with nothing, as the Westerner first supposes would be the case, because of his unconscious habit of identifying the whole of the nature of things with a determinate kind of thing, the report is that one is left with one of the most emotionally overwhelming, aesthetically ineffable experiences, with no sense either of self or of objects, which it is within the possibility of man to enjoy; and that even though this experience is indeterminate, it nonetheless has a greater emotional intensity and aesthetic ineffability and luminosity than the more determinate, differentiated experiences of the specific senses exhibit.

This helps us to understand why the Oriental insists that the giving up of the traditional Western religious belief in the immortality of the determinate human personality, for a religious belief in the indeterminate, all-embracing Brahman or Nirvana, gives a heightening, rather than a loss of human spiritual consciousness. Since the differentiations limit and inhibit consciousness, to pass into the unlimited formlessness of Brahman is to gain release. One escapes what the Maitri Upanishad terms being "beaten by qualities." This also makes clear what the Oriental Hindu means when he says that the immediately apprehended differentiations, given through the senses and introspectively, veil consciousness or Chit. The point is that the local differentiations, since they contain a portion of the undifferentiated aesthetic continuum or Chit, are emotionally and aesthetically moving; hence mind is conscious; but because they limit the overwhelming boundlessness of the otherwise undifferentiated aesthetic continuum, they at the same time lessen the intensity of its emotionally moving, aesthetic ineffability which one might enjoy.

According to the Hindu doctrine, not all people have the capacity or the inclination to apprehend the undifferentiated aesthetic continuum by itself in its purity. The select few who do are called Siddha. Those of the next most proficient group are termed Sadhaka. The latter attain the Brahman, but do it only by the help of the ritual of the religious ceremonies. It is to be noted that in the experiment previously described in which the undifferentiated aesthetic continuum was gained in its purity, no ritual was involved. A Sadhaka, the second most select type of person in the Hindu community, is one, however, who does not succeed in escaping from this dependence upon the ritual. That this does not give the pure, undifferentiated Brahman, is shown by the fact that in the ritual, limited, determinate, aesthetic symbols are used. This entails that the distinction between the worshipping subject and the object still remains. When any such distinction or differentiation is present it follows necessarily that one does not have the pure undifferentiated Brahman, however close to it the ritual may have taken one.

Even within the ritual there are different types, some of which take one nearer to the undifferentiated Brahman than do others. Certain people are so constituted psychologically that they require greater determinate symbolic aids than those provided by other and simpler forms of the ritual. In this manner people are classified in society according to their differing capacities to achieve Brahman in its purity without any differentiations. That individual or group of individuals is called the most perfect, which comes the nearest to the experience of the undifferentiated aesthetic continuum in its purity. It is in this conception that the caste system of India, in part at least, has its basis. The untouchables, some 70,000,000 in number, are orthodox Hindus with the Brahman in them, yet at the bottom of the ladder of caste. So deeply is this system rooted in India, Krishnalal Shridharani informs us, that when "some years back, Gandhi staked his life on the cause of the untouchables, the whole of India, from the Himalayas to Cape Comorin and from the Arabian Sea to the Bay of Bengal, was thrown into a terrific seizure of anguish and alarm." Recent developments are altering this attitude.

The position of this outcast group in the Indian social system is not unlike that of a similar outcast group in the Anglo-American and Western world. Both groups owe their unfortunate social status to religious and moral beliefs. Those in the West, like the untouchables of India, are not cast out because they are completely bad or completely outside the pale of religion, as the conversation of Christ with the woman at the well clearly demonstrates. The Western outcasts, like the Indian untouchables, are where they are because the divine goodness which is in them, at least potentially, is associated with so many other factors that people in a higher status in the social scale cannot associate with them without being ostracized.

Nevertheless, there is an important difference between the two groups. Whereas the criterion of the outcast group in the West is sexual in character, the untouchables of India, as we have noted, are cast out for quite different reasons. This has the effect of excluding sexual imagery from the religious symbolism in the West and of freeing erotic forms for the conveying of religious doctrine in India, especially in the Tantric sects. Thus, what is shocking to the Westerner has no evil associations for the Tantric Hindu.

A second factor leading the Hindu to an erotic symbolism is his identification of the divine and the good with the emotional aesthetic component, rather than the unseen theoretical component in the nature of things. For the Indian, and for the Oriental generally, as for the Western Spaniard, emotion or passion is of the essence of human nature and of the divine nature.

A third factor is that the undifferentiated, emotionally or passionately moving, ineffable aesthetic continuum which we have shown also to be what is meant by *tao, jen,* Nirvana, and Brahman, is often referred to throughout all Oriental religions, as the female principle. It will be recalled that the *Tao-Teh-King* asserts—

> The spirit of a valley is to be undying.
> It is what is called "the Original Female,"
> And the Doorway of the Original Female is called "the
> root from which heaven and earth sprang."

Similarly, India as a whole is referred to as "Mother India," and the Shakti doctrine of its Hinduism is by definition the doctrine of the worshippers of the emotional female principle in things. "Shakti in the highest causal sense is God as Mother, and in another sense it is the universe which issues from Her Womb." (Woodroffe)

This female divine factor, identified with the undifferentiated aesthetic component in things, may be considered in two aspects, both of which are essential to her nature. The Brahman, Chit, or Shakti may be considered in itself apart from its differentiations. When considered in this changeless aspect it is called Shiva. It may also be considered in the aspect of the source out of which its determinate, transitory differentiations come and to which in their death they return. This is the female principle in its creative, determinate, changing manifestations. The female divine principle differentiates itself, as has been previously noted, by the use of the limiting Maya principle which is "that Power by which infinite formless [Chit] . . . veils Itself to Itself and negates and limits Itself in order that it may experience Itself as Form."

In this process, as previously noted, the distinction arises between mind or the subjective differentiated personality (*purusha*) and any other natural object (*prakriti*). It is to be recalled that in the ritual even the highest of the Hindus does not escape completely from this subject-object otherness and dualism. Hence, what the ritual has to do is to exhibit the indeterminate, undifferentiated, aesthetic unity running through this difference between the personal self and its object. This is accomplished by identifying the differentiating Chit-veiling activity with one human figure in the religious symbolism, and the Chit-revealing Shiva, with another human figure, and then wedding the two male and female figures. Thus, as Sir John Woodroffe emphasizes, when the artistry and the ritual of the Tantric Hinduism are correctly understood their frankly sexual symbolism reveals a very mature and profound philosophical and religious doctrine.

A culture born of such a religion would hardly need a Freud. Even so, Hinduism is more subtle and restrained than Freudian psychology. The sexual passion, being determinate, leads to death, since all determinate aesthetic things are transitory. Nevertheless, sexual passion is the divine passion in one of its limited and veiled manifestations, since every determinate experience is a differentiation of the otherwise indeterminate aesthetic boundlessness which is Chit or Brahman. Consequently, the only lasting happiness and emotional satisfaction is obtained when one moves from this active, limited, human passion to the more passive, undifferentiated and hence timeless, ineffable, infinite self, which is the divine compassion.

Consequently, as Sir John Woodroffe emphasizes, even this Tantric ritual of Hinduism, while giving expression to the emotional, passionate nature of human beings, puts no premium or sanction upon sexual license. Only as the Tantric ritual, with its sexual symbolism, teaches one that determinate passions, being transitory, will never give permanent emotional satisfaction; and as it exhibits the indeterminate, all-embracing, compassionate aesthetic continuum common to all different things, thereby leading one on beyond the merely human portion of one's nature to the divine, is its character understood, or is the attention upon the sexual which it engenders given the sanction of either the Hindu morality or its religion.

Thus underlying the Tantric as well as all other forms of Hinduism and determining the ultimate aim and character not merely of all the Hindu treatises but also of all its art and its ritual is the same primacy and irreducible ultimacy of the indeterminate aesthetic component in things, given with immediacy, which has been found to be similarly basic in all the forms of Buddhism and in the "human-heartedness" of Confucianism as well as the *Tao* of Taoism. One is therefore able to understand what Ananda Coomaraswamy means when he writes in his *Hinduism and Buddhism*, "The more superficially one studies Buddhism, the more it seems to differ from the Brahmanism in which it originated; the more profound our study, the more difficult it becomes to distinguish Buddhism from Brahmanism, or to say in what respects, if any, Buddhism is really unorthodox."

Sir John Woodroffe adds:

To the Western, Indian Religion generally seems a "jungle" of contradictory beliefs amidst which he is lost. Only those who have understood its main principles can show them the path. . . . It has been asserted that there is no such thing as Indian Religion, though there are many Religions in India. This is not so. . . . there is a common Indian religion . . . which is an Āryan religion . . . held by all Āryas whether Brahmanic, Buddhist or Jaina.

Sir John Woodroffe and Ananda Coomaraswamy concur also in finding the same identity between the basic factor in the Chinese and Indian religions that they find in the three major indigenous religions of India alone.

It appears that jen in Confucianism, Tao in Taoism, Nirvana in Buddhism and Brahman or Atman or Chit in Hinduism and Jainism are all to be identified with the immediately apprehended aesthetic component in the nature of things, and with this in its all-embracing indeterminateness, after all sensed distinctions are abstracted. Evidently, Oriental civilization has a single predominant meaning.

CHAPTER X

THE MEANING OF EASTERN CIVILIZATION

The meaning of Oriental civilization—that characteristic which sets it off from the West—may be stated very briefly. The Oriental portion of the world has concentrated its attention upon the nature of all things in their emotional and aesthetic, purely empirical and positivistic immediacy. It has tended to take as the sum total of the nature of things that totality of immediately apprehended fact which in this text has been termed the differentiated aesthetic continuum. Whereas the traditional West began with this continuum and still returns to local portions of it to confirm its syntactically formulated, postulationally prescribed theories of structures and objects, of which the items of the complex aesthetic continuum are mere correlates or signs, the East tends to concentrate its attention upon this differentiated aesthetic continuum in and for itself for its own sake.

ORIENTAL POSITIVISM AND REALISM

As a consequence, whereas the Orient is for the most part continuously positivistic, the West tends, as S. Luria and Max Planck have noted, to be positivistic only during those revolutionary transition periods in its historical development when the traditional scientific and philosophical doctrine has broken down in the face of new evidence, and before the new, more adequate one has been put forward to take its place. And even during these positivistic periods the aim in the West has been to bring attention back from the traditional doctrine to the immediately apprehended data in order to construct afresh a more deductively fertile and extensively verified new conception of the theoretic component.

It appears therefore that the meaning of Eastern civilization in its relation to the meaning of Western civilization is as follows: *The Orient, for the most part, has investigated things in their aesthetic component; the Occident has investigated these things in their theoretic component.* Consequently, each has something unique to contribute to

375

an adequate philosophy and its attendant adequate cultural ideal for the contemporary world. The East and the West, when analyzed to determine their basic scientific and philosophical foundations, are found to be saying, not, as Ananda Coomaraswamy has suggested, the same thing; nor, as Kipling affirmed, two incompatible things; but, instead, two different yet complementary things. Thus, although the two great civilizations are different in a most fundamental and far-reaching way, there can nonetheless be one world—the world of a single civilization which takes as its criterion of the good a positivistic and theoretically scientific philosophy which conceives of all things, man and nature alike, as composed of the aesthetic component which the Orient has mastered and the theoretic component which it is the genius of the Occident to have pursued.

This means that the present meeting of the East and the West, to which individual decisions in both parts of the world have already committed mankind, may occur without conflict providing each understands the other. It means also that this can occur with genuine additions to and enrichment (aesthetically, scientifically, economically, and religiously) of the traditionally incomplete cultures of the two civilizations.

It is to be emphasized, however, that this happy possibility will not come to pass automatically. Two things are requisite: First, the specific relation between the aesthetic and theoretic components must be determined, thereby permitting the newly formulated world philosophy to specify the theoretical criterion by means of which the two differing cultures and their attendant different ideals, grounded in these two components, can be combined so that they will reinforce and sustain rather than convert, combat and destroy each other. This is by no means an easy task, as the difficulty of clarifying the relation between empirical aesthetic qualities and mathematical theoretic factors in Newton's physics and modern Western philosophy clearly indicates. This is the basic problem, and must soon concern this inquiry. Second, the aesthetic component and the specific character of the Oriental culture which is based upon it must be fully understood. This must now be determined. The Oriental more positivistic concern with things in their aesthetic immediacy has had two consequences which to a Westerner seem self-contradictory. First, there is a stark kind of realism, a this-worldly concern with the concrete, and an unflinching acceptance, in religion as well as philosophy and practical life, of the pains, disappointments, the inescapable cruelties of the struggle for existence, and the inevitable death which we observe to overtake all determinate things, whether these different things be the individual human personality or the determinate natural object. Second—and it is this second factor which distinguishes the positivism of the Orient from that of the West, especially in the modern world—there is what seems to a Westerner an excessively speculative other-worldliness. However, as was indicated in the previous chapter, this turns out instead to be as positivistically immediate and possessed of all the attendant stark realism which attaches to the transitory, determinate differentiations which come and go within it.

All this becomes clear when it is realized that what is immediately apprehended is the all-embracing differentiated aesthetic continuum, every determinate sensed or introspected quality of which is transitory, whereas its otherwise indeterminate intuited continuity is not perishable, yet, in part at least, is as positivistically and realistically given in immediate apprehension as are its differentiations (Plate XIV). That this is the case is shown by the fact that what one immediately apprehends is not merely the atomic, transitory qualities, but also the otherwise undifferentiated aesthetic continuum in which these occur, part of which is indeterminate, as William James noted, even when the determinate qualities in other parts of it are not abstracted.

Thus it is to be emphasized that when the Oriental designates the *Tao*, Nirvana, Brahman, or Chit to be something which is not given through the specific senses, he does not mean that it is a speculatively postulated, syntactically designated, and only indirectly and experimentally verified entity such as the mathematical, as opposed to the sensed, space in Newton's physics, or the unseen God the Father in the traditional Christianity of the West. He means, instead, as the previous analyses of the major religions and cultures of the Far East have indicated, something which is not inferred, not speculatively arrived at by the logical scientific method of hypothesis, but which is immediately experienced, its "transcendency" of the senses being due to the fact that the senses deliver specific, limited, determinate data within it, whereas it is indeterminate and all-embracing.

Precisely because of this the tremendous emphasis upon aesthetics and the highly ineffable and mystical quality of Oriental culture arises. What is given positivistically as pure fact, apart from all speculative hypotheses, is colors, sounds, fragrances, and flavors in the aesthetic continuum. All these are aesthetic materials. They are the kind of thing with which the novelist, the painter, the musician, and the epicure deal. Moreover, aesthetic vividness, feeling, and emotion are of their essence.

It is the beauty of the immediately apprehended aesthetic sunset which moves one, not Locke's or Berkeley's supposed mental substance. Moreover, none of these aesthetic factors can be conveyed to anyone who has not immediately apprehended them. This is precisely what is meant by the ineffable and the mystical. Thus the tremendous emphasis upon passion and aesthetics in religion and in daily life, and the obvious mystical emphasis in Oriental doctrines and in the practices of their Taoist and Cha'n Buddhist painters, is a consequence of, not in opposition to, their thoroughgoing positivism.

The positivists of the West have failed to arrive at this consequence of their position because, instead of using the immediately apprehended positivistic data to derive from them what they can give, they have used them to attempt to construct deductively formulated theory. More concretely, instead of attempting to get art from their positivism, they have attempted (unsuccessfully) to get mathematical physics and (with more success) the laws governing the movement of prices in the market place. The strength and the truth of positivism is in the realm of art of the Oriental type, and in a religion of the emotions. When one attempts to derive from it the mathematical physics and the philosophical doctrines of traditional Western culture the consequence is, as its own Western proponents insistently assert, that the basic concepts of mathematics become nothing but meaningless marks on paper, and that most of the traditional scientific and philosophical theories of Western civilization become similarly meaningless nonsense. The virtues and consequences of positivism are to be found in the East, not in the West.

This does not mean that positivism has not served a very important function in Western culture. This function has been, however, to plow under the old weeds and straw in those transition periods when, after the last season's crop has been harvested, the soil must be prepared for the planting and growing of the new. Consequently, whereas the positivism of the Orient functions positively and continuously to give its culture the religious and aesthetic, and extremely concrete realistic institutions and values which it enjoys, the positivism of the West functions more negatively, but nonetheless necessarily, during the transitional periods in its theoretically grounded culture when new empirical evidence forces a repudiation of the traditional doctrine and attendant social institutions, thereby preparing the way for the more adequate conception of the theoretic component and the attendantly more correct idea of the good for man and society which must replace the old one.

The stark realism of Oriental culture merits attention more in detail. Nowhere does it exhibit itself more notably than in the attitude of the Buddha as portrayed in Edwin Arnold's *The Light of Asia*:

> . . . But, looking deep, he saw
> The thorns which grow upon this rose of life:
> How the swart peasant sweated for his wage,
> Toiling for leave to live; and how he urged
> The great-eyed oxen through the flaming hours,
> Goading their velvet flanks: then marked he, too,
> How lizard fed on ant, and snake on him,
> And kite on both; and how the fish-hawk robbed
> The fish-tiger of that which it had seized;
> The shrike chasing the bulbul, which did chase
> The jewelled butterflies; till everywhere
> Each slew a slayer and in turn was slain,
> Life living upon death. So the fair show
> Veiled one vast, savage, grim conspiracy
> Of mutual murder, from the worm to man,
> Who himself kills his fellow; . . .

Even Darwin, with all his emphasis upon the struggle for existence, was not more unflinchingly realistic than this.

But there is more:

> . . . the taste is emptied from his mouth,
> The hearing of his ears is clogged, the sight
> Is blinded in his eyes; those whom he loved
> Wail desolate, for even that must go,
> The body, which was lamp unto the life,
> Or worms will have a horrid feast of it.
> Here is the common destiny of flesh:
> The high and low, the good and bad, must die.

Nor does the doctrine of the reappearance of life after death in transmigration help:

> . . . 'tis taught, begin anew and live
> Somewhere, somehow,—who knows?—and so again
> The pangs, the parting, and the lighted pile:—
> Such is man's round. . . .
> Since pleasures end in pain, and youth in age,
> And love in loss, and life in hateful death,
> And death in unknown lives, which will but yoke
> Men to their wheel again to whirl the round
> Of false delights and woes that are not false.
> Me too this lure hath cheated . . .

Even the appeal to the determinate, omnipotent, perfect God or gods of the later theistic Western or Middle Eastern religions, into which, according to the Buddha, the original Brahm of Hinduism had degenerated, is of no avail:

> . . . I am as all these men
> Who cry upon their gods and are not heard
> Or are not heeded— . . .
> Perchance the gods have need of help themselves
> Being so feeble that when sad lips cry
> They cannot save! I would not let one cry
> Whom I could save! How can it be that Brahm
> Would make a world and keep it miserable
> Since, if all-powerful, he leaves it so,
> He is not good, and if not powerful,
> He is not God? . . .

This disillusionment about the "Brahm" of Hinduism had arisen for the Buddha in his time because, as Paul Deussen notes, Hinduism, probably through its excessively human and realistic ritual, had become so obsessed with the determinate differentiations in the aesthetic continuum that it had come even to conceive of the Brahman in this manner, thus turning It into a determinate god of the Western theistic type. Thereby the root insight of Brahmanism, the true nature of the divine, that is, the compassionately moving, *indeterminate* aesthetic continuum, had been lost. As a consequence the Buddha takes it upon himself to return men to the initial and basic Hindu insight of the Vedas and the Upanishads. Thus the basic identity between the conceptions of the divine in Hinduism and Buddhism, together with the fact that Buddhism was a reform movement growing out of the Hindu tradition, are both explained.

The important point, however, is that the Buddha, for all his return to and more insistent emphasis upon the primacy of the indeterminate, immediately experienced, all-embracing Nirvana, was the starkest of realists. It is precisely because of this realism with respect to, and his fellow-feeling for, the immediately experienced pains and sufferings of men and animals and plants that he has attached unto himself and deservedly earned the name of the compassionate Buddha.

The realism of the Hindus, with their strikingly concrete imagery and ritual, and of the Taoists in their concern for nature, and of Confucius in his absorption with the five specific relations between men in society is equally evident. As a consequence, all the Orientals, for all their religion of the emotions, for all their mysticism, and for all their emphasis upon the ineffably indeterminate portion of man's nature and the nature of things, are the most earthly, practical, and matter-of-fact of people. So much is this the case that even the British or the Americans, for all their supposed superiority with respect to the practical virtues, are often shocked, when they find themselves in the Orient, by the excessive prevalence of these traits. This stark realism and its attendant tempering of the determinate general principle to the local circumstances and immediate intuition of the moment is so extreme in the Orientals that when the Westerner, especially the moral and religious missionary, finds himself in contact with them, his initial impression tends to be that they are the most unequivocal opportunists, without any moral principles whatever.

THE RELATIVITY OF DETERMINATE VALUES

This attitude is illustrated by the impatience with which an American missionary once voiced such an impression. A few years previously he had been a halfback carrying the ball for his Methodist college in the United States. The good old Western Christian spirit, according to which one lays down one's life if necessary in order to get that specific determinate touchdown, was still in him. In the same spirit he was now carrying the gospel in China. Neither in his morality nor in his religion was there any *wock jeh* (Perhaps!); everything was certain and determinate. A man was not a man unless he was willing to lay down his life for the determinate thesis. With this background he arrived one afternoon fresh from his contact with his Christian Chinese converts. "These Chinese," he exclaimed, "have no character. We make it clear to them that becoming a Christian involves the complete dedication of one's own life and will to the will of God. We point out specifically in terms of concrete conduct what this involves. They seem to understand and accept all that we say, becoming Christians. Then the first moment this decision becomes the least bit inconvenient for them, they drop it."

Obviously, the Christian missionary was a little excited, and undoubtedly after further reflection he would have modified this judgment considerably. But his overstatement was not his most serious error. He had in fact come into direct contact with a factor in the Oriental conception of the nature of things and in the Oriental character which is undeniably there. His only error was that, viewing this factor from the limited standpoint of the morality, religion, and culture of the West, and having not even the slightest comprehension of the different, more positivistically grounded philosophical conception of the nature of things of the East and the attendant different Oriental morality and religion which rest upon it, he had judged the behavior of his Chinese friends to be a thoroughgoing vice instead of the virtue which it is from their traditional standpoint and in part from anybody's standpoint, when the full grounds of morality and religion are properly understood.

The Westerner will undoubtedly be inclined to reply: "But how in the name of anybody's morality, whether it be Confucian or Christian, can one ever condone the failure to keep a promise, especially when the promise involves the dedication of one's life in a religious decision to one's Creator?" The answer is that one cannot; but before one jumps from this admission to the conclusion that the behavior of the Chinese in the above instance was a breach of faith, one must take into account what the initial commitment must have meant to the Chinese mind. And for this it is necessary to know the traditional Chinese standpoint on such matters.

Suppose that the Chinese or any other Oriental whose morality and religion are not of the Christian, Hebrew, Mohammedan, or Shinto theistic type, conceives of the totality of the nature of things as largely composed of nothing but what is immediately apprehended. Restricting himself thus to what is thereby certain, since it is not speculatively inferred, he would note within it the two factors previously indicated: (1) the indeterminate aesthetic continuum named "Void," Brahman, *tao*, Nirvana, or *jen*; and (2) the transitory differentiations in their transitory and relativistic associations which appear within it. Thereby, he would conceive of himself and all other things as merely instances of these two factors. Good conduct in morality and religion would then become conduct which is true to this conception of the nature of things.

As long, therefore, as an Oriental acted in accordance with this purely empirically grounded, and hence positivistically true conception of the nature of himself and things, he would be a man of principle as much as any Westerner is a man of principle. But since the Oriental grounds his religion and morality in this positivistically given aesthetic factor in things alone, whereas the Westerner tends to identify the Divine and the Good with the syntactically designated, only indirectly and experimentally verified, theoretic component in the nature of things of which, to the traditional Westerner, the aesthetic component is the mere sign or correlate, the principle underlying the Oriental's moral conduct would be different from that guiding the good conduct of the Westerner.

In precisely what, as it affects conduct, would this difference consist? An examination of the two factors, indicated above, making up the Oriental's conception of the nature of things provides the answer. These two factors are (a) the indeterminate aesthetic continuum common to all persons and all things, and (b) the immediately sensed differentiations within it. The former alone, it is to be noted, holds for all people under all circumstances, since it alone is not transitory, and does not vary from person to person and from time to time. Consequently, the only good to which one has a right to commit oneself permanently, the only good which is true for everybody, is that which in conduct gives expression to this emotionally immediate, aesthetically vivid compassionate but *indeterminate* aesthetic oneness within oneself and all things. "To preserve this *jen*," Confucius says, "the superior" or moral man "will lay down his life."

When one turns, however, to the second factor in the nature of things, the aesthetic differentiations and their determinate limited forms and relations, the situation is different. All these things are transitory. Moreover, they are relative to both the determinate natural object and the determinate individual personality. Being existent things, and part of one's nature and the nature of things as much as is the non-transitory undifferentiated aesthetic continuum, they are real and good also. Thus Confucius finds it good to allow the determinate aesthetic flavor of the bamboo sprouts to come to full expression in his conduct; and the Taoist finds it good to allow the immediate, emotionally moving, all-embracing determinate beauty of nature to come to expression in himself and in his painting. But these determinate differentiated parts of oneself and of all things, while good, are goods which vary from person to person and from time to time. Consequently, to suppose that any commitment which one makes to them is something to which a moral or religious man must remain committed for all eternity and under later, different circumstances is to be as false to the nature of oneself and to the nature of things as one would be if he failed to be true to *jen* or *tao* at all times and under all circumstances. Consequently, Confucius said, "The superior man goes through his life without any one preconceived [determinate] course of action or any taboo. He merely decides for the moment what is the right thing to do."

This is undoubtedly precisely what the Chinese convert at Canton thought was meant when he committed himself to a determinate form of Christian conduct in becoming a Christian. It would never occur to him, because of his Chinese background, to suppose that the Christian missionary meant that he must commit himself to the specific, determinate line of conduct under all circumstances, which the Christian missionary specified at the moment. Consequently, when different circumstances arising in the future seemed to make that specific form of conduct less attractive or less wise than it was under the previous circumstance, he could, in all sincerity and intellectual and moral honesty, give it up without any sense of having gone back on his initial commitment.

Certain qualifications upon this Oriental restriction of the absolute and non-transitory in morality and religion to the indeterminate must be noted. They appear in the conservatism of Confucian society, in the Indian caste system, and in the ritual and painting of Buddhism (Plate XV). With respect to Confucian society it is to be recalled, however, that Confucius taught a complete ethical relativism and opportunism with respect to determinate taboos or "any one preconceived line of action" and that he regarded the return to the society of the ancients as good only so far as the indeterminate *jen* (compassion) was embodied in it. Moreover, the Chinese Taoism unequivocally attacked the organization and rigidity of Confucian society, urging *laissez-faire* nonaction and a return to nature. With respect to the Hindu caste system and the formulism of much Buddhist ritual and art, the determinate constancies arise either because they represent different degrees of proficiency on the way to Brahman or Nirvana where they are to be dropped, as the provisional, transitory things which they are, or because of the problem of conveying the indeterminate Nirvana in terms of the determinate. In so far as the determinate symbols of the ritual or the art are taken for traits of the divine, they defeat their own end. It was precisely because this had happened in Hinduism that the Buddha inaugurated his reform movement attacking the caste system and the literalness of the ritual.

The Oriental positivism appears in other ways. Hu Shih's description of Confucius and Mo Tzu as positivists has been noted previously. Confucius taught that "true knowledge depended upon the investigation of things," and that one must have such knowledge before one can have human-heartedness or *jen*. The good for the Oriental is merely the correct theory of the positivistically, empirically true or real (*ch'eng*). But good conduct involves this theory of the positivistically true put into action. This requires the third Confucian virtue, courage. Thus Confucius taught that the three means or requirements for the good life are (1) *chih*, arrived at by *ch'eng*, *i.e.* positivistically given "realness," or truth; (2) *jen*, the indeterminate, aesthetically felt, passionately warm man-to-man-ness, continuous with and hence common to all things which realness exhibits and truth designates; and (3) courage or fortitude, to which, Confucius says, "the sense of shame" is akin.

It is to be noted, consequently, that in "the investigation of things," which must be pursued before one can know human-heartedness or *jen,* the things investigated are not the things of culture, but the things of nature. That this is true is shown by the fact that *jen* refers to the immediately apprehended, indeterminate aesthetic continuum which is in nature, as the Taoist emphasizes, and in the natural man, as Confucius emphasizes, and this fact is quite independent of the institutions of culture. Chiang Yee tells us that Lao Tzu and Chung Tzu urged man's "return to his original primitive state, where he learned the art of living from nature herself in place of fallible human laws." This is undoubtedly the reason why Confucius maintained that the true conception of the good in conduct would be found not by looking at contemporary human and social conduct and institutions, but by going back to the conception of society which men had at the very beginning of Chinese civilization, when they were confronted with approximately little more than nature, before man-made cultural institutions had come very fully into existence. In short, what Confucius was saying is that one's idea of the good for culture is identical with one's positivistically and hence scientifically descriptive concept of the true for nature and the natural man. This identification of the good for culture with action in accordance with the empirically verified, positivistically given conception of the true for nature and the natural man gives the concepts of the Confucian ethics a completely descriptive, cognitive meaning, and makes its propositions scientifically verifiable statements. It is precisely because of this that Confucius makes *ch'eng* (intuitive naturalistic truth) a prerequisite for *jen* (fellow-feeling between men in society).

But *ch'eng* and *jen* are not sufficient to give good conduct, since they insure merely the correct theory of the good but not its application in conduct. For the latter, courage or fortitude is also required; the courage namely to act as the verified theory of the true indicates. This courage, Confucius tells us, "is akin to the sense of shame." Note how this virtue also is identified with a sensation, not with a theoretical doctrine or a willful conviction.

The precise character of this sense of shame must be grasped if the concrete behavior and psychology of Oriental people are not to be misunderstood. This sense of shame is experienced by the Oriental in two forms: One, when, treating *jen, tao,* Nirvana, or Brahman as though it were a determinate transitory thing, he denies it; or, two, when, treating a determinate, transitory thing or plan of conduct as though it were a non-transitory, immortal principle, he commits himself to it for the future, for a time longer than the circumstances inherent in all transitory determinate things will warrant. It is the latter sense of shame which is at the basis of the Oriental's "loss of face." This shame is nearer to chagrin, the chagrin at failing to remember the most elementary truth drilled into one by centuries of teaching; the truth namely that all determinate things are transitory. It is also the fear of the latter sense of shame which is behind the Cantonese rickshaw boy's response with an indefinite *wock jeh* (Perhaps!) instead of a determinate "Yes, Sir"; and the traditional Oriental aristocrat's hesitation to commit himself to any determinate line of conduct for the future, unless plenty of bridges have been left standing behind so that he can retreat gracefully, should altered circumstances tomorrow make the proposed determinate plan less wise than it seems today.

THE POSITIVE ETHICAL DOCTRINE

The meaning of Oriental morality may be summarized, therefore, as follows: It identifies the real and the good with the nature of things in its empirical, positivistic, aesthetic immediacy. In this totality of immediately apprehended fact it finds two factors: the one, indeterminate, all-embracing, and not transitory; the other, determinate, relativistic, and transitory. Both, being true components of all men and all things, are good, and good conduct consists in accepting them for nothing more or nothing less than they are.

The good which is identified with the indeterminate, all-embracing factor is the only good which is absolute in the sense that it holds for all people under all circumstances. It has this absolute character because in fact it is not transitory or different in one person or thing from what it is in another. The good which is identified with the determinate, limited, differentiated factor is relative, not merely varying from person to person or from thing to thing but also, for a given person, from circumstance to circumstance and from time to time. Again, the good has these characteristics not for an *a priori*, theoretical, or hit-and-miss pragmatic reason but simply because this is what we immediately apprehended man and nature to be.

It takes as much courage to apply the relativistic portion of the principle as to apply its absolute portion. To be sure, it takes courage to retain one's common, warmly compassionate fellow-feeling for all persons and all things, in the face of the equally real, emotionally powerful differences which distinguish one person or thing from another. Shame comes upon the man who, by knowledge, has become aware of the indeterminate aesthetic continuum of feeling in all fellow-creatures, whether they be persons or other natural objects, when, in spite of this knowledge, he does not act in accordance with it. The shame arises because he realizes upon reflection that in denying the other person *in toto,* he is, in that very act, also denying and being untrue to himself, since the continuous, or field, component of his aesthetic self is in the other person as much as it is in him. But to treat the determinate portion of one's introspected convictions and the determinate portion of other persons and things for what they are, namely, factors which do not hold for everybody under all circumstances, and hence as factors which one has no right to elevate into immortal commandments, giving one the supposed moral and religious duty to force them upon other people—this also takes courage.

This is what the quoted Buddhist meant when he advised us "to giv[e] up the distinction between [determinate] virtue and vice," and "to consider with perfect equanimity and detachment the conflicting opinions and the various [differentiated] manifestations of the activity of [determinate] things." None of these determinate things is in itself either good or evil; it merely is. Evil arises with respect to them only when we treat them as if they were something other than what they actually are; just as good applies to them only when we treat them for as much as, and nothing more than, they actually are. Thus, for example, the sexual passion becomes evil only if we treat it as a non-transitory thing and the sole end of human existence, instead of merely the transitory differentiation along with countless other equally good and limited determinate transitory passions in the all-embracing and more permanently satisfying compassion of the indeterminate aesthetic manifold, out of which it arises in early youth and into which it gradually vanishes in later middle age. Similarly, to treat determinate pleasure as the sole criterion of the good, holding under all circumstances, is wrong

—not because pleasure is not good, but because such behavior involves elevating a transitory thing which exists only under certain circumstances into a rule holding under all circumstances.

Such a conception of the good is not wrong merely because it is untrue to the nature of things, but also because it defeats its own purpose by causing one to be irritated with the universe when specific sensed pleasures are not present, thereby unnecessarily increasing the amount of unpleasantness which one experiences. Likewise pain is not evil; it merely *is*. Good and evil have their origin, with respect to pain as with respect to pleasure, not in the pain itself but in one's belief about it. Pain becomes evil only when the pessimist, like the hedonist with respect to pleasure, elevates a transitory thing into a universal, immortal principle, and thereby regards it as something other than what it is. Pain can be an object of the good life as well as pleasure. It becomes this when one takes it as it comes for nothing less and nothing more than the determinate, limited, and hence partial, transitory thing which it is. It is in this courage, required to act with respect to the relative, determinate, transitory, differentiated portion of oneself and all other persons and natural things, taking them for precisely what they are—nothing more and nothing less—that the equanimity, the poise, the steady, sure peace of mind, and the all-embracing calmness and joy of the Oriental have their basis.

The good is not to be found by hunting among all the facts of experience for one determinate factor such as pleasure, mind, or personality and then selecting it, to turn it into a general criterion of the good holding under all circumstances. Instead, the good is to be found by taking all things, meaning thereby, for the Oriental, all immediately apprehended things, with the utmost realism and positivism for precisely what they are.

No objection can be found to this Oriental conception of the good as far as it goes. It is to be noted that it avoids the culturalistic fallacy which appeared in the post-Kantian philosophy of both Hegel and Marx. The only error is that of omission rather than commission. This error arises from the restrictedly positivistic conception of human knowledge, restraining it solely to the realm of the immediately apprehended, denying any component in the nature of things of which the immediately apprehended is the epistemic correlate or the sign, and tending to reject all postulationally designated, indirectly verified, theoretically known factors with mathematical and logical methods alone can determine in a trustworthy manner. The Oriental world obtained a realistic and true religion of the emotions, a realistic and true morality for that aspect of man and nature which is positivistically immediate, and a pure and true appreciation of the overwhelming beauty of immediately sensed things in and for themselves. It even obtained an excellent descriptive natural-history type of science and the beginnings of a theoretical, deductively formulated, experimentally verified science. But because of its tendency to regard the latter logically constructed type of knowledge as illusory, and only the positivistic aesthetic component in knowledge as genuine, it never followed through its initial discovery of the theoretic component to develop the deductively formulated and more pragmatically and technologically powerful, indirectly and experimentally verified science of the West with its attendant, logically and systematically formulated philosophy of the nature of things. This the Orientals themselves are now realizing, as the next chapter will show.

This suggests that one of the greatest of contemporary Western mathematical physicists, Max Planck, was correct in maintaining that positivism, when conceived as a complete philosophy of science, would "paralyze the progress of science." This consequence of positivism has been very difficult to demonstrate in the West because few creative scientists have been positivists, and because the positivists always smuggle in, in practice, the theoretically designated meanings for the terms they use, to which their own premises do not entitle them, thereby, as Planck has noted, giving their thesis that nothing exists but the immediately apprehended an apparent capacity to do justice to scientific knowledge which it does not possess. Only in the Oriental world do we have a properly controlled experiment with respect to the consequences of positivism, an experiment in which the experimenters consistently restrict themselves to the immediately apprehended, branding all logically inferred, theoretically designated reality as illusory. The result is precisely what Max Planck indicated. The purely intuitive, descriptive type of natural history science arose, and the beginnings of deductively formulated scientific theory were discovered; but because the latter type of knowledge was branded as representing nothing real and as being a mere subjective construct, it was never seriously pursued.

THE CONCEPTION OF ECONOMIC VALUE

The positivistic Oriental thesis that all determinate things are relative to the individual and to circumstance and are transitory, had interesting consequences for economics. The concept of economic value became relative from person to person and also from occasion to occasion. This shows itself in the fact that goods in the traditional stores of the Orient do not carry fixed price tags. Instead, agreement is reached upon a price which varies from one economic transaction to another for the same article in the same store, by a somewhat lengthy, human-hearted process of bargaining. In this process each party tends to exaggerate the very opposite of his major aim, the buyer attempting to impress the seller with the feeling that the purchaser wants the article less than his presence in the shop indicates, the seller similarly trying to convince the buyer that the shopkeeper has less interest in disposing of the product than his presence in business indicates. But both parties know that this is going on, and that it is merely a means by which each is trying to be sure that his own relativistic interest in the object is, under the circumstances, getting precisely the weight which it deserves. Thus the relativity of economic value is recognized, and justice is achieved in the final balance struck in the bargaining.

Through all this relativity of economic prices and determinate personal valuations and through all the relations between the buyer and the seller one additional factor must be present if the entire proceedings follow the Confucian or the Oriental ethics. There will be what to the Westerner seems a severe, almost cold-blooded bluffing; but through it all and underneath it all there must be a good humor, a human-heartedness, a man-to-man-ness—in short, there must be *jen*. Both parties must give expression not merely to the conflicting relativity of human nature and human values, but also to the non-conflicting one-ness of the indeterminate, emotionally moving continuum of sympathy and feeling which is in all persons and in all things.

THE ATTITUDE TOWARD THE LAWYER AND THE SOLDIER

This same acceptance of the determinate in all things in its relativistic character and in its transitoriness underlies the Chinese attitude toward legal conflicts and toward war. To turn one's private, determinate, introspected convictions into immortal moral and religious issues, thereby giving rise, as the moral, legal, and religious teachings of the West tend to do, to costly legal disputes to the bitter end in law courts, during which every party loses and a fair balance of justice to both parties under all the circumstances tends to be lost; and to nationalistic wars in which again, in the name of laying down one's life for one's determinate moral and religious convictions, everybody loses; the traditional Chinese believes that the existence of such Western egocentric determinate moral and religious commandments is a sign of the absence, rather than the presence, of moral and religious wisdom.

The assumption of the Western court that one side or the other must get the verdict is, to him, an expression of the fallacious notion that the determinate aspects of conduct have an absolute character holding for both parties; and that consequently the determinate conduct of one must be right for both, and the determinate conduct of the other wrong for both. For the same reason also the soldier, that person in the community who would settle disputes not by reasonableness but by force and by bloody battles to the death, was in China placed at the bottom of the social scale. But even when placed there, the traditional Chinese soldier was a very peculiar one from the Western standpoint. For in the eyes of the Westerner he lacked morale. He did not mind which cause he fought for. In fact, he did not want his enemy to be defeated too quickly or even at all, for this would mean that he would be without work. His attitude toward the cause of the battle was similar to the attitude of an ordinary laborer in the Western world as to which contractor he works for. To be sure, he preferred to be on the winning side, if there had to be a victory, since this would mean that his job would be less likely to end abruptly.

In practice, however, the soldier had a big place in the traditional China. The reason for this has to do with certain other things in the Oriental and especially the Chinese idea of the good which have been noted. First, there is the sense that all determinate relations between things are transitory. This makes it difficult for the Oriental to generate the widespread spirit of agreement necessary to construct a strong, unified state. Second, there is the tremendous primary emphasis upon the family. This family relationship does hold precisely because it can be positivistically and biologically apprehended. It does go on in time longer than do governments. But even families rise and fall. Thus, as Lin Yutang has noted, the Chinese do not expect too much constancy or idealism in social relations between men beyond the reaches of the family. This tends to make them suspicious of social reforms on a large scale. The tendency is to regard it as expecting too much of human nature to hope that a determinate social relation beyond that guaranteed by the family will maintain itself. As a consequence, the traditional governments were family or royal governments. And in between the family which provided the sovereigns and the local individual families making up the community there tended to be a vast no-man's-land. In this vast no-man's-land the soldiers and the bandits had their sway.

This rule of the bandits with their soldiers, in its relation to government, especially the local governments, tended to be a very realistic one, during those periods in which the royal sovereign and his family were weak. To be in the government, to be the governor of a province, meant that with one's paid soldiers one had the authority and the capacity to collect taxes. These taxes were collected by stopping the boats as they came down the main rivers which formed the great transportation systems of China. But the party out of power (*i.e.* the strongest bandit) also had its soldiers, not so many, to be sure, as the government; otherwise, that party would be in power. With these soldiers one also stopped boats and collected one's own taxes. The more boats one stopped, the more soldiers one could hire; and the more soldiers one could hire, the more boats one was able to stop. Thus the circle went on until finally the party out of power, called the bandit, had as many soldiers as the party in power, which was called the government. Then a war broke out.

This war was not fought with too great seriousness. The soldiers on either side did not have their hearts in it, in the Western sense. They had no interest in laying down their lives in the name of a moral or religious conviction. In fact, their morality never asked this of them, but on the contrary taught them that such an attitude is immoral and irreligious. Their moral savior was never presented to them as a leader nailed to a cross. Such a giving of one's life for a determinate human thesis on any side of any dispute would, from the standpoint of their religion and morality, be evil rather than good. Thus in the battle between the bandit and the government there would be the same stern, severe evidences of one's strength on both sides which goes on in the bargaining in the tradesman's shop; but everyone would understand that during the very noisy shooting, noses were being counted, the number of soldiers on both sides was being determined, and the battle was being fought not with the idea of one side slaying and exterminating the other, but with the much wiser purpose of deciding who was to be the government.

What tended to happen was that the governor, having profited very well by his government, lacked the interest to pursue the issue further. He, like all good Orientals, was interested in the achievement of a contented old age. This would be especially true if, while the guns were being fired off, and as a result of the counting, he found that the bandit forces had a greater number of soldiers than his own army, or even an equal number. These signs would mean that the time had come when it was proper for him to retire and to give the government over to his adversaries. Before this happened, rumor had it that it was proper and customary for him to visit the treasury. In more recent decades it became the proper practice also to remove oneself gracefully from the scene in order to leave the new governor without any sense of opposition. This was accomplished by taking up one's residence outside the province, usually in one of the foreign settlements. Thus it is that although in China the soldier was placed at the bottom of the social scale, the country was not without its soldiers. They were, however, soldiers distinctly different from their Western prototype, especially with respect to their morale. All these factors must be recognized if the difficulties in the way of the modern Chinese in their recent attempt to create a nation of the Western type are to be understood and appreciated.

THE CRITERION OF SOCIAL STATUS

The Oriental belief that all determinate things are transitory does not mean that certain things are not more permanent than others. This is a matter, however, for direct empirical, positivistic observation to determine. To precisely the extent to which, let us say, the relations of the family are observed empirically to be more constant than other relations, to this extent these relations take precedence over all others, precisely as noted in Confucius's treatment of the five distinct social relations. The matter is further complicated, in the case of India, by the hierarchic ordering of different individuals in society in accordance with the degree to which they have the natural capacity to grasp the indeterminate, all-embracing, aesthetic component of immediate experience, Brahman, in its purity. This places those members of the community who can grasp Brahman without ritual at the top of the social scale in the same manner in which Confucius and Chinese culture place the scholar there.

The positivistic Oriental emphasis upon the greater constancy of family relations over other relations resulted in the tendency to identify these ethical distinctions connected with scholarship or with pure religious intuition with social and family distinctions, thereby, in the case of India, hardening a social hierarchic ordering, based upon a definitely religious principle, into a rigid heriditary caste system, entrance into which depended in practice not upon one's capacity to achieve the higher worth defining the higher classes in the system, but instead upon the previous social status of the family into which one chanced to be born. Thus Indian culture tended in practice in its development of the caste system to deny the operation of the distinction which brought it into existence. Recognition of this fact should enable the Indians to correct the abuses which this error in application has produced, while at the same time retaining the traditional truth which the initial inception of the caste system in Indian culture envisaged.

In this respect the Chinese in their recognition of certain classes in the community being higher in the social scale than others, because their conduct exemplifies a more correct conception of the complete and true nature of things than does the conduct of other people, were more wise and consistent in their application of this principle, since the class of scholars which their culture designated as the highest class was more open to every member of the community. Here also the emphasis upon the family supported, rather than opposed, the moral principle in practice. For the individual family in China is interpreted in an exceedingly wide sense, bringing in distant cousins and uncles and even distant generations, thereby comprising literally hundreds of people. As a consequence, when even the humblest child shows signs of scholarly capacity, he has often at his disposal the resources of hundreds upon hundreds of people to provide the means to take him in traditional times to Peking for the great examination; or to take him in more recent times to the most expensive, distant and best of the Western universities. But these wise roots of a democracy which has quality as well as quantity in its conception of the good life are present throughout the entire Orient, in India and Tibet as well as in China, Japan, and Korea. And with it all is the support of a compassionate religion of the emotions and the cultivation of a refined perception of beauty.

THE PRIMARY FACTOR

Within this realistic, exceedingly positivistic Oriental philosophy and religion of the compassionately emotional and aesthetically immediate type, certain factors are regarded as more elementary, primary, and hence basic, than others. The West did this also for its theoretic component of knowledge. According to contemporary Western scientific theory, planets, tables, living organisms, protein molecules, electrons, protons, the space-time continuum, electromagnetic waves, and the electromagnetic field with its difference of potential exist. But all these scientific objects are not aggregated on the same level of importance. Some, such as the electron and the space-time continuum or the electromagnetic field, are regarded as more elementary, primary, and basic than others, such as molecules, tables, and planets; since (a), the latter scientific objects are compounded of the more elementary structures or entities; and (b), the elementary factors have greater persistence and invariance. Similarly, with the differentiated aesthetic continuum the Orient regarded that factor within it which is the indeterminate undifferentiated aesthetic continuum as more elementary and primary than the differentiations, (a) because any differentiation is always a differentiation of the continuum and hence requires the aesthetic continuum for its existence; and (b) because the indeterminate aesthetic continuum is an invariant factor having greater, even timeless persistence, whereas the differentiations come out of it in birth and fade back into it in death, and are thus temporary and transitory.

The reasons for this primacy of the undifferentiated aesthetic continuum seem to be justified. First, the totality of immediately apprehended fact is, as has been noted, not completely determinate and differentiated throughout its entirety (Plate XIV). This reveals an error in the modern Western supposition that the all-embracing continuity of the totality of immediately apprehended fact can be derived from the mere aggregation of the transitory differentiations given introspectively or through the specific senses. Thus the undifferentiated aesthetic continuum must be taken as something elementary and primary. This position has the second advantage of keeping the color of the sky in the aesthetic continuum of nature, where it obviously and realistically belongs; while at the same time not making the observer so completely other than the object of knowledge that one is left in the traditional modern difficulty, following Descartes and Locke, of being unable to make clear how the color which obviously belongs to the sky, rather than to the mind of Berkeley or Locke, can nonetheless be known by the knower. The reason is that the knower is not merely his own local differentiations given introspectively, but also the entire aesthetic continuum embracing all immediately apprehended things, of which the blue of the aesthetic sky is as immediate a differentiation as is an introspected pain of the observer.

Positivistic realism also supports this Oriental emphasis upon the primacy of the all-embracing undifferentiated aesthetic continuum. One has but to look at a landscape on a sunny day, with moving clouds in the sky, and take it solely in its aesthetic immediacy, dropping as far as is possible the suggestion of the three-dimensional, external objects of which the differentiated aesthetic continuum is the sign, to experience for oneself what the Oriental has in mind when he takes the indeterminate *tao, jen,* Nirvana, Brahman, or Chit as not merely primary, but as the source of the creation and the receptacle at the death of all transitory differentiated things. As one looks at the landscape, one sees this occur: A patch of yellow appears and then vanishes, to be replaced by a larger patch of green or of dark gray. No reference to energy transformations or to electromagnetic propagations can account for this fact. Subtle Western scientific theories may support in part prediction of the time at which the coming and going will occur. But none of them explains, nor does it pretend to explain, the miracle of the tireless, ceaseless creation of these ineffable, successive, emotionally moving aesthetic differentiations of the aesthetic manifold. For the source of this aesthetic creativity and for the source of its emotional, aesthetic content, something primary in the realm of the aesthetically immediate itself must be invoked; just as in the realm of the theoretically postulated of the West something primary and not given with aesthetic immediacy must be assumed.

As the primary factor in the aesthetic component of the nature of things, the Oriental selects the undifferentiated aesthetic continuum, because of its invariance and constancy, and conceives of all things, persons as well as natural objects, as made in part out of it; just as the Western scientist selects as the primary factor in the theoretical component of the nature of things the electron or the space-time electromagnetic field, conceiving of all things in their theoretically designated nature—persons as well as other natural objects—as made in part out of them. This does not mean for the Oriental that the differentiated aesthetic qualities and the arrow-like time to which their sequence of associations gives rise are not so real as is the indeterminate aesthetic continuum, any more than the taking of space-time relatedness or electrons and protons as primary in the science of the West entails that tables and chairs are not real.

The conception of this indeterminate, undifferentiated aesthetic continuum as an ultimate and irreducible factor in one's philosophy, religion, and practical outlook has important consequences. It makes the aesthetic immediacy, the communal, compassionate, emotional

quale of all immediately apprehended things, whether they be human
or non-human natural objects, something ultimate and primary in their
own right. This is why the poetry of Tagore, even when it is conveying
the traditional religious insight of the Orient, is laden with emotional
content and aesthetic imagery. "Who can strain the blue from the
sky?" he writes. Locke and Berkeley thought they could, dumping it
all inside the mental substance. But Tagore thinks otherwise:

> I hold her hands and press her to my breast.
> I try to fill my arms with her loveliness, to
>   plunder her sweet smile with kisses, to
>   drink her dark glances with my eyes.
>
> Ah, but where is it? Who can strain the blue
>   from the sky?
> I try to grasp the beauty; it eludes me, leav-
>   ing only the body in my hands.
> Baffled and weary I come back.
> How can the body touch the flower which
>   only the spirit may touch?

Here "body" must be interpreted as referring to the theoretically
conceived, three-dimensional physical object, which is an equally real
component of things; and "spirit" must be interpreted as the immediately apprehended, emotional, aesthetically ineffable field factor in the
equally real aesthetic component of the self and of things.

The primacy and creativity of the indeterminate, undifferentiated
aesthetic component as an irreducible factor, providing the emotional
immediacy and the aesthetic luminosity without which the differentiated, ineffable, more sharply determinate colors, sounds, flavors, and
fragrances of nature, and the determinate faculties of the human mind
would not be, are expressed best, in a religious form to be sure, in the
Kena Upanishad as translated by Charles Johnston:

> By whom impelled flies the forward-impelled
> Mind? By whom compelled does the First Life
> go forth? By whom impelled is this Voice
> that they speak? Who, in sooth, is the
> Bright One who compels sight and hearing?
>
> That which they call the Hearing of hearing,
> the Mind of mind, the Voice of voice, that is
> the Life of life, the Sight of sight. Setting
> this free, the Wise, going forth from this
> world, become immortal.

Sight goes not thither, nor does voice go
thither, nor mind. We have not seen, nor do
we know, how one may transmit the understanding of this; for this is other than the
known, other than the unknown also.

Thus have we heard from those who were
before us, who have declared this unto us.

That which by voice is not spoken, that
through whose power voice is spoken; that,
verily, know thou as the Eternal, not this
which here they serve.

That which thinks not through the power of
the mind; that by which, they have declared,
the mind is thought; that, verily, know thou
as the Eternal, not this which here they serve.

That which sees not through the power of
sight; that by which he perceives sights;
that, verily, know thou as the Eternal, not
this which here they serve.

That which hears not through the power of
hearing; that through whose power hearing is
heard here; that, verily, know thou as the
Eternal, not this which here they serve.

That which lives not through the power of
the life-breath; that through whose power the .
life-breath lives; that, verily, know thou
as the Eternal, not this which here they serve.

This Upanishad is attempting to convey the point which the Tantric
doctrine, analyzed in the previous chapter, expressed in its distinction
between mind or *purusha* and Chit. The complete differentiated personality or mind is not conscious because it is a persistent mental substance which has a mysterious faculty by means of which it reaches out
and knows the emotionally moving, aesthetically vivid sensed qualities
which a different equally mysterious faculty of this mental substance
has projected as mere appearances. Instead, the aesthetically immediate
continuum is reality. Moreover, its emotional, all-embracing ineffability
is the very stuff of which the conscious self is made. Thus, man is conscious because Chit, the indeterminate immediately felt, aesthetically
luminous continuum, is in him and is not mere appearance but the

essence of his nature. It is because human beings are made up of an ultimate, essentially ineffable stuff of this character that they have consciousness and that there is an all-embracing, emotionally and aesthetically moving world to be experienced with immediacy, and that this immediately experienced world is not a disconnected set of separated determinate items but these in a continuous, all-embracing manifold. It is the primacy of this manifold which gives to the sensed color of the sensed object in nature the same ineffable, emotional, aesthetic vividness which the one aesthetic continuum exhibits in one's own self. Thus, as the Hindu puts it, the Atman, which is the source of the psychic character of the self, is identical with Brahman, which is the cosmic principle of the universe.

Confucius expresses this primacy of the indeterminate aesthetic factor and its importance for concrete daily life in another way. The basic thesis, however, is the same. "The power of spiritual forces in the Universe—how active it is everywhere! Invisible to the eyes, and impalpable to the senses, it is inherent in all things, and nothing can escape its operation." Its practical importance appears in the following statement: "There is no one who does not eat and drink. But few there are who really know flavor." The point here is that the common-sense man, and even the Western scientific, philosophical and religious man, tends to use the aesthetically immediate merely as the springboard for arriving at his postulationally prescribed, only indirectly and experimentally verified beliefs about three-dimensional, external, common-sense objects; microscopic, atomic, scientific objects; and equally theoretically conceived religious factors such as the rational principle or *logos*, identified with God the Father or the purely spiritual, local, mental substance identified with the human soul in the traditional modern Christian religion. Thus both the common-sense man and the Western scientist, philosopher, moralist, and theologian tend to treat the aesthetically immediate merely as a means rather than as an end or as something which is good in its own right and for its own sake. Only if one realizes, Confucius believes, and the whole Orient with him, that there is a factor in the realm of the aesthetic which is not a mere sign of something beyond itself or merely transitory, but which is ultimate, irreducible, and non-transitory, will a proper appreciation of aesthetics be achieved, and a life which is good because it gives expression to and is in accord with the true nature of things be lived. The flavor of the bamboo sprout has mediately an immortal, a non-transitory value because it is but the manifestation in determinate, transitory, limited form of a non-transitory, primary, irreducible aesthetic field factor at the root of all persons and all other natural things.

Two other distinguishing characteristics of Oriental culture follow from its traditional emphasis upon the spiritual and aesthetic richness of the immediately apprehended. The one is its certainty; the other its constancy through time. Both of these follow from its essentially positivistic, purely empirical character. What is immediately apprehended is immediately apprehended. If not merely the consequences of the primitive ideas of knowledge, but also the primitive basic concepts and premises themselves are found empirically in the immediacy of experience, then this knowledge is not hypothetical in character, subject to change with further information, but categorical and certain. This is precisely the character which over the centuries the culture of the Orient exhibits. Even its reformers, such as the Buddha within the culture of Hinduism, Confucius within the culture going back to the ancient classics, and the neo-Confucianism of Wang Yang-ming within the culture of Confucianism, do not introduce new premises; nor do they force the Orientals to throw aside their old ones. Instead, they frankly say that they are merely taking contemporary people back to the old basic assumptions in their initial purity and clarity or, at most, are merely exhibiting new and fresh expressions or applications of them. As a consequence, the culture of the Orient does not exhibit the radical revolutions in the basic premises of man's scientific, philosophical, and religious thinking throughout a period of five thousand years which the culture of the West exhibits within its two thousand years or even, according to the outlook of many contemporary moderns, within the stretch of a few decades.

This constancy and its attendant sense of certainty about the continuing validity of the initial basic premises become intelligible if it is realized that the West has discovered a factor in the nature of things which is known only theoretically by hypothesis, checked only indirectly or experimentally with respect to certain of its deductive consequences, but never with respect to every one of its basic initial assumptions; and that, as a consequence, these basic assumptions, being indirectly rather than immediately known, are subject to change and reconstruction with the advent of new facts, with respect to which they turn out to be incompatible; whereas the Orient has restricted its knowledge to that factor in the nature of things which is given wholly with immediacy, and as a consequence, has been enabled to gain basic premises which are verifiable immediately and completely, rather than indirectly and only partially. Thus it is that Oriental culture maintains a comparative constancy of belief and content through time, whereas Western culture and cultural institutions are continuously undergoing reconstruction, not merely with respect to their physical, material manifestations, but even with respect to the theoretical beliefs underlying them.

This positivistic character of the knowledge and culture of the Orient also accounts for a distinguishing characteristic of the Hindu, Buddhist, Taoist, and Confucian religions. None of them in its uncorrupted form is theistic. Theism in religion is the thesis that the divine is identified with an immortal, non-transitory factor in the nature of things, which is determinate in character. A theistic God is one whose character can be conveyed positively by a determinate thesis. His nature is describable in terms of specific attributes. All of the Oriental religions which have been examined up to this point deny this characteristic of the divine. The divine is indeterminate. Theses, specific determinate properties, designate what it is not; not what it is.

Even so, these four Oriental religions are not pantheistic, as many Westerners have maintained. For pantheism is the doctrine that the universe in its totality is God. Now the followers of Hinduism, Buddhism, Taoism, and Confucianism no more identify the divine with the totality of the universe, even with everything within positivistically given reality, than do the theists of the West or the other theists of the Orient. For, as has been noted, the divine is identified not with the differentiated aesthetic continuum, which is the totality of the immediately apprehended, but merely with the indeterminate, undifferentiated aesthetic continuum within this totality.

These four major Oriental religions have one other distinguishing characteristic. None of them has, or worships, a prophet. Hinduism has no specific founder. The Buddha continuously refused to permit his followers to turn him into a divine being. He insisted again and again that he was completely unnecessary; that he was merely showing the way and pointing out a factor in the nature of things which was in the original Hinduism and which one could truly and appropriately know only when the Buddha is completely out of the way; in so far as one insisted on the presence and the teaching of the Buddha, to that extent one did not completely comprehend and have the indeterminate divine element in the nature of things. Similarly, the Taoists do not worship Lao Tzu; they immerse themselves in, and immediately apprehend, nature. Likewise, Confucius was a wise man, a purely human and natural creature like all other natural creatures, but one who was wise because he adjusted what he taught about human conduct to what the immediately apprehended facts indicate concerning the nature of man and his universe. If the nature of things for religion and ethics as well as for science is given purely positivistically and empirically with immediacy, then obviously this must be the status of the moral and religious leader.

Furthermore, none of these Far Eastern religions, except the theistic Shintoism, is a tribal, nationalistic religion. All are international religions. For none of them is the divine a God of the chosen people. To get the latter type of God it is obviously necessary to attribute to the divine, traits which belong to the leaders of one people; such traits must necessarily be restricted and determinate. Obviously a religion which identifies the divine with the indeterminate and with an all-embracing indeterminateness present in the immediately apprehended aesthetic continuum, and hence open to all and in every person naturally, cannot be a religion of a determinate tribe or of the chosen few. It is as indifferent to tribal, national, and geographical lines as are the theories of Western science. It is not an accident that a contemporary Chinese is able to point out to us that race prejudice and religious prejudice are foreign to his people. Because these Oriental religions have the basis for their authority in immediately apprehended factors open to all, the need for telling other people about them, lest otherwise they also could never gain the wisdom, is not so urgent. Thus these religions of the Far East are not characterized by the missionary spirit to the extent of the theistic religions of Mohammedan India, the Middle East, and the West. None of their founders placed an injunction upon his followers to spread the gospel to the ignorant heathen. Instead, their tendency is to remain at home, opening their arms to all foreign missionaries, hoping to learn something from them.

Nonetheless, there are theistic and missionary leaders with divinely inspired prophets in the East as well as the West. This brings us to Shintoism; to Mohammedanism, which is the second largest cultural element in India; and to the other Semitic religions of the Middle East and the West—namely, Judaism and Christianity. It will suffice for the present, however, if it is merely pointed out that the traditional Japan includes Shintoism as well as Buddhism and Confucianism; and that the traditional India can be understood only if the Mohammedan factor is included along with its Hinduism and Buddhism. As both Shintoism and Mohammedanism are exceedingly important elements in the present behavior of India and Japan, consideration of their distinguishing characteristics may properly be postponed until they arise as factors in the contemporary international situation. Also, Mohammedanism was not originally indigenous to India; instead, its presence there is the result of a foreign influence coming in from the Middle East and the West. It may be treated, therefore, in connection with the influence of the West upon the Far East.

THE AESTHETIC CHARACTER OF ORIENTAL CULTURE

It would be slightly misleading to the Western mind were this treatment of the traditional culture of the Far East to close with this excessively religious emphasis. It has this character to be sure, but the Orientals are an exceedingly concrete, practical, and realistic people; and their religion is best thought of by Westerners as something nearer to what the West regards as aesthetics than it is to what the West has regarded as religion. Although the four major religions of the East, which have been considered, bring an abiding spiritual peace and a highly refined sense of beauty into the lives of even the humblest members of the community, to a degree superior to the similarly hierarchic and ceremonial Roman Catholic Christianity of doctrine, or to the similarly humanistic but otherwise antithetical and excessively egocentric Protestant Christianity of individual enterprise and reform of the West, nevertheless they accomplish this by identifying the divine with an immediately apprehended component of the nature of things which is fundamentally aesthetic in character.

But in saying this care must be taken. For—precisely because the West has had its thought largely upon the theoretically designated, systematically indicated, indirectly verified factor in the nature of things— of which the aesthetically immediate is the mere epistemic correlate or sign—the art of the West has tended to use the aesthetic materials, not to convey those aesthetic materials in and for themselves for their own sake, but in order to convey the postulationally known, three-dimensional, external objects and the unseen, doctrinally designated divinity of the Christ-child and God the Father (Plates I, V, VII, IX, XII). It was precisely because God the Father is not in the aesthetic sense world that Christ, his Son, had to come into the world. For these tasks, an art governed by symbolic references and scientifically defined, geometrically formulated laws of perspective has been necessary in the West. Automatically, however, this separates the Western artist from the object painted and tends, as the Oriental artist points out, to cause the object to be painted from the outside in scientific and geometrical, rather than purely aesthetic terms. In saying, therefore, that the culture and even the religion of the Orient are primarily aesthetic in their roots, the aesthetic must be conceived in its Oriental sense as the aesthetically immediate for its own sake and not in its Western sense as the handmaid (a) of common-sense beliefs in external, three-dimensional, geometrically proportioned objects, or (b) of more sophisticated, experimentally verified, doctrinally formulated, scientific, philosophical, or theological objects. In short, the Oriental uses the purely aesthetic to constitute the nature of the divine (Plate XIII), instead of using the aesthetic merely as an analogical symbol to convey a divinity which is defined in some other way.

This does not prevent the Orient from having a highly developed symbolism in its art, especially in certain forms of Buddhism and in Hinduism. But this symbolism, as has been noted, points not from the aesthetic component to the theoretic component in things, as in the West, but from the one factor in the aesthetic component to another in the same component. As Chiang Yee has written of Chinese painting—

Perhaps, the most important mental process in . . . it is that movement of the sympathies where the onlooker loses his own identity and becomes one with the "observed" and eventually with the Great Spirit of the Universe, which informs everything that has life.

Nevertheless, Buddhist art and Hindu art include a theoretic component in their portrayal and use of three-dimensional objects. The latter trait, surprisingly enough, has its source in an influence from the West. In fact, it is the combination of the traditional Orient and influences from the West which has produced the contemporary Orient.

CHAPTER XI

CONTEMPORARY INDIA, JAPAN, AND CHINA

The contemporary Orient is the product of its traditional self and the influence of the West. The latter influence is not of merely recent existence. In 327 B.C. Alexander the Great invaded India. Although his military conquest and rule were of short duration, they were by no means negligible in their permanent effects. For Alexander was accompanied by Greek artists, historians, and men of science.

Through these men Greek scientific ideas, particularly in the fields of mathematics and astronomy, definitely influenced the early Indian scientific outlook. Furthermore, the Greek Megasthenes was ambassador to the Court of Bengal from 306 B.C. to 298 B.C. In his reports he describes the seven castes of Hindu society in which the philosophers, who were the Brahmans, were at the top; and the inspectors, who were sages of the forest, were included. Thus there was not merely an influence of Greek thought upon the East but a corresponding effect of Oriental thought upon the West.

WESTERN INFLUENCES IN INDIA

Nor was the influence of the Greeks upon the Hindus and the Budhists merely scientific in character. It also affected their art. The Greeks, like most of the later invaders from the Middle East, came into India from the northwest. As a consequence, their greatest influence exhibits itself in this section of India, notably in the Punjab and in Sind. Curiously enough, when one examines the art, and in particular the statuary in this region, and then moves toward the east to that part of even northern India into which the Greeks did not penetrate so deeply, one finds a phenomenon which the British author of the article on India in the *Encyclopaedia Britannica* (11th edition) describes as follows: "As we proceed eastward from the Punjab, the Greek type begins to fade. Purity of outline gives place to lusciousness of form." This difference can be understood in the light of previous analysis if it is realized that the Greek, in his art, is a Westerner who is attempting to convey the theoretically conceived, three-dimensional, geometrical, external object with its very definite, sharp outline; whereas the Oriental artist is dealing with the purely aesthetic object in its aesthetic immediacy as merely a less definite association of differentiations in the otherwise indefinite, indeterminate aesthetic continuum.

One is reminded of Rudyard Kipling's Kim, after he has passed through the turnstile into the Museum in Lahore in the heart of the Punjab:

In the entrance-hall stood the larger figures of the Greco-Buddhist sculptures done, savants know how long since, by forgotten workmen whose hands were feeling, and not unskilfully, for the mysteriously transmitted Grecian touch. There were hundreds of pieces, friezes of figures in relief, fragments of statues and slabs, crowded with figures that had encrusted the brick walls of the Buddhist *Stupas* and *viharas* of the North Country and now, dug up and labelled, made the pride of the Museum. In open-mouthed wonder the lama turned to this and that, and finally checked in rapt attention before a large alto-relief representing a coronation or apotheosis of the Lord Buddha. The Master was represented seated on a lotus the petals of which were so deeply undercut as to show almost detached. [Compare Plate XVI.]

More recently, the Frenchman René Grousset in his *Civilization of India* has made a more detailed study of this sharply cut, three-dimensional, geometrical Greek influence upon Buddhist art. He informs us of "the scruples of the earliest Indian sculptors against representing the life of the Blessed One," adding that it was "impossible . . . for the Greeks, with their instinctive anthropomorphism, to understand . . ." To portray the Buddha's indeterminate Nirvana, which is devoid of all determinate forms and qualities, with geometrically informed, sharply cut Greek statues, must indeed have seemed incomprehensible to the Orientals. Yet the very indeterminateness of their outlook has always made the East sensitive to, if not helpless before, the aggressive West. In any event, the "sculpture in the round" shows the Greek influence everywhere in Northwest India and throughout the whole of Asia, extending through Tibet and China, as carried by the silk traders, even to the silent Buddha at Kamakura in Japan. At Bankipur, near Patna, there has been unearthed, Grousset informs us, "a columned hall which seems to be more or less inspired by Darius's famous Hall of the Hundred Columns of Persepolis." At the outset, the Greek forms were "dry" in their geometrical, theoretical rigidity; and even the Buddha himself was given the head of an Apollo. But Grousset adds that to this Greek geometrical form the Indian Buddhists gave "a new fullness and fresh-

Plate XIII SAGE CONTEMPLATING NATURE.
CHINESE TAOIST OR BUDDHIST LANDSCAPE
Courtesy of the Boston Museum of Fine Arts

THE ONENESS OF KNOWER AND OBJECT IN
THE AESTHETIC CONTINUUM

Plate XIV BOAT AT ANCHOR BY REEDS.
CHINESE BUDDHIST OR TAOIST. SUNG DYNASTY
Courtesy of the Boston Museum of Fine Arts

THE UNDIFFERENTIATED AESTHETIC CONTINUUM

Plate XV   ELEVEN-HEADED KUAN-YIN.
CHINESE BUDDHIST, 16th CENTURY (TIBETAN STYLE)
Courtesy of the Boston Museum of Fine Arts

THE AESTHETIC DIFFERENTIATIONS SYMBOLIZING
THE INDETERMINATE AESTHETIC NIRVANA

Plate XVI SEATED BUDDHA.
INDIAN SCULPTURE, 150 A.D.
Courtesy of the Boston Museum of Fine Arts

THE INDETERMINATE AESTHETIC NIRVANA
NATURE OF THE BUDDHA

ness of life. The harsh realism . . . became a free and wonderfully flexible naturalism—and Indian art was born."

Of these Buddhist artistic creations, the offspring of the wedding of the sharply limited, Greek three-dimensional, geometrical form and the unlimited, indeterminate, Oriental aesthetic intuition, René Grousset writes, "What love of nature is to be seen in them, what an understand-ing of floral and animal forms! Just as our cathedrals are encyclo-paedias in stone, so the gates of Sanchi unroll before our eyes the marvellous poem of Indian nature, a very *Jungle Book*. . . . Never, even in the Greece of the classic age, has the innocent and spontaneous joy of life been so happily expressed. As we stand before these scenes, with their delicate and tender feeling for nature, Assyrian bas-reliefs seem very conventional, and even Greek bas-reliefs almost strike us cold." Nor is the reason for this difference between the Indian Buddhist art and the cold, pure Greek art difficult to state. M. Grousset puts his finger upon it: "It is precisely this brotherly sympathy with all living things, a sentiment having its source . . . in that tenderness towards the whole universe which is distinctively Buddhist and Jain, . . ."

These considerations make it clear that the symbolic and three-dimensional realism of Buddhist art, which seemed at first to put an obstacle in the way of the basic aesthetic thesis of this inquiry, turns out instead to be one of its most spectacular confirmations. This thesis is that art is always working with immediately experienced materials which may be used in two ways. The first usage has been called art in its first function; the second usage, art in its second function. Art in its first function uses the aesthetic materials to convey the materials themselves for their own sake. Art in its second function, on the other hand, uses these aesthetic materials not primarily for their own sake, but analogi-cally in order to convey some theoretically conceived factor in the nature of things, of which the aesthetic materials alone are the mere epistemic correlates or signs. The thesis is that although there are occasional excep-tions, traditional Oriental art tends to be art in its first function; and traditional Western art, to be art in its second function. Buddhist art presented a difficulty for this thesis because of its clearly symbolic, theoretical, geometrically proportioned, three-dimensional character which points clearly toward the presence of a theoretical, scien-tific, and not a purely intuitive, aesthetic component. The expert studies of René Grousset make it evident however (a) that when one finds this sharply contoured, geometrically theoretic component in Buddhist art it is due to a Western Greek influence, and (b) that even when used by the Orientals, it is used not to convey the postulated, geometrical, theoretically conceived, sharply contoured, local, external object, but to convey in all its lush aesthetic immediacy and freshness the all-embracing continuity and ineffable communal feeling which the immediately apprehended aesthetic continuum exhibits in all sensed things.

The second foreign influence upon India came in A.D. 664 with the first Mohammedan invasion. The aggressive missionary zeal which seems to characterize all traditional theistic religions, including not merely the three Semitic theisms—early Judaism, Christianity, and Mohammedanism—but also Japanese Shintoism, exhibits itself in the Mohammedan invasion of India in the fact that it occurred but thirty-two years after the death of Mohammed at Medina. During this invasion the Punjab was devastated. The victory, however, was not consolidated. Again in A.D. 771 a second decisive Mohammedan invasion of India occurred, during which Sind was captured, at the same time that the Saracens were winning a similarly remarkable victory in Spain. The Hindus succeeded, however, in again driving the Mohammedans out, and for one hundred and fifty years had their country and its culture to themselves. In 977, however, the Punjab was taken again by the Mohammedans, and twenty years later Mahmud placed himself on the throne of India after having extended the Mohammedan rule outside its homeland from Persia to the Ganges. This was the first Mohammedan invasion which succeeded in consolidating itself. Four years later a decisive victory was won in the Punjab which established this as a Mohammedan province from that day to the present moment. About one hundred years later there came a second major Mohammedan invasion, which overwhelmed the whole northern plain of India. In 1206, some seven years later, Delhi became the Mohammedan capital of India. In 1294 the third great Mohammedan conquest occurred, penetrating the center and the south of India. Approximately one hundred years later a fourth great invasion, under the Mogul Timur (Tamerlane), followed. In 1526, under Baber, the fifth Mohammedan conquest took place, during which the Mogul Empire was established, to last in name until 1857. In the last half of the sixteenth century the Mogul Empire exhibited its richest cultural flowering. Under Shah Jahan the existing city of Delhi was planned; the Peacock Throne was erected; the Shah's residence was established at Agra; and one of the world's most renowned architectural gems, the Taj Mahal, was built.

From the time of Shah Jahan onward the dominance and highly centralized control of the Mohammedans over India, or more exactly over northern India, proceeds to break up into lesser, disjunctively related parts. Hindu Rajahs revolted and established cultural and political autonomies of their own. It was the descendant of one of these who, in 1639, granted the site of Madras to the English. Shah Jahan, it is to be noted, lived just after the end of the reign of Queen Elizabeth. A century later, in 1739, the sixth and last Mohammedan conqueror swept into India. Forthwith the Mohammedan Empire proceeded to fall apart. No Mohammedan pretended to set himself up as the Sultan or Emperor of India. The Mohammedans at best maintained political dominance only in certain provinces; and Mohammedanism established itself permanently as the second largest factor in the culture of India, enrolling, according to the census of 1931, as its passionate adherents, some seventy-seven million people, or thirteen per cent. of the population of India. In a census of 1941, made by communities rather than by religious adherents, the Moslem communities number a population of some ninety-four million out of a total population for India of 389,000,000.

In properly weighing the present significance of the Mohammedan factor in contemporary India these proportions and figures must be kept continuously in mind. Also, the Mohammedan influence is not confined to India. Even as far into the South West Pacific as Java, the majority of the population is Mohammedan. One of the major islands of the Philippines is also Mohammedan. Moreover, Mohammedanism tends to have greater influence than even the numbers of its adherents suggest. This happens because of the radical difference between a religion of the aesthetic, indigenous Far Eastern type and the theistic religions of the Middle East and the West.

A few elementary facts will suffice to make this difference clear. The four major theistic religions in the world today are Japanese Shintoism and the three Semitic religions of the Middle East and the West—Judaism, Christianity, and Mohammedanism. The four major religions of the aesthetic Far Eastern type are Hinduism, Buddhism, Taoism, and Confucianism. The latter religions have several traits in common. None is a tribal religion. For the most part, they get on very well with each other. Hinduism, for example, is as much Buddhist as it is Brahman. The Tantric doctrines, expounded in Chapter IX, appear as much in the Buddhism of Tibet as they do in the Hinduism of India. Recently, Surendranath Dasgupta, the leader of contemporary Indian philosophical and religious thought, has proposed an actual practical unification of Buddhism and Hinduism. Individual Chinese or Korean families are often composed of Confucians, Taoists, and Buddhists, as Younghill Kang's *Grass Roof* indicates; and even single individuals accept all three religions at once. There is nothing eclectic or queer about this, since, as Chapter IX has shown, all four of these major Far Eastern religions are referring to the same thing, merely applying it in different ways, or giving it a different emphasis.

But these Far Eastern aesthetic, non-theistic religions merge harmoniously also with the theistic religions from the Middle East and the West. Their tendency is to welcome foreigners and missionaries in a thoroughly open-minded manner, without racial, tribal, or religious prejudice, hoping to learn something from them. As Krishnalal Shridharani has written in *My India, My America,* "Narrowness of the mind and of the spirit is hard to find among the Hindus. . . . you will never find a Hindu who consciously or unconsciously believes that the gates of heaven are open to none save the Hindus."

This cordial catholicity of spirit shows itself also in the presence of the non-theistic indeterminate aesthetic type of religion, with its "tradition of tranquil sensuality," in even the theistic religions themselves at times: Rebecca West, in *Black Lamb and Grey Falcon,* finds it in contemporary Yugoslavia. The negative theology and the cult of the Virgin at Chartres Cathedral and Guadalupe are examples within Christianity. Dr. Ananda Coomaraswamy has noted its presence in Shintoism. It is equally evident in Judaism, especially in its *Holy of Holies,* and in the sensuously immediate and emotional content of the Songs of Solomon and many other works of the Old Testament, as well as in the aesthetic sensitivity and creativity which the Jews have shown throughout their entire history. It is true, also, of Mohammedanism, as is evidenced in the sensuous and decorative painting and architecture of Mohammedan India and Java and the entire Mohammedan and Arab world. Demetra Vaka's *Haremlik* exhibits this same Oriental feeling for aesthetic immediacy for its own sake in the traditional Turkish harems.

In fact, it is precisely this conception of the divine as involving the immediately apprehended, indeterminate aesthetic continuum in all its frenzied aesthetic immediacy which moved (1) into Spain by way of Africa with the coming of the Arabs and moved from there to Mexico, to inspire the tile work at Puebla; and which (2) immersed Venice, by way of Titian and Tintoretto, to move north over the Alps into the Dutch painting of landscape, and into the Spain of Velasquez and El Greco, where it broke into two branches, one extending, as Justino

Fernández has noted, across the Atlantic to Mexico and the other Latin-American countries, to a unique fruition in the contemporary frenzied art of Orozco; the other flooding over the Pyrenees into France to inspire, much later, the modernistic French Impressionism and Abstractionism of Cézanne and Picasso.

Even this does not exhaust the tremendous range of this floodtide from the old East. In the process of immersing Venice and Spain, Constantinople also became inundated; and it is this inundation which gives rise in part to the Greek Orthodox Church with its less theoretical, more Oriental religion of passion and the aesthetic intuition which engulfed the whole of medieval Russia. It is this Oriental conception of the nature of things and of the nature of the divine as essentially immediate, passionate, and aesthetic in character, which in part generates the frenzy not merely of the traditional Russian religion, but also of the modern Russian novel and music. This element in Russia's culture should make it easy for the contemporary leaders of the Russian government, providing the war has led them to revive the old Russian love for the soil and for the traditional religious and aesthetic insights, to merge the modern scientific, technological, and economic values which are among the greatest achievements of the modern civilization of the West with the traditional intuitive, aesthetic culture of the Orient.

Unfortunately, although this aesthetic non-theistic religion merges harmoniously from its standpoint with the theistic religions, so much so that the latter have often incorporated it, the theistic religions of Shintoism, early Judaism, traditional Christianity, and traditional Mohammedanism do not, from their standpoint, get on well with the aesthetic non-theistic religions of the East, or, it may be added, with each other. The conflicts between Christians and Saracens, Christians and Jews, Jews and Arabs, Protestant Christians and Roman Catholic Christians, Shintoists and Confucianists, and Mohammedans and Hindus are historical facts. All the theistic religions are aggressive, all except recent Judaism are dominated by a missionary zeal, and all tend to regard religious views other than their own as heathen, erroneous, or inferior. Each tends to have a provincial self-righteousness which assumes that its doctrine is completely perfect, and consequently that its adherents are divinely commissioned and by duty bound to replace all other religions with "the one perfect religion." This is the reason why Mohammedanism has a far greater influence in India than its mere numbers suggest. It is an aggressive religion of the theistic type. Moreover, its adherents are difficult to convert to other religions.

Orientals brought up in a non-theistic Far Eastern religion such as Confucianism, Buddhism, Taoism or Hinduism have no difficulty in noting the cause of this aggressiveness and intolerant provincialism of the theistic religions. It centers in their tribal origins and, as Krishnalal Shridharani has noted, in the claims of the initial followers of each to be the chosen people and to possess "*The* Prophet, *The* Son of God, and *The* Way." Thus Shintoism has its Sun Goddess, from whom the Japanese emperors are the direct lineal descendants and to whom only the Japanese people have a blood relationship; the Hebrews initially were a "chosen people" and have their Moses, with his absolute, determinate commandments dictated directly to Moses by Yahweh; Christianity has the Christ, who is *the* way; and Mohammedanism has its Mohammed.

To be sure, Christianity and later Judaism took on more of a universal character when the scientific Greek philosophical element came into them, as our account of Roman Catholic culture has illustrated and the sequel will develop. Nevertheless, each of the four theistic religions began in an attempt to lead a certain restricted group of people out of certain practical difficulties; and by conferring upon this group of people certain special divine privileges which were not open to, and could not be known by, anyone else except as one accepted the authority and the specific, determinate teachings of the one divinely inspired prophet or leader. Without Christ or Mohammed one could not be saved.

As has been noted, the Far Eastern aesthetic religions are for the most part devoid of these traits. In Hinduism, Buddhism, Taoism, and Confucianism, the facts in direct experience open to everyone's inspection and quite independent of a prophet, a tribe, or a divine revelation come first, and the teacher comes afterward, if at all.

In the theistic religions, on the other hand, the divinely inspired authority of the revealed prophet appears first, and the evidence supporting his teachings must be sought out afterward, if it can be found. Moreover, if it cannot be found, *the* prophet must be given one's absolute devotion anyway, the absence of evidence supporting his teachings being taken as a spectacular confirmation of his absolute and divine authority. Usually in the theistic religions, apart from the Greek scientific and philosophical elements in them, the amount of evidence, of a character such that all people everywhere can inspect it, is so slight that one never escapes an unreasoned dependence upon the divinely inspired authority of the prophet. Thus, whereas in Buddhism one can and must find the way without Buddha, one cannot, in orthodox Christianity of either the Catholic or the Protestant form, be saved without Christ. Since the salvation provided by Christ, Mohammed, Moses, or the Sun Goddess is always perfect, because the prophet is divine; and since unqualified devotion to the particular savior in question is a minimum requirement for admission as one of his followers; one tends to be untrue to one's own religion if one admits any truths or values in any other religion which one's own theistic religion does not possess. When to this is added the injunction from the savior to spread his perfect gospel throughout the world, the cooperative spirit is not helped particularly. Instead, an aggressive missionary evangelism is added to a self-righteous religious perfectionism and provincialism.

To a follower of any one of the aesthetic non-theistic Eastern religions all this seems to be the antithesis of the religious spirit. Thus Krishnalal Shridharani writes:

The very notion [of missionary evangelism] implies a superiority complex as well as an impulse of self-righteousness. Now that might be tolerable in other fields, but when it is brought into the realm of religion and the spirit, it looks very strange to the Hindu. To the Hindu philosophers, nothing is more irreligious than a holier-than-thou attitude—an attitude which of necessity provides the driving force of evangelism. One cannot describe it as a human desire to share with fellowmen things that are found personally precious. Such a desire would turn into fellowship, into discourse, never into a drive for conversion. In this respect I feel that all the great religions of the world have one thing to learn from Hinduism [and, it may be added, from Buddhism, Taoism, and Confucianism]: a humility born of a profound philosophic insight into the relativity of knowledge of ideals. . . . I think that in this Hinduism is more in harmony with the spirit of modern science than almost any other great religion. It is forgivable to insist on *one* God, but to insist upon *The* Prophet and *The* Law is intellectually wrong. The assertion of Louis XIV that "I am The State" is quite innocent compared to anyone's assertion that "I am The Law." . . . This exclusiveness is antispiritual inasmuch as it is overweening in the light of the limitations of human perception.

Shridharani notes also that this exclusiveness is to be found in "decidedly liberal" contemporary Christian leaders as well as in the traditional fundamentalists. It is clear that if the conflicts and racial and religious prejudices of this world are to be at all ameliorated, not merely in India but in the West as well, a much deeper-going reformation than the one which occurred with the origin of Protestantism, with respect to the sufficiency and the authority of the claims of the theistic religions, must occur. One of the major causes of the ills of our world has its source in very high places.

The second thing which one notes in all the traditional theistic religions is that the teachings of their divinely inspired prophets always specified the divine to be determinate in character; and always prescribed for human conduct certain specific, determinate, absolute rules or commandments which hold for all people under all circumstances. In fact, it is precisely the doctrine that the divine does have a character which a determinate thesis can convey that defines theism. Similarly, there is the requirement also that its religious adherents must, under all circumstances, obey not merely the determinate commandments of the divinely inspired prophet but also follow the explicit, determinate behavior of this prophet. Since the prophet's commandments and behavior and the traits of his God vary from one theistic religion to another, and are in many instances definitely contradictory, as in the case of Mohammedanism, Judaism, Christianity and Shintoism, it is not a mystery that in history these religions have had difficulty not merely in getting on with each other but also in responding graciously and with mutual enrichment to the open-mindedness of the Far Eastern aesthetic non-theistic religions. Even when one of the latter Eastern religions, in its statement of the Golden Rule, asserts what Christ asserted, the tendency upon the part of the Christian is to admit merely that the Oriental sage asserted only negatively and partially what Christ asserted positively, and with absolute, complete perfection.

These traits of the theistic religions must be kept in mind if the comtemporary Orient and in particular contemporary India are to be understood. For in India resides one of the most physically militant of theistic religions, Mohammedanism, side by side with the Eastern non-theistic religions—Hinduism, Buddhism, and Jainism. What must be realized, as the above considerations have shown, is that the attitude of the Hindu toward the Mohammedan is radically different from the attitude of the Mohammedan toward the Hindu, with respect to open-minded tolerance and practical cooperation. Mohammedanism is an aggressive missionary religion of the traditional theistic type. For an orthodox Mohammedan, missionary zeal, military power, and political control go together. John Locke's contention that a religious man must never make use of force, or the circumstance that he happens to be in civil office, to impress his religious views on other people in the community, is quite foreign to the orthodox Mohammedan's mentality and to his conception of good conduct.

Consequently, since it takes both parties to any relation to insure cooperation, any statement that Mohammedans and Hindus can get on together amicably has much more weight if it comes from a Mohammedan than if it comes from a Hindu. Also, it has much more weight if it comes from an orthodox Mohammedan rather than from one who has been under marked democratic influence from modern democratic countries. The point is that the orthodoxy of the Hindu, and of any follower of a non-theistic religion of the Far Eastern aesthetic type, supports open-mindedness and friendly relations with other religious groups; whereas the orthodoxy of a theistic religion, especially one like Mohammedanism, tends not to do so.

The influence of the West upon India is complicated by other factors than the issue between the theistic Mohammedans and the non-theistic Hindus, Buddhists, and Jains. The British rule itself is compounded of two philosophically different, if not self-contradictory, components. The India Company and the Empire were built under Elizabeth. Into the building went the aristocratic, hierarchic conception of the good State and the modern, Non-Conformist Protestant, individualistic, and mercantile conception. The former goes back through Hooker and Elizabeth to Aristotle; the latter merged with Descartes and Locke. The Aristotelian heirarchic conception tends to be sympathetic with the hierarchic caste system of Hinduism and with the unity of imperialism; the individualistic Non-Conformist Protestant component would, one might suppose, support democracy. But the Non-Conformist response is mixed. It must not be forgotten that the Non-Conformists were businessmen as well as Quakers or Congregationalists. Thus their interest in India is trade, as well as the spreading of the Christian gospel or democracy.

Also, as a result of the British influence in India, many of India's best minds went to the West, and especially to England, to study its ways. Among them were Mohandas Gandhi and Jawaharlal Nehru. The former learned British law but failed to note modern Western science and philosophy. Consequently, he attempts to merge modern Western political theory with the ancient Oriental Jainist rejection of determinate action, without the mastery of the foundations of Western culture necessary to pursue so difficult an undertaking. The indeterminate intuitive religious culture of the Far East has its virtues, virtues which the West needs, as has been noted, but these Oriental virtues are not the stuff out of which modern Western nationalism for an autonomous India can be built. For this a philosophy and religion of the determinate type, grounded in the theoretic rather than the aesthetic component in the nature of things, are necessary.

Jawaharlal Nehru, on the other hand, is by birth a high-caste Brahman, reared at the top of the Hindu heirarchic social system. One of his fellow-countrymen has termed him "The Thoroughbred." Because of Mahatma Gandhi's sacrifice for India, Jawaharlal Nehru is devoted to his senior leader. But he has gone much deeper beneath the political surface of things, into the scientific and philosophical roots of the modern Western political issues, than has the Mahatma. This has brought him into contact, not merely with Locke and Bentham, but also with Karl Marx and Russian communism. The latter has so deeply impressed him that he regards it as the only constructive solution, to date, of the ills of the Western world, and important if the Indian masses are ever to escape from their present low economic standard of living, and from superstition and disease. Like Gandhi he is dedicated to autonomy and self-government for India. But, unlike Gandhi, he has been so "filled . . . with horror" at the "spectacle of what is called religion, or at least organized religion, in India and elsewhere," Shridharani informs us, that he has "frequently condemned it and wished to make a clean sweep of it." Protestant Christianity is no exception, in his opinion. Thus Nehru tends to believe that the existing religious forms and sentiments must be broken up, to allow the "something else" which was originally in them to come to expression again; and in order to remove the existing rigid, nominally religious groups who "take pride in their faiths and testify to their truths by breaking heads."

THE INDIAN PROBLEM

Need one wonder, with all these Hindu, Mohammedan, Jainist, Marxist, Lockean, Elizabethan and Mercantile ideas of the good for man and the state, contradicting each other at many points, and pushing and pulling her in opposite directions, from both within and without, that staid, intuitive, receptive, indeterminate Mother India finds it difficult to make up her contemporary mind? Nor need one wonder that there is indecision in Downing Street also. It is not an easy thing to merge the East and the West under the best of circumstances. It is doubly difficult when the East presents itself as a pyramidal Hindu caste system with "70,000,000 depressed-class peoples at its base" and the intuitive Brahman at its ideal apex, beside, or in the midst of which is a Mohammedan culture, now some dozen centuries old and 80,000,000 strong, dominated by the uncompromising determinateness of a theistic religion; and when the West has established itself under the rule of a Britain divided against herself by her Elizabethan medievalism, her Mercantile and Non-Conformist Protestantism and her Lockean urge to tolerance and democracy. Add to this an Indian nationalistic movement headed by the religious, pacifistic Gandhi on the one hand and the Marxist-inclined Nehru on the other, and the India problem appears as one of the most complicated clashes of ideals which this world of conflict exhibits. This indeed is the test case for any solution of the basic ideological issues of these times. If a criterion of the good can show the way here, it should be adequate anywhere.

WESTERN INFLUENCES IN CHINA AND THE PACIFIC ISLANDS

The Western influence in China, Japan and the East Indies is similar to that for India, even though in the case of China and Japan the political occupation and domination have not been as extensive as with the British in India, the Dutch in the East Indies, or with the United States, up to very recent times, in the Philippines. But even in China the domination has been greater than it seemed. Although the West had political and military control largely only in the foreign concessions of China's port cities, these port cities stood at the mouths of the great river systems of the whole of the country. These rivers are the transportation network of China. Consequently, anyone controlling the ports dominating these river systems, had a hold upon the entire economic life of China which was far greater than might appear to the casual observer.

Moreover, in this control, the United States has had a far greater part in recent years than its citizens have recognized. The Washington Conference held in 1922 deserves far more attention than it has received. First, it shifted Japan from its traditional alliance with Great Britain. Second, it caused the United States to cease depending upon the battleships of the British and the French, and their Civil Governors and military police to maintain order and stable conditions for banks and businessmen and even missionaries in Asia, by bringing the United States along with Japan, Great Britain, and France into the Four-Power agreement. This made the United States, as well as Japan, Great Britain, and France, financially and militarily responsible for maintaining the foreign concessions in the port cities of China. These were real changes and realignments in the relations between the nations of the world.

It is probably the first of these two changes which explains in considerable part why the Japanese were on the side of the Allies in 1918 and on the opposite side in 1941. It was a most important thing for the United States and also for Australia and New Zealand, that when the Japanese finally struck at Pearl Harbor the traditional alliance between Great Britain and Japan had been broken.

But the breaking of the British-Japanese alliance did not throw Japan out into the cold. The second accomplishment of the Washington Conference brought Japan along with Great Britain, the United States, and France into the final arrangement. If any party suffered, it was China, since the Washington Conference gave the United States, as well as France, Great Britain, and Japan, a vested interest in, and a political obligation to support, the foreign concessions in the Chinese port cities. Events, however—thanks to the fatal Japanese decision to move with the Axis powers and to break from their traditional allies— have not shown China's loss by the Washington Conference to be a serious one. On the contrary, with the recent giving up of the foreign concessions by Great Britain and the United States, and with the aid which has come to her from her allies, she has undoubtedly gained, even though the gain has been exasperatingly slow in arriving.

But the Western influence upon China and her neighbors has been more than military, political, and commercial. Western educators and missionaries have also gone there. Glimpses of the churches, medical science, educational institutions, political practices, and cultural forms of the West have been opened up to them. And these glimpses have enticed the Chinese, Koreans, and Japanese, as they have also enticed the Indians, to travel to the United States, and to a lesser extent to Latin America and to Europe, to study and observe Western culture at first hand. In one instance, as with Japan, the political nationalism, the business and banking organizations, the science, and the technology have most attracted them. In another, as with India, the legal forms have caught the imagination. And in China, both of these, along with Western religion, especially as it exhibits itself in the more pragmatically active and concrete organization of the Y.M.C.A., has wrought its influence. The number of important political and administrative leaders in China who have been Y.M.C.A. secretaries is truly remarkable; as is also the influence of Protestant Christianity in its Methodist form through the Soong family. But the Western religion has made its impress also upon Japan and upon India.

As a result of all these influences, the first and abiding characteristic of the West which stood out in the Oriental mind was the West's aggressiveness. This aggressiveness exhibited itself to the Orientals as much in the presence of Christian missionaries as in the high-pressure salesmanship, the Western gunboats, and the Governors in their midst; and in the countless wars between the Western nations on the high seas and on the battlefields of the Western hemisphere and Europe.

THE CONTEMPORARY PROBLEM OF THE ORIENT

Faced with this aggressiveness and missionary zeal, the Orientals could do one of two things to preserve their own institutions. They could attempt to put a great wall around themselves, hoping thereby to preserve from destruction their intuitively and aesthetically grounded religion of the emotions and their other cultural forms, to which the Western missionaries as well as tradesmen and soldiers were all too often quite blind; or they could respond positively by acquiring some of these Western traits and values, thereby taking on the Westerner's aggressiveness. Naturally, they began with the first policy and, with the exception of Tibet, finding it of no avail, were forced to the second.

The problem of the Contemporary Orient then took on the following form: How, with the minimum of repudiation and destruction of one's traditional Oriental beliefs and values and attendant institutions, can one, as quickly as possible, achieve a strong, independent nationalistic state of the Western type? The different answers given to this question by their respective leaders define Contemporary India, Contemporary Japan and Contemporary China.

SHINTOISM AND JAPANESE NATIONALISM

The Japanese were the only Oriental people to become a nation of the Western type quickly, with a minimum repudiation of their traditional past. The reason is that the materials out of which a strong national spirit can be built were readily at hand. It was natural, therefore, for the Japanese leaders to take advantage of them. Unfortunately the conception of man, religion, and nature upon which these means depend for their validity is erroneous, as even the Japanese themselves had recognized long before Perry sailed into Nagasaki Harbor in 1853 with the United States Navy. It is in action sustained by these resurrected erroneous beliefs that the present behavior of Japan, with its tragic consequences for the rest of the world, and especially for the Japanese people, has its basis.

Three things made relatively easy the program which Japan's leaders followed in building a strong, self-reliant, aggressive, nationalistic state. One is the insular compactness and smallness of the geography of Japan, and the racial and cultural homogeneity of its people. The second is the existence, in the almost forgotten regions of their past, of a folklore outlining a tribal, theistic religion known as Shintoism, which, because of its obviously fanciful nature, had been driven out of their lives over a period of centuries up to 1850, by the positivistically grounded religions of Buddhism and Confucianism. The third was their feudal, hierarchic, medieval society with its Emperor and privileged select orders.

This ancient Shinto religion taught that Izanagi-no-Mikoto, the Sky-God, and Izanami-no-Mikoto, the Earth-Mother, created the islands of Japan; and that Amaterasu Omikami, the Sun-Goddess, gave birth to a line of direct descendants, among whom was her great-great-great-grandson, Timmu Tenno, who, according to the tradition, became the first Emperor of Japan in 660 B.C. It taught also that because of this divine origin of their island and its civilization, their mountains and countryside were sacred and their culture, by virtue of the perfection which divine creation gives, was destined to triumph over the imperfect, because humanly created, cultures of other peoples. Also, because the Emperor is the pure and lineal descendant of the Sun-Goddess, Amaterasu Omikami, absolute obedience of all Japanese to the Emperor is as spontaneous as it is axiomatic. Having once brought this tribal, nationalistic, theistic Shintoism into the foreground and having pushed the all-embracing, truly international Buddhism and Confucianism into the background, it remained merely to make the symbol of the Sun-Goddess the flag of the New Japan and to endow one of the medieval aristocratic orders with responsibility for the Navy and another with similar responsibility for the Army, while implementing each with the industrial and military instruments of the West, to have that control by the two latter groups combined with the fanatical religious devotion to the nation as personified in its unity in the Emperor, which is the Japan that struck at Seoul, Shanghai, and Pearl Harbor.

Fortunately, the problem confronting the Japanese people, once their present misguided military leaders and their erroneous and outmoded theism and feudalism are smashed, is relatively easy to resolve. Japan is not confronted, like India, with antithetical religious groups. The Japanese need merely to do what they did centuries ago in their past; namely, push their pragmatically revived Shintoism back into the realm of folklore, where it truthfully belongs. They can then restore to the forefront of their superably aesthetic and communal life the Buddhism and Confucianism grounded in the aesthetic component of the nature of things which encourage an international compassionate fellow-feeling for all creatures. To this, in order to merge harmoniously with the West, must be added a radically reformed theism defined in terms of a contemporary scientific, rather than an ancient fanciful, conception of the theoretic component in the nature of things. Such an ideal will give Japan its own truly Oriental values; and at the same time will provide a theism with contemporary scientific content and attendant Western values far surpassing those of Shintoism.

CHINESE NATIONALISM AND THE CONFUCIAN FAMILY

To note the ease with which Japan met the problem of adjusting herself to an aggressively nationalistic Western world without breaking from her past is to appreciate the difficulties facing China. Geographically there is the tremendous area of China, tending to be pulled apart by her two major river systems and by differences in climate, linguistic dialects, and physiognomy. In the Western sense of the term, China still has no communication system, which only railways can provide, tying together the different parts of her country. For this reason political and military unity is also still very weak throughout the country as a whole. Then there is the difficulty presented by the essentially denotative, non-syntactically related, written symbolism of the traditional Chinese language. The nature of this symbolism, its lack of an alphabet and of syntactical and grammatical rules to the degree in which they occur in Western languages, tends to result in any new facts or statements being merely added on to the old ones, instead of being used through the syntactical relations tying them in with older facts, to reconstruct the original ideas. This did not bother the Japanese because, as has been noted, it was not necessary for them to break radically from their traditional ideas. Their revival of Shintoism, in order to build nationalistic sentiments, took them deeper into their past, rather than away from it.

But the Chinese have no nationalistic, provincial, tribal religion in their past even in the form of a fanciful tale; apart from what H. S. Dubs has described as the "tradition that in very ancient times the whole of China had been under the rule of one monarch." Nor did they have the unity provided by pyramidal hierarchic social institutions. Instead, as Dubs shows, their unity derived solely from a common state of mind provided by the Confucian philosophy. Thus the worshipping of the Chinese people and of the Chinese nation for its own sake, the making of this something primary, even above the importance of the individual or of the family, for which the individual will lay down his life in the name of a determinate thesis in a determinate battle—this is not easy for a group of four hundred and fifty million widely dispersed people even to understand, especially when their philosophy and their religions, Buddhist, Taoist, and Confucian alike, teach them that all determinate theses are relative and transitory, and that only the indeterminate and all-embracing *tao*, Nirvana, or *jen* is absolute and immortal.

There is another difficulty. The no-man's-land filled with bandits, between the sovereign in Peking and the individual family with its very high filial standards, has been noted. With the advent of Western Protestant religious and democratic social ideas, both of which emphasized individualism and undermined the filial family relations, giving children an independence and indifference to their parents that shocks a Confucian, and with the return of more and more young Chinese from their studies and free life in the United States and Europe, the respect for the two traditional sources of unity in China—the far-flung filial family and the Emperor—grew weaker and weaker. Thus Western influence initially, instead of unifying China, tended to destroy what few sources of feeble social unity she had. Furthermore, as the strength of the Emperor and the old far-flung Chinese family decreased, the power of the bandits, each with a private army, increased, to reach its climax when Western social practices, and even dress, finally captured the youthful leaders of the New China, and when the Revolution of 1912 under Sun Yat-sen finally eliminated the Emperor. It did not help matters particularly that one of the local military leaders in no-man's-land, termed the Christian General, made his soldiers attend several Protestant services a day and march with the German goose step, singing "Onward, Christian Soldiers." The old sources of unity were gone, and the new were as yet too verbal and too artificial to be effective.

Supporting all this was the traditional tendency of the Chinese, which their own Lin Yutang has pointed out, not to expect too much social organization and idealism beyond the filial relations of the Chinese family. If it came by the Confucian method, according to which the individual first got human-heartedness in himself and then achieved it in his family and then carried it on through the four other primary social relations until it was finally achieved in the state, well and good. But on the whole the Chinese was always inclined, due to his positivistic, concrete, intuitive realism, to believe that this was to expect too much of human nature. It was, to be sure, the ideal which their Confucius taught, but even he was not too sanguine about its actual realization in fact. Furthermore, the other religion of Chinese origin, Taoism, definitely taught non-action socially.

These were but a few of the difficulties which the leaders of the New China faced as they attempted to find a way to combine China's own traditional, indigenous truths and values with the inescapable truths and values of the culture of the West. The remarkable thing about contemporary China is not that there are obvious weaknesses and flaws or that she still has a long way to go before her problem is solved, but that she has gone as far and built as soundly as she has.

First, there had to be a genuine revolution. China could not, as did Japan, take old, indigenous Oriental elements and merely turn them to modern, aggressive, nationalistic Western uses. To accept the West at all, to keep from having her own nation completely inundated and destroyed by the invading political, religious, and military influence, she had to undergo a reconstruction in, and admit additions to, her old traditional religious, philosophical, and cultural premises. It was this revolution which came first in 1912, following the revolutionary teachings and leadership of Sun Yat-sen. The precise character of his teaching merits lengthy and serious consideration. For present purposes, however, it will suffice to note merely that it was dominated in part by traditional Oriental doctrines and, in the decisively revolutionary part, by Western nationalistic, democratic and Protestant values, and by communistic doctrines. It is the communistic portion of his teaching which made the present Madame Sun Yat-sen, who is the sister of Madame Chiang Kai-shek, assert that the Chinese government of Chiang Kai-shek in its earlier suppression of the communists has in part at least betrayed the original revolutionary principles of Sun Yat-sen, upon which the New China is based.

This revolution initially and necessarily produced disorder rather than national unity. It made the bandits and local war lords the sole *de facto* ruling elements in China. Furthermore, it had to begin in a local part of the country and to extend its power bit by bit with the conquest of one local war lord or bandit group after the other. It is to be noted that the strength and part of the power of the present Generalissimo derives from his having come up through this realistic, military schooling. Thus he represents something unique in the history of China; namely, a soldier at the top rather than at the bottom of the social scale.

But Chiang Kai-shek, as he proceeded to apply Sun Yat-sen's ideas, was very different from the traditional Chinese soldier. In 1924 at Whampoa between Canton and Hong Kong, Sun Yat-sen founded the Chinese Military Academy and placed Chiang Kai-shek in charge. This was a different military school from any which native Chinese had known before. For its students were given not merely the best military training which Chiang Kai-shek's study in Japan, and his reading and his consultation with foreign military advisers, enabled him to conceive and apply; but also they were taught a new ideology, an ideology essentially Western in character, involving specific, definite, determinate moral, political, and social theses with respect to which one must not bargain or compromise. This new Western ideology was taught with the Western thesis that a man was not true to himself morally or religiously unless he was willing to lay down his life if necessary for this determinate moral thesis. This is one reason why China no longer puts on battles which are in considerable part mere bluffing while soldiers are being counted, but is instead able to fight uncompromising wars to the death after the manner of good Westerners, as portrayed in Lin Yutang's *The Leaf in the Storm*. It is not an accident that this historical novel closes with its Chinese hero, after the battle of Hankow, saying "Greater love hath no man than this, that a man lay down his life for his friends," and with the Buddhist priest leaving the calm of his monastery to go about the battlefield taking care of the wounded and urging the youth to give their lives for the nation.

This shows that in the transformation which is producing the New China there is a typical Protestant Christian religious element. Protestantism and militant nationalism are sustaining each other in China as they have since Luther and Henry VIII in the West. Upon this point, Generalissimo and President Chiang Kai-shek is explicit. Writing of his having become "a follower of Jesus Christ," he adds: "This makes me realize more fully than ever that the success of our revolution depends upon men of faith, men of character who, because of their faith, will not sacrifice principle for personal safety under circumstances of difficulty and crisis." He had found, as Emily Hahn has written, that "the best of his officers were Christians! Certainly a large number of the generals and officials of the Government were members of the Church." Evidently any effective attack upon the problems of war must look not merely at science as its cause but at the humanities and in particular the Christian religion itself.

But, it will be asked, how can this be? Did not Christ proclaim Himself to be "the Prince of Peace"? What is overlooked in asking such a question is that the symbol of Christianity is Christ nailed to the Cross. This is the symbol of a man who sacrifices his own life for a determinate thesis and a theistic God with determinate attributes. The latter type of religious leadership and ideal is at once both the glory and the tragedy of the Western world.

It is this conception of the nature of things as something determinate, holding for everybody, that has given the Western man faith in the actualization of determinate social ideals beyond the family in the community at large, the state as a whole, and even, as a hope, throughout the world. It is this which has given the inspiration and provided the determinate political principles cutting across family lines to impress the entire nation, which has enabled the West to reap the fruits of organized *national* life, and to pursue its sequence of social reforms. Nor has this asset, with its source in considerable part in the Christian religion, failed to impress the Orient. In a broadcast from Hankow on April 15, 1938, republished in *The Generalissimo Speaks*, the President of Nationalistic China said: "I have come to the conviction that, if we wish to regenerate the Chinese people and introduce a social reform we must adopt as our own the universal love and spirit of sacrifice of Jesus. . . . To this end all revolutionists must accept struggle and sacrifice as their daily duty."

But it is this same confidence in a theistic God with determinate immortal characteristics and in a national social ideal, blueprinted almost to the last determinate detail and supported by a Christ on the Cross who teaches His followers to lay down their lives for their determinate ideals, which also generates the tragic battles between nation and nation in which no genial spirit of bluffing, bargaining and compromise is possible. This also has impressed the Orient. The head of the Sanskrit College of Calcutta, Pandit Narendranath Dasgupta, as reported by W. E. Hocking, has declared that "Christianity has shown itself a failure, in view of the inability of Christian nations to keep peace with one another." The point to note, however, is that Christianity has not merely failed to prevent war among its followers; it has in part, as contemporary China indicates, produced the required spirit of sacrifice in military battle necessary to make and preserve the modern nationalistic states.

This does not mean—notwithstanding all the bloodshed that has occurred throughout the entire history of the West and which, thanks to Western religious, economic, and other cultural influences, has now spread to Asia—that Chiang Kai-shek and Sun Yat-sen made a mistake in introducing Christian Western moral and religious ideals into the morale of the Chinese Army, and into the sentiments and outlook of the Chinese people. Nor does it mean that either the Christian religion or Western civilization is wholly evil and erroneous. It does mean, however, that any serious attempt to remove the present causes of war must concentrate on the roots of the Christian religion and of Western idealism as one of the major causes; and that the presuppositions of both must be tested against immediately apprehended and logically inferred, scientifically controlled and verified theory, so that the truth in them, holding for everybody and under all circumstances, may be separated from the falsehood having a purely tribal, limited, transitory, historical origin; to the end that the goodness which is the consequence of the truth in the culture and religion of the West may be retained, and the evil which is the consequence of its falsehood may be removed.

But all this was not enough to provide even the beginnings of a nationalistic China. To be sure, when the graduates of China's West Point went out into the Chinese villages, an entirely new type of soldier, spreading doctrinal propaganda and a fanatical devotion to the nationalistic China, confronted the people. But even these men would not have been as effective as they were, nor would the cause of the nationalistic government have won out to the extent, still incomplete, that it has, after a tremendous conflict not merely between Chiang Kai-shek's forces and the rival generals and bandit groups, but also between different emotional pulls within every solitary Chinese soul, had it not been for the fact that the way had been prepared by the *Chinese Renaissance,* led by Hu Shih, the development of a Chinese alphabet, and the beginnings of a vast system of mass education under James Yen and others, which brought to the people the new doctrines, political as well as religious, and the attendant reconstruction and revolution in thought. To all this the national and provincial universities, the mission schools, the Western medical institutions, the Chinese New Life Movement, and the returning Westernized Chinese students going into every province and countless villages throughout the whole of China, added their weight.

Even so, the main difficulty still remained to be surmounted. To some, at least, this is the greatest difficulty of all. Those acquainted with China know, as has been indicated previously, that even in local communities social organizations, such as business partnerships which attempt to bring together individuals from more than one family, tend to break down. This goes back to the Confucian emphasis upon the filial relations within the family as the basis for everything else, and to the Chinese inclination to conclude that social idealism and organization going beyond the family tends to place too great demands upon human nature. "People of the outer world [writes the Generalissimo Chiang Kai-shek] . . . have grown up with national consciousness fully developed around and about them, whereas the Chinese people have been deliberately forcibly bereft of it, and, therefore, know nothing of those sentiments and impulses that so quickly move the Occidental peoples when matters concerning their country come forward for consideration or action" (Hahn). How then can a national government be established, with the financial integrity of the different officials in the partnership sufficient to make it function in the face of the traditional Chinese attitude toward social organization, when it extends beyond the range of the individual family? This was the New China's basic practical problem.

China's solution to this problem is in terms of her tradition: the unifying factor in the national givernment has been the Soong family.

Not only is one of the Soong sisters the widow of Sun Yat-sen, and another sister the wife of the Generalissimo and President of China, Chiang Kai-shek, and a third the wife of H. H. Kung, who has shifted between the Ministry of Finance and that of Foreign Affairs, over a period of several decades, but also the brother, T. V. Soong, has usually held the one of the two latter posts not occupied by his brother-in-law H. H. Kung, and very recently he has become Premier. Examination of the personnel of the national government over a surprisingly long period of its history will show shifts in the particular post which any one of these individuals occupied, but nonetheless the surprising degree to which the control of the Army, the Treasury, the Office of Foreign Affairs, the revolutionary political ideology, and the government as a whole has been, either directly by birth or indirectly by marriage, in the hands of one closely knit family. This is the major reason, since it represents something indigenous in the traditional social life of China, why the revolutionary movement toward nationalism in that country has succeeded to the present extent. The family tie has the authority of some thousands of years of Confucian culture behind it. Even in the New China and its very Christian Soong family, Confucius is being followed.

It appears that each of the three major countries of Asia, in order to preserve its own traditional cultural values, faced the problem of building a strong nationalistic state on the Western model in its own unique way and in terms of its own philosophical background and attendant cultural materials. In India these cultural materials from within and from without are so diverse and conflicting that its people have been unable yet to find the answer. Thus, there, the world is confronted today not with a New India but with the India problem— one of the most baffling and complicated of cultural conflicts between diverse ideals, in the world. Japan, unfortunately for herself and her neighbors, had an answer too readily at hand in the potential sources of national unity of her medieval feudal society and the religion of individual sacrifice of her theistic Shintoism. Thus, Japan was able to become a militant nationalistic state of the Western type, without breaking from her past, and by going farther back into it. This is why she found a temporary solution of the problem first and so quickly. China, unlike India, had no cultural conflicts from within, apart from the Western influence; and, unlike Japan, she lacked within herself the cultural materials for building a militant national unity. Thus, instead of going back into her past, as did Japan, China had to break from her past in the Revolution of 1912; and instead of having within herself the religion of individual sacrifice to the nationalistic state, she, or at least some of her most important leaders, had to import it in the form of Protestant Christian theism from without. But even so she had to operate practically through the sole traditional instrument of unity available; namely, the tie of the Confucian family.

Once the philosophical and attendant cultural backgrounds of the Asiatic peoples are understood in relation to the impact of the different philosophical doctrines and cultural values of the West, the specific contemporary individual response of each people begins to become intelligible. *This suggests that it is not the so-called realism of power politics, which because of its neglect of ideas and values is blind and stupid rather than realistic, but the informed realism of philosophical and cultural understanding which is the key to international relations.*

More specifically, to appreciate the concrete philosophical and cultural problem facing China is not to be shocked because her present highly centralized family form of government is so far from popular democratic government, but instead to express wonder that she is so far along the way. Other peoples must not expect China to achieve this end very quickly. The price of too much speed in such deep-seated matters, as Japan clearly demonstrates, is eventual retreat and tragedy. The problem involves nothing less than a reconstruction in one's basic philosophy of the nature of things, and a shifting of one's traditional conception of what is good and divine. This, even for Westerners who are much more accustomed to it, as the analysis of Western culture has shown, than are Easterners, is not an easy task. Gradually, however, by education and other means the beliefs necessary to build political unity in China on a national scale will shift the seat of sovereignty from the present family leadership to the people.

Many obstacles must be met. There is the rift between the National Government and the Communists in the northwest provinces. Tremendous linguistic difficulties due to many spoken dialects and the absence of an alphabet in the traditional written symbolism must be overcome. Although an alphabet has been introduced, opposition to the phonetic system necessary to make it effective still goes very deep. Also, as D. N. Rowe has emphasized, a vast railway network permitting communication between the different provinces is an elementary necessity if even military unity is to be achieved. And training in science and technology is essential. But even more important, as Chancellor Chiang Mon-lin of National Peking University and Dean Chen Su-ching of Nankai University emphasize, there must be a thorough grounding in the philosophy of Western science. Otherwise, as the failure of the recent emphasis on applied science and technology has demonstrated, the Chinese people will look at these Western scientific instruments from the standpoint of the traditional Oriental philosophy of the *aesthetic component*, instead of from the standpoint of the Western philosophy of the *theoretic component*. When this occurs, as recent experience in China has demonstrated, the people fail to understand the scientific apparatus and technological instruments in their hands, and as a consequence fail to care for them or to repair them properly or use them effectively. This brings us to the question of the influences of the West upon the East which are likely to be permanent.

CONCERNING THE PERMANENCE OF WESTERN INFLUENCES

There is great difference of opinion among Orientals upon this question, especially with respect to the humanities. Jawaharlal Nehru concludes that Asia "has little to learn from the West, much to teach about the philosophy of life and the art of living." Mahatma Gandhi tends to believe that with regard to religion the Orient has more to give than to receive, even with respect to Christianity. In Japan there are relatively few Christians. Only in China does the theistic religion of the West give promise of significant permanent influence. Madame Chiang Kai-shek writes of the Christian missionaries as follows: "Back in the United States it is the fashion to condemn them. China knows better. . . . As the General and I have traveled from one end of the country to the other, we have been astonished again and again at the devotion of these missionaries and the hardships they endure. . . . I frankly do not believe we can save China without religion. Political force is not enough." Madame Kung and her husband share the same sentiments. On the other hand, the other Soong sister, Madame Sun Yat-sen, tends to be neutral if not negative with respect to the importance of Christianity, having more interest in the handicraft of the people and in communism.

Also, the acceptance of Christianity in the Orient presents dangers as well as political advantages. For no one in either the East or the West has yet shown how it is possible to convert Oriental people to the Christian religion without at the same time destroying the intuitive aesthetic unique cultural values of the East.

So serious is this danger that the Dutch Government, in order to preserve the artistic achievements of the natives of the East Indies, has prohibited in many instances the entrance of Christian missionaries. William Ernest Hocking reports a conversation with a Dutch Protestant missionary who persuaded the Dutch government to depart from its rule in his case because of his intense interest in encouraging the preservation of the remarkable artistic sense of the natives. He found to his dismay that as his converts became more and more serious Christians, they proceeded to drop their traditional aesthetic interests and values. When he asked them why this was the case in spite of his admonitions to the contrary, they wondered why he had not realized that the acceptance of the Western Christian religious teachings, in destroying the native religious doctrine, thereby took from the native aesthetic and emotional cultural forms and practices the philosophical and Oriental religious basis which is their source and their inspiration. Similarly, Marco Pallis in *Peaks and Lamas* indicates that the inroads of Western culture have destroyed the high aesthetic standards of traditional India and are fast corrupting those of Tibet.

What must be realized is that nothing in any culture is more dangerous and destructive than the acceptance of new philosophical and religious beliefs, no matter how true and valuable, at the cost of the rejection of native beliefs which may be equally true and valuable. Yet this is precisely what the Christian gospel with its neglect of the aesthetic component in things and its claim of complete perfection requires and all too often achieves. To suppose that one can replace the traditional Oriental religions with the Christian religion in its present form without destroying the aesthetic values of the Orient rooted in the native religion, is to imagine that one can take the foundations from under a building and not have that building fall.

Nor is it merely Oriental art which suffers. Oriental intuitive religion, which the whole world needs, suffers also. Rebecca West noted this in Bosnia when she compared her Christian Bosnian guide with his Mohammedan Bosnian neighbors. "The lad," she writes, "was worse off for being a Christian; he had not that air of being sustained in his poverty by secret spiritual funds that is so noticeable in the poverty-stricken Moslem."

There is no reason, of course, why the release from poverty fostered by modern Western theism and science, grounded in the theoretic component of things, should not also be present. But if this is to occur the claims of theistic religion with respect to complete perfectibility must be given up, so that the virtues of its truths and values can come to the Orient without destroying the equally important truths and values of Oriental religion and culture, rooted in the aesthetic component.

This is why the problem of determining the relation between the aesthetic component in things upon which the Oriental religions are based, and the theoretic component of things upon which the theistic Western religions rest (with which the next chapter will be concerned), is so important. Until this problem is solved and the conception of the good and the divine in morality and religion is brought into accord with the solution, Western missionary activity for all its undeniable merits will continue to be a very dangerous and destructive thing for the Oriental people, unless those people are content to see their own culture lose most of its own unique values and individuality and turn into a mere second-rate imitation of the West; also, informed Orientals who understand the philosophical foundations of culture are going to be wary of Western influences.

It must not be forgotten that a major factor in the recent Oriental acceptance of Western ways has been the need for gaining independence of action in order to preserve Oriental values. Hence, once this independence is gained by means of a strong nationalism the Western religious, and other instruments thereto may be discarded. Also, there is the traditional Chinese and Oriental tendency to regard all determinate theses as transitory, and consequently as principles of action which one accepts when this acceptance seems appropriate and discards as quickly when different circumstances render their acceptance less urgent.

What of the permanence of the Western political influences? The need for independence seems to guarantee their persistence. Here is a factor supporting the continuance of the Western religious influences. Analysis of the Western cultures has shown the political and religious doctrines to be derived from common philosophical and scientific foundations. Thus, the Western political values may very well require the Western religious doctrines for their support, as Generalissimo and Madame Chiang Kai-shek insist. The fact that both Japan and China, which have achieved political independence, found it necessary to appeal to theistic religious values supports this conclusion.

In the political influence from the West there are two major doctrines, democracy and communism. The importance of the former is evident. The effect of the latter upon the Oriental mind requires further attention.

The communist influence in China dates back to Sun Yat-sen. It continues down to the present moment through such leaders as Chu Teh, Mao Tseh-tung and Chou En-lai. It enters, as has been noted, into the Soong family itself through Madame Sun Yat-sen. So strong is this factor that in 1927, when Generalissimo Chiang Kai-shek and the Nationalist Government broke with the communists, Madame Sun Yat-sen withdrew her support from her brother-in-law's government. She wrote:

We have reached a point where definition is necessary and where some members of the party executive are so defining the principles and policies of Dr. Sun Yat-sen that they seem to me to do violence to Dr. Sun's ideas and ideals. Feeling thus, I must disassociate myself from active participation in carrying out the new policies of the party. In the last analysis, all revolutions must be social revolutions, ... Without . . . [the support of the working classes and the peasants] the Kuomintang, as a revolutionary party, becomes weak and chaotic and illogical in its social platform; . . . If we adopt any policy that weakens these supports, we shake the very foundation of our party, betray the masses and are falsely loyal to our leader. . . .

The communist influence was equally strong in Japan before it was crushed by the War Lords. The tremendous famines which occur throughout the entire Orient and the exceedingly low economic level of life of so large a portion of its population provide a rich soil in which the communist doctrine can grow. But its power in the Orient is much greater than this. During the two decades following Versailles, the wisest minds in the Orient have been objectively watching the course of affairs in the nations of the Western world. Some of them have sat at Geneva and seen Western Europe move step by step, but surely, toward disagreement and war. In this entire movement communistic Russia has not suffered in comparison with the other Western nations in the capacity to act with wisdom, cooperation, and upon a basis of principle. Jawaharlal Nehru has expressed his appraisal as follows:

Much in Soviet Russia I dislike—the ruthless suppression of all contrary opinion, the wholesale regimentation, the unnecessary violence (as I thought) in carrying out various policies. But there was no lack of violence and suppression in the capitalist world, and I realized more and more how the very basis and foundation of our acquisitive society and property was violence. . . . A measure of political liberty meant little indeed when the fear of starvation was always compelling the vast majority of people everywhere to submit to the will of the few, . . . Violence was common in both places, but the violence of the capitalist order seemed inherent in it; while the violence of Russia, bad though it was, aimed at a new order based on peace and co-operation and real freedom for the masses. With all her blunders, Soviet Russia had triumphed over enormous difficulties and taken great strides toward this new order. While the rest of the world was in the grip of the depression and going backward in some ways, in the Soviet country a great new world was being built up before our eyes. Russia, following the great Lenin, looked into the future and thought only of what was to be, while other countries lay numbed under the dead hand of the past and spent their energy in preserving the useless relics of a bygone age. In particular, I was impressed by the reports of the great progress made by the backward regions of Central Asia under the Soviet regime. In the balance, therefore, I was all in favor of Russia, and the presence and example of the Soviets was a bright and heartening phenomenon in the dark and dismal world. . . . With all my instinctive dislike for much that has happened there, I feel that they offer the greatest hope to the world.

Considerations such as these make one suspect, as recent events have confirmed, that the truce reached by the National Government of China with the Chinese communists in 1935, when both were motivated primarily, probably, by a common fear of Japan, is but a temporary stopgap rather than a permament solution of the basic, inescapable political and economic issues of the Orient. There, as in the West, the problem of reconciling democratic and communistic doctrines will persist and become more pressing.

However, upon the permanence and value of one factor in the culture of the West, most leaders of Oriental thought are in agreement. This factor is science.

THE PERMANENT VALUE OF WESTERN SCIENCE

Younghill Kang in *East Goes West* makes this clear for Korea. It is even more evident in the case of Japan. Sun Yat-sen, in his Principle of Livelihood, made science applied to the soil and society one of the three basic values (the others being nationalism and democracy) upon which the New China rests. Upon this point, President Chiang Kai-shek of the National Government and the communist leaders in the northwest provinces are in agreement, notwithstanding their differences on other points. The former Chinese Ambassador to Washington, Dr. Hu Shih, expresses the opinion of his countrymen when he writes, "The highly developed scientific method in all its phases of operation and the historic or revolutionary view of humanity . . . I consider the most important contributions of modern philosophy in the Western world." Similarly, the sensitive and cultivated humanist Jawaharlal Nehru speaks for the younger Indians and other Orientals when he affirms, "Asia is learning rapidly what the West has to teach of science and its applications and is trying to harmonize them with her old-time genius."

This genius has consisted in the formulation of a philosophy in terms of the *aesthetic component* of things and the development of religious and other cultural forms in terms of such a philosophy. To learn the science of the West and to understand it, is to discover the indirectly verified, unseen *theoretic component* in things upon which the philosophy and culture of the West are based. To harmonize the genius of Asia with the science of Europe and America entails therefore nothing less than the construction of a new world civilization in which a philosophy grounded in both the aesthetic component and the theoretic component of things as equally primary, defines the idea of the good.

But this task is not peculiar to Asia. As Chapter VIII indicated, the West, in order to clarify the relation between empirical and theoretic factors in its knowledge, is being forced to the discovery of the primacy of the aesthetic component which sustains Oriental values and to the problem of relating this aesthetic component to the traditional Western concern with the theoretic component in things.

Thus, the basic philosophical problem of the East and the West is the same. It is the problem of determining the relation between the aesthetic and the theoretic components in things. To this problem attention must now turn. If it can be solved, the guilding principle for merging the cultures of the Orient and the Occident should be at hand.

CHAPTER XII

THE SOLUTION OF THE BASIC PROBLEM

The task of the contemporary world falls into four major parts:
(1) the relating of the East and the West; (2) the similar merging of
the Latin and the Anglo-Saxon cultures; (3) the mutual reinforcement
of democratic and communistic values; and (4) the reconciliation of the
true and valuable portions of the Western medieval and modern worlds.
Running through all these special tasks is the more general one, made
imperative with the advent of the atomic bomb, of harmonizing the
sciences and the humanities.

THE BASIC PROBLEM

Examination of the Latin-American culture of Mexico has shown
that the solution of the first problem will in part resolve the second.
For what impresses as novel in Mexican culture is its highly developed
appreciation of the aesthetic and its religion of the emotions; and what
the Mexicans fear in the merging of their culture with that of the United
States is that the latter excessively pragmatic, economically centered
culture will, in its zeal for its own values, overwhelm and destroy the
cultural assets of the Indian-and-Latin world. But this task of relating
aesthetic and emotionally immediate religious values to scientific, doctrinal, and pragmatic values is precisely what constitutes the fundamental problem of correctly and safely merging the East with the West.

Another issue in Pan-Americanism will be resolved when the problem of reconciling democracy and communism is solved. This should
provide foundations for a constructive solution of the ideological portion
of the German problem, since the issue between democracy and communism turns in considerable part around the purely modern issue
between the Pre-Kantian British empirical philosophy of Locke, Berkeley, Hume, Bentham, Mill and Jevons and the Post-Kantian German
philosophy of Fichte, Hegel, Feuerbach, Marx, and Nietzsche. Similarly, the final difficulty in Pan-Americanism which also is at the heart
of the issue between medieval Roman Catholic and modern Protestant

and democratic values in the United States, Latin America, and Europe will be met, when the principle is discovered for relating the truths and attendant virtues in the modern and pre-modern components of Western civilization.

Analysis of each of these cultural and political elements and issues has revealed its basic assumptions. These assumptions turn out in every instance to be philosophical in character. Thus, cultures with differing political, economic, aesthetic and religious ideals or values are grounded in differing philosophical conceptions of the nature of man and of the universe. These diverse philosophical conceptions fall into two groups: those which differ because they refer to different factors in the nature of things, and those which conflict because they are affirming contradictory things of the same factor. The philosophy of the Orient with its attention upon things in their aesthetic immediacy in contrast with the philosophy of the West with its emphasis upon the theoretically designated and inferred factor in things exemplifies the first group; the medieval and modern worlds or traditional communistic and democratic economic and political theory are instances of the second.

In the case of the former group, the task of relating the differing cultures is, in considerable part, that of removing the notion of each people that *nothing but* its theory is correct, thereby permitting each party to add to its own traditional ideals the equally perfect values of the other culture. Only in the field of Western religion, with its traditional claim to complete perfection, does this present any difficulty. The greater difficulty rests with the second group where real contradictions appear. Nevertheless, the foregoing analysis enables the inquirer to understand the origin of these conflicts and to find the correct method for resolving them.

It will be recalled that cultures such as Confucianism, Taoism, Buddhism and Hinduism, which are reared almost exclusively on a philosophy grounded predominantly in the aesthetic component alone, merge quite happily. Those cultures on the other hand, such as medieval Aristotelianism, Lockean Anglo-American democracy, Post-Kantian German voluntarism or idealism and Marxian communism, which emphasize the theoretic component in knowledge, are in conflict. Since this component is not immediately apprehended, but instead, as the chapter on the meaning of Western civilization has shown, is known only by the speculative scientific method of hypothesis confirmed indirectly and experimentally through its deductive consequences, this conflict is easy to understand: the scientific and philosophical founders of these cultures have been led by the empirical evidence or the theoretical difficulties at hand to postulate different, and in part at least even contradictory, conceptions of the specific character of this theoretic component. The chapter on Roman Catholic culture has shown, for example, that the later Greek and medieval science was led quite correctly, considering the empirical evidence at its disposal, to Aristotle's and St. Thomas's conception of man and nature. When this theory led to deductive consequences which were out of accord with the motion of projectiles, Galilei and Newton were forced to replace this Aristotelian conception with the modern Newtonian conception of the theoretic component. Thus, medieval and modern values in the West came into conflict. Even so, the Aristotelian theory has persisted, in Roman Catholicism and the Church of England, as a vital ideological factor up to the present moment, because when the philosophical consequences of Galilei's and Newton's physics were made articulate, especially by Locke, contradictions within it were revealed by Berkeley, Leibnitz, and others, and to escape these difficulties the subsequent philosophies of the modern world were developed, each of which, for all its virtues, turned out to be inadequate, as previous analysis has indicated. Consequently, even though the medieval Aristotelian Thomism was unequivocally invalidated by the evidence of physical science and subsequent investigations in logic and mathematics, its modern successors showed equally fatal, even though more theoretical weaknesses; hence, one more inadequate philosophy of the theoretic component from the medieval world hardly made any difference. With each of these rival and conflicting philosophies an important culture in the West was identified: Roman Catholic culture with Aristotelian Thomism; French and Anglo-American democracy and Protestantism initially with Descartes's and Locke's theory of mental and material substances; Anglo-American economic theory with Hume's, Bentham's, Mill's and Jevons's empiricism; the Kaiser's Germany with Hegel's dialectical idealism; Hitler's Germany with Fichte's romantic voluntarism, reinforced with Nietzsche's superman; and Russian communism with Marx's dialectic materialism. Thus, the ideological conflicts of the modern West are to be understood. Each culture has believed in some scientifically and philosophically formulated conception of the theoretic component, and no conception met the facts without getting into inescapable contradictions or inadequacies.

But to understand these contradictory and conflicting ideologies is to have the clue to the method for resolving the issues of our civilization which they define. We must go back behind them to the facts and distinctions at the beginning of modern science and the modern Western world which brought them into existence. Somewhere on the way, in passing from the scientific facts and distinctions to the traditional philosophical foundations of modern Western culture, a mistake was made. We must find this mistake.

It happens, by good fortune, when this is done that *the problem underlying the conflicting Western cultures is identical with the one involved in relating correctly the compatible cultures of the East and the West.* This occurs because both problems have their basis in the relation between the aesthetic and theoretic components in knowledge. This has been established already in the case of the East and the West. It will be recalled also that Locke's philosophy of mental and material substances which gave rise through its internal contradictions and inadequacies to the rival ideological issues of the modern West, arose in order to clarify the relation between the immediately apprehended aesthetic qualities in sensed space and time and the theoretically designated physical atoms in public mathematical space and time of Newton's physics.

The evidence for the latter distinction must now be examined. Galilei's statement that the sensed heat does not belong to the object and Newton's emphasis upon the difference between sensed space and time and mathematical space and time have been noted in Chapter III. Additional evidence for this difference between nature as immediately apprehended and nature as mankind is forced to conceive it in indirectly and experimentally verified scientific theory appears in Einstein's current identification of the simultaneity of spatially separated events in nature, not with the immediately apprehended simultaneity of sensed events, but with a postulationally designated, directly unobserved simultaneity which is checked as to its existence through its deductive, experimentally tested, consequences by recourse to light propagation and immediately sensed events which are not spatially separated. Similarly, even the layman does not regard two loud explosions distant from each other as occurring at the same time even though he hears them at the same instant, if he knows he is standing near the place where the one occurs and distant from the place where the other occurs; instead, he corrects for the speed of sound in reaching him, thereby theoretically conceiving of the distant event as happening earlier than the near one. Such considerations indicate that while there are many identities, there are also many differences between ourselves and nature as immediately apprehended and ourselves and nature as theoretically and scientifically understood.

No alternative remains, therefore, but to accept Galilei's and Newton's distinction between sensed, and mathematically designated, indirectly verified, nature; the distinction between what is termed the aesthetic component and the theoretic component in things. This being admitted, the inescapable question then arises concerning the relation between these two components.

THE RELATION BETWEEN THE AESTHETIC AND THEORETIC COMPONENTS

One answer to this question was given by the scientists who drew the distinction initially. Sensed space and time, said Newton, are "apparent"; the theoretically known space and time are "absolute, true, and mathematical." Sensed warmth, colors, sounds and odors are, wrote Galilei, "on the side of the object in which they seem to exist, nothing else than mere names," and if the observer were removed, "every such quality would be abolished and annihilated." Put more concretely and with precision, this means that the immediately apprehended aesthetic factors were conceived by Galilei and Newton to be related to the theoretically known factors in knowledge by a three-termed relation of appearance in which the material object in the "true, real and mathematical" space and time of the theoretic component is one term, the observer is a second term, and the apparent sensed qualities in the apparent relative sensed space and time of the aesthetic component are a third term.

The question then arose, as the reader will recall from Chapter III, concerning the nature of this observer. Hobbes's proposal that the observer, entering into this three-termed relation, is a collection of material atoms, like the external physical object, broke down when it was pointed out, upon the basis of the principles of Newton's physics, that were an observer nothing but such an entity, then all that could possibly happen as the result of the atoms of the table acting upon the atoms of the observer would be that the latter atoms would merely undergo certain accelerations, and that consequently there should not be colors or sounds or pains or pleasures even as appearances. Thus Locke was led, still assuming the validity of the three-termed relation of appearance, to use this three-termed relation to define the nature of the observer; a procedure which is inescapable provided the validity of the three-termed relation joining the aesthetic to the theoretically designated factor in knowledge is once admitted. The Lockean mental substance followed immediately, since this mental substance is merely the kind of observer who can satisfy this three-termed relation of appearance; in other words, it is an entity such that, when the material atoms of physics in public mathematical space and time act upon it, it has an awareness of colors, sounds, odors, pains, and pleasures in private, sensed space and time as mere appearances.

This necessitated the Lockean theory of ideas, according to which every portion of human knowledge in any field of inquiry has to be built up out of nothing but the directly inspected colors, sounds, odors, pains, and pleasures and their inspected associations, since these are the sole products of the action of the material atoms upon the otherwise blank observer or mental substance. Forthwith, all the problems of modern philosophy and psychology arose; and the skeptical, positivistic, purely empirical philosophy of Hume, Bentham and Mill, with no theoretic component of knowledge and an attendant inadequacy, with respect to the sciences of mathematics and mathematical physics, as well as with respect to common-sense and religious beliefs and historical knowledge, followed.

The difficulties into which the assumption of the three-termed relation of appearance led modern thinkers should have made them suspicious of its validity long ago. It may be added that in recent times Alfred Whitehead, because of these attendant insoluble philosophical difficulties, has been led to question not merely the validity of the three-termed relation of appearance, but also the distinction made by Galilei and by Newton between the sensed and the mathematically postulated in nature. This has led Whitehead to reject not merely the dualism of mental and material substances propounded by Descartes and by Locke, but also the distinction between sensed space and time and mathematically defined, postulated public space and time emphasized by Galilei, Newton and Einstein. This forces him to identify nature with "the terminus of sense awareness" and to go back to the thesis, similar to Aristotle's, that all scientific concepts are derived from this terminus by "extensive abstraction." It has been shown, however, that the Galilean and Newtonian distinction between the purely empirically given component in knowledge, and the postulationally prescribed, theoretic component in knowledge, is still required not merely by Galilei's and Newton's physics but also by the most recent experimentally verified theories of Einstein and Planck, as well as by common sense. Thus it is not permissible to reject the Galilean and Newtonian contention that there are two components in any scientific knowledge: the one empirical, *a posteriori*, and directly observed; the other theoretical, hypothetically *a priori*, and neither directly observed nor abstracted from the directly observed.

Furthermore, Alfred Whitehead's attempt to derive the theoretic factor by extensive abstraction from the immediately apprehended aesthetic component has forced him to place a greater burden upon the deliverances of sense awareness than they are capable of carrying. Also, his solution of the fundamental philosophical difficulty at the basis of modern science, philosophy and culture is much more radical than is required. For what causes the difficulty, as has been indicated, is the assumption that the empirical factor in knowledge is related to the theoretically designated factor by a three-term relation of appearance. Thus all that is required to meet the difficulty is the rejection of this account of the relation between the sensed and the postulated. This way out has the merit of making it possible to retain the distinction which Galilei and Newton introduced, and which the contemporary experimentally verified theories of Planck and Einstein still require.

In any event, there is no need of speculation upon this point. For the relation between the empirical factor in knowledge and the theoretical factor is specified by the method of Western science itself. That this is the case is demonstrated by the fact that the theoretical factor proposed hypothetically *a priori* is only confirmed or rejected by means of scientific method because this method in some manner relates this factor to the directly observable, empirical items of the aesthetic component. Otherwise the theories would not be theories proposed *a priori* and tested indirectly *a posteriori*. Thus the scientific method which provides the *a posteriori*, indirect, empirical test for the postulated, *a priori* theory must contain within itself the relation which joins the empirical, aesthetic component in scientific knowledge to the inferred theoretic component. It is therefore necessary only to analyze the scientific method in question in order to specify this relation.

Elsewhere Henry Margenau, Ernst Cassirer, Philipp Frank, Hans Reichenbach, and the author of this book have quite independently carried through this analysis. These results show that the empirical factor in knowledge is related to the theoretic factor, not by a three-termed relation of appearance but by a two-termed relation which in some cases, but not in all, is one-one. These two-termed relations Henry Margenau terms "correspondencies"; the present writer terms them "epistemic correlations."

They are termed epistemic correlations—the word "epistemic" referring to the science of epistemology, or knowledge—because they relate a thing known empirically in its aesthetic component to what is in some sense that same thing known postulationally in its theoretic component. In short, the epistemic correlations join the empirical component of any complete object of knowledge to its theoretic component. Thus the relation between the immediately sensed factors in knowledge and the postulationally prescribed, deductively formulated, theoretical factors in knowledge, to which Galilei and Newton referred, is unambiguously and unspeculatively prescribed by the nature of scientific method itself when this method is analyzed, to reveal the two-termed epistemic correlations.

The answer to the basic problem underlying the ideological issues of these times is, therefore, as follows: *the aesthetic, intuitive, purely empirically given component in man and nature is related to the theoretically designated and indirectly verified component,* not as traditional modern Western science and philosophy supposed, by a three-termed relation of appearance, but instead *by the two-termed relation of epistemic correlation.* As Albert Einstein has written: "Science is the attempt to make the chaotic diversity of our sense-experience correspond to a logically uniform system of thought. In this system single experiences must be correlated with the theoretic structure in such a way that the resulting coordination is complete and convincing." It is to be noted that in this description of science Einstein is careful to indicate in both sentences that the relation between the theoretically designated component and the immediately experienced aesthetic component is neither that of a three-termed relation of appearance nor that of a one-termed relation of identity but instead a two-termed relation of correspondence or correlation.

So important is this conclusion, not merely for the understanding of scientific method but also for this entire inquiry that it merits examination in greater detail. Consider the famous Wilson cloud-chamber experiment in which the modern experimental physicist comes the nearest to what approximates to an experimental confirmation of the existence in nature of that scientific object which the deductively formulated theory of electromagnetics postulationally defines as an electron. This scientific object cannot be immediately observed. How, then, is the scientist able to be assured that such an entity exists; and how is the engineer, basing his practices upon such assurances, able to provide the United States Navy with instruments by means of which it can destroy

Japanese ships when they are miles away, shrouded by the blackness of night?

In this experiment there is a vertical chamber into which a tube opens, from which are projected the hypothetical particles which are designated by the theoretical physicist's deductively formulated theory. The cylindrical chamber into which these particles are projected is filled with a gas. This gas, according to the physicist's theory, is composed of molecules, and these molecules in turn, by hypothesis, are conceived as made up of electrically charged particles. The gas which is chosen is one having molecules with electrical properties such that when the designated particles projected into it collide with these molecules, an event occurs which the theoretical physicist terms an "ionization." Beneath this chamber is placed a magnet, thereby insuring that the particles shot into the chamber will be moving in a magnetic field. If the elementary particle is negative in its charge, and of a certain mass, that is, if it is an electron, it follows from the deductively formulated theory that in such a magnetic field it will move in a different path from one in which it would move were it neutral in its charge, or were it positive in charge. Thus it follows from the deductively formulated theory of electromagnetics that this specific Wilson cloud-chamber experiment should enable one to decide the question whether electrons exist.

It should be noted, however, that in the entire experiment, from one end to the other, one sees neither a molecule nor an electron, nor an ionization. All that one immediately apprehends is a fuzzy aesthetic continuum in which there are certain aesthetic differentiations termed "flashes" following one another in a certain order to exhibit a differentiable path. Now this fuzzy aesthetic continuum and this path are aesthetic objects. They are not three-dimensional, external, public, scientific objects.

As Berkeley and Hume in the West and the Hinayanistic Buddhists in the East make one aware, and as a careful description of what is actually seen in this Wilson cloud-chamber experiment confirms, we do not immediately apprehend even gross common-sense objects in their three-dimensional, external, public character independent of the awareness of the observer; to say nothing about observing such unseen things as electrons, molecules, ionizations, or electromagnetic waves moving with the velocity of hundreds of thousands of miles per second. But how, then, if the physicist, even in this experiment, sees merely a fuzzy aesthetic continuum with an aesthetically differentiated curved line in 'it, is he able to have such confidence in his deductively formulated theory that electrons, molecules, and electromagnetic fields with their spectacularly fast propagations exist?

The answer is that in his scientific method, ahead of time, he sets up the two-termed relations, which have here been termed epistemic correlations, joining the postulated, theoretically designated electrons, molecules and ionizations which he does not see, to the immediately apprehended colored line in the fuzzy aesthetic continuum which he does see. Thus the unseen ionization (the collision between the electron and the molecule) which is an event known only by means of postulationally formulated theory, is joined to the aesthetic differentiation in the fuzzy aesthetic continuum which is directly inspected. Consequently, when, having deduced from his theoretical assumptions defining the character of the gas, the apparatus, and the projected particles, that a collision or ionization must exist; and when having set up epistemic correlations between this theoretically designated ionization and the directly sensed aesthetic flash in the fuzzy aesthetic continuum; and having, by means of the deduction plus these epistemic correlations, established the conclusion that if the theoretically conceived projected entity is in fact a negatively charged particle, these flashes must appear as an immediately sensed path with a certain immediately sensed curved shape and character; then, if this predicted directly inspected association of sense impressions occurs, the scientist asserts his deductively formulated theory to be verified and he regards the scientific objects, which the postulates of this theory syntactically define, as existing.

One suggestion which may arise from the above analysis must be avoided. It was such a suggestion which led Galilei, Newton, and Locke to relate the theoretic and aesthetic components in knowledge by the three-termed relation of appearance instead of the two-termed relation of epistemic correlation. In the above analysis the immediately inspected colored curved line in the fuzzy aesthetic continuum was distinguished from the molecule, the electron, and the ionization. It is easy at this point to fall into the error of supposing that the flashes, *i.e.* the aesthetic objects, are the mere appearances of unseen and unaesthetic molecules and electrons. Once this is done, we turn the aesthetic flash of the aesthetic continuum into a mere appearance of the supposedly non-aesthetic molecules and electrons, and forthwith require an observer such as Locke's or Descartes's mental substance to clarify the relation between the aesthetic appearances and the supposedly non-aesthetic molecules, electrons, and ionizations. But it must be remembered that in some previous experiment the scientist has had to establish the existence of molecules and of ionizations. Moreover, when one examines the deductively formulated theories in electromagnetics which designate the character of these entities or events, it is found that the notion of stuff or substance is quite gratuitous. All that appears are certain symbols such as "ε." Moreover, these symbols have no denotatively given content. The only properties which they possess, so far as the theoretical scientist is concerned, are those which they acquire through the relations specified by the postulates which join them to the other terms or entities, which are equally without an intuitively or denotatively given content. Thus the theoretic component of the nature of things so far as the theoretical physicist is concerned is purely formal, mathematical, abstract, or logical in its character. This means that the unseen or theoretically designated component of the molecule, the electron, or the ionization·is an abstract, logical structure or a term in such a structure. Such an abstract, logical structure, although it designates completely the theoretic component of human knowledge, gives, by itself, nothing concrete and existent. It provides the universal character of a potential particular; but it needs something added to it before any fully concrete thing exists.

From what source does this particularizing concrete component of any completely known thing come? Clearly it must come from the purely empirically given, non-theoretically designated aesthetic component of human knowledge. Thus even in the case of the molecules in the cylinder of the Wilson cloud-chamber apparatus the student is confronted with an epistemic correlation of the theoretic component with the immediately apprehended aesthetic component. Consequently, not merely does the relation between the immediately sensed flashes in the fuzzy aesthetic continuum and the postulationally prescribed ionizations which are known theoretically involve the two-termed relation of epistemic correlation; but even the notion of a specific electron itself or a specific molecule or a gross common-sense, molar object such as a table, a chair, the physicist's apparatus, or a person, involves this same epistemic correlation. Any fully known concrete thing whatever has these two aesthetic and theoretic components in it, joined by a two-termed relation.

In this manner justice is done to the valid element in Kant's philosophy—to the thesis that all full knowledge involves a correlation or synthesis of empirical and systematic theoretical factors. Consequently, this solution of the basic philosophical problem of contemporary Western culture does not force the Post-Kantian Germans and Russians to return to the scientifically and philosophically inadequate political and economic ideology of the Pre-Kantian French and Anglo-American Cartesian dualists or British empiricists. But neither are the French and Anglo-Americans forced to deny British empirical positivism, for there is the purely empirically known aesthetic component as well as the postulated, indirectly verified theoretic component. And to the extent that the empiricism of Hume described accurately this aesthetic component, it is a valid factor in any adequate philosophy of culture. The basis is now prepared for combining correctly these Pre-Kantian and Post-Kantian elements in modern culture.

To this end, it will be a great aid to have different names for the two types of concepts referring to the aesthetic and theoretic components in things. Those concepts which refer to the aesthetic component for their *complete* meaning may be termed "concepts by intuition." A concept by intuition, therefore, is one the complete meaning of which is given by something immediately apprehendable. Analysis of the cultures of the East and the West indicates that there are several such concepts. There is the totality of the immediately apprehended. This is the aesthetic component of all things in its entirety, with nothing neglected or abstracted. It is more accurately described as the differentiated aesthetic continuum. Within this total differentiated aesthetic continuum attention can be directed, as it is by the Oriental positivists, upon the continuum in its all-embracing continuity and indeterminacy neglecting the transitory differentiations (Plate XIV); or it can be directed, as it has been by Hume and the modern Western positivists, upon the specific determinate differentiations (images and sense data) neglecting the continuum (Plate IX). The former method leads to Jen, Tao, Nirvana, Brahman, Atman and Chit; the latter, to the specific particular colors, sounds, odors and their transitory relative sensed relations of Galilei's and Newton's sensed space and time and to the introspected wants and preferences of Anglo-American economic theory. Following C. I. Lewis, the latter concepts by intuition which refer to the determinate sensed or introspected differentiations may be termed concepts by inspection.

Concepts, one the other hand, which refer to the theoretic component in knowledge, shall be termed concepts by postulation. A concept by postulation is one, therefore, designating some factor in man or nature which, in whole or in part, is not directly observed, the meaning of which may be proposed for it postulationally in some specific deductively formulated theory.

The difference between the East and the West may now be stated more precisely. Previously, it has been said that the East concerned itself with the immediately apprehended factor in the nature of things whereas the West has concentrated for the most part on the doctrinally designated factor. More precisely, however, as has been shown in *Philosophy—East and West* (Chapter VIII), the East used doctrine built out of concepts by intuition, whereas Western doctrine has tended to be constructed out of concepts by postulation.

"Blue" in the sense of the sensed color is an example of a concept by intuition. "Blue" in the sense of the number for the wave-length for light in experimentally confirmed deductively formulated electromagnetic theory is an example of a concept by postulation. The factor in things denoted by "blue" in the sense of the concept by intuition is related to the factor in things designated by "blue" in the sense of the concept by postulation by the two-termed relation of epistemic correlation. The presence of these two-termed relations in knowledge has been obscured because both common sense and science have used the same word, "blue," for example, for the two different factors.

A very important difference is to be noted between concepts by intuition referring to the aesthetic component and concepts by postulation which designate the indirectly verified theoretic component in things. As Galilei, Berkeley, Hume and the Oriental sages have indicated, concepts by intuition are mere names for particulars. That this is the case is shown by the fact that no amount of syntactical discourse can convey what such a concept means unless one has immediately apprehended and experienced that to which it refers. Helen Keller had no difficulty in comprehending "blue" in the sense of a concept by postulation which is the number for a wave-length, but this was of no help in enabling her to know what "blue" in the sense of the concept by intuition means. The Nirvana, Brahman, Jen, or Tao concept in Oriental intuition has precisely the same chaacter. It is a denotatively given particular, not a syntactically designated universal. Concepts by postulation, on the other hand, are universals. This is shown negatively by the fact that what they mean is not to be found denotatively in any particular aesthetic intuition or experience. It is shown positively by the fact that they gain their meaning only syntactically by virtue of the logical and grammatical relations in which they stand to each other in the postulates of some deductively formulated theory. Such postulates are always general propositions referring to all instances. Moreover, they are independent of temporal qualification. Newton's first law of motion, for example, does not assert, "Bodies not acted upon by external forces keep their velocity constant between 1590 and 1885"; it asserts instead, "Bodies not acted upon by external forces keep their velocity constant." Thus, it is a consequence of Newton's physics that any body moving in space with a certain velocity will move with that velocity forever, providing no external force acts upon it. This characteristic of elementary concepts by postulation of being systematically and syntactically defined and of holding, so far as their meaning is concerned, for all instances and all time, makes them universals rather than particulars.

It is one of the errors of traditional science and of traditional philosophy that most of their adherents felt constrained for some inexplicable reason to regard all concepts as either universal or particlar. This had the effect of making cultures grounded on Platonic or Aristotelian Greek and medieval science and philosophy or upon modern continental rationalism or Post-Kantian idealism, all of which affirmed concepts to to be universals, incompatible with cultures based upon modern British empiricism or Oriental intuition. By the same token, when the relation of epistemic correlation joins concepts by intuition which are particulars to concepts by postulation which are universals, and when it requires both types of concepts to refer to two factors in the nature of all things which are both real, ultimate, and meaningful, it indicates each of the diverse modern, medieval, Eastern and Western cultures to be giving expression to something which is in part true, and it shows precisely how to relate and reconcile them all without conflict or contradiction so that a peaceful comprehensive world civilization approximating more closely to the expression of the whole truth is possible.

With this preparation, it is possible to appreciate the tremendous transformation in the attitude toward ourselves and nature which the substitution of the two-termed relation of epistemic correlation for the traditional modern Western three-termed relation of appearance entails. In the Cartesian and Lockean foundations of traditional modern Western culture both the material substances and the mental substances are theoretically inferred rather than immediately apprehended factors. This, Berkeley and Hume in the West and the Hinayanistic Buddhists in the Orient have made abundantly clear. Consequently, when modern Protestant and Anglo-American culture, following Descartes and Locke, was led to conceive the directly experienced aesthetic continuum with its colors, sounds, odors, pains, and pleasures, as the mere effect of the action of the material substances upon the mental substances, the modern world was led into the serious mistake of attempting to derive the empirical aesthetic component in man and nature completely from an interaction between the postulated material and mental substances of the theoretic component. This is not merely logically impossible, since it confuses concepts by intuition with concepts by postulation, either type of concept being logically underivable from the other, because of the nature of their differing characteristics and definitions; but it also destroys the primacy and importance of art for its own sake by making all the emotionally moving aesthetic materials which one directly inspects, and which are an essential part of human nature and the nature of all things, the mere phenomenal by-products and appearances of the supposedly more basic, real, and ultimate postulated material and mental substances. Thereby, the aesthetic and emotional factors in man's nature, and in the nature of things, were designated as mere appearances and trivial; and the emotional and aesthetic foods which the nature of man needs for its sustenance were deprecated and ignored. The Greek and medieval Roman Catholic cultures had somewhat the same effect, when following Democritus and Plato they branded the sense world as giving spurious knowledge, and when following Plato and Aristotle they identified the undiffereniated aesthetic continuum of the aesthetic component (termed by Plato "the indeterminate dyad," and by Aristotle "prime matter") with the principle of evil; restricting trustworthy knowledge and the idea of the good and the divine to the unseen theoretic component. This had the effect also of making the cultures of East and West incompatible.

When it is found, however, that the aesthetic factor is related to the theoretic component in things by the two-termed relation of epistemic correlation rather than by the three-termed relation of appearance, the last ground is removed for regarding the aesthetic component as a mere appearance of the theoretic factor, or as the principle of evil. Both components are equally real and primary, and hence good, the one being the complement of the other. Forthwith the ineffable emotional aesthetic luminosity which is immediately experienced in oneself and nature is restored to the essential nature of all things. In fact, any complete thing whatever must be regarded as made up of (a) the ineffable, emotional, aesthetic materials of the equally ineffable and emotional aesthetic continuum common to oneself and all things, and (b) the unseen theoretic component which can be adequately designated only by thought and postulationally prescribed theory checked through its deductive consequences. Thus to be any complete concrete thing is to be not merely an immediately experienced, aesthetically and emotionally felt thing, but also to be what hypothetically conceived and experimentally verified theory designates. It is to be recalled that not merely in mathematical physics and in the unseen immortal soul and the unseen God the Father of the theistic religions, but even in ordinarily common-sense beliefs in external tables and chairs and persons as existing independently of one's awareness and sense impressions of them, the inferred postulated and indirectly verified theoretic component is present.

So far it has been indicated merely that the aesthetic factor is related to the theoretic component by the two-termed relation of epistemic correlation. This basic fact must never be forgotten in what follows. Actually, however, the relationship is much more complicated than this. The complication arises because of two facts: First, the two-termed relation joining the aesthetic to the theoretic component is not always one-one. Second, sensed qualities are joined to the rest of nature by many-termed relations.

A two-termed relation is one-one when it relates the one term to one and only one other term, and conversely. For example, the points on a map are joined to the cities of a country, of which the map is a correct delineation, by a two-termed relation which is one-one. Were the relation of epistemic correlation always one-one the form given by postulation which designates the structure of the theoretic component could be completely identical with the form which is directly inspected in the aesthetic component. That this is not the case is clearly demonstrated by the previously noted distinction between sensed and mathematical space and time, pointed out by Galilei and Newton and required by Einstein. Also, were the forms of the aesthetic and theoretic components identical, it would be hard to understand why the East and the West in their independent investigation of these two components did not come out with identical conclusions and cultures. Furthermore, in contemporary quantum mechanics, as Henry Margenau and the present writer have shown, the presence of many-one or one-many, rather than one-one epistemic correlations, is especially notable. When this occurs the epistemic correlation joining the aesthetic to the theoretic component is still a two-termed relation, but not a one-one two-termed relation. It is this which permits sensed nature to differ from experimentally verified, mathematically defined, theoretically conceived nature. This is also why, by the method of hypothesis and its indirect mode of verification, we are able to learn of structures and orders and entities in ourselves and nature which have a character other than, and different from, the relatedness and ordering of the immediately sensed qualities in the immediately apprehended aesthetic continuum.

The second factor, adding to the complexity of the situation, arises from the first. This factor has been stated by Alfred Whitehead as follows: "Sensed objects ingress into nature in many-termed relations." This again is a fact which anyone can verify. It appears most obviously even to common sense in the case of color blindness. In this instance the quality which one sees upon the rose cannot be regarded as an intrinsic property of the rose. It is a function also of the rods and cones in the observer's eyes. And even in the case of the person with normal vision, he can be made to see a different color by wearing colored glasses. Such considerations force us to conclude that the relation of a sensed quality to the, in part, theoretically designated object which it is seen apparently to qualify, is not a two-termed relation of intrinsic prediction, but a many-termed relation in which the color is one term, the aesthetically-theoretically known rose is another term, the aesthetically-theoretically known observer is the third term, and the aesthetically-theoretically known continuum in which all are embedded is a fourth term. There is a sense, therefore, in which the Lockean, Berkeleyan, and Cartesian theories had an element of truth in them; the sense, namely, that the actual character of sensed qualities does depend not merely upon the object which the color appears to qualify, but also upon the bodily character of the observer.

It is to be emphasized, however, that the fact of the ingression of sensed qualities into nature by many-termed relations, and the fact that the two-termed relation of epistemic correlation is not always one-one, in no way necessitates Descarte's, Locke's or Berkeley's theory of mental substances, or Leibnitz's theory of monads, and the attendant thesis that colors are mere appearances for a mind. The color of the rose is, to be sure, a function of the observer, but it is equally surely a function also of the character of the rose. Thus it belongs to the one as much as it belongs to the other. Moreover, it is a function, not of any hypothetical mental substance with which the observer is supposed to be identified, but, as Galilei initially explicitly indicated, of the observer's bodily sense organs. This also has been noted. For it is not by altering the mental substance but by altering the effect upon the rods and cones in a normal person's eye that he can be made to see a different color upon the rose than the one he normally sees. Thus the relativity to the observer is a relativity to the observer's body, not a relativity to any supposed mental substance, the introduction of which merely gets one into insuperable epistemological and psychological difficulties. Put more fully and concretely, the relativity of the sensed quality in the aesthetic continuum to both the rose and the observer (which in their aesthetic component are also in the aesthetic continuum) is the result of a naturalistic relation between the rose which is an aesthetically immediate-theoretically designated object, the intervening medium which is also an aesthetically immediate-theoretically designated object, and the observer who in turn is an aesthetically immediate-theoretically designated object. Consequently, the concatenation of factors which is an awareness of the rose as red is not the result of an unaesthetic material substance by some mysterious activity jumping out of space across a metaphysical gulf to act upon an equally unaesthetic blank mental substance which in some mysterious way projects out of itself the color which is observed, as a mere appearance; instead, all occurrences in human awareness and in human knowledge are a result of natural relations between entities which in their aesthetic character and in their theoretic character are in the same world of discourse. It is an aesthetic-theoretically designated rose in its aesthetic and theoretically designated relation to the aesthetic and theoretically knowable observer, which constitutes the actual occasion which is the seeing of the rose as red.

The following diagrams represent the difference between relating the aesthetic and theoretic components by the two-termed relation of epistemic correlation (Figure II) instead of the three-termed relation of appearance (Figure I):

Figure I

(1) The material substance
(2) The mental substance
(3) The aesthetic continuum with its differentiated sensed qualities as mere appearance.

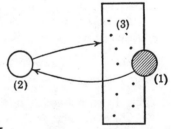

Figure II

(a) The person
(b) The object
(c) The intervening medium

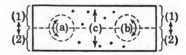

In Figure II, it is to be noted that the object (b), the person (a), and the intervening medium (c) are all in the same aesthetic-theoretic world of discourse. Consequently, no problem arises, as in the Cartesian and Lockean theory of material and mental substances, concerning the manner in which a material object in mathematical space and time can act upon a mental substance or knower, who is not in space and time; instead the event which is knowledge is the purely naturalistic interaction between one factor in the aesthetically immediate-theoretically designated complex of things and other such factors. In this manner, the distinctions and advances of modern science are not merely developed so that the difficulties and attendant ideological conflicts of traditional modern philosophy and culture are escaped, but the achievements of modern science are also reconciled with certain merits of the Greek and medieval psychology and philosophy, noted in the chapter on Roman Catholic culture. There, it will be recalled, was cited Aristotle's assertion that the study of the soul falls within the science of nature, and that the act of gaining knowledge of the external object is a naturalistic process in which the form of the object passes into the intervening medium to affect the form of the knower's living body, which, according to Aristotle, is the soul. It appears that scientific and philosophical foundations for the reconciliation of the correct and valuable elements in the medieval and modern portions of the Western world are at hand.

THE RECONCILIATION OF THE EAST AND THE WEST

At the same time the traditional opposition between the Orient and the Occident, as voiced by Kipling, is removed.

> East is East and West is West,
> And never the twain shall meet.

This situation arose because the East in its intuition and contemplation of things in their aesthetic immediacy, and the West in its pursuit of the theoretically known component, tended to brand the knowledge other than its own as illusory and evil. When the preceding analysis reveals both factors to be ultimate and irreducible the one to the other, and related by the two-termed relation of epistemic correlation, thereby insuring that the one cannot be regarded as the mere appearance of the other, the two civilizations are shown to supplement and reinforce each other. They can meet, not because they are saying the same thing, but because they are expressing different yet complementary things, both of which are required for an adequate and true conception of man's self and his universe. Each can move into the new comprehensive world of the future, proud of its past and preserving its self-respect. Each also needs the other.

The practical consequences of taking the relation of epistemic correlation as a guiding principle for the relating of the East and the West are far-reaching. It means that Western religious leaders with an adequate idea of the good and the divine will go to the East more to acquire its religion of intuition and contemplation than to convert the Easterner to the Western theistic religion of doctrine and reform; just as Easterners come to Europe and America to acquire Western science and its more theoretically grounded determinate economic, political and religious values. It means also that no claim to a completely perfect religion can be made in either portion of the world until the unique insights of the religion of the East and those of the West are combined. In purely Western terms, this entails that the Virgin Mary representing the emotional female aesthetic principle in things becomes as divine in her own right, after the actual practice in Chartres Cathedral and at Guadalupe, as is the Christ representing the unseen male rational principle in the nature of things. These consequences follow because the relation of epistemic correlation not merely distinguishes its two end-terms which are at the basis respectively of the East and the West, thereby giving each portion of the world something unique to contribute to the enrichment of the world's civilization, but it also unites them.

With respect to the Orient the consequences are equally specific. In the previous chapter, contemporary India was shown to present the most difficult problem in traditionally conflicting cultural ideals and institutions. It is selected therefore as the test case.

To begin with, all attempts, after the manner of Gandhi, to return India to nothing but its traditional past are misguided. There is the theoretically known component of things to which Western culture gives predominant expression as well as the aesthetic component of the East; and the relation of epistemic correlation prescribes that each must be cultivated and both must be related. Each type of culture is already present in India; the theoretic component being represented in an early outmoded form by the theism of Mohammedan Indian as well as by the British from the West; the aesthetic component being present in part in Mohammedanism and unequivocally in Hindu and Buddhist India.

The character of knowledge of the theoretic component in things, with which all theistic religions identify the divine, requires that this component, and hence Mohammedan theism, be conceived in terms of the content of contemporary scientific knowledge instead of in terms of that of Mohammed's time. This follows, because, as was shown previously, all knowledge referring to inferred rather than immediately apprehended factors is a hypothesis *a priori* checked only indirectly *a posteriori* and hence must be continuously reconstructed with the increase of empirical information.

This is a rule holding for all cultures grounded in the theoretic component, and for economic and political as well as religious doctrines in such cultures. This is the case, it is to be re-emphasized, because of the method of hypothesis which alone justifies knowledge concerning unseen inferred theoretically designated factors in the nature of things. One fact with which a traditional conception of the theoretic component is incompatible is enough to show that conception to be false; all the facts so far known in support of it are, on the other hand, not enough to show it to be absolutely certain. The best that can be said of any doctrine concerning an unseen theistic God the Father or concerning any other instance of the theoretic component in things is that the doctrine consistently and deductively takes care of all the directly observable data known to date. But even this can be said only if the conception of the theoretic component is identified with the latest deductively formulated experimentally verified scientific knowledge concerning its nature. Consequently, a theism which identifies the Divine and the soul of man with the theoretic component as conceived in the time of Democritus, Plato, Aristotle, Christ, Mohammed, St. Thomas, Locke or Hegel, is quite untrustworthy as a criterion of the divine and the good in the twentieth century.

Such a reform in Mohammedan India would accomplish two things: First, it would make its people aware of the tentative character of its beliefs, such as those of theism, which refer to the theoretic component in man and nature. Thereby, the absolutism, fanaticism and intolerance characteristic of much of traditional Mohammedanism would be softened down and its theism would take on more of the open-mindedness of Hinduism and the *wock jeh* (Perhaps!) of the Cantonese Chinese, making possible a peaceful mutual enrichment of Hindu and Mohammedan India. Second, it would bring into India the latest Western scientific knowledge, and provide the mentality necessary to use it to remove the unspeakable disease and squalor existing at present, thereby generating an indigenous merging of the values of the traditional East and the contemporary West. Such a reform in Mohammedan India, given the proper Mohammedan leadership, is by no means beyond the range of practical possibility since such a transformation has occurred already in the Mohammedan culture of Turkey.

Our theory indicates also that a correct solution of the India problem must provide for the aesthetic component in man and nature. This component is already present in the Hindu and Buddhist portion of India's people and culture. But here also a reform is necessary in which the aesthetic intuition frees itself, at least temporarily, from the determinate social forms of the caste system and the religious ritual, to take itself back to its original insight with respect to the real and the divine as immediately experienced and as indeterminate. This follows as a matter of principle because it is only as one goes back behind the forms of culture and reflective thought and social habits to the primitive pure intuition that one gets the aesthetic component in its purity and with life-giving freshness and vitality. Once the social rigidity is broken by this means, the natural tendency, noted in the preceding chapter, of Hinduism and other Oriental religions of the intuitive aesthetic type to welcome doctrines and cultures other than their own, will render equally possible the merging of Eastern intuitive and contemporary Western scientific and theoretical values in Hindu India. Such a reform within Hinduism, taking it away from its present rigid hierarchic social forms back to the original aesthetic intuition of the indeterminate Brahman, is quite within the range also of practical possibility, since there is a very old tradition in support of it, dating back to the Buddha in 660 B.C.

A similar reform in British India is also required. This is best treated as an instance of the reconstruction prescribed for the West by the principle which provides the solution of the basic problem of contemporary civilization. Certain parts of this reconstruction have been noted already; others pertaining to the ground of human freedom and the reconciliation of democracy and communism remain to be designated. But since the philosophy which defines these required reforms in the West is the one which has prescribed the required reforms in both Mohammedan and Hindu India, there is no difficulty *in principle* in finding a solution of the problem of reconciling the Mohammedan, Hindu and British portions of India.

Such an ideal three-fold reform is by no means easy, or something which can be accomplished quickly. However, it is not with the easy or the quick, but with a principle defining the ideal and the good, that this entire inquiry is concerned. Moreover, the question is whether anything short of a basic reconstruction in the present ideals of all parties to the India problem gets to the heart of the basic difficulty, and hence offers any hope of a genuine solution. In any event, the policy based on the indicated philosophical criterion of the good offers more hope of success than many current proposals, based as they are on foreign values local to the traditional modern Anglo-American West, since it builds on indigenous Mohammedan, Hindu and Buddhist foundations within India herself.

What must be realized is that in the India problem, as in all the other national and international ideological issues of this time, we are confronted, not with a simple issue between the good and the bad, but with a complex conflict between different conceptions of what is good. It is in the provincialism and inadequacy of the traditional ideals that the trouble in considerable part centers. Similarly it is in the solution of the philosophical problem underlying the traditional partial or out-moded conflicting ideals—a solution defining a more comprehensive and adequate idea of the good for our world—that an essential part at least of the prescription for the cure of the ills of these times is to be found. Since the stated solution of this philosophical problem alters basic conceptions in both the East and the West, it is hardly to be won-dered at that reforms in the ideals of all—Christians, Hebrews and Americans as well as Mohammedans, Hindus and the British—are called for.

THE CRITERIA OF CULTURAL REFORM

An interesting contrast appears between the rule for reforming a culture based on the aesthetic component and the rule for improving one grounded in the theoretic component. In the former case, the more the contemporary institutions and practices conform to the original aes-thetic intuition of the ancient and primitive past the better; in the latter case, the more they conform to the most technical scientific conceptions of the present the better. The reasons for this contrast are clear: Since the aesthetic component is immediately apprehended, and since mature reflection and the attendant social habits tend to obscure the original pure intuition, a society grounded in this component is likely to be more correct to the extent that its returns, as the Buddha, Confucius, and Lao Tzu counseled, to the original experience of its ancient past. Because the theoretic component is known only by hypothesis, and one's hypothesis becomes more and more trustworthy to the extent that it is reconstructed to bring under its domain more and more facts, which accumulate with passage of time, a society resting on this component comes nearer the ideal to the extent that it conceives of it in terms of the latest and technically formulated experimentally verified scientific theory.

But our philosophical principle prescribes that both the aesthetic and theoretic components are required. Thus the ideal society must return to the primitive intuition of the past with respect to its aesthetically grounded portion and advance to the sophisticated science of the present with respect to its theoretically based part. This has one very radical consequence for Westerners. It means that the traditional Western tendency to regard the primitive as inferior or evil must be rejected with respect to the aesthetic component in culture. A people leaves the primitive aesthetic intuitions of its past at its peril. It must move forward to the scientific theory of the future, taking along the primitive aesthetic intuition of the past. But rare is the individual who can master both components. Thus every society needs those who cultivate intuition and contemplation with respect to things in their naïve aesthetic immediacy as well as those who pursue science to the philosophical articulation of the theoretically known factor in things. It is precisely at this point that the native Indians of the entire American continent and the Negroes in the United States can take their place immediately in the good society, with something of their own to offer, leading and teaching with respect to the things of intuition and feeling, just as the white people can lead and teach them with respect to those things which must be known by inference and by theoretically constructed, and scientifically verified, doctrine.

The rule that the part of culture grounded in the theoretic component must reform its idea of the good by identifying it with the latest scientific conceptions, moving away from ancient doctrines, is important for the theistic religions such as Shintoism, Mohammedanism, Judaism and Christianity. Because they affirm the determinate personality to be immortal when the immediately apprehended determinate self is seen to die, and because they affirm the divine to be determinate and immortal when all immediately apprehended determinate factors are mortal, these religions rest on the inferred, unseen theoretically designated component in ourselves and nature. Consequently, unless these theistic religious concepts are identified with the technical theoretical content of present scientifically verified knowledge, they degenerate, on the one hand, into mere verbiage, as is the case with much of contemporary Protestantism, or, on the other hand, into an arbitrary, provincial, intolerant, dictatorial and inquisitorial absolutism and obscurantism above all evidence and all criticism, as is the case with contemporary Japanese Shintoism.

More specifically, this means that *determinate* moral and religious commandments or theses arrived at by nomadic tribes in the Mediterranean region in the time of Moses or the time of Christ simply cannot be taken as perfect and sufficient determinate theses for the definition of the good life in the twentieth century, even in the West, to say nothing of the Orient. Remarkable and adequate as they were for the times in which they were uttered, and permanently valid as a rough approximation as certain of their insights remain, they simply do not represent, nor do they adequately designate what the present stage of human knowledge indicates the theoretic component in man and nature to be. Only if this is first recognized and then actually realized by the construction of a theistic theology in which all its concepts are identified with the content of present scientific knowledge of the theoretic component in things, after the manner of St. Thomas with respect to the scientific knowledge of the thirteenth century, can the theistic religions of the world slough off their tribal provincialisms and their obscurantism and take on the more universal character and the more universal validity which is their birthright, thereby eliminating the still persisting religious prejudice between Christian and Jew, Protestant and Catholic, Jew and Arab, and Mohammedan and Christian which are such obviously outmoded evils in our contemporary world.

But of equal importance with this reform in the theistic religions and in all other parts of culture which are grounded in the theoretic component, is the addition of the religious and cultural values of the Orient which are rooted in the aesthetic component. The analysis of the culture of the Orient in which this immediately apprehended part of oneself and all things is pursued for its own sake, has led to description of this aesthetic component in its totality as the differentiated aesthetic continuum. This complex aesthetic continuum is made up of two factors: one the determinate sensed or introspected differentiations which are transitory; the other, the undifferentiated aesthetic continuum, within which the determinate differentiations come and go. Since time has to do with the transitory differentiations, the Oriental affirms the undifferentiated aesthetic continuum to be outside time and hence not transitory.

It has previously been established that the two-termed relation of epistemic correlation has the consequence of making the aesthetic component an ultimate real and essential part of the self and all things. Consequently, human beings, all natural objects other than human beings, and the medium joining them must be regarded as in part constituted of the aesthetic differentiations which are transitory and the otherwise indeterminate all-embracing aesthetic continuum which is not transitory. In terms of concrete appreciation, what does this mean?

THE SELF IN ITS AESTHETIC NATURE

The aesthetic self is a continuum which is as much, and with precisely the same immediacy, in the aesthetic sky, the aesthetic other person, the aesthetic table, the aesthetic flower, the aesthetic molecule, the aesthetic electron, and the aesthetic ionization, as it is in the aesthetic self. This explains how it is possible for one to apprehend in his own self-consciousness the blueness of the sky and the color of the rose and the moving beauty of the sunset with precisely the same immediacy with which the pain of one's own local toothache is apprehended. It is only with respect to the differentiations in this all-embracing aesthetic continuum that the aesthetic self is different from the aesthetic sky, the aesthetic flower, or any other human or non-human natural object. Thus, it is quite erroneous to conceive of a person, after the manner of the Lockean mental substance and traditional modern Anglo-American culture, as a completely local, independent thing having nothing in common with all other persons and things. There is an all-embracing indeterminate continuum of feeling common to all creatures in their aesthetic immediacy.

It must be remembered also that all these aesthetic materials, including the all-embracing aesthetic continuum, are the kind of thing which can be known only by being immediately experienced. No syntactically formulated, mathematically or logically abstract, indirectly and experimentally verified theory can ever designate them. They are, by virtue of this very character, ineffable. They are also emotionally moving. In short, the aesthetic continuum within the essential nature of all things is, to use the language of Shakespeare, "Such stuff as dreams are made on." But there are other differentiations in this ineffable, all-embracing aesthetic component than the introspected images which constitute dreams. There are also the equally immediately inspected images which constitute the colors, fragrances, and flavors of the sky, the earth, the flowers, the sea, and other natural objects. The aesthetic component is therefore also the stuff that these are made of.

Now it is precisely this ineffable, emotional, moving quale that constitutes what is meant by spirit and the spiritual. Thus in order to do justice to the spiritual nature of human beings and of all things it is not necessary to have recourse to idle speculations, by means of which one tries to pierce through the glass beyond which we now see darkly, to supposedly unaesthetic material substances behind, or into some unreachable and unknowable realm where mental substances are supposed to be. On the contrary, the spiritual, the ineffable, the emotionally moving, the aesthetically vivid—the stuff that dreams and sunsets and the fragrance of flowers are made of—is the immediate, purely factual portion of human nature and the nature of all things. This is the portion of human knowledge that can be known without recourse to inference and speculative hypotheses and deductive logic, and epistemic correlations, and rigorously controlled experiments. This we have and are in ourselves and in all things, prior to all theory, before all speculation, with immediacy and hence with absolute certainty. One is able to say with the Spaniards, the Mexicans and the Tantric Hindus that in part at least the essence of the soul is passion.

Consequently, the relating of the aesthetic or sensed, to the theoretical in scientific knowledge, by the two-termed relation of epistemic correlation makes the recourse to Locke's and Descartes's troublesome mental substances quite unnecessary in order to account for the spiritual, aesthetic, and emotional religious character of man, and of all other natural objects. Here, in this conception of the spiritual and in this conception of religion, are the intuitive and contemplative, indeterminate, aesthetic and emotional religion of the Orient, the negative theology of the West, the mysticism of San Juan de la Cruz, and the cult of the Virgin at Chartres and Guadalupe; rather than the theoretical, doctrinal, orthodox religion of the male Moses, Christ, or Mohammed and their determinate unseen Yahweh or God the Father. We have also the basis for understanding the individualistic philosophy of the Spaniard Unamuno, and the *existence* philosophy of Kierkegaard and Heidigger. But this is precisely what any adequate philosophy must have if it is to do justice to certain unique insights and cultural achievements of the Orient, Spain and Latin America, and merge them with the equally unmatched but different values of the traditional orthodox West, without bloodshed, devastation, and tragedy. Also, it explains why, throughout the history of Catholicism, as Henry Adams notes in Chartres

Cathedral and as can be seen even today in Mexico, surreptitiously or explicitly, men have instinctively insisted upon taking the aesthetic emotional Virgin Mary and the Virgin of Guadalupe as Divine in Her own right, and not simply because she is the earthly Mother of Christ and merely through Him a sensuous symbol of the theoretically and doctrinally known, but unseen, God the Father.

The theory also restores to natural objects their aesthetically rich luminous quality. The earth, as any farmer boy who has followed the plow in the springtime knows, is a warm and fragrant earth. It is, as the Orientals and all peoples close to the soil have clearly seen, the mother of us all. From her come the creation and the nourishment of all living things both plants and animals. Thus it is that she has been appropriately and properly named "Mother Earth," or "the Good Earth." So strong is the feeling of this inseparable bond between man and nature that the experienced explorer of China's soil and geography G. B. Cressey, and the informed student of Chinese culture Lucius C. Porter, have affirmed that "Perhaps the finest summary of Chinese philosophy is the desire to be 'in tune with nature.'"

As Tagore and the Taoist painters and the Americans Emerson and Thoreau have seen, nature fairly presses her beauty upon us always on all occasions. And as the Taoist painters have noted in their quiet contemplation, the all-embracing aesthetic continuum which is nature is the same emotionally moving aesthetic continuum which is man in the aesthetic ineffable spiritual component of his being (Plate XIII). In the language of Hinduism, Brahman (the cosmic principle in the universe) and Atman (the psychic principle in man) are one.

It is for these reasons that there will be no religion nor culture which adequately meets the spiritual as well as the intellectual needs of men until the traditional Western theism, after being reformed to bring it abreast of contemporary knowledge of the theoretic component in things upon which it rests, is also supplemented with the primitive traditional Oriental religion of intuition and contemplation with its cultivation of the aesthetic component. And before this is possible there must be an art in the West, like that of the Orient, but our own, in which the female aesthetic intuitive principle in things speaks in its purity, conveying itself for its own sake. Only if such an art is created can the West break itself of the habit of regarding feelings and emotions and the immediately given portion of man's nature and the nature of all things as mere superficial appearance, or mere symbol of the theoretic component beyond. Only then can we grasp the positive experience that the ineffable spiritual immediately felt part of oneself and all things is something ultimate, elementary, and good. Such is the importance of the painting of Georgia O'Keeffe (Plate XI).

Having accounted for the emotional, aesthetic, ineffably spiritual nature of man and the universe, with the aesthetic component or end-term in the two-termed relation of epistemic correlation, it is no longer necessary in the conception of the other end-term, the theoretic component, to include within it an inferred or postulated mental substance. Instead, the theoretic component of human knowledge can be restricted to precisely what the expert natural scientists with their scientific methods of hypothesis, deduction, and experimental confirmation indicate it to be. This means, in the case of man, that in the theoretic component of his nature he is precisely what experimental physicists, chemists, biologists, and psychologists find him to be. Thus the theoretic component of man is man conceived as a physical-chemical system, an electrodynamic field, with the particular structure which exhibits itself in man's body and especially in his nervous system and its cortex.

Man in this sense we do not immediately apprehend. The reader has but to inspect himself with all the immediacy of which he is capable, to realize that he does not immediately apprehend himself either in the data of sense or in the images of the imagination as a being with a cortex or a complicated nervous system involving electromagnetic and chemical relations with the electromagnetic field of the rest of nature. Man in this sense is known by postulated theory which is checked through its deductive consequences against the aesthetic component of oneself which is immediately apprehended, by recourse to the two-termed epistemic correlations. Thus one knows himself to be a creature with a physical-chemical-electromagnetic-biological body by indirectly verified theory, rather than by immediate inspection or observation alone. But this factor in man's nature is nonetheless real, and it is no less an essential part of his nature, because it is known in this logically inferred, scientifically and experimentally verified manner.

At this point, the theory provides the valid part of Russian communism. For the basic, unique factor in Russian communistic theory is precisely the thesis indicated just above that the physically, chemically, biologically, thermodynamically, physiologically, and anatomically known man is the essential man, and hence the economic and political person. This unique valid element in the philosophy of Karl Marx and in Russian communism, it will be recalled, came from Hobbes and Feuerbach. It is provided in the theory of epistemic correlation by what is termed the theoretic component of man's nature, since the theoretic component of anything is that thing precisely as it is known by the natural scientists' postulationally designated, indirectly and experimentally confirmed theory. In this respect and also in its emphasis upon aesthetics the theory has much in common with the philosophy of W. P. Montague.

Since it has been shown that the culture of the traditional Orient is grounded in the aesthetic component, and since the Feuerbachian unique, basic element in Marxian communism is provided by the theoretic component, the two-termed relation of epistemic correlation joining these two components specifies the manner in which the traditional Oriental culture and the valid Feuerbachian element in Russian communism can be related without conflict.

THE SYNTHESIS OF RUSSIAN COMMUNISM AND TRADITIONAL DEMOCRACY

Furthermore, the aesthetic component in the nature of things has been shown to be the differentiated aesthetic continuum. Now this differentiated aesthetic continuum contains not merely the indeterminate aesthetic continuity which the Orient and its religions have emphasized, but also the local, more atomic differentiations such as colors, sounds, pains, pleasures, and immediately introspected wants, which Hume and Bentham noted. But, as Chapter III demonstrated, it is precisely the latter specific sensed items and the immediately inspected relations of preference joining them, upon which traditional Anglo-American economic science is based. Thus, the local differentiations in the aesthetic component of the nature of things provide the assumptions of the Jevonian and Austrian foundations of the Anglo-American economic theory, just as the theoretic component of the nature of things provides the Feuerbachian element in the Marxian theory. It appears, therefore, that an economic science which is adequate to and in accord with the nature of man and the universe must combine both elements. A study of the epistemic correlations joining the introspected psychological wants in the aesthetic component of the nature of things to the theoretic component of their nature as defined by physiochemical, thermodynamic, electromagnetic, and neurological science, should specify precisely how such a comprehensive and adequate economic science, reconciling, amending and combining the truth of the Anglo-Americans and the Russians, is to be achieved. It will be recalled that the Marxian labor theory of economic value differs from the Anglo-American psychological theory of economic value because the two groups came to the formulation of economic science with different philosophical assumptions. Since these philosophical assumptions include both, and more besides, they should provide the foundations for a correspondingly more comprehensive and adequate theory of value for economic science. Thus, the way of harmoniously uniting Soviet Russia and the traditional democracies is suggested.

One consequence of such an economic and political theory of the nature of a person should be noted. As has been indicated above, thermodynamic science in part defines the theoretic component of any person's nature. According to biology and thermodynamics any living organism is not in thermodynamic equilibrium. This entails, because of the second law of thermodynamics, that no living creature can exist unless energy comes into it from outside. To believe in such a political concept of a person entails thereby that any good state, *i.e.* any state resting on a correct theory of the nature of its citizens, must make it its primary concern to insure the requisite supply of energy (*i.e.* food) from without. Thus, there is all the difference in the world, morally and politically, whether one believes Locke's theory that a person is a mental substance, or Hume's theory that he is a mere association of sense data, or Buddha's theory that he is primarily the indeterminate aesthetic continuum, or the theory to which this long inquiry has led; the theory, namely, that a person, like anything else in the universe, is the aesthetic component of the nature of things joined to the theoretic component of the nature of things by the two-termed relation of epistemic correlation.

The Russians should have no difficulty in supplementing the scientific, theoretically designated portion of man's nature, which the Feuerbachian element of their Marxian communism emphasizes, with the equally essential and irreducible aesthetic component. At this point, in fact, their medieval past and their communistic present can combine, as has happened undoubtedly in the recent war, so that the one supplements and reinforces, rather than destroys and attacks the other. For, as has been noted, the intuitive component in the nature of things, with respect to which the Orient is most proficient, appears in European Russia through the Greek Orthodox Church, as well as in Middle Eastern and Asiatic Russia. The genius of the Russians—their proficiency in the arts of the novel and of music—renders this union of the scientific-theoretical with the intuitive-aesthetic easy, if not inevitable. That it is happening, the contemporary Russian music of Shostakovich clearly demonstrates. In his Symphonies the passion of Asia has not perished, nor has it been turned into a mere tertiary quality kept at a safe distance from the essence of the human soul.

Nevertheless, before Russia can have a correct ideology and thereby become a thoroughly safe neighbor for the rest of the world, certain unjustified portions of her Marxian philosophy must be dropped. One is the determinism of her dialectic theory of history and the application of this dialectic to nature itself, rather than merely to theories of nature. The fallacy in these Hegelian and Marxian doctrines was indicated in Chapter VI. The essential point in the error is the supposition that the negation of any theory or thesis gives one and only one antithesis, and one and only one attendant synthesis. This supposition is necessary if the inevitability and economic determinism of any one of these steps by negation and synthesis in the dialectical process of history are to follow. And yet it should be clear to anyone that the denial of one theory does not specify the new theory which must inevitably take its place. Moreover, the most elementary knowledge of the character of any theory, as revealed in recent studies of the logic of deductive systems, indicates that a given theory can be negated in a large number of ways, depending on whether one denies one or another or several of its basic postulates. This is clearly manifest in the case of Euclidian geometry. There are many, in fact one may say an infinite number of non-Euclidian geometries at which one can arrive by negating Euclidian geometry in different ways. Thus, neither culture nor history has in it the inevitability with respect to the present and the future which Hegel and Marx assumed; and as a consequence nobody has the right to affirm with dogmatic certainty that he is giving expression either to the nature of the historical process or to the dialectic achievement of greater and greater good, when he selects a given utopian social hypothesis such as the traditional communistic theory and forthwith proceeds to ram it down the throats of mankind in the name of the determinism of history.

This does not mean, however, that in their recognition of the role of negation in cultural history and the attendant emphasis upon revolution rather than gradual social evolution which it entails, the Hegelians and the Marxians have not noted something which is true. The point is merely that this role of negation and revolution does not occur with the inevitability and attendant uniqueness which the Hegelians and Marxians attributed to it. The negations themselves, however, do occur and the revolutions also, not merely for Hegelians and Marxians but even for the rest of mankind, especially in the West. The modern world itself and the American Revolution, as its name explicitly indicates, are the result of a ´negation and attendant revolution against the medieval thesis of St. Thomas and Aristotle. Similarly, even within Roman Catholic culture, the present orthodoxy of St. Thomas is a negation of, and came only after the most heart-rending conflict with, the previous Roman Catholic orthodoxy of Plato, St. Augustine, and William of Champeaux. Sun Yat-sen likewise founded the New China by means of a revolution. The thesis of this book, when it negates the three-termed relation of appearance as the basis for joining the aesthetically immediate, purely empirical component in knowledge to the theoretic component, and substitutes for it the two-termed relation of epistemic correlation, is a similar example of negation with its attendant revolution not merely in man's thinking, but in his conception of what is adequate economic and political science and religion, and attendantly good personal, national, and international conduct.

This negation and attendant revolution apply to man's theories about nature, but not to nature itself, and to man's culture so far as the character of man's culture follows the pattern of, and the reconstructions in, man's theory of himself and nature. It is human theory, and the cultural values and institutions which are built upon and follow from human theory, that are subject, with the accumulation of human knowledge—especially when those human theories refer to the theoretic component in the nature of things—to the operation of the principle of negation and the attendant revolution which follows upon the operation of this principle. Thus, there is not an inevitable determinism in history, with respect to which man and his thoughts and theories are mere puppets, which defines the nature of man, the physical universe, and the course of historical events; instead it is the change in man's conception of the theoretic component in nature and the natural man with the increase of empirical knowledge, which determines in considerable part the character of, and the changes in, the historical cultural process.

That this is the case, analysis of the major cultures of the world has shown. The traditional modern Lockean and Voltairean theory of man and nature as an aggregate of mental and material substances in interaction, arose not from a study of the cultural historical process, nor from the class conflict, but as a consequence of the necessity of clarifying the distinction between the sensed component and the theoretic component in nature, which Galilei's and Newton's physics had revealed. This theory arose in the seventeenth century. The transformation by means of it of the traditional Spanish Catholic colonial historical, religious, educational, and poltical institutions of Mexico did not come until much later, in the Revolutions of 1810, 1857, and 1910. Thus it was a philosophical theory of nature and man arrived at in the sciences of physics and epistemology, rather than in the social sciences, which determined the actual changes and historical developments in Mexico in the nineteenth century, and not the inevitable dialectical develop- ment of a deterministic history supposedly pushing man and nature about.

Similarly, in China the basis of its traditional cultural forms is to be found in Taoism, Confucianism, and Buddhism. The basic philosophi- cal thesis common to all three refers to nature and man as immediately apprehended. The theory that the nature of things is an immediately apprehended aesthetic continuum which contains transitory differentia- tions is a thesis which does not need culture for its justification nor does it need the historical process. In fact, both Confucius and Lao Tzu unequivocally opposed the factual cultural institutions and forms of their time; Lao Tzu, in fact, maintaining that the ideal culture is one in which there is no human or social action at all. In so far as Confucius tended to identify the good with even the traditional forms of the ancient past instead of grounding his moral philosophy solely in the immediately apprehended aesthetic continuum and its differentiations, we see that he gains a conception of the good which is relative, pro- vincial, and transitory, which the Chinese of the twentieth century found it necessary to destroy in the Revolution of 1912. Furthermore, the basis of the scientific character of man's nature which is the unique element in the Marxian philosophy is to be found completely within natural science, and is quite independent of any study by social scien- tists of history or cultural institutions. Its justification is rooted in the immediately apprehended character of the natural man and nature and the theoretically designated character of the same, which the natural scientist, by established logical and experimental methods, infers from the immediately apprehended. Thus both types of knowledge are quite independent of the study of history or a study of culture; they depend on nothing more than immediately apprehended and logically inferred nature.

In this manner the previously established criterion of the good does justice to the rich and manifold humanistic, as well as to scientific cultural forms which Oriental and Western civilizations exhibit; while at the same time providing a criterion for distinguishing the good from the bad in actual culture. Thereby, it escapes falling into the culturalistic fallacy, committed by German Hegelian idealists, by the Russian communists, and to a lesser extent by the American pragmatists and legal realists when they identify the good for society or history with its present or future "is."

Also, because this criterion of the good for man and society has its roots (a) in the immediately apprehended component of man and nature which holds for everybody, and (b) in the theoretically designated component in man and the nature of things as determined by natural scientists whose methods give the same results for everybody, it is a theory of the good which in both of its components may be said to be valid for everybody. Thus one is not left in a thoroughgoing ethical relativism in which one man's conception of the good is as correct as that of anyone else. *That conception of good conduct and the good state is the correct one, valid for everybody, which rests upon the conception of man and nature as determined by immediate apprehension with respect to the aesthetic component and by the methods of natural science with respect to the theoretic component;* procedures which, when correctly applied, give the same results for one person that they give for another.

There is nothing particularly novel about this thesis; it is only unorthodox for the recent Post-Kantian Western world. The great moral leaders of the past have always maintained that good conduct and religious conduct consist in being true to one's real nature. Thus the bad man is one who acts from a partial or incorrect conception of the nature of himself or his universe. Since actual culture is the product, not merely of men acting upon the basis of a correct and complete conception of themselves and the universe, but also of the conduct of men, perhaps a majority of whom act upon a faulty, impulsive, partial, or incorrect conception, the "is" of culture cannot be taken as the criterion of the good for culture. This is the basic reason why the culturalistic fallacy is an error. But when, in the case of the post-Kantian idealists and the Marxians, the determinism in their conception of history is removed, making their commission of this culturalistic fallacy impossible, there still remains the Hegelian emphasis upon the importance of the spiritual, the aesthetic, and the religious, which the aesthetic component and the invariant element in the theoretic component provide, and the Marxian insistence upon the inclusion of the scientific character of man within the legal and economic concept of a person, which the scientifically determined theoretic component in knowledge guarantees.

Human freedom has its basis in part, as was noted in connection with the Buddhist culture of the Orient, in the aesthetic component of human nature. Two things are to be recalled: First, the aesthetic component is an irreducible and essential component in man's nature. Second, this aesthetic component is in part indeterminate. It is in this aesthetically immediate, basic, irreducible indeterminism in man's nature that the basis of his freedom is located. Man is in part free because he, in his essential nature, is in part indeterminate. At any time man can withdraw into the indeterminate aesthetic component of his nature, giving up any commitment to determinate, transitory, aesthetic qualities, or to determinate, inferred, theoretical theses, thereby in part escaping the determinism which attaches to all determinate things; and, because of this capacity, he may also *freely* accept the determinate, taking all its causal consequences, as Orozco and the Spanish have so truly seen. Thus, a philosophy which conceives of man as the correlation of aesthetic and theoretic components provides the required meaning for human creativity, fancy, and potentiality, and for freedom with its human choice, which is man's glory and which human responsibility and human remorse require if they also are to be real.

Moreover, all this is made meaningful entirely within a purely positivistically given and logically inferred scientific philosophy. Thus, the need for Kant's and Fichte's spurious "practical reason," and the attendant gulf between the sciences and the humanities to which it gives rise, is escaped. Also recourse to a provincial kind of moral or religious way of knowing *sui generis,* vouchsafed in some miraculous unverifiable manner to a chosen few, is rendered unnecessary and avoided. Furthermore, because of the spiritually and aesthetically enriching yet sobering effect upon the moral ego of having to adjust his conception of what is beautiful and divine and good, to the aesthetically immediate, and the scientifically inferred and factually tested theoretic components in the nature of things, all risk is avoided of letting loose upon the world all the provincially romantic demands and wars in the name of morality and religion of the recent nationalist Germans and the ancient traditional tribal Christian, early Jewish, Mohammedan, and Shintoistic theists. Before any individual or people can put forward one line of conduct as good or divine in the name of morality and religion, he or they must specify a positivistic aesthetic item immediately apprehendable and common to everybody, or a scientifically inferred and verified theoretical item in the nature of man or the universe which anyone can confirm; and show that without the conduct in question either the aesthetic or the theoretic factor in man's true nature would be falsely denied and not given expression with the precise degree of relativity or constancy which its character justifies.

As cultivated by the Orient, the indeterminate aesthetic continuous component in man's nature and in the nature of all things has demonstrated itself to be a factor which pacifies men, giving them a compassionate fellow-feeling not merely for other men but for all nature's creatures, and serving to keep them more at peace with each other, rather than to send them off on wild, impulsive, ill-considered and ill-grounded aggressive private, nationalistic, or religious military escapades. Thus, while setting man free, because of its ultimate and irreducible indeterminateness, the indeterminate aesthetic continuum, because of its all-embracing oneness and continuity, also tends to make man a sensitive compassionate human being. Moreover, since the indeterminate element in man's nature is the indeterminate aesthetic continuum common to all natural objects in their aesthetic nature, this indeterminate aesthetic source of human freedom engenders an intuitive sensitivity and religious compassion for all nature's creatures, precisely as the Buddha saw.

But man in the aesthetic component of his nature is *not completely indeterminate*. He is also differentiated by specific aesthetic qualities. These qualities, as Plato, Galilei, Berkeley, and Confucius saw, vary from person to person and circumstance to circumstance. Thus, in addition to the good which may be said to be valid for everybody, the theory also provides for the relative goods, which do not hold for everybody. Consequently, in designating an idea of the good which is absolute in the sense that it can be verified by anybody, the theory by no means denies the relative goods which differ from individual to individual, from people to people, and from one circumstance to another. It merely shows that all "goods" are not of the latter, merely relativistic character, thereby providing a basis for the moral and political agreement between men necessary to insure the majority opinion which democracy requires for its existence and effective functioning, while also recognizing the differences of preference and of attitude between men, and the emotive meanings which, as Charles Stevenson has recently shown, play such a large role in ethical issues. Nor, as Confucius has seen, as well as many Western moralists and sociologists, are the latter relative goods any the less good because they are relative. In this manner plenty of scope is provided for individuality, for the cultural richness and the spice of life which diversity and variety insure, and for the poetic imagination.

THE SOCIAL NATURE OF MAN

Western science has shown that the pains and pleasures and colors and flavors in one's aesthetic nature, besides being determinate and in part relative, are also in part determined by fixed laws which indirect experimental verification has shown to govern the comings and goings of their epistemic correlates in the theoretic component. For example, the sharp pain which one immediately apprehends may be the epistemic correlate of the scientifically inferred acidity of one's physicochemical digestive processes. Similarly, the dark round patch in the aesthetic continuum may be an epistemic correlate of the astronomical body termed the moon, when, as governed by the indirectly verified laws of celestial mechanics, this moon moves into a certain relation with the sun and the earth, which we call an eclipse of the sun. Thus an adequate comprehension of human nature must consider not merely the differentiated aesthetic component, but also the relation of its sensed qualities to the scientifically inferred theoretic component in all things. This theoretic component has one very important characteristic. Since it is not immediately apprehendable as a local particular, and since any part of it, such as a person, can be defined only relationally and syntactically by the postulates of systematic deductively formulated scientific theory, it is of necessity relational and systematic in character. Thus, by no stretching of the imagination can one's legal, political, economic or religious concept of a person in the theoretic component of its definition and essential nature be conceived, after the manner of Locke's mental substance and the traditional modern laissez-faire economic and political theory, as a self-sufficient, completely independent, purely local thing, free of all essential and internal relations to other persons and things. Instead, man in the theoretically inferred and scientifically verified part of his nature is a determinate relationally defined, and hence a social being. Again, Aristotelian, Elizabethan, and medieval truths and values are reconciled with those of contemporary modern science.

Moreover, the theoretic component in man as designated by contemporary biological and psychological science is defined systematically and relationally by the same laws which define the theoretic component in all other natural objects. Thus the social nature of man, as constituted by the theoretic component of his nature, is, like the indeterminate, all-embracing, undifferentiated continuum in the aesthetic component of his nature, a communal nature which, in a basic and systematic and fundamental sense, makes him one not merely with all human beings, as Christ taught, but also with all other natural objects —plants, animals, the good earth, and the most distant stars—as Buddha, Lao Tzu and Confucius taught. Again, traditional Christian and contemporary Western scientific values are reconciled with and supplemented to include Oriental values.

Furthermore, without the earth and the energy of the sun and the creative photosynthesis of the plants, man as we know him scientifically in the theoretic component of his nature would not be. This being the communal social nature of man in both the aesthetic and the theoretic components of his nature, clearly the old Lockean theory of the person as an absolutely free and independent mental substance, having no governmental need of his fellow men, except to preserve his private property, is a figment of the imagination as erroneous and untenable in theory as it has turned out to be inadequate and outmoded in practice before the inescapable social and international problems of the contemporary world. Consequently, to be a person, in a much more far-reaching sense than even Aristotle conceived, is to be, in one's very nature in the all-embracing aesthetic component and in the systematically defined, equally all-embracing theoretic component of one's being, a social natural object, a political animal. Hence, to have a good government is to have one which gives expression not merely to man's social nature as a human being and a living animal but also to man's social nature as part of the system of all natural objects. In this respect also justice is done to the social and systematic character of man and nature which was the merit of the Hegelian and Anglo-American idealistic social philosophy and the Marxian dialectic materialism.

But this does not occur to such an extreme degree that freedom is denied and the social becomes identical with the absolutely determined and the regimented. For it is only the theoretic component in things which is both determinate and socially systematic in character, and even knowledge of this is by hypothesis and hence, tentative and subject to change with further information. Consequently, in practice there is freedom here and open-mindedness, tempered always with the recognition that though the inferred part of human nature and things is determinate, social and systematic in character, any human being's knowledge of precisely what specific content it has, is at best approximate and probable rather than absolutely certain. With respect to the aesthetic component, not merely knowledge of it, but it in itself is in part indeterminate. This is unqualifiedly true with respect to that portion of it—namely the undifferentiated aesthetic continuum—which is the common all-embracing immediately experienced factor in all things. Thus, justice is done to the independence, integrity and freedom of the individual, which it is to the everlasting credit of Descartes, Locke, Hume, Bentham and Mill and traditional modern Protestantism and democracy to have fostered.

But this integrity and freedom of the individual is carried far beyond the traditional modern conception of it. Man in the theoretic component of his nature is not a blank tablet but his specific character as designated by the investigations of the most recent science. According to this science men vary tremendously because of determinate differences in their genes, their glandular secretions, and the structure of their nervous systems. Thus, men have individual integrity not because of a blank uniformity or because they are all mental substances but because each has in the theoretically known, scientifically verified component of his nature a unique, specific character. A free society, therefore, must do more than allow each person to vote, it must also as far as is possible allow the unique determinate traits of each person to come to fulfillment. Thus, to Anglo-American political freedom to vote and to Marxist economic freedom from want there must be added individual physiological freedom to be oneself.

The most important ground of· freedom, however, as has been noted, is in the aesthetic component of man's nature. This is not merely in part irreducibly indeterminate, thereby introducing potentiality into the essence of man's nature; it is also emotional, ineffable and luminous in character. With respect to this type of freedom of the sentiments and the emotions the traditional modern Anglo-American cultures have been weak; as Grant Wood's portraits (Plate IX) show, and as the spiritually mature British author Rebecca West indicates, when she writes of "the grey ice that forms on an Englishman's face" and of "the mean and puny element in the Gentile nature, at its worst among the English, which cannot stand up to anything abundant and generous." Even Thomas Jefferson wrote of the United States: "This country, which has given to the world the example of physical liberty, owes to it that of moral [and it should be added, emotional] emancipation also, for as yet it is but nominal with us. The inquisition of public opinion overwhelms, in practice, the freedom asserted by the laws in theory." One could expect little else from a people brought up in a philosophy and religion which removed the emotional and aesthetic factor in one-self and things from the essential natures of both the self and the natural object to turn it into mere appearance and the principle of evil. To regard the aesthetic component as possessing reality and irreducibility on an equal footing with the theoretic component, as the substitution of the two-termed relation of epistemic correlation for the traditional modern three-termed relation of appearance requires, is to change all this. Then, to be one's true self is to give expression to the ineffable emotional spontaneity and indeterminacy of the aesthetic component of one's essential nature, as well as to bring the more determinate theoretically known constitution of oneself to expression. Thus, to political, economic and physiological freedom there is also added psychological freedom of the emotions and the sentiments. In this manner justice is done to the Latin, Mexican, Spanish, Freudian, Middle Eastern and Oriental concept of freedom as well as to the more purely political freedom of the French, and English-speaking, modern West.

It is at this point also that previous emphasis upon leaving, or reconstructing, the traditional precepts which may have been reasonable in ancient times, or even in the eighteenth century, in the light of contemporary scientific and philosophical knowledge becomes important. Because of failure to bring the traditional moral doctrines referring to the theoretic component into accord with the advance in scientific knowledge, not only do outmoded provincial beliefs and practices persist in the name of morality, religion, economic science and politics but men are actually held morally responsible for items in their conduct which a scientific study of the biological, psychological, and psychiatric character of man indicates to be factors over which the individual has no control. If moralists are to insist that freedom is the precondition for a meaningful moral life, then they must also accept the corollary of this thesis, and not pass moral judgments upon human beings with respect to matters in their conduct over which the specific beings in question have in fact no control.

This must also be a guiding principle in the passage of laws in the nation and throughout the world. The community has a right to prescribe for everybody in it only laws referring to those factors which a correct, intuited and theoretically designated knowledge of the nature of man and his universe indicates to hold for everybody. There is plenty of scope for the operation of universal, unqualified laws, and for the pressing of our good works upon other people, in this realm of the nature of things alone. With respect to those matters in ourselves and the universe which a positivistic and scientific study of the aesthetic and theoretic components in the nature of things shows to be different from person to person, time to time, circumstance to circumstance, and nation to nation, both the layman and the governmental official must keep hands off in passing moral judgments upon other people and nations.

And by the same token a person or a government guided by a correct conception of man and nature has the right to affirm certain principles which hold for everybody. Otherwise, even the local individual would not be true to himself, since he would not be free to express the communal factors in his own nature; nor would the public agreement of at least a majority, necessary to prevent political freedom from destroying itself, be present. For man is not merely his own local, differentiated, aesthetic self, and his own local, differentiated, scientifically verified, theoretically known self. He is also (1) the indeterminate, otherwise undifferentiated aesthetic continuum common to all other persons and things in the aesthetic component of their nature and (2) the systematic, essentially social relatedness of the entire theoretic component of all things, apart from which his own more local theoretically known nature cannot be defined or conceived. Hence, these two factors insure positivistic and scientifically verifiable philosophical foundations for a limited application of the federal principle in international as well as national affairs.

PHILOSOPHICAL FOUNDATIONS FOR WORLD SOVEREIGNTY

Just as the relative local differentiations, both aesthetic and theoretic, which distinguish individuals and peoples from each other, provide for the limited absolute independence and freedom of the individual and for the limited sovereignties of local self-government, so the indeterminate aesthetic continuum and the determinate, theoretically designated systematic relatedness which are common to all men, guarantee the limited sovereignty of a world self-government. It is to be noted that a world government or a federal government is as much a self-government as is a village government or a government of an individual by himself alone, since the factors which are the same in all men are as much a part of the self as are the factors which distinguish that self from other persons and things. Thus, a philosophy of the state seems to be at hand with the specific criterion of private, local and world sovereignties that is required if the full freedom and integrity of the individual, which is one source of every great creative advance in civilization, is to be preserved, and if at the same time the sanctions for "one world" are to be guaranteed, which are so obviously required to solve by sympathetic, intelligent, lawful and peaceful means the inescapable national and international problems of these times.

It appears, therefore, when the paradoxically confusing and tragic conflicts of the world are analyzed one by one and then traced to the basic philosophical problem underlying them, and when this problem of the relation between immediately apprehended and theoretically inferred factors in things is then solved by replacing the traditional three-termed relation of appearance by the two-termed relation of epistemic correlation, that a realistically grounded, scientifically verifiable idea of the good for man and his world is provided in which the unique achievements of both the East and the West are united and the traditional incompatible and conflicting partial values of the different parts of the West are first reconstructed and then reconciled, so that *each* is seen to have something unique to contribute and *all* are reformed so as to supplement and reinforce instead of combat and destroy each other.

CHAPTER XIII

PRACTICAL WISDOM

The realism which underlies the criterion of the good society at which this study has arrived cautions against expecting it to come into the lives of men and nations too easily. Also, it was noted at the outset of this inquiry that philosophical, political, economic and religious beliefs are not the only things making society and history what they are. There are famines, disease, climate and countless other non-ideological factors. Also there are the ignorance, the lassitude and the bursts of impulsive, misguided frenzy in each one of us and in mankind. And there are the hardened habits, institutions and sentiments formed by the partial, inadequate and often outmoded values of the past. A wise realism must be as realistic about what is in fact the case in society as it is about what ought to be the case. Consequently, as was emphasized in Chapter I, there must be the more descriptive purely factual social science, as well as the investigation of the correct norms for man and society with which this investigation has been primarily concerned. And practical wisdom presupposes that both types of social knowledge—the ideal and the actual—be kept in mind continuously and not confused, or corrupted the one by the other.

REALISM WITH RESPECT TO IDEALS

It is to be emphasized, however, that a genuine realism with respect to the *de facto* situation of a given people must take into account, as even the leaders of communism clearly recognize, the ideological beliefs to which that people has been conditioned by its traditional education, political propaganda, artistic creations, and religious ceremonies. These traditional ideological factors embodied in the institutions and emotions of the people are just as much a part of the *de facto* situation as are pestilences, the dyspepsia of the Prime Minister, the climate, the ethnology, or the course of pig iron prices in the market place.

Furthermore, unless observable novel ideologies are at work from within, or inescapable external pressure is upon a people from without, the realistic thing to expect of it is that it will react as its traditional ideas of the good prescribe. Thus, with respect to Russia's leaders at the present writing, unless unequivocal empirical evidence to the contrary is at hand, the realistic conclusion to draw, when they affirm democracy, is the meaning prescribed for the word in the doctrine of Marx and Lenin, indicated in Chapter VI, rather than the meaning for British and Americans, indicated in Chapters III and IV. Similarly, it is the utmost folly to suppose that 80,000,000 Mohammedan Indians who have been instilled over the centuries with the dictatorial frenzied, aggressive militant theism of a Mohammed will act like good democrats electing their own representatives and behaving toward Hindus and Buddhists with the sober tolerance of a John Locke or a Thomas Jefferson, if only the British will get out of India. On the contrary, unless a reform such as that suggested in the previous chapter has occurred, the reasonable assumption is that they will behave in the future as their ideology has led them to behave in the past, namely convert and conquer by military and political dictatorship as much of India as they can. There is nothing cynical about such a view. It assumes that people will follow the ideals they have, unless they acquire other ideals or external pressure to the contrary is brought upon them from without. It is equally fallacious to assume that the German people will behave properly if only the Nazi leaders and the Junker Generals are removed and everything is made comfortable economically so that their feelings will not be hurt by poor trade. They are likely to pursue the unbridled romanticism of a moral philosophy of the practical reason derived from Kant and Fichte, and given a frenzied boost by Nietzsche, with its moral and political demands unconnected with, and hence unsobered by, scientific fact and the attendant consideration for other people, until some other and more adequate idealism is put in its place. Furthermore, until unequivocal evidence of such an adequate ideology appears, wisdom with respect to ideals prescribes that unless one wants the German people to burst forth upon the world in aggressive fury again a decade or two hence, the Germans must be kept under the most rigid supervision from without. Thus, a proper understanding of the role of ideals and ideas in society fits, rather than unfits, one to look at the *de facto* world realistically, taking it for precisely what it is.

Also, the mere knowledge of the correct idea of the good goes a considerable way toward the improvement of the *de facto* situation. One cause of the ills of these times has been the demoralization and paradoxical confusion of men with respect to their economic doctrines, political aims, and moral and religious ideals. The resultant conflicting motives within the individual and the contradictory contentions of the nations concerning what is good, tended to leave informed and sensitive men and peoples floundering at cross purposes, incapable of positive action to meet the internal schisms and the outer dangers which threatened them. As Eugene O'Neill, Jr., has indicated, "Obviously we ought to teach values, but what values shall we teach? The weakness of our education on the side of values is not the cause, but the effect of our uncertainty concerning values." Consequently, to have solved the ideological or normative portion of the social problem is to know what gives life meaning, to know what we believe, to know what is the criterion of sound economics and good political action; it is in short to know what we stand for and what we are working toward.

It is also to have gone a long way toward removing the initial discouragement, cynicism and pessimism left by the equally necessary realistic knowledge of the *de facto* state of society and the *de facto* traditional ideals of men. Consider again Mohammedan India and the present German people. A realistic facing of these two groups left one, a few pages back, a bit depressed. Yet the criterion of the good of the previous chapter, when applied to Mohammedan India showed, in terms of principle valid for all people, what factors already exist there as in any country, upon which to build spontaneously from within, and precisely what reform needs to be made in these factors. Similarly, with respect to German culture, the analysis of its ideological basis has revealed many valid partial elements such as the Kantian thesis that all knowledge is a synthesis of empirically given and systematic theoretically designated components, and such as Fichte's sense of the problem of freedom even though he gave the wrong account of its basis. Thus, here also a proper criterion of the good suggests that instead of trying to make the German people repudiate Kant, Fichte and Hegel completely by going back to Pre-Kantian laissez-faire Lockean and Humean individualism, we encourage them to take the valid element in their Kantianism, in their Hegelian sense of the systematic with respect to the theoretic component, and in their Fichtean sense of the primacy of freedom, and either amend these doctrines or provide for them in other more satisfactory ways, precisely as our theory of the aesthetic and theoretic components in things, joined by the two-termed relation of epistemic correlation, indicates. Thus, to have realistic knowledge with respect to what is in fact the case in society, including the traditional ideological as well as the non-ideological elements, and to have an equally realistic and scientifically determined criterion which is valid for everybody, of the ideal society, such as that to which this lengthy inquiry has led, is to know how to take advantage, from within, of the valuable assets of a given people or culture in order to move spontaneously from the actual situation *toward* the ideal.

Even so, if success is to occur, not merely philosophy and government but religion and perhaps even economics must bring art to their aid. For only by means of the vivid, emotionally moving materials of the artist can man's sentiments and determinate emotions, which are attached to the old, outmoded theories and the limited values be reconstructed, so that his feelings and spontaneous actions will take him where his present knowledge tells him it is good to go. As Wendell Willkie wisely said of war, "It is not simply a technical problem of task forces. It is also a war for men's minds. We must organize for our side not simply the sympathies but also the active, aggressive, offensive spirit of the peoples of the world." What is true of the military instruments of war is equally true of the religious, political and economic instruments of peace. Fortunately, in the problems of peace, all people, if they are wise, can be on the same side. For this, however, a more adequate religion and a very much more varied and vital art are essential.

THE INSTRUMENTS OF PEACE

Religious reform is essential because the traditional forms of education, political oratory, literature, and religious ceremonies have conditioned the attitudes, feelings, preferences, and spontaneous reactions of men to the old ideology. Consequently, even if one's scientific and philosophic intelligence puts old doctrines behind one, one's emotions, feelings, and habits, and even one's conscience, carry them on. It is precisely for this reason that religious conversion, as well as education, is necessary in society. The old man must be made new. Education aims primarily at the empirical and rational mind. Religion extends that of which science and philosophy persuade the intellect, from the intellect to the heart, the emotions, and the culturally conditioned habits, and from the habits of the individual to the communal habits of the group.

By means of science and natural philosophy—provided they include the intuitive as well as the theoretic component of all things—we learn what is true; or, more exactly, what is the most trustworthy conception of themselves and the total nature of things which it is possible for human beings to attain with all the aids at their disposal. Given this scientific and philosophical knowledge, theology, when it proceeds in a non-sophistic, trustworthy manner, then identifies the objects of religion with certain items in the natural philosopher's scientifically verified account of nature and the natural man. In the case of the major Far Eastern religions, the Divine and the "true self" are identified with the all-embracing, indeterminate, undifferentiated, and hence positively indescribable portion of the aesthetic component; in the case of the theistic religions, the Divine and the human soul are identified with certain primary factors in the theoretic component of the nature of things. A perfect religion will conceive of God as embracing both of these divine components. Once these identifications are made, the scientifically verified philosophical theory automatically prescribes the relations existing between God and the human soul. Thus religious doctrine is defined.

It might appear that such a method for determining theology would not do justice to the spontaneous religious response of men generally, apart from technical scientific knowledge, to the genius of the great religious leaders, or to the revealed elements in religion. Such a conclusion, however, does not follow. Much of the force of this supposition derives from the neglect of the empirical aesthetic component in scientific knowledge. This, the preceding analysis of scientific knowledge has corrected. Also, the identification of theological objects with verified factors in philosophically analyzed scientific theory is necessary if religion is to talk about the existence of God and the soul, as opposed to a mere aspiration or hope for their existence. Moreover, such an identification does not deny the natural religious inclinations of men, nor the genius of the great religious prophets; it merely insures that the people direct their aspirations and their conceptions of what the great religious leaders in part mean to the proper religious objects, thereby preventing tribal, provincial, temporary, and transitory objects from being mistaken for the Divine root principles out of which and by means of which all things are created.

Also, the reader will recall from the analysis of Roman Catholic culture in Chapter VII that even with St. Thomas both human scientific reason and revelation referred to the Aristotelian rational principle or Unmoved Mover as determined by Greek science; the difference between them was that revelation presented this principle as a human aim, known completely only by a perfect science, whereas reason designates it only as known partially in the specific human scientific knowledge we already possess. The philosophy to which the present inquiry has led permits precisely this distinction. It informs that there is a theoretic component in the nature of things which is ultimate, real, and irreducible. Following the tradition of all theistic religions, it identifies the Divine (in part, but not completely) with the invariant element in this theoretic component. It tells also that although this determinate theoretic component is known to exist with what amounts to absolute certainty, its specific character is only partially and tentatively approximated in human knowledge, due to the indirect methods of verification which it, because of its very nature as not immediately apprehended, forces upon one. The other part of the Divine which, following the Orient, has been identified with the all-embracing, indeterminate, undifferentiated field portion of the aesthetic component, is present now, when its differentiations are abstracted from it. Thus this method and theory for theology provide for the traditional theistic distinction between the aims and aspirations of life which revelation sustains and the actual, partial, specific knowledge which reason gives; at the same time it improves upon St. Thomas's distinction by adding the immediate, irreducibly imminent, purely intuitive, aesthetic type of religious knowledge which the religion of the Orient provides.

The theologians having, by this method, determined the correct religious doctrines, applied religion, or what many contemporary people call "living religion," then converts the old sentiments, emotions, and culturally conditioned habits of men from the form made determinate by the old, outmoded doctrine to the form made necessary by the new. For this task preaching is important, since, when expressing scientifically grounded philosophy and theology, it carries auditory education beyond the school and university into adult life. But art, and especially communal ritualistic art, is even more important.

There are many reasons for this. In the first place, the vast majority of people cannot follow the technical theological doctrine in its literal meaning. They must take it because of their faith in the expert theologians, just as they accept on faith the mechanism of their automobiles or radios. The important thing is that if the person has the interest and the intelligence to know the immediately apprehendable or scientifically inferable grounds for his religious faith, they can be pointed out to him by the experts in question, just as in the case of the automobile, the radio, and television. Moreover, even if the doctrine is grasped literally, it will often seem to many people (just as does the theology of St. Thomas, or just as did the idea of the good to Plato's sophistic humanists, when he released them from their chains in the cave) too abstract, dry, and cold. It takes time for people to realize that when they admit God to be omniscient they mean that He knows all the sciences and is a thinker. The rational component in God's nature can become vital in man's life in its literal, theoretical meaning only when men, by proper logical training, learn to think thoughts rather than merely to feel them, and thereby become rational, like unto God, themselves.

But there is an even more serious difficulty for a religion, especially a theistic religion, which hopes to do its important work by mere teaching and preaching. Even if the doctrines are understood and accepted intellectually, it is by no means likely, because of the old, culturally conditioned emotions, feelings, and reflexes, guided by the old, outmoded doctrine, that the new doctrine will be followed emotionally and spontaneously. Clearly, the instrument for the persuasion of the emotions is art, and the means for the conditioning of new habits is ceremonial, communal ritual. This is the reason why my colleague Charles Stevenson is quite right when he insists that emotive meanings and persuasive definitions play a much larger role in social science, religion, aesthetics, art, and ethics than the traditional modern moralists, with their concentration of attention upon cognitive meaning, have been inclined to recognize.

But it is not merely to convert men to a religious conception of the nature of man and all things, which is intuitively and scientifically grounded, that art is necessary. It is equally essential for man himself and for society. For when the scientific knowledge of these times has captured a man's mind, so that his intelligence tells him one thing and pushes him one way, and his emotions and habits attached to outmoded, incompatible scientific, philosophical, and theological doctrines push him another way, then he is a frustrated man, divided against himself. Such a man does not need to wait until after death to know what hell means.

Such is the stuff, also, of which the fall of France was made. For what modern France did was to accept modern science and philosophy with their attendant democratic, political ideology, while at the same time retaining the medieval Roman Catholic religious forms that require for their justification the Aristotelian scientific and philosophical principles, which contradict those of modern science and philosophy at many points. The intelligent Frenchman, because of French logic, knew this was the case; and as a result he often winked at his non-Catholic friends when he or his wife attended divine service. But this is to play with fire; for when one trifles with one's basic beliefs in this manner, there is in the long run a grave risk of losing all confidence in one's capacity to believe anything, either about modern democracy or about medieval religion. When this happens the will to make a stand in times of danger is not there, and all the things one really cherishes go by default.

Jacques Maritain is quite right when he suggests that France's tragedy is in considerable part due to her loss of her medieval religious faith. Certainly this time Joan of Arc did not rise again. And she failed to rise because Frenchmen no longer believed in her. But the cure for this tragedy is to be found not in taking one's scientific and philosophical beliefs back to those of medieval times, but in bringing one's medieval religious insights abreast of contemporary scientific and philosophical knowledge.

But let no one suppose that this is a task merely for France and the Roman Catholics. The traditional Anglo-American Lockean and Humean laissez-faire philosophy and the Kantian and post-Kantian moral, "idealistic" philosophy of the practical reason are as outmoded as Aristotle.

Precisely because deep-seated emotions everywhere are involved, art is indispensable. With art, however, this task should present no serious difficulty, since the Protestants, by their oldest tradition, are reformers; nor for the Roman Catholics, since they have an even older tradition, dating back behind Luther to the thirteenth century, when St. Thomas rejected the old orthodoxy to define the present one.

Moreover, both (a) art in its first function, which conveys the aesthetic component for its own sake (Plates XI and XIV) and (b) art in its second function, which uses the aesthetic component symbolically to convey the theoretic component (Plates I, V, VII, and XII), must be cultivated. Without the former, man will not receive the ineffable aesthetic, emotional, and spiritual sustenance which the aesthetic component of his spirit needs. Without art in its second function the correct contemporary conception of the theoretic component in man's nature will seem to him dry, abstract, cold, and excessively formal; and thus he will not receive the adequate intellectual food which the rational component of his spirit requires. For a properly nourished man, art in either of its two functions is not a luxury, or an afterthought, or something in which a blank, empty, traditional modern ethics tells him he ought to believe because of goodness, beauty, and truth in general; instead it is a concrete absolute and elementary necessity, as much the daily bread of his emotional and intellectual, spiritual nature as sufficient scientifically balanced calories are the daily bread of what science indicates the physiochemical theoretic component of his nature to be.

Also, for such a truly spiritual man, art in its first function is not a mere handmaid for religion; instead, what it conveys is the ineffable, emotional, spiritual stuff of which the religion which identifies the Divine with a factor in the aesthetic component of all things is made. Nor is such an art the mere handmaid of man; instead, even though it introduces no shapes suggesting the visage of a bodily person, what it conveys, nonetheless, is man. For in presenting the aesthetic component in and by itself, for its own sake, art in its first function is conveying the very stuff also of which man in one part of his nature is made. Only in this way can it be brought home to all the West that the aesthetically and emotionally immediate and the spiritually ineffable represent something irreducible, primary, and in part indestructible in the nature of man and the universe.

Even though much, if not most, of the art which he examined was art in its second function, no one in the West has expressed the unique character of art in its first function better than Benedetto Croce, when, restricting art entirely to the latter type, he writes:

Art . . . is *intuition,* in so far as it is a mode of knowledge, not abstract, but concrete, and in so far as it uses the real, without changing or falsifying it. In so far as it apprehends it immediately, before it is modified and made clear by the concept, it must be called *pure intuition.*

The strength of art lies in being thus simple, nude, and poor. Its strength . . . arises from its very weakness. Hence its fascination. If . . . we think of man, in the first moment that he becomes aware of theoretical life, with mind still clear of every abstraction and of every reflexion, in that first purely intuitive instant he must be a poet. He contemplates the world with ingenuous and admiring eyes; he sinks and loses himself altogether in that contemplation. By creating the first representations and by thus inaugurating the life of knowledge, art continually renews within our spirit the aspects of things, which thought has submitted to reflexion, and the intellect to abstraction. Thus art perpetually makes us poets again. . . . Art is the root of all our theoretic life. To be the root, not the flower or the fruit, is the function of art.

These words of Croce are superbly true. It is to be noted, however, that they are true only of art in its first function; that is, art which conveys the aesthetic component for its own sake. There is also art in its second function; and in it, art is the flower and fruition of thought, rather than its root. Lucretius's *De Rerum Natura* is an example. It gives expression in the intuitive language of the poet to the theoretic component of the nature of things as conceived according to the atomic theory of Democritus and Leucippus, who lived centuries before the Roman Lucretius. Dante's *Divine Comedy* is another example of art in its second function—an art which, to continue Croce's metaphorical language, is the fruition, rather than the root of thought. For Dante's great creation gives expression in the moving, more immediately apprehendable imagery of the poet to the conception of the theoretic component of the nature of things in its bearing on human destiny as technically formulated by St. Thomas in the logically constructed *Summa Theologica*, which Dante had previously studied. Similarly, when Queen Elizabeth's poet, in *Troilus and Cressida*, has Ulysses say—

> The heavens themselves, the planets, and this centre,
> Observe degree, priority, and place,
> Insisture, course, proportion, season, form,
> Office, and custom, in all line of order—

Shakespeare is but giving expression to the Aristotelian conception of the theoretic component and its attendant hierarchic, social idea of the good which the Tudors and Hooker and the English have always cherished.

These considerations make it evident that art in its second function must remain, and retain a primacy and importance equal to that of art in its first function. There is the theoretic component in the nature of things which art in its second function is designed to convey, as well as the aesthetic component in their nature which art in its first function is devised to present in its purity. If this book has seemed to put greater stress upon the latter, it is merely because such art and the immediately apprehended aesthetic continuum to which it restricts itself are less well known or appreciated in the West. Nor should the conclusion be drawn that all Oriental art is art in its first function. The tremendous and lasting influence of Greek art upon much of the sculpture and painting of the entire Orient—especially that of Hinduism and Buddhism, noted in the chapter on India—must be kept continuously in mind.

The necessity and importance of art in its second function has been expressed by Oscar Wilde in an essay concerning Pater, when Wilde notes that "to convey ideas through the medium of images has always been the aim of those who are artists as well as thinkers in literature"; and by George Sand in a letter to Flaubert, quoted by Wilde, where she writes, "I am aware that you are opposed to the exposition of personal doctrine in literature. Are you right? Does your opposition proceed rather from a want of conviction than from a principle of aesthetics? If we have any philosophy in our brain it must needs break forth in our writing."

The answer to George Sand's question is that it depends upon whether one is talking about art in its first function, or art in its second function. If it is the latter, then George Sand was right and Flaubert was wrong; if it is the former, then Flaubert was right and George Sand was wrong. In any event, however, George Sand has made it clear why art must be the fruition as well as the root of theory, especially for any culture which bases its idea of the good upon the inferred theoretic, rather than upon the immediately apprehendable aesthetic component in the nature of things. Conversely, the Orient must supplement its traditional emphasis upon art in its first function with a contemporary art in its second function such as Diego Rivera has inaugurated in Mexico and John Steuart Curry has started in his Wisconsin murals.

This development of an art in its second function which conveys contemporary rather than traditional doctrine is very important for all humanists. It means that at last they should be able to have their heads attached to their bodies in a normal way, enabling them to look forward where they are going, instead of having them rigidly fixed the wrong way around, so that, as has been the case in recent centuries, they have had to stand still intellectually or to stumble forward blindly, not seeing where they are stepping, because of their inability to look anywhere but behind into the past. The time is here when a man can be a competent humanist by using his artistry to convey contemporary and prospective, as well as past, often outmoded, traditional doctrines concerning the determinate nature of the theoretic component in things. This means also that humanists in education can escape from the present attachment of their emotions exclusively to the past, and from the resultant timidity with respect to consistently developed, logically disciplined proposals for the introduction of order and integrity into present education; thereby offering some hope of taking education away from the confused and incompatible eclectic hodge-podge which characterizes so much of it at present.

Thus, the art, the religion, and the other humanities of both the East and the West of the future will have twice the richness of the traditional humanities of either the East or the West. For to each part of the world an entirely new dimension of its subject matter in each one of the humanities will be opened up, provided by the addition of the traditional mode of treatment of the other civilization. To the intuitive, indeterminate aesthetic religion of the Orient will be added the determinate, contemporary, theistic type of religion of the West; and conversely, to the theistic, determinate religion of the West will be added the indeterminate, intuitive, contemplative, more aesthetic religion of the Orient. The same will be true in all the other humanities. For painting, this means that in both the East and the West there will be both the more Eastern type of art in its first function and the more Western type of art in its second function.

Once the respective technique for each type of art is mastered independently, and the public has learned to appreciate each by itself, then the two types can again be combined. The possible combinations constitute a spectrum of artistic possibilities which are infinite in their diversity.

THE SPECTRUM OF ARTISTIC POSSIBILITIES

This spectrum begins at the one extreme with a pure art in its first function, which conveys the aesthetic continuum without any suggestion of its theoretic correlate (Plate XI). It ends at the other extreme with pure art in its second function, which uses the minimum aesthetic materials solely to convey the theoretic component of things (Plate I).

The beauty of an abstract, analytical, mathematical proof, because of the large amount of the formal and theoretical, and the minimum amount of the intuitive and the ineffable in its content, stands very near the extreme purely theoretic end of the aesthetic spectrum; just as a painting like Georgia O'Keeffe's Abstraction No. 3 (Plate XI) into which it is difficult to read an inferred theoretic reference stands near the other extreme, purely aesthetic, end of the spectrum. In between the two extremes are to be located all the actual art of the past, and the potential art of the present and future, with the traditional art of the West (Plates XII, IX, VII, and V) toward the former of the two extremes, and most of the traditional art of the Orient (Plates XIV, XIII, XV, and XVI) toward the latter.

The three-dimensional statues of the Buddha (Plate XVI), in which, as René Grousset has shown, the Greek geometrical and the Eastern intuitive types of art are wedded, are instances of the middle portion of the aesthetic spectrum. Thus, to say that Oriental art, apart from the Greek influence, is art in its first function, and that Western art, before the Impressionists, is art in its second function, expresses what is true to a first approximation, but not an absolute distinction for the middle portion of the spectrum. Because traditional art in the West was art in its second function, located toward the middle portion of the spectrum, it is probable that what interested most Western artists, as artists, in their creative work, was the more pure aesthetic component in it, rather than the geometrically clear-cut pot of flowers or the humanistic or theological doctrine which their aesthetic materials were used analogically to convey.

It is to be re-emphasized that when our age has developed an independent art in its first function, following Georgia O'Keeffe and others such as Paul Gill in his *Red Flag* in the West and the Chinese landscape painters in the East (Plates XIII and XIV), and when it has created a *contemporary* art, in its second function, using the method, but not the traditional content of the traditional art in the West and the Greek element in Oriental art, then these two independent forms of art can and must be combined. For only in this manner will contemporary man have the intuitive and the scientifically rational components of his nature satisfied at one and the same time, without the danger which exists at present, in both the East and the West, and in Latin America as well as Anglo-America, of the one surviving at the expense of the other. Only by such means also can man's heart, as well as his head and his hands, be captured by the intuitively and scientifically adequate and trustworthy idea of the good for government, religion, and personal conduct which our time so desperately needs.

It will make the latter task very much easier, if contemporary science finds the field physics of Einstein, which stems from Faraday and Maxwell, to be a more adequate conception of the theoretic component in man's nature than is the particle physics theory, which stems from Galilei, Newton, and Dalton. The Oriental sages and painters (Plates XIII and XIV) and William James and the Gestalt psychologists have shown that the aesthetic component in man and nature has a field character. Hence, if the theoretic component in man, as determined by the indirectly verified theory of experimental science, has a field character also, the unity of man's aesthetic and theoretic nature will be easier to feel and comprehend.

THE THEORETIC COMPONENT AS CONCEIVED BY FIELD PHYSICS

The necessity of field physics assumptions to account for the theoretic component in inorganic objects was established by Maxwell, when he made it clear that were particle physics the whole truth, which it purported to be, the wave properties of light and experimental facts such as interference, in which the converging of two rays of light produces darkness, should not exist. Moreover, although Einstein has not yet succeeded in his quest for a generalized field physics which will account for subatomic phenomena as well as for the space-time structure of nature as a whole, contemporary physicists are agreed that Einstein's field physics is correct for nature in the large. Thus, the field physics theory of the theoretic component does seem to be reasonably well established for macroscopic nature.

Considerations such as this have suggested to H. S. Burr and the writer that since field physics assumptions are required for the understanding of inorganic systems, it is reasonable to suppose that they may be required also for living organisms, including man. Operating upon this hypothesis concerning the theoretic component in man's nature, H. S. Burr and his scientific colleagues have used Maxwell's electromagnetic equations to construct an experimental apparatus for putting this electromagnetic field physics theory of life to an experimental test. In thousands of experimental determinations covering some fifteen years of investigation, the expectations to which this theory leads one have been confirmed.

It must be said, however, that none of the findings is so conclusive as to prevent other theoretical interpretations from being put upon them, even though most of them are not so easily or plausibly interpreted from the standpoint of particle physics. There is nothing surprising about this situation. The field physics theory of the theoretic component of nature was in the same position initially with respect to its validity for inorganic systems, even after the convincing experiments of Faraday. Nevertheless, Clerk Maxwell showed Faraday's field physics theory to be correct in the end.

Recently, by this experimental technique, H. S. Burr has found suggestions of the same form of electrical response in many apparently non-sensitive plants, which appears to the naked eye in the sensitive plant, thereby confirming the findings of the Indian physicist Bose, to the same effect. Moreover, H. S. Burr's findings to date indicate that the form of the response in plants is the same as that in nervous tissue in human beings. This suggests the continuity of the form of sensitivity between human beings and plants. It was precisely because of the greater compatibility of such an electrical and field physics concept of the scientifically determined theoretic component in man's nature with the obviously field character of the aesthetic component of his nature, that the Oriental physicist Bose was led, as Sir John Woodroffe states, to perform his experiments upon plants.

It appears, therefore, that the field character may apply to the theoretic as well as to the aesthetic component of man's nature, as effectively as Einstein's physics has shown it to apply to nature as a macroscopic whole. If this turns out, upon further investigation, to be confirmed, then the number of epistemic correlations which are not one-one will be less than was the case in particle physics, thereby making the difference between aesthetically immediate man and scientifically conceived man less than it was previously, and thereby in turn making the unity of man's aesthetic and theoretic nature the easier to comprehend. The precise manner in which this will permit the psychology of the East and the West to supplement each other should be obvious. It should be noted, however, that the philosophical theory of things as composed of aesthetic and theoretic components, has been so formulated that it permits and requires one to accept the specific content of the theoretic component to which science is led.

The field physics of Faraday and Maxwell is important for one other reason. It, together with the theoretical physical-chemistry of Willard Gibbs, has enabled the modern man to lift a great portion of the drudgery and painful labor of the world off the shoulders and the muscles of men, to place it upon the oil wells, the mines, the dynamos, and the waterfalls. Because of the tremendous power of man's scientific knowledge of the theoretic component in the nature of things, to enable man to make nature do much of man's work, we have been able to produce more goods than the small buying power in the form of wages of the people could move. Thus, before this war, due to the failure of our political and economic thinking to reconstruct our monetary theory and our economic theory of distribution in accordance with the tremendous transformation in the production of economic goods wrought by modern theoretical science, we found ourselves in the paradoxical position of having millions upon millions of our inhabitants faced with starvation, apart from governmental doles, while the food that would have assuaged their hunger rotted in the granaries. Such is the stupid and terrific price that has been paid for keeping moral and political philosophy and economic theory in water-tight compartments, isolated from the theory of natural science. Somehow we must find a means, as the advances of natural science make it possible for fewer and fewer men to be hired as laborers tending the machines which produce the goods adequate in supply for the whole of mankind, of devising an economic theory of finance and distribution which will nonetheless create, throughout the whole of the population, the buying power necessary to move and to distribute these goods.

This is a problem entirely too difficult and technical for the present inquiry to attempt to resolve. Nonetheless, the philosophy resulting from this inquiry lays down certain general principles which must govern the more technical solution. The first principle is that the thermodynamical and physiochemical nature of man, requiring energy from without in the form of daily food, is as essential, and hence as moral and political a part of man's nature, as is his more emotionally vivid, aesthetic, spiritual component. Thus, good government will take as axiomatic the meeting of this need of man's nature, which depends clearly upon social factors as well as individual initiative. Hence, whatever the final economic theory is, it must be one which starts with the obvious capacity of science, the available natural resources of the world, and the thermodynamical needs of men as a basic premise, and permits these factors to get together and function with the minimum of theoretical inhibitions. Second, the development of the more comprehensive theory of economic value and of economic science, combining the valid elements of the Anglo-American and the communistic theories, which the previous chapter showed to be required and possible, should indicate how to do this upon a basis of sound economic principles.

ECONOMICS AND ART

Even so, it may be the case that the solution of the economic problems of our time, such as unemployment, is to be found in the aesthetic component. Upon one point, in any event, this philosophy is clear: No good state or no good life can be conceived, as the traditional Anglo-Americans and as the Russian communists have tended to conceive it, in restrictedly economic terms. The usual economic needs are, to be sure, one factor in the nature of man. But there is also the aesthetic component; and an adequate society, with adequate laws, must give as much attention to the feeding of this portion of man's nature as it gives to the provision of food and clothing to satisfy the needs of the theoretically known factor in his nature. Moreover, the theoretically designated component emphasizes as much theoretical, scientific inquiry for its own sake, born out of intellectual wonder, as it does the pragmatic applications of this theory in industry and in politics. Thus, this philosophy prescribes that men pursuing theoretical, scientific, philosophical, and theological inquiry are meeting the needs of men and are as essential members of a good society as is an economist, a labor leader, or a businessman. Furthermore, artists who pursue the aesthetic component, both for its own sake and as a means of conveying the scientifically known theoretic component, are as essential to the barest, most elementary needs of men as are the theoretical scientist, the theoretical philosopher, the theoretical theologian, or the practical engineer.

All these considerations suggest that one of the major causes of failure to solve the problem of unemployment and of poverty in a land of scientific ability and of plenty is that we have been conceiving of the economic problem in entirely too restrictedly economic terms. Thus, perhaps instead of economics being the key to the humanities, the humanities are, in part at least, the key to the solution of the problems of economics. For it well may be that it is only because we have had too narrow an economic idea of the good, and consequently have not brought forth the demands for creative work in art in both of its functions, in empirically verified scientific, philosophical, and theological theory, and in the teaching, preaching, and artistic conveying of such trustworthy theory, that the buying power has not been placed in the pockets of those not required to tend the machines, which is essential to distribute the goods sufficient for all, which the comparatively few men directing the automatic machinery are able to produce.

This, to be sure, is but a suggested possibility. But it is one nonetheless which follows from the nature of the concept of the good life for man, the national state and the world, which the philosophy of the theoretic and aesthetic components of the nature of all things prescribes. It would certainly be in accord with everything else that this inquiry has revealed, if, when an economic theory of finance and distribution, adequate to this time, is constructed, it turns out that its success depends as much upon the pursuit of art and the other humanities as upon economics and technology.

In any event, the scientific, theoretic component and the aesthetic component supplement each other in society in a remarkable manner. For as the mastery of modern scientific theory makes it possible more and more to lift the labor of the world from man to the machine and the waterfall, and thereby to meet the more material needs of mankind with fewer and fewer workmen, it thereby releases in society an increasing proportion of men who can give their time to the investigation of the theoretic component, continuously improving the conception of it and the scientific technology which flows from it, and to the artistic pursuit, portrayal, and analogical use of the aesthetic component. Thus, providing the continuous intuitive factor in the aesthetic, and the systematic unifying factor in the theoretic parts of our nature, which make all men and things one, are fostered, so that the equally real and important differences between men do not lead them to their mutual destruction, it should eventually be possible to achieve a society for mankind generally in which the higher standard of living of the most scientifically advanced and theoretically guided Western nations is combined with the compassion, the universal sensitivity to the beautiful, and the abiding equanimity and calm joy of the spirit which characterize the sages and many of the humblest people of the Orient.

REFERENCES

(References, including their page numbers, are in the order in which they, or the subjects which they treat, occur in the text.)

CHAPTER I

Pallis, Marco. *Peaks and Lamas.* Alfred Knopf, New York, 1940.

Kang, Younghill. *The Grass Roof.* Charles Scribner's Sons, New York, 1931.

Madariaga, Salvador de. *Englishmen, Frenchmen, Spaniards.* Oxford University Press, London, 1931.

Wolfe, Bertram D. *Diego Rivera, His Life and Times.* Alfred Knopf, New York, 1939.

Fernández, Justino. *José Clemente Orozco: Forma e Idea.* Librería de Porrua Hnos. y Cia., Argentina y Justo Sierra, Mexico, D.F., 1942.

Maritain, Jacques. *France, My Country Through Disaster.* Longmans, Green and Company, New York, 1941.

Dubs, H. H. "The Present Significance of Oriental Philosophies." *Philosophical Review,* May 1939.

Turner, Ralph E. *The Great Cultural Traditions.* The McGraw-Hill Book Company, New York, 1941.

Morris, Charles. *Paths of Life.* Harper and Brothers, New York, 1942.

Sorokin, Pitirim A. *Social and Cultural Dynamics.* American Book Company, New York, 1937.

Kluckhohn, Clyde, and Kelly, W. H. "The Concept of Culture" in *The Science of Man in the World Crisis.* Ed. by Ralph Linton. Columbia University Press, New York, 1945.

Whorf, B. L. "Science and Linguistics." *The Technology Review,* Vol. XLII, Apr. 1940.

———. "Languages and Logic." *Ibid.,* Vol. XLIII, Apr. 1941.

Lee, D. D. "Conceptual Implications of a Primitive Language." *Philosophy of Science,* Vol. V, 89–102, 1938.

———. "A Primitive System of Values." *Ibid.,* Vol. VII, 355–378, 1940.

———. "Linguistic Reflection of Wintu Thought." *Int. Jour. of Am. Linguistics,* Vol. X, Oct. 1944.

Frank, L. K. "Man's Multidimensional Environment." *Scientific Monthly,* Vol. LVI, 1943.

Bidney, David. "On the Concept of Culture and Some Cultural Fallacies." *The American Anthropologist,* Vol. 46, No. 1, 1944.

Perry, R. B. *Puritanism and Democracy.* The Vanguard Press, New York, 1944, p. 23.

Cassirer, Ernst. *An Essay on Man.* Yale University Press, 1944.

CHAPTER II

Spinden, H. J. *Ancient Civilization of Mexico and Central America.* American Museum of Natural History Handbook Series No. 3. New York, 1928.

Diaz del Castillo, Captain Bernal. *A True History of the Conquest of Mexico.* Trans. by Maurice Keatinge. Robert M. McBride and Company, New York, 1927.

Prescott, William H. *History of the Conquest of Mexico.* The Modern Library, New York.

Fernández, Justino. *José Clemente Orozco: Forma e Idea.* Librería de Porrua Hnos. y Cia., Argentina y Justo Sierra, Mexico, D.F., 1942, pp. 60–61.

———. *El Arte Moderno en Mexico.* Jose Porrua e Hijos, Mexico, D.F., 1937.

———. *Prometeo: Ensayo sobre Pintura Contemporánea.* Editorial Porrua, Mexico D.F., 1945.

Teotihuacan. Official Guide of the Instituto Nacional de Antropologia e Historia, pp. 16–17.

Caso, Alfonso. *The Religion of the Aztecs.* American Book Store. Mexico, D.F., 1937, p. 21.

———. *El Paraíso Terrenal en Teotihuacán.* Cuadernos Americanos, No. 6, 1942.

Von Wuthenau, Alexander. *Tepotzotlan.* Trans. from the Spanish by E. W. Hathaway. Von Stetten, Fotocolor, Mexico, D.F., 1941, p. 4.

Brenner, Anita. *Your Mexican Holiday.* Revised edit., G. P. Putnam's Sons, New York, 1941–42, pp. 208, 212.

———. *The Wind that Swept Mexico.* Harper and Brothers, New York and London, 1943.

The Apparitions of Our Lady of Guadalupe. Imprimatur Saturnino Pineda, Pro Vic. Gen., Mexico, D.F.

Toor, Frances. *Guide to Mexico.* 3d edit., Mexico, D.F., p. 81.

Ramos, Samuel. *El Perfil del Hombre y la Cultura en Mexico.* Editorial Pedro Robredo, Mexico, D.F., 1938, pp. 54, 58, 66, 56, 120.

———. *Historia de la Filosofia en Mexico.* Imprenta Universitaria, Mexico, D.F., 1943.

Reyes, Alfonso. *Ultima Tule.* Imprenta Universitaria, Mexico, D.F., 1942, pp. 135, 136.

———. *Critica en la Edad Ateniense.* El Colegio de Mexico, Mexico, D.F., 1941.

Zea, Leopoldo. *El Positivismo en Mexico.* El Colegio de Mexico, Mexico, D.F., 1943.

———. *Apogeo y decadencia del positivismo en Mexico.* El Colegio de Mexico, Mexico, D.F., 1944, pp. 213, 214, 213, 72, 206, 72–73.

Vasconcelos, José. *Historia del Pensamiento Filosofico.* Ediciones de la Universidad Nacional de Mexico, Mexico, D.F., 1937.

Caso, Antonio. *La Filosofia de Husserl.* Imprenta Mundial, Mexico, D.F., 1934.

Husserl, Edmundo. *Meditaciones Cartesianas.* Prólogo y traducción de José Gaos. El Colegio de Mexico, Mexico, D.F., 1942.

Rangel, Nicolás. *Preliminar a los precursores ideológicos de la Independencia, 1789–1794.* Publicaciones del Archivo General de la Nación, Mexico, D.F., 1929. As quoted by Samuel Ramos, pp. 55, 56.

Ortega y Gasset, José. *Toward a Philosophy of History.* W. W. Norton and Company, New York, 1941.

Borchard, Edwin. "The 'Minimum Standard' of the Treatment of Aliens." *Proceedings of the 33rd Annual Meeting of the American Society of International Law,* Washington, D. C., April 27–29, 1939, p. 62.

Heidegger, Martin. (Introducción) "El Ser y el Tiempo." Trad. de José Gaos. *Filosofia y Letras,* 8, Mexico, D.F., 1942.

O'Gorman, Edmundo. *Fundamentos de la Historia de America.* Imprenta Universitaria, Mexico, D.F., 1942.

Adams, Henry. *Mont-Saint-Michel and Chartres.* Houghton Mifflin Company, Boston and New York, 1933.

CHAPTER III

Reyes, Alfonso. *Ultima Tule.* Imprenta Universitaria, Mexico, D.F., 1942, pp. 93, 115, 123.

Andrews, Charles M. *The Colonial Background of the American Revolution.* Yale University Press, New Haven, 1924.

Townsend, Harvey. *Philosophical Ideas in the United States.* American Book Company, New York, 1934, p. 13.

Franklin, Benjamin. *Autobiography.* Harvard Classics, Vol. I, Collier and Son, New York, 1909, p. 121.

Nicolay, John G. and Hay, John. *Abraham Lincoln: A History.* Century Company, New York, 1904. Vol. I, p. 58; Vol. III, p. 299.

Lawrence, D. H. *Studies in Classic American Literature.* Martin Secker, London, 1933, p. 32.

Jefferson, Thomas, Living Thoughts of. Edit. by John Dewey. Longmans, Green and Company, New York, 1940, pp. 61–62, 69–70, 109.

Miller, John C. *Origins of the American Revolution.* Atlantic Monthly—Little, Brown Company, Boston, 1943, pp. 170, 492.

Madariaga, Salvador de. *Englishmen, Frenchmen, Spaniards.* Oxford University Press, London, 1931.

Gabriel, Ralph. *The Course of American Democratic Thought.* The Ronald Press, New York, 1943.

Wolfers, Arnold. *Britain and France Between Two Wars.* Harcourt, Brace and Company, New York, 1940.

Driver, Cecil. *Social and Political Ideas of Some English Thinkers of the Augustan Age. A.D. 1650–1750.* Edit. by F. J. C. Hearnshaw. G. G. Harrap and Company, Ltd., London, 1928, Ch. IV.

Gooch, G. P. See References of Chapter IV.

Voltaire, François M. A. *Letters on the English.* Harvard Classics, Vol. 34. Collier and Son, New York, 1910, p. 71.

Galilei, Galileo. As quoted by E. A. Burtt in *Metaphysical Foundations of Physics.* Harcourt, Brace and Company, New York, 1925, pp. 75, 78.

Newton, Isaac. *Principia.* Cajori Edit. University of California Press, Berkeley, 1934, p. 6.

Locke, John. *Essay Concerning Human Understanding.* Edit. by A. C. Fraser. Clarendon Press, Oxford, 1894.

———. *Letter Concerning Toleration.* Edit. by C. L. Sherman. Appleton-Century Company, New York, 1937, pp. 186–7, 190, 185–6, 181, 178–9, 173, 175–6.

———. *Of Civil Government.* Everyman's Library, E. P. Dutton and Company, New York, 1940, pp. 164, 118–9, 179–80, 187, 182–6, 190–2.

Perry, R. B. *Puritanism and Democracy.* The Vanguard Press, New York, 1944, pp. 150, 73.

Bainton, R. H. "The Struggle for Religious Liberty." *Church History,* Vol. X, No. 2, p. 21.

MacLean, Kenneth. *John Locke and English Literature of the Eighteenth Century.* Yale University Press, New Haven, 1936.

McTaggart, J. M. E. *Studies in Hegelian Cosmology.* Cambridge University Press, Cambridge, 1918, Ch. VII.

Laski, Harold. *Authority in the Modern State.* Yale University Press, New Haven, 1927, p. 35.

———. *Political Thought from Locke to Bentham.* Thornton Butterworth, London, 1920.

Brecht, Arnold. *Prelude to Silence.* Oxford University Press, New York, 1944.

Washington, George. *Farewell Address.* Harvard Classics, Vol. 43. Collier and Son, New York, 1910, pp. 258–9.

Rukeyser, Muriel. *Willard Gibbs, American Genius.* Doubleday, Doran and Company, New York, 1942, pp. 73, 74, 76.

Jay, John. *The Federalist.* Harvard Classics, Vol. 43. Collier and Son, New York, 1910, pp. 217–8.

Millar, S. J., Moorhouse, F. X. "The Establishment of American Federalism and Its Lessons for Broader Federalisms" in *Approaches to World Peace.* Ed. by L. Bryson, L. Finkelstein and R. McIver. New York, 1944. Distributed by Harper and Brothers.

Brooks, Van Wyck. *The World of Washington Irving.* The Blakiston Company, Philadelphia, 1944, Ch. II.

Turner, Ralph. *The Cultural Setting of American Agricultural Problems.* Yearbook Separate No. 1772. U. S. Department of Agriculture, 1941.

Berkeley, Complete Works of. Edit. by A. C. Fraser. Clarendon Press, Oxford, 1901.

Hume. *Selections.* Edit. by Charles W. Hendel, Jr. Charles Scribner's Sons, New York, 1927.

Naturalism and the Human Spirit. Ed. by Y. H. Krikorian. Columbia University Press, New York, 1944.

Prall, David. *Aesthetic Judgment.* T. Y. Crowell, New York, 1929.

———. *Aesthetic Analysis.* T. Y. Crowell, New York, 1936.

Bentham, Jeremy. *An Introduction to the Principles of Morals and Legislation.* W. Pickering, London, 1823, p. 1.

Mill, John Stuart. *Principles of Political Economy.* Longmans, Green and Company, London, 1904.

———. *On Liberty.* See Oakeshott, Michael.

———. *Representative Government.* See Oakeshott, Michael.

Oakeshott, Michael. *Social and Political Doctrines of Contemporary Europe.* Cambridge University Press, Cambridge, 1939, pp. 6–7, 11–12, 18, 9, 24, 13.

Jevons, W. S. *The Theory of Political Economy.* Macmillan Company, London, 1911, pp. 3, 11–12, 23–24, 37–39, 43–45; Introd., pp. 11–12; pp. 76–78; p. xlvii.

Perry, R. B. *General Theory of Value.* Longmans, Green and Company, New York, 1926.

Robbins, Lionel. *Nature and Significance of Economic Science.* Macmillan Company, London, 1935.

"Kant, Immanuel, Natural Science and the Critical Philosophy of." See *The Heritage of Kant.* Edit. by G. T. Whitney and D. F. Bowers. Princeton University Press, Princeton, 1939, pp. 39–64.

Einstein, Albert. *The World As I See It.* Covici Friede, New York, 1934, pp. 48–9.

Margenau, Henry. *Journal of the Philosophy of Science,* I, 133 (1934).

———. *Reviews of Modern Physics,* 13, 1941, pp. 176–189.

———. *Monist,* XLII, 161, 1932.

Bidney, David. *Psychology and Ethics of Spinoza.* Yale University Press, New Haven, 1940.

Wilson, Woodrow. *Constitutional Government in the United States.* Columbia University Press, New York, 1921, pp. 54–55.

Veblen, Thorstein. *Theory of the Leisure Class.* Macmillan Company, New York and London, 1899.

Dewey, John. *The Quest for Certainty.* Milton Balch and Company, New York, 1929.

Feibleman, James K. "Peirce's Use of Kant." *The Journal of Philosophy,* Volume XLII, pp. 365–377.
Justice Holmes, The Mind and Faith of. His Speeches, Essays, Letters and Judicial Opinions. Selected and Edited by Max Lerner. Little, Brown & Co., Boston, 1943.
Arnold, Thurman. *Symbols of Government.* Yale University Press, New Haven, 1935.
Llewellyn, K. N. *The Bramble Bush: Some Lectures on Law and Its Study.* New York, 1930.
Cohen, Morris. *Reason and Nature.* Harcourt, Brace & Company, New York, 1931.
Lewis, C. I. *Mind and the World-Order.* Charles Scribner's Sons, New York, 1929.
Whitehead, A. N. *Process and Reality.* The Macmillan Company, New York, 1929.
Montague, W. P. *The Ways of Things.* Prentice-Hall, New York, 1940.
Sheldon, W. H. *America's Progressive Philosophy.* Yale University Press, New Haven, 1942.
————. *Process and Polarity.* Columbia University Press, New York, 1944.
Curry, John Steuart. See *John Steuart Curry's Pageant of America,* by L. E. Schmeckebier, American Artists Group, New York, 1943.
Santayana, George. *The Sense of Beauty.* Charles Sricbner's Sons, New York, 1896.
Modern Masters. Museum of Modern Art, New York, 1940, p. 23.
The Impressionists. Oxford University Press, New York.
Modern American Painting, Peyton Boswell, Jr. Dodd, Mead and Company, New York, 1940.
Primer of Modern Art. Sheldon Cheney. Tudor Publishing Company, New York, 1939.
America and Alfred Stieglitz. Edit. by Waldo Frank and Others. Doubleday, Doran and Company, New York, 1934.

CHAPTER IV

Struther, Jan. *Mrs. Miniver.* Harcourt, Brace and Company, New York, 1940.
Whitehead, Alfred North. *The Aims of Education and Other Essays.* Macmillan Company, New York, 1929, p. 115.
Luther, Martin. *Cambridge Modern History.* Edit. by A. W. Ward, G. W. Prothero, Stanley Leathes. University Press, Cambridge, 1903, Vol. II, Ch. IV.
Carter, George. *History of England.* Relfe Brothers, London. Part II, pp. 43, 51, 61, 75–6, 177–8, 179, 182, 186, 197–8, 210, 207, 213.
Trevelyan, O.M., G. M. *English Social History.* Longmans, Green and Company, New York, 1942, pp. 191, 181, 255, 257–8, 190, 229, 278, 229–30, 245–6, 351, 230–1.
Hooker, Richard, *The Works of.* J. Vincent, Oxford, 1843.
Chesterton, G. K. *Short History of England.* Chatto and Windus, London, 1930.
Woodhouse, A. S. P. *Puritanism and Liberty.* Dent, London, 1938.
Gooch, G. P. *English Democratic Ideas in the Seventeenth Century.* Sec. Ed. With Supplementary Notes and Appendices by Professor H. J. Laski. Cambridge At The University Press, 1927.
————. *Political Thought in England from Bacon to Halifax.* Home University Library, London, 1914/1915.
Halévy, Elie. *The Growth of Philosophic Radicalism.* Trans. by Mary Morris. Faber & Gwyer, London, 1928.
Lindsay, A. D. *Religion, Science, and Society in the Modern World.* Yale University Press, New Haven, 1943, pp. 52, 61.

Temple, William, Archbishop of Canterbury. *Christianity and Social Order.* Penguin Books, New York, 1942, p. 34.

Green, T. H. *Prolegomena to Ethics.* The Clarendon Press, Oxford, 1883.

Moore, G. E. *Principia Ethica.* Cambridge University Press, Cambridge, 1922.

Webb, Beatrice. *My Apprenticeship.* Penguin Books, New York, 1938.

Haldane, J. B. S. *The Marxist Philosophy and the Sciences.* George Allen and Unwin, London, 1939.

Laski, H. J. *Reflections on the Revolution of our Time.* Viking Press, New York, 1943.

Beveridge, Sir William. *Social Insurance and Allied Services.* H. M. Stationery Office, 1942.

——. *Full Employment in a Free Society.* Allen and Unwin, 1944.

The Economist (London), Nov. 11, 1944. "Beveridge on Employment," pp. 628–30.

Barker, Ernest. *Britain and the British People.* Oxford University Press, 1942, pp. 89, 135.

CHAPTER V

Vaihinger, H. *The Philosophy of 'As If.'* Trans. by C. K. Ogden. Harcourt, Brace and Company, New York, 1924.

Dewey, John. *The Quest for Certainty.* Milton Balch and Company, New York, 1929.

Kant, Immanuel. *Critique of Pure Reason.* Trans. by N. K. Smith. Macmillan Company, London, 1929.

——. *Theory of Ethics.* Trans. by Abbott. Longmans, Green, Reader and Dyer, London, 1873.

——. *Critique of Judgment.* Trans. and Introd. by J. H. Bernard. Macmillan Company, London and New York, 1892.

Immanuel Kant's Werke. Herausgegeben von Ernst Cassirer. Verlag Bei Bruno Cassirer, Berlin, 1912.

Cassirer, Ernst. *Kants Leben und Lehre.* Verlegt bei Bruno Cassirer, Berlin, 1921.

Fichte, J. G. *Vocation of Man.* Trans. by William Smith. Open Court Publishing Company, Illinois, 1940, pp. 102–3.

Neumann, Sigmund. *Die Stufen des preussischen Konservatismus im 19 Jahrhundert.* E. Ebering, Berlin, 1930. Especially the appendix on romanticism.

Lewis, C. I. *Mind and the World-Order.* Charles Scribner's Sons, New York, 1929, p. 46.

Sheldon, W. H. *America's Progressive Philosophy.* Yale University Press, New Haven, 1942, Ch. II.

Hegel's Science of Logic. Trans. by W. H. Johnston and L. G. Struthers. George Allen and Unwin, London, 1929, Vols. I and II.

Hegel, G. W. F. *Lectures on the History of Philosophy.* Trans. by E. S. Haldane. Kegan Paul, London, 1892, pp. 34, 116.

Zea, Leopoldo. *Apogeo y decadencia del positivismo en Mexico.* El Colegio de Mexico, Mexico, D.F., 1944, pp. 127, 128.

Riess, Curt. *New York Times,* Feb. 25, 1945.

Rogers, A. K. *Student's History of Philosophy.* Macmillan Company, New York, 1916.

Royce, Josiah. *Lectures on Modern Idealism.* Yale University Press, New Haven, 1919.

Hocking, W. E. *Man and the State.* Yale University Press, New Haven, 1926.

CHAPTER VI

Feuerbach, Ludwig. *The Essence of Christianity*. Trans. by Marian Evans. Trübner & Co., London, 1881.

Oakeshott, Michael. *Social and Political Doctrines of Contemporary Europe*. Cambridge University Press, 1939, pp. 101, 103–5, 109, 84, 92, 124–5, 140, 130, 145, 99, 132, 148, 136.

Marx, Karl, and Engels, Friedrich. *Manifesto of the Communist Party* (1848).

Lenin, Vladimir. *The Teachings of Karl Marx* (1920).

———. *State and Revolution*. Chs. I and V (1917).

Marx, Karl. *Critique of the Gotha Programme* (1875).

Engels, F. *Ludwig Feuerbach and the Outcome of Classical German Philosophy*. Martin Lawrence, London, 1888.

———. *Dialectics of Nature*. International Publishers, New York, 1940.

Trotsky, L. Article on Lenin in *Encyclopaedia Britannica* (14th edit.).

———. *My Life*. Charles Scribner's Sons, New York, 1930.

Stalin, Joseph. *Dialectical and Historical Materialism*. International Publishers, New York, 1940.

The New Constitution of 1936. Trans. by Mrs. Anna Louise Strong, in *The Truth About Soviet Russia* by Sidney and Beatrice Webb. Longmans, Green and Company, New York, 1942.

Webb, Sidney and Beatrice. *Soviet Communism: A New Civilization. Ibid.*, 1935. pp. 429–30, 413, 414.

Webb, Beatrice. *The New Civilization* in *The Truth About Soviet Russia* by Sidney and Beatrice Webb. Longmans, Green and Company, New York, 1942, pp. 55, 56, 75, 71–2.

Balz, Albert G. A. *The Value Doctrine of Karl Marx*. King's Crown Press, New York, 1943.

Hook, Sidney. *The Political and Social Doctrine of Communism*. Worcester, Mass., and New York City. Carnegie Endowment for International Peace. Division of Intercourse and Education, 1934.

———. "Dialectic and Nature." *Marxist Quarterly*, Vol. I, No. 2, pp. 253–84.

———. *From Hegel to Marx*. John Day, Reynal and Hitchcock, New York, 1936.

Northrop, F. S. C. "Impossibility of a Theoretical Science of Economic Dynamics." *Quarterly Journal of Economics*, November, 1941, pp. 1–17.

Dobb, Maurice. *Political Economy and Capitalism*. Routledge and Sons, London, 1937.

CHAPTER VII

Maritain, Jacques. *The Degrees of Knowledge*. G. Bles, The Centenary Press, London, 1937.

———. *A Preface to Metaphysics*. Sheed and Ward, New York, 1939.

———. *Education at the Crossroads*. Yale University Press, New Haven, 1944.

Gilson, Etienne. *The Unity of Philosophical Experience*. Charles Scribner's Sons, New York, 1937.

———. *La philosophie au moyen âge*. Payot & Cie, Paris, 1922.

———. *The Spirit of Medieval Philosophy*. Trans. by A. H. C. Downes. Charles Scribner's Sons, New York, 1936.

Lovejoy, A. O. *The Great Chain of Being*. Harvard University Press, Cambridge, 1936.

McKeon, Richard. *Selections from Medieval Philosophers*. Vols I and II. Charles Scribner's Sons, New York, 1929.

Compayré, Gabriel. *Abelard and the Origin and Early History of Universities.* Charles Scribner's Sons, New York, 1893.

Buchanan, Scott. *The Doctrine of Signatures.* Harcourt, Brace and Co., New York, 1938.

Hutchins, Robert M. *The Higher Learning in America.* Yale University Press, New Haven, 1936.

Adler, Mortimer. *What Man Has Made of Man.* Longmans, Green and Company, New York, 1937.

Eliot, T. S. *The Idea of a Christian Society.* Faber and Faber, London, 1939.

Llewellyn, K. N. "Some Realism about Realism." *Harvard Law Review,* 44: pp. 1222–64.

———. *The Bramble Bush: Some Lectures on Law and Its Study.* New York, 1930.

Frank, Jerome. *Law and the Modern Mind.* Brentano's, New York, 1930.

Cohen, Morris R. *Reason and Nature.* Harcourt, Brace and Company, New York, 1931.

———. *American Law School Review,* 1928, pp. 231–9.

Northrop, F. S. C. "The Criterion of the Good State." *Ethics,* LII, No. 3, April 1942, pp. 309–22.

Moore, Underhill. "Law and Learning Theory." *Yale Law Journal,* Vol. 53, 1943.

Euclid's Elements, The Thirteen Books of. Edit. by T. L. Heath. Cambridge University Press, 1908, Vol. III, pp. 14–16.

Parmenides and Zeno. See *Source Book of Ancient Philosophy* by C. W. Bakewell. Charles Scribner's Sons, New York, 1907.

Empedocles, Fragments of. Trans. by W. E. Leonard. Open Court Publishing Company, Chicago, 1908.

Aristotle, The Works of. Edit. by W. D. Ross. The Clarendon Press, Oxford, 1928.

Thompson, D'Arcy. *The Legacy of Greece.* Edit. by R. W. Livingstone. The Clarendon Press, Oxford, 1921, p. 143.

Osbourn, J. C. *The Maritain Volume of the Thomist.* Sheed and Ward, New York, 1943, pp. 23–54.

McWilliams, J. A. "The Bond Between Physics and Metaphysics of St. Thomas." *The Modern Schoolman,* November 1944.

Sheldon, W. H. "Can Philosophers Cooperate?" *The Modern Schoolman,* January and March 1944. See also the reply by Jacques Maritain and Prof. Sheldon's response. *Ibid.,* November 1944 and January 1945.

Pope Leo XIII. *Immortale Dei* (1885). As given in *Social and Political Doctrines of Contemporary Europe,* by Michael Oakeshott. Cambridge University Press, 1939, pp. 50–1.

Kennedy, Walter B. "Portrait of the New Supreme Court." *Fordham Law Review,* Vol. VIII, No. 1.

Ford, John C., Rev. "The Fundamentals of Holmes Juristic Philosophy." *Ibid.,* Vol. XI, No. 3.

CHAPTER VIII

Reyes, Alfonso. *Ultima Tule.* Imprenta Universitaria, Mexico, D. F., 1942, pp. 93, 89, 94.

O'Gorman, Edmundo. *Fundamentos de la Historia de America.* Imprenta Universitaria, Mexico, D. F., 1942.

Ramos, Samuel. *El Perfil del Hombre.* Editorial Pedro Robredo, Mexico, D. F., 1938.

Seneca. *Medea.* ll. 375–9.

References 505

Plato. *Critias.*
———. *Republic,* l. 540.
Ortega y Gasset, J. *El Tema de Nuestro Tiempo.* Colección Austral, Mexico, D.F.
———. *Ideas y creencias.* Colección Austral, Mexico, D. F.
Einstein, Albert. *The World As I See It.* Covici Friede, New York, 1934, p. 60.
Whitehead, Alfred N. *Adventures of Ideas.* Macmillan Company, New York, 1933.
———. *Process and Reality.* Macmillan Company, New York, 1929.
———. *Concept of Nature.* University Press, Cambridge, 1920.
James, William. *Principles of Psychology.* Henry Holt and Company, New York, 1890.
———. *Varieties of Religious Experience.* Longmans, Green and Company, New York, 1902.
Bergson, Henri. *Time and Free Will: An Essay on the Immediate Data of Consciousness.* Macmillan Company, New York, 1910.
de Tolnay, Charles. *History and Technique of Old Master Drawings.* H. Bittner and Company, New York, 1944.
Mayor, A. Hyatt, *Jefferson's Enjoyment of the Arts.* Bulletin of Metropolitan Museum of Art, New York, December 1943.
Prall, David. *Aesthetic Judgment.* T. Y. Crowell, New York, 1929.
———. *Aesthetic Anyalysis.* T. Y. Crowell, New York, 1936.
Gautier, Théophile. *Mademoiselle de Maupin.* Modern Library, New York, pp. xxii–xxv.
Shakespeare. *Coriolanus.* Yale University Press, New Haven, 1924, p. 3.
Northrop, F. S. C. *El sentido de la civilización occidental.* Traducción de Edmundo O'Gorman. Filosofia y letras, Mexico, D.F., 1945, pp. 17 and 18.

CHAPTER IX

Edgerton, Franklin. "Sources of the Filosofy of the Upanishads." *JAOS,* 36, p. 197.
———. "The Upanishads: What Do They Seek and Why?" *JAOS,* 49, pp. 97–121.
Dubs, H. H. "'Nature' in the Teachings of Confucius." *JAOS,* Vol. 50, No. 3, pp. 233–7.
———. *Hsüntze, the Moulder of Ancient Confucianism.* Probsthain, London, 1927.
———. "Dominant Ideas in the Formation of Indian Culture." *JAOS,* Vol. 62, No. 3 (1942), pp. 151–6.
———. *Hsüntze, The Works of.* Trans. Probsthain, London, 1928.
Dasgupta, Sarendranath. *History of Indian Philosophy.* Cambridge University Press, 1922, Vol. I, pp. 10, 11, 12, 13–14, 45.
Kang, Younghill. *The Grass Roof.* Charles Scribner's Sons, New York, 1931, pp. 7, 12.
———. *East Goes West.* Charles Scribner's Sons, New York, 1937, p. 233.
Pallis, Marco. *Peaks and Lamas.* Alfred Knopf, New York, 1940, pp. 365, 348, 349, 370, 373, 374, 379.
Lin Yutang. *My Country and My People.* John Day Company, New York, 1939, pp. 83, 306, 309.
Confucius, The Wisdom of. Trans. and Edit. by Lin Yutang. Modern Library, New York, 1938, pp. 162, 168, 171, 139–40, 173, 200–1, 203–4, 196, 195, 165, 162–3, 157, 220, 117.
Lao Tsu. *Tao-Teh-King.* Trans. by Paul Carus. Open Court Publishing Company, Chicago, 1898, pp. 99, 102.
Chiang Yee. *Chinese Calligraphy.* Methuen & Co. Ltd., London, 1938, p. 207.

Chiang Yee. *The Chinese Eye*. F. A. Stokes Company, New York, 1937, pp. 86, 30, 103.

Chinese Philosophy in Classical Times. Edit. and Trans. by E. R. Hughes. Everyman's Library. E. P. Dutton and Company, New York, 1942, pp. 144, 38, 41, 156, 153, 150, 152, 150–1, 41–2, 147, 51.

Shao Chang Lee. *The Development of Chinese Culture*. Honolulu, T. H., 1930.

Latourette, K. S. *The Chinese, Their History and Culture*. Macmillan Company, New York, 1934.

Shridharani, Krishnalal. *My India, My America*. Duell, Sloan and Pearce, New York, 1941, pp. 156, 332.

Hu Shih. *Development of the Logical Method in Ancient China*. Oriental Book Company, Shanghai, 1928, pp. 13, 27.

Chan, Wing Tsit. *The Spirit of Oriental Philosophy*. Mimeographed Outline as used in lectures at University of Hawaii, Summer Session, 1939. See also *Philosophy: East and West*. Edit. by Charles A. Moore. Princeton University Press, Princeton, 1944.

Takakusu, Junjiro. *Buddhist Philosophy*. Mimeographed lectures as used in course at University of Hawaii, Summer Session, 1939. See also *Philosophy: East and West*. Edit. by Charles A. Moore. Princeton University Press, Princeton, 1944.

Philosophy: East and West. Edit. by Charles A. Moore. Princeton University Press, Princeton, 1944.

David-Neel, Madame Alexandra. *Magic and Mystery in Tibet*. Claude Kendall, New York, 1932, pp. 268–9.

World Almanac, 1938 and 1944. Population of India, pp. 586–8 and 679–80.

Moore, C. A. See *Philosophy: East and West* above, Ch. X.

Coomaraswamy, Ananda. *Hinduism and Buddhism*. Philosophical Library, New York, 1943, pp. 48–9, 45.

———. "Eastern Religion and Western Thought." *Review of Religion*, January 1942.

———. "Tantric Doctrine of Divine Biunity." *Bhandarkar Oriental Research Institute*, Annals, 19, pp. 173–83.

———. *History of Indian and Indonesian Art*. E. Weyhe, New York, 1927.

———. *Rajput Painting*. Oxford University Press, London, 1916.

Woodroffe, Sir John. *Shakti and Shâkta*. Luzac and Company, London, 1929, pp. 429, 431, 432, 247–8, 316, 240–1, 255, 290, 25, 10, 18, 1, 212.

Luria, S. *Quellen u. Studien zur Geschichte der Mathematik, Astronomie, und Physik*. Bd. 2, Abt. B. s. 106–85.

Hume, Robert E. *The Thirteen Principal Upanishads*. Oxford University Press, London, 1921, pp. 243, 242, 397, 419, 403.

Johnston, Charles. *The Great Upanishads*. The Quarterly Book Department, New York, 1927, Vol. I, pp. 83, 222.

Hocking, W. E. *Living Religions and a World Faith*. Lecture II. The Macmillan Company, New York, 1940.

CHAPTER X

Luria, S. *Quellen u. Studien zur Geschichte der Mathematik, Astronomie, und Physik*. Bd. 2, Abt. B. s. 106–85.

Coomaraswamy, Ananda K. "Eastern Religions and Western Thought." *The Review of Religion*, January 1942, pp. 129–45.

Arnold, Edwin. *The Light of Asia*. Roberts Brothers, Boston, 1891, pp. 20, 77, 78–80.

Deussen, Paul. *The System of the Vedanta*. Open Court Publishing Company, Chicago, 1912, p. 456.

Deussen, Paul. *The Philosophy of the Upanishads.* T. and T. Clark, Edinburgh, 1906.

Hahn, Emily. *The Soong Sisters.* Doubleday, Doran and Company, New York, 1943, p. 136.

Chinese Philosophy in Classical Times. Edit. and Trans. by E. R. Hughes. Everyman's Library, E. P. Dutton and Company, New York, 1942, pp. 20, 32.

Confucius, The Wisdom of. Trans. and Edit. by Lin Yutang. Modern Library, New York, 1938, pp. 187, 192, 108–9, 106.

Planck, Max. *Universe in the Light of Modern Physics.* W. W. Norton, New York, 1931, p. 13.

——. *The Philosophy of Physics.* W. W. Norton, New York, 1936, p. 114.

Northrop, F. S. C. "The Complementary Emphases of Eastern Intuitive and Western Scientific Philosophy." *Philosophy: East and West.* Edit. by Charles A. Moore. Princeton University Press, Princeton, 1944.

Lin Yutang. *My Country and My People.* John Day Company, New York, 1939, pp. 68, 175, 180–9, 203–13.

Tagore, Rabindranath. *Collected Poems and Plays.* Macmillan Company, New York, 1937, pp. 122–3.

Johnston, Charles. *The Great Upanishads.* Quarterly Book Department, New York, 1927, Vol. I, pp. 59–60, 210–11.

Wang Yang-ming, The Philosophy of. Trans. by F. G. Henke. Open Court Publishing Company, Chicago, 1916.

Chiang Yee. *The Chinese Eye.* F. A. Stokes, New York, 1937, pp. 86, 105.

CHAPTER XI

Kipling, Rudyard. *Kim.* Doubleday, Page and Company, New York, 1914, pp. 9–10.

Grousset, René. *Civilization of India.* Tudor Publishing Company, New York, 1931, pp. 113, 87, 86, 89, 115, 90, 100, 102.

Fernández, Justino. *Prometeo: Ensayo sobre Pintura Contemporánea.* Editorial Porrua, Mexico, D.F., 1945.

Dasgupta, Sarendranath. As reported by W. E. Hocking in *Living Religions and a World Faith.* The Macmillan Company, New York, 1940, pp. 79–80.

Shridharani, Krishnalal. *My India, My America.* Duell, Sloan and Pearce, New York, 1941, pp. 339, 340, 338, 337.

West, Rebecca. *Black Lamb and Grey Falcon.* The Viking Press, New York, 1943, p. 298.

Coomaraswamy, Ananda. *Hinduism and Buddhism.* Philosophical Library, New York, 1943, p. 49.

Vaka, Demetra. *Haremlik.* Houghton, Mifflin Company, Boston, 1909.

Nehru, Jawaharlal. *Toward Freedom.* John Day Company, New York, 1941, pp. 240, 229–30 and 350.

——. "Nehru Flings a Challenge." *New York Times,* July 19, 1942.

Asakawa, K. *The Documents of Iriki Illustrative of the Development of the Feudal Institutions of Japan.* Yale University Press, 1929.

——. *The Founding of the Shogunate by Minamoto-No-Yoritomo.* In Seminarium Kondakovianum VI Institut Kondakov. Praha, 1933.

Holtom, D. C. *Modern Japan and Shinto Nationalism.* University of Chicago Press, 1943.

Sakamaki, Shunzo. "Shinto: Japanese Ethnocentrism." *Philosophy: East and West.* Edit. by Charles A. Moore. Princeton University Press, 1944. Ch. VI.

Sansom, G. B. *Japan; A Short Cultural History.* The Century Company, New York, 1931.

Lin Yutang. *My Country and My People.* John Day Company, New York, 1939, pp. 172 ff.

Dubs, H. H. *The Concept of Unity in China.* Annual Report of the American Historical Association, 1942, Vol. III. Reprint, Washington, 1944, p. 18.

Hahn, Emily. *The Soong Sisters.* Doubleday, Doran Company, New York, 1943, pp. 163, 181, 163–4, 23, 258, 199–200, 132.

Chiang Kai-shek, Generalissimo. *New York Times,* April 13, 1943.

———. *Generalissimo Chiang Speaks.* Pacific Publishing Co., Hong Kong, 1939.

———. *China Fights On.* Vol. I. Trans. by F. W. Price. China Publishing Company, Chungking and Hong Kong.

Chiang Kai-shek, Madame. *China Shall Rise Again.* Harper & Brothers, New York, 1940.

———. *China in Peace and War.* Hurst & Blackett, London, 1940.

———. *We Chinese Women.* The John Day Company, New York.

Sun Yat-sen. *San Min Chu I.* Trans. by F. W. Price. The Commercial Press, Shanghai, 1929.

Hsü, Leonard S. *Sun Yat-Sen.* His Political and Social Ideals. University of Southern California Press, Los Angeles, 1933.

Buck, Pearl. *The Good Earth.* Modern Library, New York.

Gandhi, Mahatma. *Freedom's Battle.* Ganesh and Company, Madras, 1921.

Hu Shih. *Development of the Logical Method in Ancient China.* Oriental Book Company, Shanghai, 1928, pp. 5–7.

———. *The Chinese Renaissance.* The University of Chicago Press, 1934.

Rowe, D. N. *China Among the Powers.* Harcourt, Brace & Co., New York, 1945.

Kang, Younghill. *East Goes West.* Charles Scribner's Sons, New York, 1937.

CHAPTER XII

Einstein, Albert. *Science,* Vol. 91, p. 488.

———. *The World As I See It.* Covici Friede, New York, 1934, pp. 60 ff.

Whitehead, Alfred N. *Concept of Nature.* Cambridge University Press, 1920. Especially Chapter II.

Margenau, Henry. *Journal of the Philosophy of Science,* II, 48 (1935); II, 164 (1935).

———. *Reviews of Modern Physics.* Vol. 13, 1941, pp. 176–89.

Northrop, F. S. C. "Philosophical Significance of the Concept of Probability in Quantum Mechanics." *Journal of the Philosophy of Science,* Vol. 3, 1936, pp. 215–32.

———. "Whitehead's Philosophy of Science." *Library of Living Philosophers,* Vol. III. Edit by P. A. Schilpp. Northwestern University, Evanston, 1941.

———. "Complementary Emphases of Eastern Intuitive and Western Scientific Philosophy." *Philosophy: East and West.* Edit. by Charles A. Moore. Princeton University Press, 1944.

———. "The Method and Theories of Physical Science in Their Bearing upon Biological Organization." *Growth,* 1940, pp. 127–154.

Cassirer, Ernst. *Substance and Function.* Authorized translation by W. C. and M. C. Swabey. Open Court Publishing Co., Chicago, 1923.

Adams, Henry. *Mont-Saint-Michel and Chartres.* Houghton Mifflin Company, Boston, Chapter XIII.

Bachofen, Johann J. *Das mutterreckt.* Krais and Hoffman, Stuttgart, 1881.

Garcia Bacca, Juan David. *El sentido de la Nada en Heidegger y San Juan de la Cruz.* Cuadernos Americanos, 1944, 6, 87–100.

References

Pallis, Marco. *Peaks and Lamas.* A. Knopf, New York, 1940.

Montague, W. P. *The Ways of Things.* Prentice Hall, New York, 1940.

Cressey, G. B. *China's Geographic Foundations.* McGraw-Hill Book Company, New York, 1934, p. 5.

West, Rebecca. *Black Lamb and Grey Falcon.* The Viking Press, New York, 1943, pp. 401, 406.

Jefferson, Thomas, *Living Thoughts of.* Edit. by John Dewey. Longmans, Green and Company, New York, 1940, p. 111.

CHAPTER XIII

Urban, W. M. *Language and Reality.* George Allen and Unwin, Ltd., London, 1939.

O'Neill, Jr., Eugene. "Values from Above." *New York Times,* Book Review Section, Feb. 25, 1945, p. 20.

Stevenson, Charles. *Ethics and Language.* Yale University Press, New Haven, 1944.

Maritain, Jacques. *France, My Country Through Disaster.* Longmans, Green and Company, New York, 1941.

Northrop, F. S. C. "The Functions and Future of Poetry." *Furioso,* No. 4. New Haven, 1941, pp. 71–82.

———. "Causality in Field Physics in Its Bearing on Biological Causation." *Journal of the Philosophy of Science,* Vol. 5, 1938, pp. 166–80.

Croce, Benedetto. *Aesthetics.* Trans. by D. Ainslie. Macmillan Company, London, 1909, pp. 385–6.

Shakespeare, William. *Troilus and Cressida.* Yale University Press, New Haven, 1927, p. 21.

Wilde, Oscar, Essays of. Albert and Charles Boni, New York, 1935, pp. 409, 394.

Einstein, Albert, and Infeld, L. *The Evolution of Physics.* Simon and Schuster, New York, 1938, Ch. III.

Burr, H. S., and Northrop, F. S. C. "The Electrodynamic Theory of Life." *Quarterly Review of Biology,* Vol. 10, 1935, pp. 322–33.

———. "Experimental Findings Concerning the Electrodynamic Theory of Life." *Growth,* Vol. I, 1927, pp. 78–88.

———. *Proceedings of National Academy of Sciences,* Vol. 25, 1939, pp. 284–8.

Burr, H. S. "Electrometric Study of Mimosa." *Yale Journal of Biology and Medicine,* Vol. 15, No. 6.

Woodroffe, Sir John. *Bharata Shakti.* Ganesh and Company, Madras, 1921, p. 115.

INDEX

Abad, 38
Abelard, 30, 58, 59, 264, 294
Abelardo Rodriquez Market, 64
Absolute, the, 210–213; ego, 212; mind,
  217; self, 249; spirit, 213; will, 210
Absolutism, 153, 456, 460
Abstractionism, 119
Acoustics, 262
Act of Supremacy, 168
Adams, H., 59, 462, 498, 508
Adams, John, 70, 99
Adams, John Q., 102
Adler, 254, 255, 259, 504
Aesthetic analogy, 287; component, 61,
  162, 163, 300 ff., 333, 353, 372, 376,
  383, 389, 429, 434, 439–455, 461–471,
  475, 481–486, 491, 494; continuum, 119,
  160, 304, 307, 317, 318, 332–343, 349–
  354, 364–371, 377, 395, 398, 399, 444,
  451, 453, 469, 488; continuum (differentiated), 58, 447, 460, 465, (undifferentiated), 450, 460, 475, 477; differentiations, 335, 354, 383; emotional principle in the nature of things, 62; female
  component, 62; field component, 352,
  400; immediacy, 318, 327, 330, 331,
  332, 376, 410, 461; intuition, 60, 457;
  manifold, 330, 331, 334, 336, 340, 341,
  354, 357, 396; materials, 56, 450, 461;
  object, 323, 334, 340; unity, 372; values
  and science, 307
Aesthetics, 18, 21, 29, 63, 64, 118–120,
  160–163, 217, 287–288, 292, 302, 303–
  310, 314, 315–322, 323–324, 330–341,
  346–347, 351, 356–358, 359–360, 372,
  377, 397, 399, 403–404, 405–408, 410–
  411, 431, 461–464, 484–485, 486–491,
  495–496. *Also see* Art.
Africa, 410
Agama, 365
Aggressiveness of West, 419
Agnosticism, 365
"Agony of Christianity," 63
Agra, 408
Albertus Magnus, 264, 265
Alegre, 38
Alexander the Great, 188, 405
Aliens, minimum treatment of, 44
"All-embracingness," 364
All-Russia Central Committee, 222
Amaterasu Omi Kami, 420

America, defined, 66; its relation to Europe,
  291 ff.; the spectacle of, 292
American Bar Association, 258
American education, 260
"American Gothic," 55, 160
American law schools, 258
American Philosophical Association, 257
American Revolution, 216, 468
American universities, 259
Americans, practicality of, 73
Analects, 325, 326, 328 ff.
Analogical relation, 287
Ancestors, worship of, 337
Andrews, 67, 499
Anglicans, 82
Anglo-American culture, 38, 39, 53, 54,
  Ch. III, 253, 304, 449, 466, 475, 494;
  economic theory, 120, 211. *See also* Eco-
  nomics
Anglo-American Soul, 54
Anglo-American West, 458
Animists, 358
Anthropomorphism, 406
A priori forms of sensibility, 210
Apollo, 406
Appearance, three-termed relation of, 78,
  80, 81, 283, 440–452, 468, 476, 478
Arab(s), 5, 63, 263, 264, 410, 411
Arab scientists, 261
Arabian Sea, 371
Aranyakas, 360
Argentina, 4
Aristotle, 17, 28, 30, 36, 58, 59, 61, 70,
  82, 108, 111, 173, 174, 186, 192, 214,
  219, 249, 254–287, 291, 292, 294, 296,
  300, 305, 310, 362, 415, 438, 454, 456,
  468, 474, 486, 488, 504
Aristotle's biology, 271 ff.; four causes,
  270; epistemology, 274 ff.; philosophy,
  254, 259 ff.; politics, 70, 71, 87; phys-
  ics, 261 ff., 283; predictables, 272; psy-
  chology, 274 ff.; theory of value, 280
Aristotelian Thomism, 261 ff., 310; invalidity of, 438
Aristotelianism, 38, 57
Arithmetic, 267
Arnold, Edwin, 379, 506
Arnold, Thurman, 152, 501
Art, 482 ff.; and modern theory of the
  individual, 90, 91; as intuition, 487;
  and thought, 487 ff.; and morality, 487

511

Index